The Psychology of Sex Differences

Volume II: Annotated Bibliography

The Psychology of Sex Differences

ELEANOR EMMONS MACCOBY &
CAROL NAGY JACKLIN

Volume II: Annotated Bibliography

STANFORD UNIVERSITY PRESS

STANFORD, CALIFORNIA

Stanford University Press
Stanford, California
© 1974 by the Board of Trustees of the
Leland Stanford Junior University
Printed in the United States of America
Cloth ISBN 0-8047-0859-2
Paper ISBN 0-8047-0974-2 (Volume I),
0-8047-0975-0 (Volume II)
Original edition 1974
Paperback edition, in two volumes, 1978
Last figure below indicates year of this printing:
87 86 85 84 83 82 81 80 79 78

The Psychology of Sex Differences

Volume II: Annotated Bibliography

Annotated Bibliography

Works cited in the text (or in the summary tables) in Volume I, excluding works bearing the superscript letter R, are listed here. Works bearing the superscript are listed in the References Cited section of Volume I, pp. 377–91. The distinction is explained in the Introduction, Volume I, p. 8.

Some of the entries in this bibliography are not included in the summary tables or treated in the corresponding text. The nature of these entries is explained in the Introduction, Volume I, p. 10.

Ables, B. The three wishes of latency age children. *Developmental Psychology*, 1972, *6*, 186 (brief report and extended unpublished report).
    Subjects: $N = 128$; 7–12 yrs. **Measures:** Each S was asked what he would wish for if he had 3 wishes. **Results:** (1) Girls more often than boys wished for another person. (2) Boys more often than girls wished for material possessions and money. (3) There were no sex differences in percentage of wishes relating to pets, activities, personal, miscellaneous, or more wishes.

Abney, C. W. A comparative study of creative thinking ability in three student groups at the University of Arkansas as measured by the Remote Associations Test. *Dissertation Abstracts International*, 1970, *30*, 2717a.
    Subjects: $N = 168$; 18–21 yrs (college). **Measures:** The Remote Associations Test (RAT) was administered to 3 groups: honors students, students with comparable grade-point averages (GPA), and a control group with lower GPA's. **Results:** In the honors group, women scored higher than men on the RAT.

Abravanel, E. The development of intersensory patterning with regard to selected spatial dimensions. *Monographs of the Society for Research in Child Development*, 1968, *33*.
    Subjects: $N = 200$; 3–14 yrs. **Measures:** (1) After handling, but not looking at, wooden bars of varying sizes, Ss estimated the length of each bar on a measuring tape. (2) Ss tried to adjust 2 unseen brass rings to equal the distance marked off on a visually perceived rod. (3) After touching, but not looking at, grooves of varying lengths cut into masonite, Ss estimated the length of each on a measuring tape. (4) Tactile stimulation was applied at 2 distinct points along Ss' forearms. Ss estimated the distance between the 2 points on a measuring tape. (5) Ss touched, but did not look at, lines of tacks of standard lengths driven into a wooden board. Following each presentation Ss viewed 2 lines constructed in a similar manner. Ss judged which of the 2 lines was equal in length to the standard. (6) After looking at, but not touching, a standard cylinder, Ss handled 2 other cylinders, 1 of which was equal in size to the standard. Ss' task was to pick out the matching cylinder. **Results:** Among 4- and 12-14-year-old Ss, girls showed greater accuracy on tasks 2 and 6 than boys. Among 7-, 8-, and 9-year-old Ss, girls showed greater accuracy on task 4 than boys.

Achenbach, T. M. Cue learning, associative responding, and school performance in children. *Developmental Psychology*, 1969, *1*, 717–25.
    In 3 experiments, multiple-choice analogy tests were administered in which half the items had incorrect alternative words with high-frequency associations as the third word of the analogy ("foils") whereas the correct alternative was a low-frequency associate. For the other half of the items, the third word of the analogy had no high-frequency associates. D scores equal the difference between the number of "foil" responses made by S and the number of his "nonfoil" errors.
    EXPERIMENT I: **Subjects:** $N = 191$; 10 yrs. **Measures:** E administered a 50-item analogy test to all Ss. Teachers rated each S on intellectual independence and learning effectiveness. Two weeks later, the 10 highest and 10 lowest D scorers of each sex were individually tested on the Matching Familiar Figures test and on a discrimination-learning task (cues provided at increasing intervals after each trial began). **Results:** No sex differences.
    EXPERIMENT II: **Subjects:** $N = 159$; 10, 11 yrs. **Measures:** E administered a 54-item anal-

ogy test to all Ss. Teachers rated each S on learning effectiveness and physical activity. The 16 highest and 16 lowest D scorers were assigned to groups by sex, grade, D score, and type of learning task. Two versions of discrimination learning task were administered: (1) same as Experiment I with randomized cues presented, and (2) delayed cues presented with only correct responses being cued. Information and Vocabulary subjects of the Weschler Intelligence Scale for Children (WISC) were administered to each S. **Results:** Among 10-year-old Ss boys were rated more physically active than girls. No other sex differences in traits, learning task, or cognitive tests were found.

EXPERIMENT III: **Subjects:** $N = 164$; 11 yrs. **Measures:** E administered a 68-item analogy test to all Ss. Teachers rated each S on learning effectiveness and physical activity. The 24 highest and 24 lowest D scorers were assigned to groups by sex, D score, and learning condition. Learning conditions varied by delayed cue format (Experiment II) and control condition (no cue provided). Information and vocabulary subtests of the WISC and the Matching Familiar Figures test preceded the learning task. **Results:** Girls performed better than boys on the WISC vocabulary subtest.

Achenbach, T. M. Standardization of a research instrument for identifying associative responding in children. *Developmental Psychology*, 1970, *2*, 283–91.
  Subjects: $N = 1,085$; 10–13 yrs. **Measures:** Ss completed a multiple-choice analogy Children's Associative Responding Test. Half of the items had an incorrect response alternative (foil) that was a frequent association to the third word of the analogy. The other half had no alternatives that were frequent associations. Associative responding was measured by foil minus nonfoil errors (D score). **Results:** (1) Among 11- and 12-year-old Ss, boys made more nonfoil errors than girls. (2) Among 10- and 11-year-old Ss, girls had higher achievement test percentiles than boys. (3) Girls had higher IQs and grade averages than boys at all ages. (4) There were no sex differences in analogy errors or foil errors at any age. (5) Among 12-year-old Ss, girls had higher D scores than boys.

Achenbach, T. M. The Children's Associative Responding Test: a two-year follow up. *Developmental Psychology*, 1971, *5*, 477–83.
  Subjects: $N = 561$; 12, 13 yrs. **Measures:** Otis-Beta IQ scores, SRA achievement scores, and grade-point averages were obtained from school records. **Results:** No sex differences.

Achenbach, T. M., and Zigler, E. Cue-learning and problem learning strategies in normal and retarded children. *Child Development*, 1968, *39*, 827–48.
  EXPERIMENT I: **Subjects:** $N = 120$; 7, 9 yrs (normals), 12–13, 17–18 yrs (noninstitutionalized retardates), 20–21, 25–26 yrs (institutionalized retardates). **Measures:** On each trial of a discrimination-learning task, Ss were presented with 3 squares that varied in color and size. Ss' task was to determine which of the 3 squares was "correct." Ss were assigned to 1 of 2 conditions. In the experimental condition, a light went on above the correct square after a short interval of time. As the experiment progressed, this interval became longer. The criterion of learning for Ss in this group was correct responses on 5 consecutive trials before the onset of the light. The learning criterion for Ss in the control condition (no light cue) was 5 successively correct choices within the time limit imposed on Ss in the experimental condition. **Results:** No sex differences.
  EXPERIMENT II: **Subjects:** $N = 120$; 7, 11–12 yrs (normals, noninstitutionalized retardates). **Measures:** Similar to Experiment I. **Results:** No sex differences.

Adams, W. V. Strategy differences between reflective and impulsive children. *Child Development*, 1972, *43*, 1076–80.
  Subjects: $N = 80$; 6, 8 yrs. **Measures:** Impulsive and reflective Ss (as determined by the Matching Familiar Figures test) performed a 3-choice learning task using a marble game apparatus. Correct choices were randomly rewarded 33% of the time. Perseveration and 3 kinds of pattern guessing strategies were analyzed. **Results:** No sex differences.

Aiello, J. R., and Jones, S. E. Field study of the proxemic behavior of young school children in three subcultural groups. *J. Personality & Social Psychology*, 1971, *19*, 351–56.
  Subjects: $N = 420$; 6–8 yrs (white, black, Puerto Rican). **Measures:** Dyadic interactions during recess periods and lunch hours were observed. Each pair of Ss engaged in verbal interaction and were relatively stationary. The distance apart (inches) and axis of orientation (directness of shoulder orientation) were measured. **Results:** (1) Among white Ss, boys stood farther apart than girls did. (2) Overall axis scores combining all cultures showed that girls were less direct in orientation than boys. However, no sex differences were found within cultures.

Akamatsu, T. J., and Thelen, M. H. The acquisition and performance of a socially neutral response as a function of vicarious reward. *Developmental Psychology*, 1971, 5, 440–45.
Subjects: N = 48; 7–8 yrs. Measures: Ss viewed a videotaped adult male model pressing a button, with either predetermined verbal reward or no reward. They were then given the same task with the same instructions as the model, but with no reward (performance measure). Ss were asked to show everything they could remember about the way the man played, and were praised for correct responses (acquisition measure). Results: No sex differences.

Alderman, D. Effects of anticipating future interaction on the preference for balanced states. *J. Personality & Social Psychology*, 1969, 11, 214–19.
Subjects: N = 268; 18–21 yrs (college). Measures: Ss rated each of 8 hypothetical situations involving themselves, another person, and an impersonal entity for experienced pleasantness or unpleasantness. Results: No sex differences.

Ali, F., and Costello, J. Modification of the Peabody Picture Vocabulary Test. *Developmental Psychology*, 1971, 5, 86–91.
Subjects: N = 108; 4–5 yrs (black, low SES). Measures: Two comparable samples were given the PPVT and a modified version of the PPVT (MPPVT) that was designed to identify and modify aspects having adverse effects on disadvantaged preschoolers' performances. Results: No sex differences.

Allaman, J. D., Joyce, C. S., and Crandall, V. C. The antecedents of social desirability response tendencies of children and young adults. *Child Development*, 1972, 43, 1135–60.
Experiment I: Subjects: N = 95; tested at 0–80 mos and 6–10 yrs, and their mothers and fathers. Measures: (1) Until Ss reached 80 months of age, semiannual home observations were made of their mothers' behavior toward them. Mothers were rated on the following bipolar scales: Affectionateness: hostility-affection; Direction of Criticism: criticism-praise; Restrictiveness: permissive-restrictive; Severity of Punishment: mild-severe; Coerciveness of Suggestions: optional-mandatory; Acceleration Attempts: retardatory-acceleratory. The amount of praise or criticism Ss received for intellectual performance was also recorded. (2) Standards held by mother and father for intellectual performance were assessed from their responses to a questionnaire. (3) When Ss were between 6 and 12 years of age, they completed the Children's Social Desirability Scale. Results: (1) No differences were found between mothers of boys and mothers of girls. (2) There were no sex differences in standards held by mothers or fathers for intellectual performance. (3) Younger girls (6–9½ yrs) had higher CSD scores than younger boys (p < .05). No sex difference was found among older Ss.
Experiment II: Subjects: N = 65; tested at 0–40 mos, 41–80 mos, 80 mos–10 yrs, 18–26 yrs, and their mothers. Measures: (1) Until Ss were 10 years old, home observations were made of them and their mothers; 7 scales were used to rate mothers' behavior: Affectionateness, Direction of Criticism, Restrictiveness, Severity of Punishment, Coerciveness of Suggestions, Acceleration Attempts, and Intensity of Contact (indifference–high involvement). (2) When they were between 18 and 26 years of age, Ss were measured on the Marlowe-Crowne Social Desirability Scale. Results: (1) During each of the 3 age periods (0–40 mos, 41–80 mos, and 80 mos–10 yrs), no differences were found between mothers of boys and mothers of girls. (2) No sex differences were found in Ss' MC-SD scores.

Allen, C. N. Individual differences in delayed reaction of infants. *Archives of Psychology*, 1931, 19, 1–40.
Subjects: N = 100; 1 yr and mothers. Measures: S sat on his mother's lap while a desired toy was hidden in one of 3 small boxes placed on a table before him. The table was withdrawn far enough to place the boxes out of S's reach (distraction technique). After measured time intervals of 10, 20, 30, 45, and 60 seconds, the table was pushed back toward S. Speed of reaction was recorded. Results: No sex differences.

Allen, M. K., and Liebert, R. M. Effects of live and symbolic deviant modeling cues on adoption of a previously learned standard. *J. Personality & Social Psychology*, 1969, 11, 253–60.
Experiment I: Subjects: N = 24; 8–9 yrs. Measures: After receiving instructions from E to use a stringent self-reward standard when playing a bowling game, Ss were exposed to a lenient model. The performance measure was Ss' subsequent self-rewarding behavior. Results: No sex differences.
Experiment II: Subjects: N = 32; 7–9 yrs. Measures: Same as Experiment I, with Ss also exposed to a stringent model. Results: No sex differences.

Allen, S. A., Spear, P. S., and Johnson, J. Experimenter role effects on children's task performance and perception. *Child Development*, 1970, *40*, 1–9.

Subjects: $N = 256$; 10, 11 yrs. Measures: Ss played a marble-sorting game with either a warm or cold, male or female E. After a baseline period of 1 minute, Ss were verbally reinforced by E for a period of 6 minutes. Reinforcement was delivered on a fixed-interval schedule. Measures were taken of the number of marbles Ss sorted. Difference scores were also obtained (number of marbles sorted during each minute of reinforcement minus Ss' baseline rate of responding). Afterward, Ss were asked to describe E, using 23 pairs of bipolar adjectives. Results: (1) Boys and girls did not differ in their performances in the marble-dropping task. (2) Boys perceived Es as more masculine than did girls.

Allen, S. A., Spear, P. S., and Lucke, J. R. Effects of social reinforcement on learning and retention in children. *Developmental Psychology*, 1971, *5*, 73–80.

Subjects: $N = 192$; 6–7, 10–11 yrs. Measures: Ss were given either easy or difficult 2-choice simultaneous discrimination tasks under 1 of 3 reinforcement conditions—approval, disapproval, or silence. Retention was measured 8 days later. Results: There were no sex differences in response latency, total number of trials, or total task time.

Allen, V. L., and Newtson, D. Development of conformity and independence. *J. Personality & Social Psychology*, 1972, *22*, 18–30.

Subjects: $N = 366$; 6, 9, 12, 15 yrs. Measures: Ss were assigned to 1 of 3 conditions in an Asch-type conformity experiment—unanimous group, social support, and adult pressure. 3 types of stimuli were used: visual judgments, opinion statements, and delay of gratification preferences. For each S, a mean conformity score was calculated for each of the 3 types of stimuli. Results: No main sex differences.

Amatora, M. Comparisons in personality self-evaluation. *J. Social Psychology*, 1955, *42*, 315–21.

Subjects: $N = 1,000$; 9–13 yrs. Measures: Ss rated themselves on the Child Personality Scales. Results: Girls evaluated themselves more favorably than boys did on all but 3 scales.

Ammons, R. B., and Ammons, H. S. Parent preferences in young children's doll-play. *J. Abnormal & Social Psychology*, 1949, *44*, 490–505.

Subjects: $N = 48$; 3–5 yrs. Measures: Ss were asked parental preference during free play. In the doll-play measure, E had a child doll (same sex as S) go through actions of S's daily routine. S was repeatedly asked which parent he wanted to help him or to do things with him. Mother and father dolls were equally rewarding and punishing. S was observed during free play with dolls and then questioned on preference. The session was repeated a few days later. Parents were questioned about participation in activities with the child. Results: Overall, girls showed a preference for their mothers, boys showed a preference for their fathers. When separate age analyses were done, the difference between the sexes was found to be significant only among 4-year-olds.

Amster, H., and Wiegand, V. Developmental study of sex differences in free recall. *Proceedings*, 80th Annual Convention, American Psychological Association, 1972.

Subjects: $N = 64$; 7, 11 yrs. Measures: Ss heard, saw, and repeated words from 2 36-item lists, sorting each word card without regard to meaningful grouping on first 2 sorting trials. They were given either categorizing or sequential (no meaningful grouping) sorting instructions for the third trial, and categorizing for the fourth. Free recall was tested after the first 3 trials and after the fourth. Results: (1) There were no sex differences in the first recall. (2) Girls showed higher overall recall than boys.

Anders, T. R., Fozard, J. L., and Lillyquist, T. D. Effects of age upon retrieval from short-term memory. *Developmental Psychology*, 1972, *6*, 214–17.

Subjects: $N = 10$; 19–21 yrs. Measures: Ss saw a short list of visually presented digits (containing 1, 3, 5, or 7 items) 1 at a time, with instructions to memorize. Then Ss were presented with test digits and were asked to decide whether or not each digit had appeared in the previous list. Results: No sex differences in response latency.

Anderson, H. H. Domination and integration in the social behavior of young children in an experimental play situation. *Genetic Psychology Monographs*, 1937, *19*, 341–408.

Subjects: $N = 128$; 2–6 yrs (65 of the children were from an orphanage; 34 attended nursery school, 31 did not. These 31 Ss constituted the control group). Measures: Ss were taken in same-sex or opposite-sex pairs to a testing room where they were allowed to play for 5 minutes. Dominance behaviors (e.g. verbal demands or forceful attempts to secure materials from partner, verbal commands or forceful attempts to direct partner's behavior, etc.) and integrative behaviors (e.g. verbal requests to secure materials or direct partner's behavior, suggestions, attempts to share or participate in partner's activity, etc.) were recorded. **Results:** (1) Girls exhibited more dominance behaviors and fewer integrative behaviors than boys. (2) Among orphanage Ss, girl-girl (GG) pairs were more dominative than boy-boy (BB) pairs (for nursery school Ss, $p. < .01$; for control Ss, NS). No differences were found between boys in BG pairs and girls in GB pairs. Differences in integration scores between boys in BB pairs and girls in GG pairs or between boys in BG pairs and girls in GB pairs were also not significant. (3) No detailed analysis was made of the data from the nonorphanage sample.

Anderson, H. H. Domination and integration in the behavior of kindergarten children in an experimental play situation. *J. Experimental Education*, 1939, *8*, 123–31.
> **Subjects:** $N = 38$; 5 yrs. **Measures:** Ss in same-sex and opposite-sex pairs were observed in play for 5-minute periods. Ss were scored for dominance and integration. **Results:** (1) Boys in boy-boy (BB) pairs exhibited more dominance behaviors than girls in girl-girl (GG) pairs. Boys in BG pairs exhibited more dominance behaviors than girls in GG pairs. Girls in GB pairs exhibited more dominance behaviors than girls in GG pairs. (2) There were no differences between boys in BB pairs and boys in BG pairs, boys in BB pairs and girls in GB pairs, or boys in BG pairs and girls in GB pairs. (3) No sex differences were found in number of integrative behaviors displayed.

Anyan, W. R., Jr., and Quillian, W. W., II. The naming of primary colors by children. *Child Development*, 1971, *42*, 1629–32.
> **Subjects:** $N = 605$; 1–8 yrs. **Measures:** Ss were asked to (a) name colors presented on cards and (b) to copy several simple figures. **Results:** (1) Among 4-5-year-old Ss, girls named yellow more accurately than boys ($p < .025$). Among 5-6-year-old Ss, girls named each color more accurately than boys (red, $p < .001$; blue, $p < .001$; yellow, $p < .005$). (2) There were no sex differences in figure copying.

Appel, L. F., Cooper, R. G., McCarrell, N., Sims-Knight, J., Yussen, S. R., and Flavell, J. H. The development of the distinction between perceiving and memorizing. *Child Development*, 1972, *43*, 1365–81.
> **Subjects:** $N = 100$; 4, 7, 11 yrs. **Measures:** Ss looked at colored stimulus drawings and were asked to remember the names of pictures, under different conditions. During 1.5 minutes of each task, Ss' behavior was observed. A recall test was administered after each task. **Results:** (1) Among 7-year-old Ss, girls recalled more than boys ($p < .01$). (2) There were no sex differences among 4- and 11-year-old-Ss.

Argyle, M., and Dean, J. Eye-contact, distance, and affiliation. *Sociometry*, 1965, *28*, 289–304.
> **Subjects:** $N = 24$; 22–26 yrs (graduate students). **Measures:** Ss individually discussed TAT cards with confederates at different conversational distances. Confederates were instructed to gaze continually at Ss. The response variables were amount of eye contact and average length of each glance. **Results:** (1) No sex differences were found in amount of eye contact or length of glance. (2) Less eye contact was observed between mixed-sex confederate-S pairs; the difference was most marked at the shortest conversational distance ($p < .001$).

Arkoff, A., Meredith, G., and Iwahara, S. Dominance-deference patterning in Motherland-Japanese, Japanese-American, and Caucasian American students. *J. Social Psychology*, 1962, *58*, 61–66.
> **Subjects:** $N = 252$; 18–21 yrs (college). **Measures:** A dominance-deference scale, consisting of 10 dominance and 10 deference items, was administered. Ss were instructed to select the 10 items that best described themselves. The response measure was the number of dominance items chosen. **Results:** Among Caucasian American and Japanese Ss, men scored higher than women ($p < .01$, $p < .05$). No sex differences were found among Japanese-American Ss.

Armentrout, J. A., and Burger, G. K. Children's reports of parental child-rearing behavior at five grade levels. *Developmental Psychology*, 1972, *7*, 44–48.
> **Subjects:** $N = 635$; 9–13 yrs (low SES). **Measures:** Ss completed the revised Child's Report of Parental Behavior Inventory for each parent. **Results:** (1) Among 11- and 13-year-old Ss, girls reported greater parental acceptance than boys. (2) Boys reported greater overall parental psychological control than girls. (3) There were no sex differences in parental firmness of control.

Arnold, C. R. Role of discriminative stimuli in the formation of functional response to classes. *J. Experimental Child Psychology*, 1970, 9, 470–88.
    Subjects: $N = 96$; 7–8 yrs. **Measures:** Ss learned to say animal names while pushing buttons corresponding to chemical symbols or learned responses, separately. Then Ss simultaneously performed verbal and motor responses to various stimuli. **Results:** There were no sex differences in acquisition, transfer, or effect of different training conditions.

Aronfreed, J. The nature, variety, and social patterning of moral responses to transgression. *J. Abnormal & Social Psychology*, 1961, 63, 223–40.
    Subjects: $N = 122$; 11 yrs (low, middle SES). **Measures:** A projective story completion device was individually scored for the presence of a number of independently defined forms of moral response. **Results:** (1) Regardless of social status, boys emphasized external responsibility less than girls ($p < .05$), and were less dependent on an external initiation of their own moral reactions ($p < .05$ for middle SES Ss, $p < .01$ for low SES Ss). (2) Among middle SES Ss, girls showed a greater tendency than boys to display their moral reactions through expressions of remorse and promises of conformity ($p < .05$).

Aronson, E., and Cope, V. My enemy is my friend. *J. Personality & Social Psychology*, 1968, 8, 8–12.
    Subjects: $N = 80$; 18–21 yrs (college). **Measures:** Ss were treated either harshly or pleasantly by an E, and were then allowed to overhear E being treated either harshly or pleasantly by his supervisor. Ss were asked if they'd be willing to make some phone calls for the supervisor. Number of phone calls made was recorded. Ss also indicated how much they enjoyed working with E. **Results:** (1) No sex differences were found in number of phone calls made. (2) Men liked E more if he was pleasantly treated by the supervisor; women liked E more if he was harshly criticized by the supervisor ($p < .005$).

Aronson, E., and Gerard, E. Beyond Parkinson's Law: the effect of excess time on subsequent performance. *J. Personality & Social Psychology*, 1966, 3, 336–39.
    Subjects: $N = 32$; 18–21 yrs (college). **Measures:** Ss were allowed either too much time or a minimum of time to prepare a speech. Ss then worked at their own pace while preparing a second speech. Amount of time Ss used in preparing the second speech was recorded. **Results:** No sex differences.

Ashear, V., and Snortum, J. R. Eye contact in children as a function of age, sex, social and intellective variables. *Developmental Psychology*, 1971, 4, 479.
    Subjects: $N = 90$; 3–5, 7, 10, 13 yrs. **Measures:** Ss' speech patterns and eye contact with female E were recorded during an interview about interests and aspirations. **Results:** Girls showed more eye contact with E than boys while speaking and overall (including silence). There were no sex differences in eye contact during listening.

Ashton, R. Behavioral sleep cycles in the human newborn. *Child Development*, 1971, 42, 2098–100.
    Subjects: $N = 22$; 3 days (bottle-fed). **Measures:** Following feeding, Ss were observed for a period of 2–3 hours. Sleep cycles were studied. Measures were taken of the durations of the successive epochs of sleep and of the frequency of startling in these epochs. **Results:** No sex differences.

Ault, R. L., Crawford, D. E., and Jeffrey, W. E. Visual scanning strategies of reflective, impulsive, fast-accurate, and slow-inaccurate children on the Matching Familiar Figures Test. *Child Development*, 1972, 43, 1412–17.
    Subjects: $N = 29$; 8–10 yrs. **Measures:** Ss were given 30 problems to solve from the Matching Familiar Figures Test (MFF), during which time their visual scanning strategies were recorded. 4 weeks later, teachers rated Ss on an attention scale, a motivation scale, and a hyperactivity scale (irrelevant talk or play). **Results:** (1) There were no sex differences in performance on the MFF. (2) There were no sex differences in teachers' ratings of Ss on the attention scale. (3) Teachers rated boys more hyperactive than girls ($p < .01$).

Axtell, B., and Cole, C. W. Repression-sensitization response mode and verbal avoidance. *J. Personality & Social Psychology*, 1971, 18, 133–37.
    Subjects: $N = 96$; 18–21 yrs (college). **Measures:** After completing the Health and Opinion Questionnaire, a measure of R-S, Ss were asked to discuss themselves positively or negatively. Half of the Ss were exposed to prerecorded verbal feedback during their discussion. The response measure was the duration of S's verbalization. **Results:** No sex differences.

Babad, E. Y. Person specificity of the "social deprivation satiation effect," *Developmental Psychology*, 1972, 6, 210–13.
    Subjects: $N = 40$; 8 yrs. **Measures:** Ss were given a 10-minute treatment in which the stimulus word "good" was received either 2 times (deprivation) or 16 times (satiation), followed by a discrimination-learning task in which each correct response was reinforced with "good." **Results:** No main sex differences were found in number of correct responses. Girls performed better than boys in the deprivation condition, whereas the reverse was true among Ss in the satiation condition ($p < .05$).

Backman, M. E. Patterns of mental abilities: ethnic, socioeconomic, and sex differences. *American Educational Research Journal*, 1972, 9, 1–12.
    Subjects: $N = 2,925$; 17 yrs (participants from Project TALENT: Jewish white, non-Jewish white, black, Oriental). **Measures:** 60 information achievement and aptitude tests were administered to Ss; 6 mental ability factors were examined: Verbal Knowledge, English Language, Mathematics, Visual Reasoning, Perceptual Speed and Accuracy, and Memory. **Results:** Sex was related to both shape and level of performance patterns ($p < .001$). Girls scored higher than boys on ENG, PSA, and MEM; boys scored higher than girls on VKN, MAT, and VIS.

Baldwin, C. P., and Baldwin, A. L. Children's judgments of kindness. *Child Development*, 1970, 41, 29–47.
    Subjects: $N = 696$; 5, 7, 9, 11, 13, 18–21 yrs (college). **Measures:** Ss read pairs of stories with pictures and were asked to choose the picture in which they thought the child involved was kinder. The subjects of stories were both girls or both boys. All Ss were asked to explain their choices, and responses were coded. **Results:** (1) There were no sex differences for the adult sample. (2) On only one story boys gave more adult responses than girls did ($p < .05$).

Baldwin, T. L., McFarlane, P. T., and Garvey, C. J. Children's communication accuracy related to race and socioeconomic status. *Child Development*, 1971, 42, 345–57.
    Subjects: $N = 96$; 10 yrs (white and black, low and middle SES). **Measures:** Ss were arranged in matched sex, SES, and race pairs. One S had 7 pictures and the other had 1. The task was to verbally communicate which of the 7 pictures the 1 matched. **Results:** No sex differences.

Balint, M. Individual differences of behavior in early infancy and an objective method for recording them. *J. Genetic Psychology*, 1948, 73, 57–117.
    Subjects: $N = 100$; 1 day–9 mos. **Measures:** The number of sucks in each 10-second interval was recorded. **Results:** (1) No sex differences were found in basic frequency, restart frequency, or second frequency. (2) Quivering was observed in more girls than boys.

Baltes, P. B., and Nesselroade, J. R. Cultural change and adolescent personality development. *Developmental Psychology*, 1972, 7, 244–56.
    Subjects: $N = 1,249$; 12–16 yrs. **Measures:** Cattell's (1964) High School Personality Questionnaire was administered to Ss twice (once in 1970 and again in 1971) for assessment of ontogenetic (age-related) vs. generational (cohort-related) change in adolescent personality development. **Results:** (1) Boys were more reserved, detached, dominant, surgent, adventurous, and self-sufficient than girls. Boys had greater ego strength than girls. (2) Girls scored higher in general intellectual ability, had greater superego strength, and were more sensitive, zestful, guilt-prone, and tense than boys. (3) There were no sex differences on the lax-controlled dimension or the phlegmatic temperament–excitability dimension.

Baltes, P. B., and Wender, K. Age differences in pleasantness of visual patterns of different variability in late childhood and adolescence. *Child Development*, 1971, 42, 47–55.
    Subjects: $N = 120$; 9, 11, 13, 15 yrs (Germany). **Measures:** Ss viewed 2 sets of 70 stimuli (random dots and random shapes). As S viewed 1 set, each stimulus appeared for 3 seconds, then for 7 seconds, followed by a 10-second interval during which Ss were asked to indicate on a 9-point scale how they liked the stimulus. **Results:** No sex differences.

Baltes, P. B., Schaie, K. W., and Nardi, A. H. Age and experimental mortality in seven-year longitudinal study of cognitive behavior. *Developmental Psychology*, 1971, 5, 18–26.
    Subjects: $N = 280$; 21–70 yrs. **Measures:** The 5 subtests of the Intermediate Form of the Primary Mental Abilities Test (Verbal Meaning, Space, Reasoning, Arithmetic, and Word Fluency) and Schaie's Test of Behavioral Rigidity were administered to Ss. Estimated factor scores for 3 second-order ability factors (General Intelligence, Cognitive Flexibility, and Visuo-motor Flexibility) were analyzed for sex differences. **Results:** No sex differences were

found in General Intelligence or Cognitive Flexibility. The direction of the significant sex difference in Visuo-motor Flexibility was not specified.

Ban, P. L., and Lewis, M. Mothers and fathers, girls and boys: attachment behavior in the one-year-old. Paper presented at the meetings of the Eastern Psychological Association, New York, April 1971.

Subjects: $N = 20$; 1 yr. Measures: On 2 different occasions, Ss were observed in a free-play situation. Ss were tested once in the presence of their mothers and once in the presence of their fathers. Parents were told to respond to their children, but not to initiate any interaction; 4 attachment behaviors were recorded: time spent touching parent, time spent looking at parent, time spent vocalizing to parent, and time spent in proximity to parent. Results: (1) No main sex differences were found. (2) Boys spent more time looking at their fathers than at their mothers; no such difference was found for girls. (3) Both sexes directed more proximal behavior toward their mothers than toward their fathers ($p < .01$ for touching; $p < .001$ for proximity-seeking). (4) Both sexes spent more time vocalizing to their mothers than to their fathers ($p < .05$).

Bandura, A., and Harris, M. B. Modification of syntactic style. *J. Experimental Child Psychology*, 1966, *4*, 341–52.

Subjects: $N = 100$; 7 yrs. Measures: The roles of appropriate modeling cues, reinforcement variables, and strong attentional responses in the modification of syntactic style were derived from sentences Ss composed using stimulus words scored for frequency of passives and prepositional phrases. Results: During baseline, more boys than girls produced at least 1 passive sentence. No other sex differences were found.

Bandura, A., and Huston, A. C. Identification as a process of incidental learning. *J. Abnormal & Social Psychology*, 1961, *63*, 311–18.

Subjects: $N = 48$; 3–5 yrs. Measures: Ss performed diverting, 2-choice discrimination problem with a female model, who exhibited explicit, but functionless behavior. Ss experienced either a rewarding interaction or a cold, non-nurturant relationship with the model prior to the task. The measure of performance was the extent to which Ss reproduced the model's behavior. Results: No sex differences.

Bandura, A., and Jeffery, R. W. Role of symbolic coding and rehearsal processes in observational learning. *J. Personality & Social Psychology*, 1973, *26*, 122–30.

Subjects: $N = 88$; 18–21 yrs (college). Measures: Ss observed a filmed model perform complex movement configurations. Observational learning and retention were measured. Results: No sex differences.

Bandura, A., and Kupers, C. J. Transmission of patterns of self-reinforcement through modeling. *J. Abnormal & Social Psychology*, 1964, *69*, 1–9.

Subjects: $N = 160$; 7–9 yrs. Measures: Ss self-reinforcement patterns were assessed after exposure to either peer or adult models who exhibited either a high or a low criterion for self-reinforcement. Results: No sex-of-subject or sex-of-model effects were found.

Bandura, A., and Menlove, F. L. Factors determining vicarious extinction of avoidance behavior through symbolic modeling. *J. Personality & Social Psychology*, 1968, *8*, 99–108.

Subjects: $N = 48$; 3–5 yrs. Measures: Ss were initially given a test of avoidance behavior to identify those Ss fearful of dogs. Ss were then exposed to a graduated series of films in which a model interacted nonanxiously with a dog. Following completion of the treatment series, Ss were given the same avoidance test twice (immediately afterward and approximately 1 month later). Results: No sex differences were found in the effectiveness of the treatment series.

Bandura, A., and Mischel, W. Modification of self-imposed delay of reward through exposure to live and symbolic models. *J. Personality & Social Psychology*, 1965, *2*, 698–705.

Subjects: $N = 120$; 9–10 yrs. Measures: From a larger group of approximately 250, children who exhibited predominately either immediate-reward or delayed-reward patterns of behavior were assigned to 1 of 3 treatment conditions. One group of Ss was exposed to a live adult model who exhibited delay-of-reward responses counter to their predominate response patterns, while a second group of Ss was exposed to a symbolic model. Ss in a third group had no exposure to any models. Immediately afterward and again 1 month later, Ss chose between less valuable immediate rewards and more valuable delayed rewards. Results: No sex differences.

Bandura, A., and Perloff, B. Relative efficacy of self-monitored and externally imposed reinforcement systems. *J. Personality & Social Psychology*, 1968, 7, 111–16.
    Subjects: $N = 80$; 7–10 yrs. **Measures:** Ss performed a task in which progressively higher scores could be achieved by turning a wheel on a mechanical device. After selecting their own performance standards, Ss in 1 group were instructed to reward themselves with tokens whenever they attained their self-imposed standards. For Ss in a second group, the same performance standards were externally imposed and the reinforcers were automatically delivered. **Results:** (1) No sex differences were found in self-imposed performance standards. (2) Boys performed more responses than girls ($p < .05$).

Bandura, A., and Whalen, C. K. The influence of antecedent reinforcement and divergent modeling cues on patterns of self-reward. *J. Personality & Social Psychology*, 1966, 3, 373–82.
    Subjects: $N = 160$; 8–11 yrs. **Measures:** Ss were exposed to a same-sex model who either (a) adopted a high criterion for self-reward and performed the experimental task (a bowling game) at a superior level, (b) adopted a low criterion for self-reward and performed at an inferior level, or (c) adopted a moderately high criterion for self-reward and performed at a moderately high performance level. Ss then performed the game in the model's absence. Measures were taken of the performance scores for which Ss rewarded themselves. **Results:** (1) No sex differences were found in the number of reinforcers Ss administered to themselves for low and superior performance scores. Girls rewarded themselves with more reinforcers than boys did for moderately high performance scores ($p < .001$). (2) No sex differences were found in frequency of self-reinforcement. (3) With the exception of the superior model condition, where there was no sex difference, boys displayed a greater amount of verbal self-reinforcement than girls did.

Bandura, A., Grusec, J. E., and Menlove, F. L. Observational learning as a function of symbolization and incentive set. *Child Development*, 1966, 37, 499–506.
    Subjects: $N = 72$; 6–8 yrs. **Measures:** Children watched a movie in which an adult male model exhibited a series of novel behavior patterns. They were randomly assigned to 1 of 3 conditions: (1) facilitative symbolization—Ss were instructed to verbalize every action of the model as it was being performed in the movie, (2) passive observation—Ss were simply instructed to pay close attention to the movie, and (3) competing symbolization—Ss were instructed to pay close attention to the movie while counting repeatedly. Half of the Ss were assigned to the incentive-set condition, in which they were told they would be asked to demonstrate what they learned in the movie, and half of the Ss were placed in the no-incentive-set condition, in which they were told they would return to class immediately following the movie. After the movie, each S was asked to demonstrate all of the model's responses they could recall. **Results:** Boys produced a higher number of matching responses than girls did.

Bandura, A., Grusec, J. E., and Menlove, F. L. Some social determinants of self-monitoring reinforcement systems. *J. Personality & Social Psychology*, 1967, 5, 449–55.
    Subjects: $N = 128$; 7–11 yrs. **Measures:** Ss were initially exposed to a same-sex adult model who performed a task (bowling game) at a consistently superior level and adopted a high criterion of self-reward. Afterward, Ss either did or did not observe a peer model perform less well and adopt a lower standard of self-reward. Ss then played the bowling game alone, receiving instructions to reward themselves with tokens whenever they felt they had performed well. **Results:** No sex differences were found in either the number of rewards Ss administered to themselves or in the percentage of trials Ss rewarded themselves for performances below the criterion adopted by the adult model.

Banikiotes, F. G., Montgomery, A. A., and Banikiotes, P. G. Male and female auditory reinforcement of infant vocalizations. *Developmental Psychology*, 1972, 6, 476–81.
    Subjects: $N = 16$; 3 mos. **Measures:** Infants' vocalizations were counted after baseline (non-reinforced) and conditioning stages. Each S received auditory reinforcement for vocalizations from a male in 1 conditioning stage and from a female in the other conditioning stage. **Results:** No sex differences.

Barclay, A. M. The effect of female aggressiveness on aggressive and sexual fantasies. *J. Projective Techniques & Personality Assessment*, 1970, 34, 19–26.
    Subjects: $N = 55$; 18–21 yrs (college). **Measures:** After being angered by a hostile female E, Ss wrote stories to 2 male-dominant (MD) and 2 female-dominant (FD) TAT pictures. **Results:** (1) Men expressed more aggressive imagery than women did. More aggression was expressed toward FD pictures than toward MD pictures. (2) Men expressed more sexual

imagery than women did. (3) No sex differences were found in aggressive defensiveness imagery. More aggressive defensiveness imagery was expressed toward FD pictures than toward MD pictures. (4) As assessed by a postexperimental questionnaire, no sex differences were found in level of arousal.

Barnard, J. W. The effects of anxiety on connotative meaning. *Child Development*, 1966, 37, 461–72.
Subjects: $N = 220$; 10 yrs. Measures: Ss who received either high or low scores on the Test Anxiety Scale for Children were asked to rate concepts related to school on the semantic differential (SD). The SD was administered under either evaluative or nonevaluative conditions. Results: Girls rated the concepts more positively than boys.

Barnes, K. E. Preschool play norms: a replication. *Developmental Psychology*, 1971, 5, 88–103.
Subjects: $N = 42$; 3–5 yrs. Measures: Play behavior categories of unoccupied, solitary, onlooker, parallel, associative, and cooperative were scored during 10 minutes of free-play observation. Results: No sex differences.

Barthol, R. P. Individual and sex differences in cortical conductivity. *J. Personality*, 1958, 26, 365–78.
Subjects: $N = 106$; 18–21 yrs (college). Measures: Measurements of the movement-simultaneity threshold (phi phenomenon) were correlated with measures of the kinesthetic figural aftereffect for men and women. Movement refers to a report of a single light moving back and forth; simultaneity refers to a report of 2 stimuli appearing rapidly and approximately at the same time. Results: No sex differences.

Bartol, C. R., and Pielstick, N. L. The effects of ambiguity, familiarization, age, and sex on stimulus preference. *J. Experimental Child Psychology*, 1972, 14, 21–29.
Subjects: $N = 45$; 7, 11, 18–21 yrs (college). Measures: During the slide presentation of pairs of ambiguous-unambiguous figures, looking time was recorded. Results: (1) There were no main sex differences. (2) Among 7- and 11-year-old Ss, boys viewed ambiguous stimuli longer than girls did. (3) Among 18 to 21-year-old Ss, women viewed ambiguous stimuli longer than men did.

Barton, K. Block manipulation by children as a function of social reinforcement, anxiety, arousal, and ability pattern. *Child Development*, 1971, 42, 817–26.
Subjects: $N = 64$; 9–10 yrs (half of the Ss were high verbal–low spatial (HV-LS) and half were high spatial–low verbal (HS-LV) on the basis of Thurstone's Primary Mental Abilities Test). Measures: Baseline Palmer Sweat Index (PSI) was established for each S. S played with blocks during either social reinforcement or no reinforcement. Number and complexity of structures were measured, as were PSI and state of anxiety (State-Trait Anxiety Inventory). Results: Girls were more anxious than boys on the questionnaire ($p < .01$) during 2 of 3 administrations.

Batchelor, T. R., and Tesser, A. Attitude base as a moderator of the attitude similarity-attraction relationship. *J. Personality & Social Psychology*, 1971, 91, 229–36.
Subjects: $N = 406$; 18–21 yrs (college). Measures: After completing an attitude questionnaire, Ss were given information about other individuals, including each other's attitude on a topic (similar-dissimilar) and the reason given for holding this attitude. Ss then recorded their impressions of each other on a modified version of the Byrne Interpersonal Judgment Scale. Results: No sex differences.

Battle, E. S. Motivational determinants of academic task persistence. *J. Personality & Social Psychology*, 1965, 2, 209–18.
Subjects: $N = 74$; 12–14 yrs. Measures: Ss indicated on a 10-point scale the personal importance of doing well in math. Results: No sex differences.

Battle, E. S. Motivational determinants of academic competence. *J. Personality & Social Psychology*, 1966, 4, 634–42.
Subjects: Approximately 500; 12–14 yrs. Measures: For 2 subject areas, English and mathematics, Ss indicated (a) the lowest grade they could get and still be satisfied, (b) how certain they were that they could achieve that grade, (c) the grade they expected to receive on their next report card, and (d) the importance to them of doing well in that area. Ss also listed their favorite academic subject and the 2 school subjects they thought they were "best"

in. **Results:** (1) Boys thought it was more important to do well in mathematics than girls did ($p < .001$). (2) Boys expected to perform better in English than girls did ($p < .001$). The lowest grade that boys reported they would be satisfied with was higher than the grade girls reported ($p < .001$). Girls were more certain than boys, however, that they would achieve the grade they indicated ($p < .001$). Girls thought it was more important to do well than boys did ($p < .001$). (3) Boys chose English as their favorite subject and listed it as their "best" subject less frequently than girls did ($p < .01$, $p < .001$). No sex differences were found in the frequency with which math was chosen as the favorite subject.

Battle, E. S., and Lacey, B. A context of hyperactivity in children, over time. *Child Development*, 1972, *43*, 757–73.
> **Subjects:** $N = 74$; 18–26 yrs. **Measures:** Observational data for Ss had been collected at 6-month intervals from birth to 6 years at home, and from 6 to 12 years at the Fels Day Camp. Interview data were available for 60 of 74 Ss at ages 12–18. 65 out of the 74 Ss were assessed in interviews at ages 18–26 concerning motivational and behavioral variables. Data were divided into 5 age periods and rated for evidence of hyperactivity. **Results:** Among 6-10-year-old Ss, boys were rated more hyperactive than girls were ($p < .05$).

Baumrind, D. Current patterns of parental authority. *Developmental Psychology Monograph*, 1971, *4*.
> EXPERIMENT I: **Subjects:** $N = 238$; 3, 4 yrs. **Measures:** Episodes of interpersonal and social behavior were recorded while Ss engaged in activities in nursery school. In addition, each S was observed and rated while taking the Stanford-Binet. **Results:** Boys displayed more hostility to peers and more resistiveness to adult supervision than girls ($p < .01$, $p < .01$). Boys were also more domineering; girls, on the other hand, were more tractable. No sex differences were found in dominance, purposiveness, independence, or achievement orientation.
>
> EXPERIMENT II: **Subjects:** $N = 293$; parents of 3- and 4-year-old children. **Measures:** Parent's behavior toward their children was recorded. **Results:** (1) Fathers were more firm with their sons than with their daughters. No differences were found between fathers of boys and fathers of girls on the following dimensions: encouragement of independence and individuality; passiveness and acceptance; rejection; encouragement of nonconformity; authoritarianism. (2) No differences were found between mothers of boys and mothers of girls on the following dimensions: firm enforcement; encouragement of independence and individuality; passiveness and acceptance; rejection; self-confident, secure, potent parental behavior. (3) No differences were found between parents of boys and parents of girls on the following dimensions: expectation of participation in household chores; enrichment of child's environment; directiveness; discouragement of emotional dependency; discouragement of infantile behavior.
>
> EXPERIMENT III: **Subjects:** $N = 415$; parents of 3- and 4-year-old children. **Measures:** Parents' child-rearing attitudes and values were assessed in individual interviews. **Results:** (1) No differences were found between mothers of boys and mothers of girls or between fathers of boys and fathers of girls on the following dimensions: early maturity demands; values conformity; anger over lack of control; firm enforcement; encouragement of nonconformity; discouragement of infantile behavior; authoritarianism. (2) No differences were found between mothers of boys and mothers of girls on the following dimensions (these dimensions did not appear for fathers): impatience; consistent, articulated child-rearing philosophy.

Baumrind, D., and Black, A. E. Socialization practices associated with dimensions of competence in preschool boys and girls. *Child Development*, 1967, *38*, 291–327.
> **Subjects:** $N = 103$; 3-4 yrs and their mothers and fathers. **Measures:** (1) Ss were observed in their classrooms by a pair of psychologists who used a 95-item Q-sort to describe each child's behavior. (2) 95 of the 103 families were visited at home. After being interviewed separately, mothers and fathers were rated on their attitudes and child-rearing practices. **Results:** (1a) On the Q-sort, boys were rated higher on "high energy level," "good sense of humor," "contentedness," "does not seek assurance that he is liked," "explores environment," and "takes initiative in making friends," while girls were rated higher on "acts too mature," "enjoys aesthetic experiences," "exploits dependent state," "interested in pre-primer skills," "guileful and manipulative," and "chatters to obtain attention." (1b) No sex differences were found on the following items: alienates vs. attracts other children; able vs. not able to form close friendships; uses vs. does not use persuasion to get what he wants; affiliative, supportive vs. negativistic; irritable vs. even-tempered; obstructive vs. helpful; becomes hostile vs. does not become hostile when hurt or frustrated; helps vs. does not help other children adapt;

impulsive vs. self-controlled; impetuous vs. deliberate; thoughtless, inconsiderate vs. thoughtful, considerate; disrespectful vs. courteous demeanor with adults; provokes vs. avoids conflict with adults; responsible vs. irresponsible about following rules; affectionate vs. unaffectionate with nursery school staff; submits to group consensus vs. takes independent stand; conforming vs. willing to risk adult disapproval; suggestible vs. has mind of own; listens vs. actively participates in discussions; an interesting, arresting child vs. uninteresting and bland; imaginative; emotionally expressive vs. bland; produces stereotyped vs. original work; curious vs. lacks curiosity; gives up vs. perseveres when adversity is encountered; stretches to meet vs. retreats from performance demands; sets easy vs. hard goals to achieve; hazards failure vs. avoids difficult tasks; withdraws vs. stands his ground when hurt or frustrated; high vs. low self-confidence; at ease vs. ill at ease at nursery school; apprehensive vs. nonapprehensive; self-abasive vs. self-valuing; indecisive vs. resolute about making decisions; does not vs. does regret wrong-doing; dependable, trustworthy vs. undependable, untrustworthy; bullies vs. avoids forcing will on other children; managerial and bossy vs. tactful and modest; permits self to be dominated vs. will not submit; not easily vs. easily intimidated or bullied; seldom vs. often spends time in withdrawn fantasy; poorly vs. well oriented in his environment; does not vs. does become pleasurably involved in tasks; gives his best vs. expends little effort; enjoys vs. avoids new learning experiences. (2a) Mothers of boys were rated higher than mothers of girls on "negative sanctions: deprivation of privileges" and "tolerance of verbal protest." Mothers of girls were rated higher than mothers of boys on "strictness regarding neatness," "demands for obedience," "negative sanctions: withdrawal of love," "control of verbal and/or physical aggression toward parent," and "maturity expectations: does not reward dependency." No differences were found between fathers of boys and fathers of girls on the above items. (2b) Fathers of boys were rated higher than fathers of girls on "negative sanctions: corporal punishment," "positive sanctions as reinforcers: tangible reward," and "directiveness: restrictions on child's initiative." No differences were found between mothers of boys and mothers of girls on the preceding items. (2c) No differences were found between mothers of boys and mothers of girls or between fathers of boys and fathers of girls on the following items: strictness in care of family property, in responsibilities about orderliness, in aggression toward other children, and in television; negative sanctions on isolation and on frightening the child; parents' feeling of control over the child; lack of internal conflict about disciplinary procedures; parent's appraisal of his/her general influence on child; consistency: follow-through in discipline; consistency: child-rearing practices; consistency of discipline: parental agreement; reason for restrictions; an absolutist ethical imperative; maturity expectation; household responsibilities; maturity expectation, rewarding of self-sufficiency, and intellectual achievement expected; independence, encouraging contact with other adults, and introducing child to new experiences; communication, attentiveness to child's communication, and expression of negative feelings to child; individual character of child perceived; warmth, presence of loving relationship, demonstrativeness, approval, absence of hostility, empathy, and sympathy; conscientiousness, keeping track of child, sacrificing own needs to those of children, and acceptance of responsibility.

Bayley, N. Data on the growth of intelligence between 16 and 21 years as measured by the Wechsler-Bellevue Scale. *J. Genetic Psychology*, 1957, *90*, 3–15.
Subjects: $N = 33$; tested at 16, 18, 21 yrs (Berkeley Growth Study). Measures: Wechsler-Bellevue Adult Intelligence Scale. Results: Both sexes showed similar increases in intelligence over the 5-year period.

Bayley, N., and Oden, M. The maintenance of intellectual ability in gifted adults. *J. Gerontology*, 1955, *10*, 91–107.
EXPERIMENT I: Subjects: $N = 768$; tested at 29, 41 yrs (Ss were taken from Terman's Study of the Gifted). Measures: At each testing, Ss were given the Concept Mastery Test. The test is composed of 2 subtests: (1) Synonyms and Antonyms and (2) Analogies. Results: At the initial testings, men scored higher on the Analogies subtest than women. At the later testing, men scored higher than women on the Analogies subtest and on both subtests combined.
EXPERIMENT II: Subjects: $N = 334$, tested at 29, 41 yrs (Ss were the spouses of the men and women in the sample above). Measures: Concept Mastery Test. Results: At the initial testing, men scored higher on the Analogies subtest than women. At the later testing, men had higher Analogies subtest and overall scores than women.
EXPERIMENT III: Subjects: $N = 168$; 29 yrs (Ss were originally part of Terman's Study). Measures: Concept Mastery Test. Results: No sex differences were found in overall scores.
EXPERIMENT IV: Subjects: $N = 227$; 41 yrs (Ss were originally part of Terman's Study). Measures: Concept Mastery Test. Results: Men had higher overall scores than women.

Beckwith, L. Relationships between attributes of mothers and their infants' IQ scores. *Child Development*, 1971, *42*, 1083–97.
Subjects: $N = 24$; tested at 8, 10 mos (adopted infants). **Measures:** S was given the Cattell Infant Intelligence Scale and motor items from the Gesell Developmental Schedules at each of 2 visits. Mother and S were observed during 1 hour of spontaneous interaction and care-taking activities. **Results:** No sex differences (even though female Ss' natural mothers were more educated).

Beckwith, L. Relationships between infants' social behavior and their mothers' behavior. *Child Development*, 1972, *43*, 397–411 (and personal communication).
Subjects: $N = 24$; tested at 7–9 mos (session 1), 8–11 mos (session 2). **Measures:** Mothers and their adopted children were observed in their homes for 2 1-hour sessions. Measures were taken of the frequency with which mothers touched and talked to their infants and of the amount of freedom they gave their infants to explore objects and places. Two infant measures were also recorded: number of social approaches to mother, and ratio of number of 30-second intervals Ss responded to mother to number of 30-second intervals in which mother initiated contact. At the end of each session, Ss' reactions to the observer were assessed in 4 standard-ized situations (Rheingold Social Responsiveness Scale). **Results:** (1) No differences were found between mothers of boys and mothers of girls in the amount they touched or talked to their infants. (2) Mothers with only a high school education treated boys particularly restric-tively. (3) No sex differences were found in number of social approaches to mother. (4) Girls were more socially responsive to their mothers in the second session than boys were ($p < .05$, one-tailed test). No difference was found in the first session. (5) Boys were more responsive to the observer on the Rheingold Social Responsiveness Scale than girls ($p < .05$).

Bedell, J., and Sistrunk, F. Power, opportunity costs, and sex in a mixed-motive game. *J. Personality & Social Psychology*, 1973, *25*, 219–26.
Subjects: $N = 90$; 18–21 yrs (college). **Measures:** Ss played the Prisoner's Dilemma game in same-sex or opposite-sex pairs. On every fifth trial, S was given the opportunity to either add or subtract 4 points from his partner's score. A third response also available ("none") did not affect the other's score. **Results:** (1) No differences were found between male and mixed-sex dyads in number of mutually cooperative responses. Both were more cooperative than female dyads ($p < .01$). (2) Both male and mixed-sex dyads showed an increase in number of mutually cooperative responses across trial blocks; female dyads showed no change ($p < .05$). (3) Following DC, CC, or DD trials, Ss in the male and mixed-sex dyads made cooperative responses more often than Ss in the female dyads. No differences were found following CD trials. (The first letter represents S's response, the second represents partner's response; C = cooperative, D = competitive.) (4) Ss in mixed-sex dyads rewarded their partners more often than Ss in the female dyads. No differences were found between male and mixed-sex dyads or between male and female dyads. (5) Ss in the mixed-sex dyads punished their partners less frequently than Ss in the female dyads. No differences were found between male and mixed-sex dyads or between male and female dyads.

Bee, H. L. Parent-child interaction and distractibility in 9-year-old children. *Merrill-Palmer Quarterly*, 1967, *13*, 175–90 (and unpublished doctoral dissertation, Stanford University, 1964).
Subjects: $N = 36$; 9 yrs and parents. **Measures:** Initially, Ss were assigned to distractible and nondistractible groups based upon the difference in their problem-solving performance under conditions of distraction and no distraction. All Ss were then observed in problem-solving interaction with their parents. **Results:** (1) No sex differences were found in the specificity of the suggestions or in the amount of positive or negative encouragement given to them by their parents. Mothers of nondistractible boys gave less negative encouragement than mothers of distractible boys did; for girls, the reverse was true ($p < .05$). (2) There were no sex differences in rate of suggestive and nonsuggestive interaction. Among parents of distractible Ss, boys' parents gave the greatest relative number of suggestions; among parents of non-distractible Ss, girls' parents gave the greatest relative number of suggestions ($p < .001$). (3) There were no sex differences in number of bids for help or attention. (4) More boys than girls spoke first in the presence of their parents (not tested for significance).

Bee, H. L., Van Egeren, L. F., Streissguth, A. P., Nyman, B. A., and Leckie, M. S. Social class differences in maternal teaching strategies and speech patterns. *Developmental Psychology*, 1969, *1*, 726–34 (and personal communication).
Subjects: $N = 114$; 4–5 yrs and their mothers (76 black and white low SES, 38 white middle

SES). **Measures:** Mothers were observed in an unstructured "waiting room" situation and in a structured problem-solving situation with the child. The waiting room response measures were mother's rates of control statements, suggestions, approval, ignoring, disapproval, questions, information statements, and attention; child's rates of acceptance, rejection, general seeking, ignoring, questions, demands, information statements, toy shifts, and space shifts. The problem-solving response measures were mother's rates of nonquestion suggestions, question suggestions, positive feedback, negative feedback, and nonverbal intrusions; mean specificity of mother's suggestions; child's rates of acceptance, rejection, and dependency bids; and total time spent on problem. **Results:** (1) No main sex-of-child effects were found. (2) Mothers of middle SES girls gave more information and positive feedback than mothers of middle SES boys; in the low SES sample, mothers of girls gave less information and positive feedback than mothers of boys. (3) Mothers of low SES boys expressed disapproval of their child's actions more often than mothers of low SES girls. No difference was found among middle SES mothers. (4) During the problem-solving session, middle SES mothers of boys and low SES mothers of girls interacted with their child to a greater extent than their SES counterparts did (overall measure).

Beilin, H. Feedback and infralogical strategies in invariant area conceptualization. *J. Experimental Child Psychology*, 1966, *3*, 267–78.
   Subjects: $N = 236$; 6, 7 yrs. **Measures:** There was an attempt to improve performance in a quasi-conservation task where high rate of error was previously reported. Translocation, iteration, and feedback training methods were used. Number of correct quasi-conservation responses and classified verbal reports was analyzed (categorized in terms of infralogical strategies used). **Results:** There were no sex differences before or after conservation performance training, or in use of infralogical strategies.

Beilin, H., and Kagan, J. Pluralization rules and the conceptualization of number. *Developmental Psychology*, 1969, *1*, 697–706.
   EXPERIMENT I: **Subjects:** $N = 78$; 4 yrs (private nursery school). **Measures:** (1) Pluralization rules were tested for nouns, possessives, and verbs. (2) Number of conceptualizations was assessed from a discrimination task using quantitative propertives. If S reached criterion in 45 trials, he was shifted to reverse concept. **Results:** (1) There were no sex differences in proportion of Ss among concept attainers and reversers. (2) There were no sex differences in trials to concept attainment. (3) Girls did better than boys did in attaining reversal criterion.
   EXPERIMENT II: **Subjects:** $N = 96$; 4 yrs (private nursery school). **Measures:** Ss were divided into 5 training groups and a control group: 3 training groups consisted of Ss who failed both the verb pluralization and concept attainment pretests, and were trained in number conceptualization, pluralization, or both; 2 other training groups consisted of Ss who passed 1 of pretest and received training on the pretest they failed. The control Ss failed both pretests and received no training. **Results:** No sex differences.

Beiswenger, H. Linguistic and psychological factors in the speech regulation of behavior in young children. *J. Experimental Child Psychology*, 1971, *11*, 63–75.
   Subjects: $N = 48$; 2–4 yrs. **Measures:** Ss were given 2 sets of verbal commands, the first consisting of conditional and nonconditional commands to respond to a sequence of visual signals ("When the blue light comes on, get a blue marble and put it in the dish"), the second requiring mental transformation of the spatial relationship of the target ("Touch the toothbrush with the spoon"). **Results:** No sex differences.

Bell, R. Q., and Costello, N. S. Three tests for sex differences in tactile sensitivity in the newborn. *Biologica Neonatorium*, 1964, *7*, 335–47.
   EXPERIMENT I: **Subjects:** $N = 21$; 4 days (bottle-fed infants born to primiparae). **Measures:** A weighted index of observed movements was obtained before and after removal of a covering blanket. **Results:** Girls showed a higher movement index than boys after removal of the blanket ($p < .05$).
   EXPERIMENT II: **Subjects:** $N = 17$; 3 days (bottle-fed infants born to primiparae). **Measures:** Time-sampled observations of movements of eyeballs, mouth, face, head, and hands were recorded. When all Ss reached a comparable level of arousal, several skin surfaces were stimulated by an air jet. The threshold of the flow of air was measured at the time the infant responded. Each S was tested twice in 2 testing sessions, separated by at least 16 minutes. **Results:** Girls showed lower thresholds for abdomen areas than boys.
   EXPERIMENT III: **Subjects:** $N = 74$; 3 days (breast-fed and bottle-fed infants born to multiparae). **Measures:** Observations were made from the time immediately following feeding through to awakening. Time samples of movements (Experiment II), numbers of respirations,

number of mass movements, and number of cries after being offered a sterile nipple filled with cotton were obtained. When arousal criteria were met (Experiments I and II), tactile sensitivity was tested twice using aesthesiometer (initially near 74 hours, and retested near 87 hours). **Results:** (1) Breast-fed boys and bottle-fed girls showed highest thresholds on both initial test and retest. (2) Breast-fed boys and bottle-fed girls were leaner.

Bell, R. Q., and Darling, J. F. The prone head reaction in the human neonate: relation with sex and tactile sensitivity. *Child Development*, 1965, *36*, 943–49.

> **Subjects:** $N = 75$; 3 days (breast- and bottle-fed, second- or later-born). **Measures:** Each S's general bodily movements and respiration were observed for 3½ hours on two occasions. During sleep, tactile sensitivity was measured with a set of nylon filaments. Prone head reaction was tested when the infant was awake (extent and duration of chin lift at the highest point during a 60-second period). **Results:** (1) On the first test, there were no sex differences in prone head reaction. Breast-fed boys and bottle-fed girls had the highest prone head reaction scores. (2) On the retest, boys' prone head reaction scores were higher than those of girls.

Bell, R. Q., Weller, G. M., and Waldrop, M. F. Newborn and preschooler: organization of behavior and relations between periods. *Monographs of the Society for Research in Child Development*, 1971, *36*, series no. 142.

> EXPERIMENT I: **Subjects:** $N = 75$; newborns (second- or later-born). **Measures:** On 2 separate occasions, Ss were observed for a 3½-hour interfeeding period covering a complete cycle of sleep and waking. During sleep, measures were taken of number of mouth movements, number of closed-eye movements, tactile threshold, highest respiration rate, and lowest respiration rate. While the infants were awake, the following measures were obtained: degree of arousal, prone-head reaction, number of sucks preceding the first or second pause in nonnutritive sucking, average size of a suck group (the initial suck group was not included in this calculation), nonnutritive suck rate, formula consumption relative to birth rate, and latency of response and number of cries following removal of the nipple. **Results:** (1) Boys lifted their heads higher than girls on the prone head reaction test. (2) Breast-fed boy infants had higher tactile thresholds than breast-fed girl infants. No difference was found between bottle-fed boy and girl infants. (3) Families of girl infants were lower in educational and occupational level, larger in size, and had shorter intervals between births than families of boy infants.
>
> EXPERIMENT II: **Subjects:** $N = 74$; 2½ yrs (including 55 follow-up cases from Experiment I. **Measures:** Ss were rated by their nursery school teachers on the following behaviors: contact with female teacher; contact with male teacher; vigor in play; friendliness with peers (involvement); friendliness with peers (positive); negative interaction; interest in bells (Bell Pull situation); active coping, object block; active coping, peer block; seeking help, peer block; tractability (cooperativeness with teacher's suggestions to change activities); geographic orientation; speech development; gross motor coordination; interest in attending school; manipulative skill, excitability; verbal originality; rhythmic response to music; reaction to teacher contact, child upset; seeking admiration. **Results:** Girls were rated higher than boys in speech development, gross motor coordination, seeking admiration, and tractability. No other sex differences were found.

Bell, S. M., and Ainsworth, M. D. S. Infant crying and maternal responsiveness. *Child Development*, 1972, *43*, 1171–90.

> **Subjects:** $N = 26$; 1–54 wks. **Measures:** Ss were observed in their homes at 3-week intervals. Duration and frequency of crying were recorded. **Results:** No sex differences.

Beloff, H. Two forms of social conformity: acquiescence and conventionality. *J. Abnormal & Social Psychology*, 1958, *56*, 99–104.

> **Subjects:** $N = 60$; 18–21 yrs (college). **Measures:** Ss completed a shortened version of the Thurston-Chave War Scale. After a 3-week interval, Ss again responded to the T-C statements under simulated group conditions. (Stooges presented strongly agreeing, neutral, and strongly disagreeing positions.) Acquiescence was defined as the difference between Ss' first and second response sets with respect to the group report. From Eysenck's Inventory of Social Attitudes and Ss' preferences for pictures of teapots, 2 indexes of conventionality (defined as the degree of agreement between an individual S and the mean or modal response of the rest of the group) were obtained. **Results:** (1) There were no sex differences in acquiescence scores. (2) There were no differences in aesthetic conventionality (teapot preference). (3) On political conventionality, women's conformity scores were higher than those of men (Eysenck's Inventory).

Bem, S. L. Sex-role adaptability: one consequence of psychological androgyny. *J. Personality & Social Psychology*, 1974, in press.

EXPERIMENT I: Subjects: $N = 54$; 18–21 yrs (college). **Measures:** Ss described themselves on the Bem Sex-Role Inventory. The BSRI includes both a masculinity and femininity scale; the 2 scales yield logically independent scores. Among the Ss selected for the experiment, one-third of each sex were masculine, one-third feminine, and one-third androgynous. After being assigned to same-sex groups of 4, Ss were tested in an Asch-type conformity situation. The number of trials in which Ss conformed was recorded. **Results:** No sex differences.

EXPERIMENT II: Subjects: $N = 66$; 18–21 yrs (college). **Measures:** 3 groups of Ss were chosen on the basis of their responses to the BSRI; one-third of each sex were masculine, one-third feminine, and one-third androgynous. Ss were first asked to build something with 60 plastic disks (this activity served to equalize mood across Ss). A kitten was then brought into the room and placed in an enclosed playpen. Instructions were given to interact with the kitten (forced play period). For their third activity, Ss were given a game of skill. Finally, the kitten was again placed in the playpen. Ss were told they could do anything they liked (spontaneous play period). The room contained a number of interesting magazines, games, and puzzles. The response measures were the amount of time Ss spent in spontaneous play with the kitten, the extent to which they touched the kitten during forced play, and their self-reported enjoyment of the forced-play interaction. **Results:** (1) No overall sex differences were found. (2) Among masculine males and females, females scored higher on a combined measure of the above-listed responses.

Benton, A. A. Productivity, distributive justice and bargaining among children. *J. Personality & Social Psychology*, 1971, *18*, 68–78.

Subjects: $N = 96$; 9–12 yrs. **Measures:** Same-sex pairs of friends, nonfriends, and neutrals were formed: 1 member of each pair (choice determined randomly) passed a reading test that made toys (previously rank-ordered by each S) available for play; 5 pairs of toys were presented to each group. Ss' first choice was paired with other's fifth choice (1:5), Ss' second choice was paired with other's fourth choice (2:4), etc. Ss rated the acceptability of each of the 5 options. Ss then decided between themselves which of the 4 pairs of toys they would like to play with. (In order to avoid an easy middle choice, each S's fifth-choice toy was removed.) **Results:** (1) No sex differences were found in the acceptability of toy allocations. (2) Female pairs agreed to an equity solution (1:4, 2:3) more often than male pairs did ($p < .025$). (3) Female nonfriends made lower evaluations of one another and saw each other as less friendly than male nonfriends did ($p < .05$). No sex differences were found for friends and neutrals.

Benton, A. A., Gelber, E. R., Kelley, H. H., and Liebling, B. A. Reactions to various degrees of deceit in a mixed-motive relationship. *J. Personality & Social Psychology*, 1969, *12*, 170–80.

Subjects: $N = 80$; 18–21 yrs (college). **Measures:** Ss played a 2-person, 2-choice, mixed-motive game with simulated same-sex partners. Each trial involved the following sequence: Ss picked the top card from a deck of (40 red and 40 black) shuffled cards. After noting its color, Ss passed the card through an opening in a partition to their partners (actually E, who henceforth will be referred to as declarer). Declarer informed Ss whether or not their cards were of the same color as the card that he had picked from a similar deck of red and black cards. Ss had the option of either accepting or doubting declarer's message. Accepting declarer's message that the cards were of the same color resulted in S receiving 2 points and declarer 0. Accepting declarer's message that the cards were different resulted in S receiving 0 points and declarer 2. Doubting the declarer on trials in which declarer had given Ss correct information resulted in a mutual loss to both players. Doubting the declarer on trials in which declarer deceived Ss (in an attempt to improve his own score at Ss' expense) resulted in 1 point being added to Ss's score and 1 point being deducted from declarer's score. Depending on the treatment condition to which they were assigned, declarer lied to Ss in either 0%, 25%, 50%, or 75% of the trials when it was to his advantage to present inaccurate information to Ss. After the last trial, Ss completed a postexperimental questionnaire. **Results:** (1) As assessed by a questionnaire administered just prior to the beginning of the game, men expressed a greater feeling of power in their role than women did ($p < .05$). Women indicated a preference for the declarer role; men indicated no role preference ($p < .05$). No sex differences were found in Ss' expected trustworthiness ratings of declarer. (2) No sex differences were found in Ss' doubting behavior. (3) On the postexperimental questionnaire, (a) women indicated they were less successful in affecting the declarer's behavior than men did ($p < .05$); (b) women reported they felt less responsible ($p < .05$) for their scores than men did (in the

75% rate-of-deception condition only); no sex differences were found when the deception rate was 0%, 25%, or 50%; (c) women reported they felt more tension ($p < .01$) than men did (in the 75% rate-of-deception condition only); no sex differences were found when the deception rate was 0%, 25%, or 50%; (d) women reported less satisfaction with the relationship they established with the declarer ($p < .05$) and indicated a greater preference for a new partner than men did ($p < .05$); (e) women reported less satisfaction with catching the declarer at lying than men did ($p < .05$); when asked if they would have preferred to face the declarer during the task, women indicated less desire to do so than men did ($p < .05$); (f) men rated the declarer more potent than women did in the 0% ($p < .10$), 25% ($p < .01$) and 50% ($p < .05$) conditions.

Bergan, A., McManis, D. L., and Melchert, P. A. Effects of social and token reinforcement on WISC Block Design performance. *Perceptual & Motor Skills*, 1971, *32*, 871–80.
> **Subjects:** $N = 48$; 9 yrs. **Measures:** Ss were given the Block Design subtest of the WISC and assigned to 1 of 3 treatment groups that were matched on the basis of total score and time score. Assignment to groups was randomly determined within each sex. 3 weeks later, Ss were retested under 1 of 3 conditions: (1) control (standard instructions), (2) social reinforcement (positive verbal statement made after each correct response), and (3) token reinforcement (chips given for each correct response). **Results:** (1) Boys exceeded girls in accuracy on each test. (2) There were no sex differences in relative improvement in accuracy under control and token reinforcement. Girls showed a greater gain in accuracy under social reinforcement than boys. (3) Boys showed a decrease in absolute percentage of time required from pretest to post-test, whereas girls showed an increase in percentage of time. (4) Boys performed with greater speed under social reinforcement than girls. No sex differences were found for other treatment groups. (5) Under social reinforcement, boys made greater gains in speed than girls did, but not under other conditions.

Berger, S., and Johansson, S. L. Effect of a model's expressed emotions on an observer's resistance to extinction. *J. Personality & Social Psychology*, 1968, *10*, 53–58.
> **Subjects:** $N = 144$; 18–21 yrs (college). **Measures:** After observing a model guess either 25% or 100% of the answers correct in a guessing game, Ss played the game with E. Ss were always told their guesses were wrong. Performance measure was the number of trials Ss played until they expressed a desire to quit. **Results:** No sex differences.

Berk, L. E. Effects of variations in the nursery school setting on environmental constraints and children's modes of adaptation. *Child Development*, 1971, *42*, 839–69.
> **Subjects:** $N = 72$; 2–5 yrs. **Measures:** Ss' encounters with positive and negative environmental force units (EFUs) in nursery school were observed. EFUs were defined as any actions or constraints imposed upon the child by the environment that were directed to some specifiable end that the child was aware of. **Results:** (1) Boys encountered more EFUs than girls did. (2) Boys' actions were more frequently disrupted by their teachers than were girls'. (3) A higher percentage of boys' than girls' responses to EFUs were categorized as compliant. There were no sex differences in responses categorized as offensive-combative.

Berkowitz, H., and Zigler, E. Effects of preliminary positive and negative interactions and delay conditions on children's responsiveness to social reinforcement. *J. Personality & Social Psychology*, 1965, *2*, 500–505.
> **Subjects:** $N = 80$; 7 yrs. **Measures:** Ss received intermittent verbal praise for inserting marbles into holes. Ss played until they expressed a desire to stop or until they did not insert a marble for 30 seconds. **Results:** No sex differences were found in task persistence.

Berkowitz, H., Butterfield, E. C., and Zigler, E. The effectiveness of social reinforcers on persistence and learning tasks following positive and negative social interactions. *J. Personality & Social Psychology*, 1965, *2*, 706–14.
> **Subjects:** $N = 240$; 7 yrs. **Measures:** (1) Ss received intermittent verbal praise for inserting marbles into holes. Ss played until they expressed a desire to stop. Ss' persistence at the task was measured. (2) Ss turned off colored lights by pushing either of 2 buttons beneath the lights. After a baseline period, Ss received verbal praise for pressing the least preferred button. The number of responses to the reinforced stimulus was recorded. **Results:** No sex differences.

Berman, P. W., Rane, N. G., and Bahow, E. Age changes in children's learning set with win-stay, lose-shift problems. *Developmental Psychology*, 1970, *2*, 233–39.
> **Subjects:** $N = 32$; 4, 6, 8, 10 yrs. **Measures:** Ss performed 2-trial object-discrimination prob-

lems. A single stimulus presented on trial 1 was rewarded on half of the problems and not rewarded on the remaining ones. The stimulus was presented again on trial 2, paired with a new stimulus. Ss were required to respond according to a win-stay, lose-shift principle. A criterion of correct responses was set. Results: There were no sex differences among 4- and 6-year-old Ss (only groups tested).

Bermant, G., Starr, M., and Trowbridge, B. Are men more inclined than women to take risks? *Personnel Psychology*, in press.

Subjects: $N = 112$; 18–21 yrs (college). Measures: Ss were randomly placed in 24 mixed-sex discussion groups of 4–5 members each. Each S was given the short form of the Kogan-Wallach Choice Dilemmas Questionnaire. After individual tests, each problem was discussed in a group until consensus was reached. After the discussion, Ss individually solved the problems. Results: (1) There were no sex differences in pregroup risk taking or postgroup shift to risk. (2) Women's post-group scores were more varied than men's ($p. < .02$).

Bernstein, R. C., and Jacklin, C. N. The 3½-month-old infant: stability of behavior, sex differences, and longitudinal findings. Unpublished master's thesis, Stanford University, 1973.

EXPERIMENT I: Subjects: $N = 18$; 3½ mos and mothers. Measures: Responses measured were: tactile threshold; prone head reaction; first fixation time, total fixation time, and number of smiles to slides of faces and scrambled faces; and number of alerts to voices and auditory controls for voices. Mothers reported the amount of time the infant slept during the day. Results: (1) Girls were more responsive to (combined) auditory stimuli than boys ($p < .05$). There were no sex differences in responsiveness to social versus nonsocial auditory stimuli. (2) There were no other sex differences.

EXPERIMENT II: Subjects: $N = 20$; tested at birth, 3½ mos. Measures: Response measures at birth were prone head reaction and tickle sensitivity (pressure aesthesiometer). Response measures at 3½ months were the same as for Experiment I. Results: (1) At birth, boys raised their heads higher than girls ($p < .05$). (2) Mothers reported that, at 3½ months, boys slept more than girls ($p < .05$). (3) There were no other sex differences.

Berry, J. W. Temne and Eskimo perceptual skills. *International J. Psychology*, 1966, *1*, 207–29.

Subjects: $N = 366$; 10–15, 15–20, 21–30, 31–40, over 40 yrs (Temne of Sierra Leone, Eskimo, Scots). Ss in the Temne and Eskimo samples were from either traditional or transitional societies. Ss in the Scottish sample were from either a rural or an urban area. Measures: 4 tests of spatial skills were administered to Ss—(1) Kohs Blocks, (2) Witkin's Embedded Figures Test, (3) Morrisby Shapes, and (4) Raven Matrices. In each sample, comparisons were made between men and women from the same area (e.g. rural Scottish men were compared only with rural Scottish women). This yielded a total of 24 comparisons, 6 for each of the 4 measures. Results: (1) In 4 of 8 comparisons in the Temne sample, men were superior to women. (2) In 4 of 8 comparisons in the Scottish sample, men were superior to women. (3) No sex differences were found in the Eskimo sample.

Biaggio, A., and Rodrigues, A. Behavioral compliance and devaluation of the forbidden object as a function of probability of detection and severity of threat. *Developmental Psychology*, 1971, *4*, 320–23.

Subjects: $N = 39$; 7 yrs (Brazil). Measures: Ss were left alone for 10 minutes and instructed not to play with 1 of 4 attractive toys (always child's second preferred toy). Conditions varied as to level of threat and probability of detection: severe threat/high probability of detection, severe threat/low probability of detection, mild threat/high probability, or mild threat/low probability. Results: No sex differences.

Biber, H., Miller, L. B., and Dyer, J. L. Feminization in preschool. *Developmental Psychology*, 1972, *7*, 86 (brief report).

Subjects: N = 14 classes (size 13 to 20); 4 yrs and their female teachers. Measures: Videotape records of classes in 4 different types of school programs were observed. Results: (1) Girls received more instructional contact (requests for information by teacher and information given individually to child) than boys did. (2) Girls received more positive reinforcement for instruction (feedback for correct or adequate academic performance) than boys did in the Montessori, enrichment-type preschool programs, and in a program emphasizing attitudes as well as abilities. (3) There were no sex differences in amount of positive reinforcement in the structured academic program.

Bickman, L. Sex and helping: interaction and ingratiation. Paper presented at Symposium on Sex and Helping Behavior, 80th Annual Convention of the American Psychological Association, Hawaii, 1972.

EXPERIMENT I: **Subjects:** $N = 200$; 18 yrs (college). **Measures:** Ss were telephoned by an E who said either he was a freshman or he was a senior. E asked the S to help him by participating in a psychology experiment. S's helping behavior was noted. Sex of E and sex of S were varied. **Results:** No sex differences.

EXPERIMENT II: **Subjects:** $N = 223$; 18–21 yrs (college). **Measures:** Same as Experiment I, except E said he needed subjects for either a male or a female friend. **Results:** No sex differences.

EXPERIMENT III: **Subjects:** $N = 300$; 18–21 yrs (college). **Measures:** Ss received a letter asking them to participate in an experiment. The letter was signed by a male or female E. **Results:** No sex differences.

EXPERIMENT IV: **Subjects:** $N = 298$; 18–21 yrs (college). **Measures:** Same as Experiments I–III, except (male or female) Es asked Ss for help, face to face. **Results:** No sex differences.

Bieri, J. Parental identification, acceptance of authority and differences in cognitive behavior. *J. Abnormal & Social Psychology*, 1960, *60*, 76–79.

Subjects: $N = 60$; 18–21 yrs (college). **Measures:** Embedded Figures Test. **Results:** No sex differences.

Bieri, J., Bradburn, W., and Galinsky, M. Sex differences in perceptual behavior. *J. Personality*, 1958, *26*, 1–12.

EXPERIMENT I: **Subjects:** $N = 110$; 18–21 yrs. **Measures:** An 8-item form of the Embedded Figures Test was administered to Ss. **Results:** Men located the figures faster than women did.

EXPERIMENT II: **Subjects:** $N = 112$; 18–21 yrs. **Measures:** (1) Ss were given the Barron-Welsh Art Scale, a measure of Ss' preference for complex, asymmetrical line drawings vs. simple, symmetrical drawings. (2) Ss were assigned an External-Construct Score based on their responses to a modified version of Kelly's Role Construct Repertory Test. **Results:** No sex differences.

EXPERIMENT III: **Subjects:** $N = 111$; 18–21 yrs. **Measures:** Ss were asked to list possible uses of a brick (Bricks Test). **Results:** No sex differences.

EXPERIMENT IV: **Subjects:** $N = 76$; 18–21 yrs. **Measures:** SAT. **Results:** Men had higher quantitative scores than women. No sex difference was found in verbal scores.

Bigelow, G. Field dependence–field independence in 5- to 10-year-old children. *J. Educational Research*, 1971, *64*, 397–400.

Subjects: $N = 160$; 5–10 yrs. **Measures:** Children's Embedded Figures Test. **Results:** No sex differences.

Birch, D. Evidence of competition and coordination between vocal and manual responses in preschool children. *J. Experimental Child Psychology*, 1971, *12*, 10–26.

Subjects: $N = 35$; 3½–6½ yrs. **Measures:** To extinguish a light, Ss were required to perform either a manual or a vocal response, or both. Start times, reach times, target times (sum of start and reach times), and voice times were recorded. **Results:** No sex differences.

Birnie, L., and Whitely, J. H. The effects of acquired meaning on children's play behavior. *Child Development*, 1973, *44*, 355–58.

Subjects: $N = 32$; 5 yrs. **Measures:** E told Ss 2 activities that a boy doll did or did not like to engage in when he visited a toy farm. 1 of the activities was 1 of 4 behaviors designated as a high-probability response, the other was 1 of 2 behaviors designated as a low-probability response (probabilities were determined by two Ss' free-play activity during the pilot study). Afterward, Ss were presented with the toy doll and the toy farm and were observed for 5 minutes. The number of times Ss exhibited each of the 4 high-probability and 2 low-probability responses was recorded. **Results:** No sex differences.

Birns, B. Individual differences in human neonates' responses to stimulation. *Child Development*, 1965, *36*, 249–56.

Subjects: $N = 30$ (24 girls, 6 boys); tested at 2, 3, 4, 5 days. **Measures:** Each of 4 stimuli (soft tone, loud tone, cold disk, and pacifier) was applied to Ss 3 times at each session. Intensity of response (consisting primarily of changes in body movement) was recorded. **Results:** No sex differences.

Bisett, B. The effects of age and incentive value on discrimination learning. *J. Experimental Child Psychology*, 1966, 3, 199–206.

    Subjects: $N = 120$; 6–7, 10–11 yrs. **Measures:** Ss' relative preferences for 8 reward objects (paper clips, metal washers, small white rocks, pennies, miniature cars, small tin birds, trinkets, and Beatle cards) were assessed. **Results:** (1) Boys' choices of reward objects differed from girls' choices ($p < .001$). (2) Girls had a preference for the pennies more than boys did ($p < .05$).

Bishop, B. R., and Beckman, L. Developmental Conformity. *Developmental Psychology*, 1971, 5, 536 (brief report).

    Subjects: $N = 144$; 7–11 yrs. **Measures:** Confederates gave erroneous prearranged responses about line length to naïve Ss. Number of yieldings by Ss was recorded. **Results:** No sex differences.

Blanchard, E. B., and Price, K. C. A developmental study of cognitive balance. *Developmental Psychology*, 1971, 5, 344–48.

    Subjects: $N = 120$; 6, 8, 13, 18 yrs. **Measures:** Nonconserving 6-year-old Ss and conserving 8-year-old Ss, 9-year-old Ss who failed and 13-year-old Ss who passed tests of formal operational thought, and 18-year-old Ss were orally presented with 8 triadic situations of the form "You (like, dislike) (name of person)"; "You (like, dislike) (different person)"; "You see that (first person) and (second person) (like, dislike) each other." Ss were asked to indicate feelings regarding each situation on 2 5-point scales anchored by good-bad, happy-sad. **Results:** No sex differences.

Blayney, G. Sex differences in father protectiveness toward their preschool children. Unpublished senior honors thesis, Stanford University, 1973.

    Subjects: $N = 29$; 4 yrs and fathers. **Measures:** To assess their basic level of timidity, Ss were initially tested on an elevated balance beam mounted on springs (Phase 1). Fathers were then brought to the experimental room and the beam was raised 1 foot. Ss were allowed to cross the beam if they desired (Phase 2). Next, 3 wooden blocks were placed along the beam. Both the father's and the child's reactions to this challenge were recorded (Phase 3). In the final phase of the study (Phase 4), Ss and their fathers were given the opportunity to manipulate the toy's challenge by either adding or removing blocks. Measures were taken of the following: latency to begin crossing the beam; time spent crossing the beam; time spent in the sitting and crawling positions while on the beam; child reaches for father; child touches father; father reaches for child; father touches child; father's proximity to child; number of blocks added or removed by father or child (Phase 4). A timidity rating was assigned to each child based on the time it took him to cross the beam and on whether or not a crossing was completed in both directions. In addition, all verbalizations and communicative gestures (both child's and father's) were recorded, tallied, and then classified into the following categories: *child*—(a) requests father's help; (b) agrees to follow father's instructions; (c) refuses to perform expected act; (d) seeks father's encouragement and attention; (e) rejects father's help, accepts challenge, praises self; *father*—(a) withdraws aid, demands child assume self-direction; (b) withdraws aid, requests child to assume self-direction; (c) withdraws aid, presents child with challenging situation to overcome; (d) warns child of danger, suggests that child decrease degree of challenge; (e) offers aid, encourages parental reliance; (f) expresses affection or approval; (g) criticizes or complains about child's performance; (h) submits to child's demands or requests. **Results:** No differences were found between boys and girls. During the final phase of the study, fathers of girls made more independent-encouraging commands (withdraws aid, demands child assume self-direction) than fathers of boys did. No other differences were found between fathers of boys and fathers of girls.

Bledsoe, J. C. Sex differences in mental health analysis scores of elementary pupils. *J. Consulting Psychology*, 1961, 25, 364–65.

    Subjects: $N = 197$, 9–12 yrs. **Measures:** Ss were given the Elementary Form of Mental Health Analysis; 5 personality "liabilities" (behavioral immaturity, emotional instability, feelings of inadequacy, physical defects, and nervous manifestations) and 5 personality "assets" (close personal relationships, interpersonal skills, social participation, satisfying work and recreation, and adequate outlook and goals) were assessed. **Results:** Girls scored higher than boys on total assets, close personal relationships, and adequate outlook and goals, and lower on total liabilities, behavioral immaturity, and feelings of inadequacy. Overall, girls' mental health scores were superior to those of boys.

Bledsoe, J. C. Self-concepts of children and their intelligence, achievement, interests, and anxiety. *Childhood Education*, 1967, *43*, 436–38.
> **Subjects:** $N = 271$; 9, 11 yrs. **Measures:** A 30-item self-concept, adjective checklist was administered to Ss. **Results:** Girls had more positive self-concepts than boys ($p < .01$).

Block, J. H. Conceptions of sex role: some cross-cultural and longitudinal perspectives. Unpublished manuscript (to be revised and submitted to *American Psychologist*), 1972.
> **Subjects:** $N = 90$; 3 yrs and parents. **Measures:** Using the Child-rearing Practices Report, parents described their child-rearing attitudes and behaviors. **Results:** (1) Mothers of boys scored higher on the following items than mothers of girls: I think competitive games are good for a child; I encourage my child always to control his feelings; I don't think young children should see each other naked; I teach my child punishment will "find" him when he's bad. (2) Fathers of boys scored higher on the following items than fathers of girls: I think competitive games are good for a child; I encourage my child to always do his best; I think a child must learn early not to cry; I have firm rules for my child; I don't allow my child to get angry with me; I don't want my child looked upon as different. (3) Mothers of girls scored higher on the following items than mothers of boys: I find it difficult to punish my child; I like some time to myself away from my child; I give up some of my own interests for my child. (4) Fathers of girls scored higher on the following items than fathers of boys: I encourage my child to wonder and think about life; I feel a child should have time to daydream and loaf; I encourage my child to talk about her troubles; I encourage my child to be independent of me.

Blum, J. E., Fosshage, J. L., and Jarvik, L. F. Intellectual changes and sex differences in octogenarians: a twenty-year longitudinal study of aging. *Developmental Psychology*, 1972, *7*, 178–87.
> **Subjects:** $N = 54$; tested at 64 yrs, 84 yrs (mean). **Measures:** In 1947 and again in 1967, Ss were given 5 tests from the Wechsler-Bellevue Intelligence Test (Similarities, Digits Forward, Digits Backward, Digit Symbol Substitution, Block Design), a vocabulary test from the Stanford-Binet Scale (1916), and a paper-and-pencil tapping test. **Results:** (1) In 1947, women scored higher than men on the Digit Symbol Substitution and Tapping tests. (2) In 1967, women scored higher than men on the Vocabulary, Similarities, Tapping, and Digit Symbol Substitution tests. (3) For each of the 7 tests, no sex difference was found in annual rate of decline in performance over the 20-year period.

Blumenfield, W. S., and Remmers, H. H. Research note on high school spectator sports preference of high school students. *Perceptual & Motor Skills*, 1965, *20*, 166.
> **Subjects:** $N = 2,000$; 14–17 yrs. **Measures:** Ss were asked which of 11 sports was their favorite high school spectator sport. **Results:** Girls chose basketball and baseball more frequently than boys did; boys chose football more frequently than girls did.

Blurton Jones, N. Categories of child-child interaction. In N. B. Jones, ed., *Ethological Studies of Child Behaviour*. London: Cambridge University Press, 1972, pp. 97–127.
> **Subjects:** $N = 25$; 2, 3–4 yrs. **Measures:** Ss were observed in a playroom well equipped with toys. Frequencies of rough-and-tumble, aggressive, and social play were recorded. **Results:** (1) Among younger Ss, girls engaged in more rough-and-tumble play than boys did. No sex differences were found in the older sample. Most displays of rough-and-tumble play by the older girls occurred when the slide was put out; this was not so true for older boys ($p < .001$). (2) When the slide was not available, boys engaged in more wrestling and hitting during rough-and-tumble play than girls did ($p < .04$). (3) No sex differences were found in aggressive or social play. (4) Among older Ss, girls displayed more kinds of behavior toward their teacher than boys did.

Blurton Jones, N., and Leach, G. M. Behaviour of children and their mothers at separation and greeting. In N. B. Jones, ed., *Ethological Studies of Child Behaviour*. London: Cambridge University Press, 1972, pp. 217–47.
> **Subjects:** $N = 73$; 2–4 yrs and mothers. **Measures:** Data on whether a child cried when his mother left him at nursery school were obtained from a variety of sources: arrival and departure records; teacher's logbook; teacher's and author's memories. **Results:** No sex differences.

Bogo, N., Winget, C., and Gleser, G. C. Ego defenses and perceptual styles. *Perceptual & Motor Skills*, 1970, *30*, 599–604.
> **Subjects:** $N = 97$; 18–21 yrs (college). **Measures:** (1) Rod and Frame test (portable model), (2) Figure-drawing test, (3) Defense Mechanisms Inventory: a paper-and-pencil measure

assessing the relative strength of 5 different defense mechanisms, (4) Autokinetic Effect: Ss sat in a darkened room and watched a pinpoint of light. Ss' task was to trace the path of any apparent movement of the light. Measure of autokinesis was the length of the line(s) Ss produced. **Results:** (1) Men were more field-independent than women on the RFT ($p < .005$). (2) No sex differences were found in FDT scores. Women drew larger figures of both sexes than men did. (3) No sex differences were found in Autokinetic Effect Scores. Women's scores were more varied than men's ($p < .01$). (4) On the Defense Mechanisms Inventory, men demonstrated more turning against an object ($p < .01$) and less turning against self ($p < .001$) than women. No sex differences were found in reversal, principalization, or projection.

Bokander, I. Semantic description of complex and meaningful stimulus material. *Perceptual & Motor Skills*, 1966, 22, 201–2.
   Subjects: $N = 29$; 18–21 yrs (college). **Measures:** Ss rated each of 7 photographs of male faces on 22 different semantic scales. **Results:** No sex differences.

Borke, H. Interpersonal perception of young children. *Developmental Psychology*, 1971, 5, 263–69.
   Subjects: $N = 20$; 3–8 yrs. **Measures:** Ss heard stories about another child and indicated how the story child felt by picking a happy, sad, afraid, or angry face. 8 more stories were told in which Ss behaved toward story children in ways that might make story children feel happy, sad, or angry. Ss chose the face that best indicated each story child's feelings. **Results:** There were no sex differences in ability to identify other people's feelings.

Bortner, R. W., and Hultsch, D. F. Personal time perspective in adulthood. *Developmental Psychology*, 1972, 7, 98–103.
   Subjects: $N = 1,292$; 20–88 yrs. **Measures:** After defining in their own terms the worst and best possible lives they could imagine for themselves, Ss were asked to rate their past, present, and future status with respect to these extremes. 2 scores were derived from Ss' ratings: a retrotension score (S's rating of his present status was compared with his assessment of his past status) and a protension score (S's rating of his future status was compared with his assessment of his present status). **Results:** No sex differences.

Bosco, J. The visual-information-processing speed of lower- and middle-class children. *Child Development*, 1972, 43, 1418–22 (and personal communication).
   Subjects: $N = 180$; 6, 8, 11 yrs. **Measures:** Ss viewed a test stimulus (square, circle, star, or triangle) on a tachistoscope. A variable interstimulus interval was followed by presentation of a masking stimulus. Processing speed (i.e. the minimum time necessary for recognition of the stimulus) was measured. **Results:** No sex differences.

Bourne, L. E., and O'Banion, K. Conceptual role learning and chronological age. *Developmental Psychology*, 1971, 5, 525–34.
   Subjects: $N = 288$; 7, 9, 11, 13, 15, 19 yrs. **Measures:** Ss solved 3 conceptual rule-learning problems (relevant attributes of concept given, rule unknown) based on 1 of 4 rules: conjunctive (and), disjunctive (and/or), conditional (if, then), or biconditional (if and only if). **Results:** Girls were superior to boys on number of trials to last error. Authors say this effect is constant over all variables (grade and type of rule), and therefore imposes no qualifications on interpretation of other variables.

Bowers, K. S., and van der Meulen, S. J. Effect of hypnotic susceptibility on creativity test performance. *J. Personality & Social Psychology*, 1970, 14, 247–56.
   Subjects: $N = 60$; 18–21 yrs (college). **Measures:** 9 creativity measures were derived from Ss' responses to Guilford's Consequences Test, the Holtzman Inkblot Test, and a free association test. The 3 tasks were administered while Ss were either awake or hypnotized. A third group of Ss feigned hypnosis to a naïve E. **Results:** In every comparison, 4 of which were significant, women achieved higher creativity scores than men.

Bowers, P., and London, P. Developmental correlates of role-playing ability. *Child Development*, 1965, 36, 499–508.
   Subjects: $N = 40$; 5, 7, 9, 11 yrs. **Measures:** (1) A Dramatic Acting Test was used to measure ability to portray another person. E described a situation to S and asked him to respond in ways appropriate to mother, father, friend, bully, and teacher. (2) The Children's Hypnotic Susceptibility Scale, used to measure S's ability to portray himself in an unfamiliar role, was administered without hypnotic induction or relaxation. **Results:** No sex differences.

Brackbill, Y. Cumulative effects of continuous stimulation on arousal level in infants. *Child Development*, 1971, 42, 17–26.
> **Subjects:** $N = 24$; 1 mo. **Measures:** S was tested on 5 consecutive days under 5 different randomly ordered conditions: no extra stimulation, continuous stimulation of 1, 2, 3, and 4 sensory modalities including auditory stimulation (tape-recorded heartbeat), visual stimulation (combination of fluorescent and incandescent bulbs), swaddling, and temperature stimulation. Heart rate, respiration regularity, motor activity, and general state were measured. **Results:** No sex differences.

Brackbill, Y., Adams, G., Crowell, D., and Gray, M. L. Arousal level in neonates and preschool children under continuous auditory stimulation. *J. Experimental Child Psychology*, 1966, 4, 178–88.
> **EXPERIMENT I: Subjects:** $N = 41$; 3 yrs. **Measures:** Ss heard 4 continuously presented auditory stimuli at nap time for an hour every day. The stimuli were no sound, paired heartbeats, beating of a metronome, and unfamiliar lullabies in a foreign language. Number of minutes until S fell asleep was recorded. **Results:** No sex differences.
> **EXPERIMENT II:** $N = 24$; 2 days. **Measures:** Ss heard 4 consecutive 15-minute presentations of no sound, heartbeat, metronome beating, and unfamiliar lullabies in a foreign language. Amount of crying, general motor activity, heart rate, regularity of heart rate, and regularity of respiration were recorded. **Results:** No sex differences.

Braginsky, D. D. Machiavellianism and manipulative interpersonal behavior in children: two explorative studies. Unpublished doctoral dissertation, University of Connecticut, 1966.
> **Subjects:** $N = 48$; 10 yrs. **Measures:** Ss responded to a modified version of Christie's Likert-type Machiavellianism (Mach) scale. Ss classified as either low Machs or high Machs were then paired with a middle Mach of the same sex. Their task was to persuade their middle partners to eat as many crackers strongly flavored with quinine as possible. Ss were promised a reward for every cracker they could persuade their partners to eat. **Results:** No sex differences were found in Mach scores or in the effectiveness of Ss' persuasive attempts.

Braginsky, D. D. Machiavellianism and manipulative interpersonal behavior in children. *J. Experimental Social Psychology*, 1970, 6, 77–99.
> **Subjects:** $N = 225$ (on the Mach test), 96 (for the behavioral measures); 10 yrs. **Measures:** The Christie Mach Scale was adapted for suitability to 10-year-old children. On the basis of Mach scores, pairs of Ss were chosen such that the subject child in each pair had either a high or a low score while his partner (the "target child") had a Mach score in the middle range. On the pretext of wanting to test the palatibility of a new "health cracker," E asked each subject child to see how many quinine-flavored crackers he could get his partner to eat, and offered to pay the subject 5¢ for every cracker his partner consumed. Tape recordings were made of the interactions during the persuasive session. **Results:** There were no sex differences on the Mach test, or in the number of crackers consumed by the targets of boy and girl Ss. High-Mach boys told more direct lies, whereas high-Mach girls more often failed to mention unpleasant truths. However, the reverse pattern was found among low-Mach children, so there was no overall sex difference in the persuasive strategies employed.

Brainerd, C. J. The development of the proportionality scheme in children and adolescents. *Developmental Psychology*, 1971, 5, 469–76.
> **Subjects:** $N = 72$; 8, 11, 14 yrs. **Measures:** Ss with conservation of number and length were given conservation tests of density, solid volume, and liquid volume. **Results:** No sex differences.

Brainerd, C. J. The age-stage issue in conservation acquisition. *Psychonomic Science*, 1972, 29, 115–17 (and personal communication).
> **Subjects:** $N = 155$; 4–6 yrs. **Measures:** Ss were pretested and post-tested on conservation of number tasks with or without intervening training. **Results:** No sex differences.

Brainerd, C. J. Order of acquisition of transitivity, conservation, and class inclusion of length and weight. *Developmental Psychology*, 1973, 8, 105–16.
> **EXPERIMENT I: Subjects:** $N = 120$; 7–8 yrs (Canada, U.S.). **Measures:** Ss were tested in 2 concept areas (length and weight) for 3 concrete-operational skills (transitivity, conservation, and class inclusion). **Results:** In the U.S. sample, there were no sex differences in correct tran-

sitivity, conservation, or class inclusion judgments of weight and length. In the Canadian sample, boys found conservation more difficult than girls did ($p < .05$).

EXPERIMENT II: Subjects: $N = 180$; 5, 6, 7 yrs (Canada). Measures: Same as Experiment I. Results: No sex differences.

Brainerd, C. J., and Huevel, K. V. Development of geometric imagery in five- to eight-year-olds. *Genetic Psychology Monographs*, 1974, *86*, in press.

Subjects: $N = 120$; 5, 6 yrs. Measures: Ss were presented with 3 3-dimensional objects (a cube, a box, and a cylinder). Ss picked from among 21 drawings the 3 that accurately represented what the objects would look like if they were "opened up." Results: No sex differences.

Brannigan, G. G., and Tolor, A. Sex differences in adaptive styles. *J. Genetic Psychology*, 1971, *119*, 143–49.

Subjects: $N = 333$; 18–21 yrs (college). Measures: Ss completed a modified version of the Future Events test (a measure of personal future-time perspective) and Rotter's Internal-External Scale (a measure of Ss' generalized expectations about how reinforcement is controlled). Results: (1) Women were less futuristically oriented, having more constricted scores on a greater number of items than men. (2) Women were more external in their expectancy, scoring higher than men on the Rotter scale ($p < .001$).

Braun, C., and Klassen, B. A transformational analysis of oral syntactic structures of children representing varying ethnolinguistic communities. *Child Development*, 1971, *42*, 1859–71.

Subjects: $N = 216$; 6, 9, 11 yrs (German-, French-, English-speaking). Measures: Ss were divided into ability groups by the Pintner-Cunningham Primary Test (grade 1) and the Pintner General Ability Test (grades 4, 6). Ss viewed a film, after which they summarized the story and answered questions. Ss viewed another soundless film that was interrupted; they were asked to tell the story of the film and to conjecture what might have happened. Linguistic indexes were measured. Results: Girls used more noun plus relative clause transformations and object transformations than boys did. No sex differences were found on the 29 other indexes (e.g. number of subordinate clauses, redundancies, etc.).

Bresnahan, J. L., and Blum, W. L. Chaotic reinforcement: a socioeconomic leveler. *Developmental Psychology*, 1971, *4*, 89–92.

Subjects: $N = 60$; 6 yrs (low, high SES). Measures: Ss were given a concept acquisition problem after either 0, 6, or 12 random reinforcement trials. Results: No sex differences.

Bresnahan, J. L., Ivey, S. L., and Shapiro, M. M. Developmentally defined obviousness and concept formation tasks. *Developmental Psychology*, 1969, *1*, 383–88.

Subjects: $N = 64$; 5–6 yrs (white and black, Head Start program). Measures: Ss were given 4 concept-formation tasks: (a) number as the relevant dimension with size as a partial cue, (b) number without size, (c) size as the relevant dimension with number as a partial cue, and (d) size without number. Results: No sex differences.

Bridges, K. M. B. Occupational interests of three-year-old children. *J. Genetic Psychology*, 1927, *34*, 415–23.

Subjects: $N = 6$ boys, 4 girls; 2–3 yrs. Measures: Ss were observed in nursery school during free-play period. Results: Boys' favorite activities were building with large bricks, fitting cylinders into holes, color pairing, naming objects in picture postcards, and cube construction. Girls' favorite activities were fitting cylinders into holes, threading beads, writing on the blackboards, and fastening buttons.

Brimer, M. A. Sex differences in listening comprehension. *J. Research & Development in Education*, 1969, *3*, 72–79.

Subjects: $N = 8,324$; 5–8 yrs (test 1), 7–11 yrs (test 2). Measures: Ss took 1 of 2 versions of the orally administered English Picture Vocabulary Test (a modification of the Peabody Picture Vocabulary Test). Results: Among 6-8-year-old Ss, boys scored higher than girls (test 1). No other sex differences were found.

Brissett, M., and Nowicki, S., Jr. Internal vs. external control of reinforcement and reaction to frustration. *J. Personality & Social Psychology*, 1973, *25*, 35–44.

EXPERIMENT I: Subjects: $N = 80$; 18–21 yrs (college). Measures: Ss were given the Child and Waterhouse Frustration Reaction Inventory to assess Ss' claimed reactions to frustration in terms of 7 behavioral tendencies: preoccupation, pessimism, striving, vindication, aggression, self-blame, and nondistractibility. Ss' reported reactions to frustration were classified as either generally constructive or generally unconstructive. **Results:** Men scored higher in aggression than women ($p < .05$). No sex differences were found for striving, vindication, or self-blame. No mention was made of preoccupation, pessimism, or nondistractibility. There were no sex differences in generally constructive versus unconstructive reactions to frustration.

EXPERIMENT II: **Subjects:** Same as Experiment I. **Measures:** On an angle-matching task, Ss judged which of several angles matched a standard (none actually did). The measure was the amount of time Ss took to reach a decision. **Results:** No sex differences.

EXPERIMENT III: **Measures:** Ss responded to 4 TAT cards suggesting achievement situations. Ss' stories were scored for positive, negative, and doubtful outcomes, need for achievement, achievement imagery (task and general), and imagery unrelated to achievement. **Results:** No sex differences.

Brockman, L. M., and Ricciuti, H. N. Severe protein-calorie malnutrition and cognitive development in infancy and early childhood. *Developmental Psychology*, 1971, 4, 312–19.
Subjects: $N = 39$; 1–3½ yrs. **Measures:** 20 protein-calorie-deficient children and 19 controls without a history of malnutrition were administered 10 sorting tasks. After 12 weeks of nutritional treatment, the tasks were readministered to the experimental Ss. Highest-level serial ordering and highest-level similar-object grouping were assessed. **Results:** (1) No sex differences were found when experimental and control Ss' scores at the initial testing were compared. (2) An analysis of the experimental Ss' data from both testings showed that girls' overall task performance was superior to that of the boys.

Bronfenbrenner, U. Reaction to social pressure from adults versus peers among Soviet day school and boarding school pupils in the perspective of an American sample. *J. Personality & Social Psychology*, 1970, 15, 179–89.
Subjects: $N = 353$; 12 yrs (USSR). **Measures:** Ss responded to a series of conflict situations, each of which presented Ss with the choice of engaging in either antisocial behavior being urged by peers or behavior acceptable to adults and society. **Results:** Boys chose the "antisocial" alternatives more often than girls.

Bronson, G. W. Fear of visual novelty: developmental patterns in males and females. *Developmental Psychology*, 1970, 2, 33–40.
Subjects: $N = 60$; tested monthly from 1 to 15 mos, at increasing intervals from ages 15 mos to 8½ yrs. **Measures:** At each testing, Ss completed various measures of mental ability and physical and motor development. A record was kept during the first 15 sessions of the percentage of time each child cried. When Ss were between 4 and 36 months of age, judgments were made as to whether or not the strangeness of the experience had made them cry. Beginning at age 10 months, and continuing until the age of 8½ years, Ss were rated on the amount of shyness they had exhibited. **Results:** No sex differences.

Bronson, G. W. Infants' reactions to unfamiliar persons and novel objects. *Monographs of the Society for Research in Child Development*, 1972, 37.
Subjects: $N = 32$; tested at 3, 4, 6½, 9 mos (white, Oriental). **Measures:** (1) During the first home visit at 3 months, Ss were rated on a 5-point persistency-of-crying scale ranging from "no crying, or baby quickly quieted" to "baby recurrently cried unless being held in mother's arms." Mothers were also asked to describe their infants' reactions to being bathed during the first and second months of their lives. (2) At 3 and 6½ months, mothers' behaviors toward their infants were rated on 2 5-point scales, yielding an overall measure of quality of maternal care. (3) At 3, 4, 6½, and 9 months, the frequency with which Ss smiled at their mothers was recorded. (4) At 3, 4, 6½, and 9 months, a red-patterned paper parasol was rapidly opened and closed in front of Ss. Incidences of blinking responses were recorded. (5) At 4, 6½, and 9 months, Ss' responses to an encounter with a male stranger were rated on a 5-point scale of affect ranging from "smiled with delight" to "cried." (6) At 6½ months, a large beeping object was placed near Ss. The number of infants who reached out and grabbed the object was recorded. **Results:** No sex differences.

Bronson, W. C. Exploratory behavior of 15-month-old infants in a novel situation. Paper read at the meeting of the Society for Research in Child Development, Minneapolis, 1971.
Subjects: $N = 40$; 15 mos and mothers. **Measures:** Mother and infant entered a room containing 2 chairs, a small toy dog, and a novel object. After showing the novel object to the infant, the mother walked over to a chair, taking the infant with her. The infant was then set on the floor; if he did not spontaneously approach the object within 30 seconds, the mother began encouraging the child to do so until an approach was effected (Episode 1).

Next, a young woman who was a stranger to Ss entered the room and sat down, remaining silent for 60 seconds (Episode 2). After the minute had elapsed, she began speaking to both the mother and the infant. Moving over to the object, she continued to attend to the baby. For the remainder of the time, she responded to the infant's approaches, but did not initiate interaction (Episode 3). **Results:** (1) In Episodes 2 and 3, boys attended to the novel object more frequently than girls did ($p < .05$, $p < .001$). In Episode 1, boys spent more time near the object than girls did ($p < .01$). In Episodes 1 and 3, girls gazed at the object more than boys did ($p < .01$, $p < .01$). In Episodes 1, 2, and 3, boys pulled the stick and observed the contingent effects more frequently than girls did ($p < .05$, $p < .001$, $p < .05$). No sex differences were found in the amount of time Ss spent examining or playing with the object. (2) In Episode 1, girls attended to and spent more time near their mothers than boys did ($p < .05$, $p < .05$). (3) In Episodes 1, 2, and 3, girls attended to the toy dog more frequently than boys did ($p < .01$, $p < .01$, $p < .01$). (4) In Episode 2, girls reacted more positively to the stranger than boys did ($p < .01$). No sex differences were found in the amount of attention Ss directed toward the stranger. (5) No sex differences were found in overall ratings of motor activity and affect.

Brooks, J., and Lewis, M. Attachment behavior in thirteen-month-old, opposite-sex twins. *Child Development*, 1974, 45, 243–47.
   Subjects: $N = 17$ pairs of opposite-sex twins; 11–15 mos. **Measures:** Each child and mother were observed for 15 minutes in a room containing the following toys: a set of blocks, a pail, a cornpopper, a rubber dog, a stuffed cat, a set of quarts, a wooden mallet, a pegboard, and a pull toy. **Results:** (1) Girls looked at their mothers more frequently than boys did ($p < .001$). (2) Girls spent more time in proximity to their mothers than boys ($p < .02$). (3) No sex differences were found in frequency of touching mother, number of pleasant vocalizations to mother, number of toy changes, or amount of sustained play. (4) No sex differences were found in Ss' preferences for the various toys.

Brooks, R. L., Brandt, L., and Weiner, M. Differential response to two communication channels: socioeconomic class differences in response to verbal reinforcers, communicated with and without tonal inflection. *Child Development*, 1969, 40, 453–70.
   EXPERIMENT I: **Subjects:** $N = 80$; 5, 6 yrs (low, middle SES). **Measures:** Ss played a marble-dropping game in which they were free to drop marbles into either of 2 holes. Following an initial baseline period, Ss were reinforced (good-fine or right-correct) for dropping a marble into the hole they had chosen less frequently during baseline. The reinforcers were said in either a positive or neutral tone of voice. The number of reinforced responses Ss performed and the total number of marbles they dropped were recorded. **Results:** No sex differences.
   EXPERIMENT II: **Subjects:** $N = 168$; 5–6 yrs. **Measures:** Procedures similar to Experiment I were followed. The reinforcers E used (good-right or bad-wrong) were said in either a positive, neutral, or negative tone of voice. **Results:** No sex differences.

Brotsky, S., and Kagan, J. Stability of the orienting reflex in infants to auditory and visual stimuli as indexed by cardiac deceleration. *Child Development*, 1971, 42, 2066–70.
   Subjects: $N = 79$; tested at 4, 8, 13 mos. **Measures:** At 4 and 8 months of age, Ss were exposed to a series of achromatic slides. At 8 months, infants also heard 4 different recitations read by a male voice. At 13 months of age, 3 3-dimensional figures were shown to Ss, 1 at a time. Afterward, auditory stimuli (identical to the set of stimuli used at 8 months) were presented. At each session, cardiac deceleration to the first stimulus in the visual or auditory series was assessed. **Results:** No sex differences.

Brown, F. An experimental and critical study of the intelligence of Negro and White kindergarten children. *J. Genetic Psychology*, 1944, 65, 161–75.
   Subjects: $N = 432$; 5–6 yrs. **Measures:** Stanford-Binet Intelligence Test, Form L. **Results:** No sex differences.

Brown, H. Children's comprehension of relativized English sentences. *Child Development*, 1971, 42, 1923–36.
   Subjects: $N = 96$; 3–5 yrs. **Measures:** Ss heard a sentence describing 1 of 2 pictures and were asked to choose the matching picture. **Results:** No sex differences.

Brown, L. Developmental differences on the effects of stimulus novelty on discrimination learning. *Child Development*, 1969, 40, 813–22.
   Subjects: $N = 64$; 4–5 yrs (middle-high SES). **Measures:** Ss initially learned a constant posi-

tive–constant negative, 2-choice discrimination learning problem to criterion. Ss were then presented with 1 of 4 shift problems. For half the Ss, the positive stimulus was replaced either by a new constant positive stimulus or by a series of new positive stimuli, a different one of which appeared on each trial. For the other half of the Ss, similar replacement procedures were followed with the constant negative stimulus. **Results:** No sex differences were found in number of trials needed to reach criterion on the initial constant positive–constant negative problem or in number of correct responses made on the shift problems.

Brown, R. A. Interaction effects of social and tangible reinforcement. *J. Experimental Child Psychology,* 1971, *12,* 289–303.

Subjects: $N = 60$; 4–6 yrs. **Measures:** Ss performed a bar-pressing task under either tangible, social, or alternated tangible and social reinforcement. Difference scores were derived by subtracting Ss' base rates from their average response rates in each of the 5 experimental trial blocks. **Results:** (1) Over trials, girls showed a greater increase in performance than boys ($p < .01$). Tests for sex differences within each block of trials showed that girls responded to the reinforcement in trial blocks 3, 4, and 5 more than boys did ($p < .05$). (2) During extinction, no sex differences were found.

Brownfield, M. K. Sex and stimulus time difference in afterimage durations. *Perceptual & Motor Skills,* 1965, *21,* 446.

Subjects: $N = 30$; 18–20 yrs (college). **Measures:** In a dark room, Ss viewed a stimulus of .2 candlepower, 1 square centimeter in area. The durations of Ss' afterimages were recorded. **Results:** Men's afterimages lasted longer than women's.

Bruning, J. L. Direct and vicarious effects of a shift in magnitude of reward on performance. *J. Personality & Social Psychology,* 1965, *2,* 278–82.

Subjects: $N = 144$; 5 yrs. **Measures:** Ss received rewards each time they performed a lever movement response. In 1 condition, Ss played 2 sets of 30 trials each. In a second condition, 1 group of Ss (models) performed 30 trials while a second group of Ss (observers) watched. Observer Ss then played 30 trials by themselves. **Results:** (1) There were no main sex differences. (2) The presence of an observer facilitated the performance of female models, but inhibited the performance of male models ($p < .025$).

Bruning, J. L., and Husa, F. T. Given names and stereotyping. *Developmental Psychology,* 1972, *7,* 91 (brief report).

Subjects: $N = 60$; 5, 8, 11 yrs. **Measures:** 2 male stickfigures were presented, 1 with an active and 1 with a passive name; statement to Ss: "These are two little boys. This one's name is —— and this one's name is ——. Which one do you think would ——?" 25 active and 25 passive behavioral statements were used. Number of correct matches of behaviors with names was recorded. **Results:** Among 11-year-old Ss, boys made more correct matches than girls.

Bryan, J. H., and Walbek, N. H. Preaching and practicing generosity: children's actions and reactions. *Child Development,* 1970, *41,* 329–53.

EXPERIMENT I: **Subjects:** $N = 91$; 8, 9 yrs. **Measures:** Ss observed a same-sex adult model win gift certificates while playing a bowling game. On winning trials, the model either did or did not always donate a proportion of his certificates to charity. On no-win trials, one-third of the Ss in each group heard the model preach generosity, and one-third heard the model preach selfishness; the remaining third heard the model make neutral comments. All Ss then played the game in the model's absence. The number of Ss who donated in each condition was recorded. **Results:** No sex differences.

EXPERIMENT II: **Subjects:** $N = 168$; 8, 9 yrs. **Measures:** Same as Experiment I, except videotapes of peer models were used instead of live adult models. After playing the bowling game, Ss evaluated the model's attractiveness. **Results:** No sex differences were found in Ss' donating behavior or their attractiveness ratings.

EXPERIMENT III: **Subjects:** $N = 132$; 8, 9 yrs (white and black). **Measures:** Same as Experiment II, with 2 exceptions: (1) the model's appeals to Ss to be either charitable or selfish were personalized, and (2) Ss were asked to comment into a microphone while playing the game. Ss were rated for the emphasis they placed upon generosity. **Results:** (1) No main sex differences were found in Ss' attractiveness ratings. (2) Among black Ss, boys preached more generosity than girls. No sex difference was found among white Ss. (3) The authors did not report whether tested for sex differences in donating behavior.

Bryan, J. H., Redfield, J., and Mader, S. Words and deeds about altruism and the subsequent reinforcement of the model. *Child Development*, 1971, *42*, 1501–8.

Subjects: $N = 96$; 7–8 yrs. Measures: Ss initially observed a videotape of an adult female model playing a bowling game. On selected trials, the model won gift certificates and either donated all of them to charity or kept them for herself. On no-win trials, the model either urged Ss to be charitable or selfish or made neutral comments. When the film ended, the model entered the experimental room where Ss were seated. Ss then played a lever-pressing game. On each trial, Ss could choose to press either a lever that yielded an M&M candy or 1 that illuminated a bright light. Half the Ss in each treatment condition were verbally reinforced by the model whenever the blue light came on. The remaining Ss received no social reinforcement. Afterward, Ss related the model's attractiveness. Results: No sex differences were found in Ss' attractiveness ratings or in the number of times they pressed the lever associated with the blue light.

Bryden, M. P. Auditory-visual and sequential-spatial matching in relation to reading ability. *Child Development*, 1972, *43*, 824–32.

Subjects: $N = 40$; 11 yrs. Measures: Ss were given a same-different matching task in which patterns were presented in 3 modes: auditory, visual-sequential, and dot patterns. Each of 20 pairs of patterns was presented once in each combination. Ss had to decide if 2 patterns were the same or different. Results: No sex differences.

Buck, M. R., and Austrin, H. R. Factors related to school achievement in an economically disadvantaged group. *Child Development*, 1971, *42*, 1813–26.

Subjects: $N = 100$; 14–16 yrs (black). Measures: Pairs of adequate achievers and underachievers were established on the basis of the Iowa Tests of Basic Skills. Ss were given Crandall's Intellectual Achievement Responsibility questionnaire. Teachers rated Ss on classroom behavior, attitudes, personality characteristics, and performance. Mothers rated their own attitudes and Ss' attitudes. Results: (1) Among adequate achievers, teachers rated girls less deviant in behavior than boys ($p < .01$). (2) Among adequate achievers, girls received higher scores on IAR total ($p < .05$) and on IAR negative ($p < .01$) than boys; i.e. girls in this group were more internal, especially for negative events. (3) There were no sex differences for total positive teacher rating. (4) Mothers of girls were more reactive concerning daughters' intellectual achievement than mothers of boys ($p < .05$). (5) Mothers of girls expressed higher expectancy levels, higher degree of satisfaction with accomplishments, and higher minimal academic standards than mothers of boys ($p < .01, p < .01, p < .05$).

Buck, R. W., Savin, V. J., Miller, R. E., and Caul, W. F. Communication of affect through facial expressions in humans. *J. Personality & Social Psychology*, 1972, *23*, 362–71.

Subjects: $N = 38$; 18–21 yrs (college). Measures: 1 subject (sender) in each pair of like-sex Ss watched slides designed to elicit affect, while the other subject (observer) viewed the sender subject's face over television. After each slide, both observer and sender Ss made judgments about the strength and pleasantness of the emotional response experienced by sender Ss. Skin conductance and heart rate were recorded. Results: (1) No sex differences were found in the physiological responses of senders. (2) Among observer Ss, women had higher heart rates than men ($p < .01$). Men had more numerous skin-conductance responses than women ($p < .05$).

Bugenthal, D. E., Kaswan, J. W., and Love, L. R. Perception of contradictory meanings conveyed by verbal and nonverbal channels. *J. Personality & Social Psychology*, 1970a, *16*, 647–55.

Subjects: $N = 160$; 5–12 yrs and parents. Measures: Ss evaluated videotaped messages that varied on 3 dimensions: vocal channel (voice), visual channel (facial expressions, etc.), and verbal channel (script). Each channel contained either positive-evaluative (friendly) or negative-evaluative (unfriendly) content. Results: Women speakers were rated more negatively than men ($p < .01$); the difference was greater for conflicting messages than for messages that were either uniformly positive or uniformly negative.

Bugenthal, D. E., Kaswan, J. W., Love, L. R., and Fox, M. N. Child versus adult perception of evaluative messages in verbal, vocal, and visual channels. *Developmental Psychology*, 1970b, *2*, 367–75.

Subjects: $N = 120$; 5–18 yrs and parents. Measures: Ss rated televised parent-child interaction scenes on a 13-point scale representing degrees of positive and negative evaluation. Scenes were either positive (friendly), neutral, or negative (unfriendly) in content, voice tone, and/or facial expression. Results: (1) There were no sex differences in ratings of male actor scenes or female actor scenes. (2) Female actors were evaluated more favorably in positive scenes and more unfavorably in negative scenes than male actors.

Burton, G. M. Variations in the ontogeny of linear patterns among young children. Unpublished doctoral dissertation, University of Connecticut, 1973.
Subjects: $N = 111$; 4–7 yrs (inner-city schools). **Measures:** 3 tasks involving linear patterns (reproduction, identification, and extension) in 3 cognitive modes (enactive, iconic, and symbolic) were used to assess patterning ability. **Results:** No sex differences.

Burton, R. V. Correspondence between behavioral and doll-play measures of conscience. *Developmental Psychology*, 1971, 5, 320–32.
Subjects: $N = 60$; 4 yrs (2 studies). **Measures:** In each of 2 doll-play sessions, Ss completed 4 deviation story stems. Ss' responses were scored for the presence of the following: reparations (actions whereby the deviation is repaired), punishment (e.g. verbal censure, isolation, physical punishment, etc.), and confession (admission of the deviation). Between doll-play sessions, Ss were taught the rules of beanbag game, after which Ss were left alone for 3 minutes to play the game. The number of Ss who conformed to the rules and the number who deviated were recorded. In the second study, 2 temptation story stems were added in each doll-play session. **Results:** (1) When both samples were combined, girls were found to deviate from the rules more often than boys. (2) No sex differences were found in Ss' Session 1 or Session 2 doll-story completions. (3) No sex differences were found in changes in Ss' doll-story completions between Session 1 and Session 2.

Burton, R. V., Allinsmith, W., and Maccoby, E. E. Resistance to temptation in relation to sex of child, sex of experimenter, and withdrawal of attention. *J. Personality & Social Psychology*, 1966, 3, 253–58.
Subjects: $N = 112$; 4 yrs. **Measures:** Ss were taught the rules of a beanbag game by either a same-sex or opposite-sex E. Ss then performed an intervening task, receiving either continuous or interrupted attention from E. Following E's departure, Ss played the beanbag game for attractive toys. For each act of breaking the rules, Ss were rewarded with a "hit." The number of bags Ss threw correctly before deviating from the rules was recorded. **Results:** (1) No main sex differences were found. For boys, continuous attention from E produced greater resistance to deviation than interrupted attention from E ($p < .01$). No treatment effect was found for girls. (2) Ss assigned to opposite-sex Es threw more bags before deviating from the rules than Ss who were assigned to same-sex E's ($p < .05$).

Bush, L. E., II. Individual differences multidimensional scaling of adjectives denoting feeling. *J. Personality & Social Psychology*, 1973, 25, 50–57.
Subjects: $N = 762$; 18–21 yrs (white and black, college). **Measures:** Using Ss' judgments of the similarity of adjective pairs, 264 adjectives were scaled by the Individual Differences Multidimensional Scaling method (INDSCAL). **Results:** No sex differences.

Buss, A. H. Instrumentality of aggression, feedback, and frustration as determinants of physical aggression. *J. Personality & Social Psychology*, 1966, 3, 153–62.
Subjects: $N = 240$; 18–21 yrs (college). **Measures:** Ss administered shocks to either same-sex or opposite-sex victims. **Results:** Men administered higher intensities of shock to victims than women did. Ss administered more intense shocks to men than women ($p < .001$).

Butter, E. J., and Zung, B. J. A developmental investigation of the effect of sensory modality on form recognition in children. *Developmental Psychology*, 1970, 3, 276 (brief report).
Subjects: $N = 144$; 5–8 yrs. **Measures:** Ss could see, feel, or see and feel each stimulus form while trying to find the matching cutout on a formboard containing 58 cutouts of varying size, shape, and orientation. Number of recognition errors was recorded. **Results:** No sex differences.

Byrne, D., Clore, G. L., Jr., and Worchel, P. Effect of economic similarity-dissimilarity on interpersonal attraction. *J. Personality & Social Psychology*, 1966, 4, 220–24.
Subjects: $N = 84$; 19 yrs (college). **Measures:** Using the Interpersonal Judgment Scale, Ss evaluated strangers on the basis of the strangers' responses to attitude items and to items dealing with "spending money." **Results:** No sex differences were found in attraction to stranger.

Byrne, D., Lamberth, J., and Ervin, C. R. Continuity between the experimental study of attraction and real-life computer dating. *J. Personality & Social Psychology*, 1970, 16, 157–65.
Subjects: $N = 88$; 18–21 yrs (college). **Measures:** Men and women were paired on the basis of maximal or minimal similarity of responses on an attitude-personality questionnaire. After

spending 30 minutes together, Ss evaluated each other on the Interpersonal Judgment Scale. Two to three months later, further information was obtained from Ss, including whether each S's evaluation of his or her date was influenced more by physical attractiveness or by attitude similarity. **Results:** (1) No sex differences were found in Ss' responses to the IJS. (2) 18 men and 17 women indicated that their evaluations were influenced more by either physical attractiveness or attitude similarity. The remaining Ss (53) indicated either that both factors were equally important or that neither factor was important. Of the 35 Ss who selected one or the other, most of the men ($N = 14$) indicated that their evaluations were more influenced by physical attractiveness, while most women ($N = 16$) indicated that their evaluations were more influenced by attitude similarity ($p. < .001$).

Cairns, R. B. Informational properties of verbal and nonverbal events. *J. Personality & Social Psychology*, 1967, *5*, 353–57.
   Subjects: $N = 40$; 9 yrs. **Measures:** Ss were given a modified version of the Wisconsin Card-Sorting Test. During the first 50 trials (acquisition phase), Ss were reinforced for choosing the correct response. During the last 20 trials (extinction phase), no reinforcement was administered. **Results:** No sex differences.

Cairns, R. B. Meaning and attention as determinants of social reinforcer effectiveness. *Child Development*, 1970, *41*, 1067–82.
   EXPERIMENT I: **Subjects:** $N = 120$; 6, 7 yrs. **Measures:** During the first phase of the experiment Ss were instructed to put cards into the "mouth" of a machine. On 16 of the 43 trials Ss received an M&M candy after responding. Depending on the condition to which they were assigned, on each trial the delivery of an M&M was either preceded or not preceded by a signal (for half the Ss, the signal was the word "right"; for the remaining Ss, the signal was a bell-light combination). After Ss completed trial 43, no M&M's were delivered. Every subsequent response was followed by a signal. The number of cards Ss put into the machine during a 5-minute period was recorded. During the second phase of the experiment, Ss were tested on a discrimination-learning problem. On each trial, Ss were presented with a red and a blue token. Selection of the "correct" color was always followed by either the word "right" or a bell-light combination. The response measure was number of times Ss chose the reinforced color. **Results:** No sex differences.
   EXPERIMENT II: **Subjects:** $N = 20$; 6, 7 yrs. **Measures:** Similar to Experiment I. **Results:** No sex differences.
   EXPERIMENT III: **Subjects:** $N = 40$; 8, 9 yrs. **Measures:** Similar to Experiment I. **Results:** No sex differences.

Caldwell, E. C., and Hall, V. C. Concept learning in discrimination tasks. *Developmental Psychology*, 1970, *2*, 41–48.
   Subjects: $N = 144$; 4–5, 7–8 yrs. **Measures:** Ss under 1 of 3 sets of instructions picked which of several transformed figures were the same as a standard form. Some Ss were allowed to rotate the standard form, others were not. **Results:** There were no sex differences in percentage of correct matches with line-to-curve transformations, rotation and reversal transformations, perspective transformations, or break-and-close transformations. Instructions to rotate affected the two sexes equally.

Calhoun, W. Stanford Research Institute, Menlo Park, California. Personal communications, 1972.
   Subjects: $N = 12,350$; 8, 9 yrs. **Measures:** Raven's Coloured Progressive Matrices (abbreviated form). **Results:** Boys scored higher than girls.

Callard, E. D. Achievement motive of four-year-olds and maternal achievement expectancies. *J. Experimental Education*, 1968, *36*, 15–23.
   Subjects: $N = 80$; 4 yrs and mothers (low, high SES). **Measures:** (1) 4 achievement tasks (bead designs, picture memory, basket throw, drawing forms) were administered to Ss. After performing each task, Ss were given the opportunity to repeat either an easy, difficult, or challenging version of the task. The number of times Ss chose to repeat a challenging task was recorded. (2) Torgoff's Parental Developmental Timetable was used to assess the age at which mothers thought it appropriate (a) to start to teach, encourage, or train a child to adopt new, more mature modes of behavior (Achievement Inducing Scale); and (b) to allow the child to engage in activities requiring autonomy and independence of action and decision (Independence-Granting Scale). A controlling score was calculated by dividing the mean age recommended on the IG scale by the mean age on the IA scale. **Results:** (1) Girls chose to resume more challenging tasks than boys did. (2) The mean age recommended by mothers of boys on

the IG scale was younger than the mean age recommended by mothers of girls. No differences were found in AI or controlling scores.

Cameron, P. The generation gap: beliefs about sexuality and self-reported sexuality. *Developmental Psychology*, 1970a, 3, 272 (brief report).
Subjects: $N = 317$; 18–25, 40–55, 65–79 yrs. **Measures:** Ss responded to a questionnaire assessing their beliefs about their own and the 3 generations' sexual knowledge, desire, skill, capacity, attempts, opportunities, access, and frequency. **Results:** No sex differences.

Cameron, P. The generation gap: which generation is believed powerful versus generational members' self-appraisals of power. *Developmental Psychology*, 1970b, 3, 403–4.
Subjects: $N = 317$; 18–25, 40–55, 65–79 yrs. **Measures:** Ss completed a questionnaire assessing their beliefs about their own wealth and power, and the differences in wealth and power among the 3 generations. **Results:** Men tended to judge themselves as more powerful and wealthy than women did (no statistics given).

Campione, J. C. The effects of stimulus redundancy on transfer of stimulus pretraining. *Child Development*, 1971, 42, 551–59.
Subjects: $N = 64$, 3–5 yrs. **Measures:** Ss performed high- or low-redundancy tasks from a modified version of the Wisconsin General Test Apparatus. Verbal and perceptual stimulus pretraining were given; task involved discrimination-learning transfer. **Results:** No sex differences.

Campione, J. C., and Beaton, V. L. Transfer of training: some boundary conditions and initial theory. *J. Experimental Child Psychology*, 1972, 13, 94–114.
Experiment IIIa: **Subjects:** $N = 36$; 3–6 yrs. **Measures:** After verbal pretraining, Ss were given a simultaneous 2-choice discrimination-learning task. **Results:** No sex differences.
Experiment IIIb: **Subjects:** $N = 48$; 3–6 yrs. **Measures:** Ss were divided into 2 groups. One-half were pretrained on a successive discrimination-learning problem, while the other half were pretrained on a simultaneous discrimination problem. After reaching the learning criterion, Ss in both groups were tested on a simultaneous 2-choice discrimination problem involving either an intradimensional (ID) or extradimensional (ED) shift. **Results:** No sex differences.
Experiment IV: **Subjects:** $N = 128$; 5–6 yrs. **Measures:** Same as Experiment IIIb. **Results:** No sex differences.
Experiment V: **Subjects:** $N = 64$; 3–6 yrs. **Measures:** After verbal pretraining, Ss were tested on a successive discrimination-learning task. **Results:** No sex differences.

Canavan, D. Field dependence in children as a function of grade, sex, and ethnic group membership. Paper received at the APA Meeting, Washington, D.C., 1969.
Subjects: $N = 1,510$; 5–11 yrs (white, black, Mexican). **Measures:** Man in the frame test (adaptation of Witkin's Rod-and-Frame Test). **Results:** When scores were adjusted to control for differences in IQ (as measured by the Full Scale WISC), boys were more field-independent than girls.

Canon, L. K. Motivational state, stimulus selection, and distractibility. *Child Development*, 1967, 38, 489–96.
Subjects: $N = 40$; 10 yrs. **Measures:** (1) 10 boys and 10 girls were assigned to isolation or nonisolation conditions. Nonisolated Ss spent time with E in casual conversation prior to the task; isolated Ss waited alone for 20 minutes prior to the task. (2) All Ss worked under the influence of a social distractor involving a female voice relating a nurturant story as well as an impersonal distractor involving nonhuman sound effects. All Ss worked on 2 forms of a concept-utilization task in which they were required to select symbols out of several alternatives that identically matched a standard. **Results:** No sex differences.

Cantor, G. N. Effects of a "boredom" treatment on children's simple RT performance. *Psychonomic Science*, 1968, 10, 299–300.
Subjects: $N = 60$; 6 yrs. **Measures:** Ss were given alternating blocks of trials on a picture-viewing and a reaction-time (RT) task. On the picture-viewing task, half of the Ss viewed different colored slides of high-interest value (nonbored group), while the remaining Ss were repeatedly exposed to the same geometric form (bored group). On the RT task, Ss had to move their finger off a start button and depress a response button upon representation of a light stimulus. Response measures were start (time from onset of light to the moment Ss removed their fingers from the start button) and travel speed (time from the moment Ss removed their fingers from the start button to the moment they depressed the response button). **Re-**

sults: (1) No sex differences were found in start speed. (2) For travel speed, boys were faster than girls ($p < .01$). Nonbored girls were faster than bored girls; bored boys were faster than nonbored boys ($p < .04$).

Cantor, G. N. Effects of context on preschool children's judgments. *J. Experimental Child Psychology*, 1971, *11*, 505–12.
Subjects: $N = 40$; 4–5 yrs. Measures: Ss saw 10 slide pictures of either happy or unhappy faces and then rated ambiguous slides of an individual infant or young child on a 5-point happy-unhappy continuum. Results: No sex differences.

Cantor, G. N. Effects of familiarization on children's ratings of pictures of whites and blacks. *Child Development*, 1972a, *43*, 1219–29.
Subjects: $N = 80$; 9–12 yrs. Measures: Ss were initially exposed to photographs of 3 black boys and 3 white boys. Ss then rated these pictures and those of 6 other boys (3 black, 3 white) on the extent to which they "would like to bring the boy home to spend time with them and their families." Results: Boys gave more favorable ratings to black boys than girls did ($p < .01$). No sex differences were found in Ss' ratings of white boys.

Cantor, G. N. Use of a conflict paradigm to study race awareness in children. *Child Development*, 1972b, *43*, 1437–42 (and personal communication).
Subjects: $N = 60$; 7–8 yrs. Measures: Ss viewed pairs of photographs of boys in which both were black, both were white, or one was black and one was white. A story was read describing behaviors of the boys in the photographs, and Ss were asked to choose which of the 2 boys was the "good" or the "bad" boy. Response latencies and choices were measured. Results: Boys had greater response latencies for choosing the "good" boy ($p < .05$), whereas girls had greater latencies for choosing the "bad" boy ($p < .05$).

Cantor, G. N., and Whitely, J. H. Effects of rewarding children's high- and low-amplitude motor responses. *Psychonomic Science*, 1969, *16*, 211–12.
Subjects: $N = 48$; 4–5 yrs. Measures: Ss were presented with a wooden mallet and a padded metal plate that served as a response target. On baseline trials, Ss were informed they could hit the target either "hard" or "soft." Response amplitudes were recorded. Subsequently, a series of 36 training trials were administered; half the Ss were reinforced for response amplitudes exceeding their baseline scores while the remaining Ss were reinforced for amplitudes lower in magnitude than their baseline scores. Response amplitudes were again recorded. Results: (1) No sex differences were found in either baseline or training response amplitudes. (2) When difference scores were computed by subtracting baseline scores from training scores, no main sex differences were found. Boys' response amplitudes decreased between baseline and the first block of 4 trials; girls showed an increase ($p < .05$).

Carey, G. L. Sex differences in problem-solving performance as a function of attitude differences. *J. Abnormal & Social Psychology*, 1958, *56*, 256–60.
Subjects: $N = 144$; 18–21 yrs (college). Measures: Before and after participating in a discussion, the disguised intent of which was the promotion of a more favorable attitude toward problem solving, Ss were administered problem sets and a scale designed to measure their attitudes toward problem solving. Results: (1) Men had more favorable attitudes toward problem solving than women. (2) Following the discussion, women performed better on the second problem set than on the first set ($p < .02$); men showed no improvement ($p < .05$). (3) There were no sex differences in attitude score improvement following the discussion.

Carlson, R. Stability and change in the adolescent's self-image. *Child Psychology*, 1965, *36*, 659–66.
Subjects: $N = 49$; tested at 11, 17 yrs. Measures: Ss were given parallel forms of a self-descriptive questionnaire at both ages. Self and ideal-self descriptions were included. Kelley's Role Construct Repertory Test was administered at age 17. Results: (1) There were no sex differences at the preadolescent level. (2) Among 17-year-old Ss, girls were more socially oriented than boys ($p < .02$). (3) There were no sex differences in level or stability of self-esteem.

Carlson, R. Sex differences in ego functioning: exploratory studies of agency and communion. *J. Consulting & Clinical Psychology*, 1971, *37*, 267–77.
EXPERIMENT I: Subjects: $N = 76$; 18–21 yrs (college). Measures: Carlson's Adjective Checklist. Results: A greater number of women than men checked interpersonal adjectives (e.g.

friendly, persuasive) more frequently than individualistic adjectives (e.g. ambitious, idealistic).

EXPERIMENT II: **Subjects:** $N = 41$; 18–21 yrs (college). **Measures:** A modified version of Kelley's Role Construct Repertory Test. **Results:** When asked to choose from among 3 persons (1 of whom was the self) the 2 who were most alike and different from the third, more women than men included themselves with another person ($p < .05$).

EXPERIMENT III: **Subjects:** $N = 82$; 18–21 yrs (college). **Measures:** Ss were asked to write a brief personality sketch of a friend. The first sentence of each sketch was scored for the presence or absence of demographic constructs. **Results:** More men than women included demographic constructs in their first sentence ($p < .01$).

EXPERIMENT IV: **Subjects:** $N = 48$; 18–21 yrs (college). **Measures:** Ss were asked to describe the physical-geographic environment of their childhood. Responses were classified as either proximal (inclusion of personal memories, attention to details that only a person who has lived in a neighborhood would know about) or distal (demographic description of the town, its climate, size of population, SES levels, etc.). **Results:** More women than men gave proximal responses ($p < .05$).

EXPERIMENT V: **Subjects:** $N = 55$; 18–21 yrs (college). **Measures:** Ss were asked the following questions: What sort of person do you expect to be in 15 years? What will you be doing? How might have you changed? Ss' responses were scored on whether mention was made of work, family, physical change, or inner psychological change. **Results:** More men than women mentioned work ($p < .05$), whereas more women than men mentioned inner psychological change ($p < .01$) and family ($p < .01$).

EXPERIMENT VI: **Subjects:** $N = 43$; 18–21 yrs (college). **Measures:** Ss were asked to recall emotional incidents in their lives. Ss' responses were coded as agentic (concerned with achievement, success, separateness, or aloneness), communal (concerned with social acceptance, togetherness, or dependence), or mixed (having both agentic and communal themes). **Results:** More men than women gave agentic responses (in reporting negative affects, $p < .05$; overall, $p < .02$).

Carlson, R., and Levy, N. Brief method for assessing social-personal orientation. *Psychological Reports*, 1968, *23*, 911–14.
  Subjects: $N = 133$; 18–45 yrs. **Measures:** Ss completed an adjective checklist measuring social-personal orientation. **Results:** Men were more frequently personally oriented, women more socially oriented ($p < .001$).

Carlson, R., and Levy, N. Self, values, and affects: derivations from Tomkins' polarity theory. *J. Personality & Social Psychology*, 1970, *16*, 338–45.
  EXPERIMENT I: **Subjects:** $N = 202$; 18–21 yrs (college, black). **Measures:** Ss completed the Carlson adjective checklist and were classified as either socially or personally oriented. **Results:** No sex differences.
  EXPERIMENT II: **Subjects:** $N = 80$; 18–21 yrs (college, black). **Measures:** Ss were presented with 25 pictures and asked to judge whether each picture portrayed a pleasant or unpleasant experience. **Results:** No sex differences.

Carlson, R., and Price, M. A. Generality of social schemas. *J. Personality & Social Psychology*, 1966, *3*, 589–92.
  Subjects: $N = 158$; 7–11, 25–50 yrs. **Measures:** Ss were asked to arrange 9 sets of stimulus figures on a felt-covered board (man, woman, child; man, woman, dog; man, child; woman, child; man, woman, 2 rectangles; 3 men, 3 rectangles; 3 women, 3 rectangles; 3 rectangles; square, circle, triangle). For each set, E recorded the order of arrangement and the distance between the figures. **Results:** (1) Males were more likely than females to produce a vertical arrangement of the square, circle, and triangle ($p < .01$). (2) Both sexes centered the like-sexed figure in the man, woman, dog set ($p < .02$).

Caron, A. J. Far transposition of intermediate-size in preverbal children. *J. Experimental Child Psychology*, 1966, *3*, 296–311.
  Subjects: $N = 192$; 3–4 yrs. **Measures:** Multiple discrimination training and far transposition administered to preverbals to test for abstraction of middle size. **Results:** (1) Girls trained faster than boys. (2) Girls were superior to boys in transposition.

Caron, R. F., and Caron, A. J. Degree of stimulus complexity and habituation of visual fixation in infants. *Psychonomic Science*, 1969, *14*, 78–79.
  Subjects: $N = 96$; 14–16 wks. **Measures:** Ss were presented with 15 20-second trials of visual stimuli. Geometric designs were shown on trials 1–4 and 10–12, 1 of 3 red-and-white checker-

board patterns on trials 5–9 and 13, and abstract art photos on trials 14 and 15. Fixation times were recorded. **Results:** (1) On trials 1–4 and 5–9, no sex differences were found in fixation times. The slope of the fixation curve over trials 5–9 was steeper for girls than for boys ($p <$ .025). (2) The decline in fixation time between trial 5 and trial 13 was greater for girls than for boys ($p < .005$). (3) Girls showed a greater increase in fixation time from trial 13 to trial 14 than boys ($p < .005$).

Caron, R. F., Caron, A. J., and Caldwell, R. C. Satiation of visual reinforcement in young infants. *Developmental Psychology*, 1971, 5, 279–89.
    Subjects: $N = 98$; 3½ mos. **Measures:** After a conditioning period in which head turning was continuously reinforced with abstract pictures, Ss were exposed to an interval of variable reinforcement, redundant reinforcement (repeatedly presented 4 x 4 or 24 x 24 checkerboards, or checkerboards alternating in either color, pattern, or both), and recovery (reconditioning of head turning with variable reinforcement). **Results:** (1) There were no sex differences in head-turn rate in the minute prior to onset of redundancy. (2) Girls' head turning declined faster than boys' in the minute prior to redundancy, plus 3 minutes of redundancy ($p < .001$). (3) During each minute of redundancy, the response rate of girls was lower than that of boys ($p < .01$, $p < .001$, $p < .05$). (4) There were no sex differences in recovery of the head-turn response. (5) There were no sex differences in hard crying during any of the 3 intervals.

Carpenter, T. R., and Busse, T. V. Development of self-concept in Negro and White welfare children. *Child Development*, 1969, 40, 935–39.
    Subjects: $N = 80$; 6, 10 yrs (father-absent welfare families). **Measures:** Ss were asked to rate themselves on a 5-point scale for 7 bipolar dimensions of positive-negative qualities. **Results:** Among blacks, girls had a more negative self-concept than boys. No sex difference was found in the white sample.

Carrigan, W. C., and Julian, J. W. Sex and birth-order differences in conformity as a function of need affiliation arousal. *J. Personality & Social Psychology*, 1966, 3, 479–83.
    Subjects: $N = 96$; 11 yrs. **Measures:** One group of Ss initially rated fellow classmates on a sociometric questionnaire; the remaining group of Ss did not. 4 different stories were then presented with each of 10 TAT cards. Ss' task was to pick the story that provided the best description of each TAT picture. Before responding, Ss were informed which stories had received the most votes in another class. The number of times Ss picked the popular choice was recorded. **Results:** Girls made more popular choices than boys ($p < .01$). This sex difference was greater among those Ss who completed the sociometric questionnaire than among those who did not ($p < .05$).

Carroll, W. R. Response availability and percentage of occurrence of response member in children's paired associate learning. *J. Experimental Child Psychology*, 1966, 4, 232–41.
    Subjects: $N = 80$; 10–11 yrs. **Measures:** Ss learned a paired-associates list by either the conventional anticipation method or by having the responses of the to-be-learned list presented in a vertical array next to each stimulus during the anticipation interval. Under both methods, the specific response to each stimulus word appeared on either 33% or 100% of trials. **Results:** There were no main sex differences. Girls gave more correct responses than boys on the first trial block; boys gave more correct responses on several of the later trial blocks.

Carroll, W. R., and Penney, R. Percentage of occurrence of response member, associative strength, and competition in paired associate learning in children. *J. Experimental Child Psychology*, 1966, 3, 258–66.
    Subjects: $N = 56$; 11 yrs. **Measures:** Ss were assigned either to a typical paired-associates task or to one in which the second member of the pair occurred only 33% of the time. Each S learned word pairs of high or low associative strength. One-half learned a competitional list, the other half a concompetitional. **Results:** No sex differences.

Castore, C. H., and Stafford, R. E. The effect of sex role perception on test taking performance. *J. Psychology*, 1970, 74, 175–80.
    Subjects: $N = 462$; 18 yrs (college). **Measures:** Ss were given the Identical Blocks Test and 1 of 3 forms of a spatial visualization test: (a) a neutral form entitled "Pattern Development," (b) a masculine form entitled "Drafting Aptitude Test" (the instructions to this form were read by a male E; performance on the test was related to ability in engineering, architecture, and sheet-metal work), or (c) a feminine form entitled "Fashion Design Aptitude Test" (the instructions were read by a female E; scores on the test were related to success in the fields

of fashion design, pattern-making, and dressmaking). **Results:** Men performed better than women on the Identical Blocks Test and on all 3 forms of the spatial visualization test. The magnitude of the sex differences on the spatial test did not vary among forms.

Cathcart, W. G. The relationship between primary students' rationalization of conservation and their mathematical achievement. *Child Development*, 1971, *42*, 755–65.
> **Subjects:** $N = 120$; 7, 8 yrs. **Measures:** An 8-item conservation test was administered to Ss. Ss were asked to provide a rationale for each of their responses. **Results:** No sex differences were found in the frequency of different modes of rationalization.

Chandler, M. J., Greenspan, S., and Barenboim, C. Judgments of intentionality in response to videotaped and verbally presented moral dilemmas: the medium is the message. *Child Development*, 1973, *44*, 315–20.
> **Subjects:** $N = 80$; 7 yrs. **Measures:** Ss were preesnted with 1 videotape of children and adults portraying a moral dilemma and 1 verbal account of a moral dilemma; intention and seriousness of consequence were varied. Ss were asked to judge which character was the naughtiest and which should be punished the most. **Results:** No sex differences.

Charlesworth, R., and Hartup, W. W. Positive social reinforcement in the nursery school peer group. *Child Development*, 1967, *38*, 993–1002.
> **Subjects:** $N = 70$; 3, 4 yrs. **Measures:** Ss were observed in their preschool over a period of 5 weeks. Measures were taken of the frequency of occurrence of the following types of positive social reinforcement: gives attention and approval to peer; gives affection, shows acceptance of peer; submissively reinforces peer. The total number of other children that each child reinforced was also recorded. **Results:** (1a) Among 3-year-olds, boys scored higher than girls on "gives affection, shows acceptance of peer" and "submissively reinforces peer" ($p < .01$, $p < .05$). Boys also reinforced a greater number of other children than girls did ($p < .001$). Overall, girls gave less positive reinforcement ($p < .02$). (1b) Among 4-year-olds, no sex differences were found. (2) When both age groups were combined, both boys and girls were found to reinforce same-sex peers more frequently than opposite-sex peers.

Cheyne, J. A. Effects of imitation of different reinforcement combinations to a model. *J. Experimental Child Psychology*, 1971, *12*, 258–69.
> **Subjects:** $N = 30$; 8 yrs. **Measures:** Ss performed a word-choice task (2 response alternatives, no feedback) after observing a same-sex peer perform the same task under 3 reinforcement conditions: feedback for right and wrong choices, feedback for right only, and feedback for wrong only. Ss were then instructed to perform the model's choices, under no feedback conditions. **Results:** No sex differences.

Christie, R. Scale construction. In R. Christie and F. L. Geis, eds., *Studies in Machiavellianism*, pp. 10–34. New York: Academic Press, 1970a.
> **Subjects:** $N = 1,596$ (white), 148 (nonwhite); 18–21 yrs (college). **Measures:** Ss were given the Likert-type and forced-choice versions of the Machiavellianism scale. **Results:** Among white Ss, men scored higher than women on both scales. Among nonwhite Ss, men scored higher than women only on the Likert-type scale.

Christie, R. Social correlates of Machiavellianism. In R. Christie and F. L. Geis, *Studies in Machiavellianism*, pp. 314–36. New York: Academic Press, 1970b.
> **Subjects:** $N = 72$; 11 yrs (Puerto Rican, black, Chinese, and European ancestry). **Measures:** A children's version of Christie's Likert-type Machiavellianism Scale was administered to Ss. **Results:** No sex differences.

Cicirelli, V. G. Sibling constellation, creativity, IQ, and academic achievement. *Child Development*, 1967, *38*, 481–90.
> **Subjects:** $N = 609$; 11 yrs. **Measures:** The California Short-Form Test of Mental Maturity, the California Arithmetic Test, the California Language Test, the Gates Basic Reading Tests, and the Minnesota Tests of Creative Thinking, Verbal and Nonverbal Forms A were administered to Ss. An analysis of Ss' scores on the creativity tests yielded 4 factors: (a) verbal fluency-flexibility-originality, (b) verbal elaboration, (c) nonverbal fluency-flexibility-originality, and (d) nonverbal elaboration. **Results:** (1) Girls scored higher in language achievement and verbal elaboration than boys. (2) In 2-child families, girls scored higher in reading achievement than boys.

Clapp, W., and Eichorn, D. Some determinants of perceptual investigatory responses in children. *J. Experimental Child Psychology*, 1965, *2*, 371–87.

Subjects: $N = 24$; 4–5 yrs. **Measures:** 32 stimuli cards were tachistoscopically exposed during 3 experiments: incongruity, redundancy (geometric figures), and redundancy (meaningful objects). The response measure was the mean number of times a card was looked at. **Results:** No sex differences.

Clark, A. H., Wyon, S. M., and Richards, M. P. M. Free play in nursery school children. *J. Child Psychology & Psychiatry*, 1969, *10*, 205–16.

Subjects: $N = 40$; 2–4 yrs. **Measures:** Observations were made of Ss during their morning free play session. **Results:** (1) Boys spent more time than girls playing with blocks, drinking milk, and playing with toys on which they sat and propelled themselves. Girls spent more time than boys painting, playing with dolls, and engaging in table activities (cutting, gluing, sewing, crayoning, etc.). No sex differences were found in the amount of time Ss spent playing with cars, trucks, puzzles, old car parts, sand, plasticine, clay, or musical instruments; or in the amount of time they spent playing house, sawing and hammering, getting out/putting back toys, or climbing up and playing in the balcony. (2) No sex differences were found in average length of time between activity changes or in the amount of time Ss spent in supervised work. (3) More boys than girls exhibited the tendency to have a few close friends ($p < .01$). More children were observed with whom boys never played than girls ($p = .02$). (4) No sex differences were found in average number of companions, in the number of times Ss were observed alone or with teacher, or in the number of times they initiated contact with the teacher.

Clarke-Stewart, K. A. Interactions between mothers and their young children: characteristics and consequences. *Monographs of Society for Research in Child Development*, 1973, *38*, no. 153.

Subjects: $N = 36$; tested at 9–18 mos (black and white low-SES firstborns), and their mothers. **Measures:** *The capital letters following many of the measures listed below refer to the factors on which the measures load. The 5 infant factors (Competence, C; Object Orientation, O; Early Test Talent, E; Physical Attachment, P; and Irritability, I) and 3 maternal factors (Optimal Care, O; Effectiveness, E; and Restrictiveness, R) reported here were among the 11 factors with eigenvalues greater than 1 that emerged from factor analyses of the data.* 12 home visits were made to each mother-child pair. (1) At the initial home visit, interviews were conducted with mothers to assess their attitudes toward their children. (2) During 7 of the visits, naturalistic observations were made of a variety of infant and maternal behaviors. Infants were assessed on the following: schema development (C); attachment to mother (P); positive involvement with mother (C); number of vocalizations to mother (C); number of looks to mother (C); number of prolonged involvements with objects (O); stimulation by materials (looks at or plays with toys or other objects) (O); number and variety of objects played with (0); frequency of negative behavior (cries, fusses, whines, frets when not hurt) (I); physical attachment to mother (P); frequency of giving, offering, or taking object to mother; number of 10-second intervals spent eating or sleeping; frequency of vocalizations; number of interactions with observer; activity level. Mothers were assessed on the following: verbal stimulation (O); frequency of giving, showing, or placing toy near child (O); social stimulation (O); rejectingness (O); responsiveness to infant's distress and demand behaviors (O); responsiveness to infant's social signals (O); appropriateness (selectivity of mother's response, appropriateness for infant's age) (O); referential speech ratio (O); frequency of looking to infant (O); frequency of giving food, object, or toy to infant (O); directiveness; physical contact with infant; restrictiveness (R); frequency of nonresponsive speech; effectiveness of physical contact; effectiveness of stimulation with materials (O); effectiveness of instrumental speech (E); effectiveness of social behavior (E). Also recorded during these observation sessions were the number of times mother and child were present in the same room, the number of times they were in eye-to-eye contact, the number of times they interacted, and the number of times they played together. At 17 months, the number, functional availability, variety, and age appropriateness of the infant's toys were assessed. When the data from these sessions were analyzed, scores from the first 3 visits were summed together to yield a combined score, as were the scores from the final 3 visits. (3) The Bayley Mental and Motor Scales were given to the infants when they were 10½–12½ months old, and again when they were 17–18 months old. Infants' scores on the Motor Scale were combined with the ratings observers assigned to them on a developmental checklist to yield an overall measure of motor development. Their scores on the Mental Scale loaded on the factor Early Test Talent. (4) After a brief home observation session at 11–13 months of age, mother-infant pairs were brought to the laboratory for further testing. As they arrived, Ss were led to a group of attractive toys, while their mothers were directed to chairs in the corner of the room. The infants were then exposed to a sequence of events consisting of varying episodes of free play, stranger intrusion, and mother absence. The episodes were arranged in an order designed to be increasingly stressful for the infant. 5 measures were assessed during this session: intensity of attachment to mother (P); positive social responsiveness to the female stranger (P); variety of toys played with (O); average length of involvement with individual toys (C); "play level." The latter 3 variables were assessed only during the mother-present free-play episodes. (5) When Ss were 12–14 months old, items for assessing cognitive development from 4 of the Uzgiris-Hunt series were administered; 3 scores were obtained: objective permanence (C); schema development (E); and object relations (E). (6) At 17 months of age, Ss completed several tests designed to assess language competence (C). (7) At the final home visit, mothers completed a questionnaire assessing their attitudes toward their children and their knowledge of child rearing and child development. Results: (1) During the first 3 home observation sessions, no sex differences were found on any measure (2) During the last 3 sessions in the home, girls spent more time eating and sleeping, exhibited more positive involvement with their mothers, received higher scores on the measures of language competence, exhibited fewer prolonged involvements with objects, and looked at and played with toys and other objects less frequently than boys did. (3) When all visits were taken into consideration, white boys were found to be more object-oriented than white girls; no difference was found between black boys and black girls. No sex differences were found among Ss of either race on the other 4 factors—Competence, Early Test Talent, Physical Attachment, and Irritability. (4) Among white Ss, mothers of boys scored higher than mothers of girls on 2 measures: "plays with infant" and "gives, shows, or places toy near infant"; among black Ss, the reverse was true. On the questionnaire administered at the final home session, boys' mothers expressed more positive attitudes toward their children than girls' mothers. No sex differences were found on any other measure of maternal behavior or on any of the 3 maternal factors—Optimal Care, Effectiveness, or Restrictiveness.

Clement, D. E., and Sistrunk, F. Judgments of pattern goodness and pattern preference as functions of age and pattern uncertainty. *Developmental Psychology,* 1971, 5, 389–94.
Subjects: $N = 96$; 9–10, 13–14, 17–18, 20–21 yrs. Measures: Ss rated dot patterns of known pattern uncertainty for "goodness" (how well formed they were) and for their own preference. Results: No sex differences.

Clore, G. L., and Jeffery, K. M. Emotional role playing, attitude change, and attraction toward a disabled person. *J. Personality & Social Psychology,* 1972, 23, 105–11.
Subjects: $N = 76$; 18–21 yrs (college). Measures: Ss in one group played the role of a person confined to a wheelchair for an hour, while Ss in a second treatment group walked behind role players, observing their experiences. Afterward, Ss responded to affective ratings and attitude scales and indicated their attraction to E (who appeared to be confined to a wheelchair). Ss also provided written descriptions of their experiences, which were analyzed for emotional content. Results: (1) Women described themselves as feeling weaker ($p < .01$) and more anxious ($p < .01$) than men did. (2) Women expressed a more favorable attitude toward disabled students than men did ($p < .01$). (3) No sex differences were found in attraction to E or in Ss' written descriptions of their experiences.

Coates, B. White adult behavior toward Black and White children. *Child Development,* 1972, 43, 143–54.
Subjects: $N = 48$; 18–23 yrs. Measures: Ss were asked to instruct a black or white male child how to perform a discrimination task. The child's responses were fixed so that each adult thought his pupil had a slow learning curve. Ss could make 5 negative-to-positive statements about the child's behavior. Ss also filled out a questionnaire on their attitudes toward the child. Results: When teaching the black child, men used more negative statements than women did ($p < .025$). No other sex differences were found.

Coates, B., and Hartup, W. W. Age and verbalization in observational learning. *Developmental Psychology,* 1969, 1, 556–62.
Subjects: $N = 72$; 4–5, 7–8 yrs. Measures: Ss observed a filmed male model perform novel behaviors. In the induced verbalization (IV) condition, Ss were told to repeat E's description of the model's action while watching the movie. In the free verbalization (FV) condition, Ss were asked to describe the model's behaviors in their own words. In the passive observation (PO) condition, no instructions related to verbalizing were given. After viewing the film, Ss were asked to demonstrate their learning of the model's actions. Results: While watching the

movie, girls in the IV and FV conditions emitted more accurate verbalizations than boys ($p < .05$). No sex differences were found in number of correct matching responses on the acquisition test.

Coates, B., Anderson, E. P., and Hartup, W. W. Interrelations in the attachment behavior of human infants. *Developmental Psychology*, 1972, *6*, 218–30.

Subjects: $N = 23$; tested at 10, 14 mos, and their mothers. $N = 23$; tested at 14, 18 mos, and their mothers. Measures: Mother-infant pairs were observed in a testing room with several toys. After an initial 3-minute period of nonseparation, mothers left the room for 2 minutes. A reunion phase then followed. Frequency of (a) visual orientation to mother, (b) touching mother, (c) proximity to mother, and (d) vocalizing to mother was recorded preceding and following the separation phase. Frequency of crying was recorded during all 3 periods (preseparation, separation, reunion). Results: No sex differences.

Coates, S. W. Preschool Embedded Figures Test. Consulting Psychologists Press, Inc., Palo Alto, California, 1972.

Subjects: $N = 247$; 3–5 yrs. Measures: Preschool Embedded Figures Test. Results: Girls' performance was superior to boys' ($p < .05$).

Coates, S. W. Field dependence, autonomy striving, and sex differences in preschool children. Unpublished manuscript, State University of New York, Downstate Medical Center, 1973.

Subjects: $N = 53$; 4–5 yrs. Measures: (1) S's scores on the Preschool Embedded Figures Test, the WPPSI Block Design test, and the Geometric Design test were converted to Z scores and added together to yield a composite field dependence score. (2) Each S was rated by his teacher on Beller's Autonomous Achievement Striving Scale. Results: No sex differences were found in composite field dependence scores. Teachers rated girls higher than boys in autonomous achievement striving ($p < .05$).

Cohen, B. D., and Klein, J. F. Referent communication in school age children. *Child Development*, 1968, *39*, 597–609.

Subjects: $N = 240$; 8, 10, 12 yrs. Measures: Pairs of Ss matched by age and sex were tested. One S was assigned the role of speaker, the other S was assigned the listener role. Both Ss were presented with 30 word pairs. On the speaker's list 1 word of each pair was underlined. The speaker was instructed to give the listener cues so he could identify which of the 2 words was underlined. Results: No sex differences in communication skills.

Cohen, L. B. Attention-getting and attention-holding processes of infant visual preferences. *Child Development*, 1972, *43*, 869–79.

Subjects: $N = 36$; 3–4 mos. Measures: Ss viewed red-and-white checkerboard patterns that varied in size and number of checks. Latency and fixation were measured. Results: No sex differences.

Cohen, L. B., Gelber, E. R., and Lazar, M. A. Infant habituation and generalization to differing degrees of stimulus novelty. *J. Experimental Child Psychology*, 1971, *11*, 379–89.

Subjects: $N = 64$; 4 mos. Measures: Ss were exposed to simple geometric patterns, followed by test trials of 2 exposures to the same pattern, 2 to patterns with the same form but with a novel color, 2 to a novel form but the same color, or 2 to both novel form and color. Fixation times were measured. Results: (1) Both sexes initially attended to the simple pattern at similar levels, but fixation times decreased over trial blocks for boys and not for girls. (2) During the test trials, girls had greater overall fixation time than boys ($p < .01$). (3) During the 2 trial blocks and for the first test trial, girls had greater fixation times than boys ($p < .01$, $p < .01$).

Cohen, S. E. Infant attentional behavior to face-voice incongruity. Paper presented at meeting of Society for Research in Child Development, Philadelphia, March 1973.

Subjects: $N = 96$; 5, 8 mos and mothers. Measures: With mother and a female stranger in full view, Ss were twice presented with 4 taped stimulus conditions, each emanating from a speaker held at shoulder level of a supposed person speaking: mother speaking with mother's voice, mother speaking with stranger's voice, stranger speaking with stranger's voice, and stranger speaking with mother's voice. Visual fixation behaviors were recorded. Results: There were no main sex differences. Girls looked more to the sound source under all conditions; boys deployed their attention more widely, especially when the mother was the sound source ($p < .001$).

Cole, M., Frankel, F., and Sharp, D. Development of free recall learning in children. *Developmental Psychology*, 1971, *4*, 109–23.
> EXPERIMENT II: **Subjects:** $N = 120$; 6, 8, 13 yrs. **Measures:** Ss either heard and repeated the names of 20 objects or saw and named the actual objects. Ss were later tested for recall of the stimuli. **Results:** No sex differences.
> EXPERIMENT III: **Subjects:** $N = 82$; 6, 9, 11, 14 yrs. **Measures:** After learning and repeating the names of 20 objects, Ss were asked to recall as many of the names as possible. **Results:** No sex differences.

Collins, D., Kessen, W., and Haith, M. Note on an attempt to replicate a relation between stimulus unpredictability and infant attention. *J. Experimental Child Psychology*, 1972, *13*, 1–8.
> **Subjects:** $N = 48$; 2, 4 mos. **Measures:** Ss were presented with 3 patterns of flashing lights varying in complexity. Limb movement and sucking behavior were recorded. **Results:** No sex differences.

Collins, W. Learning of media content: a developmental study. *Child Development*, 1970, *41*, 1133–42.
> **Subjects:** $N = 168$; 8, 11, 12, 14 yrs. **Measures:** Ss viewed an old situation-comedy that included both male and female family members. Afterward, Ss were tested for recall of essential and nonessential content. **Results:** (1) Girls showed better learning of essential content than boys did. (2) No sex differences were found in learning of nonessential content. (3) Difference scores (number of essential items correct minus one-half the number of correct nonessential items) were larger for girls than for boys.

Connell, D. M., and Johnson, J. E. Relationship between sex-role identification and self-esteem in early adolescents. *Developmental Psychology*, 1970, *3*, 268 (brief report).
> **Subjects:** $N = 143$; 13 yrs. **Measures:** Gough Femininity Scale, Coopersmith Self-Esteem Inventory. **Results:** (1) Among high sex-role identification Ss, boys had greater feelings of self-esteem than girls ($p < .05$). (2) Low sex-role identification boys had lower feelings of self-esteem than girls, regardless of girls' sex-role identification level ($p < .05$).

Conners, C. K., Schuette, C., and Goldman, A. Informational analysis of intersensory communication in children of different social class. *Child Development*, 1967, *38*, 251–66.
> **Subjects:** $N = 80$; 5, 6, 9, 12 yrs (low, middle SES). **Measures:** 27 geometric forms were constructed, which varied by orthogonal combinations of 3 levels of size, shape, and angle. Ss reached beneath a panel and felt a hidden form. Ss were asked to identify each form in a visual display. The 27 forms were presented 3 times, for a total of 81 trials. **Results:** Among 5-year-old, lower-class Ss, girls performed more poorly than boys.

Constantinople, A. Perceived instrumentality of the college as a measure of attitudes toward college. *J. Personality & Social Psychology*, 1967, *5*, 196–201.
> **Subjects:** $N = 353$; 18, 20 yrs. **Measures:** Ss rated each of the following items on its importance to them as a goal and on the degree to which college either helped or hindered their progress toward that goal: (1) learning how to learn from books and teachers, (2) acquiring an appreciation for ideas, (3) establishing their own personal, social, and academic values, (4) developing relationships with the opposite sex, (5) contributing in a distinguished and meaningful manner to some campus group, (6) developing ability to get along with different kinds of people, (7) becoming self-confident, (8) personal independence, (9) finding a spouse, (10) achieving academic distinction, (11) having many good friends, (12) discovering their own strong points and limitations, (13) preparing for a career that begins right after graduation, and (14) preparing for a career that requires further study beyond the BA or BS. **Results:** (1) The following goals were more important to women than to men: 2, 3, 4, 6, 9, and 13. The following goals were more important to men than to women: 10 and 14. (2) Women more than men perceived college as helping in their progress toward the following goals: 1, 2, 3, 4, 7, 8, 9, and 13.

Constantinople, A. Some correlates of average level of happiness among college students. *Developmental Psychology*, 1970, *2*, 447 (brief report).
> **Subjects:** $N = 58$; tested at 18, 21 yrs. **Measures:** At each testing, Ss completed both the Inventory of Psychosocial Development (IPD) and a 10-point bipolar scale measuring average level of happiness during the academic year. **Results:** (1) Men showed a significant increase in happiness from their freshman to their senior year; women showed a nonsignificant decrease

$(p < .01)$. (2) On the IPD, both sexes showed significant changes in the direction of greater maturity on the following scales: Autonomy, Identity, Shame and Doubt, and Guilt.

Cook, H., and Smothergill, D. W. Racial and sex determinants of initiative performance and knowledge in young children. *Educational Psychology*, 1973, *65*, 211–15.
    Subjects: $N = 154$; 4 yrs (low SES white and black). **Measures:** Ss observed a white or black adult model choose the picture he liked best in each of 12 picture pairs. Afterward, Ss were asked (1) to indicate their own preferences (imitative performance phase) and (2) to try to recall the model's choices (imitative knowledge phase). **Results:** (1) In the imitative performance phase, no main sex differences were found in the number of times Ss' choices were identical to the model's responses. Both sexes imitated same-sex models more than opposite-sex models. (2) No sex differences were found in the imitative knowledge phase. Black Ss had higher recall scores with a female model than with a male model.

Cook, T. D., Bean, J. R., Calder, B. J., Frey, R., Krovetz, M. L., and Reisman, S. R. Demand characteristics and three conceptions of the frequently deceived subject. *J. Personality & Social Psychology*, 1970, *14*, 185–94.
    Experiment I: Subjects: $N = 63$; 18–21 yrs (college). **Measures:** After participating in an experiment involving deception, Ss completed a questionnaire designed to assess their reactions to the experiment. **Results:** (1) Women liked the experiment more $(p < .02)$, perceived the deception as more legitimate $(p < .001)$, and were less annoyed by the deception $(p < .05)$ than men were. (2) No sex differences were found in how truthful Ss perceived E to be, in how much they tried to figure out what the experiment was about, in how much they tried to understand and follow instructions, or in how much they considered the experiment to be scientific and valuable.
    Experiment II: Subjects: $N = 113$; 18–21 yrs (college). **Measures:** After listening to a persuasive message, Ss evaluated the source and completed an attitude questionnaire. **Results:** No sex differences were found in Ss' perceptions of the source or in the extent to which Ss agreed with the source.

Coombs, C. H. Thurstone's measurement of social values revisited forty years later. *J. Personality & Social Psychology*, 1967, *6*, 85–91.
    Subjects: $N = 369$; 18–21 yrs (college). **Measures:** Ss were presented with pairs of criminal offenses, and were asked to judge which of the 2 crimes was more serious. **Results:** (1) Women considered abortion to be a more serious crime than men did. (2) Men judged offenses against property to be more serious crimes than women did. (3) Men were more homogeneous in their evaluations than women were.

Coopersmith, S. A method for determining two types of self-esteem. *J. Abnormal & Social Psychology*, 1959, *59*, 87–94.
    Subjects: $N = 87$; 10–12 yrs and their teachers. **Measures:** Ss completed a 50-item Self-Esteem Inventory. Teachers rated Ss on behaviors presumed to be related to self-esteem. **Results:** (1) No sex differences were found on the Self-Esteem Inventory. (2) Teachers rated girls more favorably than boys $(p < .001)$.

Coopersmith, S. *The antecedents of self-esteem.* San Francisco: W. H. Freeman & Co., 1967.
    Subjects: $N = 1,748$; 10, 11 yrs and teachers. **Measures:** (1) Coopersmith's Self-Esteem Inventory. (2) Teachers were asked to rate each child on a set of behaviors that were presumed to be related to self-esteem. **Results:** No sex differences were found in self-esteem scores. Teachers' ratings of girls were more favorable than those of boys.

Corah, N. L. Differentiation in children and their parents. *J. Personality*, 1965, *33*, 300–308.
    Subjects: $N = 60$; 8–11 yrs and parents. **Measures:** The Full-Range Vocabulary Test, Form A, and the Draw-A-Person (DAP) test were administered to Ss and their parents. IQ equivalents were derived from vocabulary scores. In addition, Ss were given the Children's Embedded Figures Test (CEFT); parents were given Witkin's Embedded Figures Test (EFT). **Results:** (1) Boys achieved higher vocabulary IQ scores than girls $(p < .02)$; fathers achieved higher vocabulary IQ scores than mothers $(p < .05)$. (2) Girls achieved higher DAP scores than boys $(p < .05)$; no difference was found between mothers and fathers. (3) Fathers discovered the solutions to the EFT more quickly than mothers $(p < .001)$; no difference was found between boys' and girls' CEFT scores.

Corah, N. L., and Boffa, J. Perceived control, self-observation, and response to aversive stimulation. *J. Personality & Social Psychology*, 1970, *16*, 1–4.
Subjects: $N = 40$; 18–21 yrs (college). **Measures:** Ss rated the amount of discomfort they experienced after being exposed to aversive white noise. Galvanic skin responses were recorded. **Results:** Women rated the sounds as producing more discomfort than men did ($p < .05$). There were no sex differences in GSR.

Corter, C. M., Rheingold, H. L., and Eckerman, C. O. Toys delay the infant's following of his mother. *Developmental Psychology*, 1972, *6*, 138–45.
Experiment I: Subjects: $N = 10$; 9–10 mos and mothers. **Measures:** After placing their children alone in a room, mothers went into an adjoining room out of the infants' sight. **Results:** Boys followed their mothers into the adjoining room more quickly than girls did.
Experiment II: Subjects: $N = 26$; 9–10 mos and mothers. **Measures:** Same as Experiment I, except children were left alone with either 1 or 6 toys. **Results:** In the 1-toy group boys followed their mothers more quickly than girls did, and girls spent more time in touching the toy than boys did. No sex differences were found in the 6-toy group.

Coryell, J. Children's lateralizations of self, other, and object images. Unpublished manuscript, Boston University, 1973.
Subjects: $N = 90$; 5, 7, 9 yrs. **Measures:** (1) A pencil was placed in S's hand. He was then shown a photograph of himself and was asked to point to the hand (in the picture) with which he had held the pencil. (2) E stood on S's left side, holding a pencil in his hand. S was then shown a photograph of E and was asked to point to the hand E had used to hold the pencil. (3) A model TV set with an antenna in one corner was placed next to S. S was then shown a photograph of a model TV set with no antenna, and was asked to point to the corner of the TV set where the antenna should be. S's responses were classified either as mirror or diagonal. **Results:** No sex differences were found in number of diagonal responses.

Costanzo, P. R., and Shaw, M. E. Conformity as a function of age level. *Child Development*, 1966, *37*, 967–75.
Subjects: $N = 96$; 7–9, 11–13, 15–17, 19–21 yrs (college). **Measures:** 4 Ss of the same age and sex were in each experimental session. Ss were subjected to erroneous judgments in a simulated conformity situation in which they were asked to match comparison lines to standard. Each S sat in a booth containing lights that he expected to reflect the responses of other Ss. E controlled "response" lights and signaled erroneous responses in 16 of 24 trials. The number of times S's response agreed with an erroneous response was recorded. **Results:** No sex differences.

Cotler, S., and Palmer, R. J. Social reinforcement, individual difference factors, and the reading performance of elementary school children. *J. Personality & Social Psychology*, 1971, *18*, 97–104.
Subjects: $N = 120$; 9–11 yrs. **Measures:** Ss were divided into overachievers and underachievers on the basis of scores on the Iowa Tests of Basic Skills and the Otis Lennon Mental Abilities Test. Ss also completed the Sarason Test Anxiety Scale. Ss then read paragraphs and received either positive, negative, or no reinforcement for their reading performance. Afterward, Ss listened as E read each of the paragraphs to them. This sequence of reading-reinforcement-instruction was repeated 3 times. Reading errors were recorded on the fourth reading. **Results:** (1) Overall, girls made fewer reading errors than boys ($p < .05$). (2) Girls made fewer errors in every comparison except one: among overachieving, low-test-anxiety Ss, girls made more errors than boys ($p < .05$). (3) Although errors decreased over trials for both boys and girls, the decrease was greater for boys ($p < .01$).

Cowan, P. A., Weber, J., Hoddinott, B. A., and Klein, J. Mean length of spoken response as a function of stimulus, experimenter, and subject. *Child Development*, 1967, *38*, 191–203.
Subjects: $N = 96$; 5, 7, 9, 11 yrs (low, high SES). **Measures:** Ss were shown at least 10 pictures and asked to talk about them. E attempted to elicit a minimum of 3 responses per picture, and a total of 50 responses in all from each S. Average number of words per remark was determined. **Results:** (1) No main sex differences were found. (2) Sex differences within each age and SES group were not tested for significance.

Cowen, E. L., and Danset, A. Étude comparée des réponses d'écoliers français et américains à une échelle d'anxiété. *Revue de Psychologie Appliqué*, 1962, *12*, 263–74.
Subjects: $N = 132$; 9 yrs (France). **Measures:** Children's Manifest Anxiety Scale. **Results:**

Girls scored higher than boys on the Anxiety Scale. No sex differences were found on the lie scale.

Cowen, E. L., Zax, M., Klein, R., Izzo, L. D., and Trost, M. A. The relation of anxiety in school children to school record, achievement and behavioral measures. *Child Development*, 1965, *36*, 685–95.
Subjects: $N = 169$; 9 yrs. Measures: Children's Manifest Anxiety Scale. Results: Girls scored higher than boys on the anxiety scale. No sex differences were found on the lie scale.

Cox, H. Intra-family comparison of loving-rejecting child-rearing practices. *Child Development*, 1970, *41*, 437–48.
Subjects: $N = 100$; 11, 12, 13 yrs and parents (98 mothers, 77 fathers). Measures: Ss and parents filled out the Roe-Siegelman Parent-Child Relationship Questionnaire. Results: (1) Girls perceived fathers as more loving than boys did. (2) Girls perceived fathers as less rejecting than boys did. (3) Girls perceived mothers as less rejecting than boys perceived fathers. (4) Girls perceived fathers as less rejecting than boys perceived mothers. (5) Mothers of girls reported themselves as more loving than fathers of boys did.

Craig, K. D. Vicarious reinforcement and noninstrumental punishment in observational learning. *J. Personality & Social Psychology*, 1967, *7*, 172–76.
Subjects: $N = 80$; 18–21 yrs (college). Measures: Ss in same-sex pairs served as either performers or observers. While the observer Ss watched, performer Ss attempted to learn a complex temporal maze task. For incorrect responses, one-half of the observers and all performers received a shock; correct responses were indicated by a green light. After performer Ss were dismissed, observer Ss attempted to master the same maze task. The number of correct choices made by observer Ss was recorded. Results: (1) There were no sex differences in number of correct choices. (2) Women who were not shocked as observers learned more rapidly and required fewer trials to criterion than women who were shocked as observers; the opposite was true for men ($p < .05$). (3) Women rated the shock as being more painful than men did (assessed by a post-experimental questionnaire).

Craig, K. D., and Lowery, H. J. Heart-rate components of conditioned vicarious autonomic responses. *J. Personality & Social Psychology*, 1969, *11*, 381–87.
Subjects: $N = 56$; 22 yrs (college). Measures: 10 colored slides of common objects were shown to a confederate. Half the Ss observed the confederate being shocked whenever certain slides were presented and were led to believe that they either would or would not have to perform the confederate's task afterward. Ss in a third condition simply observed the confederate move his arm rather than being shocked. No movement was observed by Ss in the control condition. During each slide presentation, galvanic skin responses (GSRs) and heart rate were recorded. Upon completion of the slide series, a postexperimental questionnaire was administered to Ss. Results: (1) Women had fewer vicarious and conditioned GSRs than men did ($p < .01$, $p < .01$). (2) No sex differences were found in heart rate. (3) No sex differences were found in Ss' ratings of the severity of the shocks received by the confederate. Women rated their reactions to observing the confederate as being more painful than men did ($p < .01$). Women also expressed more liking for the confederate than men did ($p < .05$).

Cramer, P. A developmental study of errors in memory. *Developmental Psychology*, 1972, *7*, 204–9.
Subjects: $N = 96$; 6–7, 10–11 yrs. Measures: Ss were instructed to remember 12 words that were read to them. As a memory aid, Ss in the experimental conditions were told to think of synonyms or rhyming words for each of the words. Afterward, Ss were presented with the 12 stimulus words along with 12 generalization stimuli (6 synonyms, 6 rhymes) and 12 control words. Ss indicated which words they had heard before. Results: (1) No main sex differences were found. (2) Among 6-7-year-old Ss in the control group, girls made more correct recognitions of presentation words, whereas boys gave more false recognition responses to both generalization stimuli and control words. (3) There were no sex differences in generalization difference scores (number of errors to synonyms minus one-half the number of errors to control words; number of errors to rhyming words minus one-half the number of errors to control words).

Cramer, P., and Bryson, J. The development of sex-related fantasy patterns. *Developmental Psychology*, 1972, *8*, 131–34.
Subjects: $N = 89$; 4–6, 8–10 yrs. Measures: Ss were asked to tell stories about 4 pictures, 2

from the Thematic Apperception Test (depicting a man clinging to a rope and a boy looking at a violin), and 2 depicting either a male or female circus performer swinging on a trapeze, and a child running across a field with a bird overhead. Using May's scoring system, the number of categories of "enhancement" and "deprivation" were identified. More positive scores signified a more feminine story pattern—stories that began with deprivation and ended with enhancement or happiness; the male pattern was the reverse. **Results:** (1) There were no sex differences among younger Ss. (2) Among older Ss, girls had more positive scores than boys did ($p < .01$). (3) There were no sex differences in younger boys' and girls' scores to any pictures except male and female circus performers. Girls gave more positive responses to that picture than boys did ($p < .02$). (4) Among older Ss, girls gave more positive responses than boys did to all but 1 picture, the male and female circus performers. The 3 pictures with more positive girls' responses were the man clinging to the rope ($p < .01$), the boy looking at a violin ($p < .02$), and the child in a field with bird overhead ($p < .05$).

Crandall, V. C. Personality characteristics and social and achievement behaviors associated with children's social desirability response tendencies. *J. Personality & Social Psychology,* 1966, 4, 477–86.
    Experiment I: **Subjects:** $N = 76$; 15 yrs. **Measures:** Children's Social Desirability Scale. **Results:** No sex differences.
    Experiment II: **Subjects:** $N = 50$; 6–11 yrs. **Measures:** Children's Social Desirability Scale. **Results:** No sex differences.

Crandall, V. C. Sex differences in expectancy of intellectual and academic reinforcement. In C. P. Smith, ed., *Achievement related motives in children,* New York: Russell Sage Foundation, 1969.
    Experiment I: **Subjects:** $N = 41$; 7–12 yrs (Fels sample). **Measures:** Ss were presented with 6 tasks, each of which was graduated into 8 levels of difficulty. The most difficult level at which each S predicted he would be able to perform when tested constituted his expectancy estimate for that task. Tasks were estimating number of blocks in constructions, brain teasers (logical relations), jigsaw puzzles (spatial relations), numerical skills, memory for objects, and mazes. **Results:** (1) Boys had higher overall expectancies and higher individual task expectancies than girls did. (2) There were no sex differences in Stanford-Binet IQ scores, Children's Social Desirability Scale scores, or Intellectual-Academic Attainment Value scores.
    Experiment II: **Subjects:** $N = 380$; 18 yrs (college). **Measures:** At entrance and at each quarter's registration, Ss listed courses they were taking and the grades they expected in each course. **Results:** (1) There were no sex differences in quarter grades actually received. (2) Men had higher quarterly grade expectancies than women did. (3) Over a 5-year period, men overestimated quarterly grade they were to receive more than women did. (4) Over a 5-year period, girls made lower grade estimates than their past grades warranted, whereas boys estimated higher than their grades warranted.
    Experiment III: **Subjects:** $N = 41$; 18–26 yrs (Fels sample). **Measures:** Ss received identical predetermined schedules of verbal reinforcement from a same-sex E on a complex task requiring storage, recall, and reproduction of different geometric patterns. Estimates of success expectancy were obtained from each S before the task and after 10 trials. **Results:** (1) First expectancy estimates of women were lower than those of men. After 10 trials, women's expectancies were still lower than those of men. (2) There were no sex differences in amount of expectancy change between first and second estimates.
    Experiment IV: **Subjects:** $N = 256$; 13 yrs. **Measures:** A digit-symbol substitution task was presented to Ss as a test of intellectual competence. After expectancy of success estimates were obtained, Ss were assigned to 1 of 6 reinforcement conditions (52 Ss were dropped from the study at this point in order that groups could be matched on initial expectancy). The 6 schedules of reinforcement were: 50% positive, 50% negative, 60% positive, 60% negative, 80% positive, and 80% negative. Performance feedback was provided to Ss via a display panel of 10 lights. Each light supposedly represented 1 of 10 schools in which the test had previously been given. After each trial, 5 lights came on in the 50% reinforcement conditions, 6 lights came on in the 60% conditions, and 8 lights came on in the 80% conditions. Ss in the 3 positive groups were informed that each light signified they had "beaten the kids at that school." In the 3 negative groups, Ss were told that the onset of any light meant "the kids at that school had beaten" them. Post-task expectancies were obtained at the end of 10 trials. **Results:** (1) No sex differences were found in expectancy change scores. (2) Each S's grades and initial expectancy scores were transformed into z scores. A discrepancy (D) score was then computed by subtracting the grade z score from the expectancy z score. More boys had positive rather than negative D scores, whereas the reverse was true for girls ($p < .001$).

Crandall, V. C., and Gozali, J. The social desirability responses of children of four religious-cultural groups. *Child Development*, 1969, *40*, 751–62.
Subjects: $N = 1,474$; 9–17 yrs (U.S. non-Catholic, U.S. Catholic parochial, Norwegian State Lutheran, Norwegian Fundamentalist Lutheran). Measures: Children's Social Desirability Scale. Results: Girls gave more socially desirable responses than boys did ($p < .001$).

Crandall, V. C., and Lacey, B. W. Children's perceptions of internal-external control in intellectual-academic situations and their Embedded Figures Test performance. *Child Development*, 1972, *43*, 1123–34.
Subjects: $N = 50$; 6–12 yrs. Measures: Ss were given 10 figures from the Embedded Figures Test, the Intellectual Achievement Responsibility scale (a measure of locus of control), and the Stanford-Binet IQ test. Results: No sex differences.

Crandall, V. C., Crandall, V. J., and Katkovsky, W. A children's social desirability questionnaire. *J. Consulting Psychology*, 1965a, *29*, 27–36.
Subjects: $N = 956$; 8, 9, 10, 11, 13, 15, 17 yrs. Measures: Children's Social Desirability Questionnaire. Results: Girls gave more socially desirable responses than boys did ($p < .001$).

Crandall, V. C., Katkovsky, W., and Crandall, V. J. Children's beliefs in their own control of reinforcements in intellectual-academic achievement situations. *Child Development*, 1965b, *36* 91–109.
Subjects: $N = 923$; 8, 9, 10, 11, 13, 15, 17 yrs. Measures: Intellectual Achievement Responsibility Scale. Results: (1) Among 11-, 13-, 15-, and 17-year-old Ss, girls attributed more internal responsibility for failure than boys did. (2) Among 11- and 17-year-old Ss, girls attributed more internal responsibility for success than boys did. (3) Overall, older girls (ages 11, 13, 15, and 17) gave more internal responses than older boys did. (4) No differences were found between younger boys and girls.

Crandall, V. J., and Sinkeldam, C. Children's dependent and achievement behaviors in social situations and their perceptual field dependence. *J. Personality*, 1964, *32*, 1–22.
Subjects: $N = 50$; 6–12 yrs (Fels Day Camp). Measures: Ss were given the 10 least difficult figures of the Witkins Embedded Figures Test. Total number of seconds used attempting to solve all 10 test figures was recorded. Results: No sex differences.

Cronin, V. Mirror-image reversal discrimination in kindergarten and first grade children. *J. Experimental Child Psychology*, 1967, *5*, 567–85.
Subjects: $N = 216$; 5–6 yrs. Measures: Ss performed 1 of 3 discrimination tasks with triangles and their mirror-image reversals: same-different judgments with standard and mirror-image triangle pairs, judgments of which triangle of a triad was different (i.e. reversed), and matching a standard triangle to 1 of 2 others. Results: No sex differences.

Cropley, A. J., and Feuring, E. Training creativity in young children. *Developmental Psychology*, 1971, *4*, 105 (extended version of brief report).
Subjects: $N = 69$; 6 yrs. Measures: Ss were given the Product Improvement Test of the Torrance Tests of Creativity (child is presented with a toy and asked how it could be changed to make it more fun to play with). Instructions were either to produce as many ideas as possible (quantity) or to produce clever and unusual ideas (quality). Half of the Ss received creativity training, the other half did not. Tests were scored for fluency (total number of suggested improvements), flexibility (number of distinct principles employed in suggestions), and originality (number of clever and unusual suggestions). Results: (1) There were no sex differences in flexibility or originality. (2) Among Ss given quantity instructions, boys scored higher on fluency than girls. Under quality instructions, girls surpassed boys on fluency. (3) There were no sex differences in the effects of creativity training.

Cross, J. F., and Cross, J. Age, sex, race and the perception of facial beauty. *Developmental Psychology*, 1971, *5*, 433–39.
Subjects: $N = 300$; 7, 12, 17, 30–50 yrs. Measures: Ss rated photographic portraits of black and white males and females, ages 7, 18, and adult, on a 7-point scale of facial beauty. Results: Females rated female faces higher than males did ($p < .01$).

Crowder, A., and Hohle, R. H. Time estimation by young children with and without informational feedback. *J. Experimental Child Psychology*, 1970, *10*, 295–307.
EXPERIMENT I: Subjects: $N = 48$; 5, 7, 9 yrs. Measures: Ss attempted to estimate the time

it took a hidden toy to travel along a path to a designated point, after watching E perform the same task (but with toy not hidden at destination point). Ss received either informational feedback or no feedback. **Results:** No sex differences.

EXPERIMENT II: **Subjects:** $N = 64$; 5 yrs. **Measures:** Same as Experiment I, except that the feedback procedure was modified. One group received informational feedback with no praise for correct estimates, and the other received only praise with no information about performance. **Results:** No sex differences.

Crowne, D. P. Family orientation, level of aspiration, and interpersonal bargaining. *J. Personality & Social Psychology*, 1966, 3, 641–45.

Subjects: $N = 76$; 18–21 yrs (college). **Measures:** Ss played the Prisoner's Dilemma Game in same-sex pairs. Ss' parents were classified as to whether they were engaged in entrepreneurial occupations (farmer, small businessman, lawyer, etc.) or bureaucratic occupations (employment in a relatively large organization of complex structure). **Results:** Among Ss with entrepreneurial parents, men played more cooperatively than women did ($p < .05$). No sex differences were found among Ss with bureaucratic parents.

Crowne, D. P., Holland, C. H., and Conn, L. K. Personality factors in discrimination learning in children. *J. Personality & Social Psychology*, 1968, 10, 420–30.

Subjects: $N = 63$; 10–11 yrs. **Measures:** After completing the Children's Social Desirability Scale, Ss were given visual discrimination learning tasks. Number of trials needed to reach criterion, time between presentation of each stimulus and S's response (impulsivity), and heart rates were recorded. **Results:** No sex differences.

Croxern, M. E., and Lytton, H. Reading disability and difficulties in finger localization and right-left discrimination. *Developmental Psychology*, 1971, 5, 256–62.

Subjects: $N = 164$; 9, 10 yrs. **Measures:** Tactile stimulation was applied to Ss' fingers while their hands were either hidden from view or visible. On each trial, Ss reported which finger had been touched either by pointing to the correct finger on a numbered diagram of a right and left hand, by indicating its number, or by naming it. Ss were also tested on their ability to discriminate between the left and right sides of their bodies. **Results:** Girls performed better on the right-left discrimination task than boys did (for control group, $p < .02$; for experimental group, NS; for both groups combined, $p < .05$). No sex differences were found on the tactile stimulation task.

Cruse, D. B. Socially desirable responses at ages 3 through 6. *Child Development*, 1966, 37, 909–16.

Subjects: $N = 299$; 3, 4, 5, 6 yrs. **Measures:** A social-desirability scale was administered to each S. The child was asked to endorse or reject 20 desirable and 20 undesirable items. **Results:** At ages 4 and 6, girls gave more socially desirable responses than boys did.

Curcio, F., Kattef, E., Levine, D., and Robbins, O. Compensation and susceptibility to conservation training. *Developmental Psychology*, 1972, 7, 259–65.

Subjects: $N = 67$; 5–6 yrs. **Measures:** Ss were given the following pretests: understanding of "more" and "same," compensation of height-width dimensions, and conversation of discontinuous quantity. Conservation training was administered, followed by post-tests of discontinuous quantity conservation and transfer conservation. **Results:** No sex differences.

Curry, L., and Dickson, P. Sex differentiation by age in embedded figures test. Unpublished paper, Stanford University, 1971.

Subjects: $N = 24$; 5, 8, 11 yrs. **Measures:** The Visual Closure subtest of the Illinois Test of Psycholinguistics Abilities was used as a measure of embedded figures skill. Stanford-Binet IQ scores were collected for 8- and 11-year-old Ss. **Results:** No sex differences.

Daehler, M. W. Children's manipulation of illusory and ambiguous stimuli, discriminative performance and implications for conceptual development. *Child Development*, 1970, 41, 224–41.

Subjects: $N = 160$; 4, 5, 6 yrs. **Measures:** 4 discrimination tasks were used as measures of investigatory activity. Problems were a length, a brightness, and 2 size-discrimination tasks. Illusory arrangements of stimuli prevented correct choices unless Ss were willing to investigate the problem further. Correct responses were reinforced with a marble and a verbal comment. **Results:** Boys performed more investigatory responses than girls did ($p < .01$).

Daehler, M. W. Developmental and experimental factors associated with inferential behavior. *J. Experimental Child Psychology*, 1972, *13*, 324–38.

EXPERIMENT I: **Subjects:** $N = 192$; 4, 5, 6, 7 yrs. **Measures:** In 16 2-trial identification problems, Ss inferred positive instance from 4 alternatives (outline pictures of faces) appearing 2 at a time. **Results:** There were no sex differences in mean number of correct responses or kinds of errors.

EXPERIMENT II: **Subjects:** $N = 42$; 8 yrs. **Measures:** Ss in 3 conditions inferred positive instance in 24 2-trial problems. Dimensions were varied to determine the effect on difficulty. **Results:** There were no sex differences in mean number of corrct responses.

Darley, F. L., and Winitz, H. Comparison of male and female kindergarten children on the WISC. *J. Genetic Psychology*, 1961, *99*, 41–49.

Subjects: $N = 150$; 6 yrs. **Measures:** Wechsler Intelligence Scale for Children. **Results:** (1) Girls were superior to boys on the Performance Scale IQ ($p < .02$), the Similarities subtest ($p < .05$), and the Coding A subtest ($p < .01$). (2) No sex differences were found in Verbal Scale IQ or Full Scale IQ.

Darley, J. M., and Latané, B. Bystander intervention in emergencies: diffusion of responsibility. *J. Personality & Social Psychology*, 1968, *8*, 377–83.

Subjects: $N = 72$; 18–21 yrs (college). **Measures:** Ss overheard a person experiencing an epileptic seizure. Ss were led to believe that another subject had also overheard the seizure. Response measure was the speed in which Ss reported the emergency. **Results:** No sex differences.

Davidson, H. H., and Lang, G. Children's perceptions of their teachers' feelings toward them related to self-perception, school achievement and behavior. *J. Experimental Education*, 1960, *29*, 107–18.

Subjects: $N = 203$; 9, 10, 11 yrs. **Measures:** Ss completed an adjective checklist measuring their perceptions of teachers' feeling toward them. Teachers rated each pupil's academic achievement, behavior, and personality characteristics. **Results:** (1) Girls perceived their teachers' feeling toward them as more favorable than boys did ($p < .02$). (2) Girls were rated more favorably than boys on behavioral and personality characteristics ($p < .05$).

Davies, A. D. The perceptual maze test in a normal population. *Perceptual & Motor Skills*, 1965, *20*, 287–93.

Subjects: $N = 540$; 20–79 yrs. **Measures:** Perceptual maze tests were administered to Ss. **Results:** Among 20-59-year-old Ss, men performed better than women ($p < .01$). Among 60-79-year-old Ss, no sex differences were found.

Davies, C. M. Development of the probability concept in children. *Child Development*, 1965, *36*, 779–88.

Subjects: $N = 112$; 3–9 yrs. **Measures:** Ss played a lever-pressing marble game for prizes in which the outcomes were fixed to preclude learning the concept of probability. A verbal measure followed in which Ss judged which color marble they would be most likely to get if they chose without looking from an assortment of known proportions. **Results:** At age 7, girls performed better than boys on the verbal test ($p < .02$).

Davies, G. M. Quantitative and qualitative aspects of memory for picture stimuli. *J. Experimental Child Psychology*, 1972, *13*, 382–93.

Subjects: $N = 100$; 8–9 yrs. **Measures:** Ss were shown names or pictures of objects and were instructed to find likenesses among alternatives. Written recall and identification accuracy were assessed twice: 5 hours and 3 days after stimulus presentation. **Results:** No sex differences.

Davis, A. J. Cognitive style: methodological and developmental considerations. *Child Development*, 1971, *42*, 1147–59.

Subjects: $N = 120$; 10, 13, 16, 18–21 yrs (college). **Measures:** Ss were given Sigel's Cognitive Style Test, Form A. Responses were scored as Descriptive Part-Whole, Descriptive Global, Relational-Contextual, or Categorical-Inferential. **Results:** No sex differences.

Davis, J. H., Cohen, J. L., Hornik, J., and Rissman, A. K. Dyadic decision as a function of the frequency distributions describing the preferences of members' constituencies. *J. Personality & Social Psychology*, 1973, *26*, 178–95.

Subjects: $N = 246$; 18–21 yrs (college). **Measures:** Pairs of Ss, each acting as a representative for a hypothetical constituency, discussed and reached a decision on one of the following: the percentage of university control that should be invested with students, or the percentage of the national budget that should be spent on pollution control. **Results:** No sex differences were found in the decisions Ss reached.

Davis, O. L. Teacher behavior toward boys and girls during first grade reading instruction. *American Education Research J.*, 1967, *4*, 261–70.

> **Subjects:** $N = 238$; 6, 7 yrs. **Measures:** Ss' perceptions of pupil-teacher interactions were ascertained in individual interviews. Teachers rated each pupil's motivation and readiness for reading. Observations were made of teacher-pupil interactions during reading instruction. In addition, all Ss received the Stanford Achievement Test, Primary Battery, Form X. **Results:** Ss perceived boys as receiving more negative comments from the teacher ($p < .01$) and as being poor readers ($p < .05$). No sex differences were obtained in each of the following categories: amount of praise received from teacher, amount of opportunity to read, best reader in class. (2) Teachers assessed more boys as "less motivated and ready" than girls ($p < .01$). Teachers' mean assessment of boys and girls did not differ significantly, however. (3) No differences were found in the number of times boys and girls were called on to respond by their teachers, nor did teachers react differently to boys' and girls' responses. (4) No sex differences were found on the achievement test.

Davol, S. H., Hastings, M. L., and Klein, D. A. Effect of age, sex and speed of rotation on rotary pursuit performance by young children. *Perceptual & Motor Skills*, 1965, *21*, 351–57.

> **Subjects:** $N = 54$; 5–8 yrs. **Measures:** During each of 5 2-minute trials on a rotary pursuit task, Ss attempted to follow a revolving gold circle with the end of a stick. Performance measure was time on target. **Results:** No sex differences.

Dean, R. B., Austin, J. A., and Watts, W. A. Forewarning effects in persuasion. *J. Personality & Social Psychology*, 1971, *18*, 210–21.

> **Subjects:** $N = 161$; 18–21 yrs (college). **Measures:** Ss were either forewarned or not forewarned about the persuasive nature of a message. After reading the message, Ss responded to an attitude questionnaire (Ss' scores were compared to a control group's scores, yielding a measure of attitude change). Ss then evaluated the message in terms of its fairness, interest, forcefulness, and persuasiveness. **Results:** No sex differences.

Deaux, K. K. Honking at the intersection: a replication and extension. *J. Social Psychology*, 1971, *84*, 159–60.

> **Subjects:** $N = 123$; adult drivers. **Measures:** Ss were blocked at an intersection by either a male or a female confederate who failed to move his (her) car when the light turned green. Ss' horn-honking responses were recorded. **Results:** More drivers honked at the female confederate than at the male confederate ($p < .05$). No sex differences were found.

Debus, R. L. Effects of brief observation of model behavior on conceptual tempo of impulsive children. *Developmental Psychology*, 1970, *2*, 22–32.

> **Subjects:** $N = 320$; 8–10 yrs. **Measures:** Ss were given an 8-item form of the Matching Familiar Figures test. The 100 children with the shortest response latencies and largest number of errors were asked to return. These Ss were exposed at a later testing session to same-sex 11-year-old models who exhibited reflective and/or impulsive response patterns while taking the MFF. Models were reinforced for correct choices. Immediately after the model(s) left, Ss completed a second 8-item form of the MFF; 2½ weeks later, a third form of the MFF was administered. **Results:** No sex differences were found on either the initial pretest, the immediate post-test, or the delayed post-test.

Deci, E. L. Intrinsic motivation, extrinsic reinforcement, and inequity. *J. Personality & Social Psychology*, 1972, *22*, 113–20.

> **Subjects:** $N = 96$; 18–21 yrs (college). **Measures:** Ss either did or did not receive verbal reinforcement while attempting to solve a spatial puzzle. The amount of time Ss spent working on the puzzle during a free-choice period immediately afterward was recorded. **Results:** No sex differences.

DeFazio, V. J. Field articulation differences in language abilities. *J. Personality & Social Psychology*, 1973, *25*, 351–56.

> **Subjects:** $N = 44$; 18–21 yrs (college). **Measures:** (1) Word Beginnings and Endings Test (Ss were asked to write as many words as possible beginning with one letter and ending with another); (2) Advanced Vocabulary Test; (3) Cloze Test (Ss were presented with 6

paragraphs. Every fifth word in each paragraph was deleted. Ss' task was to guess the identities of the deleted words); (4) Shadowing Task (Ss were asked to repeat aloud sentences or strings of words that were read to them). **Results:** No sex differences.

Deffenbacher, K. A., and Hamm, N. H. An application of Brunswik's lens model to developmental changes in probability learning. *Developmental Psychology*, 1972, *6*, 508–19.
Subjects: $N = 288$; 7–8, 13–15, 19–20 yrs. **Measures:** Ss were instructed to guess what 2-digit number went best with a 2-digit number presented. Cue and criterion number were presented after Ss recorded their response. Half of the younger Ss also saw a pattern of dots close to the corresponding numerals, in order to make the task more concrete. **Results:** No sex differences.

DeLeon, J. L., Raskin, L. M., and Gruen, G. E. Sensory-modality effects of shape perception in preschool children. *Developmental Psychology*, 1970, *3*, 358–62.
Subjects: $N = 48$; 3–4 yrs. **Measures:** Ss performed shape-discrimination tasks (judging which comparison form is the same as the standard) under 4 conditions: seeing stimuli, feeling stimuli, seeing and feeling stimuli, and combination (seeing and feeling standard and only feeling comparison stimuli). Correct responses were reinforced with M & M candies. Responses and response latencies were recorded. **Results:** No sex differences.

DeLucia, L. Stimulus preference and discrimination learning. In J. F. Rosenblith, W. Allinsmith, and J. P. Williams, eds., *The Causes of Behavior*. Boston: Allyn & Bacon, 1972.
Subjects: $N = 24$; 5 yrs. **Measures:** Ss' relative preferences for each of 24 toys were determined by the method of paired comparisons. **Results:** No significance tests for sex differences were performed on a toy-by-toy basis. Girls' and boys' relative preferences, however, were considerably different, as is evident from the following list (boys' choices are ordered from most to least preferred, and the position of each item within girls' rank-ordering of preferences is given in parentheses): convertible (14), dump truck (19), tool set (23), airplane (20), racing car (22), erector set (19), football (24), wheelbarrow (21), banjo (5), tractor (17), wading pool (11), alphabet ball (12), blackboard (15), roller skates (14), rocking horse (8), teddy bear (16), telephone (7), jump rope (9), dish cabinet (6), sewing machine (10), broom set (4), doll wardrobe (3), doll buggy (2), cosmetics (1).

Denmark, F. L., and Diggory, J. C. Sex differences in attitudes toward leaders' display of authoritarian behavior. *Psychological Reports*, 1966, *18*, 863–72.
Subjects: $N = 327$; 18–21 yrs (college fraternity and sorority members). **Measures:** Part I, Scale A: All Ss were asked to describe how the leader (president) of their fraternity or sorority behaved in concrete situations. Scale B: Ss, excluding the 19 leaders, were then asked to describe how the leader should have behaved. On both scales, Ss rated the leaders on a 19-item list of authoritarian characteristics. In Part II, Ss were asked to answer yes or no to 16 propositions about the personal characteristics "necessary for good leaders." **Results:** (1) There were no sex differences among leaders or followers in mean scores on either Scale A or Scale B. (2) On Scale A, followers considered male leaders more authoritarian on 9 characteristics and female leaders more authoritarian on 2 characteristics. The leaders themselves rated 2 items more characteristic of male leaders and 1 more characteristic of female leaders. (3) On Scale B, male leaders were considered more authoritarian on 9 characteristics and female leaders more authoritarian on 4 characteristics. (4) On Part II, more men believed good leaders should oppose those who disagree with them (item 2) and good leaders usually help you with your personal problems (item 7). More women believed a good leader will be adequate in almost all types of situations (item 16).

Denney, N. W. A developmental study of free classification in children. *Child Development*, 1972a, *43*, 221–32.
Subjects: $N = 96$; 2, 4, 6, 8, 12, 16 yrs. **Measures:** Ss were given colored blocks of various shapes and were asked to arrange them under a free-grouping procedure and under a verbal-labeling (nonsense syllables) procedure. **Results:** No sex differences.

Denney, N. W. Free classification in preschool children. *Child Development*, 1972b, *43*, 1161–70.
Subjects: $N = 108$; 2, 3, 4 yrs. **Measures:** Ss were asked to place 32 cardboard figures of various shapes, colors, and sizes in groups of their own choosing. **Results:** No sex differences.

Denney, N. W., and Lennon, L. Classification: a comparison of middle and old age. *Developmental Psychology*, 1972, *7*, 210–13.

Subjects: $N = 74$; 25–55, 67–95 yrs. **Measures:** Ss arranged geometric figures varying in color, size, and shape according to instructions to group things that are alike or go together. Responses were classified as graphic (design made with stimuli), similarity (common attribute shared by stimuli in each grouping), or other (neither graphic nor similarity). **Results:** No sex differences.

Desor, J. A. Toward a psychological theory of crowding. *J. Personality & Social Psychology*, 1972, *21*, 79–83.
Subjects: $N = 70$; 18–21 yrs (college). **Measures:** Ss were presented with scaled-down rooms and human figures and asked to place as many people as possible in the rooms without overcrowding them. **Results:** No sex differences.

Devi, G. A study of sex difference in reaction to frustration situations. *Psychological Studies*, 1967, *12*, 17–27.
Subjects: $N = 220$; 16–24 yrs (Asian Indian college). **Measures:** Ss reported what their reactions would be to each of 10 frustrating situations. **Results:** (1) Men reported more overtly aggressive reactions than women did. (2) Women reported more regressive and withdrawal reactions than men did. (3) No sex differences were found in the frequency of suppressed aggressive reactions, self-aggressive reactions, anxiety, adjustment, or rationalization.

Dewing, K. The reliability and validity of selected tests of creative thinking in a sample of seventh grade West Australian children. *British J. Educational Psychology*, 1970, *40*, 35–42.
Subjects: $N = 394$; 12 yrs. **Measures:** (1) 2 verbal (Alternate uses: tin cans; Alternate uses: bricks) and two nonverbal (Circle, Squares) tests of creative thinking were administered to Ss. Each test was scored for fluency and originality. (2) 5 additional measures of creativity were also assessed: (a) teacher ratings of in-school creativity, (b) peer ratings of in-school creativity, (c) Torrance Creative Leisure Interests Checklist, (d) Golann Creative Motivation Scale, and (e) an imaginative composition on the topic "The Lion Who Couldn't Roar." **Results:** No sex differences.

Di Bartole, R., and Vinacke, W. E. Relationship between adult nurturance and dependency and performance of the preschool child. *Developmental Psychology*, 1969, *1*, 247–51.
Subjects: $N = 24$; 4 yrs (low SES). **Measures:** 2 teachers independently rated Ss for dependency on Beller's scale (1957). Within each sex, Ss were divided into high- and low-dependency groups based on these scores. For 2 weeks prior to the experimental session, Ss were allowed to play with 4 jigsaw puzzles used in the experiment. Each S was individually brought into the experimental room by a female E and asked to solve a puzzle in a nurturant situation (E adopted predetermined nurturant patterns of behavior involving permissiveness, praise, affection, verbal reward, nearness, and attention). After a rest period, Ss were asked to solve the puzzle again under conditions of continued nurturance or nurturance deprivation (E avoided nurturant behaviors and left S alone). **Results:** No sex differences.

Dickerson, D. J., Wagner, J. F., and Campione, J. Discrimination shift performance of kindergarten children as a function of variation of the irrelevant shift dimension. *Developmental Psychology*, 1970, *3*, 229–35.
Subjects: $N = 96$; 5 yrs. **Measures:** After discrimination training for color-relevance or form-relevance, Ss performed either intradimensional (ID), reversal (RV), or extradimensional (ED) shifts. Original relevant dimension remained relevant in ID shift; original irrelevant dimension became relevant in ED shift. RV Ss were assigned 2 new cues along the irrelevant dimension. **Results:** No sex differences.

Dickie, S. P. Effectiveness of structured and unstructured (traditional) methods of language training. *Monographs of the Society for Research in Child Development*, 1968, *33*, serial no. 124, 62–79.
Subjects: $N = 50$; 3–4 yrs. **Measures:** Ss were pretested on the Peabody Picture Vocabulary Test, the Stanford-Binet IQ test, tasks of color naming, counting, block-building, the Expressive Vocabulary Inventory, and the Auditory-Vocal Association subtest of the Illinois Test of Psycholinguistic Abilities. Ss underwent 5 months of language training using structured or unstructured methods of teaching. Ss were post-tested on language tests. **Results:** No sex differences.

Dienstbier, R. A., and Munter, P. O. Cheating as a function of the labeling of natural arousal. *J. Personality & Social Psychology*, 1971, *17*, 208–13.
Subjects: N = 105; 18–21 yrs (college). Measures: Ss experienced failure on a vocabulary test and were then given an opportunity to improve their scores by cheating. Results: No sex differences were found in the percentage of Ss who cheated.

Dillehay, R. C., and Jernigan, L. R. The biased questionnaire as an instrument of opinion change. *J. Personality & Social Psychology*, 1970, *15*, 144–50.
Subjects: N = 90; 18–21 yrs (college). Measures: Ss initially responded to biased questionnaires designed to elicit either harsh or lenient opinions concerning the treatment of criminals. All Ss then responded to Likert and Thurstone scales of punishment orientation. Results: No sex differences.

Dion, K., Berscheid, E., and Walster, E. What is beautiful is good. *J. Personality & Social Psychology*, 1972, *24*, 285–90.
Subjects: N = 60; 18–21 yrs (college). Measures: Ss were presented with photographs of college students who varied in physical attractiveness. Ss rated each of the students on 32 personality traits and estimated which of the stimulus persons would be most likely, and least likely, to have a number of different life experiences. Ss also indicated which of the students would be most likely to engage in each of 30 different occupations. Results: No sex differences.

Ditrichs, R., Simon, S., and Greene, B. Effect of vicarious scheduling on the verbal conditioning of hostility in children. *J. Personality & Social Psychology*, 1967, *6*, 71–78.
Subjects: N = 150; 12–13 yrs. Measures: Ss were free to use either hostile or neutral verbs in the construction of sentences. Prior to the experiment, Ss had been vicariously reinforced for choosing hostile verbs. Results: Boys constructed more sentences using hostile verbs than girls did ($p < .05$).

Dixon, J. F., and Simmons, C. H. The impression value of verbs for children. *Child Development*, 1966, *37*, 861–66.
Subjects: N = 100; 9 yrs. Measures: 45 simple past-tense verbs were presented to Ss for rating in terms of "what my teacher would think of me if I used the word about myself." Each verb was rated on a 5-point scale ranging from "would not like me at all" to "would like me very much." Results: (1) Girls scaled the following verbs more positively than boys did: trusted, helped, liked, loved, found. (2) Boys scaled the following verbs more positively than girls did: looked, lost, cried. (3) Girls rated positive and negative verbs in a more extreme direction (i.e. positive verbs higher, negative verbs lower) than boys did. (4) Boys showed greater variability in rating positive and negative verbs than girls did.

Dlugokinski, E., and Firestone, I. J. Congruence among four methods of measuring other-centeredness. *Child Development*, 1973, *44*, 304–8.
Subjects: N = 164; 10, 13 yrs. Measures: Ss were given a value scale, a test of moral understanding (Baldwin), a peer-impact scale (S rated by peers), and a behavioral measure concerning donations of money earned as subject to UNICEF under varying appeals. Results: (1) Girls had a higher relative ranking of other-centered values than boys did ($p < .01$). (2) Girls showed higher moral understanding than boys did ($p < .05$). (3) No sex differences were found in the amount of money Ss donated.

Dmitruk, M. Incentive preference and resistance to temptation. *Child Development*, 1971, *42*, 625–28.
Subjects: N = 302; 5–10 yrs. Measures: Incentive preferences were assessed. Ss were offered a preferred, nonpreferred, or no object in a resistance-to-temptation situation. Results: No sex differences.

Doctor, R. M. Awareness and the effects of three combinations of reinforcement on verbal conditioning in children. *Child Development*, 1969, *40*, 529–38.
Subjects: N = 60; 10, 11 yrs. Measures: Ss constructed sentences from stimulus pronouns and selected verbs. Correct and incorrect responses received either positive, negative, or no reinforcement in varying combinations. E checked Ss for awareness of reinforcement contingencies. Results: No sex differences in acquisition or extinction.

Dodd, B. J. Effects of social and vocal stimulation on infant babbling. *Developmental Psychology*, 1972, *7*, 80–83.
Subjects: N = 10 boys, 5 girls; 9–12 mos. Measures: Ss' spontaneous vocalizations were re-

corded for a period of 15 minutes. **Results:** No sex differences were found in the number, range, or length of Ss' utterances.

Dodd, C., and Lewis, M. The magnitude of the orienting response in children as a function of changes in color and contour. *J. Experimental Child Psychology*, 1969, 8, 296–305.

> **Subjects:** $N = 52$; 3½ yrs. **Measures:** Ss viewed achromatic and chromatic pictures of a family and of designs (curved and straight lines). Fixation, smiling, pointing, and surprise were measured. **Results:** No sex differences.

Dodge, N., and Muench, G. A. Relation of conformity and the need for approval in children. *Developmental Psychology*, 1969, 1, 67–68.

> **Subjects:** $N = 122$; 11 yrs. **Measures:** Conformity to group pressure was measured in an Asch-type situation. **Results:** No sex differences.

Dodge, W. F., West, E. F., Bridgeforth, E. B., and Travis, L. B. Nocturnal enuresis in 6- to 10-year-old children. *American J. Diseases of Children*, 1970, 120, 32–35.

> **Subjects:** $N = 1,436$; 6–8 yrs (white, black, Hispanic). **Measures:** Mothers were interviewed about their children's bed-wetting habits. **Results:** At each age, more boys than girls were enuretic ($p < .025$).

Doob, A. N., and Gross, A. E. Status of frustrator as an inhibitor of horn-honking responses. *J. Social Psychology*, 1968, 76, 213–18.

> **Subjects:** $N = 74$; adult drivers. **Measures:** Ss were blocked at an intersection by a male confederate who failed to move his car when the signal turned green. Measures were taken of the duration and latency of each honk. Total number of honks was also recorded. **Results:** Men honked faster than women did ($p < 05$).

Dorman, L., Watson, J. S., and Vietze, P. Operant conditioning of visual fixation in infants under three intensities of auditory and visual reinforcement. Submitted to *Developmental Psychology*, 1971.

> **Subjects:** $N = 48$; 14 wks. **Measures:** Visual fixation on 1 of 2 blank targets was reinforced with either visual or auditory stimuli in 1 of 3 intensity sequences: (1) low, medium high, (2) medium high, low, or (3) high, low medium. The observer, blind to the reinforced target, modality, and sequence of reinforcement, recorded the number of fixations on each target. A learning score was obtained by subtracting the number of looks at the nonrewarded side in conditioning period from the number in the base period. **Results:** No main sex differences were found.

Dosey, M. A., and Meisels, M. Personal space and self-protection. *J. Personality & Social Psychology*, 1969, 11, 93–97.

> **Subjects:** $N = 186$; 18–21 yrs (college). **Measures:** Ss approached members of the same and opposite sex. **Results:** There were no main effects of sex of S on approach distance. Female Ss approached closer to women than to men; the approach behavior of male Ss was not affected by sex of other ($p < .01$).

Dreman, S. B., and Greenbaum, C. W. Altruism or reciprocity; sharing behavior in Israeli kindergarten children. *Child Development*, 1973, 44, 61–68.

> **Subjects:** $N = 120$; 5–6 yrs (low, middle SES). **Measures:** Ss were given an odd number of candies to either share or not share with an alleged same-sex peer, who would either know or not know who gave him the candies. S thought E would not know how many he chose to share. **Results:** No main sex differences.

Dreyer, A. S., Hulac, V., and Rigler, D. Differential adjustment to pubescence and cognitive style patterns. *Developmental Psychology*, 1971, 4, 456–62.

> **Subjects:** $N = 22$; 9–16 yrs (longitudinal sample). **Measures:** The Draw-a-Person test was administered annually and scored on a 5-point scale of degree of sophistication of body concept. **Results:** No sex differences.

Droege, R. C. Sex differences in aptitude maturation during high school. *J. Counseling Psychology*, 1967, 14, 407–11.

> **Subjects:** $N = 20,541$; 14–16 yrs (retested at 17 yrs). $N = 6,167$; 17 yrs. **Measures:** General Aptitude Test Battery (U.S. Employment Service, 1958). **Results:** (1) In every comparison, boys scored higher than girls in intelligence and spatial aptitude. Girls scored higher than

boys in verbal aptitude, form perception, clerical perception, motor coordination, and finger dexterity. (2) At the initial testing, and again at 17 years, 14-year-old boys scored higher in numerical aptitude than 14-year-old girls. At the initial testing, but not at the retesting 2 years later, 15-year-old boys scored higher in numerical aptitude than 15-year-old girls. Among 17-year-olds who were tested just once, boys scored higher in numerical aptitude than girls. No differences were found among 16-year-old Ss either at the initial testing or at the retesting a year later. (3) 14-year-old boys scored higher in manual dexterity when they were retested at 17 years than 14-year-old girls did. No sex differences were found at the initial testing. Among 15-year-old Ss, girls scored higher in manual dexterity at the initial testing than boys did. No sex differences were found at the retesting 2 years later. No sex differences were found in the 16- or 17-year-old samples.

Druker, J. F., and Hagen, J. W. Developmental trends in the processing of task-relevant and task-irrelevant information. *Child Development*, 1969, *40*, 371–82.
 Subjects: $N = 240$; 9, 11, 13 yrs (black low SES). Measures: As the central task, Ss viewed cards of objects paired with animals. The cards were then covered, and a duplicate of one of the cards served as a cue. Ss were asked to point to the location of the covered card that matched the cue card. As the incidental task, Ss were asked to match objects with animals they had appeared with before. Results: (1) Boys had higher scores than girls on the central task. (2) There were no sex differences on the incidental task.

Dubanoski, R. A., and Parton, D. A. Effect of the presence of a human model on imitative behavior in children. *Developmental Psychology*, 1971, *4*, 463–68.
 Subjects: $N = 90$; 4 yrs. Measures: Ss saw films of either a female model manipulating (stimulus) objects, a hand manipulating objects, or objects moving with no visible means of locomotion (invisible nylon threads). Controls saw wooden puzzles assembled under the same conditions. Ss were given a free play period with the same toys plus others. Imitative responses were recorded. Then performance recall of taped manipulations was tested. Results: After viewing no model, boys made more imitative responses than girls did. There were no sex differences in imitation after viewing the model, or in recall scores.

DuHamel, T. R., and Biller, H. B. Parental imitation and nonimitation in young children. *Developmental Psychology*, 1969, *1*, 772.
 Subjects: $N = 63$; 5 yrs. Measures: Ss were presented with 3 non-sex-typed human figures and 3 dolls—a mother doll, a father doll, and a child doll of the same sex as S. Ss were asked 18 questions about the 3 figures. Each was similar in format to the following: "Which of these 3 people is nice?" Half of the questions contained familiar adjectives (e.g. nice, good, poor, happy); the other half contained unfamiliar adjectives (e.g. idealistic, smug, controversial, cynical). E informed Ss of the mother and father dolls' choices by placing the mother doll next to 1 of the figures and the father doll next to another. There were 3 options available to Ss: they could imitate either the mother or father doll (by moving the child doll to either of the parent dolls' selections), or they could imitate neither (by moving the child doll to the remaining figure). Results: More boys imitated the father doll; more girls imitated the mother doll ($p < .01$). When responding to questions containing familiar adjectives, more boys than girls chose not to imitate either parent doll ($p < .05$).

Duncan, C. P. Probability vs. latency of solution of an insight problem. *Psychological Reports*, 1962, *10*, 119–21.
 Subjects: $N = 1,088$; adults. Measures: Maier 2-string problem. Results: More men than women solved the problem within the specified period of time.

Dusek, J. B. Experimenter bias in performance of children at a simple motor task. *Developmental Psychology*, 1971, *4*, 55–62.
 Subjects: $N = 126$; 6–7 yrs. Measures: Ss performed a marble-dropping task under social reinforcement or nonreinforcement conditions, with either a neutral E, an E biased toward superior performance of girls, or an E biased toward superior performance of boys. The response measures were the base rate (number of marbles dropped in the first minute of the task) and a difference (D) score computed separately for each (number of marbles dropped in the first minute minus number of marbles dropped in each subsequent minute). Results: (1) Girls had a higher base rate than boys ($p < .05$). (2) No sex differences were found in D scores.

Dusek, J. B., and Hill, K. T. Probability learning as a function of sex of the subject, test anxiety, and percentage of reinforcement. *Developmental Psychology*, 1970, *3*, 195–207.
 Subjects: $N = 72$; 9, 10 yrs. Measures: Ss performed a 3-choice probability learning task in

which the "correct" response was reinforced 33% or 66% of the time. **Results:** (1) Boys gave a higher number of correct responses than girls ($p < .001$). (2) Girls showed more response patterns than boys ($p < .001$). (3) Boys showed more win-stay and less lose-shift responding than girls ($p < .001$, $p < .001$). Over trials, boys showed a greater decrease in lose-shift responding than girls ($p < .01$). No sex differences were found in Ss' display of low-side-shift responding.

Dweck, C. S., and Reppucci, N. D. Learned helplessness and reinforcement responsibility in children. *J. Personality & Social Psychology*, 1973, 25, 109–16.
   Subjects: $N = 40$; 10 yrs. **Measures:** Ss were given the Intellectual Achievement Responsibility Questionnaire, which yielded 2 subscale scores and a total score. The I+ and I− subscales measured Ss' respective tendencies to see themselves as responsible for the positive and negative reinforcement they received in intellectual academic situations. The total I score measured Ss' acceptance of responsibility for the outcomes of their achievement efforts. **Results:** (1) No sex differences were found in total I, I+, or I− scores. (2) No sex differences were found in the number of times Ss attributed success to ability or to effort. (3) No sex differences were found in the number of times Ss attributed failure to lack of ability. Men were more likely than women to attribute failure to lack of effort.

Dykstra, R., and Tinney, R. Sex differences in reading readiness—first grade achievement and second grade achievement. *Reading & Realism*, 1969, 13, 623–28.
   EXPERIMENT I: **Subjects:** $N = 3,283$; tested at 6 and 7 yrs. **Measures:** The following measures of reading readiness were administered at age 6 (the beginning of first grade): Murphy-Durrell Phonemes, Murphy-Durrell Letter Names, Murphy-Durrell Learning Rate, Thurstone-Jeffery Identical Forms, Metropolitan Word Meaning, and Metropolitan Listening. Ss also completed the Pintner-Cunningham Primary, a group test of intelligence. **Results:** (1) Girls were superior to boys in intelligence, auditory discrimination (M-D Phonemes), letter knowledge (M-D Letter Names), learning rate, visual discrimination (T-J Identical Forms), and ability to follow oral directions (Metropolitan Listening). (2) Boys were superior to girls on the orally administered test of general vocabulary (Metropolitan Word Meaning).
   EXPERIMENT II: **Subjects:** Same as Experiment I. **Measures:** The Stanford Achievement Test, Primary Battery I, was administered to all Ss at age 6 (the end of the first grade). **Results:** Girls had higher scores on 4 of the 5 subtests (Word Reading, Paragraph Meaning, Spelling, and Work Study Skills). No sex differences were found on the orally administered vocabulary test.
   EXPERIMENT III: **Subjects:** Same as Experiment I. **Measures:** The Stanford Achievement Test, Primary Battery II, was administered to all Ss at age 7 (the end of the second grade). **Results:** (1) Girls were superior to boys on 6 of the 8 subtests (Word Meaning, Paragraph Meaning, Work Study Skills, Science and Social Studies Concepts, Language, and Arithmetic Computations). (2) Boys were superior to girls on the Spelling subtest. (3) No sex differences were found on the Arithmetic Concepts subtest.

Eagly, A. H., and Manis, M. Evaluation of message and communicator as a function of involvement. *J. Personality & Social Psychology*, 1966, 3, 483–85.
   Subjects: $N = 124$; 14 yrs. **Measures:** Ss read 2 persuasive messages arguing that teenagers should be more strictly controlled by adults. One message was constructed to be relatively involving for boys but not for girls; the other was constructed to be relatively involving for girls but not for boys. Afterward, Ss evaluated the messages and the communicators. **Results:** (1) No main sex differences were found in Ss' evaluations of the messages. Boys responded less favorably to the boy's message than to the girl's message, while girls responded less favorably to the girl's message than to the boy's message ($p < .01$). This interaction was maintained when initial attitudes were held constant ($p < .01$). (2) No main sex differences were found in Ss' evaluations of the communicators. Boys responded less favorably to the communicator of the boy's message than to the communicator of the girl's message; girls responded less favorably to the communicator of the girl's message than to the communicator of the boy's message ($p < .05$). This interaction was not maintained when initial attitudes were held constant.

Eagly, A. H., and Telaak, K. Width of the latitude of acceptance as a determinant of attitude change. *J. Personality & Social Psychology*, 1972, 23, 388–97.
   Subjects: $N = 118$; 18–21 yrs (college). **Measures:** After completing an attitude questionnaire, Ss received a persuasive communication either slightly, moderately, or strongly discrepant from their initial attitude. Ss then responded to a second attitude questionnaire. Ss were also asked to evaluate the message and the source. **Results:** No sex differences.

Eagly, A. H., and Whitehead, G. I. Effect of choice on receptivity to favorable and unfavorable evaluations of oneself. *J. Personality & Social Psychology*, 1972, *22*, 223–30.
   Subjects: $N = 145$; 18–21 yrs (college). Measures: After completing tests described as measures of social sensitivity and receiving either favorable or unfavorable feedback on their
   performances, Ss rated themselves on social sensitivity. Ss' ratings were scored as deviations
   from a control group. Ss also completed 18 items from Berger's Self-Acceptance Scale.
   Results: (1) There were no main sex differences in self-ratings of social sensitivity. Men
   changed more toward the favorable than the unfavorable message in their self-ratings of
   social sensitivity; women changed equally toward both ($p < .05$). (2) No main sex differences
   were found in self-acceptance.

Eckert, H. M. Visual-motor tasks at 3 and 4 years of age. *Perceptual & Motor Skills*, 1970,
31, 560.
   Subjects: $N = 22$; tested at 3, 4 yrs. Measures: Ss performed the following visual-motor tasks:
   walking on the balance board, the Lowe rotor (with epicyclic pattern), 3 disk-sorting tasks
   (right, left, and both hands), and 4 peg-shifting tasks (right hand moving pegs away from
   body, left away, right hand moving pegs toward body, left toward). Results: No sex differences.

Edelman, M. S., and Omark, D. R. Dominance hierarchies in young children. *Social Science Information*, 1973, *12*, 103–10.
   Subjects: $N =$ approximately 270; 6–9 yrs. Measures: Ss were asked "Who is the toughest?"
   comparing their classmates with each other and with themselves. A "dyad of established
   dominance" was scored if both members agreed on who was. Results: (1) Boys were consistently ranked higher in toughness, with a few girls scoring in the masculine range. (2)
   There was a higher proportion of dyads of established dominance in boy-girl pairs than in same-
   sex pairs. In boy-girl pairs the boy was almost always recognized as dominant by both members. (3) There were no sex differences in accuracy of perception of the dominance relations
   between pairs of classmates, not including the subject.

Eimas, P. D. Information processing in problem solving as a function of developmental
level and stimulus salience. *Developmental Psychology*, 1970, *2*, 224–29.
   Subjects: $N = 192$; 7, 9, 11, 13 yrs. $N = 48$; 18–21 yrs (college women). Measures: Ss were
   shown 8- and 16-cell matrices containing 1 of 3 types of stimuli. Instructions were to find the
   correct cell as quickly as possible by asking questions answerable by yes or no. Questions
   were analyzed to provide a measure of average amount of information obtained, categorical-
   ness, and focusing. Results: No sex differences.

Eisen, M. Characteristic self-esteem, sex and resistance to temptation. *J. Personality &
Social Psychology*, 1972, *24*, 68–72.
   Subjects: $N = 125$; 11 yrs. Measures: Ss were classified as either high cheaters, low cheaters,
   or noncheaters, on the basis of the number of times they changed or falsified answers (in order
   to win a prize) in a dot-counting contest. Results: No sex differences.

Eisenberg, L., Berlin, C. I., Dill, A., and Frank, S. Class and race effects on the intelligi-
bility of monosyllables. *Child Development*, 1968, *39*, 1077–89.
   Subjects: $N = 64$; 8–10 yrs (black and white, low and middle SES). Measures: 40 teachers
   from inner-city schools listened to tapes of Ss' speech (made in an earlier study) and recorded their perceptions of what the children said. Results: Girls were better understood than
   boys were ($p < .05$).

Ekman, P., and Friesen, W. V. Constants across cultures in the face and emotion. *J. Per-
sonality & Social Psychology*, 1971, *17*, 124–29.
   Subjects: $N = 319$; children and adults (Fore linguistic cultural group of the South East
   Highlands of New Guinea). Measures: After being told a story and shown a set of 3 faces,
   Ss were asked to select the face that showed the emotion most appropriate to the story.
   Results: No sex differences.

Elder, M. The effects of temperature and position on the sucking pressure of infants. *Child
Development*, 1970, *41*, 95–102.
   Subjects: $N = 27$; 3–5 days. Measures: Infant's state was rated. Sucking strength was measured while S was supine or supported at crib temperatures of 80 or 90 degrees. Results: No
   sex differences.

Elkind, D., Van Doorninck, W., and Schwarz, C. Perceptual activity and concept attainment. *Child Development*, 1967, *38*, 1153–61.
  Subjects: $N = 120$; 5–11 yrs. Measures: Ss were given a 2-choice discrimination-learning task. The stimuli used were 27 drawings of a boy, girl, or dog engaged in 1 of 3 activities (running, eating, or playing with a ball) in 1 of 3 settings (room, yard, or beach). The response measure was the number of trials Ss needed to reach the criterion of 10 successively correct responses. Results: No sex differences.

Elkind, D., Medvine, L., and Rockway, A. S. Representational level and concept production in children and adolescents. *Developmental Psychology*, 1970, *2*, 85–89.
  Subjects: $N = 120$; 9, 14 yrs. Measures: Ss were asked to state 3 ways in which each of 10 stimulus pairs were alike. Stimulus pairs were either pictures, verbal labels of pictures, or mixed series of pictures and verbal labels. Results: No sex differences.

Elliott, R., and Vasta, R. The modeling of sharing: effects associated with vicarious reinforcement, symbolization, age and generalization. *J. Experimental Child Psychology*, 1970, *10*, 8–15.
  Subjects: $N = 48$; 5–7 yrs. Measures: After (pretest) sharing behavior was measured (putting candy in an envelope for a poor boy), Ss saw a filmed male-peer model who exhibited sharing behavior and was either nonreinforced, tangibly reinforced with no explanation, or tangibly reinforced with explanation (all by adult female E). Controls saw no film. Postmodeling sharing was measured (candy and/or pennies put in an envelope for a poor boy). Results: There were no main sex differences in sharing after observing the model. Boys shared candy more freely than pennies, whereas girls shared pennies more freely than candy.

Ellsworth, P. C., Carlsmith, J. A., and Henson, A. The stare as a stimulus to flight in human subjects. *J. Personality & Social Psychology*, 1972, *21*, 302–11.
  Subjects: $N = 216$; adults. Measures: Standing at the corner of a sidewalk, male or female Es either did or did not stare at drivers ($N = 88$) who pulled up in the near lane and stopped for a red light. When the light turned green, drivers were timed until they crossed a white line on the far side of the intersection. In a second experiment, similar procedures were followed using pedestrians ($N = 128$) as subjects. Results: No sex differences.

Emmerich, W. Continuity and stability in early social development: II. Teacher ratings. *Child Development*, 1966, *37*, 17–27.
  Subjects: $N = 53$; tested at 3, 4 yrs. Measures: At the end of each semester of nursery school, Ss were rated by their teachers on 24 social-behavior scales; 3 basic factor structures emerged from factor analyses of the data: Aggression-Dominance, Dependency, and Autonomy. Results: (1) At the end of the first semester, girls scored higher than boys on the Autonomy factor; no sex difference was found at the end of the second, third, or fourth semester. (2) Girls scored consistently higher than boys on the Dependency factor (for each semester, $p < .01$). (3) No mention was made of the Aggression-Dominance factor.

Emmerich, W. The parental role: a functional-cognitive approach. *Monographs of the Society for Research in Child Development*, 1969, *34*.
  Subjects: $N = 88$; parents (mean age of child 45 mos). Measures: Parents completed the Parental Role Questionnaire to assess attitudes concerning child-rearing: goal values, means-ends beliefs, means-ends capacities, and goal achievements. Results: No sex-of-parent or sex-of-child differences were found.

Emmerich, W. Structure and development of personal-social behaviors in preschool settings. Educational Testing Service—Head Start Longitudinal Study, November 1971.
  EXPERIMENT I: Subjects: $N = 415$; 4–5 yrs (disadvantaged black and white). Measures: After being observed in their classrooms during free-play periods, Ss were rated on 127 unipolar scales and 18 bipolar scales. Each child was observed twice, once in the early fall and once in the late fall. Results: (1) Girls were more constructive (vs. destructive), compliant (vs. rebellious), and withdrawn, and engaged in more artistic activity. Boys were more assertive, exhibited more peer orientation, and engaged in more gross motor and fantasy activity. (2) No sex differences were found in autonomous achievement; cognitive and fine manipulative activity; adult orientation; defiance-hostility; distrustfulness; submissiveness vs. dominance; purposefulness vs. aimlessness (interpersonal cooperativeness); sociableness vs. solitariness; or loving (happiness vs. unhappiness).
  EXPERIMENT II: Subjects: $N = 596$; 4–5 yrs (disadvantaged black and white). Measures: Ss were observed in their classrooms once in the early fall and once toward the end of the

school year. Since considerable overlap exists between the 2 samples, many of the early fall observations included in the data analysis in Experiment I were analyzed again in the present study. **Results:** (1) In comparison with boys, girls were more purposeful and constructive, had higher autonomous achievement scores, and engaged in more artistic, cognitive, and fine manipulative activity. (2) In comparison with girls, boys affiliated more with peers, and were more attached and more oriented to peers. Boys also engaged in more fantasy and gross motor activity and were more socially controlling with adults. (3) No sex differences were found in affiliation with adults, attachment to adults, or orientation to adults; recognition-seeking (from adults or peers); information-seeking (from adults or peers); social control of peers; assertiveness; defiance-hostility; distrustfulness; withdrawal; submissiveness vs. dominance; compliance vs. rebelliousness; sociableness vs. solitariness; dependence vs. independence; loving. (4) Overall, boys exhibited more person-oriented behavior; girls displayed more task-oriented behavior.

Emmerich, W., Goldman, K. S., and Shore, R. E. Differentiation and development of social norms. *J. Personality & Social Psychology*, 1971, *18*, 323–53.
    Subjects: $N = 680$; 8–17 yrs. **Measures:** Ss were asked to name a friend who was a boy and a friend who was a girl. Ss were then given a set of questions asking them to indicate how frequently their parents and their named friends expected them to agree with, argue with, help and seek help from others. Ss were also asked to give their own expectations concerning their behavior. **Results:** (1) Girls indicated that their parents and friends expected them to seek help from others more frequently than boys did. No sex differences were found in the frequency with which Ss indicated that their parents and friends expected them to help others, agree with others, or argue with others. (2) Girls thought they should seek help from others more frequently than boys did; boys thought they should argue with others more frequently than girls did. No sex differences were found in the frequency with which Ss thought they should help others or agree with others. (3) Girls indicated that their parents and friends expected them to show higher standards of conduct with same-sex friends than with opposite-sex friends. A similar but weaker tendency was found among boys between the ages of 8 and 13. From age 14 on, boys indicated that their parents and friends expected them to show higher standards of conduct with their girl friends than with their boy friends. (4) Girls of all ages and boys between the ages of 8 and 13 thought they should exhibit higher standards of conduct with same-sex friends than with opposite-sex friends. Among 14- and 15-year-old boys, no trend was found. Boys aged 16–17 years thought they should exhibit higher standards of conduct with their girl friends than with their boy friends.

Endler, N. S. Conformity as a function of different reinforcement schedules. *J. Personality & Social Psychology*, 1966, *4*, 175–80.
    Subjects: $N = 120$; 18–21 yrs (college). **Measures:** Before responding to multiple-choice stimulus items, Ss were subjected to social pressure via a Crutchfield-type conformity apparatus. On critical items, Ss were either positively or negatively reinforced for agreeing or disagreeing with the contrived group consensus. Ss in a neutral condition received no reinforcement. During a second session 2 weeks later, Ss responded to the stimulus items without social pressure or reinforcement. The number of times Ss agreed with the contrived group consensus was recorded. **Results:** Women conformed more than men did in both sessions ($p = .05$).

Endler, N. S., and Hoy, E. Conformity as related to reinforcement and social pressure. *J. Personality & Social Psychology*, 1967, *7*, 197–202.
    Subjects: $N = 120$; 18–21 yrs (college). **Measures:** Ss responded to multiple-choice items after being informed of the choices of simulated others. The number of times Ss agreed with the unanimous group response was recorded. **Results:** No sex differences.

Endo, G. T. Social drive or arousal: a test of two theories of social isolation. *J. Experimental Child Psychology*, 1968, *6*, 61–74.
    Subjects: $N = 96$; 8 yrs. **Measures:** Ss performed a 2-choice probability learning task (predicting which of 2 cards, in ratios of 7:3 or 3:7, would appear on the next trial) after social isolation (12 minutes alone) or nonisolation. Half of the Ss in each isolation group were verbally reinforced for correct predictions, the other half were reinforced with a buzzer and light. Total number of responses made to the more frequently occurring event were recorded, regardless of whether reinforcement occurred. **Results:** No sex differences.

Engel, M. The stability of the self-concept in adolescence. *J. Abnormal & Social Psychology*, 1959, *58*, 211–15.
    Subjects: $N = 104$; tested at 13, 15 yrs. $N = 68$; tested at 15, 17 yrs. **Measures:** Self-concept

was assessed by a set of 100 Q-sort items, half of which had positive and half negative connotations. In responding, Ss had to place each item in 1 of 11 categories, ranging from "most like me" to "least like me." Results: No sex differences were found either during the initial testing in 1954 or during retesting in 1956. No sex differences were found in stability of self-concept.

Entwisle, D. R., and Greenberger, E. Adolescents' views of women's work role. *American J. Orthopsychiatry,* 1972a, *42,* 648–56.
Subjects: $N = 575$; 14 yrs (white, black). Measures: Ss' attitudes toward women's working role were assessed. Results: Boys' attitudes were more conservative than girls', i.e. boys felt more strongly that women should not work; rather, they should center their lives around their homes and families. Girls felt more strongly than boys that women were intellectually curious ($p < .01$).

Entwisle, D. R., and Greenberger, E. Questions about social class, internality-externality, and test anxiety. *Developmental Psychology,* 1972b, *7,* 218 (brief report and extended report).
Subjects: $N = 664$; 14 yrs (inner-city black, low and medium IQ; inner-city white, medium IQ; blue-collar black, low and medium IQ; blue-collar white, medium and high IQ; rural white, medium and high IQ; middle-class white, medium and high IQ; middle-class Jewish, medium and high IQ). Measures: All Ss completed the Intellectual Achievement Responsibility (IAR) scale. 566 of the Ss were also given a test-anxiety questionnaire. Results: (1) Among inner-city and rural whites of medium IQ, girls had higher IAR success scores than boys. Among middle-class whites of high IQ, boys had higher success scores than girls. (2) Girls consistently had higher test-anxiety scores than boys.

Epstein, R. Authoritarianism, displaced aggression, and social status of the target. *J. Personality & Social Psychology,* 1965, *2,* 585–89.
Subjects: $N = 40$; 18–21 yrs (college). Measures: Ss were instructed to shock a confederate whenever he made an incorrect response in a serial learning task. The intensity of the shock delivered was recorded. Results: Men delivered higher intensities of shock than women did ($p < .01$).

Eska, B., and Black, K. N. Conceptual tempo in young grade-school children. *Child Development,* 1971, *42,* 505–16.
Subjects: $N = 100$; 8 yrs. Measures: Ss completed the Matching Familiar Figures task and the verbal subtest of the Otis-Lennon Mental Ability Test. Ss were also presented with 6 pictures and asked to tell a story about each; measures were taken of the latency and duration of Ss' responses. Results: No sex differences.

Fagan, J. F., III. Infants' recognition memory for a series of visual stimuli. *J. Experimental Child Psychology,* 1971, *11,* 244–50.
Subjects: 12 opposite-sex twin pairs; 3–8 mos. Measures: Ss' fixation times to (a) novel relative to familiar stimuli, and (b) less familiar relative to more familiar stimuli, were recorded. Results: No sex differences.

Fagan, J. F., III. Infants' recognition memory for faces. *J. Experimental Child Psychology,* 1972, *14,* 453–76.
EXPERIMENT I: Subjects: $N = 17$ same-sex twin pairs; 4–6 mos. Measures: Ss viewed pictures of unfamiliar faces (a woman, a man, and a baby). Orientation was varied, as were lengths of familiarization. Recognition memory was assessed. Results: No sex differences.
EXPERIMENT II: Subjects: $N = 52$; 3–4 mos. Measures: Same as Experiment I. Masks were introduced to assess discrimination between photos and 3-dimensional representations. Results: No sex differences.
EXPERIMENT III: Subjects: $N = 72$; 5–6 mos. Measures: Same as Experiment I. Discrimination between male, female, and baby was assessed. Results: Girls responded differentially to properly oriented photos, boys did not.
EXPERIMENT IV: Subjects: $N = 36$; 4–6 mos. Measures: Same as Experiment III. Orientation was proper; line drawings were used. Results: No sex differences.
EXPERIMENT V: Subjects: $N = 56$; 5–6 mos. Measures: Novelty problem with masks and photos was used. Orientation varied. Results: There were no sex differences in discrimination of highly lifelike masks.
EXPERIMENT VI: Subjects: $N = 24$; 5–6 mos. Measures: Homogenous gray forms, equal

to photos in reflectance and outline, were paired with photos. Preference was assessed. **Results:** No sex differences.

EXPERIMENT VII: **Subjects:** $N = 16$; 5–6 mos. **Measures:** A novelty problem with masks (as in Experiment II) was contrasted with photos of a man and a woman. Ss' fixation point was watched. **Results:** No sex differences.

Fagot, B. I., and Patterson, G. R. An in vivo analysis of reinforcing contingencies for sex-role behaviors in the preschool child. *Developmental Psychology*, 1969, *1*, 563–68.

Subjects: $N = 18$; 3 yrs (School 1). $N = 18$; 3 yrs (School 2). **Measures:** During both the fall and spring terms, observations were made of Ss, free-play activities. 28 play behaviors and 10 social consequences of these behaviors were recorded. **Results:** (1) Boys spent more time than girls (a) playing with building blocks, setting up farms and villages (School 1, both terms; School 2, fall term only); (b) playing with toy trucks, planes, boats, trains, or tractors (School 1, both terms; School 2, both terms); (c) climbing or hiding in pipes (School 1, fall term only; School 2, no difference); (d) riding trikes, cars, horses, skates, wagons, or boats (School 1, spring term only; School 2, no difference); (e) playing at the cornmeal table or sandbox outside (School 1, no difference; School 2, both terms). Girls spent more time than boys (a) painting at the easel (School 1, both terms; School 2, fall term only); (2) cutting, pasting, or drawing with crayons or chalk (School 1, both terms; School 2, both terms); (c) playing in the kitchen or large playhouse (School 1, both terms; School 2, no difference); (d) playing with the dollhouse (School 1, fall term only; School 2, no difference); (e) playing with dolls (School 1, both terms; School 2, no difference); (f) playing with clay (School 1, both terms; School 2, no difference); (g) looking at books or listening to stories (School 1, no difference; School 2, fall term only). No sex differences were found in time spent (a) playing with water, blowing bubbles; (b) playing with the design board, puzzles, tinkertoys, snakes, flannel boards or marble games; (c) stringing beads; (d) hammering; (e) playing with a steering wheel or dashboards; (f) dressing up in like-sex costumes; (g) dressing up in opposite-sex costumes; (h) using like-sex tools; (i) using opposite-sex tools; (j) singing, listening to records, or playing musical instruments; (k) playing at the science table or with dinosaurs; (l) playing with live animals or toy animals; (m) sitting and doing nothing, wandering, following the teacher around; (n) helping the teacher; (o) swinging, playing on the slide or teeter-totter, bouncing on tires; (p) throwing rocks, hitting with an object, or pushing. During the spring term, boys and girls in School 2 spent a considerable amount of time wandering. The authors noted that this accounted in part for the drop in percentage of time spent in sex-preferred activities. (2) Girls spent less time in opposite-sex behaviors than boys did. There was no sex difference in percentage of time spent in same-sex behaviors. (3) Teachers (4 women) reinforced both sexes for feminine behaviors; however, boys did not as a result become more feminine in their behavior preferences. (4) Girls were reinforced for sex-preferred behavior more frequently than boys. When neutral behaviors were included, no sex differences were found in teacher reinforcement. (5) No difference was found between boys and girls in the amount of criticism they received. (6) Ss reinforced same-sex peers more often than opposite-sex peers.

Farnham-Diggory, S. Cognitive synthesis in Negro and white children. *Monographs of the Society for Research in Child Development*, 1970, 35.

EXPERIMENT I: **Subjects:** $N = 192$; 6–9 yrs. **Measures:** Ss learned to associate verbalized words with pictures and with unrelated logographs. Ss were tested on decoding of logograph sentence and acting out its meaning. Ss performed a maplike test that required imitation of line drawings using pieces of string. Forms in the drawings were symbols for words; Ss were asked to construct a sentence with symbols. In the mathematical synthesis task, Ss matched different numbers of dots on card with cubes of varying sizes. **Results:** (1) Boys performed better than girls did on verbal synthesis. (2) On the maplike synthesis task, among white Ss, boys did better than girls. Among black Ss, girls did better than boys. (3) There were no sex differences in mathematical synthesis.

EXPERIMENT II: **Subjects:** $N = 110$; 4, 5, 7–8 yrs. **Measures:** Same as Experiment I, except with verbal and motor pretraining. **Results:** There were no main sex differences. Maplike task and training affected performance of girls but not boys ($p < .05$).

EXPERIMENT III: **Subjects:** $N = 140$; 5, 7 yrs. **Measures:** The maplike synthesis problem was given as before, except that Ss either (1) role-played the various items in the sentence before attempting the problem, (2) heard new instructions altered so as to play up their tendency to act on first word heard, or (3) attempted the problem under a perceptual shield condition in which the various steps had to be memorized (they were not always on display). The mathematical synthesis task was given with either a verbal drill on base concepts or an action drill on the various steps. **Results:** (1) Girls did better than boys on the maplike task. (2) There were no sex differences on mathematical synthesis.

Farrell, M. Sex differences in block play in early childhood education. *J. Educational Research*, 1957, *51*, 279–84.

Subjects: $N = 376$; 3–7 yrs. Measures: Teachers' observations of children's indoor play activities. Results: (1) A higher percentage of boys than girls played with blocks ($p < .01$). (2) Boys played with blocks longer than girls did ($p < .01$).

Farwell, L. Reactions of kindergarten, first- and second-grade children to constructive play materials. *Genetic Psychology Monographs*, 1930, *8*, 451–561.

Subjects: $N = 271$; 5–7 yrs. Measures: Ss were observed while working with modeling, building, drawing, painting, sewing, cardboard construction, and paper construction materials. Results: In comparison with girls, boys showed a marked preference for blocks and a lack of interest in sewing. Popular choices among both boys and girls were modeling and painting materials. A fair interest was shown by both sexes in drawing and only a slight interest in cardboard and paper construction.

Faterson, H. F., and Witkin, H. A. Longitudinal study of development of the body concept. *Developmental Psychology*, 1970, *2*, 429–38.

Subjects: $N = 53$; tested at 8, 13 yrs. $N = 60$; tested at 10, 14, 17 yrs. Measures: Ss first drew a person, then a person of the opposite sex. Pictures were scored on a 5-point articulation-of-body concept (ABC) scale, from "most articulated" to "most primitive and infantile." Results: At ages 8, 13, and 14, girls' ABC scores were higher than those of boys ($p < .025$, $p < .025$, $p < .025$).

Fauls, L. B., and Smith, W. D. Sex-role learning in 5-year-olds. *J. Genetic Psychology*, 1956, *89*, 105–17.

Subjects: $N = 38$; 4, 5 yrs. Measures: Ss were presented with sets of paired pictures depicting a child of the same sex and his parents. One picture in each pair showed the child performing a masculine activity; in the other picture the child was engaged in a feminine activity. Ss were asked 4 questions about each set: (1) "Which of these do you do?" (2) "Which do you like best?" (3) "Which does Mommy want the boy (girl) to do?" (4) "Which does Daddy want the boy (girl) to do?" Results: Boys chose the masculine activity more frequently than girls did ($p < .01$). (2) Both sexes perceived the parents as preferring the activity "appropriate" for the child's sex rather than the "inappropriate" activity.

Fay, T. Culture and sex differences in concepts of sex role and self. *Dissertations Abstracts International*, 1971, *31*, 6239.

Subjects: $N = 45$; 18–21 yrs (college: U.S., Philippines, Colombia). Measures: Ss rated each of 5 concepts (self, typical male, typical female, ideal male, and ideal female) on 25 semantic differential rating scales. Results: (1) Regardless of sex or nationality of rater, a significant difference was found between ratings of male and female stereotypes (typical and ideal). (2) Similarity between ratings or self and same-sex stereotype (whether typical or ideal) was higher for women than for men.

Feather, N. T. Level of aspiration and performance variability. *J. Personality & Social Psychology*, 1967a, *6*, 37–46.

Subjects: $N = 106$; 18–21 yrs (college). Measures: Ss were individually tested on a manual-dexterity task, which allowed E complete control over Ss' performance. Ss' scores were manipulated to be either high, medium, or low in variability. Before each of 11 trials, Ss stated both the highest and the lowest scores they expected to receive and their level of aspiration. The measures derived were (a) mean highest score expected; (b) mean lowest score expected; (c) mean goal discrepancy (difference between level of aspiration at trial $(n + 1)$ and performance at trial n); (d) mean attainment discrepancy (difference between level of aspiration at trial n and performance at trial n); (e) change in level of aspiration from trial 1 to trial 2; (f) mean change in aspiration following success; (g) mean change in aspiration following failure; and (h) number of atypical responses (number of times Ss raised their level of aspiration after failure and lowered it following success). The projective measure of n achievement, the achievement anxiety test, Radner's test of intolerance ambiguity, and Pettigrew's test of category width were also administered. Results: (1) No main sex differences were found. (2) Women in the high-variability condition showed a larger change in aspiration following either success or failure than women in the low-variability condition; women in the medium-variability condition fell in between these 2 extremes. No differences were found among the 3 male groups. (3) The difference between the mean change in aspiration following success and the mean change in aspiration following failure was greater for women in the low-variability condition than for women in the high-variability condition. Women in the medium-variability group again fell in between these 2 extremes. No differences were found among the 3 male groups. (4) No sex differences were found on any of the personality measures.

Feather, N. T. Valence of outcome and expectation of success in relation to task difficulty and perceived locus of control. *J. Personality & Social Psychology*, 1967b, 7, 372–86.
Subjects: $N = 76$; 18–21 yrs (college). Measures: Ss provided estimates of probability of success and ratings of the attractiveness of success and repulsiveness of failure for the first and last trials of a task described as involving either luck or skill. Results: No sex differences.

Feather, N. T. Change in confidence following success or failure as a predictor of subsequent performance. *J. Personality & Social Psychology*, 1968, 9, 38–46.
Subjects: $N = 60$; 18–21 yrs (college). Measures: Ss provided confidence ratings before attempting to solve each of 15 anagrams. Results: (1) Men had higher confidence ratings than women did ($p < .05$). (2) No sex differences were found in number of typical changes in confidence ratings (a typical change was one in which S either raised his confidence rating after a success or lowered it after a failure). (3) No sex differences were found in number of anagrams correctly solved.

Feather, N. T. Attitude and selective recall. *J. Personality & Social Psychology*, 1969a, 12, 310–19.
Subjects: $N = 138$; 18–21 yrs (college). Measures: One week after rating American intervention in South Vietnam on a bipolar adjective scale, Ss were asked to write arguments favoring American intervention with which they agreed or disagreed, and arguments opposing American intervention with which they agreed or disagreed. Results: (1) Men wrote down more arguments than women ($p < .05$). (2) No sex differences were found in initial attitudes, or in consistency of arguments with initial attitudes.

Feather, N. T. Attribution of responsibility and valence of success and failure in relation to initial confidence and task performance. *J. Personality & Social Psychology*, 1969b, 13, 129–44.
Subjects: $N = 167$; 18–21 yrs (college). Measures: Ss worked at a 10-item anagrams test. Before they began, Ss rated their confidence in passing the test (solve 5 or more anagrams). After they finished, Ss recorded the number of anagrams they had solved, the degree to which they felt their performance was due to ability (internal attribution) or luck (external attribution), and their degree of satisfaction with their performance. Ss also completed self-esteem and competence measures (administered prior to the anagram test) and a feeling-of-inadequacy measure (administered 1 week after the anagrams tests). Results: Women were lower in initial confidence ($p < .005$), higher in external attribution ($p < .01$), and higher in feelings of inadequacy ($p < .05$) than men were. No sex differences were found in self-esteem, competence, satisfaction, or performance scores.

Feather, N. T., and Simon, J. G. Attribution of responsibility and valence of outcome in relation to initial confidence and success and failure of self and other. *J. Personality & Social Psychology*, 1971, 18, 173–88.
Subjects: $N = 128$; 18–21 yrs (college). Measures: Like-sex pairs of Ss worked on 5 practice anagrams and then on 15 test anagrams. For both practice and test items, difficulty level was manipulated so that half of the Ss did well and half did poorly. Before beginning test items, Ss rated degree of confidence in passing for self and for other. After being informed of their test score, Ss rated the degree to which they felt their performance and that of their partner was due to luck or ability, and then rated their degree of satisfaction with their own and their partner's performance. Results: (1) There were no main sex differences. (2) Confidence ratings were higher for passing men than for passing women, but lower for failing men than for failing women ($p < .001$).

Feld, S. C., and Lewis, J. The assessment of achievement anxieties in children. In C. P. Smith, ed., *Achievement-related motives in children*. New York: Russell Sage Foundation, 1969.
Subjects: $N = 7,355$; 7 yrs (white, black). Measures: Ss completed expanded forms of the Test Anxiety Scale for Children (TASC) and the Defensiveness Scale for Children, which included original and reversed questions. Results: (1) There were no sex differences on the Poor Self-Evaluation subscale of the TASC. On Test Anxiety, Remote School Concern, and Somatic Signs of Anxiety subscales, girls had higher scores than boys (strongest on Remote School Concern and Somatic Signs of Anxiety). (2) On total scores from the original Sarason

Test Anxiety Scale for Children, girls had higher scores than boys. (3) The overall main effects for sex were due to the white sample (there were no sex differences in the black sample).

Feldman, S. S., and Ingham, M. E. Attachment behavior: a study of the concurrent validity in two age groups. Unpublished manuscript, Stanford University, 1973.
    EXPERIMENT I: Subjects: $N = 56$; 1 yr. Measures: Accompanied by either their mother, their father, or a female acquaintance, Ss were observed in the following situations: accompanying adult (AA) brings child to room with toys, then sits down (Episode 1); AA attends to child for 2 minutes, then fills out questionnaire (Episode 2); female stranger (Str) enters, sits silently for 1 minute, converses with AA for 1 minute, then plays with child (Episode 3); AA leaves, Str goes to chair (Episode 4); AA enters, Str leaves, AA plays with child (Episode 5); AA leaves, child remains alone (Episode 6); Str returns, comforts child if distressed (Episode 7); AA enters, plays with child (Episode 8). During Episodes 2, 3, 5, 6, and 7, Ss were scored for the following behaviors: manipulative play; crying; looks toward AA or Str; smiles, shows object; or speaks to AA or Str; proximity to AA or Str (this was scored only when the AA or the Str was in the chair). Activity was assessed by the number of lines Ss crossed (the room was marked off into 18-inch squares). During the reunion episodes (5 and 8), the presence or absence of the following behaviors was recorded: looks at AA; smiles, shows, or gives object to AA; talks to AA; averts looking at AA; moves toward AA; bids for comfort and physical contact; comfort derived from physical contact. Results: (1) Among those Ss accompanied by their mothers, boys exhibited less playing and more crying when left alone (Episode 6) than girls did. (2) Among those Ss accompanied by their fathers, boys exhibited more proximity to the Str, less playing, and more crying upon the stranger's return in Episode 7 than girls did. (3) Among those Ss accompanied by a female acquaintance (FA), boys exhibited more crying (Episode 2 only), more proximity to FA (Episodes 2 and 3), and less looking at FA (Episode 2 only) than girls did. (4) No other sex differences were found.
    EXPERIMENT II: Subjects: $N = 79$; 2½ yrs. Measures: Identical to Experiment I. Results: (1) Among those Ss accompanied by their mother, boys exhibited more crying than girls during Episode 7, and more girls than boys looked at their mothers during Episodes 2 and 3. (2) Among those Ss accompanied by their father, boys exhibited more crying than girls when left alone (Episode 6). (3) No differences were found between boys and girls accompanied by a female acquaintance.

Feldstein, J. H., and Witryol, S. L. The incentive value of uncertainty reduction for children. *Child Development*, 1971, *42*, 793–804 (and personal communication).
    Subjects: $N = 60$; 9 yrs. Measures: On each of 40 trials, Ss chose between a piece of bubble gum and a package that concealed either a charm, a piece of bubble gum, a bean, or a paper clip (each was presented on 25% of the trials). In one condition, Ss were informed of the contents of the package after every trial. Ss in other conditions experienced delays of either 10, 20, or 40 trials before becoming aware of the identity of the objects in the packages they had chosen. Results: No sex differences were found in the number of times the package was chosen.

Feldstone, C. S. Developmental studies of negatively correlated reinforcement in children. *Developmental Psychology*, 1969, *1*, 528–42.
    Subjects: $N = 106$; 5–6, 8–10, 11–13 yrs (Crank Experiment II). $N = 26$; 18–27 yrs (Crank Experiment III). $N = 74$; 4–6 yrs (Grip Experiment I). $N = 32$; 11–13 yrs (Grip Experiment III). Measures: In the first series of 3 experiments, Ss were asked to turn a crank. Experimental Ss were reinforced when they turned the crank slowly. Yoked control groups were reinforced the same number of times and on the same trials, but their reinforcements were not related to how rapidly they turned the crank. In a second series of 3 experiments, strength of grip was tested. Experimental Ss were reinforced for squeezing weakly, and again yoked control groups were used. In both series, 2 of the 3 experiments were analyzed for sex of S. Results: (1) Among experimental and control Ss in Crank Experiment II, boys turned the crank faster than girls did. There were no sex differences in speed of acquiring the inhibitory response. No sex differences were found in Crank Experiment III. (2) No sex differences were found in either of the Grip experiments.

Felzen, E., and Anisfeld, M. Semantic and phonetic relations in the false recognition of words by third- and sixth-grade children. *Developmental Psychology*, 1970, *3*, 163–68.
    Subjects: $N = 80$; 8, 11 yrs. Measures: On a second taped, verbal presentation of a word list, Ss indicated by saying "old" or "new" whether the word had been read on the first presentation. The second word list contained "old" words, semantically and phonetically related words, and control words. Results: (1) There were no sex differences in number of false recognition

errors. (2) Boys had longer latencies of responding "new" to new words than girls did ($p < .05$).

Fenz, W. D., and Epstein, S. Manifest anxiety: unifactorial or multifactorial composition? *Perceptual & Motor Skills*, 1965, *20*, 773–80.
Subjects: $N = 98$; 18–21 yrs (college). Measures: Ss were given a 160-item questionnaire that included the following scales: striated muscle tension, autonomic arousal, feelings of anxiety, hostility, negative attitude toward hostile expression, conflict, inhibition, and defensiveness. Results: Women scored higher than men on the autonomic arousal and negative attitude toward hostile expression scales. Men scored higher than women on the hostility scale.

Ferguson, L. R., and Maccoby, E. E. Interpersonal correlates of differential abilities. *Child Development*, 1966, *37*, 549–71.
Subjects: $N = 126$; 10 yrs. Measures: Ss were selected from a larger sample of 1,200 because of performance discrepancies between 2 out of 3 abilities—verbal, number, and space. The third area of ability was at an intermediate level. Ss were matched for total intelligence. (1) The Peer Nominations Inventory was revised to include items relating to dependency, aggression, withdrawal, mastery, and sex-typing. Each S rated same-sex peers. (2) 2 self-report scales of sex-typing were administered. The Sex-Role Differentiation Scale was used to determine whether Ss made distinctions between girls' and boys' activities. The Sex-Role Acceptance Scale consisted of a series of questions in which Ss indicated their preference for one sex role or the other (Ss could also indicate that both roles were equally attractive). Ss were scored for the number of own-sex preferences they checked. (3) 2 self-report scales of dependency measured the tendency to seek help from adults (a) in difficult problem-solving situations and (b) when sick, alone, or afraid. (4) 2 self-report scales of dependency anxiety assessed derogation of dependency and anticipation of punishment for dependency. (5) 3 self-report scales measured aggression-agression anxiety, antisocial aggression, and projected aggression. (6) A task measuring susceptibility to distraction was also administered. Results: Girls scored higher than boys on aggression anxiety and dependency when sick, alone, or afraid. Boys scored higher than girls on antisocial aggression, derogation of dependency, and sex-role acceptance. There were no other sex differences on self-report or peer-nomination measures.

Ferraro, D. P., Francis, E. W., and Perkins, J. J. Titrating delayed matching to sample in children. *Developmental Psychology*, 1971, *5*, 488–93.
Subjects: $N = 40$; 4, 5, 6, 8, 10 yrs. Measures: During pretraining, Ss were asked to press the 1 of 2 lighted comparison panels that matched the standard stimulus panel color. A criterion of 4 consecutive correct responses was set (2 at 0-second delay between termination of standard stimulus and onset of comparison stimuli, and 2 at 1-second delay); 60 experimental matchings followed, with 2-second delay, increasing 2 more seconds at each correct response and decreasing 2 seconds at each incorrect one. Results: No sex differences.

Feshbach, N. D. Sex differences in children's modes of aggressive responses toward outsiders. *Merrill-Palmer Quarterly*, 1969, *15*, 249–58.
Subjects: $N = 126$; 6 yrs (middle SES). Measures: In the first session, same-sex pairs were encouraged to play as a cohesive unit. In the second play session, half of these groups received a same-sex newcomer. Mode and frequency of aggressive behaviors were recorded by a hidden observer. Results: First session: (1) No sex differences were found in direct aggressive, indirect aggressive, or approach behaviors. (2) Boys struck the Bobo doll more frequently than girls did. Second session: (1) During the first 4 minutes of the session, girls were more indirectly aggressive to the newcomer than boys were; during the last 12 minutes, no sex differences were found. (2) No sex differences were observed in the frequency of direct aggressive or approach behaviors or in the number of times a child gave an order to another child. (3) No differences were found between boy and girl newcomers in display of direct or indirect aggression.

Feshbach, N. D. Cross-cultural studies of teaching styles in four-year-olds and their mothers: some educational implications of socialization. Draft of a paper presented at the Minnesota Symposium on Child Psychology, 1972.
Subjects: $N = 104$; 4 yrs and mothers (white and black, low and middle SES). Measures: Ss initially taught a 3-year-old how to assemble a puzzle; 1 hour later, each S's mother was asked to teach her child a similar but slightly more complex puzzle. Measures were taken of the number of times positive and negative reinforcements were administered by Ss and their mothers. Results: (1) Boys delivered more negative reinforcements to the younger child than girls did. No sex differences were found in number of positive reinforcements administered.

(2) Mothers of boys negatively reinforced their sons more often than their daughters (significant for middle SES sample only). No difference was found between mothers of boys and girls in number of positive reinforcements administered.

Feshbach, N. D., and Devor, G. Teaching styles in four-year-olds. *Child Development,* 1969, *40,* 183–90.
Subjects: $N = 204$; 3–4 yrs (black, white; low, middle SES). Measures: 4-year-old Ss initially learned how to assemble a puzzle. Afterward, they were asked to teach the task to a 3-year-old of the same or opposite sex. The number of positive and negative reinforcements administered to the 3-year-old Ss was recorded. Results: No sex of "teacher" or sex of "pupil" differences were found.

Feshbach, N. D., and Feshbach, S. The relation between empathy and aggression in two age groups. *Developmental Psychology,* 1969, *1,* 102–7.
Subjects: $N = 88$; 4–5, 6–7 yrs. Measures: Measures of empathy were obtained from Ss' responses to a series of slide sequences depicting happiness, sadness, fear, and anger. Results: No sex differences were found in overall scores. Among 4- and 5-year-olds, girls showed more empathy in response to the "sadness" stimulus than boys did ($p < .05$); however, no sex difference was found on the comprehension measure for sadness.

Feshbach, N. D., and Roe, K. Empathy in six- and seven-year-olds. *Child Development,* 1968, *39,* 133–45.
Subjects: $N = 46$; 6 yrs. Measures: Ss were presented with a sequence of slides and stories showing 4 different affective situations: happiness, sadness, fear, and anger; 2 alternate sets of the same situations were prepared, varying by sex of stimulus figure. Ss reported their feelings about the stimulus series. As an index of social comprehension, 27 Ss viewed the story-slide sequence again, and were asked to report their feelings about the central character. Results: (1) Empathy scores of girls observing girls were greater than corresponding scores of boys observing boys. (2) There were no sex differences in social comprehension scores, except in fear situations, where boys were more accurate than girls.

Feshbach, N. D., and Sones, G. Sex differences in adolescent reactions toward newcomers. *Developmental Psychology,* 1971, *4,* 381–86.
Subjects: $N = 87$; 12–13 yrs. Measures: A same-sex close-friend pair (as judged by a teacher) solved 3 social problems together. A same-sex newcomer (1 year younger) joined the pair, and 2 more social problems were solved by the triad. Latency of speaking to the newcomer, latency of newcomer speaking, frequencies of verbal rejection, and incorporation of newcomer's ideas were recorded. All Ss independently rated other 2 members on intelligence, appearance, social desirability, acceptance, and leadership. Results: (1) There were no sex differences in original dyads' ratings of each other. (2) Ratings of girls reflected a less favorable reaction to the newcomer than the ratings of boys did. (3) Girls took longer to speak to the newcomer than boys did. (4) Girl newcomers waited longer before speaking than boy newcomers did. (5) Initial sex differences in response to newcomer persisted after the instructions to the second problem were given. Girls took longer than boys to address the newcomer. Newcomer girls took longer than boys to address original-pair members. (6) There were no sex differences in frequency of direct verbal rejections of newcomer's ideas. (7) Girls demonstrated a lower frequency of incorporating newcomer's ideas than boys did.

Fiebert, M. Cognitive styles in the deaf. *Perceptual & Motor Skills,* 1967, *24,* 319–29.
Subjects: $N = 90$; 12, 15, 18 yrs (deaf). Measures: Ss were given the Rod and Frame Test, the Children's Embedded Figures Test, and the Poppelreuter Test. Ss' Paragraph Meaning scores on the Standard Achievement Test were used as a measure of reading ability. Results: Boys achieved higher scores than girls on each of the 3 embedded figures tests (RFT, $p < .05$; CEFT, $p < .01$; P-T, $p < .01$). No sex differences were found in Paragraph Meaning scores.

Figurelli, J. C., and Keller, H. R. The effects of training and socio-economic class upon the acquisition of conservation concepts. *Child Development,* 1972, *43,* 293–98.
Subjects: $N = 48$; 6 yrs (black). Measures: Ss completed the Concept Assessment Kit: Conservation once as a pretest and once after training or no training. Results: No sex differences.

Finley, G. E., and Frenkel, O. J. Children's tachistoscopic recognition thresholds for and recall of words which differ in connotative meaning. *Child Development,* 1972, *43,* 1098–1103.
Subjects: $N = 48$; 9, 12 yrs (white low-middle SES). Measures: Ss were presented with 14

stimulus words, of good or bad connotative meanings. Ss learned to recognize the words (if they did not already recognize them), and were later asked to rate and recall them. **Results:** (1) Girls rated the good words less positively and the bad words more negatively than boys did (*p* < .05). (2) Girls recalled more words than boys did (*p* < .01).

Finley, G. E., and Layne, O., Jr. Play behavior in young children. Unpublished manuscript, 1969.

Subjects: *N* = 96; 1, 2, 3 yrs (American, Mayan Indian). **Measures:** Each S was accompanied by his mother to the testing room. After setting the child down, the mother was requested not to initiate any interactions. Otherwise, she was told she could respond normally to the child's overtures. S was then observed in free play for 20 minutes with toys from both cultures present. The following measures were recorded: number of involvements with toys of less than 30 seconds duration; number of involvements with toys of more than 30 seconds duration; total number of seconds spent in prolonged involvements with toys; number of toys played with; number of squares traversed (the floor was marked off into 12 squares); number of episodes of visual exploration of toys less than 30 seconds in duration; number of episodes of visual exploration of toys more than 30 seconds in duration; total number of seconds spent in prolonged acts of visual exploration; number of looks at mother; total number of seconds spent in the 3 squares nearest mother; number of times in physical contact with mother for less than 30 seconds; number of times in physical contact with mother for more than 30 seconds; total number of seconds spent in prolonged episodes of physical contact with mother. **Results:** No main sex differences were found. Among American Ss, 3-year-old girls crossed more squares than 2-year-old girls, whereas for boys the reverse was true.

Finley, G. E., Kagan, J., and Layne, O., Jr. Development of young children's attention to normal and distorted stimuli: a cross-cultural study. *Developmental Psychology*, 1972, 6, 288–92.

Subjects: *N* = 96; 1, 2, 3 yrs (Mayan Indians, white Americans). **Measures:** Ss viewed 4 drawings of a man (normal, trunk, scrambled, free-art form) and 5 drawings of a face (normal, cyclops, blank, scrambled, free-art form). The length of Ss' first fixation to each stimulus was recorded. **Results:** No sex differences.

Fischbein, E., Pampu, I., and Manzat, I. Comparison of ratios and the chance concept in children. *Child Development*, 1970, 41, 377–89.

Subjects: *N* = 60; 5–6, 9–10, 12–13 yrs (Rumania). **Measures:** Ss were given 18 problems in which they had to choose the 1 of 2 boxes that contained a black (or white) marble. Estimates of chance could be made as Ss viewed proportion of black/white marbles before decision making. Correct answers were reinforced verbally. **Results:** No sex differences.

Fishbein, H. D., Lewis, S., and Keiffer, K. Children's understanding of spatial relations: coordination of perspectives. *Developmental Psychology*, 1972, 7, 21–33.

EXPERIMENT I: **Subjects:** *N* = 120; 3–9 yrs. **Measures:** Ss saw either 1 or 3 toys at a time, and either 4 or 8 photographs of the toy display. During familiarization, each S was to point to the photo that corresponded to what he could see from his perspective. E then turned the toy to present each remaining view that S had on photos in front of him. In the pointing task, each S was to point to the photo that corresponded to the view E had as E walked around the display. E removed photos and asked S to turn a revolving toy display to present the specified view to E. Candy was given for correct responses; incorrect responses were corrected. **Results:** No sex differences.

EXPERIMENT II: **Subjects:** *N* = 128; 5, 7 yrs. **Measures:** 2 tasks were given to Ss, the pointing task described in Experiment I plus a turning task in which E sat in turn on each of the 4 sides of the table. Pointing to 1 of the photographs, she asked Ss to turn the tray so that she could view the toys from the perspective depicted in the photograph. **Results:** (1) When scores from both tasks were combined, no mean sex differences were found. Among 7-year-olds, girls' overall scores were better than those of boys, whereas the reverse was true among 5-year-olds (*p* < .05). (2) Boys performed better than girls on the pointing task; girls performed better than boys on the turning task (*p* < .05).

Fitzgerald, H. E. Autonomic pupillar reflex activity during early infancy and its relation to social and nonsocial stimuli. *J. Experimental Psychology*, 1968, 6, 470–82.

Subjects: *N* = 30; 1–2 mos. **Measures:** S viewed photos of his mother's face, an unfamiliar female's face, checkerboard patterns, and a triangle. Diameter of pupil and pupillar activity were measured. **Results:** No sex differences.

Fitzsimmons, S. J., Cheever, J., Leonard, E., and Macunovich, D. School failures: now and tomorrow. *Developmental Psychology*, 1969, *1*, 134–46.
> **Subjects:** $N = 270$; 15–17 yrs (students with performance difficulties or dropouts). **Measures:** Ss' academic records from early elementary school through high school were studied. **Results:** More boys than girls dropped out. Boys left for alleged lack of interest in school and desire to work. Girls left for sudden, personal reasons such as marriage, pregnancy, or illness.

Flanagan, J. C., Dailey, J. T., Shaycoft, M. F., Gorham, W. A., Orr, D. B., Goldberg, I., and Neyman, C. A., Jr. Counselor's technical manual for interpreting test scores (Project Talent), Palo Alto, California, 1961.
> **Subjects:** $N = 4,545$; 14, 17 yrs. **Measures:** Project Talent Test Battery. **Results:** Boys scored higher than girls on the vocabulary, mathematics, and 2- and 3-dimensional visual spatialization tests. Girls scored higher than boys on the disguised words, English language, reading comprehension, and verbal memory tests. Ss' scores on the other tests were not analyzed for sex differences.

Flavell, J. H., Beach, D. R., and Chinsky, J. M. Spontaneous verbal rehearsal in a memory task as a function of age. *Child Development*, 1966, *37*, 283–99.
> **Subjects:** $N = 60$; 5, 7, 10 yrs. **Measures:** Each S was given 3 nonverbal, serial recall tasks: (1) Immediate recall. E pointed to series of pictures on a portable board and asked S to point to the duplicate set of pictures in the same order on another board. Sequences of 2, 3, 4, and 5 pictures were used according to age level. (2) Delayed recall. S waited 15 seconds after E pointed before beginning. (3) Point and name. Same as delayed recall procedure, except S was asked to name each picture object as E pointed to it, and name it again during the recall task. **Results:** No sex differences.

Fleener, D. E., and Cairns, R. B. Attachment behaviors in human infants: discriminative vocalization on maternal separation. *Developmental Psychology*, 1970, *2*, 215–23.
> **Subjects:** $N = 64$; 3–19 mos. **Measures:** Mother and unfamiliar female E alternated leaving the room for 60-second periods (thus leaving the infant alone with the other person). Frequency of crying was recorded. **Results:** No sex differences were found in total amount of crying or in the extent to which Ss cried during the absence of their mothers relative to the extent to which they cried during the absence of E.

Fleming, E. S., and Anttonen, R. G. Teacher expectancy as related to the academic and personal growth of primary-age children. *Monographs of the Society for Research in Child Development*, 1971, 36.
> **Subjects:** $N = 1,087$; 7 yrs (low, middle SES). **Measures:** Teachers who were classified as having high, middle, and low opinions toward IQ tests were given 1 of 4 kinds of test information for each S: Kuhlmann-Anderson IQ scores, IQs inflated by 16 points, Primary Mental Abilities percentiles without IQ equivalents, or no intelligence test information. In October, Ss completed 3 subtests of the Stanford Achievement Test (SAT) Primary I Battery, Form W: Word Meaning, Paragraph Meaning, and Arithmetic. In February and May, Ss completed 4 subtests of the Primary II Battery, Forms W and X: Word Meaning, Paragraph Meaning, Arithmetic Computation, and Arithmetic Concepts. A semantic differential self-concept measure was administered at each testing. Grades were collected in February and June. **Results:** (1) When Ss' achievement scores in October were held constant, no sex differences were found in February or June on any of the 4 SAT subtests. (2) On the self-concept measure in February and May (with October scores held constant), boys scored higher on the Potency factor than girls did. In May (with February scores held constant), girls scored higher on the Evaluative factor than boys did. The Evaluative factor did not emerge in October. (3) In February and June, girls achieved higher grades than boys in reading, spelling, and handwriting. In June, girls achieved higher arithmetic grades than boys did; no sex difference was found in February. Overall, girls earned higher grades than boys did during each marking period.

Flick, G. L. Sinistrality revisited: a perceptual-motor approach. *Child Development*, 1966, 37, 613–22.
> **Subjects:** $N = 453$; 4 yrs (black). **Measures:** Perceptual-motor functioning was measured by performance on Copy Forms (Stanford-Binet and Merrill-Palmer items) and Copy Mazes (Porteus Mazes). Hand dominance was determined by noting the preferred hand used on Copy Forms task. Eye dominance was revealed by asking S to look through a small hole in a shoe box. Stanford-Binet IQ scores were also obtained. **Results:** Girls were superior to boys on Copy Forms. No other sex differences were found.

Fling, S., and Manosevitz, M. Sex typing in nursery school children's play interests. *Developmental Psychology*, 1972, 7, 146–52.

Subjects: $N = 32$; 3–4 yrs and parents. Measures: E administered the IT Scale for Children with blank IT cards. S was asked to choose items It and S would prefer (to assess sex-role orientation and sex-role preference, respectively). S was asked whether he had pretended blank It was a boy or a girl, and was then shown Brown's It and asked to label It a boy or a girl (to assess sex labeling). E later visited S's home and asked S to show him his favorite toys, which E scored as masculine, feminine, or neuter (to assess sex-role adoption). E interviewed S's parents about the child's play interests and possible parental influences. An It test was administered in which parents indicated the It items they preferred for their child, with elaboration on omissions. Results: (1) Both boys and girls labeled standard It as boy ($p < .001$). (2) Ss labeled imaginary It as same sex ($p < .001$). (3) There were no sex differences on any of the 3 measures of sex typing (orientation, preference, adoption). Boys' scores were less variable than girls' on preference and adoption ($p < .05$, $p < .05$). (4) Boys' mothers' scores were greater than girls' mothers' scores on discouragement of sex-inappropriate interests ($p < .005$), It scores (high-sex-appropriate choices, $p < .001$), and Total (It and encouragement of sex-appropriate interests and discouragement of sex-inappropriate interests, $p < .005$). Boys' fathers' scores were greater than girls' fathers' scores on discouragement ($p < .05$), It ($p < .005$), and Total ($p < .005$). Girls' mothers' scores were greater than boys' mothers' scores on encouragement of sex-appropriate interests ($p < .01$). (5) Boys' fathers' scores were greater than boys' mothers' scores on encouragement of sex-appropriate interests ($p < .01$). Girls' mothers' scores were greater than girls' fathers' scores on the same measure ($p < .01$).

Fouts, G. T. Charity in children: the influence of "charity" stimuli and an audience. *J. Experimental Child Psychology*, 1972, 13, 303–9.

Subjects: $N = 40$; 10, 11 yrs. Measures: Ss performed a lever-pulling task, either alone or with E watching. Correct responses resulted in pennies dropping into a neutral or a "charity" box. Number of pulling responses were recorded under each condition. Results: No sex differences.

Frager, R. Conformity and anticonformity in Japan. *J. Personality & Social Psychology*, 1970, 15, 203–10.

Subjects: $N = 139$; 18–21 yrs (Japanese college). Measures: Ss judged which of 3 lines was equal in length to a fourth after exposure to the incorrect judgments of 3 confederates. E recorded the number of times Ss conformed to the inaccurate group response, and the number of times on noncritical trials Ss made the incorrect choice after confederates had made the correct choice (a measure of anticonformity). Ss also completed a Japanese values scale, measuring alienation (A) and traditionalism (T). Results: No sex differences were found in conformity or anticonformity scores. Men had higher A scores than women ($p < .02$). No sex differences were found in T scores.

France, K. Effects of "White" and of "Black" examiner voices on IQ scores of children. *Developmental Psychology*, 1973, 8, 144 (brief report).

Subjects: $N = 252$; 6–9 yrs. Measures: The Peabody Picture Vocabulary Test was administered by taped voices of black and white students reading instructions and questions. Results: Boys achieved higher scores than girls ($p < .001$).

Fraunfelker, B. S. Phonetic campatibility in paired-associate learning of first- and third-grade children. *Developmental Psychology*, 1971, 5, 211–15.

Subjects: $N = 80$; 6, 8 yrs. Measures: Ss learned 2 paired associate tasks: shape-color pairs as a warm-up task, and color-trigram (3-letter) pairs with trigrams of high and low phonetic compatibility. Response learning (number of trigrams correctly articulated and associated with correct stimulus) and retention (number of correctly articulated trigrams associated with correct stimulus at end of 12 trials) were recorded. Results: No sex differences.

Frederiksen, N., and Evans, F. R. Effects of models of creative performance on ability to formulate hypotheses. *J. Educational Psychology*, 1974, 66, 83–89.

Subjects: $N = 395$; 18 yrs (paid college volunteers). Measures: S was given findings from a research study and asked to write hypotheses that might help account for the findings. Answers were analyzed for total number of hypotheses, number of acceptable hypotheses, quality of hypotheses, value of hypotheses (independent number), and number of words per response (fluency). Other scores obtained were verbal comprehension, verbal fluency, test anxiety, and Guilford's obvious vs. remote consequences measure. Results: Women were superior to men on number of hypotheses, number of words, and number of obvious consequences. Men were superior to women on number of remote consequences.

Friedman, S. Habituation and recovery of visual response in the alert human newborn. *J. Experimental Child Psychology*, 1972, *13*, 339–49.
  Subjects: $N = 40$; 1–3 days. Measures: Infants viewed a checkerboard target ($2'' \times 2''$ or $12'' \times 12''$) until habituation was demonstrated (decrement in visual fixation time). They were then exposed to either the same or a novel target to assess effect of familiarity and novelty on recovery of habituation. Results: No sex differences.

Friedman, S., and Carpenter, G. C. Visual response decrement as a function of age of human newborn. *Child Development*, 1971, *42*, 1967–73.
  Subjects: $N = 96$; 1–4 days. Measures: Fixation time to a black-and-white checkerboard target was recorded. Results: No sex differences.

Friedman, S., Nagy, A. A., and Carpenter, G. C. Newborn attention: differential response decrement to visual stimuli. *J. Experimental Child Psychology*, 1970, *10*, 44–51.
  Subjects: $N = 40$; 2–3 days. Measures: Ss were exposed to 1 of 2 visual stimuli, a $2'' \times 2''$ or $12'' \times 12''$ black-and-white checkerboard target. Visual fixation time was recorded. Results: There were no main sex differences. Boys showed fixation decrement to the less redundant ($2'' \times 2''$) target; girls showed fixation decrement to the more redundant ($12'' \times 12''$) target ($p < .005$).

Friedman, S., Bruno, L. A., and Vietze, P. Differential dishabituation as a function of magnitude of stimulus discrepancy and sex of the newborn infant. Paper presented at the meeting of the Society for Research in Child Development, Philadelphia, 1973.
  Subjects: $N = 26$; 1–3 days. Measures: Ss were presented with 60-second exposures of 1 of 2 stimuli (either a 4-square or 144-square black-and-white checkerboard pattern). Presentation continued until evidence of decrement in looking time occurred. When Ss reached the decrement criterion, they were presented with a final 60-second exposure of either the same target stimulus to which they had shown habituation (no-discrepancy or control group) or a different target of either moderate discrepancy (a 16-square checkerboard pattern) or large discrepancy (the 144-square target for Ss who viewed the 4-square target during the habituation trials; the 4-square target for Ss who previously had viewed the 144-square target). Response measures were looking time and number of looks. Results: (1) Looking time: (a) No sex differences were found in degree of response decrement to the repeated stimulus. (b) No main sex differences were found when the mean looking time for the last 3 habituation trials was compared with looking time on the final 60-second test trial. For the moderate discrepancy group, girls showed a recovery effect, boys did not ($p < .025$). (2) Number of looks: No sex differences were reported. With introduction of the moderately discrepant stimulus, girls showed a reduction in number of looks, boys did not (significance not tested).

Friedrichs, A. G., Hertz, T. W., Moynahan, E. D., Simpson, W. E., Arnold, M. R., Christy, M. D., Cooper, C. R., and Stevenson, H. W. Interrelations among learning and performance at the preschool level. *Developmental Psychology*, 1971, *4*, 164–72.
  Subjects: $N = 50$; 3–5 yrs. Measures: Ss were presented with 16 learning and performance tasks: paired associates, serial memory, oddity learning, concept formation, observational learning, incidental learning, problem solving, object sorting, social imitation, task persistence, reactivity, motor inhibition, following instructions, variability, attention, and level of aspiration. Results: (1) There were no sex differences on the learning tasks. (2) On the performance tasks there was a sex difference in level of aspiration. Boys chose taller towers to build than girls did ($p < .01$).

Fromkin, H. L. Effects of experimentally aroused feelings of indistinctiveness upon valuation of scarce and novel feelings. *J. Personality & Social Psychology*, 1970, *16*, 521–29.
  Subjects: $N = 59$; 18–21 yrs (college). Measures: Ss received bogus test results that described them as either extreme, high, or low in uniqueness. Ss then received information about 4 "psychedelic" chambers, which were described as either available or unavailable to others, and as producing either novel or familiar feelings. The response measures were Ss' evaluation of each of the 4 different environments. Results: (1) No main sex differences were found. (2) On a postexperimental scale designed to measure the effectiveness of the novelty manipulation, men had higher expectations about the novelty of the experience than women.

Fry, C. L. A developmental examination of performance in a tacit coordination game situation. *J. Personality & Social Psychology*, 1967, 5, 277–81.
Subjects: $N = 84$; 9, 13, 18–21 yrs (college). Measures: Ss played tacit coordination games with like-aged, same-sex partners. The tacit coordination game required S to anticipate the object choice of his partner. Points were awarded when both Ss made the same object choice. Results: No sex differences.

Fryrear, J. L., and Thelen, M. H. Effect of sex of model and sex of observer on the imitation of affectionate behavior. *Developmental Psychology*, 1969, 1, 298 (brief report).
Subjects: $N = 60$; 3–4 yrs (nursery school). Measures: Ss observed a filmed male or female adult model display a sequence of 4 affectionate responses toward a small stuffed clown. Afterward, Ss were observed in free play with the clown and other toys. Imitative responses were recorded. Results: Girls imitated the female model more than boys did. No sex differences were found in the number of imitative behaviors Ss displayed after observing the male model.

Furth, H. G., Youniss, J., and Ross, B. M. Children's utilization of logical symbols: an interpretation of conceptual behavior based on Piagetian theory. *Developmental Psychology*, 1970, 3, 36–57.
Subjects: $N = 300$; 6–12 yrs. Measures: On each trial, E put an incomplete sequence on the blackboard that was to be completed by S filling in or modifying one part of the sequence. Each sequence consisted of (1) a symbol pattern expressing 2 attribute classes (letter of the alphabet standing for a thing or shape, and a color) and a logical connective (a dot meaning "and," "v" meaning "either/or" or "both"), (2) the instance pattern (a drawing of 2 attributes), and (3) the judgment by S of whether the instance pattern was a logically correct example of the symbol pattern. Results: Among 7-year-old Ss, girls made more correct judgments of whether or not symbol patterns and drawings matched than boys. There were no sex differences at other ages.

Gaertner, S. L. Helping behavior and racial discrimination among liberals and conservatives. *J. Personality & Social Psychology*, 1973, 25, 335–41.
Subjects: $N = 468$; adults. Measures: Ss received a wrong number phone call from a person in a pay telephone booth (either a black or white, male or female) whose car had broken down. Ss were asked to contact a garage for the caller (who supposedly had no more change). Results: (1) Men contacted the garage more frequently than women did ($p < .05$). (2) No difference was found between male and female victims in the frequency of eliciting help from Ss. More male than female victims experienced premature hanging up ($p < .01$).

Gaertner, S. L., and Bickerman, L. Effects of race on the elicitation of helping behavior: the wrong number technique. *J. Personality & Social Psychology*, 1971, 20, 218–22.
Subjects: $N = 1,109$; adults (white, black). Measures: Ss received a wrong number phone call from a man (either black or white) in a pay telephone booth whose car had broken down. Ss were asked to contact a garage for the caller (who supposedly had no more change). Results: (1) Men contacted the garage more frequently than women did ($p < .05$). (2) More women than men hung up prematurely ($p < .001$).

Gahagan, G. A., and Gahagan, D. M. Paired-associate learning as partial validation of a language development program. *Child Development*, 1968, 39, 1119–31.
Subjects: $N = 54$; 6–7 yrs. Measures: Ss were shown 8 cards; on each were pictures of 2 objects. After naming the items, Ss were asked to construct a sentence containing both words by linking them with a verb. Ss also completed the English Picture Vocabulary Test (EPVT). At the time of testing, 18 Ss had undergone language training for a period of 4 terms; the other 36 Ss had not. Results: No sex differences were found in EPVT scores or in number of lexically different verbs produced.

Gaines, R. The discriminability of form among young children. *J. Experimental Child Psychology*, 1969, 8, 418–31.
Subjects: $N = 30$; 4–7 yrs. Measures: Ss performed form-oddity problems, i.e. pointing to the stimulus drawing that was different from the other 4. Stimuli varied in number of sides, form perimeter, and structure (symmetrical to asymmetrical). Results: No sex differences.

Gaines, R. Variables in color perception of young children. *J. Experimental Child Psychology*, 1972, 14, 196–218.
Subjects: $N = 47$; 5–6 yrs. Measures: The effects of variations in value, chroma, and hue were studied in relation to sex, IQ, and dimensional attention; 2 measures of discrimination ability

were made on each of 54 base colors of the Munsell color matrices. **Results:** (1) There were no main sex differences. (2) Boys were more accurate in the mid-chroma range, girls were more accurate on high and low chroma stimuli ($p < .02$).

Gall, M., and Mendelsohn, G. A. Effects of facilitating techniques and subject-experimenter interaction on creative problem solving. *J. Personality & Social Psychology*, 1967, 5, 211–16.
   Subjects: $N = 120$; 18–21 yrs (college). **Measures:** Ss were given the Remote Associates Test which demands the production of remote associates in the process of the solution. After attempting each of the items, Ss were allowed to continue working on the first 5 problems they had failed to solve (continued work condition), or asked to associate to the words comprising the first 5 problems they had missed (association training condition), or diverted for a time from the problems by means of a nonverbal task (incubation condition). All Ss were then given 10 minutes to work on the missed problems. **Results:** (1) No sex differences were found in mean number of solutions. (2) The association-training condition produced more solutions for women than for men ($p < .01$).

Gallo, P. S., and Sheposh, J. Effects of incentive magnitude on cooperation in the prisoner's dilemma game: a reply to Gumpert, Deutsch, and Epstein. *J. Personality & Social Psychology*, 1971, 19, 42–46.
   Subjects: $N = 200$; 18–21 yrs (college). **Measures:** Same-sex pairs of Ss played the Prisoner's Dilemma game for real or imaginary dollars. **Results:** No sex differences were found in percentage of cooperative responses.

Gallo, P. S., Funk, S. G., and Levine, J. R. Reward size, method of presentation, and number of alternatives in a prisoner's dilemma game. *J. Personality & Social Psychology*, 1969, 13, 239–44.
   Subjects: $N = 160$; 18–21 yrs (college). **Measures:** Like-sex pairs of Ss played either the standard Prisoner's Dilemma game or a 2-, 6-, or 11-choice nonmatrix equivalent of the game. Afterward, Ss completed a 19-item semantic differential on which they evaluated their partners. **Results:** No sex differences.

Gardiner, H. W. Dominance-deference patterning in Thai students. *J. Social Psychology*, 1968, 76, 281–82.
   Subjects: $N = 199$; 18–21 yrs (college Thai). **Measures:** A dominance-deference scale, consisting of 10 dominance and 10 deference items, was administered to all Ss. Ss were instructed to select the 10 items that best described themselves. S's score was the number of dominance items chosen. **Results:** No sex differences.

Gardner, H. Children's sensitivity to painting styles. *Child Development*, 1970, 41, 813–21.
   Subjects: $N = 80$; 6, 8, 11, 14 yrs. **Measures:** Ss viewed 2 paintings by 1 artist, and were then asked to select which 1 out of 4 others was painted by the same artist. **Results:** No sex differences.

Gardner, H. Children's sensitivity to musical styles. *Merrill-Palmer Quarterly*, 1973, 19, 67–77.
   Subjects: $N = 100$; 6, 8, 11, 14, 18–19 yrs. **Measures:** Ss listened to 16 pairs of musical passages. Each pair consisted of 2 halves, 15 seconds in duration, separated by a 1-second bell; 8 of the pairs consisted of halves from the same piece, and the remaining 8 consisted of halves from different compositions by different composers. Ss' task was to indicate whether or not the 2 halves were from the same piece. **Results:** No sex differences.

Gates, A. I. Sex differences in reading ability. *Elementary School Journal*, 1961, 61, 431–34.
   Subjects: $N = 13,114$; 7–13 yrs. **Measures:** Gates Reading Survey tests: Speed of Reading, Reading Vocabulary, and Level of Comprehension. **Results:** (1) At all ages, girls had higher scores on each of the 3 tests than boys did. (2) Among 9-, 10-, and 12-year-old Ss, boys' scores on the Speed of Reading test varied more than those of girls. Among 7- and 11-year-old Ss, girls' scores varied more than those of boys. (3) At all ages (except 7), boys' scores on the vocabulary and comprehension tests varied more than those of girls.

Geer, J. H. A test of classical conditioning model of emotion: the use of nonpainful aversive stimuli as unconditioned stimuli in a conditioning procedure. *J. Personality & Social Psychology*, 1968, *10*, 148–56.

Subjects: *N* = 48; 18–21 yrs (college). Measures: Ss were assigned to 1 of 3 experimental groups. In the forward-conditioning group, exposure to the CS (a tone of 60 decibels) preceded exposure to the UCS (color photographs of dead bodies). In the backward-conditioning group, the UCS preceded the CS. Ss in the third group experienced an essentially random relationship between CS and the UCS. Graduated skin responses to the experimental stimuli were recorded and classified into 3 categories: CS responses, pre-UCS responses, and post-UCS responses. CS responses were defined as decreases in skin resistance that began 1 and 5 seconds after tone onset. Pre-UCS responses were defined and measured as the CS responses were, except that the response's inflection began between 5 and 10 seconds after the CS's onset. Post-UCS responses were measured and defined as the preceding responses were, except that response inflection began between 1 and 6 seconds after UCS onset. Results: (1) For the last minute of the rest period prior to the experimental manipulation, there were no sex differences in number of spontaneous fluctuations of skin resistance. (2) Men had larger CS responses than women did during conditioning ($p < .01$) and extinction ($p < .05$). (3) During conditioning, no sex differences were found in pre-UCS responses. During extinction, men had larger pre-UCS responses than women did ($p < .05$). Men showed a decrease in pre-UCS responding over extinction trial blocks, while women showed an increase ($p < .05$). (4) Men had larger post-UCS responses than women did during conditioning ($p < .01$) and extinction ($p < .01$). During extinction, men showed more rapid habituation than women did ($p < .01$).

Gelfand, D. M., Hartmann, D. P., Walder, P., and Page, B. Who reports shoplifters? A field-experimental study. *J. Personality & Social Psychology*, 1973, *25*, 276–85.

Subjects: *N* = 89; 16–75 yrs. Measures: Ss observed a female confederate steal store merchandise. Results: More men than women reported the incident to a store employee ($p < .05$).

Gellert, E. The effect of changes in group composition on the dominant behavior of young children. *British J. Social & Clinical Psychology*, 1962, *1*, 168–81.

Subjects: *N* = 55; 3–5 yrs. Measures: Teachers were asked to pay special attention to dominance behaviors in their nursery school classrooms. One week later, teachers ranked the children on relative dominance. Results: No sex differences.

Gelman, R., and Weinberg, D. H. The relationship between liquid conservation and compensation. *Child Development*, 1972, *43*, 371–83.

Subjects: *N* = 80; 6, 7, 8, 11 yrs. Measures: Ss performed liquid conservation and compensation operations. Results: No sex differences.

Gerace, T. A., and Caldwell, W. E. Perceptual distortion as a function of stimulus objects, sex, naïveté, and trials using a portable model of the Ames distorted room. *Genetic Psychology Monographs*, 1971, *84*, 3–33.

Subjects: *N* = 40; 25 yrs. Measures: Using a portable model of the Ames distorted room, Ss were instructed to change the length of an adjustable rod to the size of an object in the room. The response measure was the length of the rod set by S. Results: Men were more accurate in their judgments than women ($p < .001$).

Gerard, H. B., Wilhelmy, R. A., and Conolley, E. S. Conformity and group size. *J. Personality & Social Psychology*, 1968, *8*, 79–82.

Subjects: *N* = 154; 14–17 yrs. Measures: Ss participated in an Asch experiment, judging which of 3 lines was equal in length to a standard. Girls were run in groups of 3, 5, or 7; boys were run in groups of 2, 4, 6, or 8. Results: Girls were more conforming than boys ($p < .05$).

Gerst, M. S. Symbolic coding processes in observational learning. *J. Personality & Social Psychology*, 1971, *19*, 7–17.

Subjects: *N* = 72; 18–21 yrs (college). Measures: Ss observed a filmed model perform complex motor responses. The performance measure was Ss' reproduction of the model's behavior. Results: No sex differences.

Gewirtz, H. B., and Gewirtz, J. L. Visiting and caretaking patterns for kibbutz infants: age and sex trends. *American J. Orthopsychiatry*, 1968, *38*, 427–43.

Subjects: *N* = 24; 4, 8 mos. Measures: Individual chronological logs were kept for all infants. Onset and termination of typical daily events were recorded. Results: (1) Cumulative caretaking activities were found to be of longer duration for boys than for girls. (2) Feeding took longer for boys than for girls. (3) Girls fed themselves more frequently than boys did. No difference was found in the percentage of boys and girls who were classified as "eaters." (4) The mean interval between diaper changes was shorter for boys than for girls. No sex differences were found in the frequency or duration of diaper changing. (5) No sex differences were found in "total time awake" or in its components, "time alone" (no person present in Ss' background) and "social time" (1 or more persons present in Ss' background). (6) No sex differences were found in sleeping or dressing. (7) No sex differences were found in the duration of mothers', fathers', or caretakers' visits.

Ghent, L. Developmental changes in tactual thresholds on dominant and nondominant sides. *J. Comparative & Physiological Psychology*, 1961, 54, 670–73.
> Subjects: $N = 108$; 5, 6, 7, 9, 11 yrs. Measures: Tactual thresholds were determined for thumbs and upper arms. Results: (1) Among 6-, 7-, and 9-year-old girls, the nondominant thumb was more sensitive than the dominant thumb; among 6-, 7-, and 9-year-old boys, no differences in sensitivity were found ($p < .05$; $p < .01$; $p < .05$). (2) Among 11-year-old Ss, boys' nondominant thumbs were more sensitive than the dominant thumbs; no differences were found for girls. (3) No sex differences were found among 5-year-old Ss. (4) Thresholds for the upper arms did not parallel the developmental changes observed for the thumbs.

Giacoman, S. L. Hunger and motor restraint on arousal and visual attention in the infant. *Child Development*, 1971, 42, 605–14.
> Subjects: $N = 32$; 5–6 wks. Measures: Ss were observed for 2 15-minute periods while lying supine in a crib. During 1 of the periods they were swaddled. At intermittent intervals, a visual stimulus (either a red plastic ring or a red ball) was held (stationary) in front of Ss for 5 seconds, after which it was slowly moved to the left and right of their line of vision. Measures were taken of fixation (the number of Ss focused on the stationary stimulus at any time during the first 5 seconds of presentation) and pursuit (the number of seconds Ss focused on the moving stimulus during the last 15 seconds of presentation). Ss were also rated for level of arousal. Results: (1) No main sex differences were found. (2) Boys had higher pursuit scores when they were swaddled during the second 15-minute observation period; girls had higher pursuit scores when they were swaddled during the first period ($p < .05$).

Ginsburg, H., and Rapoport, A. Children's estimates of proportions. *Child Development*, 1967, 38, 205–12.
> EXPERIMENT I: Subjects: $N = 40$; 6, 11 yrs. Measures: Each S was given 4 problems that required estimating proportions of 2 categories of elements. Each problem used 40 black and white marbles. S estimated the proportion of each color after watching them drawn out of an opaque container, 1 at a time. Results: No sex differences.
> EXPERIMENT II: Subjects: $N = 36$; 6, 11 yrs. Measures: Same as Experiment I, except 3 categories of elements were used (black, white, and yellow marbles). Results: No sex differences.

Gitter, A. G., Mostofsky, D. I., and Quincy, A. J. Race and sex differences in the child's perception of emotion. *Child Development*, 1971, 42, 2071–75.
> Subjects: $N = 80$; 4–6 yrs (white, black). Measures: Ss were shown 4 cartoon-like drawings of different emotions—anger, surprise, happiness, and pain. After being trained to associate the name of each emotion with the appropriate cartoon, Ss were shown slides of black or white female models; 1 of the 4 emotions was portrayed on each slide. Ss' task was to match each slide with the appropriate cartoon. Results: No sex differences.

Glick, O. Interaction effects of sex of mother's child and child's reading performance on the mother's evaluations of the school. *J. Educational Research*, 1970, 64, 124–26.
> Subjects: $N = 92$; mothers of 8-year-old children. Measures: Mothers were asked to evaluate the school their children were attending. Results: No main sex differences were found. Mothers of girls who performed above the reading criterion for third-graders on the Metropolitan Achievement Test of Reading evaluated the school more favorably than did mothers of boys who performed above the criterion. No differences were found in the evaluations of mothers whose children performed below the reading criterion.

Gliner, C. R. Tactual discrimination thresholds for shape and texture in young children. *J. Experimental Child Psychology*, 1967, 5, 536–47.
> Subjects: $N = 160$; 5, 8 yrs. Measures: Ss made tactual judgments as to whether pairs of shapes (ellipses) and textures (sandpaper patches) were the same or different from each other. Textures were presented either without shape (texture condition) or on a constant shape (shaped-texture condition). Shapes were presented either untextured (shape condition) or with a

constant texture (textured-shape condition). **Results:** (1) With smoother sandpaper patches, girls performed better in the texture condition than in the shaped-texture condition; for boys, the reverse was true. In both conditions, girls more often employed successive exploration, whereas boys more often used simultaneous exploration. (2) No sex differences were found in the shape or textured-shape conditions.

Gliner, C. R., Pick, A. D., Pick, H. L., Jr., and Hales, J. J. A developmental investigation of visual and haptic preferences for shape and texture. *Monographs of the Society for Research in Child Development*, 1969, *34*.

EXPERIMENT I: **Subjects:** $N = 160$; 5, 8 yrs. **Measures:** Ss were visually presented with a series of either pairs of shapes or pairs of textures, and were asked whether members of each pair were alike or different. Textures were presented either without shape or on a constant shape. Shapes were presented either untextured or with a constant texture. **Results:** Among 5-year-olds, boys were more sensitive than girls to differences between textures. No other sex differences were found.

EXPERIMENT II: **Subjects:** $N = 181$; 5, 8 yrs. **Measures:** Haptic preference for shape and texture was assessed in a discrimination-learning situation. **Results:** No sex differences.

EXPERIMENT III: **Subjects:** $N = 80$; 5, 8 yrs. **Measures:** Same as Experiment II, but discriminations were made visually rather than haptically. **Results:** No sex differences.

Glinski, R. J., Glinski, B. C., and Slatin, G. T. Nonnaivety contamination in conformity experiments: sources, effects, and implications for control. *J. Personality & Social Psychology*, 1970, *16*, 478–85.

Subjects: $N = 56$; 18–21 yrs (college). **Measures:** After receiving the decisions of 3 other subjects of the same sex, Ss judged which of 3 girls was lying from the tone of her voice. Decisions of prior Ss either were in unanimous agreement or were characterized by a two-thirds majority. The response measure was the number of times Ss conformed to the majority opinion. **Results:** When Ss who admitted being previously informed of the true nature of the experiment were removed (all girls), no sex differences were found.

Glixman, A. F. Categorizing behavior as a function of meaning domain. *J. Personality & Social Psychology*, 1965, *2*, 370–77.

Subjects: $N = 36$; 20–26 yrs. **Measures:** Ss categorized sets of items. **Results:** (1) Women used a greater number of categories than men did ($p < .001$). (2) No sex differences were found in the distribution of items over categories.

Goffeney, B., Henderson, N. B., and Butler, B. V. Negro-white, male-female eight-month developmental scores compared with seven-year WISC and Bender test scores. *Child Development*, 1971, *42*, 594–604.

Subjects: $N = 626$; tested at 8 mos and 7 yrs. **Measures:** Bayley Infant Scales, Wechsler Intelligence Scale for Children, Bender-Gestalt Test. **Results:** (1) Girls' fine motor skills were superior to boys' ($p < .001$). Black boys scored the lowest, black girls the highest ($p < .05$). No sex differences were found in gross motor or mental scores. (2) No sex differences were found on the WISC or on the Bender-Gestalt Test.

Goldberg, S. Probability judgments by preschool children: task conditions and performance. *Child Development*, 1966, *37*, 157–67.

Subjects: $N = 32$; 3–5 yrs. **Measures:** Ss made probability judgments in Piagetian or decision-making conditions. **Results:** No sex differences.

Goldberg, S., and Lewis, M. Play behavior in the year-old infant: early sex differences. *Child Development*, 1969, *40*, 21–31.

Subjects: $N = 64$; tested at 6, 13 mos, and their mothers. **Measures:** At the initial session with their mothers present, Ss were exposed to visual and auditory stimuli. 2 maternal behaviors were recorded: number of vocalizations to infant and amount of physical contact (touching, playing, comforting) with infant. At the second session 7 months later, Ss were observed in a free-play situation. The testing room contained 9 toys: a set of blocks, a pail, a lawn mower, a stuffed dog, an inflated plastic cat, a set of quoits, a wood mallet, a pegboard, and a wooden pull toy. After their mothers placed them on the floor, Ss were assessed on the following measures: latency to return to mother; number of returns to mother; time spent touching mother; time spent vocalizing to mother; time spent looking at mother; number of looks to mother; time spent in the squares closest to and farthest from mother (the room was marked off into 12 squares); and time spent playing with each of the various toys. At the end of the free-play period, a barrier was constructed in the middle of the room. Each infant was placed on the opposite side by his mother. Measures were taken of the number of seconds Ss cried and of the amount of time they spent at the center and at the ends of the barrier. **Results:** (1) At 6 months of age: Mothers vocalized more to girls than to boys; more mothers of girls than mothers of boys were rated high in physical contact; more girls than boys were breast-fed. (2) In the free-play situation at 13 months of age: girls returned to their mothers more quickly and more frequently than boys; girls spent more time touching mother, vocalizing to mother, and in the squares nearest mother than boys; girls exhibited a greater preference for the blocks, the cat and the dog (combined score), and the pegboard than boys: boys banged the toys more frequently than girls; boys played more vigorously than girls (observer rating). No sex differences were found on the other free-play measures or in overall toy preferences. (3) In the barrier situation, girls spent more time at the center of the barrier; boys spent more time at the two ends. Girls cried longer than boys.

Goldrich, J. M. A study in time orientation: the relation between memory for past experience and orientation to the future. *J. Personality & Social Psychology*, 1967, *6*, 216–21.
   Subjects: $N = 80$; 25–40 yrs. **Measures:** (1) Ss' responses to the Thematic Apperception Test (cards 1, 2, 16, and 20) were scored for (a) number of stories in which the future was spontaneously mentioned, (b) prospective (future) time spans, (c) total time spans, (d) percentage of verbal output devoted to description of future events, (e) continuity of depicted events in time, (f) pleasantness of stories, and (g) degree of involvement. (2) Ss also completed a Likert-type future scale, designed to measure Ss' feelings about their future professional life, their future interpersonal relations, and their future self-evaluations. **Results:** (1) No sex differences were found in Ss' TAT scores. (2) Women were more optimistic than men on the future scale.

Goldschmid, M. L. Different types of conservation and nonconservation and their relation to age, sex, IQ, MA, and vocabulary. *Child Development*, 1967, *38*, 1229–46.
   Subjects: $N = 81$; 6–7 yrs. **Measures:** Ss were tested on a series of 10 conservation tasks. The WISC Vocabulary subtest and either the Pintner-Cunningham or the Otis IQ test were also administered to Ss. **Results:** Boys performed better on the conservation tasks than girls did. No sex differences were found in IQ or vocabulary scores.

Goldschmid, M. L. The relation of conservation to emotional and environmental aspects of development. *Child Development*, 1968, *39*, 579–89.
   Subjects: $N = 81$; 6–7 yrs. **Measures:** (1) The Children's Manifest Anxiety Scale was administered orally to each S. (2) Ss rated their actual and their ideal self on an adjective checklist. Teachers used the same set of adjectives to describe each child. (3) Popularity ratings were obtained by asking Ss to (1) indicate whether they liked or disliked each of their classmates, and (2) select the 3 children in their class they liked most and the 3 children they liked least. (4) The Parental Attitude Survey, a measure of parents' attitudes toward child-rearing methods, was given to mothers and fathers; 3 scores reflecting degree of dominant, ignoring, and possessive attitudes were derived for each parent. Differences between mothers' and fathers' scores were then computed. **Results:** No sex differences.

Goldstein, A. G., and Chance, J. E. Effects of practice on sex-related differences in performance on Embedded Figures. *Psychonomic Science*, 1965, *3*, 361–62.
   Subjects: $N = 26$; 18–21 yrs (college). **Measures:** Ss were presented with 68 embedded figures. Discovery times were recorded. **Results:** On the first 10 items, women had higher discovery times than men ($p < .05$). On the last 10 items, no sex differences were found.

Goldstein, S. B., and Siegel, A. W. Observing behavior and children's discrimination learning. *Child Development*, 1971, *42*, 1608–13.
   Subjects: $N = 48$; 8 yrs. **Measures:** Ss performed a 2-choice discrimination-learning task. Geometric figures were used as the discriminative stimuli. Response latencies and number of trials needed to reach criterion were recorded for each S. **Results:** No sex differences.

Goldstein, S. B., and Siegel, A. W. Facilitation of discrimination learning with delayed reinforcement. *Child Development*, 1972, *43*, 1004–11.
   Subjects: $N = 84$; 8, 9 yrs. **Measures:** Ss were presented with 2 geometric figures on each trial of a discrimination-learning task. Performance measures were number of trials to criterion and number of correct responses. **Results:** No sex differences.

Golightly, C., Nelson, D., and Johnson, J. Children's dependency scale. *Developmental Psychology*, 1970, *3*, 114–18.
   Subjects: $N = 219$; 9–11 yrs. **Measures:** The Children's Dependency Scale. **Results:** (1) Over-

all, girls had higher dependency scores than boys. (2) Girls had higher dependency scores than boys at ages 10 and 11. There were no sex differences at age 9.

Gonen, J. V., and Lansky, L. M. Masculinity, femininity, and masculinity-femininity: a phenomenological study of the MF scale of the MMPI. *Psychological Reports*, 1968, *23*, 183–94.
Subjects: $N = 94$; 18–21 yrs (college). Measures: Ss evaluated responses by a hypothetical man and woman to the MMPI MF scale's items as making the man or woman "more masculine," "less masculine," "more feminine," or "less feminine." When S placed a behavior along a continuum with masculine at one pole and feminine at the other, his conceptualization was termed bipolar. When S placed a behavior along a continuum with more masculine (or feminine) at one end and less masculine (or feminine) at the other, his conceptualization was termed unipolar. Results: Men responded with more unipolar patterns than women did ($p < .05$).

Goodenough, D. R., and Eagle, C. J. A modification of the Embedded Figures Test for use with young children. *J. Genetic Psychology*, 1963, *103*, 67–74.
Subjects: $N = 96$; 5, 8 yrs. Measures: A children's version of the Embedded Figures Test (CEFT). Results: No sex differences.

Goodenough, E. W. Interest in persons as an aspect of sex difference in the early years. *Genetic Psychology Monographs*, 1957, *55*, 287–323.
EXPERIMENT I: Subjects: $N = 80$; parents of children of 2–4 yrs. Measures: Interviews were conducted separately with mothers and fathers. Results: Girls were described as submissive more frequently than boys were ($p < .01$). No differences were found for the following traits: sensitive, emotional; obstinate; good-natured, happy; affectionate; aggressive; sense of humor. When parents gave illustrations of these traits, however, qualitative sex differences appeared.
EXPERIMENT II: Subjects: $N = 247$; 2–4 yrs. Measures: Pictures that Ss had drawn were collected and analyzed. Results: Girls included people in their drawings more frequently than boys did ($p < .01$).
EXPERIMENT III: Subjects: $N = 52$; 2–4 yrs. Measures: Verbalizations were elicited from Ss during the administration of the Mosaic Test. Results: Girls made more references to persons than boys did ($p < .01$).

Gorsuch, R. L., and Smith, R. A. Changes in college students' evaluations of moral behavior: 1969 versus 1939, 1949, and 1958. *J. Personality & Social Psychology*, 1972, *24*, 381–91.
Subjects: $N = 1,030$; 18–21 yrs (college). Measures: Ss rated each of 50 behaviors on a 10-point scale of wrongness (Crissman's moral behavior scale). Results: Women were more severe in their ratings than men were ($p < .0001$).

Goss, A. M. Paired associate learning by young children as functions of initial associative strength and percentage of occurrence of response members. *J. Experimental Child Psychology*, 1966, *4*, 398–407.
Subjects: $N = 60$; 3–4, 5–6 yrs. Measures: Ss were given a paired-associates task. The number of correct responses Ss made was recorded. Results: No sex differences.

Goss, A. M. Estimated versus actual physical strength in three ethnic groups. *Child Development*, 1968, *39*, 283–90.
Subjects: $N = 192$; 8, 11, 14, 17 yrs (black, Latin American, Anglo-American). Measures: Self-estimates of strength and estimates of the strength of mother, father, and an imagined opposite-sex partner were obtained from each S. Ss were then tested on a hand dynamometer. Results: (1) At all but the youngest age level, girls rated themselves lower than boys did on self-estimates of strength ($p < .001$). (2) There was a consistent reduction of girls' self-ratings across grades; the difference between girls' and boys' self-estimates tended to increase with age ($p < .001$). (3) On the dynamometer test, boys were consistently stronger than girls ($p < .001$). (4) Girls tended to rate imagined opposite-sex partner's strength higher than boys did ($p < .001$). (5) There were no sex differences in father-strength estimates. (6) Girls tended to estimate mothers' strength to be higher than boys did ($p < .05$).

Gough, H. G., and Delcourt, M. Developmental increments in perceptual acuity among Swiss and American school children. *Developmental Psychology*, 1969, *1*, 250–64.
Subjects: $N = 1,065$; 8–16 yrs (U.S., Switzerland). Measures: Ss were given the Perceptual

Acuity Test; 25 geometric illusion problems and 5 nonillusion problems were included. **Results:** No sex differences.

Grams, A., Hafner, A. J., and Quast, W. Child anxiety: self-estimates, parent reports, and teacher ratings. *Merrill-Palmer Quarterly*, 1965, *11*, 261–66.
  Subjects: $N = 110$, 9–11 yrs. **Measures:** General Anxiety Scale for Children (GASC), Children's Manifest Anxiety Scale (CMAS). **Results:** Girls had higher scores than boys did on the GASC ($p < .01$). No sex differences were found on the CMAS.

Granger, G. W. An experimental study of color preferences. *J. General Psychology*, 1955, *32*, 3–20.
  Subjects: $N = 50$; 19–36 yrs. **Measures:** 60 sets of colors, each containing approximately 7 items, were selected to represent the color spectrum with respect to hue, value, and chroma. Ss rank-ordered their preferences within each set. **Results:** No sex differences.

Grant, M. J., and Sermat, V. Status and sex of other as determinants of behavior in a mixed-motive game. *J. Personality & Social Psychology*, 1969, *12*, 151–57.
  Subjects: $N = 48$; 18–21 yrs (college). **Measures:** Ss played two consecutive 30-trial games of "Chicken" (a game similar to the Prisoner's Dilemma game) with simulated partners of the same and opposite sex. On each trial, Ss predicted whether their partners would make the cooperative or the competitive choice. Information about the partners' choice was given to Ss on 4 of the 30 trials. Before beginning, Ss recorded the number of points they expected to make in each of the 2 games. **Results:** (1) Men expected to make more points than women did ($p < .05$). (2) No sex differences were found in the number of competitive responses made. Men made more competitive responses when paired first with a male and then with a female than when the order was reversed; for women, the opposite was true ($p < .01$). (3) Ss were less competitive when paired with a female than when paired with a male ($p < .05$). (4) Women were more competitive than men when paired with a male other; men were more competitive than women when paired with a female other ($p < .05$). (5) An attempt was made to distinguish submission from cooperation and exploitation from competition. For each of the first 7 trials on which Ss predicted partners would choose the competitive response, the number of men and women who chose the cooperative response (i.e. submitted) was tabulated. Similarly, for each of the first 7 trials on which Ss predicted partners would choose the cooperative response, the number of men and women who chose the competitive response (i.e. exploited) was tabulated. Women were less submissive than men ($p < .01$). Men were more exploitive than women ($p < .05$). Women were less exploited than men ($p < .05$).

Graves, A. J. Attainment of conservation of mass, weight, and volume in minimally educated adults. *Developmental Psychology*, 1972, *7*, 223 (brief report).
  Subjects: $N = 120$; 33 yrs (minimally educated). **Measures:** Based on performance on the Adult Basic Learning Examination, Ss were assigned to 1 of 3 grade levels: 0–3, 4–6, and 7–8. Each S was tested for conservation of mass, weight, and volume. **Results:** (1) Men scored higher than women on conservation of volume. (2) There were no sex differences in conservation of quantity (total conservation score), conservation of mass, or conservation of weight.

Graves, M. F., and Koziol, S. Noun plural development in primary grade children. *Child Development*, 1971, *42*, 1165–73.
  Subjects: $N = 67$; 6–9 yrs. **Measures:** Ss were tested on 6 types of plural noun formations. **Results:** No sex differences.

Green, A. The relation of dancing experience and personality to perception. *Psychological Monographs: General and Applied*, 1955, *69*, 399.
  Subjects: $N = 60$; 17–40 yrs. **Measures:** (1) Rod-and-Frame Test, (2) Tilting-Room-Tilting-Chair test, (3) Embedded Figures Test, (4) Stabilometer. **Results:** (1) Men were more field-independent than women were on RFT series 2 ($p < .001$) and series 3 ($p < .01$). No sex differences were found on series 1. (2) Men were superior to women on series 1a ($p < .05$) and 1b ($p < .01$) of the TRTC test. No sex differences were found in series 2a or 2b. (3) No sex differences were found on the EFT. (4) Men kept the platform horizontal more often than women did. No sex differences were found in number of seconds Ss touched the surrounding guard rail in order to keep their balance.

Greenbaum, C. W. Effect of situational and personality variables on improvisation and attitude change. *J. Personality & Social Psychology*, 1966, *4*, 260–69.

Subjects: $N = 100$; 18–21 yrs (college). **Measures:** Ss were given either a choice or no choice to speak in defense of a counterattitudinal topic. After making the speech, Ss received either positive, negative, or no feedback. Attitude change was assessed immediately afterward and again 2 weeks later. **Results:** No sex differences.

Greenberg, D. J. Accelerating visual complexity levels in the human infant. *Child Development,* 1971, *42,* 905–18 (and personal communication).
Subjects: $N = 36$; tested at 8, 10, 12 wks. **Measures:** Ss' fixation time to 3 checkerboard patterns of equal area was assessed. Groups viewed either a gray stimulus or various checkerboard patterns for a 4-week period. **Results:** (1) At age 8 weeks, girls maintained longer interest in the simple $2'' \times 2''$ than boys did. (2) There were no sex differences involving more complex patterns. (3) Boys habituated after an initial surge of interest in the simple pattern; girls habituated slowly but maintained interest.

Greenberg, D. J., and O'Donnell, W. J. Infancy and the optimal level of stimulation. *Child Development,* 1972, *43,* 639–45.
Subjects: $N = 72$; 6, 11 wks. **Measures:** Ss viewed stimulus patterns in which equal black and white proportions were combined in checks, stripes, and dots, gradually increasing in complexity within each type. Each S saw 3 patterns of the same type. **Results:** Girls looked at checkerboards more than boys did ($p < .05$); no other sex differences were found.

Greenberg, D. J., and Weizmann, F. The measurement of visual attention in infants: a comparison of two methodologies. *J. Experimental Child Psychology,* 1971, *11,* 234–43.
Subjects: $N = 24$; 2, 3 mos. **Measures:** Ss' fixation times to 3 checkerboard patterns (2x2, 8x8, 24x24) of equal area were recorded twice, once with each stimulus presented singly, and once using a paired-comparisons method of presentation. **Results:** There were no overall sex differences, but girl infants looked longer at the more complex pattern than boys did. However, post hoc comparisons qualified the sex difference: in a single-stimulus presentation, girl infants looked longer at the $24'' \times 24''$ checkerboard relative to the $8'' \times 8''$ than boys did, whereas in the paired comparison, girls looked longer at both the $24'' \times 24''$ and $8'' \times 8''$, relative to the $2'' \times 2''$, than boys did.

Greenberger, E., O'Connor, J., and Sorensen, A. Personality, cognitive, and academic correlates of problem-solving flexibility. *Developmental Psychology,* 1971, *4,* 416–24.
Subjects: $N = 113$; 6–8 yrs. **Measures:** Each S was given the California Test of Mental Maturity for IQ scores, Test Anxiety Scale for Children, recall of novel information from taped stories one week later, Investigatory Activities Inventory (self-report curiosity measure), "Foolish Sayings" scale (whether or not statements made sense), teacher ratings of children's curiosity (adjective checklist, behavior profile with subscales for curiosity, achievement striving, achievement blocks), question as to "which parent best likes to answer your questions," and measure of problem-solving flexibility (giving as many reasons as possible for certain occurrences, scores for number of different categories responses fell into). **Results:** (1) There were no sex differences in problem-solving flexibility. (2) Among 6-year-old Ss, girls recalled more than boys did. There were no sex differences in recall at the other 2 age levels.

Greenglass, E. R. A cross-cultural comparison of maternal communication. *Child Development,* 1971a, *42,* 685–92.
Subjects: $N = 132$ mother-child pairs; 9–10, 13–14 yrs (Italian-Canadian and Canadian). **Measures:** Mother-child pairs were required to reach a consensus in each of 3 discussion tasks. Maternal verbalizations were recorded. **Results:** No sex of child differences were found in total amount of maternal communication or in mothers' use of demands or justifications.

Greenglass, E. R. A cross-cultural study of the child's communication with his mother. *Developmental Psychology,* 1971b, *5,* 494–99.
Subjects: $N = 132$; 9–10, 13–14 yrs (Italy, Canada). **Measures:** Each child's verbalizations were recorded during 3 discussion tasks in which the mother and child were required to reach consensus. **Results:** (1) There were no sex differences in the extent to which Italian children used requests for information. (2) Among 9-10-year-old Canadian Ss, girls used more requests for information or evaluation than boys did.

Greenglass, E. R. A cross-cultural study of the relationship between resistance to temptation and maternal communication. *Genetic Psychology Monographs,* 1972, *86,* 119–39.
Subjects: $N = 62$; 9–10 yrs and mothers. **Measures:** Ss played a game in which it was neces-

sary to violate the rules in order to win a gold star. The number of times each S cheated was recorded. Each mother-child pair engaged in three discussion tasks. Each task required that a consensus be reached. Mothers were scored for their use of demands and justifications. **Results:** No sex differences.

Greenwald, H. J. Dissonance and relative versus absolute attractiveness of decision alternatives. *J. Personality & Social Psychology*, 1969, *11*, 328–33.
Subjects: $N = 85$; 18–21 yrs (college). **Measures:** Ss initially rated 40 singers' acceptability on a 15-point scale; 2 weeks later, Ss were asked to evaluate the records of one of the singers. Half of the Ss were given a choice of which of 2 singers they were to evaluate, while the other Ss simply expressed their preference for 1 of 2 singers. In this latter condition, Ss were told a singer had already been selected for them by a random process. The singers Ss chose between were derived from Ss' preratings. Relative attractiveness was manipulated by presenting Ss with 2 singers they had previously rated either alike (high-conflict situation) or different (low-conflict situation). Immediately after selecting a singer (or expressing a preference for 1), Ss rerated both singers. "Spreading apart" was the increase in the chosen alternative's rating added to the decrease in the rejected alternative's ratings. **Results:** In the low-conflict condition, the decrease in spreading apart was greater for women than for men ($p < .02$).

Greenwald, H. J., and Oppenheim, D. B. Reported magnitude of self-misidentification among Negro children—artifact? *J. Personality & Social Psychology*, 1968, *8*, 49–52.
Subjects: $N = 79$; 3–5 yrs (white, black). **Measures:** Ss were presented with a dark brown, a mulatto, and a white doll. Ss were then asked the following series of questions: Is there a doll that (a) you like to play with best? (b) you don't want to play with? (c) is a nice color? (d) is a good doll? (e) is a bad doll? (f) is not a nice color? (g) looks like a white child? (h) looks like a colored child? (i) looks like you? **Results:** No sex differences.

Gross, F. The role of set in perception of the upright. *J. Personality*, 1959, *27*, 95–103.
Subjects: $N = 110$; 17–25 yrs. **Measures:** Rod-and-Frame Test. **Results:** Men were more field-independent than women ($p < .01$).

Gross, R. B., and Marsh, M. An instrument for measuring creativity in young children: the Gross Geometric Forms. *Developmental Psychology*, 1970, *3*, 267 (brief report).
Subjects: $N = 170$; 3–6, 10, 15 yrs. **Measures:** For 10 trials, Ss used colored geometric forms to make "something" and were asked to name and describe their creation. Creations were scored for different form constructions and names (productivity), communicability (degree to which form constructions and names matched), and richness of thinking shown in action, color, and embellishment. **Results:** No sex differences.

Gruder, C. L., and Cook, T. D. Sex, dependency and helping. *J. Personality & Social Psychology*, 1971, *19*, 290–4.
Subjects: $N = 104$; 18–21 yrs (college). **Measures:** Ss were requested to collate and staple copies of an 18-page questionnaire as a favor for either a male or female E who at the last moment had to change his schedule to go to a class meeting. The note that E left stated that he needed the questionnaire either in 2 hours (high-dependency condition) or next week (low-dependency condition). The number of questionnaires Ss stapled was recorded. **Results:** (1) There were no sex of S effects. (2) The female E received greater help in the high-dependency than in the low-dependency condition; the male E did not ($p < .05$).

Gruen, G. E., Ottinger, D., and Zigler, E. Level of aspiration and the probability learning of middle- and lower-class children. *Developmental Psychology*, 1970, *3*, 133–42.
Subjects: $N = 121$; 6, 9 yrs (lower, middle SES). **Measures:** Level of aspiration was measured by each S's estimate of how many times out of 10 he could throw a beanbag into a box 6 feet away. Probability learning was measured by the number of correct knob pushes (out of 3) S made, with 1 knob reinforced 66% of the time and the other 2 knobs never reinforced. **Results:** No sex differences.

Gruen, G. E., and Vore, D. A. Development of conservation in normal and retarded children. *Developmental Psychology*, 1972, *6*, 146–57.
Subjects: $N = 20$; 7, 10 yrs (retarded). $N = 40$; 5, 6, 8, 10 yrs (normal). **Measures:** Ss performed tasks for conservation of number, continuous quantity, and weight. **Results:** No sex differences.

Grusec, J. E. Some antecedents of self-criticism. *J. Personality & Social Psychology*, 1966, 4, 244–52.

Subjects: $N = 80$; 5–6 yrs. Measures: While playing a game with an adult female model, Ss were criticized for their performance on selected trials. The model accompanied this criticism with either withdrawal of love or withdrawal of material reward. Termination of punishment was made either contingent or noncontingent upon Ss' verbalization of the model's criticism of them. The speed with which Ss verbalized the criticism was recorded. Generalization of the model's criticism of them to a new situation and its resistance to extinction were also measured. Results: No sex differences.

Grusec, J. E. Waiting for rewards and punishments: effects of reinforcement value on choice. *J. Personality & Social Psychology*, 1968, 9, 85–89.

Subjects: $N = 40$; 8 yrs. Measures: Ss listed their preferences for immediate vs. delayed rewards and punishments. Delayed outcomes were of either equal or greater magnitude than immediate outcomes. Results: No sex differences.

Grusec, J. E. Power and the internalization of self-denial. *Child Development*, 1971, 42, 93–105.

EXPERIMENT I: Subjects: $N = 48$; 7–11 yrs. Measures: Ss experienced high or low nurturance from a model who had power or no power to administer rewards. The model played a bowling game with Ss in which the model exhibited altruism by explaining he would donate his rewards to charity. Results: No sex differences in Ss' donations to charity.

EXPERIMENT II: Subjects: $N = 40$; 7–11 yrs. Measures: Same as Experiment I, except standards of self-reward on the bowling game were enacted by the model rather than explained. Results: No sex differences.

Grusec, J. E. Demand characteristics of the modeling experiment: altruism as a function of age and aggression. *J. Personality & Social Psychology*, 1972, 22, 139–48.

EXPERIMENT I: Subjects: $N = 100$; 7, 11 yrs. Measures: Following exposure to an altruistic same-sex adult model, Ss were given the opportunity to donate marbles to charity. Results: No sex differences were found in number of marbles donated.

EXPERIMENT II: Subjects: $N = 54$; 8–9 yrs. Measures: One group of Ss observed a same-sex adult model perform a series of aggressive responses with toys. A second group of Ss simply heard a model say that aggressive behaviors were appropriate. Following the model's departure, Ss were observed with the toys and then asked to recall everything the model had either said or done. Results: There were no sex differences in number of imitative aggressive responses displayed or number of novel aggressive responses displayed. There were no sex differences in Ss' recall of the model's behavior and verbalizations.

EXPERIMENT III: Subjects: $N = 20$; 8–9 yrs. Measures: Same as Experiment II, except Ss were not observed with the toys. Results: No sex differences were found in Ss' recall of the model's behavior or verbalizations.

Grusec, J. E. Effects of co-observer evaluations on imitation: a developmental study. *Developmental Psychology*, 1973, 8, 141 (extended version of brief report).

Subjects: $N = 60$; 5, 10 yrs. Measures: Ss watched a movie of a female adult being aggressive toward a Bobo doll while hearing a female E make positive, negative, or neutral evaluations of the model's behavior. Ss were then left alone for 7 minutes in the playroom with the Bobo and other toys. Results: No sex differences were found in the number of Ss who imitated the model.

Grusec, J. E., and Brinker, D. B. Reinforcement for imitation as a social learning determinant with implications for sex-role development. *J. Personality & Social Psychology*, 1972, 21, 149–58.

EXPERIMENT I: Subjects: $N = 32$; 6, 7 yrs. Measures: Ss were shown a series of separate filmed sequences of 2 men (models A and B) performing different behaviors. After each sequence, Ss were asked to reproduce 1 of the behaviors they had seen. Half of the Ss were reinforced for imitating model A, the other half for imitating model B. The performance measure was number of trials needed by Ss to reach the criterion of 10 correct responses in succession. In the next phase of the study, a second movie of models A and B was shown and Ss' eye movements were recorded. The response measure was the number of seconds Ss spent looking at each model. Immediately afterward, Ss were asked to perform the behaviors of both models. The number of items of each model's behavior that Ss were able to recall was recorded. Results: No sex differences.

EXPERIMENT II: **Subjects:** $N = 32$; 8 yrs. **Measures:** Same as Experiment I, except new movies were made using 2 females as models and Ss' eye movements were not recorded. **Results:** (1) Girls reached the criterion of 10 correct responses in succession faster than boys did ($p < .01$). (2) No sex differences were found in Ss' recall of the model's behaviors.

EXPERIMENT III: **Subjects:** $N = 144$; 5, 7 yrs. **Measures:** Ss were shown a movie of an adult male and an adult female model, who exhibited (with the exception of 2 short sequences of nurturant and aggressive responses) mostly neutral behaviors. Afterward, Ss were rewarded for reproducing the behaviors of both models. **Results:** (1) No main sex differences were found in number of items recalled of each model's behavior. Boys remembered more of the adult male's than of the adult female's behavior, while girls remembered slightly more of the adult female's than of the adult male's behavior ($p < .001$). (2) No main sex differences were found in Ss' recall of nurturant behaviors. Girls remembered more of the female's nurturance than boys did ($p < .05$). No sex differences were found in Ss' recall of the male model's nurturance. (3) No sex differences were found in Ss' recall of aggressive behavior.

Grusec, J. E., and Mischel, W. Model's characteristics as determinants of social learning. *J. Personality & Social Psychology,* 1966, *4,* 211–15.
Subjects: $N = 28$; 3–4 yrs. **Measures:** In the context of a game, Ss observed an adult female model display both neutral and aversive behaviors. Following the model's departure, Ss were offered attractive incentives contingent upon the reproduction of as many of the model's behaviors as they could recall. **Results:** No sex differences.

Grusec, J. E., and Skubiski, S. L. Model nurturance, demand characteristics of the modeling experiment, and altruism. *J. Personality & Social Psychology,* 1970, *14,* 352–59.
Subjects: $N = 80$; 8, 10 yrs. **Measures:** After exposure to an altruistic same-sex model, Ss were given the opportunity to donate marbles to charity. **Results:** No sex differences were found in number of marbles donated.

Grusec, T., and Grusec, J. E. Information seeking about uncertain but unavoidable outcomes: effects of probability, valence, and intervening activity. *Developmental Psychology,* 1971, 5, 177 (brief report).
EXPERIMENT I: **Subjects:** $N = 48$; 11 yrs. **Measures:** Before he left for 20 minutes, E gave Ss an envelope. The envelope contained a note informing Ss whether they would later be asked to eat either some delicious or some terrible-tasting food. The speed with which they opened the envelope was recorded. **Results:** No sex differences.
EXPERIMENT II: **Subjects:** $N = 64$, 18–21 (college). **Measures:** Same as Experiment I, except that the envelope contained information on whether Ss would later have a chance to win between $10 and $25 or whether they would be asked to receive painful shocks. **Results:** Women opened the envelope more quickly than men ($p < .05$).

Guardo, C. J. Personal space in children. *Child Development,* 1969, *40,* 143–51.
Subjects: $N = 60$; 11 yrs. **Measures:** Ss placed a silhouette figure of themselves in relation to another figure. The other figure was described as a best friend, an acquaintance, a stranger, "someone you like very much," "someone you neither like nor dislike," "someone you dislike very much," an angry stranger, or as "someone you're afraid of." **Results:** Girls placed the silhouette figure of themselves closer to "best friend" and "someone you like very much" and farther away from "someone you're afraid of" than boys did ($p < .05$, $p < .05$, $p < .05$).

Guardo, C. J., and Bohan, J. B. Development of a sense of self-identity in children. *Child Development,* 1971, *42,* 1909–21.
Subjects: $N = 116$; 6–9 yrs. **Measures:** Ss were asked if they could assume the identity of each of the following: a pet, a same-sex sibling or peer, and an opposite-sex sibling or peer. Ss were also asked how long they had been a boy or a girl and whether or not they would be the same person in the near future (in the higher grades) and in the remote future (when grown up). **Results:** (1) Boys more often than girls indicated they could not assume the identity of an opposite-sexed sibling or peer (significance level not reported). (2) In answer to the question regarding how long they had been a boy or a girl, boys indicated a length of time less than their chronological age more often than girls did (significance level not reported).

Guardo, C. J., and Meisels, M. Child-parent spatial patterns under praise and reproof. *Developmental Psychology,* 1971, 5, 365 (brief report).
Subjects: $N = 431$; 8–15 yrs. **Measures:** Ss placed self-referent paper silhouettes in spatial relation to an adult male or female silhouette, described as father or mother, praising or reproving the child. Interfigure distances were measured. **Results:** (1) In the praise condition,

girls placed silhouettes closer to parental figures than boys did ($p < .01$). (2) In the reproof condition, there were no sex differences in silhouette placement.

Guinagh, B. J. An experimental study of basic learning ability and intelligence in low socioeconomic status children. *Child Development*, 1971, *42*, 27–36.

Subjects: $N = 80$; 8 yrs (white and black, low SES). Measures: Ss were given the Raven's Progressive Matrices Test of Intelligence and a digit-span test of basic learning ability: 2 groups (low DS–low RPM and high DS–low RPM) were established; 10 from each group received experimental treatment (training for RPM), 5 received the Hawthorne Treatment (training unrelated to task), and 5 received no treatment. All Ss were post-tested on RPM. Results: No sex differences.

Gummerman, L., and Gray, C. R. Age, iconic storage and visual information processing. *J. Experimental Child Psychology*, 1972, *13*, 165–70.

Subjects: $N = 48$; 7, 9, 11, 18–21 yrs (college). Measures: Tachistoscopic presentation of a T rotated to right or left was followed by a white field or a patterned masking stimulus. Ss made a verbal report of "left" or "right" at end of each trial to indicate which side of the perpendicular bar the T appeared on. Results: No sex differences.

Gutkin, D. C. The effect of systematic story changes on intentionality in children's moral judgments. *Child Development*, 1972, *43*, 187–95.

Subjects: $N = 72$; 6, 8, 10 yrs. Measures: Ss were presented with 6 stories (3 pairs) in which a "good" or "bad" child caused high or low damage, intentionally or nonintentionally. They were then asked to make judgments comparing children in the pairs of stories. Results: No sex differences.

Guttman, R., and Kahneman, I. Sex and age differences in pattern organization in a figural-conceptual task. *Developmental Psychology*, 1971, *5*, 446–53.

Subjects: $N = 57$; 2½ yrs and parents (Jerusalem). Measures: Ss individually filled form boards with red, green, and blue / circle, square, and triangle discs. Results: Women showed higher levels of organization than men did with regard to color and "goodness of pattern" (redundancy).

Guttman, R., and Kahneman, I. Age and sex-related variation in performance on a figural-conceptual task. *Developmental Psychology*, 1972, *7*, 4–9.

Subjects: $N = 128$; 2½, 3–4, 5–6 yrs and parents. Measures: Ss filled form boards with 3 colors of disks. No time limit existed, and disks could be placed in any order with respect to color and/or location on the board. Results: (1) At each age level, a lower proportion of boys than girls used all 3 colors. (2) There were no sex differences in the order in which the colors were used. (3) At each age level, girls exceeded boys in the proportion of perfectly ordered placement patterns of disks (without regard to color). (4) Among 2½-year-old Ss, more girls than boys were in a region of the scalogram profile characterized by use of 3 colors and ordered placement. (5) Among 5-6-year-old Ss, twice as many girls as boys were in a region of the scalogram where organization of several components was at a high level.

Haber, L., and Iverson, M. A. Status maintenance in communications from dyads with high and low interpersonal comparability. *J. Personality & Social Psychology*, 1965, *1*, 596–603.

Subjects: $N = 112$; 18–21 yrs (college). Measures: Same-sex pairs of Ss composed a joint letter describing the atmosphere of their college to an outsider. Ss' letters were scored for total number of words, percentage of total number of words having an occurrence frequency of fewer than 100 times per million, total number of value-oriented statements, and percentage of negative references relating to the college. Ss' verbal scores on the College Entrance Examination Boards were also obtained. Results: Women wrote longer letters than men ($p < .05$). No other sex differences were found.

Hafner, J. A., and Kaplan, A. M. Children's manifest anxiety and intelligence. *Child Development*, 1959, *30*, 269–71.

Subjects: $N = 188$; 10 yrs. Measures: Children's Manifest Anxiety Scale. Results: No sex differences found on either the anxiety scale or the L scale.

Hagen, J. W., and Huntsman, N. J. Selective attention in mental retardates. *Developmental Psychology*, 1971, *5*, 151–60.

Subjects: $N = 21$; 9, 11 yrs (institutional retardates). Measures: Ss were shown cards with a central and incidental picture on each. Ss' task was to remember the order in which the cards were presented. **Results:** No sex differences.

Hagen, J. W., Hargrave, S., and Ross, W. Prompting and rehearsal in short-term memory. *Child Development,* 1973, *44,* 201–4.

Subjects: $N = 48$; 4–7 yrs. **Measures:** Ss were shown cards of 1 of 7 animals. After exposure, cards were laid face down in a horizontal row, Ss were asked to show the position of the card that was the same as the cue card. In a second trial block, a verbal rehearsal strategy was taught to all Ss. The third trial block was presented 1 week later. **Results:** No sex differences in correct recall.

Haith, M. The response of the human newborn to visual movement. *J. Experimental Child Psychology,* 1966, *3,* 235–43.

Subjects: $N = 41$; 1–4 days. **Measures:** Responsiveness and habituation of responsiveness of newborns to an intermittent, moving, visual stimulus were assessed. Nonnutritive sucking rate was measured during experimental (visual stimulus present) and control situations. **Results:** No sex differences in amount of nonnutritive sucking and habituation rate.

Hale, G. A., Miller, L. K., and Stevenson, H. W. Incidental learning of film content: a development study. *Child Development,* 1968, *39,* 69–77.

Subjects: $N = 719$; 8–12, 18–21 yrs (college). **Measures:** An 8-minute dramatic skit, filmed in sound and color, was presented as a reward for participation in an earlier study for younger Ss. The film was presented to college Ss without comment. After the film, Ss answered questions about incidental aspects of the verbal and visual content of the film. **Results:** (1) Among 8-12-year-old Ss, girls answered more questions correctly than boys did. (2) There were no sex differences in adult scores.

Hall, J. W., and Halperin, M. S. The development of memory-encoding processes in young children. *Developmental Psychology,* 1972, *6,* 181 (brief report).

Subjects: $N = 23$; 2½ yrs. **Measures:** 2 lists of common words were read. Ss were asked to remember the first list. The second list, the recognition test, contained 3 words from first list, 3 unrelated words, 3 words associatively related to first list, and 3 superordinates of first-list words. Ss were asked to recognize words that appeared on both lists. **Results:** No sex differences.

Hall, J. W., and Ware, W. B. Implicit associative responses and false recognition by young children. *J. Experimental Child Psychology,* 1968, *6,* 52–60.

Subjects: $N = 86$; 5–7 yrs. **Measures:** Ss heard 16 words at 4-second intervals with instructions to repeat each word and try to remember it. After a 15-minute interval, Ss were asked to identify previously heard words from the 24-word list containing previous words, strong associates of them, and control words (which had not appeared and were not associates of previous words). False recognitions were recorded. **Results:** No sex differences.

Hall, V. W., Salvi, R., Segev, L., and Caldwell, E. Cognitive synthesis, conservation, and task analysis. *Developmental Psychology,* 1970, *2,* 423–28.

Experiment I: **Subjects:** $N = 40$; 3–4 yrs. **Measures:** Ss were assigned to 1 of 4 conditions. 3 of the groups were tested on their ability to translate logograph sentences (directing them to do something) into actions. (A logograph is a card that represents a word. Logograph sentences are constructed by overlapping 2 or 3 cards. To correctly translate each sentence, Ss must (1) remember the word each card represents and (2) respond to the sentence as a whole rather than to each word separately.) In the remaining condition, Ss were simply asked by E to perform each of the actions. The number of correct responses each S made was recorded. **Results:** No sex differences.

Experiment II: **Subjects:** $N = 20$; 6 yrs. **Measures:** Ss were asked to translate logograph sentences into actions. **Results:** No sex differences were found in number of correct responses.

Halverson, C. F. Personal communication, 1971.

Subjects: $N = 45$; 2½ yrs (nursery school). **Measures:** Data were obtained from an activity recorder worn by each S during a 2½-hour session of free play with his mother. The recorder was also worn by each child every day of a 4-week session in which he played with 4 other children (mixed-sex group). **Results:** There were no sex differences in activity level when Ss were alone. Boys were more active than girls in groups ($p < .05$).

Halverson, C. F., and Waldrop, M. F. Maternal behavior toward own and other preschool children: the problem of "ownness." *Child Development,* 1970, *41,* 839–45.

Subjects: $N = 42$; mothers of 2½-year-old children. **Measures:** Each mother was asked to administer 6 different tasks to her child and 1 other same-sexed child; 4 tasks were taken from the Stanford-Binet: from board, block stacking, bead stringing, and picture vocabulary. Mother also attempted to get the child to tell a story and to place marbles in designated holes of a box; 2 coders categorized tape-recordings of maternal verbalizations into 4 categories: (a) positive, encouraging statements, (b) negative, controlling statements, (c) total words, and (d) total statements. Coders also recorded time children spent vocalizing. **Results:** Mothers talked more with girls than with boys (in terms of both total words and total statements). Girls spent more time talking than boys did.

Halverson, C. F., and Waldrop, M. F. The relations of mechanically recorded activity level to varieties of preschool play behavior. *Child Development,* 1973, *44,* 678–81.
    Subjects: $N = 58$; 2½ yrs (white, middle SES). **Measures:** Activity level of each S was assessed by means of mechanical recorders attached to his jacket or shirt during outdoor free play. **Results:** Boys were more active than girls ($p < .001$).

Hamilton, M. L. Reward and punishment in child discrimination learning. *Developmental Psychology,* 1969, *1,* 735–38.
    Subjects: $N = 24$; 3–5 yrs (nursery school). **Measures:** Scores from a social desirability scale were used to divide Ss into 6 levels. Ss at each level were assigned to 1 of 4 experimental conditions in 2-alternative discrimination tasks. Ss were asked to play a marble game. For half the Ss, E rewarded choosing the nonpreferred hole; for the other half, E punished choosing the preferred hole. Half of Ss were informed that E's nonreaction did not consistently follow either the correct or incorrect response. **Results:** No sex differences.

Hamilton, M. L. Vicarious reinforcement effects on extinction. *J. Experimental Child Psychology,* 1970, *9,* 108–14.
    Subjects: $N = 28$; 3–4 yrs. **Measures:** Ss received either direct or vicarious (watching 6-year-old male model), continuous or partial reinforcement during the acquisition stage of a marble-dropping task. During the extinction stage, Ss were instructed to play the game as long as they wanted to. A week later, extinction procedure was administered again. **Results:** No sex differences.

Hamilton, M. L. Response to social reinforcement rates as a function of reinforcement history. *Developmental Psychology,* 1972, *6,* 180 (brief report).
    Subjects: $N = 24$; 4 yrs. **Measures:** Social reinforcements Ss received from adults in 12 3-minute free-play observations were recorded. Ss were divided into high- and low-reinforcement standard groups, with half of each group receiving 33% reinforcement for nonpreferred choice during the discrimination learning task and the other half receiving 100% reinforcement. **Results:** No sex differences.

Hamilton, M. L. Imitative behavior and expressive ability in facial expression of emotion. *Developmental Psychology,* 1973, *8,* 138 (brief report and personal communication).
    Subjects: $N = 72$; 3–4, 7, 10 yrs. **Measures:** Ss matched pictures of facial expressions, imitated each expression, and saw films portraying happiness and sadness. Ss' happy and sad expressions during films were recorded. **Results:** No sex differences.

Hamm, H., and Hoving, K. L. Conformity of children in an ambiguous perceptual situation. *Child Development,* 1969, *40,* 773–84.
    Subjects: $N = 192$; 7, 10, 13 yrs. **Measures:** An autokinetic stimulus was presented to same-sex triads for a series of 45 trials. For the first 15 trials, Ss' judgments of both latency and magnitude of perceived movement of the stimulus were made privately. For the last 30 trials, Ss made their judgments publicly. The extent to which the Ss in each triad agreed with each other's judgments was used as a measure of conformity. **Results:** At ages 7 and 10, girls conformed to a greater degree than boys. At age 13, no sex differences were found.

Hamm, N. H. A partial test of a social learning theory of children's conformity. *J. Experimental Child Psychology,* 1970, *9,* 29–42.
    Subjects: $N = 216$; 7, 10, 13 yrs. **Measures:** On day 1, Ss performed perceptual discrimination judgments (judging which projected figures contained the most dots) on ambiguous, unambiguous, and partially ambiguous stimuli, with either no social influences on judgments, social influence (result of peers' judgments), or partial social influence (result of 1 peer's judgment before making own decision, and one peer result afterward). On day 2 (3 weeks later), Ss viewed filmed male and female peer models perform the same task (in competition) and be either rewarded or not. A third group of Ss saw no film. Afterward, Ss performed the task.

Results: There were no overall sex differences in conformity on day 1, but girls conformed more than boys did on the unambiguous task. No sex differences were found in change in conformity from day 1 to day 2.

Hanlon, C. C. The effects of social isolation and characteristics of the model on accent imitation in fourth grade children. *J. Experimental Child Psychology*, 1971, *11*, 322–36.
Subjects: $N = 52$; 9 yrs. Measures: After either social isolation (20 minutes alone before the experimental procedure) or nonisolation (proceeding directly to the experimental situation from the classroom), American-speaking Ss learned the speaking role of either a helpless or nurturant British character in a puppet play by hearing a taped British male (if boy) or female (if girl) say lines for Ss to repeat. Accent imitation was measured by the frequency of phonetic shifts from pre-exposure reading of the script to 2 post-exposure repetitions. Results: No overall sex differences weer found in accent imitation, but girls imitated the model's accent more after isolation, whereas boys imitated more when taken directly from the classroom to the experimental condition.

Hannah, R., Storm, T., and Caird, W. K. Sex differences and relationship among neuroticism, extraversion, and expressed fears. *Perceptual & Motor Skills*, 1965, *20*, 1214–16.
Subjects: $N = 1,958$; 18–19 yrs (college). Measures: The Maudsley Personality Inventory (MPI) and the Fear Survey Schedule (FSS) were administered to Ss. On the MPI, Ss were scored for neuroticism (N) and extraversion (E). On the FSS, Ss rated each of the 73 items for its emotion-producing effect. Ss' ratings were added together to yield a total fear (F) score. The number of items checked as "very disturbing" was also recorded. Results: Women received higher N and F scores and checked more items as "very disturbing" than men did.

Hapkiewicz, W. G., and Roden, A. H. The effect of aggressive cartoons on children's interpersonal play. *Child Development*, 1971, *42*, 1583–85.
Subjects: $N = 60$; 7 yrs. Measures: Ss viewed an aggressive cartoon, a nonaggressive cartoon, or no cartoon. Same-sex pairs were then presented with a peep show in which sharing was necessary in order to see. Aggression (pushing, grabbing, hand over hole) and sharing were measured. Results: (1) Boys were more aggressive than girls. (2) Overall, boys shared more than girls. After viewing the aggressive film, boys showed a nonsignificant tendency to share less than girls.

Harmatz, M. G. Verbal conditioning and change on personality measures. *J. Personality & Social Psychology*, 1967, *5*, 175–85.
Subjects: $N = 50$; 18–21 yrs (college). Measures: Ss rated positive, negative, and neutral self-references on a 9-point true-untrue scale. Ss were reinforced for placing either positive or negative self-references toward the true end of the scale. Ss were also either reinforced or not reinforced for placing either negative or positive self-references toward the false end of the scale. Before and after conditioning, Ss completed the semantic differential, the Q sort, and 5 personality scales: Test Anxiety (TA), General Anxiety (GA), Hostility (H), Lack of Protection (LP), and Defensiveness (D). Results: (1) No sex differences were found in Ss' ratings of positive or negative self-references. (2) For each of the personality measures, Ss' initial scores were compared with their post-conditioning scores: (a) No sex differences were found on the semantic differential. (b) No sex differences were found in TA, GA, LP, or D. (c) Mean increase in Q Sort Adjustment Scores was greater for men than for women ($p < .025$). (d) On the pretest, women scored higher on the H scale than men ($p < .005$).

Harris, G. J., and Burke, D. The effects of grouping on short-term serial recall of digits by children: developmental trends. *Child Development*, 1972, *43*, 710–16.
Subjects: $N = 90$; 7, 9, 11 yrs. Measures: Ss were presented with digits that were either ungrouped, spatially grouped, or spatially and temporally grouped. Recall was measured in writing. Results: No sex differences.

Harris, L. The effects of relative novelty on children's choice behavior. *J. Experimental Child Psychology*, 1965, *2*, 297–305.
Subjects: $N = 64$; 3–5 yrs. Measures: Ss were given 1-minute familiarization trials with 2 identical toys of different colors from each of 4 different sets of toys. Ss chose 1 of 2 toys on each trial, and on every fifth trial, Ss could choose one or both of the familiarization toys or a novel toy, either damaged or undamaged; the choice was either 1 out of 3 toys or 2 familiar toys vs. 1 novel toy. All 4 combinations of the factors of damage and kind-of-choice offered were used to measure children's preferences for novelty. Results: (1) There were no sex dif-

ferences in toy choice alternation. (2) Among younger Ss, girls chose the novel toy more frequently than boys did; among older Ss, no sex differences were found.

Harris, L. Looks by preschoolers at the experimenter in a choice-of-toys game: effects of experimenter and age of child. *J. Experimental Child Psychology*, 1968, *6*, 493–500.
Subjects: $N = 40$; 3–5 yrs. Measures: Ss chose toys (locomotives, ladybugs, dump trucks, and tops) in the presence of a familiar male or female E. Looking at E was measured. Results: (1) The female E was looked at by all Ss more than the male E was. (2) There were no effects of sex of S.

Harris, L., Schaller, M. J., and Mitler, M. M. The effects of stimulus type on performance in a color-form sorting task with preschool, kindergarten, first-grade and third-grade children. *Child Development*, 1970, *41*, 177–91.
Subjects: $N = 100$; 5–8 yrs. Measures: Ss chose which of 2 pictures was more like a third (which matched in form or color). Geometric and scrambled figures were used. Results: No sex differences.

Harris, L. J., and Strommen, E. A. The role of front-back features in children's "front," "back," and "beside" placements of objects. *Merrill-Palmer Quarterly*, 1972, *18*, 259–71.
Subjects: $N = 80$; 4–7 yrs. Measures: Ss made a series of "in front," "in back," and "beside" placements of common objects. Of the 7 pairs of objects that were used, 4 pairs had front-back features and 3 pairs did not. In the object-referent condition, E placed 1 member of a pair of objects in front of the Ss and then asked them to place the other member of the pair either behind, beside, or in front of the first member. In the self-referent condition, E gave Ss an object and then asked them to place it either behind, beside, or in front of themselves. After each trial, the location and orientation of Ss' placements were recorded. Results: No sex differences were reported.

Harris, M. B. Reciprocity and generosity: some determinants of sharing in children. *Child Development*, 1970, *41*, 313–28.
Subjects: $N = 168$; 9, 10 yrs. Measures: S played a chance game with a model in which tokens were dispensed when either player was "lucky." The model always got more tokens than S. In 5 of 6 conditions the model had the opportunity to share her tokens and did so with the child or with the "charity" or refused to share. In the sixth condition there was no chance to share. Reinforcement for sharing was varied across conditions. The model and S played the game again, this time S always won more chips. The model left the room before dividing the chips. The measure of sharing was what S did with the chips. Results: No sex differences.

Harris, M. B., and Hassemer, W. G. Some factors affecting the complexity of children's sentences: the effects of modeling, age, sex and bilingualism. *J. Experimental Child Psychology*, 1972, *13*, 447–55.
Subjects: $N = 48$; 7, 9 yrs (two-thirds of Ss bilingual). Measures: Ss composed sentences about pictures before and after hearing models (speaking Spanish to half of the bilingual Ss and English to all others) compose simple and complex sentences. Scored for number of words and complexity. Results: No sex differences.

Harris, S., and Braun, J. R. Self-esteem and racial preference in black children. *Proceedings of the 79th Annual Convention of the APA*, 1971, *8*, 259–60.
Subjects: $N = 60$; 7–8 yrs (black). Measures: Ss were given a black and a white puppet and asked to choose (a) the puppet they would like to play with, (b) the puppet that is a nice puppet, (c) the puppet that is a nice color, and (d) the puppet that looks bad. Ss were also given the Piers-Harris Children's Self-Concept Test. Results: No sex differences.

Harrison, A., and Nadelman, L. Conceptual tempo and inhibition of movement in black preschool children. *Child Development*, 1972, *43*, 657–68.
Subjects: $N = 50$; 4, 5 yrs (black, middle SES). Measures: (1) Matching Familiar Figures Test, (2) Peabody Picture Vocabulary Test, (3) Draw a Line Slowly Test, (4) Walk Slowly Test. Results: (1) When requested to go slowly on the 2 motor-inhibition tests, girls performed more slowly and showed greater change in relationship to their normal speed than boys. (2) On the MFF test, girls exhibited longer response latencies and committed fewer errors than boys. (3) No sex differences were found on the PPVT.

Harrison, C. W., Rawls, J. R., and Rawls, D. J. Differences between leaders and nonleaders in six- to eleven-year-old children. *J. Social Psychology*, 1971, *84*, 269–72.

Subjects: $N = 649$; 6–11 yrs. **Measures:** Teachers rated how often each child in their classrooms had been chosen as leader by his peers. **Results:** No sex differences.

Harter, S. Discrimination learning set in children as a function of IQ and MA. *J. Experimental Child Psychology*, 1965, *2*, 31–43.
Subjects: $N = 81$; 3–14 yrs (normals, retardates). **Measures:** Ss were given a series of 4-trial object-discrimination problems each day until they reached the learning criterion. **Results:** No sex differences.

Harter, S. Mental age, IQ, and motivational factors in the discrimination learning set performance of normal and retarded children. *J. Experimental Child Psychology*, 1967, *5*, 123–41.
Subjects: $N = 160$; mental ages: 5½, 8½ yrs. **Measures:** Until they reached criterion, Ss were tested each day on a series of 4-trial object-discrimination problems. In the standard condition, E stood behind a one-way screen. In the social condition, each S was given a preliminary success experience, E and S were face to face during the discrimination task, and S's correct choices were praised by E. The number of problems to criterion was the response measure. **Results:** No sex differences.

Harter, S., and Zigler, E. Effects of rate of stimulus presentation and penalty conditions on the discrimination learning of normal and retarded children. *Developmental Psychology*, 1972, *6*, 85–91.
Subjects: $N = 80$; 6 yrs (normal), 13–15 yrs (retarded): mental age 7 yrs. **Measures:** Ss performed a 2-choice discrimination learning problem with 2 rates of stimulus presentation and 2 reinforcement conditions (reward only or reward plus penalty). **Results:** No sex differences.

Harter, S., Brown, L., and Zigler, E. The discrimination learning of normal and retarded children as a function of penalty conditions and etiology of the retarded. *Child Development*, 1971a, *42*, 517–36.
Subjects: $N = 210$; 6, 7 yrs (normal, cultural-familial retardates, mental retardates). **Measures:** Ss performed a 2-choice size-discrimination task. Penalty and reward conditions were varied across groups. **Results:** No sex differences.

Harter, S., Shultz, R. R., and Blum, B. Smiling in children as a function of their sense of mastery. *J. Experimental Child Psychology*, 1971b, *12*, 396–404.
Subjects: $N = 41$; 4, 8 yrs. **Measures:** 40 items were preselected from the Peabody Picture Vocabulary Test to represent 4 levels of difficulty: very easy, moderately difficult, very difficult, and impossible. These items were then administered to Ss; Ss' spontanous smiling responses were recorded. **Results:** No main sex differences were found in the magnitude of Ss' smiling responses.

Hartig, M., and Kanfer, F. H. The role of verbal self-instructions in children's resistance to temptation. *J. Personality & Social Psychology*, 1973, *25*, 259–67.
Subjects: $N = 261$; 3–7 yrs. **Measures:** Ss were seated with their backs to attractive toys. As E left the room for a few minutes, he instructed Ss not to look at the toys until his return. Ss were also told to verbalize either the positive consequences for nontransgression, the negative consequences for transgression, E's instructions, or a nursery rhyme. Response measures were (1) percentage of Ss who turned around within 1 minute after E left, percentage of Ss who turned around after 1 minute elapsed but before E returned, and percentage of Ss who did not turn around at all, (2) number of Ss who verbalized the self-instructions, and (3) number of Ss who denied transgressing in a postexperimental interview. **Results:** No sex differences.

Hartmann, D. P., Gelfand, D. M., Courtney, R. J., Jr., and Malouf, R. E. Successive presentation of elements of the Mueller-Lyer Figure and CA, MA, and IQ: an age extension and unsuccessful replication. *Child Development*, 1972, *43*, 1060–66.
Subjects: $N = 50$; 6–9 yrs. **Measures:** Ss made comparative decisions about 21 variations of the Mueller-Lyer figure on a tachistoscope. **Results:** No sex differences.

Hartup, W. W. Some correlates of parental imitation in young children. *Child Development*, 1962, *33*, 85–96.
Subjects: $N = 63$; 3–5 yrs. **Measures:** A forced-choice doll play interview was used to determine whether Ss preferred to imitate their like-sex parent more than their opposite-sex parent.

The It Scale for Children (ITSC) was also administered. **Results:** (1) Both sexes preferred to imitate the like-sex parent doll. No sex differences were found in the proportion of like-sex choices. (2) On the ITSC, boys obtained more masculine scores than girls.

Hartup, W. W., and Zook, E. A. Sex-role preferences in three- and four-year-old children. *J. Consulting Psychology*, 1960, *24*, 420–26.
> **Subjects:** N = 161; 3–4 yrs. **Measures:** It Scale for Children. **Results:** Boys received more masculine scores than girls did (p < .001).

Haskett, G. J. Modification of peer preferences of first-grade children. *Developmental Psychology*, 1971, *4*, 429–33.
> **Subjects:** N = 106; 6 yrs. **Measures:** Ss ranked photographs of classmates from most liked to least liked friend, and from first-best to last-best friend. They were then matched with an opposite- or same-sex peer who was neither extremely liked nor disliked. In the 3 following days, pairs either worked cooperatively on a building task, sat together but worked separately (contiguity), or sat separately and worked separately (controls). Post-treatment peer preference was measured. **Results:** (1) Almost all Ss chose as their best friend a child of the same sex; (2) no sex differences were found in change in liking for partner.

Hass, R. G., and Linder, D. E. Counterargument availability and the effects of message structure on persuasion. *J. Personality & Social Psychology*, 1972, *23*, 219–33.
> **Subjects:** N = 150; 18–21 yrs (college). **Measures:** Ss were asked to determine the guilt or innocence of a defendant on the basis of a written summary of the evidence presented at a bigamy trial. **Results:** No sex differences.

Hatfield, J. S., Ferguson, L. R., and Alpert, R. Mother-child interaction and the socialization process. *Child Development*, 1967, *38*, 365–414.
> **Subjects:** N = 40; 4–5 yrs and mothers (22–41 yrs). **Measures:** During the first half-hour session, the mother completed a questionnaire while the child played with crayons and paper. Afterward, the mother was asked to structure a telephone game in which the child was encouraged to role-play himself, a mother, a father, a deviant same-sex child, and a child of the opposite sex. During the second session, the mother was asked to have her child work with puzzles. She could help him if she wished. The child also played a fishing game in which the mother could participate. After the fishing game, the mother was asked to clean the room. Cleaning equipment was offered to both the mother and the child. **Results:** (1) Boys were rated higher than girls on verbal aggression and fantasy aggression. While playing the role of the deviant child in the telephone game, boys were more tense than girls. No sex differences were found in dependency; independence; warmth toward mother; achievement standards; disobedience; direct or indirect aggression to mother; indirectness of aggression to mother; outer-directed physical aggression; self-aggression; involvement in water play aside from fishing; tension (overall rating), activity level; willingness to adopt self-role; willingness to adopt the roles of mother, father, deviant child, and child of opposite sex; interest in adult role behavior; resistance toward adult role behavior; concern with sex appropriateness; confession (i.e. the extent to which Ss confessed to wrongdoing while playing the role of the deviant child); fixing (i.e. the extent to which Ss tried to make amends for the deviation). (2) Boys received more achievement pressure from their mothers than girls did. Mothers of girls were more concerned with water play during the fishing game than mothers of boys. No differences were found between boys' and girls' mothers in pressure for independence; restriction of independence; rewarding of independence; punishment of independence; directiveness, rewarding of dependency; punishment of dependency; warmth toward child; responsiveness to child (questionnaire situation); involvement and enjoyment (telephone game); involvement and enjoyment (fishing game); pressure for obedience; punishment of aggression; hostility toward child; rewarding of achievement; punishment of low achievement; concern with neatness and orderliness; concern with cleaning up (fishing game); pressure and reward for adult role behavior; restriction and punishment of adult role behavior; concern with sex appropriateness; use of models; use of reasoning.

Haugan, G. M., and McIntire, R. W. Comparisons of vocal imitation, tactile stimulation, and food as reinforcers for infant vocalizations. *Developmental Psychology*, 1972, *6*, 201–9.
> **Subjects:** N = 24; 3–6 mos. **Measures:** Rates of infant vocalizations were measured under 3 types of reinforcement (adult imitation, food, tactile), in 3 experimental stages (baseline, conditioning, extinction). **Results:** (1) There were no main sex differences in vocalizations before reinforcement. More boys than girls vocalized during baseline in the vocal and tactile

reinforcement groups, before reinforcement was given; more girls than boys vocalized in the food group, before reinforcement was given ($p < .05$). (2) There were no sex differences between reinforcement groups during conditioning or extinction. (3) Examination of group differences within reinforcement showed a higher vocal rate for boys than for girls in the vocal reinforcement group during conditioning and extinction ($p < .05$). (4) During extinction, girls in the tactile reinforcement group had higher vocal rates than boys ($p < .05$).

Havighurst, R. J., and Hilkevitch, R. R. The intelligence of Indian children as measured by a performance scale. *J. Abnormal & Social Psychology*, 1944, 39, 419–33.
Subjects: $N = 670$; 6–15 yrs (Navaho, Hopi, Zuni, Zia, Pappago, and Sioux Indian tribes). Measures: A shortened form of the Arthur Point Performance Scale. Results: In 10 of 11 communities, no sex differences were found. In one community, boys scored higher than girls.

Hawkins, R. P. Learning of peripheral content in films: a developmental study. *Child Development*, 1973, 44, 214–17.
Subjects: $N = 306$; 8, 10, 12, 14 yrs (parochial school). Measures: Ss viewed 1 of 2 films, a children's Western or an adult Western. Afterward, they answered questions pertaining to central or peripheral information. Results: (1) There were no sex differences on peripheral learning. (2) On central learning, girls did better than boys at ages 8, 10, and 14; boys did better than girls at age 12. (3) On central learning, boys did better than girls on the adult film ($p < .05$).

Heal, L. The role of cue value, cue novelty, and overtraining in the discrimination shift performance of retardates and normal children of comparable discrimination ability. *J. Experimental Child Psychology*, 1966, 4, 126–42.
Subjects: $N = 48$; 5 yrs (normal), adult (retardate). Measures: Ss were given 4 2-stage discrimination-learning problems. In stage 1, 1 dimension (either form or color) was relevant whereas the other was irrelevant. In stage 2, the relevant dimension was either changed (extradimensional shift) or not changed (intradimensional reversal). The performance measure was the number of errors Ss made in both stages of problems 3 and 4. Results: No sex differences.

Hebble, P. W. The development of elementary school children's judgment of intent. *Child Development*, 1971, 42, 1203–15.
Subjects: $N = 944$; 6–11 yrs. Measures: Ss read 4 variations of 7 stories involving good intent–light damage, good intent–heavy damage, bad intent–light damage, and bad intent–heavy damage. Ss rated the characters' "badness." Results: No sex differences.

Hebda, M. E., Peterson, R. A., and Miller, L. K. Aggression anxiety, perception of aggressive cues, and expected retaliation. *Developmental Psychology*, 1972, 7, 85 (brief report).
Subjects: $N = 31$; 8 yrs. Measures: Ss were presented with 30 pictures of angry, neutral, and friendly male and female faces. Instructions were given to rate each stimulus on an anger-friendliness dimension and on the intensity of retaliation expected following a hypothetical act by the S. Results: No sex differences were found.

Hecox, K. E., and Hagen, J. W. Estimates and estimate-based inferences in young children. *J. Experimental Child Psychology*, 1971, 11, 106–23.
Subjects: $N = 52$; 5–7 yrs. Measures: Ss saw visual field slides with differing proportions of red and black dots. Their task was to produce as many red and black dots on the response apparatus screen (by moving a lever to change proportions) as were projected on the display screen. Results: No sex differences.

Heider, E. R. "Focal" color areas and the development of color names. *Developmental Psychology*, 1971, 4, 447–55.
EXPERIMENT I: Subjects: $N = 24$; 3 yrs. Measures: S made 8 free color choices from each of 2 arrays of Munsell color chips of focal colors (areas of color space previously found with adults to be most exemplary of basic color names in many languages). Each focal color was embedded in 2 array types: all brightnesses of same hue as the focal chip (maximum saturation) and all lesser saturations of the same hue and value as the focal chip. Results: No sex differences.
EXPERIMENT II: Subjects: $N = 20$; 4 yrs. Measures: Ss were asked to match comparison chips of focal and nonfocal colors with color chips in 1 of 2 arrays differing in brightness and hue. Results: Girls were more accurate in overall matching than boys. There were no sex differences in relative accuracy of matching focal and nonfocal colors.

EXPERIMENT III: **Subjects:** $N = 27$; 3–4 yrs. **Measures:** Ss were asked to point to basic colors of chips when the color name was verbalized by E. Stimuli were chips of the same values, but different hues. **Results:** No sex differences.

Heilbrun, A. B., Harrell, S. N., Gillard, B. J. Perceived maternal child-rearing patterns and the effects of social nonreaction upon achievement motivation. *Child Development*, 1967, *38*, 267–81.

    Subjects: $N = 237$; 18–21 yrs (college). **Measures:** (1) Maternal child-rearing behavior was assessed by the S's impression of how his mother would answer the Parent Attitude Research Instrument; 16 scales defined perceived maternal control for males, 13 scales defined perceived maternal control for females. Ss' perception of maternal nurturance was estimated from ratings on the Parent-Child Interaction Rating Scales. (2) The achievement motivation task was a variation of a visual discrimination task in which Ss were asked to match test angles with 1 of 5 standards, none of which was actually correct. For the first trial, Ss were informed of high school students' performances, and were asked to indicate their level of aspiration under 3 reinforcement conditions (success, failure, or nonreaction). At the end of the second trial, Ss were asked to estimate their performance (without feed-back). Ss were asked to estimate their performance on the third trial; however, a third trial was never run. (3) Equal numbers of male and female Es for each of 3 reinforcement conditions were assigned; 4 child-rearing groups were high control/high nurturant (overprotected), high control/low nurturant (rejected), low control/high nurturant (accepted), and low control/low nurturant (ignored). **Results:** No main sex differences. Among Ss in the accepted and ignored groups who experienced failure on trial 1, the difference between level of aspiration prior to trial 3 and level of performance during trial 1 was greater for men than women.

Hendry, L. S., and Kessen, W. Oral behavior of newborn infants as a function of age and time since feeding. *Child Development*, 1964, *35*, 201–8.

    Subjects: $N = 19$; 1–3 days. **Measures:** Ss were observed feeding at 23 and 71 hours of age. Measures were taken of total duration and average length of contact between hand and mouth, total duration of mouthing (defined as any sucking-like movement), and total duration of contact between hand and mouth accompanied by mouthing (hand-sucking). **Results:** (1) Between 23 and 71 hours old, duration of hand-to-mouth contact and hand-sucking increased for boys but decreased for girls ($p < .05$, $p < .05$). No sex differences were found on these 2 measures at age 23 hours. (2) No sex differences were found in duration of mouthing or in average length of contact between hand and mouth.

Herbert, E. W., Gelfand, D. M., and Hartmann, D. P. Imitation and self-esteem as determinants of self-critical behavior. *Child Development*, 1969, *40*, 421–30.

    Subjects: $N = 40$; 9 yrs. **Measures:** Ss completed the P. S. Sears Self Concept Inventory and the Bledsoe-Garrison Self Concept Inventory. Ss played a bowling game with preselected scores, with or without a same-sex model (opposite-sex adult served as observer). Ss played the game by themselves, called out their own scores, and rated their own performances. **Results:** (1) When Ss were equated for self-esteem, there were no sex differences in imposing fines on self, or in self-criticism. (2) Girls had lower self-esteem ratings than boys on the Sears SCI ($p < .01$), and rated their own performance lower.

Herder, E. R. Style and accuracy of verbal communications within and between social classes. *J. Personality & Social Psychology*, 1971, *18*, 33–47.

    EXPERIMENT I: **Subjects:** $N = 143$; 10 yrs (white, low and middle SES; black, low SES). **Measures:** Ss were asked to encode (describe) abstract and face stimuli presented alongside sets of similar items, so that other children would be able to pick out the target items at a later date. Ss' statements were classified as either inferential or descriptive, referring to either all or part of the stimulus. **Results:** No sex differences.

    EXPERIMENT II: **Subjects:** $N = 141$; 10 yrs (same as Experiment I). **Measures:** Ss were recalled after several weeks to decode examples of descriptions given by each SES and sex of subject. **Results:** No sex differences.

Hermans, H. J., ter Laak, J. J., and Maes, P. C. Achievement motivation and fear of failure in family and school. *Developmental Psychology*, 1972, *6*, 520–28.

    Subjects: $N = 40$; 9–10 yrs (Dutch). **Measures:** After testing a group of 445 children, 20 boys and 20 girls were selected on the basis of their extreme scores on the achievement-motivation and debilitating-anxiety scales of the Prestatie Motivatie Test voor Kinderen (Achievement Motivation Test for Children). There were 4 groups of Ss in all: (1) high-achievement-motivated—high-debilitating-anxiety; (2) high-achievement-motivated—low-debilitating-anxiety; (3) low-achievement-motivated—high-debilitating-anxiety; and (4) low-achievement-motivated—low-debilitating-anxiety. (1) Each S performed 4 tasks at home in the presence of his parents. The following parental behaviors were recorded: (a) gives specific help; (b) gives nonspecific help; (c) gives encouragement; (d) gives positive-task-oriented reinforcement; (e) gives negative-task-oriented reinforcement; (f) gives positive-person-oriented reinforcement; (g) gives negative-person-oriented reinforcement; (h) withholds reinforcement after a correct response; (i) shows signs of good mood and enthusiasm; (j) exhibits negative expressions of tension, shows signs of irritation; (k) does not react when the child shows signs of insecurity. The following behaviors were recorded for children: (a) asks parents for help; (b) refuses parental help; (c) shows signs of good mood and enthusiasm; (d) exhibits negative expressions of tension, shows signs of irritation. Prior to 2 of the tasks, parents recorded what they expected their child's performance to be. (2) Ratings of Ss' behavior in task situations were obtained from their classroom teachers. The items on which teachers made their ratings pertained to social dependence, goal setting, attention, personal responsibility, and persistence. **Results:** (1) Parents of boys exhibited more signs of good mood and enthusiasm than parents of girls ($p < .05$). No main sex differences were found on any other measure. (2) Among low-debilitating-anxiety Ss, girls received more specific help than boys did ($p < .05$). (3) High-debilitating-anxiety girls received a relatively low frequency of positive-task-oriented reinforcements in comparison with other groups ($p < .05$). (4) There were no sex differences found in teachers' ratings.

Herriot, P. The comprehension of syntax. *Child Development*, 1968, 39, 273–82.
   Subjects: $N = 1,176$; 5–9 yrs. **Measures:** Ss were initially presented with 4 cards. On each were line drawings of either a boy and a girl or weird creatures. After E uttered a passive or an active sentence, Ss were asked to select the card that best fit the sentence. The amount of semantic content was varied by substituting nonsense words into either none, some, or all of the content word spaces of the sentence frame. **Results:** No sex differences were found in sentence comprehension, as assessed by choice of cards.

Herriot, P. The comprehension of tense in young children. *Child Development*, 1969, 40, 103–10.
   Subjects: $N = 24$; 36–48 mos. **Measures:** E showed Ss 3 toys, in moving or resting states. For each set of actions, E asked Ss questions about which toy would move, using various tenses. Ss responded to each question to indicate their understanding of the tense employed. **Results:** No sex differences.

Hertzig, M. E., Birch, M. G., Thomas, A., and Mendez, O. A. Class and ethnic differences in the responsiveness of preschool children to cognitive demands. *Monographs of the Society for Research in Child Development*, 1968, 33, 117.
   Subjects: $N = 176$; 3 yrs (U.S., middle SES; Puerto Rican, low SES). **Measures:** Ss were given Form L-M of the Stanford-Binet. During the administration of the test, Ss' responses to E's demands for cognitive performance were classified into 2 categories: work (Ss attempted to do what was asked of them) and nonwork (Ss failed to perform the task presented). Work responses (both verbal and nonverbal) were further classified according to whether or not they were limited to the defined requirements of the task. Verbal nonwork responses were also classified into 4 categories: (1) negation; (2) motor substitution (task-irrelevant physical activity); (3) motor requests for aid; (4) passive behavior (e.g. sitting still, staring straight ahead). **Results:** (1) Among American Ss, girls expressed passively a greater proportion of their nonverbal, non-work responses than boys ($p < .05$). No sex differences were found in other response categories, or in the proportion of (a) demands initially responded to with a work response; (b) initial work responses followed by a non-work response; (c) initial non-work responses followed by a work response. (2) In the Puerto Rican sample, girls had a higher proportion than boys of work responses, of demands initially responded to with a work response, and of passive, nonverbal, non-work responses ($p < .05$, $p < .05$, $p < .05$). Boys had a higher proportion than girls of initial work responses followed by a non-work response, and of nonverbal, non-work responses expressed as substitution ($p < .05$, $p < .001$). No other sex differences were found.

Hess, A. L., and Bradshaw, H. L. Positiveness of self-concept and ideal self as a function of age. *J. Genetic Psychology*, 1970, 117, 57–67.
   Subjects: $N = 175$; 16–18, 18–20, 35–50, 55–60 yrs. **Measures:** Gough's Adjective Check List. **Results:** No sex differences were found in either self-concept or ideal self.

Hetherington, E. M., and Frankie, G. Effects of parental dominance, warmth, and conflict on imitation in children. *J. Personality & Social Psychology*, 1967, 6, 119–25.
Subjects: N = 160; 4–6 yrs and parents. Measures: At the beginning of the study, interviews were conducted with Ss' parents. On the basis of their answers to questions concerning how they would handle problem situations involving their child, each parent was rated on a 6-point warmth-hostility scale. On the basis of their behavior during the interview, parents were classified as to whether the father or mother or neither was the more dominant figure. Ss then observed each of their parents perform a variety of behaviors. The frequency of Ss' subsequent imitative behavior was recorded. Results: (1) No main sex differences were found. (2) Boys imitated their fathers more than their mothers; girls imitated their mothers more than their fathers ($p < .01$). (3) In mother-dominant families, both sexes imitated their mothers more than their fathers. In father-dominant families, boys imitated their fathers more than girls did; girls imitated their mothers more than boys did. (4) Parents who were rated high on warmth were imitated by both sexes more than parents rated low in warmth. Girls imitated mothers high in warmth more than boys did; boys imitated mothers low in warmth more than girls did ($p < .05$).

Hicks, B. J., and Nicholson, R. W. Need-for-approval and peer presence in goal setting. *Perceptual & Motor Skills*, 1966, 23, 1336.
Subjects: N = 27; 18–21 yrs (college). Measures: Before each of 5 throws in a dart game, Ss were given 1 of 3 choices of distances to shoot from (6 feet, 9 feet, or 14 feet). Results: No sex differences were found in Ss' choices.

Hicks, D. J. Effects of observer's sanctions and adult presence on imitative aggression. *Child Development*, 1968, 39, 303–9.
Subjects: N = 84; 5–8 yrs. Measures: Ss were divided equally by sex into 4 experimental groups and 2 control groups. All Ss viewed a 5-minute film of a male adult model exhibiting aggressive behavior to toys. An adult male E in the room made positive or negative comments about the filmed model's actions (no comments for the control group). The Ss went to an experimental room (half being accompanied by E), where they were presented with aggressive and nonaggressive toys; 2 judges scored aggressive and nonaggressive behaviors, imitative and nonimitative, for 15 minutes. Results: Boys performed more imitative aggression than girls ($p < .001$).

Hicks, R. A., Reaney, T., and Hill, L. Effects of pupil size and facial angle on preference for photographs of a young woman. *Perceptual & Motor Skills*, 1967, 24, 388–90.
Subjects: N = 40; 18–21 yrs (college). Measures: Ss rated photographs, in which pupil size and facial angle were manipulated. Results: Women preferred small pupil more than men did.

Hildebrandt, D. E., Feldman, S. E., and Ditrichs, R. A. Rules, models, and self-reinforcement in children. *J. Personality & Social Psychology*, 1973, 25, 1–5.
Subjects: N = 96; 7–9 yrs. Measures: Ss' self-reinforcement was measured on 3 separate occasions. Ss were initially instructed to reward themselves under stringent or lenient conditions while playing a pre-programmed bowling game. After completing 1 game, Ss were twice exposed to either stringent or lenient self-reinforcing models. After each interruption, Ss played 1 game in the absence of the model. Results: No sex differences.

Hill, A. L., and Burke, D. Apparent visual size as a function of age, intelligence, and a surrounding frame of reference for normal and mentally retarded subjects. *Developmental Psychology*, 1971, 5, 349–56.
Subjects: N = 97; 4–14 yrs (normal), 9–20 yrs (retarded). Measures: Ss were presented with 2 illuminated triangles in an otherwise completely dark room and asked to judge whether the comparison or the standard was larger. In the illusion condition, Ss were equally distant from both stimuli; the frame of reference surrounding the comparison triangle was twice the size of the standard's frame of reference. In the distance control condition, the frame of reference surrounding the comparison triangle was identical in size to the standard's. The constancy control condition was identical to the distance control condition, except that Ss were seated closer to the comparison than to the standard triangle. The illusion control condition was identical to the illusion condition, with 1 exception—the room lights were never turned off. Results: No sex differences.

Hill, D. L., and Walters, R. H. Interaction of sex of subject and dependency-training procedures in a social reinforcement study. *Merrill-Palmer Quarterly*, 1969, 15, 185–98.
Subjects: N = 120; 5–7 yrs. Measures: Ss were randomly assigned to 1 of 6 conditions, each

involving 2 successive 15-minute periods of interaction with a female E. The sessions involved either consistent dependency reinforcement (DR), DR followed by solitary play (SP), DR followed by frustration (F), consistent SP, SP followed by DR, or SP followed by F. Following these treatments, Ss played a marble-dropping game with E. Ss' task was to place marbles into either of 2 holes. Ss were reinforced by E for dropping marbles into the "correct" hole. The degree of conditionability Ss displayed was noted. **Results:** No main effects of sex were found. Among Ss who experienced solitary play followed by frustration, boys conditioned to a greater extent than girls did ($p < .05$).

Hill, K. T. Social reinforcement as a function of test anxiety and success-failure experiences. *Child Development*, 1967, *38*, 723–37.

Subjects: $N = 64$; 7 yrs. Measures: On the basis of their scores on the Test Anxiety Scale for Children, the Lie Scale for Children, and the Defensiveness Scale for Children, Ss were divided by sex into high and low test anxiety groups. Ss first experienced either success on an easy puzzle or failure on an unsolvable one. Ss then performed a marble-sorting task, for which half the Ss were verbally reinforced. **Results:** No main sex differences were found in number of marbles sorted. Boys decreased in responding over the entire experimental period; girls increased in responding during the latter minutes of the task after exhibiting an initial decrease in response rate ($p < .05$).

Hill, K. T., and Dusek, J. B. Children's achievement expectations as a function of social reinforcement, sex of S and test anxiety. *Child Development*, 1969, *40*, 547–57.

Subjects: $N = 96$; 8, 9 yrs. Measures: Selection of Ss was based on scores on the Test Anxiety Scale for Children. Ss' pretraining session involved success, failure, or nonevaluative experiences. For the experimental task (angle-matching) Ss were shown contrived graphs of other children's performances, and their achievement expectation was obtained. Ss received either social reinforcement or no reinforcement. E also obtained post-test achievement expectation from S. **Results:** (1) Girls demonstrated a greater increase in achievement expectation than boys did ($p < .05$). (2) No sex differences were found in initial achievement expectation score.

Hill, K. T., and Moely, B. E. Social reinforcement as a function of task instructions, sex of S, age of S, and baseline performance. *J. Experimental Child Psychology*, 1969, *7*, 153–65.

Subjects: $N = 192$; 6, 7, 9, 10 yrs. Measures: Ss performed a marble-dropping task under test or game instructions. E was neutral or supportive. **Results:** (1) No sex differences were found in baseline scores. (2) Whereas older boys (9–10 yrs) showed little change in response rate following the first minute of play, older girls showed a decrease ($p < .05$). No sex difference was found among younger Ss.

Hill, K. T., and Sarason, S. B. The relation of test anxiety and defensiveness to test and school performance over the elementary-school years. *Monographs of the Society for Research in Child Development*, 1966, *31*, no. 104.

Subjects: $N = 323$; tested at 6, 8, 10 yrs. $N = 347$; tested at 9, 11 yrs. Measures: At each testing, Ss completed the Test Anxiety Scale for Children (TASC), the Lie Scale for Children (LSC), and the Defensiveness Scale for Children (DSC). **Results:** At ages 8, 10, and 11, girls had higher TASC scores than boys. At ages 8, 9, 10, and 11, boys obtained higher LSC and DSC scores than girls.

Hill, K. T., and Watts, G. H. Young children's performance on a two-choice task as a function of social reinforcement, base-line preference, and response strategy. *Developmental Psychology*, 1971, *4*, 487–88.

Subjects: $N = 48$; 4 yrs. Measures: After an initial 25-trial baseline period, Ss performed a 2-choice learning task. Selection of the choice less preferred during baseline was either socially reinforced or not. Response strategies and change in preference were assessed. **Results:** No sex differences.

Hill, S. D. Transfer in discrimination learning. *Child Development*, 1965, *36*, 749–60.

EXPERIMENT I: Subjects: $N = 54$; 4, 6 yrs. Measures: Ss received 2 kinds of training for an oddity problem (object discrimination, or experience with double and single objects as cues but no reinforcement). Ss were asked to "find the candy" that was hidden under the odd of 3 objects, 2 of which were identical. **Results:** No sex differences.

EXPERIMENT II: Subjects: $N = 60$; 9, 12 yrs. Measures: Same as Experiment 1, except color and position cues were introduced. **Results:** No sex differences.

Hilton, I. Differences in the behavior of mothers toward first- and later-born children. *J. Personality & Social Psychology*, 1967, 7, 282–90.

Subjects: $N = 60$; 4 yrs and mothers. **Measures:** Mothers' behavior toward their children was recorded while the children attempted a series of puzzles; it was recorded again later after E had informed them the children had performed either extremely well or extremely poorly on the tasks. **Results:** No differences were found between mothers of boys and mothers of girls in frequency of initiating work on the puzzle, number of task-oriented suggestions, amount of direct help, number of supportive and critical statements, or number of overt expressions of love and/or support (hugs, kisses, etc.).

Hilton, I. R., Lambert, N. W., Murphy, M. J., Epstein, R., and Samsky, J. Three experiments on variations in the conditions of judgments. *Monographs of the Society for Research in Child Development*, 1969, 34.

EXPERIMENT I: **Subjects:** $N = 44$; 18–21 yrs (college). **Measures:** In 16 situations, Ss were asked to judge the likelihood that another person would choose one alternative rather than another (Social Expectation Scale). Each S was told whether each alternative harmed or benefited the chooser (0) and whether it harmed or benefited S. Each S made 3 judgments on each situation: how many people would choose a designated alternative (with only S and the chooser knowing), how many would make that choice privately, and how many would make that choice publicly. Ss' judgment of the likelihood of another's choice involved assessment of 3 motivations: benevolence (desire to help rather than to harm), self-interest (strength of valence to benefit oneself rather than harm oneself), and intensity of a person's desire for equal outcomes. **Results:** There were no overall sex differences in Ss' judgments of the contributions of benevolence, self-interest, and equality of outcome to others' decisions on choice situation made publicly or privately. Boys judged a benevolent choice and a self-interested choice to be far more likely in public than in private; girls did not.

EXPERIMENT II: **Subjects:** $N = 45$; 18–21 yrs (college). **Measures:** Same as Experiment I. Ss were also asked to decide how many boys and girls, respectively, would make particular choices. **Results:** No overall differences by sex of S or sex of "other" making choice, but boys showed no different expectations of boys and girls, whereas girls expected other girls to be less benevolent and more self-interested than boys were.

Hilton, T. L., and Berglund, G. W. Sex differences in mathematics achievement—a longitudinal study. *Educational Testing Service Research Bulletin*, unpublished, 1971.

Subjects: $N = 1,859$; tested at 10, 12, 14, 16 yrs (academic and nonacademic high school programs). **Measures:** The Sequential Test of Educational Progress (STEP) and the School and College Ability Test (SCAT) were given to 10-year-old Ss, who were tested again at ages 12, 14, and 16. The Background and Experience Questionnaire (BEQ) was also administered to Ss at ages 12, 14, and 16. **Results:** (1) On the STEP-Math, there were no sex differences among 10-year-old Ss. In the academic group, boys had higher scores than girls at ages 12, 14, and 16. In the nonacademic group, boys had higher scores than girls at age 16. (2) On the SCAT, academic boys scored higher than girls at age 16. In nonacademic group, girls scored higher than boys at age 10, but boys scored higher than girls at age 16. (3) In both groups, boys read scientific books and magazines more frequently than girls at ages 14 and 16. (The difference in magazine reading was not significant among 14-year-old academic Ss.) (4) More boys than girls found math courses interesting at ages 14 and 16 in the academic group and at age 16 in the nonacademic group. More girls than boys found math courses boring at age 16 in the academic group. (5) More boys than girls thought math courses would be useful in earning a living at ages 14 and 16 in the academic group, and at age 16 in the nonacademic group. (6) In both groups, more boys than girls talked about science with friends and parents at ages 14 and 16. (7) Among 14- and 16-year-old academic Ss, more mothers of boys than mothers of girls felt that a student should continue his education beyond high school. (8) Among 16-year-old academic Ss, more fathers of boys than fathers of girls felt that a student should continue education beyond high school.

Himmelfarb, S. Studies in the perception of ethnic group members: accuracy, response bias, and anti-Semitism. *J. Personality & Social Psychology*, 1966, 4, 347–55.

EXPERIMENT I: **Subjects:** $N = 58$; 18–21 yrs (non-Jewish college). **Measures:** Ss identified individuals in photographs as being either Jewish or non-Jewish. **Results:** No sex differences were found in accuracy scores. Ss were more accurate in identifying males than females as either Jewish or non-Jewish ($p < .01$).

EXPERIMENT II: **Subjects:** $N = 99$; 18–21 yrs (non-Jewish college). **Measures:** Photographs of non-Jewish and Jewish individuals were presented to Ss in pairs. Ss were asked to select either the Jewish or the non-Jewish individual in the pair. **Results:** No sex differences were found in accuracy scores. Ss were more accurate in judging the identity of male photographs than in judging the identity of female photographs.

Hochreich, D. J., and Rotler, J. B. Have college students become less trusting? *J. Personality & Social Psychology*, 1970, *15*, 211–14.

Subjects: $N = 4,605$; 18–21 yrs (college). **Measures:** Interpersonal Trust Scale. **Results:** No sex differences were found in mean scores.

Hoemann, H. W. The development of communication skills in deaf and hearing children. *Child Development*, 1972, *43*, 990–1003.

Subjects: $N = 80$; 8, 11 yrs (deaf, normal). **Measures:** Ss were required to communicate information to peers of the same hearing group. The 3 tasks were (1) describe a variety of pictured referents, (2) describe the referents from the receiver's perspective, and (3) explain the rules of a game. Response measures for the first task were a sending score based on the percentage of messages rated as adequate, a receiving score based on the percentage of messages that resulted in correct choices by the receiver, and an overall accuracy score. The perspective task was evaluated as to which perspective the sender took and whether he communicated this information. Performance on the game task was evaluated according to rules communicated. **Results:** No sex differences.

Hoffman, L. R., and Maier, M. R. Social factors influencing problem solving in women. *J. Personality & Social Psychology*, 1966, *4*, 382–90.

Subjects: $N = 502$; 18–21 yrs (college). **Measures:** The following problem was given to Ss twice: "A man bought a horse for $60, sold it for $70, bought it back for $80, and then sold it for $90. How much money did the man make in the horse business?" Masculine and feminine versions of 8 reasoning problems were also administered. Men answered the problems in the presence of a male E. Women responded in the presence of either a male or a female E, who either did or did not attempt to motivate them to do well on the problems. **Results:** (1) On both administrations of the horse-trading problem, more men than women solved the problem correctly under a male E. No difference was found between the performance of men under a male E and women under a female E. (2) 8 reasoning problems: (a) Under a male E, men solved more of the masculine versions of the problems than women did; when mathematical aptitude was held constant (as measured by the quantitative section of either the Graduate Record Examinations or the American Council on Education Tests of Intelligence), there were no sex differences. (b) There were no sex differences on the feminine versions of the problems. (c) No difference was found between men's performance on the feminine problems and women's performance on the masculine problems. (d) Men had higher scores than women on the quantitative sections of the aptitude tests.

Hoffman, M. L., and Saltzstein, H. D. Parent discipline and the child's moral development. *J. Personality & Social Psychology*, 1967, *5*, 45–57 (and personal communication).

Subjects: $N = 444$; 12 yrs (low, middle SES) and parents. **Measures:** Parents' disciplinary practices were assessed in individual interviews with 270 middle SES children, 174 lower SES children, 129 middle SES mothers, and 75 middle SES fathers. A measure of parents' affection for their child was obtained from rating scales completed by each child and parent. **Results:** (1) Middle SES Ss' reports: girls viewed their mothers and fathers as expressing more affection ($p < .01$, $p < .001$) and less power assertion ($p < .05$, $p < .01$) than boys. No sex differences were reported in mothers' or fathers' use of love withdrawal techniques. (2) Middle SES parents' reports: no differences were found between boys' and girls' mothers or fathers. (3) Lower SES Ss' reports: girls reported both parents as expressing more affection than boys did ($p < .01$). Girls viewed their fathers as using more induction than boys ($p < .01$). No other sex differences were found.

Hokanson, J. E., and Edelman, R. Effects of three social responses on vascular processes. *J. Personality & Social Psychology*, 1966, *3*, 442–47.

Subjects: $N = 28$; 18–24 yrs. **Measures:** In response to being shocked by a same-sex confederate, Ss were free to perform either an aggressive (shock), a friendly, or an ignoring counterresponse. Systolic blood-pressure levels were recorded at 20-second intervals during most of the experiment. **Results:** (1) No differences were found between men and women in their use of the available responses. (2) For the first 2 20-second intervals after making a shock counterresponse, men had lower systolic blood-pressure levels than women ($p < .05$).

Hollander, E. P., and Marcia, J. E. Parental determinants of peer orientation and self-orientation among preadolescents. *Developmental Psychology*, 1970, 2, 292–302.
Subjects: $N = 52$; 10 yrs. **Measures:** Ss were asked a series of direct and open-ended questions designed to assess their parents' peer orientation, differential parent power (i.e. whether their mother or father was dominant in matters pertaining to them), and sibling alliance. Ss were then presented with 6 problematic situations. These required Ss to choose between peer values on the one hand and either their own or their parents' values on the other. Of the 6 items, 3 required a self vs. peer choice, and 3 a parent vs. peer choice. In the analysis of the test results, self vs. peer-orientation and parent vs. peer-orientation scores were added together to yield a measure of total peer orientation. Finally, Ss rated all other same-sex children in their class on the following items: (a) this is a classmate who does things independently; (b) this is a classmate who gets other children to do things; (c) this is a classmate who goes along with what the other children are doing; (d) this is a classmate who does what grown-ups think is right; (e) this is a classmate who gets along with other children. **Results:** (1) No sex differences were found in parents' peer orientation or in the relationship between parents' and child's peer orientation. (2) A majority of members of both sexes saw their fathers as more dominant than their mothers; however, this tendency was more pronounced for boys, since girls indicated a greater number of mother-dominant families than boys did ($p < .05$). (3) Boys were more peer- vs. self-oriented than girls. Boys also achieved higher total peer-orientation scores. (4) Peer-oriented boys and self-oriented girls were seen as "getting other children to do things"; peer-oriented girls were seen as "not getting other children to do things" ($p < .025$). (5) Boys who claimed an older sibling as an ally and girls who did not were seen as "doing what grown-ups think is right" ($p < .025$).

Hollander, E. P., Julian, J. W., and Haaland, G. A. Conformity process and prior group support. *J. Personality & Social Psychology*, 1965, 2, 852–58.
Subjects: $N = 112$; 18–21 yrs (college). **Measures:** Ss judged which of 3 lights went off first after being informed of the (inaccurate) judgments of same-sex others. The number of trials on which Ss conformed to the inaccurate group response was recorded. **Results:** Women conformed more often than men ($p < .01$).

Holloway, H. D. Reliability of the Children's Manifest Anxiety Scale at the rural third grade level. *J. Educational Psychology*, 1958, 49, 193–96.
Subjects: $N = 121$; 8 yrs. **Measures:** Children's Manifest Anxiety Scale. **Results:** No sex differences.

Holstein, C. B. Moral change in early adolescence and middle age: a longitudinal study. Paper presented at the meetings of the Society for Research in Child Development. Philadelphia, March–April, 1973.
Subjects: $N = 53$; tested at 13, 16 yrs, and their parents. **Measures:** At both testings, Ss were given 5 of Kohlberg's Moral Judgment Dilemmas (situations I, III, IV, VII, and VIII). At the second testing, a liberalism questionnaire was administered to assess social-political attitudes. **Results:** (1) At 13 years of age, girls were modally stage 3, whereas boys were modally stage 2. By age 16, boys were modally stage 4, whereas girls were still modally stage 3. (2) At both testings, fathers were modally stage 4 or a mixture of 4 and 5 (with no use of stage 3 thinking). Mothers' scores reflected a combination of stage 3 and stage 4 thinking. (3) Females in both age groups exhibited more liberal attitudes than males on the liberalism questionnaire.

Hooper, F. H. Piaget's conservation tasks: the logical and developmental priority of identity conservation. *J. Experimental Child Psychology*, 1969, 8, 234–49.
Subjects: $N = 108$; 6, 7, 8 yrs. **Measures:** Ss performed Piagetian tasks of identity and equivalence conservation. **Results:** Boys conserved more than girls did across all conditions and age levels.

Hopkins, K. D., and Bibelheimer, M. Five-year stability of intelligence quotients from language and non-language group tests. *Child Development*, 1971, 42, 645–49.
Subjects: $N = 354$; tested at 8, 10, 12, 13 yrs. **Measures:** The California Test of Mental Maturity, language and nonlanguage tests. **Results:** No sex differences.

Horai, J., and Tedeschi, J. T. Effects of credibility and magnitude of punishment on compliance to threats. *J. Personality & Social Psychology*, 1969, 12, 164–69.
Subjects: $N = 90$; 18–21 yrs (college). **Measures:** Ss played the Prisoner's Dilemma Game with a simulated partner (SP). Intermittently, the SP threatened Ss with a loss of points (5, 10, or 20) if Ss did not perform the cooperative response on the next trial. Ss were required

to reply to each threat with 1 of 3 available messages: (1) I will make the cooperative choice on the next trial, (2) I will make the competitive choice on the next trial, or (3) I do not wish to reveal my intentions on the next trial. If noncompliance occurred, the threat was enforced or unenforced depending on the condition to which Ss were assigned. **Results:** (1) Using total number of threats sent to assess compliance (thereby satisfying the criterion of 10 unsuccessful threats per game), no main sex differences were found. (2) Using the delay of first testing the veracity of the SP's message as a secondary measure of compliance, no main sex differences were found. Men delayed testing longer than women in the intermediate-punishment condition, whereas women delayed testing longer than men in the severe-punishment condition ($p < .05$). (3) No sex differences were found in Ss' use of the 3 available messages. Men lied more frequently than women did ($p < .02$). (4) No sex differences were found in the proportion of cooperative choices.

Horner, M. S. Femininity and successful achievement: basic inconsistency. In Bardwick, J. M., Douvan, E., Horner, M. S., and Gutman, D. *Feminine Personality and Conflict.* Belmont, California: Brooks Cole Publishing Company, 1970, 45–74.
 Subjects: $N = 178$; 18–19 yrs (college). **Measures:** Men were asked to write a story based on the cue "After first-term finals, John finds himself at the top of his medical school class." The cue was changed for women: "Anne" was substituted for "John." Ss' stories were scored for fear-of-success imagery. **Results:** More women than men wrote stories that were high in fear-of-success imagery ($p < .005$).

Horowitz, F. D. American and Uruguayan infants: reliabilities, maternal drug histories, and population differences. Paper presented at the Society for Research in Child Development Conference, 1973 (and personal communication).
 Subjects: $N = 44$; newborns (U.S. sample only). **Measures:** Observations were made of Ss for the first 10 days of life and again at 4 weeks of age. The Brazelton Neonatal Scale was also administered. **Results:** No sex differences were found in response decrements to light, rattle, bell, and pinprick; orientation to inanimate and animate visual and auditory stimuli; alertness; general tonus; motor maturity; pull-to-sit; cuddliness; defensive movements; consolability; peak of excitement; rapidity of build-up; irritability; activity level; tremulousness, startle responses; lability of skin color; lability of state; self-quieting activity; hand-mouth facility; number of smiles.

Horowitz, F. D., and Armentrout, J. Discrimination-learning, manifest anxiety, and effects of reinforcement. *Child Development*, 1965, *36*, 731–48.
 Subjects: $N = 48$; 9–11 yrs. **Measures:** Ss were designated high or low anxiety on the Children's Manifest Anxiety Scale. Ss were given either a simultaneous discrimination task in which the object was to press a button every time a certain colored light appeared regardless of its position, or a successive discrimination task in which all these positions showed the same color, and Ss had to press a different button for every color. Ss were reinforced for correct responses by either a buzzer or a verbal "right." **Results:** No sex differences.

Horowitz, L. M., Lampel, A. K., and Takansishi, R. N. The child's memory for unitized scenes. *J. Experimental Child Psychology*, 1969, 8, 375–88.
 EXPERIMENT I: **Subjects:** $N = 72$; 3–5 yrs. **Measures:** Ss were initially shown a display of pictures of objects. E hid the items after Ss named them; 1 item was then removed and the remaining ones exposed. Ss' task was to name the missing object. **Results:** No sex differences.
 EXPERIMENT II: **Subjects:** $N = 12$; 3 yrs. **Measures:** Same as Experiment I, with minor procedural changes. **Results:** No sex differences.
 EXPERIMENT III: **Subjects:** $N = 12$; 3–5 yrs. **Measures:** Ss were shown the displays used in Experiment II and asked to describe each. Ss' descriptions were scored for (1) total number of words and (2) total number of verbs and prepositions. **Results:** No sex differences.
 EXPERIMENT IV: **Subjects:** $N = 24$; 3–5 yrs. **Measures:** Same as Experiment II, except that Ss were asked to name each item before E hid it. **Results:** No sex differences.

Hoving, K. L., and Choi, K. Some necessary conditions for producing reinstatement effects in children. *Developmental Psychology*, 1972, 7, 214–17.
 Subjects: $N = 40$; 6–8 yrs. **Measures:** Ss learned 10 picture pairs, and 4 weeks later received exposure to either stimulus items only, response items only, stimulus items paired with response items, original 10 stimulus items plus 10 new items, or no treatment; 8 weeks after initial learning, the same task was relearned. **Results:** No sex differences.

Hoving, K. L., Coates, L. Bertucci, M., Riccio, D. C. Reinstatement effects in children. *Developmental Psychology*, 1972, 6, 426–29.
Subjects: $N = 72$; 5–11 yrs. Measures: Two-thirds of the Ss in each age group learned a paired-associates task; 8 weeks later they relearned (reinstated) the same task. Pairs were repeated in a story 4 weeks after the initial learning for these reinstatement groups. One-third of the Ss received only reinstatement training (story, but no initial learning), followed 4 weeks later by formal learning of the pairs. Results: No sex differences.

Hurley, J. R., and Hohn, R. L. Shifts in child rearing attitudes linked with parenthood and occupation. *Developmental Psychology*, 1971, 4, 324–28.
Subjects: $N = 75$; 24–27 yrs (retested 6 years after original testing as undergraduates). Measures: Ss were retested on a child-rearing attitude measure consisting of items relating to manifest rejection (tendency to assume negative and punitive stance toward children), over-protection (pervasive overconcern), and achievement pressure (variety of ways in which children might be pushed toward acquisition of social skills). Results: No sex differences.

Hutt, C. Curiosity in young children. *Science Journal*, 1970, 6, 68–71.
Subjects: $N = 59$; preschool. Measures: On 6 different occasions, Ss were individually exposed to a novel toy and 5 familiar toys. The novel toy was a rectangular metal box with a lever mounted on the top. Pushing the lever in different directions sounded a bell or buzzer, lit up lights, or had no effect. Each S's behavior was cine-recorded for later analysis. Results: (1) More girls than boys failed to explore in the presence of the novel toy. (2) More boys than girls engaged in creative or inventive play with the new toy (creative play was defined as use of the toy in an unusual or unconventional manner for longer than 20 seconds). (3) Boys and girls did not differ in number of manipulations of the novel toy on the first day.

Immergluck, L., and Mearini, M. C. Age and sex differences in response to embedded figures and reversible figures. *J. Experimental Child Psychology*, 1969, 8, 210–21.
Subjects: $N = 120$; 9, 11, 13 yrs (Italian). Measures: Embedded Figures and Reversible Figures tasks. Results: (1) Among 9-year-old Ss, girls disembedded better than boys did. There were no sex differences at ages 11 and 13. (2) Among 9-year-old Ss, boys gave more reversal responses on the Reversible Figures test than girls did. There were no sex differences at ages 11 and 13. (3) Rate of reversal responses increased with age for girls, but not for boys.

Insko, C. Verbal reinforcement of attitude. *J. Personality & Social Psychology*, 1965, 2, 621–23.
Subjects: $N = 70$; 18–21 yrs (college). Measures: Ss were contacted by telephone and either positively or negatively reinforced for agreement or disagreement with a series of opinion statements relating to the creation of a special week. One week later, Ss answered a questionnaire assessing Ss' attitudes toward the creation of the special week. Results: No sex differences.

Insko, C. A., and Cialdini, R. B. A test of three interpretations of attitudinal verbal reinforcement. *J. Personality & Social Psychology*, 1969, 12, 333–41.
Subjects: $N = 152$; 18–21 yrs (college). Measures: Ss were contacted over the telephone and asked to either "strongly agree," "agree," "disagree," or "strongly disagree" with each of a series of 12 opinion statements regarding pay TV. Ss were reinforced for either pro or con statements. Results: No sex differences.

Insko, C. A., Thompson, V. C., Stroebe, W., Shaud, K. F., Pinner, B. E., and Layton, B. D. Implied evaluation and the similarity-attraction effect. *J. Personality & Social Psychology*, 1973, 25, 297–308.
Subjects: $N = 300$; 18–21 yrs (college). Measures: After examining an attitude scale completed by a same-sex or opposite-sex stranger, Ss completed the Interpersonal Judgment Scale. Liking the stranger and preference for the stranger as a co-worker were measured. Ss also provided answers to the following questions: "How rewarding would it be for you to interact with this person?" and "How much do you think this person is like you?" Results: No sex-of-subject effects were found. Ss preferred women as co-workers and anticipated more future rewards from interactions with female than with male strangers.

Ireton, H., Thwing, E., and Gravem, H. Infant mental development and neurological status, family socioeconomic status, and intelligence at age four. *Child Development*, 1970, 41, 937–45.
Subjects: $N = 536$; 8 mos. Measures: Bayley Mental Scale. Results: No sex differences.

Irwin, D. M., and Moore, S. G. The young child's understanding of social justice. *Developmental Psychology*, 1971, 5, 406–10.

Subjects: $N = 65$; 3–5 yrs. Measures: Ss were asked to choose just or unjust endings for 6 stories describing accidental and intentional misdeeds, 6 involving apology and restitution, and 6 involving situations in which 1 character was guilty of a transgression and another was innocent. Results: No sex differences were found in the number of times Ss chose just endings.

Irwin, M., Tripodi, T., and Bieri, J. Affective stimulus value and cognitive complexity. *J. Personality & Social Psychology*, 1967, 5, 444–48.

EXPERIMENT I: Subjects: $N = 115$; 18–21 yrs (college). Measures: Ss rated 4 liked, 4 neutral, and 4 disliked housemates on each of 10 construct dimensions (e.g. outward-decisive, etc.). Ss' responses were scored for the degree to which they differentiated among liked, disliked, and neutral others. Results: Women differentiated among neutral and disliked others more than men did ($p < .05$).

EXPERIMENT II: Subjects: $N = 80$; 18–21 yrs (college). Measures: Ss listed 2 persons of each sex they liked and 2 persons of each sex they disliked. Ss then rated each person on a different construct dimension. Ss' ratings were again scored for the degree to which they differentiated among liked and disliked others. Results: Women differentiated more among disliked others than men did ($p < .01$).

Isen, A. M. Success, failure, attention, and reaction to others: the warm glow of success. *J. Personality & Social Psychology*, 1970, 15, 294–301.

Subjects: $N = 30$; 18–21 yrs (college). Measures: After either succeeding or failing on a series of tasks, Ss were exposed to a female confederate. Performance measures were helpfulness and attentiveness to the confederate. Helping was measured by whether Ss offered to help the confederate with the armload of items she was carrying, whether they picked up the book she had dropped, and whether they offered to open a door for her. Attentiveness was measured by Ss' recall and recognition of confederate's behavior. Results: No sex differences.

Iverson, M. A., and Schwab, H. G. Ethnocentric dogmatism and binocular fusion of sexually and racially discrepant stimuli. *J. Personality & Social Psychology*, 1967, 7, 73–81.

Subjects: $N = 80$; 18–21 yrs (college). Measures: Ss (previously classified as either high or low in ethnocentric dogmatism based on their scores on the Rokeach's Dogmatism Scale E and the California Ethnocentrism Scale) viewed 3 sets of facial sketches by means of a stereoscope. The sets were pairs of (a) male with mustache–male with glasses, (b) white male–white female, and (c) black male–white male faces. Ss then selected from 3 comparison sketches the stimulus they had just viewed in the stereoscope; 2 of the comparison pictures were the same as the stereoscopic targets, while the third was a composite. Selection of the composite was recorded as an instance of binocular fusion. Results: (1) No sex differences were found in the frequency of fusion judgments. (2) When the data for each set of faces was analyzed separately, high ethnocentric-dogmatic women were found to be less inclined than other groups to select the comparison picture that fused the pair of faces in Set A (male with mustache–male with glasses). No sex differences were found in the other two sets.

Iwawaki, S., Sumida, K., Okuno, S., and Cowen, E. L. Manifest anxiety in Japanese, French, and United States children. *Child Development*, 1967, 38, 713–22.

Subjects: $N = 155$; 9 yrs (Japanese). Measures: Children's Manifest Anxiety Scale. Results: No sex differences were found on the anxiety scale. Girls scored higher than boys on the lie scale.

Jacklin, C. N., Maccoby, E. E., and Dick, A. E. Barrier behavior and toy preference: sex differences (and their absence) in the year-old child. *Child Development*, 1973, 44, 196–200.

EXPERIMENT I: Subjects: $N = 40$; 13–14 mos. Measures: In the first phase of the study, the mother placed her child on the floor either next to her chair or 2.4 meters away. Across the room were 6 toys, 3 masculine (2 robots and a Playskool workbench) and 3 feminine (2 stuffed animals and a ferris wheel decorated with pink ribbons). After playing for 5 minutes, S was brought back to his initial starting place and exposed to a loud, angry male voice (beginning of Phase II). After the fear stimulus was terminated, the child was observed for 4½ minutes. During the first 2 phases, the percentage of time S spent with each of the toys, the amount of sustained play he engaged in, and the number of toy changes he exhibited were recorded. In Phase III, each mother interacted with her child for 3 minutes. The number of times the child offered each of the toys to his mother and the number of times the mother offered each of the toys to her child were counted. In Phase IV, the child was placed behind 1 of 2 barriers located at the far corners of the room. Location (center, edge), activity (push-pull, manipulate, cling), and crying at barrier were recorded. **Results:** (1) Boys spent a greater percentage of their time with the robots than girls did ($p < .05$). No sex differences were found in percentage of time Ss spent with the cuddly or activity toys. (2) Girls who were placed near their mothers cried more than boys ($p < .05$); no sex difference was found in the far condition. (3) All other sex differences were nonsignificant.

EXPERIMENT II: **Subjects:** $N = 40$; 13–14 mos. **Measures:** Procedures were identical to the first 2 phases of Experiment I. **Results:** Boys played with the robots more than girls did ($p < .01$).

Jackson, J. P. Development of visual and tactual processing of sequentially presented shapes. *Developmental Psychology*, 1973, *8*, 46–50.
  Subjects: $N = 120$; 6, 8, 10 yrs. **Measures:** Ss were asked to recognize shapes under cross-modal (visual to tactual, tactual to visual) or intramodal (visual to visual, or tactual to tactual) conditions. **Results:** No sex differences.

Jacobs, P. I., and Vandeventer, M. The learning and transfer of double-classification skills: a replication and extension. *J. Experimental Child Psychology*, 1971, *12*, 240–57.
  Subjects: $N = 61$; 6 yrs. **Measures:** Ss performed 57 double-classification tasks involving determinations of which of 4 stimuli belonged in the empty cell of 2×2 or 3×3 matrices. The 57 matrices were grouped into 12 sets based on the relationships involved. Within each set, color and shape were each paired with 1 of 9 basic relations: size, shading, elements of a set, number series, addition, added element, reversal, flip-over, and movement in a plane. **Results:** No sex differences.

Jacobson, L. I., Berger, S. E., and Millham, J. Self-esteem, sex differences, and the tendency to cheat. *Proceedings* of the 77th Annual Convention of the American Psychological Association, 1969, *4*, 353–54.
  Subjects: $N = 276$; 18–21 yrs (college). **Measures:** Before taking a modified version of the WAIS Digit Symbol subtest, Ss answered the following questions: "How many squares do you expect to complete?" (expectancy of success) and "How many squares would you like to complete?" (level of aspiration). Self-esteem was defined as the discrepancy between level of aspiration and expectancy of success. **Results:** No sex differences.

Jacobson, L. I., Berger, S. E., and Millham, J. Individual differences in cheating during a temptation period when confronting failure. *J. Personality & Social Psychology*, 1970, *15*, 48–56.
  Subjects: $N = 276$; 18–21 yrs (college). **Measures:** After being given an unrealistically high estimate of the average college student's score, Ss were presented with a modified version of the Digit Symbol test of the WAIS, and were either given or not given an opportunity to cheat. Ss also completed the Marlowe-Crown Social Desirability Scale and a self-satisfaction measure. Self-satisfaction was defined as the discrepancy between Ss' level of aspiration and Ss' expectancy of success on the Digit Symbol test. **Results:** (1) Among those Ss who were not given an opportunity to cheat, no sex differences were found in number of squares completed. Among those Ss who were given an opportunity to cheat, women completed more squares than men did ($p < .03$). However, women in the temptation condition did not complete significantly more squares than women in the control condition. (2) Men demonstrated a greater expectancy of success ($p < .001$) and a greater level of aspiration ($p < .031$) than women did. No sex differences were found in self-satisfaction scores.

Jacobson, L. I., Berger, S. E., Bergman, R. L., Millham, J., and Greeson, L. E. Effects of age, sex, systematic conceptual learning sets, and programmed social interaction on the intellectual and conceptual development of preschool children from poverty backgrounds. *Child Development*, 1971, *42*, 1399–1415.
  Subjects: $N = 46$; 3–4 yrs (low SES). **Measures:** Ss were trained on the Conceptual Development Program developed by the authors. The acquisition conditions were reinforcement, modeling, and feedback. The Stanford-Binet Intelligence Scale was administered to all Ss.

Results: For the first 5 concept problems, boys required fewer trial blocks to concept attainment than girls did. By the sixth problem, there were no sex differences.

James, S. L., and Miller, J. F. Children's awareness of semantic constraints in sentences. *Child Development*, 1973, *44*, 69–76.
Subjects: $N = 32$; 4–5, 6–7 yrs. **Measures:** Ss were presented with meaningful and anomalous sentences associated with pictures of an "okay" lady and a "silly" lady. Ss were asked to identify sentences as meaningful or anomalous, to explain their choices, and to convert the sentence into whatever type it was not. **Results:** No sex differences.

Jensen, L., and Hughston, K. The effect of training children to make moral judgments that are independent of sanctions. *Developmental Psychology*, 1971, *5*, 367 (brief report).
Subjects: $N = 72$; 4–5 yrs. **Measures:** Ss heard 5 stories involving good and bad acts followed by punishment. Ss were then randomly assigned to either a discussion group (told a story of an act followed by punishment, discussed the goodness or badness of the act, and why sanctions occurred), a verbal discrimination group (same story, with reward given if Ss judged act correctly, ignoring sanction), or a control group (question and answer session unrelated to sanctions). Ss were post-tested 3–8 days later on judgments of situations. **Results:** No sex differences.

Jensen, L., and Rytting, M. Effects of information and relatedness on children's belief in imminent justice. *Developmental Psychology*, 1972, *7*, 93–97.
Subjects: $N = 25$; 7 yrs. **Measures:** E told each S 6 stories, 2 in which an accident resulted directly from a misdeed, 2 in which an accident was in some way related to a misdeed, and 2 in which an accident was completely unrelated to a misdeed. E asked S, "Why did this happen?" "Would it have happened if the child had been naughty?" "Do you know if the child was naughty?" and whether the S had ever experienced the particular situation. **Results:** No sex differences.

Jersild, A. T., and Holmes, F. B. Children's fears. *Child Development Monographs*, 1935, *20*.
 EXPERIMENT I: **Subjects:** $N = 136$; 0–8 yrs. **Measures:** For a period of 21 days, parents were asked to record instances in which their child exhibited fear. **Results:** No sex differences were found in the average number of fears Ss displayed or in the nature of the situations that aroused fear in them.
 EXPERIMENT II: **Subjects:** $N = 398$; 5–12 yrs. **Measures:** Ss were asked in private interviews to describe their fears. **Results:** No sex differences.
 EXPERIMENT III: **Subjects:** $N = 105$; 2–5 yrs. **Measures:** Ss' reactions to 8 potentially fearful experimental situations were recorded. To obtain a different measure of fearfulness, Ss' nursery school teachers were asked to rate each child on a 20-point fear scale. **Results:** (1) Whereas no sex differences were found in the number of Ss who showed fear in response to the situations, girls exhibited more intense fear than boys. (2) No sex differences were found in teachers' ratings.

Jeruchimowicz, R., Costello, J., and Bagur, J. S. Knowledge of action and object words: a comparison of lower and middle class Negro preschoolers. *Child Development*, 1971, *42*, 455–64.
Subjects: $N = 79$; 4 yrs (black, low and middle SES). **Measures:** Ss completed the Peabody Picture Vocabulary Test (Form A) and the Expressive Language task (verbal description of pictures). Responses were scored for action and object words, action and object phrases, number of words, and number of phrases. **Results:** No sex differences.

Johnson, C. D., and Gormly, J. Academic cheating: the contribution of sex, personality, and situational variables. *Developmental Psychology*, 1972, *6*, 320–25.
Subjects: $N = 113$; 10 yrs. **Measures:** After completing a math test, Ss were allowed to correct their own papers. 2 techniques were used to determine the frequency with which Ss changed their initial answers to agree with the correct ones. Measures of n Ach and internal-external control (as assessed by the Intellectual Achievement Responsibility Questionnaire) were also obtained. **Results:** (1) No main sex differences were found in the number of Ss who cheated in n Ach, IAR, or exam scores. Girls who cheated had lower achievement motivation than

girls who did not cheat; the opposite relationship was found for boys ($p < .05$). Girls who cheated had higher IAR scores than girls who did not; a similar but not nearly so strong a relationship was found for boys ($p < .05$). (2) Girls had higher course grades than boys did ($p < .05$).

Johnson, P. J., and White, R. M., Jr. Concept of dimensionality and reversal shift performance in children. *J. Experimental Child Psychology*, 1967, 5, 223–27.
Subjects: $N = 30$; 5–7 yrs. Measures: Ss were presented with 6 squares varying only in brightness. Their task was to arrange the 6 items from brightest to least bright. Results: No sex differences.

Jones, E. E., Rock, L., Shaver, K. G., Goethals, G. R., and Ward, L. M. Pattern of performance and ability attribution: an unexpected primacy effect. *J. Personality & Social Psychology*, 1968, 10, 317–40.
Subjects: $N = 140$; 18–21 yrs (college). Measures: Ss were informed of a female stimulus person's (SP) performance on an initial set of 30 problems. Ss then observed a film of the SP in the act of solving a second set of problems. Before the SP attempted each problem, Ss predicted whether she would succeed or fail. Afterward, Ss rated her intelligence and recalled her performance on the initial set of problems. Results: (1) Men predicted a lower level of SP performance than women did ($p < .01$). (2) No sex differences were found in Ss' intelligence ratings or in Ss' recall of the SP's performance.

Jones, S. E., and Aiello, J. R. Proxemic behavior of black and white first-, third-, and fifth-grade children. *J. Personality & Social Psychology*, 1973, 25, 21–27.
Subjects: $N = 192$; 6, 8, 10 yrs (white, black). Measures: Observations were made of the interpersonal distance and axis orientation of same-sex pairs of children in conversation. Results: (1) No sex differences were found in interpersonal distance. (2) Boys were less direct in axis orientation than girls ($p < .005$).

Jones, S. J. Children's two-choice learning of predominantly alternating and repeating sequences. *J. Experimental Child Psychology*, 1970, 10, 344–62.
Subjects: $N = 122$; 3–5 yrs. Measures: Ss guessed which of 2 lights would come on for 100 acquisition and 100 transfer trials. During acquisition, repetition probability was set at .10 for half Ss, and at .90 for the other half. During the transfer trials, repetition probabilities were reversed for half of Ss in both probability groups. Results: (1) Boys made more response-repetition responses than girls did during acquisition and transfer, i.e. made the same prediction as was made on the preceding trial, regardless of outcome. (2) There were no sex differences in even-repetition responses during acquisition or transfer, i.e. making the same prediction as the preceding prediction, based on a successful preceding outcome.

Jones, S. J., and Moss, H. A. Age, state, and maternal behavior associated with infant vocalizations. *Child Development*, 1971, 42, 1039–51.
Subjects: $N = 28$; tested at 2 wks, 3 mos. Measures: Ss were observed in their home on 4 separate days, 2 days at the earlier testing and 2 at the later. The percentage of time infants vocalized in each of 5 states (active awake, passive awake, drowsy, active sleep, and passive sleep) was recorded. During each of the 2 awake states, measures were also taken of percentage of vocalizations in mother's presence and in her absence. Results: No sex differences.

Jones-Molfese, V. J. Individual differences in neonatal preferences for planometric and stereometric visual patterns. *Child Development*, 1972, 43, 1289–96.
Subjects: $N = 40$; 7–48 hrs. Measures: Ss viewed planometric and stereometric black squares against a white background. The stimuli were presented in pairs, within each dimensional set, for 30 seconds each. Fixation time was the measure of stimulus preference. Results: No sex differences.

Jourard, S. M., and Friedman, R. Experimenter-subject "distance" and self-disclosure. *J. Personality & Social Psychology*, 1970, 15, 278–82.
EXPERIMENT I: Subjects: $N = 48$; 18–21 yrs (college). Measures: Ss disclosed personal information to a male E who either (a) avoided eye-contact or (b) offered continuous eye-contact. Ss in a third condition spoke into a tape recorder, with E out of the room. Average time spent in self-disclosure was recorded. Results: (1) When E was out of the room, no sex differences were found in time spent in self-disclosure. (2) When E was present, men spent more time in self-disclosure than women did.
EXPERIMENT II: Subjects: $N = 64$; 18–21 yrs (college). Measures: In individual inter-

views, Ss were asked to discuss 4 intimate and 4 nonintimate topics. "Distance" between E (male) and subjects varied from E being present but silent, to E making physical contact with and making himself known to Ss. Time spent talking on each of the 8 topics was recorded. Before and after being interviewed, Ss gave their impressions of E on a 40-trait questionnaire. Results: No sex differences.

Julian, J. W., Regula, C. R., and Hollander, E. P. Effects of prior agreement by others on task confidence and conformity. *J. Personality & Social Psychology*, 1968, 9, 171–78.
   Subjects: N = 240; 18–21 yrs (college). Measures: Ss judged which of 3 lights went off first. The response measure was the number of trials Ss conformed to the erroneous judgments of 4 same-sex others (phase 2) after previously experiencing agreement on an initial set of trials with either 100%, 75%, 50%, 25%, or 0% of the group (phase 1). Results: (1) Women conformed more often than men did (p < .01). (2) Men had more confidence in their performance than women did (p < .01). No sex differences were found in Ss' perceptions of the difficulty of the task (which had been assessed by a questionnaire administered between phase 1 and phase 2).

Kaess, D. W. Measures of form constancy: developmental trends. *Developmental Psychology*, 1971a, 4, 296 (brief report).
   Subjects: N = 54; 6, 8, 10 yrs. Measures: Ss viewed sandpaper forms 105 mm high and either 145, 160, or 176 mm wide from a distance of 5 feet. Forms varied by angle of orientation. Ss were required to identify the objective shape of the form by pressing 1 of 3 buttons. Results: No sex differences.

Kaess, D. W. Methodological study of form constancy development. *J. Experimental Child Psychology*, 1971b, 12, 27–34.
   Subjects: N = 80; 7, 9, 11, 18 yrs. Measures: Ss compared widths of 3 rectangular turned forms with a comparison series of 19 similar forms. Results: No sex differences.

Kagan, J. Individual differences in the resolution of response uncertainty. *J. Personality & Social Psychology*, 1965, 2, 154–60.
   Subjects: N = 113; 7–8 yrs. Measures: Incongruous pictures were tachistoscopically presented to Ss at successively increasing exposure times. After each exposure, Ss were asked to describe the picture in detail. When Ss accurately described a picture for 3 consecutive trials, the series was terminated. Measures were taken of the latency from the presentation of the stimulus to Ss' first significant verbalization. Results: No sex differences.

Kagan, J. On the meaning of behavior: illustrations from the infant. *Child Development*, 1969, 40, 1121–34.
   Subject: N = 150; tested at 4, 8, 13 mos. Measures: At each testing, Ss were exposed to 4 3-dimensional lady faces, the features of which were either normal, scrambled, partially missing, or totally absent. The length of time Ss vocalized to each of the stimuli was recorded. At 8 months, Ss were exposed to a set of 4 taped stimuli read by a male voice. Measures were taken of cardiac deceleration vocalization rate and vocalization time. Results: No sex differences.

Kagan, J. *Change and continuity in infancy*. New York: Wiley, 1971 (and personal communication).
   Subjects: N = 180; tested at 4, 8, 13, 27, 48 mos (low, middle SES). Measures: At age 4 months, Ss were presented with 16 achromatic slides of human faces (half were photographs, half were schematic representations) and 4 3-dimensional clay faces painted flesh color. The features of the 2-D faces were either normal or scrambled; the features of the 3-D faces were either normal, scrambled, or missing. Fixation time, vocalization time, frequency of smiling, time spent crying, and heart rate were recorded; 66 of the infants were also scored for gross motor activity. During home visits, mothers' behavior toward their children was recorded. At age 8 months, identical procedures were followed, with the following 2 additions: (1) Ss heard a tape recording of 4 different recitations read with either high or low inflection by a male voice. Duration or orientation to the speaker, vocalization time, frequency of smiling, time spent crying, and heart rate were recorded. (2) Ss and their mothers were taken to a room marked off into squares. Mothers were seated in a corner of the room while the infants were placed in the middle of a set of toys. Measures were taken of the number of squares Ss traversed and the number of times they changed activities (put down one toy, picked up another). At the end of the session, mothers left the room for 2 minutes. The number of infants of each sex who cried or fretted during this period was recorded. When the infants were

13 months old, the 3-dimensional clay faces and the 4 recitations were again presented. The infants were also exposed to 7 12-inch-high male dolls. During the administration of these visual and auditory stimuli, the vocalization time, frequency of crying, time spent smiling, heart rate, and fixation time (visual episodes only) were recorded. Ss were also rated for motor activity, general alertness, positive and negative affect, and speed of habituation. The procedures at 13 months also included assessment of Ss' free-play behavior in the room marked off into squares. At age 27 months, mothers and infants were brought to a large room decorated as a living room. In the middle of the room were 10 toys arranged on a rug. Mothers were asked to remain on the couch, while infants were allowed to roam about freely. Measures were taken of locomotor movement (number of squares traversed in each of 7 5-minute time periods), amount of time spent in physical contact with mother, number of times each toy was played with, duration of each play activity, frequency of smiling, and number of verbalizations. Ss were then shown a series of colored slides accompanied by narration; 10 of the 23 slides contained discrepant information (e.g. a man wearing a dress). Fixation time, number of vocalizations, frequency of smiling, heart rate, number of times Ss turned toward their mothers and toward the examiner were recorded. Ss were then presented with 2 types of perceptual problems. The first required Ss to pick from among a set of pictures the one that was identical to a standard. The second was an embedded figures test. Measures were taken of the accuracy of Ss' responses, the length of time Ss looked at the stimulus before making their initial response, the length of time Ss looked at each stimulus before answering, the occurrence of any smiling or laughing responses, and the degree of cardiac deceleration to the first scanning of the stimulus. After Ss completed the embedded figures task, a discrimination-learning problem was administered. On each trial Ss had to decide whether to touch a red or yellow light. Ss were rewarded with an M & M only when they touched the yellow light. When Ss made 5 correct responses in succession, a series of conflict trials was initiated. These involved exposure to either a pair of red lights or a pair of yellow lights. On the final conflict trial, 2 yellow and 2 red lights were presented simultaneously, 1 light of each color on each side. The accuracy of Ss' responses and the duration of their fixations to the lights were recorded. The final measure at 27 months involved the presentation of the 3-dimensional clay faces and 4 of the male dolls. Fixation time, frequency of smiling, number of vocalizations, and heart rates were recorded. Within 2 weeks after the testing, 2 home visits were made, each of which lasted approximately 6 hours. All sequences involving a child's violation of a socialization standard set by his mother or classified a priori by the experimenters as a socialization standard were recorded, as were the mother's reactions to the child's counterreactions. During 1 of the 2 home visits, a vocabulary-recognition test and a vocabulary-naming test were administered. At 4 years of age, 30 of the Ss were given 3 different memory tasks. The first 2 tested their ability to remember pictures they had seen. The third required Ss to imitate pointing sequences demonstrated by E. **Results:** (1) At age 4 months, upper-middle-class mothers issued more distinct vocalizations to their daughters than to their sons. No sex differences were found in amount of physical affection or number of general vocalizations received. (2) At age 13 months, boys were more likely than girls to become quiet when the stimuli appeared. (3) During the free-play observation period at 27 months, girls spent more time in physical contact with their mothers than boys did (no test of significance reported). (4) During the 2 home visits, mothers were more likely to reprimand or prohibit their sons than their daughters (no test of significance reported). (5) Interviews with mothers at 27 months revealed that more girls than boys owned dolls, and more boys than girls owned guns. Sex differences in toy preference were reported.

Kagan, J., and Lemkin, J. Form, color and size in children's conceptual behavior. *Child Development*, 1961, *32*, 25–28.
> **Subjects:** $N = 69$; 3–8 yrs. **Measures:** Ss paired geometric stimuli that differed in form, color, or size. **Results:** Among older Ss, boys were more likely than girls to use color as a basis for similarity ($p < .05$).

Kagan, J., and Lewis, M. Studies of attention in the human infant. *Merrill-Palmer Quarterly*, 1965, *11*, 95–137.
> EXPERIMENT I: **Subjects:** $N = 32$; 6 mos. **Measures:** Ss were presented with: (a) filmed pictures of faces and designs (each picture was presented for 12 seconds, 5 times in 5 different orders), (b) 3 patterns of blinking lights (each pattern was presented for 30 seconds, 4 times in 4 different orders), (c) auditory stimuli consisting of an intermittent tone, modern jazz, and 3 human voices (a male, a female, and S's mother), each reading the same paragraph (each of the 5 stimuli was presented for 30 seconds 4 times in 4 different orders). Response mea-

sures for the visual episodes were fixation time (the total time during which Ss oriented their eyes toward the visual arrays), number of arm movements, frequency of vocalization, and cardiac deceleration (assessed by subtracting the heart rate during the rest period preceding each stimulation from the heart rate during the stimulation period). Response measures for the auditory episode were number of arm movements, frequency of vocalization, and cardiac deceleration. **Results:** (1) Film episode: (a) No sex differences were found in fixation time when all 5 trials were considered. When only the first 3 trials were considered, girls had longer fixation times than boys did ($p < .05$). (b) No sex differences were found in arm movements, frequency of vocalization, or cardiac deceleration. (2) Blinking lights episode: (a) No sex differences were found in fixation time, arm movements, or cardiac deceleration. (b) Boys emitted more vocalizations than girls did ($p < .05$). (3) Auditory episode: (a) No sex differences were found in arm movements. (b) Girls emitted more vocalizations than boys did to each of the 5 stimuli ($p < .05$, sign test). When all the stimuli were pooled, no significant sex difference was found. (c) Boys showed greater cardiac deceleration than girls did to the intermittent tone ($p < .05$); girls showed greater deceleration than boys did to the jazz music ($p < .05$). When the auditory episode was repeated on a new group of 6-month-old infants, no sex differences were found.

EXPERIMENT II: **Subjects:** $N = 30$; 13 mos (same as Experiment I). **Measures:** (1) Ss were presented with tape recordings of paragraphs read with or without inflection; 2 paragraphs were constructed—1 containing words and sentences that Ss most likely would be familiar with and 1 containing nonsense words. Cardiac deceleration was recorded. (2) Ss were also presented with the same 3 patterns of lights that they had been exposed to at 6 months of age. Fixation times were recorded. (3) As a final measure, Ss were brought into a room containing numerous toys. The room was marked off into 12 equal rectangles with white tape. The number of rectangles Ss traversed during a 15-minute free-play period was recorded. **Results:** (1) Auditory stimulation: For boys, the mean cardiac deceleration for trials 1 and 2 was greater than the mean deceleration for the last 2 trials, 15 and 16. For girls, the mean decelerations for the first 2 and for the last 2 trials were similar. The authors did not report whether or not this interaction was significant. Girls showed more cardiac deceleration to the low meaning–high inflection paragraph than boys ($p < .05$). (2) Blinking lights: On the last 3 trials, girls exhibited longer fixation times than boys did ($p < .05$). (3) Free play: No sex differences were found in number of rectangles traversed.

Kagan, J., Rosman, B. L., Day, D., Albert, J., and Phillips, W. Information processing in the child: significance of analytic and reflective attitudes. *Psychological Monographs: General and Applied*, 1964, 78, whole no. 578.

EXPERIMENT II: **Subjects:** $N = 180$; 7 yrs. **Measures:** Ss were given the Conceptual Style Test(CST), the Design Recall Test (DRT), and the Hidden Figures Test (HFT). Before each was administered, Ss were instructed either to delay before answering or to respond quickly. The CST was employed to assess Ss' preference for analytic conceptualizations. On each trial, Ss were presented with 3 pictures of common stimuli. After examining them, Ss were asked to pick the 2 that were alike or went together. The number of analytic responses Ss made was recorded. On each trial of the DRT, Ss were instructed to select from among an array of geometric designs the 1 that was identical to a standard. Measures were taken of the number of correct responses Ss made on the first attempt. On each trial of the HFT, Ss attempted to find a familiar object embedded in a patterned background. The response measure was the number of correct identifications Ss made on the first attempt. **Results:** No sex differences.

EXPERIMENT III: **Subjects:** $N = 135$; 7–8 yrs. **Measures:** Ss were given the CST, the Draw-a-line Slowly Test (DAL), 2 forms of the DRT, the Picture Discrimination Test (PDT), the Draw-a-face Test (DAF), and 2 verbal fluency tests. The CST was scored for number of analytic responses and mean response time. On the DAL, Ss were told to draw a straight line as slowly as possible. The time Ss took to complete the line was recorded. The DRT was administered as in Experiment II, except that Ss were told to respond neither quickly nor slowly. Measures were taken of mean response time, number of major errors, number of minor errors, and numbers of responses that were correct on the first attempt. On each trial of the PDT, Ss were asked to detect the difference between 2 similar pictures. 3 response measures were obtained: time to solution, number of incorrect solution hypotheses, and number of items for which Ss' first response was correct. On the DAF, Ss were told to draw a human face. The number of face parts included and the order in which they appeared were recorded. On the verbal fluency tasks, Ss were given 2 minutes to think of things that were round, and 2 minutes to think of things that were square. The response measure for each task was the number of appropriate items Ss named. **Results:** (1) Boys produced more analytic responses (CST), had higher verbal fluency scores, and gave more incorrect solution hypotheses (PDT) than girls. Among 8-year-olds, boys made fewer major errors on both forms of the DRT and took a longer time to draw the straight line. (2) Girls' average response latency on the CST and average latency to first response on the DRT were both higher than boys. Girls also included a greater number of face parts on the DAF. (3) No other sex differences were found.

EXPERIMENT V: **Subjects:** $N = 113$; 8, 9 yrs. **Measures:** The Matching Familiar Figures Test and 2 visual analysis (VA) tasks were administered to Ss. Both VA tasks required Ss to first learn to associate 4 nonsense syllables with each of 4 designs. Ss were then presented with cards containing the nonsense syllables and stimuli illustrating the separate components of each design. Each design that was used contained 3 component parts—the ground component was a repetitive pattern and the figural component portrayed the form into which the individual element components fell. Ss' task was to match each component part to the correct set of nonsense syllables. **Results:** (1) On the MFF test, no sex differences were found in errors or average response time. (2) On the VA tasks, boys were more likely than girls to (a) analyze the stimuli during learning (no level of significance reported) and (b) correctly label the figural, ground, and element components. No sex differences were reported in average response time or number of trials to criterion.

EXPERIMENT VIII: **Subjects:** $N = 76$; 7–8 yrs. **Measures:** Restless behavior was recorded while Ss sat at their desks. **Results:** No sex differences.

Kagan, J., Henker, B. A., Hen-Tov, A., Levine, J., and Lewis, M. Infants' differential reactions to familiar and distorted faces. *Child Development*, 1966, 37, 519–32.

EXPERIMENT I: **Subjects:** $N = 34$; 4 mos. **Measures:** Each S was shown 4 different 3-dimensional faces (regular, scrambled, no-eyes, and blank face). Stimuli were presented individually in randomly ordered blocks, on 4 consecutive trials. A continuous record was kept of incidence and duration of S's fixation on the stimulus, smiling, and vocalizations. **Results:** Total and first fixation time scores were longer for boys than for girls on all 4 faces ($p < .05$).

EXPERIMENT II: **Subjects:** $N = 32$; 4 mos (different sample). **Measures:** Same as Experiment I, except that the order of presentation was held constant. Since earlier appearing stimuli were more likely to elicit larger decelerations, the specific order favored larger deceleartion to the scrambled face than to the regular face. Fixation time scores and continuous cardiac records were obtained. **Results:** There were no main sex effects. For girls, the cardiac deceleration was greater in response to the regular face than to the scrambled face. This was not true for boys.

Kagan, S., and Madsen, M. C. Cooperation and competition of Mexican, Mexican-American, and Anglo-American children of two ages under four instructional sets. *Developmental Psychology*, 1971, 5, 32–39.

Subjects: $N = 320$; 4–5, 7–9 yrs (Anglo-American, Mexican-American, Mexican). **Measures:** Same-sex pairs used a circle matrix board (competition-cooperation game) under conditions of 1 of 4 sets of instructions: neutral (instructions did not stress individual or group orientation), "I" set (instructions stressed possessiveness), "we" set (no goals indicated for Ss). Number of moves, number of prizes won, and types of moves made were analyzed. **Results:** No sex differences.

Kagan, S., and Madsen, M. C. Experimental analyses of cooperation and competition of Anglo-American and Mexican children. *Developmental Psychology*, 1972a, 6, 49–59.

EXPERIMENT I: **Subjects:** $N = 160$; 7–9, 10–11 yrs (U.S., Mexico). **Measures:** Same-sex pairs of Ss were instructed to open a "cooperation box." To accomplish this task, the simultaneous use of 4 hands was necessary. In the cooperation condition, E placed 2 toys in the box and told the children they each would receive 1 of the toys if they succeeded in opening the box. In the help condition, only 1 toy was placed in the box. E then indicated which child would receive the prize if the box was opened. **Results:** There were no overall sex differences in time required to open the box. On Trial 1, American boys were faster than American girls ($p < .05$) and Mexican girls were faster than Mexican boys ($p < .01$). No sex differences were found on subsequent trials.

EXPERIMENT II: **Subjects:** $N = 128$; 7–9 yrs (U.S., Mexico). **Measures:** Same-sex pairs of Ss were tested on the author's circle matrix board. After the children were seated, a present was given to 1 of them (child A). The second child (child B) was then given a marker to move. By reaching the "take" circle, B could take away A's present and either keep it for himself (competition condition) or relinquish it to E (rivalry condition). By moving his marker to the "let keep" circle, or by reaching neither the "let keep" nor the "take" circle, B allowed A to keep the present. **Results:** No sex differences were found in the frequency with which Ss chose each of the possible outcomes.

EXPERIMENT IV: **Subjects:** $N = 64$; 7–9 yrs (U.S., Mexico). **Measures:** Ss were seated on opposite sides of the circle matrix board. Each was given 1 marker. Before alternating turns, Ss were informed that a prize would be given to the child whose marker first reached the circle initially occupied by his partner's marker. Each child could choose to either block the other child's approach or move aside. No prize was awarded if neither child reached his goal. **Results:** No sex differences were found in willingness to block.

Kagan, S., and Madsen, M. C. Rivalry in Anglo-American and Mexican children of two ages. *J. Personality & Social Psychology*, 1972b, *24*, 214–20.

Subjects: $N = 96$; 5–6, 8–10 yrs (U.S., Mexico). **Measures:** Ss distributed marbles between themselves and their same-sex partners. Condition 1 offered S the choice either of taking 3 marbles for himself and giving 3 to his partner or of taking 2 for himself and giving 1 to his partner. Condition 2 offered S the choice either of taking 3 marbles for himself and giving 3 to his partner or of taking 3 for himself and giving 1 to his partner. Condition 3 offered S the choice either of taking 3 marbles for himself and giving 4 to his partner or of taking 2 for himself and giving 1 to his partner. Condition 4 offered S the choice either of taking 3 marbles for himself and giving 2 to his partner or of taking 3 for himself and giving 1 to his partner. In all cases, the rivalrous distribution was the choice that left fewer rewards to the partner. **Results:** (1) No main sex differences were found. (2) Among the younger Ss, boys were more rivalrous than girls in condition 3. Among the older Ss, boys were more rivalrous than girls in condition 2. (3) Among the American Ss, boys were more rivalrous than girls in condition 1. No sex differences were found in the Mexican sample. (4) Among the older American Ss in conditions 1 and 2, more boys than girls were always rivalrous, whereas more girls than boys were never rivalrous. No sex differences were found among younger American Ss or among younger or older Mexican Ss.

Kahn, A. Reactions to generosity or stinginess from an intelligent or stupid work partner: a test of equity theory in a direct exchange relationship. *J. Personality & Social Psychology*, 1972, *21*, 116–23.

Subjects: $N = 120$; 18–21 yrs (college). **Measures:** Same-sex pairs of Ss earned money after working on 2 proofreading tasks. Each S initially received either more (overpay), less (underpay), or the same amount of money as O (S's partner) from O's distribution of their earnings from the first task. After the second task was completed, S was given the money to distribute. **Results:** (1) Men kept more money for themselves than women did when distributing earnings in the underpay condition ($p < .01$). Men felt more strongly than women that the other S kept too much money for himself ($p < .01$). (2) No sex differences were found in the equal-pay and overpay conditions. (3) Men were more concerned with the financial aspects of the study than women were (as assessed by a postexperimental questionnaire).

Kahn, A., Hottes, J., and Davis, W. L. Cooperation and optimal responding in the Prisoner's Dilemma game. *J. Personality & Social Psychology*, 1971, *17*, 267–79.

EXPERIMENT I: **Subjects:** $N = 40$; 18–21 yrs (college). **Measures:** Ss played the Prisoner's Dilemma game in same-sex pairs. For half the Ss (the contingent group), the cooperative response led to higher earnings. For the remaining Ss (the noncontingent group), the competitive response was optimal. The number of cooperative responses made by each S was recorded. After the game, Ss were asked: "How much did you feel you influenced your partner's choices?"; "How much did you feel your partner's choices influenced your own choices?"; "How much control did you have over how many points you earned?" Ss then rated their liking for their partner on 30 bipolar adjective scales. **Results:** Women liked their partners more than men did ($p < .05$). No other sex differences were found.

EXPERIMENT II: **Subjects:** $N = 80$; 18–21 yrs (college). **Measures:** Same as Experiment I. **Results:** No main sex difference was found in number of cooperative responses. Men were more cooperative than women in the contingent condition; women were more cooperative than men in the noncontingent condition ($p < .05$).

Kaminski, L. R. Looming effects on stranger anxiety and toy preferences in one-year-old infants. Unpublished master's thesis, Stanford University, 1973.

Subjects: $N = 48$; 1 yr and mothers. **Measures:** Mothers and their infants were brought to a testing room marked off into 18-inch squares. In the middle of the room were 6 toys: a baby doll that could be easily cuddled, a young child doll that had movable parts, 2 pick-up trucks (the back of 1 was covered with rabbit fur, the other was covered with aluminum foil), a ring stack toy, and a Fisher Price musical merry-go-round. Once in the room, Ss were observed in the following sequence of 3-minute episodes: (1) After placing their infants on the floor facing the toys and a folding door, mothers returned to their seats. (2) The folding door was opened, revealing either a seated female stranger (non-loom condition) or a stranger standing against the far wall who subsequently walked forward and sat down (loom condition). (3) The stranger got up, smiled at and talked to the child, and then offered him toys to play with (the musical merry-go-round was always the first toy offered). Afterward, she departed, closing the folding door behind her. (4) Mothers remained quietly seated as in episode 1. (5) Same as episode 2, except that a different female stranger was employed. (6) Same as episode 3, except that toward the end of the episode, the stranger took 2 green toy turtles out of her pockets and presented them to the child—1 with its toy wheels up and moving, the other with its wheels down and silent; (7) Same as episode 4. Measures were taken of the frequency of the following behaviors: (a) looks to the mother; (b) touches mother; (c) proximity to mother; (d) looks to the stranger; (e) touches stranger; (f) smiles at the stranger, shows or gives toy to the stranger; (g) proximity to stranger; (h) looks to the toys; (i) touches toys; (j) manipulates toys; (k) non-distress vocalizations; (1) fusses or cries; and (m) self-oral behaviors. Latencies to moving within proximity to mother and to stranger, latency to moving out of proximity of mother, latency to smile at or show a toy to stranger, and latency to play with the toys were also recorded. **Results:** (1) Girls looked at their mothers more than boys did ($p < .01$). (2) Girls looked at the stranger more in the non-loom condition than in the loom condition; for boys, the reverse was true ($p < .025$). (3) Boys approached the stranger more frequently than girls did ($p < .02$). Boys' proximity to the stranger greatly declined in episode 6, while girls' proximity slightly increased though it was still less than the boys' ($p < .005$). (4) No sex differences were found in toy preference during the first 2 episodes. Over all episodes, no sex differences were found in the frequency with which Ss played with any individual toy. Boys played with both dolls (combined scores) more often than girls did ($p < .05$). (5) Mothers reported boys had more friction toys and girls had more dolls.

Kanareff, V. T., and Lanzetta, J. T. The acquisition of imitative and opposition responses under two conditions of instruction-induced set. *J. Experimental Psychology*, 1958, 56, 516–28.
   Subjects: $N = 48$; 18–21 yrs (college). **Measures:** Ss were asked to indicate whether the second of a pair of identical tones (in a series of 60 paired tones) was higher than the first. Before responding, Ss were provided with a simulated same-sex partner's judgment. "Partner's" choices were programmed to be correct either 20%, 50%, or 80% of the time. **Results:** No sex differences were found in number of imitative responses.

Kanareff, V. T., and Lanzetta, J. T. Effect of success-failure experiences and probability of reinforcement upon the acquisition and extinction of an imitative response. *Psychological Reports*, 1960a, 7, 151–66.
   Subjects: $N = 48$; 18–21 yrs (college). **Measures:** Ss predicted whether a red or green light would go on after being provided with a simulated partner's judgment. During the acquisition phase (first 80 trials) the partner's predictions were correct either 50% or 80% of the time. During extinction (the final 30 trials) 50% of partner's selections were correct. The performance measure was the number of imitative responses. **Results:** When paired with a partner who was correct 50% of the time, women imitated more than men did ($p < .01$). When paired with a partner who was correct 80% of the time, there were no sex differences in number of imitative responses.

Kanareff, V. T., and Lanzetta, J. T. Effects of task definition and probability of reinforcement upon the acquisition and extinction of imitative responses. *J. Experimental Psychology*, 1960b, 60, 340–48.
   Subjects: $N = 48$; 18–21 yrs (college). **Measures:** Ss predicted whether a red or a green light would go on after being exposed to a simulated partner's judgment. The partner's choices were correct either 50% or 80% of the time. The performance measure was the number of imitative responses. **Results:** No sex differences.

Kanareff, V. T., and Lanzetta, J. T. Effects of congruent social and task reinforcement upon acquisition of imitative responses. *Psychological Reports*, 1961, 8, 47–57.
   Subjects: $N = 72$; 18–21 yrs (college). **Measures:** Ss predicted whether a red or a green light would go on after being provided with a simulated partner's judgment. Partner's predictions were correct either 50% or 80% of the time. After each of S's choices, E responded with

either "good" or "okay." The performance measure was the number of imitative responses. **Results:** Men imitated more often than women did (*p* < .05).

Kangas, J., and Bradway, K. Intelligence at middle age: a thirty-eight year followup. *Developmental Psychology*, 1971, 5, 333–37.
    Subjects: *N* = 48; 39–44 yrs (tested in 1931, 1941, 1956, 1969). **Measures:** The Stanford-Binet IQ test was administered at all 4 sessions. The Adult Intelligence Scale was administered in 1956 and 1969. **Results:** Over the 38-year period, men made greater IQ gains than women did (*p* < .025).

Kaplan, H. B. Self-derogation and social position: interaction effects of sex, race, education, and age. *International J. Social Psychiatry*, 1973 (forthcoming).
    Subjects: *N* = 500; over 21 yrs (white, black). **Measures:** Ss rated 10 global self-descriptive statements on a 4-point scale ranging from "strongly agree" to "strongly disagree." Ss' responses were analyzed to yield a measure of self-derogation. **Results:** (1) There were no main sex effects. (2) Among white Ss without college education, women had higher self-derogation scores than men did (*p* < .01). (3) Among black Ss with a high school education or better, women had higher self-derogation scores than men did (*p* < .025).

Kato, N. A fundamental study of rod-frame test. *Japanese Psychological Research*, 1965, 7, 61–68.
    Subjects: *N* = 60; 18–21 yrs (college). **Measures:** Rod and Frame Test. **Results:** Women had higher error scores than men did (*p* < .05).

Katz, J. M. Reflection-impulsivity and color-form sorting. *Child Development*, 1971, *42*, 745–54.
    Subjects: *N* = 67; 3–5 yrs. **Measures:** Ss were given a color-form test in which a standard shape and 2 comparisons were presented; 1 comparison matched the standard in form, 1 in color. Ss were given 3 series of figures (which varied in saliency of color and form cues) and were asked to choose the comparison most like the standard. Ss were then given Matching Familiar Figures Test and were divided into impulsive and reflective groups. **Results:** On the third series of the color-form tests (color cue more salient), impulsive boys made more comparison glances than impulsive girls did (*p* < .05). Reflective girls made more comparison glances than reflective boys did.

Katz, P. A. Stimulus predifferentiation and modification of children's racial attitudes. *Child Development*, 1973, *44*, 232–37.
    Subjects: *N* = 96; 7, 11 yrs (white, black). **Measures:** Prejudiced Ss were chosen on the basis of racial-ethnic attitude scale scores. Ss received either distinctive-labeling training with photographs of other-race faces, perceptual-differentiation training to make same-different judgments of facial pairs, or no training, i.e. they observed faces without labels. E was black or white. After training, attitude scales were readministered. **Results:** There were no main sex differences in either prejudice or perceptual judgment scores.

Katz, P. A., and Zigler, E. Self-image disparity: a developmental approach. *J. Personality & Social Psychology*, 1967, 5, 186–95.
    Subjects: *N* = 120; 10, 13, 16 yrs. **Measures:** Ss' ratings of their real self, ideal self, and social self were assessed by a questionnaire and an adjective checklist. **Results:** (1) There were no sex differences in Ss' real or ideal self ratings on either measure. (2) There were no sex differences in Ss' social self ratings as assessed by the questionnaire. (3) At age 10, boys' social self ratings (as assessed by the adjective checklist) were lower than girls'; at age 13, girls' social self ratings were lower than boys' (*p* < .01). At age 16, no sex differences were found.

Katz, P. A., Albert, J., and Atkins, M. Mediation and perceptual transfer in children. *Developmental Psychology*, 1971, 4, 268–76.
    EXPERIMENT I: **Subjects:** *N* = 60; 6, 11 yrs. **Measures:** Ss judged the degree of similarity of 52 pairs of random geometric forms. Ss indicated their decision by moving the lever of a perceptual similarity apparatus. **Results:** No sex differences.
    EXPERIMENT II: **Subjects:** *N* = 240; 6, 11 yrs. **Measures:** Ss in 3 verbal labeling conditions were presented with 3 nonsense forms of either high, intermediate, or low similarity. Distinctive-label Ss were taught to associate different nonsense syllables (of either 40% or 95% association value) to each of the forms. Common-label Ss were taught to associate an identical label (again high- or low-association value) to 2 forms, and a different label to the third.

Control Ss counted aloud and learned what forms looked like. Ss then made degree-of-similarity judgments for pairs of previously employed forms. Similarity responses for pairs associated with a common label were analyzed. **Results:** There were no sex differences in verbal learning of labels or perceptual judgment scores.

Kaufman, A. S. Piaget and Gesell: a psychometric analysis of texts built from their tasks. *Child Development,* 1971, *42,* 1341–60.
Subjects: $N = 103$; 5–6 yrs. **Measures:** Ss were given the Gesell School Readiness Tests and the Lorge-Thorndike Intelligence Tests. Teething level was used as measure of physiological age. Ss also performed a battery of Piaget number tasks (conservation of length and number, addition and subtraction, discrimination, insertion, numeration, constructing and perceiving a straight line, sorting, class inclusion, multiple class membership, and seriation). **Results:** Girls scored higher than boys on the Piagetian tasks and on the GSRT ($p < .01$, $p < .05$).

Kaugmann, H., and Marcus, A. M. Aggression as a function of similarity between aggressor and victim. *Perceptual & Motor Skills,* 1965, *20,* 1013–20.
Subjects: $N = 64$; 18–21 yrs (college). **Measures:** After reading a criminal's case history, high and low scorers on a modified version of Siegel's Manifest Hostility Scale were asked to suggest an appropriate sentence for him. **Results:** No sex differences.

Keasey, C. B. Sex differences in yielding to temptation: a function of the situation. *J. Genetic Psychology,* 1971a, *118,* 25–28.
Subjects: $N = 108$; 11 yrs. **Measures:** After E explained the game and departed, Ss rolled the ball 10 times in a miniature bowling game. The score Ss earned on each roll was programmed so that the total number of pins Ss knocked over fell short of the number they needed to win a toy. Measures were taken of the number of times Ss falsified their scores, of the number of points Ss added to their scores, and of the turn on which Ss first cheated. **Results:** More girls than boys cheated. Girls cheated more frequently, added more points to their scores, and yielded to temptation earlier than boys did.

Keasey, C. B. Social participation as a factor in the moral development of preadolescents. *Developmental Psychology,* 1971b, *5,* 216–20.
Subjects: $N = 144$; 10, 11 yrs. **Measures:** E administered Kohlberg's Moral Judgment Interview to each S. Teachers and peers rated Ss' leadership and popularity relative to same-sexed classmates. Ss indicated past and present membership and leadership in clubs or social organizations. Peers nominated classmates who were their best friends. **Results:** (1) Among Ss rated as leaders by their teachers, boys had higher moral judgment scores than girls did ($p < .05$). (2) Among Ss rated popular by teachers, boys had higher moral judgment scores than girls ($p < .01$).

Keasey, C. B. The lack of sex differences in the moral judgments of preadolescents. *J. Social Psychology,* 1972, *86,* 157–58.
Subjects: $N = 155$; 11 yrs. **Measures:** 5 interview situations from Kohlberg's Moral Judgment Interview were administered to each S. **Results:** No sex differences.

Keating, D. P., and Stanley, J. C. Extreme measures for the exceptionally gifted in mathematics and science. Study of the Mathematically and Scientifically Precocious Youth, 1972 (correspondence from Johns Hopkins University Department of Psychology).
EXPERIMENT I: **Subjects:** $N = 396$; 12, 13 yrs. **Measures:** Ss volunteered to participate in a contest for students exceptionally gifted in math. The quantitative section of the SAT and the Mathematics Level I Achievement Test were administered. **Results:** 20% of the boys scored above the top-scoring girl on the SAT Math section; 10% of the boys scored above the top-scoring girl on the Math Achievement Test.
EXPERIMENT II: **Subjects:** $N = 192$ (130 boys, 62 girls); 12, 13 yrs. **Measures:** The Science section of the Sequential Tests of Education Progress was administered to Ss who were exceptionally gifted in science. **Results:** 17% of the boys scored above the top-scoring girl.

Keenan, V. Effects of Hebrew and English letters on children's perceptual set. *J. Experimental Child Psychology,* 1972, *13,* 71–84.
Subjects: $N = 48$; 7, 9, 11 yrs. **Measures:** A tachistoscopic slide presentation (.2 second) was made of the alphabetic pattern of 7 randomly generated letters (Hebrew and English) and 15 binary patterns (rows of blackened or nonblackened zeros). Ss filled in response sheets to match projected patterns. Number of elements recorded in correct serial position was analyzed. **Results:** No sex differences.

Keillor, J. S. The effects of experimentally induced consciousness expansion and conscious control upon intellectual functioning. *Dissertation Abstracts International*, 1971, 31-B, p. 4339.
  Subjects: $N = 22$; 18–21 yrs (college). **Measures:** After listening to a description of an LSD experience, a Stelazine experience, or a visit to the Stratford Shakespeare Festival, Ss were administered the Remote Associates Test. **Results:** Girls obtained higher scores than boys.

Kellaghan, T., and MacNamara, J. Family correlates of verbal reasoning ability. *Developmental Psychology*, 1972, 7, 49–53.
  Subjects: $N = 500$; 11 yrs (Irish). **Measures:** Drumcondra Verbal Reasoning Test. **Results:** No sex differences.

Kellogg, R. L. A direct approach to sex-role identification of school-related objects. *Psychological Reports*, 1969, 24, 839–41.
  Subjects: $N = 47$; 9 yrs. **Measures:** Ss were given a list of 24 common objects and were asked to decide whether each object was more suitable for masculine or feminine use. Of the 24 items, 8 were considered more appropriate for boys, 8 were considered more appropriate for girls, and the remaining 8 were related to scholastic activities. **Results:** Of the school-related items, both sexes labeled book, blackboard, library, and chalk more appropriate for feminine use; map and pencil were labeled more appropriate for masculine use. Girls considered school to be a feminine item; boys showed no consistent tendency. Boys considered desk a masculine item; girls were equally divided in their choices.

Kempler, B. Stimulus correlates of area judgments: a psychophysical developmental study. *Developmental Psychology*, 1971, 4, 158–63.
  Subjects: $N = 59$; 6, 8, 10, 12 yrs. **Measures:** Ss made "large-small" judgments on each of 100 rectangles, which varied in height, width, and area. Ss were retested 1 week later. **Results:** No sex differences.

Kendler, H. H., Glasman, L. D., and Ward, J. W. Verbal-labeling and cue-training in reversal-shift behavior. *J. Experimental Child Psychology*, 1972, 13, 195–209.
  Subejcts: $N = 80$; 4–5 yrs. **Measures:** Ss were given a reversal-shift discrimination-learning problem. **Results:** No sex differences were found in either preshift or postshift task performance.

Kenney, J. B., and White, W. F. Sex characteristics in personality patterns of elementary school teachers. *Perceptual & Motor Skills*, 1966, 23, 17–18.
  Subjects: $N = 100$; adults (school teachers). **Measures:** Cattell and Stice's Sixteen Personality Factor Questionnaire, Form A. **Results:** (1) Men were more emotionally stable, independent, enthusiastic, realistic, tough-minded, adventurous, and socially responsive, and scored higher in "ego strength" than women. (2) Women were more inclined toward changeable attitudes, general emotionality, evasiveness, and neurotic fatigue, were more sober, taciturn, introspective, sensitive, shy, and restricted in their interests than men.

Keogh, B. K. Pattern copying under three conditions of an expanded spatial field. *Developmental Psychology*, 1971, 4, 25–31.
  Subjects: $N = 135$; 8, 9 yrs. **Measures:** Ss made pencil copies of 10 simple and complex patterns. Within a week, Ss walked these same patterns under 1 of 3 conditions: on an unmarked floor, on an unmarked linoleum mat, or on sand. **Results:** (1) No sex differences were found in the accuracy of Ss' drawings. (2) Boys walked the simple and complex patterns more accurately than girls did ($p < .01, p < .05$).

Keogh, B. K., and Ryan, S. R. Use of three measures and field organization with young children. *Perceptual & Motor Skills*, 1971, 33, 466.
  Subjects: $N = 44$; 7 yrs. **Measures:** Rod-and-Frame Test (portable model), Children's Embedded Figures Test, Pattern Drawing Test, and Pattern Walking Test. **Results:** (1) Boys were more field-independent than girls on the RFT ($p < .05$). (2) Boys were superior to girls on the PWT ($p < .01$). (3) No sex differences were found on either the CEFT or the PDT.

Kershenbaum, B. R., and Komorita, S. S. Temptation to defect in the Prisoner's Dilemma game. *J. Personality & Social Psychology*, 1970, 16, 110–13.
  Subjects: $N = 96$; 18–21 yrs (college). **Measures:** After receiving cooperative instructions, same-sex pairs of Ss played 2 Prisoner's Dilemma games simultaneously. Feedback was controlled so that Ss were never sure whether their partner had defected or not. The temptation

to defect was high or low for self and other. The main response measure was the trial on which Ss first defected. **Results:** No sex differences.

Kershner, J. R. Children's acquisition of visuo-spatial dimensionality: a conservation study. *Developmental Psychology*, 1971, 5, 454–62.
Subjects: $N = 160$; 6 yrs. **Measures:** Ss were tested on their ability to remember the orientation and directional movement of elements in a previously seen field configuration. **Results:** No sex differences.

Kidd, A. H. Closure as related to manifest anxiety and rigidity. *Perceptual & Motor Skills*, 1965, 20, 1177–81.
Subjects: $N = 100$; 18–20 yrs (college). **Measures:** The Stanford-Gough Rigidity Scale and a shortened version of Taylor's Manifest Anxiety Scale were administered to Ss. Ss were also tachistoscopically presented with incomplete geometric designs (e.g. triangles with an opening along their perimeters, simple dot designs, and line drawing of angles). Immediately after exposure, Ss were asked to reproduce each figure. Ss' drawings were scored for closure (reproducing an angle smaller than the one presented, reproducing an opening taking up a smaller percentage of the perimeter than did the opening in the original figure, etc.) and elaboration (drawing more than the correct number of lines, dots, arcs, or gaps). **Results:** Men had higher elaboration scores than women ($p < .05$).

Kidd, A. H., and Cherymisin, D. G. Figure reversal as related to specific personality variables. *Perceptual & Motor Skills*, 1965, 20, 1175–76.
Subjects: $N = 100$; 18–21 yrs (college). **Measures:** Ss were given a shortened version of the Taylor Manifest Anxiety Scale, the Draw-a-Person test, the Stanford-Gough Rigidity Scale, and a reversal rate test. **Results:** Women had higher DAP scores and higher average reversal times than men.

Kimball, M. Women and success—a basic conflict? In M. Stevenson, ed., *Women in Canada*. Toronto: New Press, 1973.
Subjects: $N = 187$; 13, 17 yrs (Canadian). **Measures:** (1) Ss were asked to write stories based on projective cues of the following nature: "Susan (John) finds at the end of the school year that she (he) has been named first in the class." There were 2 cues given to each S—1 contained a male name and 1 contained a female name. Ss were scored for the number of fear-of-success stories they wrote. (2) Ss were then presented with descriptions of moderately and highly successful persons. Each description of a moderately successful person was paired with that of a person highly successful in the same field. Ss answered the following questions about each set: (a) Who is happier? Why? (b) Who do you like better? Why? (c) Who would you rather be? Why? **Results:** (1) Among 17-year-olds, girls wrote more fear-of-success stories than boys did. Among 13-year-olds, no sex differences were found. (2) No sex differences were found in Ss' responses to the questions about the moderately and highly successful persons.

Kimura, D. Functional asymmetry of the brain in dichotic listening. *Cortex*, 1967, 3, 163–78.
Subjects: $N = 142$; 5–8 yrs (low-middle SES). **Measures:** 2 different digits were presented simultaneously through earphones, 1 digit to the left ear, the other to the right. Ss were asked to report all the numbers they had heard. **Results:** With the exception of the 5-year-old boys, all age-sex groups accurately reported more digits presented to the right ear than to the left ear.

Kimura, D., Spatial localization in left and right visual fields. *Canadian J. Psychology*, 1969, 23, 445–58.
EXPERIMENT I: **Subjects:** $N = 38$; 18–21 yrs (college). **Measures:** A stimulus field was constructed consisting of 2 squares situated to the right and left of a central point. On each trial of the experimental task, a single dot was presented in 1 of 25 positions in either the right or left square. Ss were then asked to locate the dot on a spatial map of the stimulus field. **Results:** No main sex differences were found. Men were more accurate when the dot was presented to their left visual field than when it was presented to their right visual field; women showed no difference ($p < .01$).
EXPERIMENT II: **Subjects:** $N = 46$; 18–21 yrs (college). **Measures:** Same as Experiment I, except that the exposure time for which the dot was presented varied. **Results:** No main sex differences.
EXPERIMENT III: **Subjects:** $N = 28$; 18–21 yrs (college). **Measures:** Each dot was presented

at increasing exposure times until Ss accurately identified it in either left or right square. The position of the dot within the square was unimportant. **Results:** No sex differences.
EXPERIMENT IV: **Subjects:** $N = 34$; 18–21 yrs (college). **Measures:** Same as Experiment I, except that the pre-exposure field consisted of a single large circle instead of 2 squares. **Results:** No sex differences.
EXPERIMENT VI: **Subjects:** $N = 20$; 18–21 yrs (college). **Measures:** Same as Experiment III except that (a) the pre-exposure field consisted of a single circle, and (b) each dot was presented just once. After every presentation, Ss were asked whether they had seen the dot or not. **Results:** No sex differences.
EXPERIMENT VII: **Subjects:** $N = 32$; 18–21 yrs (college). **Measures:** Same as Experiment VI except that the stimulus dot was presented at increasing exposure times. Ss were asked to indicate whether the dot had appeared on the left or on the right side. **Results:** No sex differences.

King, W. Learning and utilization of conjunctive and disjunctive classification rules: a developmental study. *J. Experimental Child Psychology*, 1966, *4*, 217–31.
  Subjects: $N = 32$; 6, 9, 12, 18–21 yrs (college). **Measures:** Ss performed an attribute-identification task (to the criterion of 10 consecutive correct responses), and then received 6 conjunctive and disjunctive rule-learning problems. After the last problem, Ss were asked to describe the 2 different rules. **Results:** (1) On the attribute identification task, no main sex differences were found. Among 6-year-olds, boys made more errors than girls; among 12-year-olds, girls made more errors than boys ($p < .05$). (2) On the rule-learning problems, girls made fewer errors than boys ($p < .05$). The authors noted that "the significant effect for 'sex' cannot be interpreted as indicating that females perform better than males since sex was deliberately confounded with other variables."

King, W. L. A non-arbitrary behavioral criterion for conservation of illusion-distorted length in five year olds. *J. Experimental Child Psychology*, 1971, *11*, 171–81.
  Subjects: $N = 47$; 4–6 yrs. **Measures:** By means of a Mueller-Lyer illusion, the apparent length of 2 unequally long sticks was perceptually reversed. After showing S a dot indicating the longer stick, each S was tested on which stick was longer (both with and without Mueller-Lyer arms) and which looked longer (with arms). If S's response was correct, S was asked to make a bridge between the 2 blocks, choosing the physically longer or shorter of the 2 sticks. **Results:** No sex differences.

Kirchner, E. P., and Vondracek, S. I. What do you want to be when you grow up? Vocational choice in children aged three to six. Paper presented at the Society for Research in Child Development Conference, Philadelphia, 1973.
  Subjects: $N = 282$, 3–6 yrs (white and black, low SES). **Measures:** Ss were asked what they would like to be when they grow up. **Results:** (1) More boys than girls expressed aspirations that were classified as adult (i.e. mention of a nonoccupational status; e.g. "be a man") or as fantasy (e.g. "be Batman," "be a princess"). (2) More girls than boys expressed aspirations that were classified as parent (e.g. "be a father") or as older child (e.g. "be a Girl Scout," "be older"). (3) No sex differences were found in the number of responses that fell into the following categories: same child (lack of projection into more mature roles, e.g. "be a boy just like me"), specific occupation (e.g. "be a doctor"), nonhuman (e.g. "be a dog"), and all-adult (a category that encompasses adult, specific occupation, and parent). (4) Boys' occupational choices were more evenly distributed across occupations than those of girls (significance not tested).

Klaus, R. A., and Gray, S. W. The early training project for disadvantaged children: a report after five years. *Monographs of the Society for Research in Child Development*, 1968, *33*, Serial No. 120.
  Subjects: $N = 88$; tested at 3, 4, 5, 6, 7 yrs (black, low SES). **Measures:** Ss were divided into 4 groups. Groups 1 and 2 participated in enrichment programs designed to offset some of the negative consequences of growing up in a culturally deprived environment. Specifically, the acquisition of attitudes and aptitudes relating to achievement was stressed. Groups 3 and 4 served as the control groups. Several times each year Ss were given the Peabody Picture Vocabulary Test and either the Stanford-Binet or the WISC. Other tests administered were the Matching Familiar Figures test and a social schemata measure (age 5); the Illinois Test of Psycholinguistic Abilities (ages 5, 6, and 7); the Metropolitan and the Gates Reading Readiness tests (age 6); a peer nomination measure assessing reputation (general social effectiveness, aggression, withdrawal) among peers (age 6); the Metropolitan Achievement Test

and a self-concept scale (ages 6 and 7); the Stanford Achievement Test (age 7). Measures of delay of gratification and achievement motivation were administered at various unspecified times. **Results:** At 5 years of age, boys used more words in their descriptions of 3 pictures than girls did. At the same age, boys were superior to girls on certain unspecified subtests of the ITPA. No other sex differences were found.

Klausmeier, J., and Wiersma, W. Relationship of sex, grade level, and locale to performance of high IQ students on divergent thinking tests. *J. Educational Psychology*, 1964, 55, 114–19.
    Subjects: $N = 320$; 10–12 yrs (IQ > 115). **Measures:** 10 divergent thinking tests, 4 convergent thinking tests. **Results:** (1) On 5 of the 10 divergent thinking tests (Object Uses–Fluency, Plot Titles–Fluency, Expressional Fluency, Plot Questions, Object Improvement), girls scored higher than boys ($p < .05$). No sex differences were found on the other 5 tests (Object Uses–Fluency, Word Uses–Flexibility, Plot Titles–Cleverness, Sentence Improvement–Metaphor, Sentence Improvement–Onomatopeia). (2) On 3 of the 4 convergent thinking tests (Current Events, Analogies, Problem Solving–Judgment), boys had higher scores than girls ($p < .05$). No sex differences were found on the fourth test (Work-Study Skills).

Klein, E. B., Gould, L. J., and Corey, M. Social desirability in children: an extension and replication. *J. Consulting & Clinical Psychology*, 1969, 33, 128.
    Subjects: $N = 1,008$; 7–14 yrs. **Measures:** Children's Social Desirability Scale. **Results:** At every age level (except 12 years old), girls gave more socially desirable responses than boys.

Kleinman, R. A., and Higgins, J. Sex of respondent and Rorschach M production. *J. Projective Techniques*, 1966, 30, 439–40.
    Subjects: $N = 92$; 18–21 yrs (college). **Measures:** Rorschach Inkblot Test. **Results:** Women produced more human movement responses (M) than men ($p < .025$).

Knott, P. D., and Drost, B. A. Sex-role identification, interpersonal aggression, and anger. *Psychological Reports*, 1970, 27, 154.
    Subjects: $N = 80$; 18–21 yrs (college). **Measures:** Ss were divided into 4 groups—masculine males, feminine males, masculine females, and feminine females—based on their extreme scores on the MF dimensions of the Guilford-Zimmerman Temperament Survey. After being shocked by a confederate, Ss were free to deliver shocks in return. **Results:** Masculine males delivered a greater number of shocks ($p < .05$) and more intense shocks ($p < .05$) than either feminine males, masculine females, or feminine females.

Knox, C., and Kimura, D. Cerebral Processing of nonverbal sounds in boys and girls. *Neuropsychologia*, 1970, 8, 227–37.
    Experiment I: Subjects: $N = 80$; 5–8 yrs. **Measures:** Different digits were simultaneously presented to Ss' left and right earphones. On each trial, Ss were asked to report what they had heard; 2 weeks later, similar procedures were followed using a variety of environmental sounds (i.e. sounds made by common objects). **Results:** Boys accurately identified more environmental sounds than girls did ($p < .05$). No sex differences were found on the digits task.
    Experiment II: Subjects: $N = 120$; 5–8 yrs. **Measures:** Digits, environmental sounds, and animal sounds were dichotically presented to Ss during the first session. As in Experiment I, Ss were asked to report what they had heard; 2 weeks later, Ss performed 2 additional dichotic listening tasks, both of which utilized a nonverbal method of report. **Results:** Boys correctly identified a greater number of animal sounds than girls did ($p < .05$). No sex differences were found on the other 4 tasks.
    Experiment III: Subjects: $N = 36$; 7, 8 yrs. **Measures:** The 2 tasks employed during the second session of Experiment II. **Results:** No sex differences.
    Experiment IV: Subjects: $N = 27$; 2–5 yrs. **Measures:** 18 animal sounds were individually presented to Ss through the speakers of a tape recorder. After each sound was played, Ss were asked to name or describe the animal they had heard. **Results:** Boys correctly identified more animal sounds than girls did ($p < .03$).

Koen, F. Codability of complex stimuli: three modes of representation. *J. Personality & Social Psychology*, 1966, 3, 435–41.
    Subjects: $N = 72$; 18–21 yrs (college). **Measures:** (1) Verbal codability: Ss were presented with 24 different photographs of the same individual. Ss were instructed to write a description of each photograph accurate to the extent that others could identify which of the 24 pictures each description applied to. Afterward, Ss' descriptions were decoded by a second group of

Ss. Performance measures were number of successful transmissions (by encoders) and number of successful identifications (by decoders). (2) Enactive codability: 2 subjects (either of the same or opposite sex) were seated across from each other at a table: 1 subject in each pair attempted to duplicate the expression of 1 of the 24 photographs. The second subject's task was to identify the picture being imitated. Ss served alternatively as senders and receivers of the expressions. The number of correct transmissions made by each pair of Ss was recorded. (3) Recognition: Ss were exposed to 2 of the 24 photographs for 2.5 seconds. Then Ss either imitated the expressions in the pictures (enactive condition), described the expressions aloud (verbal condition), or counted backward (iconic condition). Following this, Ss attempted to identify the 2 pictures they had seen. (4) Discrimination: All 24 photographs were put on display in front of Ss. Ss were then given a duplicate print of 1 of the photographs. Ss' task was to match the duplicate with the original print in the shortest possible time. Response measure was the number of seconds required by Ss to find the original print. **Results:** (1) On the recognition test, women performed better than men did in the enactive and verbal conditions ($p < .05$); no sex differences were found in the iconic condition. (2) No sex differences were found on the discriminability or codability tasks.

Koenig, K. P. Verbal behavior and personality change. *J. Personality & Social Psychology,* 1966, 3, 223–27.

> **Subjects:** $N = 40$; 18–21 yrs (college). **Measures:** Ss were asked to talk about their academic work. Ss were reinforced for either positive or negative self-statements. Both before and after the interview task, Ss completed the Test Anxiety and General Anxiety scales. Pretask scores were subtracted from post-task scores to yield a difference (D) score for each S. **Results:** (1) No sex differences were found in the frequency of verbalization of positive, negative, or ambiguous self-statements. (2) No sex differences were found in D scores.

Kohen-Raz, R. Mental and motor development of kibbutz, institutionalized and home-reared infants in Israel. *Child Development,* 1968, 39, 489–504.

> **Subjects:** $N = 35$; 3, 6, 12, 27 mos (reared in institutions). $N = 94$; 3, 6, 12, 18, 24, 27 mos (reared in kibbutzim). $N = 128$; 1, 3, 4, 6, 8, 10, 12, 15, 18, 27 mos (reared in private homes). **Measures:** Ss were given the Bayley Infant Scales of Mental and Motor Development. **Results:** Among 6-month-old kibbutz ($N = 22$) and institution ($N = 10$) infants, boys scored higher than girls on the Mental Scale. No other sex differences were found.

Kohlberg, L., Yaeger, J., and Hjertholm, E. Private speech: four studies and a review of theories. *Child Development,* 1968, 39, 691–736.

> EXPERIMENT II: **Subjects:** $N = 112$; 4–10 yrs. **Measures:** Ss made sticker designs with an adult male and then with an adult female. Adults were instructed to minimally respond in a friendly fashion to Ss' verbalizations, but not to initiate conversation. Sentence-like verbal remarks made by Ss were recorded. **Results:** No sex differences were found in percentage of egocentric speech.
>
> EXPERIMENT IV: **Subjects:** $N = 34$; 4–5 yrs (U.S., Norway). **Measures:** Ss were individually presented with a series of 4 sensorimotor tasks (bead-stringing, easy jigsaw puzzle, tower building, hard jigsaw puzzle). Ss' verbalizations were recorded while performing the tasks. **Results:** No sex differences were found in amount of egocentric speech.

Komorita, S. S. Cooperative choice in a Prisoner's Dilemma game. *J. Personality & Social Psychology,* 1965, 2, 741–45.

> EXPERIMENT I: **Subjects:** $N = 72$; 18–21 yrs (college). **Measures:** Ss played the Prisoner's Dilemma game with simulated same-sex partners. Conditional probabilities of cooperative and competitive responses by the simulated partner were varied so that competitive behavior was optimal in a majority of the conditions. **Results:** (1) Women were more cooperative than men ($p < .05$). (2) Women were more cooperative with more cooperative partners; no such relationship was found for men ($p < .05$).
>
> EXPERIMENT II: **Subjects:** $N = 40$; 18–21 yrs (college). **Measures:** Ss played the PD game with simulated same-sex partners. Partner's response always matched S's previous response. Cooperative behavior was therefore optimal. **Results:** Men were more cooperative than women ($p < .05$).

Komorita, S. S., and Mechling, J. Betrayal and reconciliation in a two-person game. *J. Personality & Social Psychology,* 1967, 6, 349–53.

> **Subjects:** $N = 64$; 18–21 yrs (college). **Measures:** After receiving instructions to cooperate, Ss were led to believe they were betrayed twice by their same-sex partners in the Prisoner's Dilemma game. Response measures were the number of cooperative choices made by Ss on

the first 5 trials following the initial betrayal and the number of trials needed by Ss to reach the criterion of 5 consecutive cooperative responses following the second betrayal. **Results:** No sex differences.

Kopfstein, D. Risk-taking behavior and cognitive style. *Child Development*, 1973, *44*, 190–92.
    Subjects: $N = 60$; 9 yrs (white, middle SES). **Measures:** Ss were given Kagan's Matching Familiar Figures task and then Slovic's "toggle-switch" risk-taking task. In the latter task Ss could lose all their prizes if they pulled 1 too many switches. A male or a female E administered the tasks. **Results:** (1) Girls took more risks than boys did in presence of male experimenter ($p < .05$). There were no sex differences in the presence of a female experimenter. (2) On the MFF, no sex differences were found in errors or response latencies.

Korner, A. F. Neonatal startles, smiles, erection, and reflex sucks as related to state, sex and individuality. *Child Development*, 1969, *40*, 1039–53.
    Subjects: $N = 32$; 3–5 days. **Measures:** Ss were observed for a total of 140 minutes. Most observations took place before and after feeding. Frequency of 3 spontaneous behaviors (startles, reflex smiles, and bursts of rhythmical mouthing) were recorded during each of 3 states (drowsiness, irregular sleep, and regular sleep). **Results:** No sex differences.

Korner, A. F. Visual alertness of neonates: individual differences and their correlates. *Perceptual & Motor Skills*, 1970, *31*, 499–509.
    Subjects: $N = 32$; 2–3 days. **Measures:** Ss were observed over a 9-hour span. Frequency and duration of alert inactivity were recorded. During this time, Ss were also exposed for 10-second periods to a moving object. Visual pursuit scores were calculated by giving Ss 1 point for each fixation, 2 points for each visual pursuit, and 3 points for each visual pursuit accompanied by a head-turning movement. **Results:** No sex differences.

Korner, A. F. Sex differences in newborns with special reference to differences in the organization of oral behavior. *J. Child Psychology & Psychiatry*, 1973, *14*, 19–29.
    Subjects: $N = 32$; 3–5 days. **Measures:** Films of infant's hand and mouth interactions were assessed. Categories were hand approached mouth, mouth approached hand, mouth opened when hand was closed, mouth strained after hand to maintain already established contact. **Results:** Girls engaged in more mouth-dominated approaches than boys did ($p < .01$).

Korner, A. F., and Thoman, E. B. Visual alertness in neonates as evoked by maternal care. *J. Experimental Child Psychology*, 1970, *10*, 67–78.
    Subjects: $N = 40$ (crying), 24 (sleeping); 2–3 days. **Measures:** Ss experienced 6 interventions, each of which entailed either contact, vestibular stimulation, or a combination of both. During each intervention, Ss were rated for level of alertness. **Results:** No sex differences.

Korner, A. F., and Thoman, E. B. The relative efficacy of contact and vestibular-proprioceptive stimulation in soothing neonates. *Child Development*, 1972, *43*, 443–53.
    Subjects: $N = 40$; 2 days. **Measures:** Ss experienced 6 physical interventions. Crying time was recorded during and after each intervention. **Results:** No sex differences.

Korner, A. F., Chuck, B., and Dontchos, S. Organismic determinants of spontaneous oral behavior in neonates. *Child Development*, 1968, *39*, 1145–57.
    Subjects: $N = 32$; 3–5 days. **Measures:** Each S was observed for 32 minutes over a 5-hour period. Measures were taken of the frequency of hand-mouth contacts, hand-face contacts, finger sucking, and mouthing. **Results:** No sex differences.

Kossuth, G. L., Carroll, W. R., and Rogers, C. A. Free recall of words and objects. *Developmental Psychology*, 1971, *4*, 480 (brief report).
    Subjects: $N = 80$; 11 yrs. **Measures:** Ss saw either 20 unrelated nouns or their object counterparts. Half of the Ss were required to pronounce words and name objects, the other half were not. Recall was tested immediately. **Results:** (1) Girls showed more clustering of words or objects in their recall responses than boys did. (2) Girls clustered better with objects, boys clustered better with words. (3) Girls had better overall recall than boys did.

Kranzler, G. D. Some effects of reporting Scholastic Aptitude Test scores to high school sophomores. *School Counselor*, 1970, *17*, 219–27.
    Subjects: $N = 154$; 15 yrs. **Measures:** Self-acceptance scale of Bill's Index of Adjustment and Values, high school form. **Results:** No sex differences.

Kravitz, H., and Boehm, J. J. Rhythmic habit patterns in infancy: their sequence, age of onset and frequency. *Child Development*, 1971, *42*, 399–413.
Subjects: $N = 200$; newborn–1 yr. Measures: Rhythmic habit patterns were observed. Patterns were considered established if they lasted for more than 2 days. Results: (1) Boys showed more body-rocking behavior than girls did. (2) There were no sex differences in toe-sucking or head-rolling.

Kraynak, A. R., and Raskin, L. M. The influence of age and stimulus dimensionality on form perception by preschool children. *Developmental Psychology*, 1971, *4*, 389–93.
Subjects: $N = 64$; 3–4 yrs. Measures: Ss performed a matching task with 2- and 3-dimensional objects: animal stimuli during pretraining, and geometric stimuli during testing. Instructions were to tap appropriate shelf when either of the comparison forms matched standard form, or to tap blank shelf when no match existed. Results: No sex differences.

Kreitler, H., and Kreitler, S. Children's concepts of sexuality and birth. *Child Development*, 1966, *37*, 363–78.
Subjects: $N = 185$; 4–5 yrs (Israeli-Oriental or Western origin). Measures: Ss were interviewed about their views on sex differences and birth. Results: (1) Both Oriental and Western boys were better informed than girls about location and function of sexual organs. Boys seemed to have more exact information about sexual organs of girls than girls had about sexual organs of boys. (2) More girls than boys thought that fathers' task in birth consisted of helping the mother after birth.

Kreitler, H., and Kreitler, S. Dependency of laughter on cognitive strategies. *Merrill-Palmer Quarterly*, 1970, *16*, 163–77.
Subjects: $N = 92$; 5–6 yrs (European, Oriental). Measures: Ss were asked to express their opinions about 15 pictures depicting absurd situations. Ss' verbal responses and facial expressions were recorded. Classification of the verbal responses yielded 9 categories of cognitive strategies. Results: (1) Verbal responses of more Oriental girls than boys fell into category 1, description by enumerating various items in the situation, without pointing out the theme or the absurdity ($p < .001$). Verbal responses of more Oriental boys than girls fell into category 4, pointing out the absurdity in the depicted situation and directing criticism at it ($p < .001$). (2) Verbal responses of more European girls than boys fell into category 4 ($p < .01$). (3) The percentage of verbal answers accompanied by smiling was higher for Oriental boys than girls ($p < .05$). No sex differences were found in the European sample. (4) No sex differences were found in percentage of verbal answers accompanied by laughter.

Kubose, S. K. Motivational effects of boredom on children's response speeds. *Developmental Psychology*, 1972, *6*, 302–5.
Subjects: $N = 60$; 7 yrs. Measures: Ss responded to 8- and 18-second colored picture or square stimuli with instrumental or noninstrumental lever-pulling. Response and movement times were measured. Results: No sex differences.

Kubzansky, P. E., Rabelsky, F., and Dorman, L. A developmental study of size constancy for two- versus three-dimensional stimuli. *Child Development*, 1971, *42*, 633–35.
Subjects: $N = 64$; 3–6 yrs. Measures: Ss performed a size constancy task with 2- and 3-dimensional stimuli. Results: No sex differences.

Kuhn, D. Mechanisms of change in the development of cognitive structures. *Child Development*, 1972, *43*, 833–44 (and personal communication).
Subjects: $N = 87$; 4, 6, 8 yrs. Measures: Ss were pretested for concept of class and classification. A week later, a modeling task was given. The stage at which the model sorted the objects was either 1 below, 1 above, 2 above, or equal to S's previously established stage of development. After the model completed her sortings, S was told it was his turn, and was asked to sort the objects and give explanations for his sortings. A second post-test was given 1 week later. S was again asked to sort the objects, recall the way the model had sorted them, recognize a sketch of the model's sorting, and tell which sketch showed the best way of sorting the objects (preference). Results: No sex differences.

Kurtz, R. M. Body attitude and self-esteem. *Proceedings* of the 79th Annual Convention of the APA, 1971, *8*, 467–68.
Subjects: $N = 40$; 18–21 yrs (college). Measures: Ss were given the Ziller Self-Esteem Scale and the Body Attitude Scale. The latter assessed Ss' attitudes toward the outward form of their bodies on 3 dimensions: evaluative, potency, and activity. Results: (1) Women had higher

evaluative mean scores than men ($p < .001$). (2) Men had higher potency mean scores than women ($p < .001$). High self-esteem men had higher potency mean scores than low self-esteem men; high self-esteem women had lower potency mean scores than low self-esteem women ($p < .05$). (3) Men had higher activity mean scores than women ($p < .005$).

L'Abate, L. Personality correlates of manifest anxiety in children. *J. Consulting Psychology*, 1960, *24*, 242–48.
Subjects: $N = 96$; 9–13 yrs. Measures: Children's Manifest Anxiety Scale. Results: (1) No sex differences were found in anxiety or lie scores (CMAS). (2) Girls checked the following items more frequently than boys did: I am secretly afraid of a lot of things ($p < .05$); My feelings get hurt easily ($p < .001$); It is hard for me to go to sleep at night ($p < .05$); and I am afraid of the dark ($p < .001$). (3) Boys checked the following items more frequently than girls did: I wish I could be very far away from here ($p < .025$); I never get angry ($p < .05$); and I would rather win than lose in a game.

Lalljee, M., and Cook, M. Uncertainty in first encounters. *J. Personality & Social Psychology*, 1973, *26*, 137–41.
Subjects: $N = 10$; 18–21 yrs (college). Measures: Ss discussed both anxiety-arousing and non-anxiety-arousing topics with E. The response measures were speech rate, filled pause ratios, and non-ah speech-disturbance ratios. Filled-pause ratios were calculated by summing the number of filled pauses during each minute of speech and dividing by the number of words spoken during that time. Non-ah speech-disturbance ratios were calculated by summing instances of sentence change, repetition, sentence incompletion, stutter, slip of the tongue, omission, and intruding incoherent sound, and then dividing by the number of words spoken. Results: (1) Filled-pause ratios were higher for men than for women. (2) No sex differences were found in speech rate or non-ah speech-disturbance ratios.

Lamal, P. A. Imitation learning of information-processing. *J. Experimental Child Psychology*, 1971, *12*, 223–27.
Subjects: $N = 72$; 8, 10, 12 yrs. Measures: Each S tried to solve "20 questions" type problems after observing E solve a sample problem using either a hypotheses-scanning approach (testing specific hypotheses such as "Is it the apple?") or a constraint-seeking approach (more efficient strategy such as "Is it an animal?"). Results: No sex differences.

Lambert, W., and Levy, L. H. Sensation seeking and short-term sensory isolation. *J. Personality & Social Psychology*, 1972, *24*, 46–52.
Subjects: $N = 40$; 18–21 yrs (college). Measures: The Sensation-Seeking Scale (SSS) was initially administered to all Ss in order to predict Ss' need for visual stimulation during a subsequent 2-hour period of sensory isolation. Ss' rate of using freely available visual stimuli during isolation was sampled across the 2 hours. Digital skin resistance was also measured. Results: No sex differences were found in scores on the SSS in rate of using visual stimuli or in skin resistance. Women had higher skin resistance levels at the beginning of the 2-hour period of sensory isolation, while men had higher levels during the last hour.

Lambert, W. E., Yackley, A., and Hein, R. N. Child training values of English Canadian and French Canadian parents. *Canadian J. Behavioral Science*, 1971, *3*, 217–36.
Subjects: $N = 73$; parents of 6-year-old children (French-Canadian, English-Canadian). Measures: (1) Parents' reactions to a tape recording of various incidents and behaviors that are frequent occurrences in a child's life were recorded and coded. (2) Parents also completed a questionnaire assessing (a) their perceptions of similarities or differences in the behavior of boys and girls and (b) their opinions as to whether sex-role differences in behavior should exist. Results: (1) No differences were found between boys' and girls' parents' reactions to (a) requests for help; (b) displays of insolence; (c) conflicts between a child and a baby, a child and a guest, or a child who is hurt and a baby; (d) requests to go outside and play. (2) Parents of boys were harsher than parents of girls in their reactions to anger. (3) In response to the child's request to invite a friend home, parents of girls were more restrictive than parents of boys (French-Canadian sample only). (4) In response to the child's comfort-seeking requests, parents of girls were more likely to comply than parents of boys. (5) In response to the conflict between the child and a guest, fathers of boys sided more with the guest than fathers of girls. In the FC sample, mothers of girls sided more with the guest than mothers of boys. (6) Fathers of boys responded more harshly to insolence than fathers of girls, whereas mothers of boys were less harsh than mothers of girls. This result was true only among FC parents. (7a) EC mothers were harsher in their reactions to insolence than EC fathers. No difference was found between FC mothers and fathers; (7b) EC fathers sided more with the

baby after the baby hurt the child than EC mothers did. No difference was found between FC mothers and fathers; (7c) Differences between mothers and fathers on the other items were not significant. (8) Questionnaire findings: (a) No differences were found between boys' and girls' parents' perceptions of sex-role differences in behavior. FC fathers perceived more sex-role differences in behaviors than FC mothers did. No differences were found between EC mothers and fathers. (b) Parents of boys thought sex-role differences in behavior should exist more than did parents of girls. No differences were found between mothers and fathers.

Landauer, T. L., Carlsmith, J. M., and Lepper, M. Experimental analysis of the factors determining obedience of four-year-old children to adult females. *Child Development*, 1970, *41*, 601–11.

Subjects: $N = 33$; 3–4 yrs and mothers. Measures: Each mother asked 3 Ss (1 her own child) to perform 1 of 3 obedience tasks. The latency of the first disobedience, the number of times the request was repeated, the length of time the child was obedient, and a description of the session were recorded. Results: No sex differences.

Landsbaum, J. B., and Willis, R. H. Conformity in early and late adolescence. *Developmental Psychology*, 1971, *4*, 334–37.

Subjects: $N = 64$; 13–14, 18–21 yrs (college). Measures: Systematically varied fake feedback was given to paired same-sex Ss regarding their own and partner's supposed performance on line length judgments. Ss and partners then performed a slightly different line length judgment task. After making his own response, S was allowed to see his partner's response (which was actually E's response pre-planned to disagree 50% of the time) before S made his final judgment. The number of times S changed his initial judgment to agree with partner's judgment was recorded. Results: No sex differences.

Lane, E. A. Childhood characteristics of black college graduates reared in poverty. *Developmental Psychology*, 1973, *8*, 42–45.

Subjects: $N = 22$; 27–46 yrs (black college graduates from low SES backgrounds). Measures: Group IQ tests were administered in the second grade (Kuhlman-Anderson), the sixth grade (Cleveland Classification Test), and the eighth grade (McNemar Test), with same-sex scores obtained for individually matched controls and for as many siblings as possible. Results: There were no sex differences in IQ increase from second to eighth grade.

Lane, I. M., and Coon, R. C. Reward allocation in preschool children. *Child Development*, 1972, *43*, 1382–89.

Subjects: $N = 80$; 4, 5 yrs (white, middle SES). Measures: S was told he was playing a game with a (fictitious) partner in another room. S was asked to paste gummed stickers on a special work sheet as fast as possible. S and his "partner" worked as a team, i.e. the more stickers they pasted the more rewards they would get. Time and "partner's" performance were manipulated so that S pasted many less, many more, or the same number of stickers compared with his partner. Afterward, S could distribute the rewards as he wished. Results: No sex differences.

Lane, I. M., and Missé, L. A. Equity and the distribution of rewards. *J. Personality & Social Psychology*, 1971, *20*, 1–17.

Subjects: $N = 128$; 18–21 yrs (college). Measures: Ss were given unilateral power to determine their rewards and those of 1 other person. Ss chose between a standard and an alternative distribution. Results: Men more often than women chose distributions more favorable to themselves than to other partners.

Langhorne, M. C. The effects of maze rotation on learning. *J. General Psychology*, 1948, *38*, 191–205.

Subjects: $N = 102$; 21–22 yrs. Measures: On the first day, Ss traced through a maze with a stylus until they reached the criterion of 2 consecutive, errorless trials. On the following days, the maze was successively rotated in a counterclockwise direction through the 90°, 180°, 270°, and 360° positions. Results: (1) On the first day, men averaged fewer trials, fewer errors, and less time than women did. (2) On successive days, similar gains in performance were exhibited by men and women.

Langlois, J. H., Gottfried, N. W., and Seay, B. The influence of sex of peer on the social behavior of preschool children. *Developmental Psychology*, 1973, *8*, 93–98 (and personal communication).

Subjects: $N = 32$; 3, 5 yrs (black). Measures: Same-sex and opposite-sex pairs of Ss were observed in free play for 4 15-minute sessions. **Results:** First two sessions: (1) Girls talked with and touched their partners more frequently than boys did ($p < .01$; $p < .05$). (2) Boys hit their partners with objects more frequently than girls did ($p < .01$). (3) Among 3-year-old Ss, girls exhibited more nonword vocalizations than boys did; among 5-year-old Ss, the reverse was true ($p < .05$). (4) 3-year-old girls threw blocks more frequently than 3-year-old boys and 5-year-old girls did; 5-year-old boys threw blocks more frequently than any other age-sex group did ($p < .05$). Overall, boys threw blocks more frequently than girls did ($p < .01$). (5) No sex differences were found in the following behaviors (some of which had a low frequency of occurrence): hitting partner with hand and foot; moving from within to beyond or from beyond to within 1 foot of partner; being within 1 foot of partner; smiling; frowning, manipulating partner with hand; throwing, sitting on, manipulating, or embracing objects; oral contact with objects; standing; riding toy truck; touching own body or clothing. Second two sessions: (1) Girls spent more time talking with their partners and touching their own bodies and clothing than boys did ($p < .05$, $p < .05$). (2) Ss with same-sex partners displayed more hitting, more touching, less talking, and kept within 1 foot of their partners more frequently than Ss with opposite-sex partners did.

Lansky, L. M. The family structure also affects the model: sex-role attitudes in parents of preschool children. *Merrill-Palmer Quarterly*, 1967, *13*, 139–50.
  Subjects: $N = 196$; parents of preschool children. **Measures:** Ss completed the Sex-Role Attitude Test (SRAT); 2 forms were available, 1 for boys' parents and 1 for girls' parents. For each item, Ss judged a same-sex parent's reaction to a child's preference for 1 of 2 sex-linked objects, names, or activities. **Results:** (1) Fathers and mothers expressed more negative attitudes toward boys' than toward girls' cross-sex choices ($p < .001$, $p < .01$). (2) No differences were found in fathers' and mothers' attitudes toward boys' and girls' same-sex choices.

Lansky, L. M., and McKay, G. Independence, dependence, and manifest and latent masculinity-femininity: some complex relationships among four complex variables. *Psychological Reports*, 1969, *24*, 263–68.
  Subjects: $N = 36$; 5–6 yrs. **Measures:** 2 teachers independently rated Ss' overall-school behavior on the Beller's scales for dependent behavior (DEP) and independence or autonomous achievement-striving behaviors (AAS). Manifest masculinity-femininity was measured by a modified version of the IT Scale for Children (ITSC). Latent masculinity-femininity was measured by Franck's Drawing Completing Test (DCT). **Results:** (1) Boys scored higher (more masculine) on the ITSC than girls did. (2) No sex differences were found on the DCT or the DEP. (3) Girls scored higher (showed more independent, autonomous achievement-striving) on the AAS than boys did ($p < .05$).

Laosa, L. M., and Brophy, J. E. Effects of sex and birth order on sex-role development and intelligence among kindergarten children. *Developmental Psychology*, 1972, *6*, 409–15.
  Subjects: $N = 93$; 5–7 yrs. **Measures:** (1) Sex-role orientation: IT Scale for Children, draw-a-person task (own sex first, then sex differentiation). (2) Sex-role preference: forced- and free-choice toy preference, forced-choice game preference, occupational preference naming, peer preference naming. (3) Sex-role adoption: teacher ratings of child behaviors. (4) Other: sociometric play observations by teachers, child questionnaire of parental dominance, Primary Mental Abilities test. **Results:** (1) The sexes differed in the expected direction on all measures of sex typing: role orientation, preference, and adoption ($p < .001$, $p < .001$, $p < .001$). (2) Ss more often chose members of their own sex as playmates (interview measure and play behavior observation). (3) Girls played in pairs more often than boys did. (4) There were no sex differences in seeing fathers as dominant in decision making and competence and mothers as dominant in a limited setting. (5) Girls saw mothers as more nurturant than fathers; boys saw parents as more nearly equal.

Lapidus, D. Differential socialization of male and female preschoolers: competition versus cooperation. Psychology Honors Thesis for Dr. Eleanor Maccoby, Stanford University, 1972.
  Subjects: $N = 30$; 3–4 yrs and their mothers. **Measures:** Each mother-child pair played 30 trials on Madsen's marble-pull game. **Results:** (1) No differences were found between boys and girls or their mothers in (a) number of marbles obtained; (b) number of marbles taken out of turn (taking a marble out of turn was defined as winning a marble after having won a marble on the previous trial); (c) number of interaction episodes in which verbalization occurred. (2) Boys and their mothers made self-deprecatory narrative statements in more

interaction episodes than did girls and their mothers. No differences were found between boys and girls or their mothers in the frequency of the following types of verbalizations: cooperative permissive; cooperative submissive; cooperative receptive; competitive general; competitive aggressive; competitive threatening/teasing; narrative, praise of other; narrative, praise of self; narrative, suggestions/explanations. (3) Boys laughed in more interaction episodes after they had won a marble than girls did.

Lapouse, R., and Monk, M. A. Behavior deviations in a representative sample of children: variation by sex, age, race, social class, and family size. *American J. Orthopsychiatry,* 1964, *34,* 436–46.
Subjects: $N = 482$; 6–12 yrs and mothers. Measures: Mothers were interviewed about their children's behavior and adjustment by means of a structured schedule. Reports of behavior deviations were recorded. Results: (1) More boys than girls were reported as displaying a high frequency of bed-wetting, masturbation, physical inactivity, and daydreaming. More girls than boys were reported as showing a high frequency of daydreaming. (2) No sex-of-child differences were found in maternal reports of deviations in speech, bedtime behavior, awaking behavior, elimination, sex behavior, eating behavior, eating habits, sleeping behavior, or body management. In addition, no differences were reported in wild behavior, overactivity, temper loss, restless behavior, tension phenomena, tics, compulsive behavior, or teachers' complaints about the child's behavior. (3) Overall, more boys than girls were reported as displaying a high incidence of behavior control problems (a category encompassing temper loss, wild behavior, overactivity, and teachers' complaints).

Larder, D. L. Effect of aggressive story content on nonverbal play behavior. *Psychological Reports,* 1962, *11,* 14.
Subjects: $N = 15$; 4 yrs. Measures: Ss played with an aggressive toy and a nonaggressive toy. The aggressive toy was a striking doll apparatus in which a 6-inch boy hit another doll when a lever was pressed. The nonaggressive toy was a dog that came from behind swinging doors when a lever was pressed. Results: A greater proportion of boys' than girls' responses were aggressive ($p = .02$).

Larsen, K. S., and Minton, H. L. Attributed social power—a scale and some validity. *J. Social Psychology,* 1971, *85,* 37–39.
Subjects: $N = 106$; 18–21 yrs (college). Measures: Ss were presented with a scale designed to measure attributed power (AP). The scale consisted of 5 power relationships: policeman-citizen, professor-student, general-private, foreman-worker, and king-subject. Ss were asked to rate each relationship on 15 7-step dichotomous power-laden adjectives (e.g. powerful-weak, restraining-noninterfering, arbitrary-reasonable, etc.). Results: Women attributed more power to power relationships than men did ($r = .25$, $p < .05$).

Larsen, K. S., Coleman, D., Forbes, J. and Johnson, R. Is the subject's personality or the experimental situation a better prediction of a subject's willingness to administer shock to a victim? *J. Personality & Social Psychology,* 1972, *22,* 287–95.
Subjects: $N = 213$; 18–21 yrs (college). Measures: Willingness of Ss to shock a victim within a learning-study paradigm was assessed. Ss were assigned to 1 of 5 conditions: control, model, conformity, female learner, or high model. Results: (1) When exposed to a model who shocked his victim at maximal level, men shocked their victims at a higher voltage and for a longer period of time than women did ($p < .05$). No sex differences were found in total voltage administered or in Ss' estimates of the maximum voltage they had reached. (2) No sex differences were found in the control, conformity, high model, or female learner conditions.

Laughlin, P. R., and McGlynn, R. P. Cooperative versus competitive concept attainment as a function of sex and stimulus display. *J. Personality & Social Psychology,* 1967, *7,* 398–402.
Subjects: $N = 192$; 18–21 yrs (college). Measures: Same-sex pairs of Ss performed a visual discrimination-learning task. The response measures were number of trials to solution, percentage of untenable hypotheses, and time to solution. Ss' responses were also scored for focusing and scanning strategy. Results: Men required more time to reach a solution than women did ($p < .05$).

Laughlin, P. R., Moss, I. L., and Miller, S. M. Information-processing in children as a function of adult model, stimulus display, school grade and sex. *J. Educational Psychology,* 1969, *60,* 188–93.
Subjects: $N = 216$; 8, 10, 12 yrs. Measures: Ss played a modified game of "20 questions,"

attempting to determine which of 42 objects E had in mind. Performance measures were number of questions to solution, percentage of constraints (questions that referred to 2 or more objects), and average number of items included per question. **Results:** No sex differences.

Laughlin, P. R., Branch, L. G., and Johnson, H. H. Individual versus triadic performance on a unidimensional complementary task as a function of initial ability level. *J. Personality & Social Psychology*, 1969, *12*, 144–50.
    Subjects: *N* = 528; 18–21 yrs (college). **Measures:** Part 1 (Synonyms and Antonyms) of Form T of the Terman Concept Mastery Task. **Results:** No sex differences.

Laurence, M. W., and Trotter, M. Effect of acoustic factors and list organization in multi-trial free recall learning of college age and elderly adults. *Developmental Psychology*, 1971, *5*, 202–10.
    Subjects: *N* = 72; 23, 75 yrs. **Measures:** 36 words were presented to Ss on a memory drum. The 36 words included 6 homophone pairs (e.g. idol, idle), 6 pairs of acoustically similar words (e.g. jacket, jagged), and 12 acoustically and semantically unrelated words. Afterward, Ss were asked to recall as many words as possible. **Results:** No sex differences.

LeCompte, G. K., and Gratch, G. Violation of a rule as a method of diagnosing infants' levels of object concept. *Child Development*, 1972, *43*, 385–96.
    Subjects: *N* = 36; 9, 12, 18 mos. **Measures:** Ss were familiarized with a toy, which was then hidden and replaced by another toy to assess object transformation level. **Results:** No sex differences.

Lefebvre, A., and Bohn, M. J., Jr. Occupational prestige as seen by disadvantaged black children. *Developmental Psychology*, 1971, *4*, 173–77.
    Subjects: *N* = 300; 9–13 yrs (black). **Measures:** Ss ranked 12 high and low SES occupations from most admired to least admired. **Results:** Among 9-11-year-old Ss, girls ranked elementary school teachers first more often than boys did.

Leff, R. Effects of punishment intensity and consistency on the internalization of behavioral suppression in children. *Developmental Psychology*, 1969, *1*, 345–56.
    Subjects: *N* = 107; 6–8 yrs. **Measures:** Ss were asked to choose between a small, unattractive toy and a larger, attractive toy. Ss were either intermittently or continuously punished for choosing the more attractive toy. Punishment consisted of exposure to a high- or low-volume noise followed by a verbal expression of disapproval from E. **Results:** No sex differences in number of times Ss were punished.

LeFurgy, W. G., and Woloshin, G. W. Immediate and long-term effects of experimentally induced social influence in the modification of adolescents' moral judgments. *J. Personality & Social Psychology*, 1969, *12*, 104–10.
    Subjects: *N* = 53; 12–13 yrs. **Measures:** Ss were initially presented with a 10-item form of the moral realism scale, a measure designed to assess Ss' position along the moral realism–moral relativism dimension. Each of the 10 items was a story, describing a moral dilemma in which the protagonist, confronted with extenuating circumstances, had to decide whether to obey (realistic response) or disobey (relativistic response) legal or social norms. On the following day, Ss responded to 20 stories of a similar nature after being exposed to the (prerecorded) choices of same-sex confederate. Confederates' responses were consistently contrary to Ss' initial position (realistic or relativistic). Immediately following this social influence phase and again one week later, Ss were presented with a new 10-item form of the moral realism scale. Approximately 3 months later, Ss were given the original 10-item pretest. **Results:** (1) On the initial 10-item form of the moral realism scale, girls made more realistic choices than boys did ($p < .001$). (2) No sex differences were found in the difference between Ss' scores on the pretest and social influence forms of the moral realism score. (3) At each of the post-test phases, no sex differences were found in change from initial orientation.

Lehman, E. B. Selective strategies in children's attention to task-relevant information. *Child Development*, 1972, *43*, 197–209.
    EXPERIMENT I: **Subects:** *N* = 60; 5, 7, 9 yrs. **Measures:** Ss performed a haptic matching task with a standard and 2 comparison stimuli. One comparison object was identical to the standard in shape but different in texture; the other was identical in texture but different in shape. On half the trials, Ss were instructed to pick as quickly as possible the comparison that was the same shape as the standard; on the remaining trials, Ss were told to match on the basis of texture. A record was kept of the frequency with which Ss explored only the relevant

dimension (i.e. either texture or shape) and of the number of times Ss felt only 1 of the 2 comparison stimuli. **Results:** No sex differences.

EXPERIMENT II: **Subjects:** $N = 30$; 5, 7, 9 yrs. **Measures:** Same as Experiment I, with the following exceptions: (1) On each trial, both comparison stimuli were identical to the standard in shape (texture), but only 1 matched the standard in texture (shape); (2) no specific instructions were given regarding which dimension was relevant. **Results:** No sex differences.

EXPERIMENT III: **Subjects:** $N = 120$; 5, 7, 9, 11 yrs. **Measures:** As in Experiments I and II, Ss performed a haptic matching task with a standard and 2 comparison stimuli (wooden crosses); 1 comparison was exactly the same size as the standard, while the other was considerably larger or smaller. Half the Ss were trained to realize that the crosses were of equal length horizontally and vertically; the other half were not. Instructions were given to match the crosses on the basis of size "in the fastest possible way." The frequency with which Ss performed only 1 hand movement (i.e. felt or spanned either 1 dimension or 1 quadrant of each cross) and the frequency with which they touched only 1 comparison stimulus were recorded. **Results:** No sex differences.

Leiderman, P. H., Leifer, A. D., Seashore, M. J., Barnett, C. R., and Grobstein, R. Mother-infant interaction: effects of early deprivation, prior experience and sex of infant. *Early Development*, 1973, *51*, 154–75.
Subjects: $N = 66$ infants (premature, full-term) and their mothers; tested at time of discharge from the hospital and at 1 week, 1 mo, and 3 mos postdischarge. **Measures:** (1) Selected mother and infant behaviors were observed during caretaking in the home at 1 week postdischarge and again in the pediatrics clinic at 1 month postdischarge. During both observation sessions, mothers fed and held their infants. (2) At time of discharge and again 3 months later, the Bayley Tests of Mental and Motor Development were administered. (3) Physical growth was assessed by recording the infant's weight at discharge and again at his physical examination 1 month later. (4) Each mother's confidence in her ability to care for her infant was assessed immediately preceding her infant's discharge from the hospital and again 1 month later. A paired comparison questionnaire was used. **Results:** (1) At 1 week and at 1 month postdischarge, mothers of girls showed more ventral contact with their infants than mothers of boys ($p < .05$, $p < .05$). At 1 month but not at 1 week postdischarge, mothers of boys affectionately touched their infants more than mothers of girls ($p < .025$). At both observation sessions, no sex differences were found in the frequency of the following maternal attachment behaviors: holding, looking, talking, laughing, or smiling. (2) No sex differences were found on the Bayley Tests or on the physical growth measures. (3) No difference was found between boys' and girls' mothers in maternal self-confidence.

Leifer, A. D., Collins, W. A., Gross, B. M., Taylor, P. H., Andrews, L., and Blacknert, E. R. Developmental aspects of variables relevant to observational learning. *Child Development*, 1971, *42*, 1509–16.
Subjects: $N = 60$; 4, 7, 10 yrs. **Measures:** Ss observed a filmed adaptation of a fairy tale. Afterward, they were questioned on memory and understanding of feelings and motivation attributed to male and female characters. **Results:** No sex differences.

Lekarczyk, D. T., and Hill, K. T. Self-esteem, test anxiety, stress, and verbal learning. *Developmental Psychology*, 1969, *1*, 147–54.
Subjects: $N = 114$; 10, 11 yrs. **Measures:** Ss completed a revised Coopersmith's Self-Esteem Inventory, the Test Anxiety Scale for Children (TASC), the Lie Scale for Children (LSC), the Defensiveness Scale for Children (DSC), the Kuhlmann Anderson IQ test (Forms E and F), and the Stanford Achievement Test. The 5% of Ss with the highest LSC and DSC scores were eliminated from the sample. **Results:** (1) Boys scored higher than girls on the LSC and the DSC. (2) Girls had higher test anxiety, achievement, and IQ scores than boys. (3) There were no sex differences in self-esteem scores.

Lepper, M. R. Dissonance, self-perception, and honesty in children. *J. Personality & Social Psychology*, 1973, *25*, 65–74.
Subjects: $N = 129$; 7 yrs. **Measures:** (1) Ss initially indicated their relative preferences for 6 attractive toys. Before leaving Ss alone for a short period of time, E told each child in the experimental condition not to play with his second-ranked toy; in the control condition, no prohibition was given. At the end of this temptation period, a second E asked Ss to rerank the 6 toys. The response was the new rank Ss assigned to the toy they had initially ranked second. (2) Half of the Ss were then given the following tasks: (a) a self-perception measure in which Ss were presented with 12 adjectives, 4 of which were chosen to fall on a dimension of honesty-

dishonesty and 8 on a more general positive-negative continuum. Ss were asked to place each adjective in 1 of 5 categories (ranging from "very much like me" to "not at all like me"); (b) an attitude-toward-moral-offenses measure in which Ss were presented with 2 brief stories of children yielding to temptation. After each story, Ss indicated how bad they thought the protagonist was and how bad they thought the protagonist felt about what he had done; (c) measure of how much they liked the first E. (3) 3 weeks later, a third E asked Ss to play a game in which they could only obtain attractive prizes by falsifying their scores. The response measure was the number of points Ss added to their scores. **Results:** No sex differences.

Lerner, M. J. Observer's evaluation of a victim: justice, guilt, and veridical perception. *J. Personality & Social Psychology*, 1971, *20*, 127–35.
   Subjects: $N = 61$; 18–21 yrs (college). **Measures:** Ss observed a victim receive apparently painful shocks from making incorrect responses, after which they rated the victim on 15 bipolar adjective scales. Only in 1 of 3 conditions were Ss informed that the victim was acting. **Results:** No sex differences were found in Ss' ratings.

Lerner, R. M., and Gellert, E. Body build identification, preference, and aversion in children. *Developmental Psychology*, 1969, *1*, 456–62.
   Subjects: $N = 45$; 5 yrs. **Measures:** E rated the body build of every student as chubby to average, average or muscular, thin to average, thin and linear. Ss were presented with same-sex photographs of chubby, average, and thin peers and were asked to indicate the pictures they most resembled, those they would most like to look like, and those they would least like to look like. Ss were also asked to name same-sex classmate who looked like stimulus picture. All tasks were administered twice. **Results:** (1) No sex differences were found in the percentage of Ss who correctly matched their own body builds. (2) A similar number of boys and girls showed an aversion to chubbiness. (3) A higher proportion of girls than boys correctly matched peers to each of the 3 body builds (level of significance not reported).

Lerner, R. M., and Schroeder, C. Kindergarten children's active vocabulary about body build. *Developmental Psychology*, 1971a, *5*, 179 (brief report).
   Subjects: $N = 76$; 5 yrs. **Measures:** Ss were asked questions about fat and thin children (e.g. "What does it mean to be a fat boy?" and "What would a thin boy be like?"). Ss' responses were categorized into 1 of 3 content categories (physique and physical, social, personal) or into an irrelevant-statement category. **Results:** No sex differences.

Lerner, R. M., and Schroeder, C. Physique identification, preference, and aversion in kindergarten children. *Developmental Psychology*, 1971b, *5*, 538 (brief report).
   Subjects: $N = 140$; 5 yrs. **Measures:** Ss were presented with same-sex figure drawings of fat, average, and thin peers, and were asked to point to the figure they most resembled, the one they most wanted to look like, and the one they least wanted to look like. **Results:** No sex differences.

Leskow, S., and Smock, C. D. Developmental changes in problem solving strategies. *Developmental Psychology*, 1970, *2*, 412–22.
   Subjects: $N = 96$; 12, 15, 18 yrs. **Measures:** Ss performed permutations on 4 sets of 4 stimuli, under instructions to find all possible arrangements without repetition. Performance measures were number of unrepeated permutations (NP), frequency of first-position items held constant from 1 trial to the next (IMC), and number of sequentially subgrouped transformations (GT) that were then scored on type of strategy. **Results:** No sex differences.

Lesser, G. S., Fifer, G., and Clark, D. H. Mental abilities of children from different social-class and cultural groups. *Monographs of the Society for Research in Child Development*, 1965, *30*.
   Subjects: $N = 320$; 6–7 yrs (Chinese, Jewish, Negro, Puerto Rican). **Measures:** Ss were given a modified version of the Hunter College Aptitude Scales for Gifted Children, which included (1) Verbal scale (picture vocabulary, word vocabulary), (2) Reasoning scale (picture analogies, picture arrangement, jump peg), (3) Numerical scale (enumeration, addition, subtraction, multiplication, division), and (4) Space scale (object completion, estimating path, jigsaw puzzles, perspective). **Results:** (1) Boys performed better than girls on the picture vocabulary and jump peg subtests and on the total Space scale. (2) Among Chinese, black, and Puerto Rican Ss, boys performed better than girls on both the Verbal and the Space scales; among Jewish Ss, the reverse was true (Verbal scale, $p < .01$; Space scale, $p < .05$).

Lessler, K. Sexual symbols, structured and unstructured. *J. Consulting Psychology*, 1962, *26*, 44–49.

Subjects: N = 120; 9, 14, 18–21 yrs (college). **Measures:** Ss' task was to sort 20 structured and 20 unstructured (texture) symbols into 2 piles, masculine and feminine. The measure of performance was the percentage of symbols sorted in agreement with the previous ratings of 5 judges with knowledge of psychoanalytic theory. **Results:** (1) There were no sex differences in percentage of correct identifications for structured symbols. (2) Females identified more unstructured symbols consistent with the judges' ratings than males did ($p < .05$).

Leventhal, D.B., and Shemberg, K. M. Sex role adjustment and nonsanctioned aggression. *J. Experimental Research in Personality*, 1969, *3*, 283–86.

Subjects: N = 80; 18–21 yrs (college). **Measures:** Ss were divided into 4 groups (masculine males, masculine females, feminine females, and feminine males) based on their extreme scores on the MF dimensions of the Guilford-Zimmerman Temperament Survey. Ss were instructed to teach a confederate a concept by flashing a light for each response or shocking him for each incorrect response. Ss were given ambiguous sanctions for aggressive behavior, i.e. they were informed that experiments had not yet determined whether strong or weak shocks produced faster learning. The mean intensity of the shocks Ss administered was recorded. **Results:** No sex differences were found.

Leventhal, D. B., Shemberg, K. M., and van Schoelandt, S. K. Effects of sex-role adjustment upon the expression of aggression. *J. Personality & Social Psychology*, 1968, *8*, 393–96.

EXPERIMENT I: **Subjects:** N = 40; 18–21 yrs (college). **Measures:** Ss were divided into 4 groups (masculine males, feminine males, masculine females, and feminine females) based on their extreme scores on the MF dimension of the Guilford-Zimmerman Temperament Survey. Ss were instructed to shock a male confederate every time he made an error. The response measure was the mean intensity of the applied shock. **Results:** There were no main effects of sex or sex-role identification. Masculine males and feminine females had higher mean aggression scores than feminine males and masculine females ($p < .0001$).

EXPERIMENT II: **Subjects:** N = 40; 18–21 yrs (college). **Measures:** Ss were divided into high and low need for approval groups based on their scores on the Marlowe-Crowne Social-Desirability Scale. As in Experiment I, all Ss were told to shock a male confederate whenever he made an error. **Results:** No sex differences.

Leventhal, G. S., and Anderson, D. Self-interest and the maintenance of equity. *J. Personality & Social Psychology*, 1970, *15*, 57–62.

Subjects: N = 144; 5 yrs. **Measures:** Ss were told their performance on a task (pasting gummed stars on a worksheet) was either superior, equal, or inferior to that of a fictitious same-sex partner. Ss were then rewarded with colorful picture seals that they were requested to divide between themselves and their partners. Ss were also asked to recall their own performance and their partners' performance scores. **Results:** (1) In the superior condition, boys took a larger number of seals for themselves than girls did. No sex differences were found in the equal or inferior condition. (2) No sex differences were found in the number of stars Ss attributed to self or to partner.

Leventhal, G. S., and Lane, D. W. Sex, age, and equity behavior. *J. Personality & Social Psychology*, 1970, *15*, 312–16.

Subjects: N = 61; 18–21 yrs (college). **Measures:** Ss worked with a fictitious same-sex partner on a task for which their dyad received monetary reward. Ss were told their performance was either superior or inferior to that of their partner. The performance measure was Ss' allocation of the group reward. **Results:** (1) Men took a larger share of the group reward than women did ($p < .01$). (2) On a postexperimental questionnaire, women in the superior performance condition attributed a lower level of performance to themselves and judged their performance to be more similar to that of their partner than men did. No sex differences were found in the inferior performance condition.

Leventhal, G. S., and Whiteside, H. D. Equity and the use of reward to elicit high performance. *J. Personality & Social Psychology*, 1973, *25*, 75–83.

Subjects: N = 28; 18–21 yrs (college). **Measures:** After being given information about the aptitude and examination performance of several hypothetical students, Ss assigned a midterm grade to each student. **Results:** No sex differences.

Leventhal, G. S., Michaels, J. W., and Sanford, C. Inequity and interpersonal conflict: reward allocation and secrecy about reward as methods of preventing conflict. *J. Personality & Social Psychology*, 1972, *23*, 88–102.

> **Subjects:** $N = 44$; 18–21 yrs (college). **Measures:** Ss gave their opinions about the best way to divide group earnings among the members of a hypothetical group. Ss divided group rewards twice, once under the assumption that all members would know what others were receiving and once under conditions of secrecy. Afterward, Ss rated how reluctant they would be in the secrecy condition to provide group members with information about their allocation of the group rewards. **Results:** No sex differences.

Leventhal, H., and Fischer, K. What reinforces in a social reinforcement situation— words or expressions? *J. Personality & Social Psychology*, 1970, *14*, 83–94.

> **Subjects:** $N = 96$; 5–9 yrs. **Measures:** After an initial base period, Ss received either positive reinforcement or no reinforcement for placing marbles into 1 of 2 holes. Performance measures were rate of marble insertion and hole preference. Additionally, Ss' expressive behavior was rated for anxiety, physical activity, and attentiveness. **Results:** No sex differences.

Levin, G. R., and Maurer, D. M. The solution process in children's matching-to-sample. *Developmental Psychology*, 1969, *1*, 679–90.

> EXPERIMENT I: **Subjects:** $N = 19$; 5–6 yrs. **Measures:** Ss were given matching-to-sample problems using slides of familiar objects and animals. Response measures were choice latency and the time between observing response and choice response. **Results:** No sex differences.
>
> EXPERIMENT III: **Subjects:** $N = 63$; 4–5 yrs. **Measures:** Ss were randomly assigned to "matching" or "oddity" groups. Same as Experiment I, except that slides of black and white drawings and color slides of common geometric forms were used. Color, size, and form were used separately as criteria for matching and oddity problems. **Results:** No sex differences.

Levinger, G., and Moreland, J. Approach-avoidance as a function of imagined shock threat and self-other similarity. *J. Personality & Social Psychology*, 1969, *12*, 245–51.

> **Subjects:** $N = 96$; 18–21 yrs (college). **Measures:** Ss placed figures representing the self in relation to standing silhouette representing 4 "others" of the same sex: (a) a good friend, (b) a stranger, (c) a "similar" stranger, and (d) a "dissimilar" stranger. In 1 condition, Ss were asked to imagine both self and other waiting to receive a shock from E. Distances between Ss' placement of self and other were measured. **Results:** No sex differences.

Levinger, G., and Schneider, D. J. Test of the "risk is a value" hypothesis. *J. Personality & Social Psychology*, 1969, *11*, 165–69.

> **Subjects:** $N = 250$, 18–21 yrs (college). **Measures:** For each of the 12 items from Kogan and Wallach's choice-dilemmas instrument, Ss indicated (a) the minimum odds of success they would want before choosing the more attractive alternative, (b) the minimum odds of success they believed their fellow students would want before choosing the more attractive alternative, and (c) the choice of odds they considered most admirable. **Results:** No sex differences.

Levinger, G., and Senn, D. J. Disclosure feelings in marriage. *Merrill-Palmer Quarterly*, 1967, *13*, 237–49.

> **Subjects:** $N = 32$; married couples. **Measures:** Ss indicated the proportion of their pleasant and unpleasant feelings that they disclosed to their spouses. Ss also estimated what proportion of pleasant and unpleasant feelings their spouses disclosed to them. **Results:** No sex differences were found between husbands' and wives' reports of the proportion of feelings they disclosed to their spouses. Husbands' estimates of the proportion of unpleasant feelings their wives disclosed were higher than their wives' estimates of the proportion of unpleasant feelings their husbands disclosed ($p < .01$).

Levitin, T. E., and Chananie, J. D. Responses of female primary school teachers to sex-typed behaviors in male and female children. *Child Development*, 1972, *43*, 1309–16.

> **Subjects:** 40 female first- and second-grade school teachers. **Measures:** Ss read about 2 hypothetical children who were described as either aggressive, dependent, or achieving. Ss then rated their liking for each child, their approval of his behavior, and the degree to which he was typical of children his own age and sex. **Results:** (1) The achieving girl was liked more than the achieving boy ($p < .05$). No sex differences were found in teachers' typicality or approval ratings. (2a) The aggressive boy and the dependent girl were seen as more typical than the aggressive girl and the dependent boy ($p < .05$). (2b) Teachers' approval ratings of the aggressive boy and the dependent girl were not significantly different from their approval ratings of the dependent boy and the aggressive girl. Overall, teachers exhibited equal approval

of boys and girls. (2c) The dependent girl was liked more than the aggressive girl ($p < .05$); however, the aggressive boy was not liked more than the dependent boy (interaction, $p < .05$). Overall, boys and girls were liked equally well.

Levy, P., Lundgren, D., Ansel, M., Fell, D., Fink, B., and McGrath, J. E. Bystander effect in a demand-without-threat situation. *J. Personality & Social Psychology*, 1972, *24*, 166–71.

> **Subjects:** $N = 110$; 18–21 yrs (college). **Measures:** Ss' responses to an intrusion were recorded while Ss completed a questionnaire either alone or in the presence of 1 or 2 same-sex confederates. Intrusions were 1 or 3 nonemergency, nonthreatening demands for action by a male. The main performance measure was latency of Ss' response. Ss also completed the Rotter Internal-External Control Scale. **Results:** (1) Women had lower response latencies than men; the differences arose mainly from the alone situation. (2) No sex differences were found on the Rotter Scale.

Lewis, M. Social isolation: a parametric study of its effect on social reinforcement. *J. Experimental Child Psychology*, 1965, *2*, 205–18.

> **Subjects:** $N = 150$; 8 yrs. **Measures:** Ss were preesnted with 30 2-choice probability learning tasks after either 0, 3, 6, 9, or 12 minutes of social isolation. Correct responses were verbally reinforced, incorrect responses were not. **Results:** No sex differences.

Lewis, M. Infants' responses to facial stimuli during the first year of life. *Developmental Psychology*, 1969, *1*, 75–86.

> **Subjects:** $N = 120$; 12, 24, 36, 57 wks. **Measures:** Ss were presented with 4 variations of a male face (regular, cyclops, schematic, scrambled). Response measures were length of first fixation, smiling, vocalization, and fret/cry behavior. Only behaviors emitted during or immediately after a fixation were analyzed. **Results:** (1) At all age levels (except 57 weeks), boys looked at stimuli longer than girls did. (2) At all age levels, girls vocalized more than boys did. Girls' smiles differentiated among stimuli, boys' did not.

Lewis, M. State as an infant-environment interaction: An analysis of mother-infant behavior as a function of sex. *Merrill-Palmer Quarterly*, 1972, *18*, 95–121.

> **Subjects:** $N = 32$; 3 mos (white, black) and mothers. **Measures:** Home observations were made of 15 mother and infant behaviors. **Results:** (1) No sex differences were found in the frequency of the following infant behaviors: vocalizing, playing, fretting/crying, smiling, noise-making, gross motor movement. (2) Mothers of boys held their infants more and vocalized to them less than mothers of girls ($p < .05$, $p < .05$). No sex-of-infant differences were found in the following maternal behaviors: touching, looking, smiling, playing, rocking, vocalizing to others, reading/watching TV. (3) Mothers of boys were equally likely to respond in either a proximal (touch-hold) or distal (vocalize-look) modality to their infants' gross motor movements; mothers of girls responded most often in a distal modality ($p < .50$).

Lewis, M., and Freedle, R. Mother-infant dyad: the cradle of meaning. Paper presented at a Symposium on Language and Thought: Communication and Affect, Erindale College, University of Toronto, March 1972.

> **Subjects:** $N = 40$; 3 mos (black, white) and mothers. **Measures:** Mothers and infants were observed in their homes. **Results:** (1) Mothers of girls vocalized to their infants more than mothers of boys did. (2) Mothers of boys responded to vocalizations initiated by their infants more than mothers of girls did. Girls vocalized more in response to mother-initiated behaviors than boys did. (3) Boys spent more time in their mothers' laps than girls did. No sex differences were found in amount of time spent in or on crib/bed, jumper, couch/sofa, playpen, floor, infant seat, diaper-changing table or bath tub.

Lewis, M., Kagan, J., Campbell, M., and Kalafat, J. The cardiac response as a correlate of attention in infants. *Child Development*, 1966, *37*, 63–71.

> **Subjects:** $N = 64$; 6 mos. **Measures:** Fixation time and cardiac rate were measured as Ss viewed varied patterns of lights in a matrix. **Results:** No sex differences.

Lewis, M., Rausch, M., Goldberg, S., and Dodd, C. Error, response time and IQ: sex differences in cognitive style of preschool children. *Perceptual & Motor Skills*, 1968, *26*, 563–68.

> **Subjects:** $N = 57$; 3 yrs. **Measures:** Ss were shown 4 line drawings and were asked to identify which of the 4 was identical to a standard. If Ss did not initially make the correct choice, they were allowed to respond a second time. E recorded Ss' choices and the time between the

presentation of the standard and Ss' initial response. Form L-M of the Stanford-Binet Intelligence Scale was also administered to Ss. **Results:** No sex differences were found in number of errors or mean response time. Girls had higher IQs than boys ($p < .02$).

Lewis, M., Wilson, C. D., and Baumel, M. Attention distribution in the 24-month-old child: variations in complexity and incongruity of the human form. *Child Development*, 1971a, *42*, 429–38.

  Subjects: $N = 60$; 2 yrs. **Measures:** Ss viewed achromatic pictures of human forms varying in complexity and incongruity. Response measures were fixation time, heart rate, arm movement, smiling, pointing, and vocalizations. **Results:** No sex differences.

Lewis, M., Baumel, M., and Groch, A. Infants' attentional distribution across two modalities. Paper presented at meetings of Eastern Psychological Association, New York, 1971b.

  Subjects: $N = 22$; 3 mos. **Measures:** In 2 visits, 1 week apart, Ss were exposed to visual and auditory episodes separated by a test of cognitive development. Visual stimuli consisted of 3 colored lines (simple) and 20 colored lines (complex). Auditory stimuli were a C-tone (simple) and C-chord (complex). Response measures were length of first fixation to visual episode, and heart rate and activity (stabilimeter) recorded for both auditory and visual episode. **Results:** No sex differences.

Lewit, D. W., and Virolainen, K. Conformity and independence in adolescents' motivation for orthodontic treatment. *Child Development*, 1968, *39*, 1189–1200.

  Subjects: $N = 129$; 13 yrs. **Measures:** Desire for Orthodontic Treatment to Children's Social Desirability Scale, Need for Peer Approval, Test Anxiety for Children Scale, Bailer's Locus of Control Scale. **Results:** Girls scored higher on the Desire for Orthodontic Treatment Scale than boys ($p < .01$).

Lichtenwalner, J. S., and Maxwell, J. W. The relationship of birth order and socioeconomic status to the creativity of preschool children. *Child Development*, 1969, *40*, 1241–47.

  Subjects: $N = 68$; 4–6 yrs (low, middle SES). **Measures:** The Starkweather test of creativity. **Results:** No sex differences.

Liebert, R. M., and Baron, R. A. Some immediate effects of televised violence on children's behavior. *Developmental Psychology*, 1972, *6*, 469–75.

  Subjects: $N = 136$; 5–6, 8–9 yrs. **Measures:** After watching 3½ minutes of "The Untouchables" or a videotaped sports sequence, Ss were given the opportunity to either help (by pressing a red button) or hurt (by pressing a green button) a child in an adjacent room. Ss were then taken to a room containing aggressive and nonaggressive toys. Ss were told they could play with any of the toys. The occurrence of each of the following aggressive responses was recorded: plays with knife, plays with gun, and assaults doll. **Results:** (1) No differences were found in the duration of boys' and girls' helping or hurting responses. (2) Boys exhibited more aggressive play responses than girls.

Liebert, R. M., and Fernandez, L. E. Imitation as a function of vicarious and direct reward. *Developmental Psychology*, 1970, *2*, 230–32.

  Subjects: $N = 48$; 4–6 yrs. **Measures:** After watching an adult male model choose the less popular of 2 alternatives and receive verbal reward in 1 condition or no reward in the other condition, S indicated his preference for each of 12 slide pairs. S performed the task again under instructions to match the model's responses. **Results:** No sex differences.

Liebert, R. M., and Ora, J. P. Children's adoption of self-reward patterns: incentive level and method of transmission. *Child Development*, 1968, *39*, 537–44.

  Subjects: $N = 72$; 8–10 yrs. **Measures:** Ss learned to play a bowling game (with preset scores) that they later had a chance to play under self-reward conditions; 1 group of Ss were shown a variety of prizes and told they could win these items if they earned enough tokens in the self-reward trial. The low-incentive group was shown a selection of dull textbooks during the length of time required for the high-incentive manipulation. The scores for which Ss took self-rewards when playing the game alone were recorded. **Results:** No sex differences.

Liebert, R. M., and Swenson, S. A. Association and abstraction as mechanisms of imitative learning. *Developmental Psychology*, 1971a, *4*, 289–94.

  Subjects: $N = 48$; 4 yrs. **Measures:** Ss observed a female model choose all single or all double items projected on slides (common dimension condition), or half single and half double items (no common dimension condition). Ss were then instructed to make the choices the model had made. **Results:** (1) Girls showed better recall of the model's choices than boys ($p < .05$). (2) There were no sex differences in latency of imitative recall.

Liebert, R. M., and Swenson, S. A. Abstraction, inference, and the process of imitative learning. *Developmental Psychology*, 1971b, 5, 500–504.
> **Subjects:** $N = 32$; 6 yrs. **Measures:** Ss watched a model choose single items or double items from slide pictures (common dimension condition), or equal numbers of single and double items (no common dimension condition). Ss were asked to recall the model's choices when the slides were presented again, and to guess model's preferences in novel slide set. **Results:** (1) In accuracy of immediate forced recall of model's choices, boys performed better than girls in the no common dimension condition. There were no sex differences in accuracy of recall in the common dimension condition. (2) There were no sex differences on latency of imitative recall measures. (3) There were no sex differences in response latencies of predicting model's choice behavior.

Liebert, R. M., Hanratty, M., and Hill, J. H. Effects of rule structure and training method on the adoption of a self-imposed standard. *Child Development*, 1969a, 40, 93–101.
> **Subjects:** $N = 48$; 7 yrs. **Measures:** Before a bowling game, half the Ss received direct instructions, while the other half observed self-reward standards exhibited by a training agent. After learning the game, each S individually played for prizes, which were earned by acquiring self-reward tokens. The game had fixed scores for all trials. The number of tokens self-administered when S played alone was the measure recorded. **Results:** No sex differences.

Liebert, R. M., Odom, R. D., Hill, J. H., and Huff, R. L. Effects of age and rule familiarity on the production of modeled language constructions. *Developmental Psychology*, 1969b, 2, 108–12.
> **Subjects:** $N = 14$; 5, 8, 14 yrs. **Measures:** Ss were assigned to 1 of 2 conditions: (1) the English rule condition in which Ss were exposed to and rewarded for production of sentences containing familiar prepositional phrases, and (2) the new rule condition in which Ss were exposed to and rewarded for production of sentences containing ungrammatical prepositional phrases. All Ss were given 10 base-rate trials and 20 training trials. Difference scores were computed by doubling each S's base-rate production of relevant prepositional constructions and subtracting it from his training score. **Results:** No sex differences.

Liebert, R. M., McCall, R. B., and Hanratty, M. A. Effects of sex-typed information on children's toy preference. *J. Genetic Psychology*, 1971, 119, 133–36.
> **Subjects:** $N = 40$; 6–8 yrs. **Measures:** Ss were asked to indicate which of 2 toys they preferred. Before responding, Ss were told 1 of the following: (a) that both boys and girls prefer toy A, (b) that both boys and girls prefer toy B, (c) that boys prefer toy A, whereas girls prefer toy B, or (d) that girls prefer toy A, whereas boys prefer toy B. The response measure was the number of times Ss chose the toy preferred by members of their own sex. **Results:** No sex differences.

Light, C. S., Zax, M., and Gardiner, D. H. Relationship of age, sex and intelligence level to extreme response style. *J. Personality & Social Psychology*, 1965, 2, 907–9.
> **Subjects:** $N = 240$; 9, 13, 17 yrs. **Measures:** Ss rated each of 10 Rorschach inkblots on 15 semantic differential scales. Ss were scored for the number of extreme, intermediate, and neutral ratings made. **Results:** No sex differences.

Linder, D. E., Cooper, J., and Jones, E. E. Decision freedom as a determinant of the role of incentive magnitude in attitude change. *J. Personality & Social Psychology*, 1967, 6, 245–54.
> **Subjects:** $N = 53$; 18–21 yrs (college). **Measures:** After writing essays in favor of a speaker ban they were actually opposed to, Ss rated the degree to which they were either in favor of or opposed to the ban. **Results:** No sex differences.

Lindskold, S., Cullen, P., Gahagan, J., and Tedeschi, J. T. Developmental aspects of reaction to positive inducements. *Developmental Psychology*, 1970, 3, 277–84.
> **Subjects:** $N = 144$; 10, 11 yrs. **Measures:** The Prisoner's Dilemma game was modified so that Ss paid a simulated player, who communicated occasonal promises of an extra reward if the cooperative choice was made on the next trial. The 4 manipulated variables were (1) 10%, 50%, and 90% credibility of the simulated player's promises (probability of bribe being paid as promised), (2) $5, $10, and $20 play money reward levels, (3) overall game strategies of 50% or 90% cooperative choices made by the simulated player, and (4) sex of subject. **Results:**

(1) Overall, boys were more cooperative than girls ($p < .001$). (2) Girls and boys were equally cooperative when the simulated player cooperated 50% of the time. When the simulated player was highly cooperative (90%), boys cooperated more often. Girls responded to both strategy levels the same way. (3) Girls won more often than boys ($p < .001$). (4) Neither sex won very often when the simulated player played a 50% strategy, but girls won more than boys when strategy used was 90% cooperative ($p < .004$).

Lipsitt, L. P., and Jacklin, C. N. Cardiac deceleration and its stability in human newborns. *Developmental Psychology*, 1971, 5, 535 (brief report and personal communication).
   Subjects: $N = 20$; 2 days. Measures: Ss' heart rates were analyzed for 10 beats before and 20 beats after 10 5-second presentations of either an odorant stimulus on 2 successive days, or a nonodorant 1 day and an odorant the next day. Results: No sex differences.

Lipton, C., and Overton, W. F. Anticipatory imagery and modified anagram solution: a developmental study. *Child Development*, 1971, 42, 615–23.
   Subjects: $N = 80$; 7, 9, 11, 13 yrs (high and low reading-achievement groups). Measures: An anagram test was administered to Ss. Number of correct solutions and average solution time were recorded. Results: No sex differences.

Littenberg, R., Tulkin, S. R., and Kagan, J. Cognitive components of separation anxiety. *Developmental Psychology*, 1971, 4, 387–88.
   Subjects: $N = 24$; 11 mos and mothers. Measures: After 10 minutes together, the infants watched their mothers leave from an exit in the home that was normally used (1 trial) or rarely used (other trial). For 2 minutes after the mother's exit, the infant was observed for vocalizations, fretting, crying, staring at the exit, and crawling to the exit. Results: No sex differences.

Little, K. B. Cultural variations in social schemata. *J. Personality & Social Psychology*, 1968, 10, 1–7.
   Subjects: $N = 432$; 18–21 yrs (college: U.S., Sweden, Greece, Italy, Scotland). Measures: Ss placed doll figures (always the same sex as S) in positions appropriate for each of 19 different social interactions. Results: (1) No overall sex differences were found in average distance between placement of doll figures. Among Italian and Greek Ss, women placed figures closer together than men did. Among American and Scottish Ss, women placed figures farther apart than men did. (2) Women perceived neutral topics as being discussed at greater distances than men did. Women perceived unpleasant topics as being discussed at closer distances than men did. (3) Women perceived intimate transactions as occurring at closer distances than men did. (4) Women perceived interactions with authority figures or superiors as taking place at greater distances than men did.

Lloyd, B. B. Studies of conservation with Yoruba children of differing ages and experience. *Child Development*, 1971, 42, 415–28.
   Subjects: $N = 80$; 3–8 yrs (Yoruba). Measures: 2 types of materials, bricks and sweets, were used to test for conservation of number. Results: When bricks were used, boys' performance was superior to that of girls. When sweets were used, no sex differences were found.

Lodge, A., Armington, J. C., Barnet, A. B., Shanks, B. L., and Newcomb, C. N. Newborn infants' electroretinograms and evoked electroencephalographic responses to orange and white light. *Child Development*, 1969, 40, 267–93.
   Subjects: $N = 20$; 1–2 days. Measures: Electroretinogram and electroencephalogram data were recorded while Ss viewed a series of orange and white light flashes. Response measures were (1) peak latencies and amplitudes of the x- and b-waves of the ERG, and (2) peak latency and peak-to-trough amplitude of the first positive component of the occipital response. Results: No sex differences.

London, P., and Cooper, L. M. Norms of hypnotic susceptibility in children. *Developmental Psychology*, 1969, 1, 113–24.
   Subjects: $N = 240$; 5–16 yrs. Measures: Ss were given the Children's Hypnotic Susceptibility Scale. Results: No sex differences were found in total susceptibility scores or item difficulty.

Long, A. B., and Looft, W. R. Development of directionality in children. *Developmental Psychology*, 1972, 6, 375–80.
   Subjects: $N = 144$; 6–12 yrs. Measures: Each S was given a battery of 125 directionality

items taken from those used by Piaget, Swanson and Benton, Wapner and Cirillo, and some generated by the authors. **Results:** No sex differences.

Long, B. H., and Henderson, E. H. Social schemata of school beginners: some demographic correlates. *Merrill-Palmer Quarterly*, 1970, *16*, 305–24.

> **Subjects:** $N = 192$; 6 yrs (white and black, low and middle SES). **Measures:** A modified version of the preschool Children's Self-Social Constructs Test was administered. Measures assessed were (a) self-esteem: S was presented with a column of circles representing other children and asked to select 1 of the circles to represent himself. Selection of positions closer to the top was assumed to represent a higher level of self-esteem; (b) social interest or dependency: Ss were presented with a diagram in which 3 circles (representing other children) were arranged as the apexes of a triangle. Each S was given a gummed circle (representing himself) to paste anywhere on the sheet of paper. Placement of the gummed circle within, rather than outside, the boundaries of the triangle was assumed to indicate greater social interest or dependency; (c) identification: Ss were presented with a row of circles, with the circle to the extreme left representing either father, mother, teacher, or friends. Each S was asked to select 1 of the remaining circles to represent himself. Fewer circles intervening between self and other was assumed to indicate greater identification with the other; (d) preference for others: Ss were presented with pages on which all possible pairs of 4 stimulus figures appeared (mother, father, teacher, friends). On each page, S was asked to paste a figure representing himself next to 1 of the 2 stimulus persons. The response measure was the number of times each stimulus person was selected; (e) realism size: Ss were presented with an array of circles of 3 sizes. Ss first selected 1 circle to represent father and then 1 circle to represent self. The choice of a smaller circle was assumed to indicate a more realistic conception of one's size; (f) minority identification: Ss were presented with an array of plain circles in a rectangle, accompanied by a plain and a shaded circle to the right. Circles within the rectangle represented other children. Ss were asked to pick 1 of the 2 circles to the right to represent themselves. The selection of the shaded circle was assumed to indicate minority identification. **Results:** (1) There were no sex differences in self-esteem. (2) There were no main sex differences in social interest or dependency. Middle SES girls and lower SES boys had higher scores than their male and female counterparts ($p < .05$). (3) There were no sex differences in identification with mother, teacher, or friends. Boys placed the self closer to the father than girls did ($p = .05$). (4) On the preference-for-others measure, boys placed the self less often with teacher and more often with father than girls did ($p < .005$, $p < .001$). (5) There were no sex differences in realism for size. (6) There were no sex differences in minority identification. Among middle SES blacks, boys chose the shaded circle more often than girls did ($p = .02$).

Long, B. H., Henderson, E. H., and Ziller, R. C. Developmental changes in the self-concept during middle childhood. *Merrill-Palmer Quarterly*, 1967, *13*, 201–15.

> **Subjects:** $N = 312$; 6–13 yrs. **Measures:** (1) Ss were administered the Children's Self-Social Constructs Test, a measure consisting of the following tasks: (a) Ss viewed a large circular area containing an array of smaller circles representing "other children." Each S was asked to select 1 of 2 other circles (one shaded, one not) to represent himself. The choice of the circle different from those representing peers (i.e. shaded) was assumed to indicate a higher degree of individuation. (b) Ss viewed a row of circles representing other children. Each S was asked to select 1 of the circles to represent himself (herself). Positions to the left were assumed to represent a higher level of self-esteem. (c) Ss viewed a diagram in which 1 circle (representing the self) was surrounded by a semicircle of other circles. Other circles were directly above, diagonally above, even with, diagonally below, and directly below the circle representing the self. Ss were asked to select 1 of the 5 other circles to represent certain authority figures (father or teacher). Ss' responses were scored from 1 to 5, with a higher score indicating a lower position for the other person. (d) Each S was presented with 2 gummed circles, 1 representing himself and 1 representing a friend. Ss were asked to place them on a sheet of paper in any way they liked. Distance between circles was measured, with less distance assumed to represent more identification with friends. (e) Ss were presented with a row of circles, with the circle to the extreme left representing an adult other (mother, father, or teacher). Each S was asked to select 1 of the remaining circles to represent himself. The number of circles intervening between self and other was counted, with less distance assumed to indicate more identification with the adult other. (f) Ss were presented with a diagram in which 3 circles (representing parents, teachers, and friends) were arranged as the apexes of an equilateral triangle. Each S was given a gummed circle to represent himself and was asked to paste it anywhere on the sheet of paper. Placement of the

self within rather than outside the triangular area was assumed to reflect a perception of the self as dependent upon, or as a part of, the group of others. (2) Ss were also presented with a list of activities and were asked to indicate whether they would rather do them alone or with a group of friends. **Results:** (1) Individuation: a higher proportion of boys than girls represented the self as "different" from others. (2) Self-esteem: no sex differences. (3) Power of self in relation to father: no sex differences. Power of self in relation to teacher: no sex differences. (4) Identification with friends: no sex differences. (5) (a) Identification with teacher: girls identified more with their teachers than boys did ($p < .05$). Little difference was found between the sexes on this measure in the first grade. Henceforth, the sex difference increased until the sixth grade, where it declined again (possibly because the only male teacher in the sample taught a sixth-grade class). (b) Identification with mother: girls identified more with their mothers than boys did ($p < .05$). (c) Identification with father: no sex differences. (d) Boys did not identify more with their fathers than with their mothers; girls identified more with their mothers than with their fathers ($p < .05$). Boys were less closely identified with their fathers than girls were with their mothers ($p < .05$). (6) Dependency on others: no sex differences. (7) Girls chose to pursue more group activities than boys did ($p < .001$).

Long, B. H., Henderson, E. H., and Ziller, R. C. Self-ratings on the semantic differential: content versus response set. *Child Development*, 1968, *39*, 647–56.
Subjects: $N = 312$; 6–13 yrs (white, rural, middle SES). A random sample of 52 was studied for sex effects. **Measures:** All Ss rated self on 6 pairs of adjective-opposite in 2 scales, evaluative and power. Responses were scored from 1 to 5, with a high score indicating high self-rating in power or value. Scores were summed to provide content scores for each scale. Responses were also scored for extremity in response set. **Results:** (1) Boys rated self higher on the power scale than girls did ($p < .001$). (2) Girls rated self higher on evaluative scale than boys did ($p < .001$). (3) Set scores declined over grade level except for 10-year-old boys and 11-year-old girls (evaluative $p < .05$, set scores $p < .01$). (4) Boys made more extreme responses and fewer qualified responses than girls did ($p < .01$, $p < .05$). (5) 10-year-old girls and 11-year-old boys made relatively less use of extremes and greater use of neutral positions than their opposite sex counterparts did ($p < .05$, $p < .05$).

Long, B. H., Ziller, R. C., Kanisetti, R. V., and Reddy, V. E. Self-description as a function of evaluative and activity ratings among American and Indian adolescents. *Child Development*, 1970, *41*, 1017–24.
Subjects: $N = 200$; 10–14 yrs (U.S., India). **Measures:** Ss rated themselves on 81 adjectives from the Thorndike-Lorge Teachers' Word Book. **Results:** (1) Boys checked more words than girls did ($p < .05$). (2) There was greater concordance between cultures for girls than for boys ($p = .001$).

Longstreth, L. E. Birth order and avoidance of dangerous activities. *Developmental Psychology*, 1970, *2*, 154.
Subjects: $N = 130$; 18–21 yrs (college). **Measures:** Ss retrospectively rated themselves on a 7-point scale on the dangerous activities and rough games they avoided at age 12. **Results:** Boys rated themselves as having been more daring than girls rated themselves ($p < .02$).

Loo, C., and Wenar, C. Activity level and motor inhibition: their relationship to intelligence-test performance in normal children. *Child Development*, 1971, *42*, 967–71.
Subjects: $N = 40$; 5–6 yrs. **Measures:** Ss' classroom activity levels were measured by actometers attached to their dominant wrists and ankles. Inhibition of movement was measured by the Draw a Line Slowly Test and the Walk Slowly Test. The Primary Mental Abilities Test was also administered. Teachers rated the Ss on activity and impulsivity. **Results:** Sex of subject was not significantly correlated with actometer scores, IQ scores, or motor-inhibition scores. Teachers rated more boys than girls as active and impulsive, and as having less inhibiting control.

Looft, W. R. Sex differences in the expression of vocational aspirations by elementary school children. *Developmental Psychology*, 1971, *5*, 366 (brief report).
Subjects: $N = 66$; 6–8 yrs. **Measures:** Each S was asked, "What would you like to be when you grow up?" and "What do you think you *really* will do when you grow up?" The response measure was S's first choice. **Results:** (1) In response to the first question, boys named 18 different occupations, the most frequent being football player and policeman. Other desirable occupations included doctor, dentist, priest, scientist, airline pilot, and astronaut. Girls named 8 different occupations, the most frequent being teacher and nurse. Other desirable occupa-

tions included housewife, mother, airline stewardess, and salesgirl. (2) In response to the second question, more boys than girls changed from their initial response to other vocations.

Looft, W. R., and Charles, D. C. Modification of the life concept in children. *Developmental Psychology*, 1969, *1*, 445 (brief report).
Subjects: $N = 35$; 7–9 yrs. Measures: Before and after viewing an instructional film on the biological nature of life, Ss indicated whether each of 18 familiar phenomena was living or nonliving. Results: No sex differences.

Lott, A. J., and Lott, B. E. Liked and disliked persons as reinforcing stimuli. *J. Personality & Social Psychology*, 1969, *11*, 129–37.
Subjects: $N = 100$; 14 yrs. Measures: On each trial of a visual discrimination learning task, Ss were presented with 2 figures that varied on 3 dimensions: shape, size, and color. Only 1 dimension (size) was relevant. The choice of the large stimulus was correct for half the Ss, while the choice of the small stimulus was correct for the remaining Ss. Following a correct response, Ss were presented with either a card on which the word "right" was printed, a photo of a liked same-sex peer, a photo of a neutrally regarded peer, or a photo of a disliked peer. Ss in a fifth condition were shown a photo of a disliked peer following an incorrect response. Results: There were no sex differences.

Lott, A. J., Bright, M. A., Weinstein, P., and Lott, B. E. Liking for persons as a function of incentive and drive during acquisition. *J. Personality & Social Psychology*, 1970a, *14*, 66–76.
Subjects: $N = 31$; 18–21 yrs (college). Measures: Attitudes toward two different E's were measured by semantic differential, personal feelings, and the like-dislike scales; 1 E had been present when Ss attained high scores on an intelligence test, the other E had been present when Ss performed poorly. For each S, a difference score was obtained for each measure: liking for the E who was present during high achievement minus liking for the E who was present during low achievement. Results: No sex differences.

Lott, A. J., Lott, B. E., and Walsh, M. L. Learning of paired associates relevant to differentially liked persons. *J. Personality & Social Psychology*, 1970b, *16*, 274–83.
Subjects: $N = 52$; 18–21 yrs (college). Measures: Ss learned to associate nonsense syllables with the names of well-liked, neutral, and disliked acquaintances. The performance measure was the number of errors made before reaching the criterion of 2 consecutive errorless trials. Results: No sex differences.

Lott, A. J., Lott, B. E., Reed, T., and Crow, T. Personality-trait descriptions of differentially liked persons. *J. Personality & Social Psychology*, 1970c, *16*, 284–90.
EXPERIMENT I: Subjects: $N = 50$; 18–21 yrs (college). Measures: Ss were asked to name 3 persons: a well-liked friend, a disliked acquaintance, and a neutrally regarded acquaintance. Ss were then presented with a list of personality traits. Ss were asked to indicate which of the 3 persons was most appropriately described by each trait. Results: No sex differences.
EXPERIMENT II: Subjects: $N = 60$; 18–21 yrs (college). Measures: Same as Experiment I. Results: In describing their friends, women chose adjectives that were higher in "likableness" value than men did ($p < .05$). No other sex differences were found.

Lott, B. E., and Lott, A. J. The relationship of manifest anxiety in children to learning task performance and other variables. *Child Development*, 1968, *39*, 207–20.
Subjects: $N = 233$; 9, 10 yrs (white, black). Measures: Ss were given the Children's Manifest Anxiety Scale. Results: No sex differences were found in either Anxiety-scale or Lie-scale scores.

Loughlin, K. A., and Daehler, M. W. The effects of distraction and added perceptual cues on the delayed reaction of very young children. *Child Development*, 1973, *44*, 384–88.
Subjects: $N = 51$; 2–4 yrs. Measures: Ss performed a delayed reaction task (toy lamb hidden in each of 4 boxes). During the delay, S either remained looking at the boxes or interacted with E. Distraction was provided by placing pictures in front of the boxes. Results: No sex differences.

Lunneborg, P. W., and Rosenwood, L. W. Need affiliation and achievement; declining sex differences. Bureau of Testing, University of Washington, 1972.
Subjects: $N = 465$; 18–21 yrs (college). Measures: Ss answered the following questions: (1) "What would make you happy?" (2) "What makes you sad?" and (3) "What makes you an-

gry?" Ss' responses were scored for *n* affiliation and *n* achievement. **Results:** In response to question 1, women showed more *n* affiliation than men did ($p < .01$).

Luria, Z., and Rebelsky, F. Children's conceptions of events before and after confessions of transgression. *Child Development*, 1969, *40*, 1055–61.
    Subjects: $N = 80$; 10–13 yrs. **Measures:** Ss were given 4 transgression stories to read. All 4 ended with the protagonist (always of the same sex as S) confessing the crime to the person transgressed against. After each story, Ss indicated how likely it would be before confessing for the protagonist to feel (a) unhappy, (b) afraid of being found out, (c) afraid of being punished, (d) anxious and worried, (e) sorry, and (f) guilty. Ss also indicated the probability after confessing that the protagonist would be (a) forgiven, (b) praised, (c) punished, (d) scolded, (e) reasoned with, (f) hit, and (g) deprived of something, with the probability of "things getting better" and of "things getting worse." **Results:** No sex differences.

Lynn, D. B., and Lynn, R. The structured doll play test as a projective technique with children. *J. Projective Techniques*, 1959, *23*, 335–44.
    Subjects: $N = 49$; 4, 6 yrs. **Measures:** Structured Doll Play Test. **Results:** (1) Among 4-year-old Ss, a higher proportion of boys than girls picked the bottle (immature choice) instead of the cup (mature choice) ($p < .05$). (2) Among 6-year-olds, boys received lower dependency scores than girls; among 4-year-olds, no sex differences were found.

MacArthur, R. Sex differences in field dependence for the Eskimo. *International J. Psychology*, 1967, *2*, 139–40.
    Subjects: $N = 167$; 9–15 yrs (western Eskimo). **Measures:** Vernon's Embedded Figures Test. **Results:** No sex differences.

McBain, W. N., Fox, W., Kumura, S., Nakanishi, M., and Tirado, J. Quasi-sensory communication: an investigation using semantic matching and accentuated affect. *J. Personality & Social Psychology*, 1970, *14*, 281–91.
    Subjects: $N = 22$; 18–21 yrs (college). **Measures:** 1 subject in each pair of same-sex or opposite-sex Ss concentrated on 1 of 5 symbols, without communicating with his partner. The partner's task was to guess which 1 of the 5 symbols had been concentrated on. **Results:** The guesses of like-sex pairs of Ss were more accurate than those of opposite-sex pairs of Ss. ($p < .001$).

McCall, R. B., and Kagan, J. Attention in the infant: effects of complexity, contour, perimeter, and familiarity. *Child Development*, 1967, *38*, 939–52.
    Subjects: $N = 36$; 4 mos. **Measures:** Ss were presented with slides of 9 solid black, random shapes, having 5, 10, or 20 turns and 3 different contour lengths. Response measures were first fixation time, total fixation time, number of fixations, average fixation time, nonfretful vocalization, smiling frequency, resting cardiac level, and magnitude of cardiac deceleration. Each infant's height and weight were also recorded. Information on feeding was obtained from parent interviews. **Results:** Girls were more likely to be nursed than boys. No other sex differences were found.

McCall, R. B., and Kagan, J. Individual differences in the infant's distribution of attention to stimulus discrepancy. *Developmental Psychology*, 1970, *2*, 90–98.
    Subjects: $N = 72$; 4 mos. **Measures:** Ss were repeatedly exposed to a standard of 3 objects. Intermittently, either 1, 2, or 3 new objects were substituted for those in the standard set. Fixation times were recorded. **Results:** No sex differences.

McCall, R. B., Hogarty, P. S., Hamilton, J. S., and Vincent, J. M. Habituation rate and the infant's response to visual discrepancies. *Child Development*, 1973, *44*, 280–87.
    Subjects: $N = 120$; 12, 18 wks. **Measures:** Ss viewed a stimulus pattern until visual fixation reached habituation criterion. A discrepant stimulus varying in magnitude of discrepancy was then introduced. Rate of habituation and fixation were measured. **Results:** No sex differences.

McCarson, C., and Daves, W. F. Free recall of object names in preschool children as a function of intracategory variation. *Developmental Psychology*, 1971, *4*, 295 (brief reports).
    Subjects: $N = 20$; 4, 5 yrs. **Measures:** Each S, tested individually, was shown 48 common objects, comprising 12 different categories. For 6 categories the same object was repeated 4 times; for the other 6 categories, 4 different specimens were used. The objects, randomly arranged

on 2 turntables, were exposed for 2 seconds each. Then E asked S to recall what he saw. **Results:** No sex differences.

McCarthy, J. J., and Kirk, S. A. *The construction, standardization, and statistical characteristics of the Illinois Test of Psycholinguistic Abilities.* Urbana: University of Illinois Press, 1963.

> **Subjects:** $N = 700$; 28–32, 34–38, 40–44, 46–50, 52–56, 58–62, 64–68, 70–74, 76–80, 82–86, 88–92, 94–98, 100–104, 106–110 mos. **Measures:** The Illinois Test of Psycholinguistic Abilities. **Results:** (1) Among 40-44- and 82-86-month-old Ss, girls scored higher than boys in auditory decoding ($p < .05$; $p < .05$). (2) Among 52-56-, 100-104-, and 106-110-month-old Ss, boys scored higher than girls in visual decoding ($p < .05$; $p < .01$; $p < .01$). (3) Among 58-62- and 70-74-month-old Ss, girls scored higher than boys in auditory vocal association ($p < .05$; $p < .05$). The opposite was true among 106-110-month-old Ss ($p < .01$). (4) Among 40-44- and 94-98-month-old Ss, girls scored higher than boys in visual-motor association ($p < .01$; $p < .05$). (5) There were no sex differences on the vocal encoding and the auditory vocal automatic tests. (6) Among 64-66- and 106-110-month-old Ss, boys scored higher than girls in motor encoding ($p < .05$; $p < .05$). (7) Among 88-92-month-old Ss, girls scored higher than boys in auditory-vocal sequencing ($p < .01$). (8) Among 82-86-month-old Ss, girls scored higher than boys in visual motor sequencing ($p < .01$; $p < .01$).

McCarver, R. B. A developmental study of the effect of organizational cues on short-term memory. *Child Development*, 1972, *43*, 1317–25.

> **Subjects:** $N = 160$; 5, 7, 10, 18–21 yrs (college). **Measures:** Ss were shown 8 colored drawings of familiar objects, 1 at a time, for a period of 1 or 2 seconds each. Each picture was turned over and placed in a horizontal row after it was presented. A drawing identical to 1 of the 8 was then given to Ss, with instructions to find its duplicate. The percentage of Ss' first-choice responses that were correct was recorded. **Results:** No sex differences.

McCarver, R. B., and Ellis, N. R. Effect of overt verbal labeling on short-term memory in culturally deprived and nondeprived children. *Developmental Psychology*, 1972, *6*, 38–41.

> **Subjects:** $N = 60$; 5–6 yrs (low, middle SES). **Measures:** Ss completed the Peabody Picture Vocabulary Test, a digit-span test, and a short-term-memory task with or without verbal labeling of stimuli by Ss. **Results:** No sex differences.

Maccoby, E. E., and Feldman, S. S. Mother-attachment and stranger-reactions in the third year of life. *Monographs of the Society for Research in Child Development*, 1972, *37*.

> AMERICAN STUDY: **Subjects:** $N = 64$; 2 yrs. 35 Ss were retested at 2½ yrs, 38 at 3 yrs. **Measures:** At each testing, Ss were observed in the following sequence of events involving the presence or absence of their mother and/or a stranger in a room with toys: Episode 1: Mo and Ch brought to testing room by E. E leaves. Episode 2: Mo sits in chair, then gets down on floor to play with Ch. Mo returns to chair. Episode 3: Str enters, greets Mo, sits quietly for 1 minute, converses with Mo, then plays with Ch. Mo leaves. Episode 4: Str gradually disengages from play with child. Episode 5: Mo returns, Str leaves. Mo calls to child, waits for a moment, then plays with Ch. Mo leaves. Episode 6: Ch remains alone for 3 minutes. Episode 7: Str enters, stands quietly for a moment, then moves to chair. Episode 8: Mo enters, then talks to Ch. Mo and Ch collect belongings in preparation for leaving. **Results:** (1) No sex differences were found in manipulative play during Episode 2, 3, or 6. During Episodes 4 (at age 2½ only) and 7 (at age 2 only), boys exhibited manipulative play more frequently than girls did. No sex differences were found in duration of longest manipulation of single toy before shifting to another (personal communication). (2) No sex differences were found in activity level during Episode 3, 6, or 7. During Episodes 2 (at age 3 only) and 4 (at age 2 only), boys were more active than girls. Overall, 2-year-old boys had a higher activity level than 2-year-old girls. (3) During Episodes 2 and 3, no sex differences were found in proximity to Mo, total looks at Mo, or total number of speaks, smiles, or shows item to Mo. (4) During Episodes 4 and 7, no sex differences were found in proximity to Str. During Episodes 3, 4, and 7, no sex differences were found in total number of speaks, smiles, or shows item to Str. (5) During Episodes 4, 6, and 7, no sex differences were found in crying. (6) When left alone during Episode 6, more boys than girls banged on the door. (7) No difference was found between 2-year-old boys and girls in the amount of time that elapsed before they made their first approach to Mo during Episode 2. No analysis was made of the data at 2½ and 3 years of age.
>
> KIBBUTZ STUDY: **Subjects:** $N = 20$; 2 yrs. **Measures:** Procedures were identical to those followed in the American study. The amount of crying and manipulative play Ss exhibited during

Episodes 4 and 6 and the amount of proximity to mothers displayed during Episode 3 were added together to yield a summary attachment score. Manipulative play was given a negative value in the sum. **Results:** No sex differences.

Maccoby, E. E., and Jacklin, C. N. Stress, activity and proximity seeking: sex differences in the year old child. *Child Development*, 1973, *44*, 34–42.

EXPERIMENT I: **Subjects:** $N = 40$; 13, 14 mos. **Measures:** Ss were observed in an unfamiliar room with their mothers. The room was marked off into 18-inch squares and contained 6 toys. At the beginning of each of 2 phases, half the Ss were placed in the square adjacent to where their mothers were seated, while the other half were placed 8 feet away. Phase 1 was free-play period lasting 5 minutes. Phase 2 began with exposure to a loud, angry male voice, followed by a free-play period of 4 minutes. **Results:** (1) Boys crossed more squares than girls did (Phase 1, $p < .05$; Phase 2, $p < .05$). Boys showed a decrease in activity from Phase 1 to Phase 2; girls did not ($p < .01$). (2) Boys made more trips to their mothers during Phase 1 than girls did ($p < .05$). (3) Following presentation of the fear stimulus, boys had longer latencies to first movement than girls did ($p < .01$). (4) No sex differences were found in time spent in proximity to or in physical contact with mother, in frequency of looking at mother, or in frequency of crying.

EXPERIMENT II: **Subjects:** $N = 40$; 13, 14 mos. **Measures:** Same as Experiment I, except that (a) all Ss were placed 8 feet away from their mothers at the beginning of both phases, (b) the angry male voice was presented either at a high or at a moderate level of intensity. **Results:** No sex differences.

McCormick, C. C., Schnobrich, J., and Footlik, S. W. IE Arrow-Dot performance in different adolescent populations. *Perceptual & Motor Skills*, 1966, *22*, 507–10.

Subjects: $N = 72$; 14–17 yrs (black). **Measures:** The Arrow-Dot subtest of the IES (Impulse, Ego, Superego) Test was administered to Ss (mean $IA = 66$). **Results:** Girls had lower E scores and higher S scores than boys ($p < .0005$; $p < .0005$). No sex differences were found in I scores.

McCullers, J. C. Associative strength and degree of interference in children's verbal paired-associate learning. *J. Experimental Child Psychology*, 1967, *5*, 58–68.

Subjects: $N = 144$; 11 yrs. **Measures:** Ss were given a verbal paired-associates learning task. The number of trials Ss needed to reach criterion was recorded. **Results:** No sex differences.

McCullers, J. C. Size-discrimination difficulty and verbal paired-associate learning in children. *Developmental Psychology*, 1969, *1*, 447–48 (brief report).

EXPERIMENT I: **Subjects:** $N = 120$; 11 yrs. **Measures:** A size-discrimination task and a verbal paired-associates learning task were administered to Ss concurrently. **Results:** No sex differences.

EXPERIMENT II: **Subjects:** $N = 40$; 9 yrs. **Measures:** Same as Experiment I. **Results:** No sex differences.

McCullers, J. C., and Martin, J. A. A reexamination of the role of incentive in children's discrimination learning. *Child Development*, 1971, *42*, 827–37.

EXPERIMENT I: **Subjects:** $N = 24$; 9 yrs. **Measures:** Ss rated their preference for 12 objects and then made forced choices between objects having the same value. Ss were allowed to select and keep any objects they wanted. **Results:** Boys selected more objects to keep than girls ($p < .001$).

EXPERIMENT II: **Subjects:** $N = 72$; 9 yrs. **Measures:** 2 high-incentive (bubblegum, chocolate kiss) and 2 low-incentive (paper clip, slip of paper) objects from Experiment I were selected. Ss rated objects, and made forced choices as in I. Ss performed a discrimination-learning task, with the value of the reinforcing object varied. **Results:** No sex differences.

McDavid, J. W. Imitative behavior in preschool children. *Psychological Monographs: General and Applied*, 1959, *73*.

EXPERIMENT I: **Subjects:** $N = 32$; 3–5 yrs. **Measures:** Ss were reinforced for imitating the response of either an adult male or an adult female model in a 2-choice discrimination-learning problem. To make the correct response on each trial, Ss had to avoid paying attention to irrelevant environmental cues. **Results:** No main sex differences were found in (a) tendency to imitate on trial 1, (b) total number of imitative responses, or (c) deviation from chance imitation scores (calculated by recording the difference between the number of imitative responses made by Ss in each 4-trial block and the value 2). Among older Ss (above 56 months), girls made more imitative responses than boys did; among younger Ss (45–56 months), boys made more imitative responses than girls did.

EXPERIMENT II: **Subjects:** $N = 26$; 3–5 yrs. **Measures:** Stanford-Binet Intelligence Test, Form L. **Results:** No sex differences.

MacDonald, A. P., Jr. Birth order and religious affiliation. *Developmental Psychology,* 1969, *1*, 628 (brief report).
Subjects: $N = 393$; 18–21 yrs (college). **Measures:** After indicating their religious preference (Catholic, Jewish, Protestant, other, or none), Ss rated their church attendance on a 6-point scale. **Results:** (1) There were no sex differences in church attendance among Ss who indicated no religious preference. (2) Among Ss who did indicate a preference, Catholic women who were only children attended church more frequently than Catholic men who were only children.

MacDonald, A. P., Jr. Anxiety, affiliation, and social isolation. *Developmental Psychology,* 1970, *3*, 242–54.
Subjects: $N = 149$; 18–21 yrs (college). **Measures:** Ss reported to the testing session in small mixed-sex groups. After being told that a series of electric shocks would be given to them later in the experiment, Ss rated their uneasiness on a 100-point scale and indicated their preference to be alone or with others. Ss were then assigned to 1 of 2 conditions without regard to their stated preference. Groups in the affiliation condition were sent to an adjacent room where they remained for 5 minutes. In the isolation condition, Ss remained alone in separate cubicles in the experimental room for an identical period of time. Afterward, Ss in the affiliation condition were returned to the experimental room. Then, the uneasiness scale was readministered and the option to drop out was given. **Results:** (1) On the initial administration of the uneasiness scale, women reported higher levels of anxiety than men ($p < .005$). (2) No sex differences were found in preference to wait alone or with others. (3) On the second administration of the uneasiness scale, no main sex differences were found in change in anxiety scores. Men who preferred waiting alone and women who preferred waiting with others showed more anxiety reduction than men who preferred affiliation and women who preferred isolation ($p < .025$). (4) Firstborn women were more likely to drop out of the experiment than firstborn men ($p < .05$). No sex differences were found among later-borns. (This result can be found in an article by A. P. MacDonald, Jr., entitled "Manifestations of Differential Levels of Socialization by Birth Order," *Developmental Psychology,* 1969, *1*, 485–92.)

McDonald, R. L. Effects of sex, race, and class on self, ideal-self and parental ratings in southern adolescents. *Perceptual & Motor Skills,* 1968, 27, 15–25.
Subjects: $N = 528$; 17 yrs (white, black). **Measures:** Self, parental, and ideal-self ratings were obtained on the Interpersonal Checklist. **Results:** (1) Self ratings: men had higher dominance and lower love scores than women. (2) Ideal-self ratings: Women had higher love scores than men. (3) Parental ratings: Women described their fathers as higher in love than men did. No sex differences were found in Ss' descriptions of their mothers.

MacFarlane, J. W., Allen, L., and Honzik, M. P. *A developmental study of the behavior problems of normal children between 21 months and 14 years.* Berkeley: University of California Press, 1962.
Subjects: $N = 116$; mothers (children 21 mos–14 yrs). **Measures:** Interviews regarding child's behavior. **Results:** (1) Mothers of boys reported a greater incidence of the following problem behaviors than mothers of girls: diurnal enuresis, excessive emotional dependence, irritability (21 months); temper tantrums (5 years); stealing (7 years); hyperactivity, temper tantrums, lying (8 years); excessive demanding of attention (9 years); lying, excessive demanding of attention, jealousy, competitiveness (11 years); overactivity, lying (12 years); overactivity, selfishness in sharing (13 years). (2) Mothers of girls reported a greater incidence of the following problem behaviors than mothers of boys: excessive modesty, specific fears (3 years); thumb-sucking (4 years); thumb-sucking, physical timidity (5 years); food fussiness, oversensitiveness, mood swings (6 years); excessive emotional dependence, shyness, excessive reserve (7 years); excessive modesty, excessive reserve (8 years); shyness, somberness (9 years); excessive reserve (10 years); shyness (11 years); disturbing dreams, physical timidity (12 years); specific fears (13 years).

McIntyre, A. Sex differences in children's aggression. *Proceedings* of the 80th Annual Convention of the APA, 1972, 7, 93–94.
Subjects: $N = 27$; 2–4 yrs. **Measures:** Ss were observed at their preschool. Response measures were frequency of verbal and nonverbal activities with peers and/or adults (social activity rate) and frequency of each of 4 classes of aggressive behavior (direct physical aggression, indirect physical aggression, direct verbal aggression, and indirect verbal aggression). **Results:**

(1) More boys than girls had high social activity rates. (2) More boys than girls scored high in physical aggression. No sex differences were found in verbal aggression, direct aggression, or indirect aggression.

McKinney, J. D. Problem solving strategies in impulsive and reflective second graders. *Developmental Psychology*, 1973, 8, 145 (brief report).
   Subjects: $N = 60$; 7 yrs. **Measures:** Reflective and impulsive Ss (as determined by the Matching Familiar Figures Test) were asked to determine the "correct" stimulus (out of 16) by asking questions answerable by "yes" or "no." Problem-solving strategies were assessed. **Results:** No sex differences were found in amount of information obtained from questions.

McKitrick, K. G. Bodily activity and perceptual activity. *Perceptual & Motor Skills*, 1965, 20, 1109–12.
   Subjects: $N = 200$; 18–21 yrs (college). **Measures:** Ss were tested for the autokinetic illusion. **Results:** Latency to perceiving autokinesis was greater for women than for men.

McMains, M. J., and Liebert, R. M. Influence of discrepancies between successively modeled self-reward criteria on the adoption of a self-imposed standard. *J. Personality & Social Psychology*, 1968, 8, 166–71.
   Subjects: $N = 48$; 9 yrs. **Measures:** While playing a bowling game, Ss were trained to employ a stringent self-reward standard by a model who subsequently adhered to the standard or deviated from it. Ss then performed in the model's absence. Afterward, Ss were exposed to a second model, who displayed either the same stringent self-reward criterion that the Ss had previously been taught or a more lenient standard. Ss then played the game alone for a second time. The response measure was the number of times Ss did not adhere to the stringent self-reward criterion. **Results:** (1) No sex differences were found in Game 1. (2) Boys were more lenient than girls in Game 2 ($p < .05$).

McManis, D. L. Pursuit-rotor performance of normal and retarded children in four verbal-incentive conditions. *Child Development*, 1965, 36, 667–83.
   Subjects: $N = 96$; 10–11 yrs (normal intelligence), 12–13 yrs (retardates). **Measures:** Ss' base levels of pursuit-rotor performance were established under neutral incentive; 4 mixed-ability treatment groups were established: neutral E response, praise, reproof, and competition. Ss performed the task again in presence of a same-sex peer. Task persistence was measured. **Results:** (1) There were no sex differences in accuracy or response to treatments. (2) Boys were more persistent in continuing tasks than girls ($p < .05$).

McManis, D. L. Marble-sorting rate of elementary school children as a function of verbal-incentive and performance-level pairings. *Perceptual & Motor Skills*, 1966, 23, 499–507.
   Subjects: $N = 240$; 9–11 yrs. **Measures:** Ss performed alternate trials on a marble-sorting task with same-sex partners whose performance rates in baseline were either similar or different. Each dyad experienced 1 of 3 treatments: (1) S_1 was criticized by E while S_2 was praised; (2) S_1 was criticized while S_2 was told to try as hard as he could to beat his partner's score on the previous trial; (3) S_1 was praised while S_2 was told to be competitive. Response measures were changes in rate of response between baseline and the experimental sessions. **Results:** Boys showed larger increases in response rates than girls ($p < .05$).

McMichael, R. E., and Grinder, R. E. Children's guilt after transgression: Combined effect of exposure to American culture and ethnic background. *Child Development*, 1966, 37, 425–31.
   Subjects: $N = 114$; 12–13 yrs (rural and urban Japanese Americans, Hawaiian Americans, and Caucasian Americans). **Measures:** 5 stories describing common transgressions were presented to Ss. After reading each story, Ss indicated how they would feel and behave if they were the protagonist. The multiple-choice questions they responded to assessed remorse, confession, and restitution. **Results:** Among rural Japanese Americans ($N = 23$), girls scored higher than boys on confession and restitution. No other sex differences were found.

MacMillan, D. L., and Keogh, B. K. Effect of instructional set on twelve-year-old children's perception of interruption. *Developmental Psychology*, 1971a, 4, 106.
   Subjects: $N = 60$; 11 yrs. **Measures:** Ss were asked to duplicate 6 designs pictured on cards using 9 blocks given to them by E. Ss were allowed to complete 3 of the designs. While working on the other 3, they were interrupted before completion (interruption was attributed either to success or to failure). In a third condition, interruption was defined as a neutral event.

Afterward, Ss were asked to pick 1 design to try again. They were also asked to explain why they did not complete 3 of the designs. **Results:** No sex differences were found in Ss' choice of designs to repeat or in their placement of blame for not completing 3 of the designs.

MacMillan, D. L., and Keogh, B. K. Normal and retarded children's expectancy for failure. *Developmental Psychology*, 1971b, 4, 343–48.
Subjects: $N = 120$; 8 yrs (normal, retarded). **Measures:** Ss performed 6 block design tasks; 3 were interrupted before completion. Instructions prior to the task defined interruption as an indication of success, failure, or neutral. After the task, Ss were asked which design they would like to do over and why some tasks had not been completed. **Results:** No sex differences.

McNamara, J. R., and Porterfield, C. L. Levels of information about the human figure and their characteristic relationship to human figure drawing in young disadvantaged children. *Developmental Psychology*, 1969, 1, 669–72.
Subjects: $N = 78$; 5–6 yrs (black disadvantaged). **Measures:** Human Figure Drawing Test. **Results:** No sex differences.

McNeel, S. P., McClintock, C. G., and Nuttin, J. M. Effects of sex role in a two person mixed-motive game. *J. Personality & Social Psychology*, 1972, 24, 372–80.
Subjects: $N = 144$; 18–21 yrs (college). **Measures:** Ss in like-sex and mixed-sex pairs played a modified version of the Prisoner's Dilemma game. Competitive choices reflected a single motive (relative gain maximization), while the remaining 2 choices reflected either own gain or joint gain considerations. **Results:** (1) Mixed-sex pairs were less competitive than like-sex pairs. No difference was found between male and female pairs. (2) Men in mixed-sex pairs were less competitive than men in like-sex pairs ($p < .02$). No differences were found for women.

Madsen, C. Nurturance and modeling in preschoolers. *Child Development*, 1968, 39, 221–36.
Subjects: $N = 40$; 4–5 yrs. **Measures:** Ss were assigned for 6 weeks to male teachers trained to be either nurturant or nonnurturant. During weeks 7 and 8, Ss viewed 2 films; the actor in each film was either their teacher or an unfamiliar adult male. In the aggression film, novel physical and verbal aggressive behaviors toward a Bobo doll were modeled. After watching the film, Ss were taken to an experimental room where they were observed for 5 minutes. Measures were taken of imitative, partially imitative, and nonimitative aggression. Ss were then asked to perform all the behaviors they had observed in the film. Matching responses were praised and rewarded with candy. In the toy-rejection film, the model made disparaging comments about a mechanical dog and pleasurable comments about a robot while playing exclusively with the latter. Ss were allowed to play with the 2 toys at the completion of the film. The time they spent playing with the robot minus the time they spent playing with the dog was recorded. **Results:** (1) Boys exhibited more imitative physical aggression, more non-imitative verbal aggression, and less nonimitative Bobo-directed aggression than girls. Boys who were exposed to the familiar model exhibited more imitative aggression than boys exposed to the unfamiliar model; no such difference was found among girls. No sex differences were found in Ss' display of partially imitative aggression, imitative verbal aggression, or total verbal imitation (aggressive and nonaggressive). In the recall task, no sex differences were found in number of novel aggressive behaviors performed. (2) No difference was found between boys and girls on the measure "time spent on robot minus time spent on dog."

Madsen, C. H., and London, P. Role playing and hypnotic susceptibility in children. *J. Personality & Social Psychology*, 1966, 3, 13–19.
Subjects: $N = 42$; 7–11 yrs. **Measures:** Children's Hypnotic Susceptibility Scale, Hypnotic Simulation Test, Dramatic Acting Test. **Results:** No sex differences.

Madsen, M. C., and Shapira, A. Cooperative and competitive behavior of urban Afro-American, Anglo-American, Mexican-American, and Mexican village children. *Developmental Psychology*, 1970, 3, 16–20.
EXPERIMENT I: **Subjects:** $N = 144$; 7–9 yrs (Afro-, Anglo-, and Mexican American). **Measures:** Same-sex groups of 4 were tested on Madsen's Cooperation board. Rewards were received first on a group (trials 1–3) and then on an individual basis (trials 4–6). Owing to the nature of the apparatus, cooperation was adaptive. For each group, the change in amount of cooperation between trials 3 and 4 was recorded. **Results:** No sex differences.
EXPERIMENT III: **Subjects:** $N = 156$; 7–9 yrs (Afro-, Anglo-, and Mexican-American; Mexi-

can). **Measures:** Procedures similar to Experiment I were followed, with 1 exception: throughout the testing session, rewards were received on an individual basis. **Results:** No differences were found in the amount of cooperation exhibited by boys and girls.

Maehr, M. L., and Stallings, W. M. Freedom from external evaluation. *Child Development*, 1972, *43*, 177–85.
  Subjects: $N = 154$; 13 yrs. **Measures:** For each of 10 problems, Ss judged which of 4 geometric designs was different from the other 3. In the external evaluation condition, Ss were informed that the task was a test of their ability and that the results would be given to their teachers. In the internal evaluation condition, Ss were told to complete the task in a spirit of fun and interest, since no one but themselves would see their scores. Afterward, Ss' willingness to return to perform a similar task at a later date was assessed. **Results:** (1) No sex differences were found in task performance. (2) Girls indicated a greater willingness to return than boys did ($p < .01$).

Maier, N. R. Male vs. female discussion leaders. *Personnel Psychology*, 1970, *23*, 455–61.
  Subjects: $N = 384$; 18–21 yrs (college). **Measures:** Ss participated in the Changing Work Procedure Problem, a role-playing situation in which a foreman attempts to get 3 workers to change their work method. Foremen were given the facts of the problem and were either supplied (Standard Condition) or not supplied (Facts Only Condition) with a rather obvious solution. There were 3 outcomes possible: (1) workers successfully resist the change, (2) leader succeeds in getting his solution adopted, or (3) workers and leader compromise on an alternative solution. **Results:** (1) With males as foremen, differences between the 2 experimental conditions were nonsignificant; with females as foremen, more groups accepted the leader's solution in the Standard Condition than in the Facts Only Condition ($p < .01$). (2) More groups with a male rather than a female as foreman accepted the leader's solution in the Facts Only Condition ($p < .01$). No sex differences were found in the Standard Condition.

Maier, N. R., and Burke, R. J. Response availability as a factor in the problem solving performance of males and females. *J. Personality & Social Psychology*, 1967, *5*, 304–10.
  Experiment I: Subjects: $N = 173$; 18–21 yrs (college). **Measures:** Ss were given the standard version of the horse-trading problem. **Results:** Men chose the correct answer more often than women ($p < .01$). Women chose the incorrect "broke even" answer more often than men ($p < .01$).
  Experiment II: Subjects: $N = 126$; 18–21 yrs (college). **Measures:** Same as Experiment I, except that a rationale was provided for each alternative answer. **Results:** Same as Experiment I.
  Experiment III: Subjects: $N = 114$; 18–21 yrs (college). **Measures:** Same as Experiment I, except that the broke even alternative was eliminated. **Results:** No sex differences.
  Experiment IV: Subjects: $N = 114$; 18–21 yrs (college). **Measures:** Ss were told that a man bought a secondhand car for his wife. Since she didn't like it, he sold it. Ss were asked whether the man lost money, broke even, made a small profit, or made a large profit. No financial figures were given to influence Ss' choices. **Results:** Men chose the lost money alternative more often than women ($p < .01$). Women chose the broke even alternative more often than men ($p < .01$).
  Experiment V: Subjects: $N = 69$; 18–21 yrs (college). **Measures:** Same as Experiment IV, except that the roles of the husband and wife were reversed. **Results:** Men chose the lost money alternative more often than women ($p < .05$). Women chose the broke even alternative more often than men ($p < .01$).
  Experiment VI: Subjects: $N = 88$; 18–21 yrs (college). **Measures:** The horse-trading problem was modified to make the broke even alternative correct. **Results:** No sex differences.

Mallick, S. R., and McCandless, B. R. A study of catharsis of aggression. *J. Personality & Social Psychology*, 1966, *4*, 591–96.
  Experiment I: Subjects: $N = 48$; 8–9 yrs. **Measures:** After being either frustrated or not frustrated by a same-sex confederate, Ss were given the opportunity to administer shocks to the confederate. **Results:** No sex differences.
  Experiment II: Subjects: $N = 60$; 8–9 yrs. **Measures:** Ss were either frustrated or not frustrated by a same-sex confederate (first phase). Ss then either engaged in aggressive play, talked with E, or received a reasonable interpretation of the confederate's behavior (second phase). Afterward, Ss were given the opportunity to either impede (by pressing a "slowing" button) or facilitate (by pushing a "helping" button) the confederate's performance on a block-building task. Ss provided like-dislike ratings of the confederate after the first and second phases. **Results:** (1) No sex differences were found in the number of times Ss pressed the

"slowing" button. (2) After the first phase, boys expressed more dislike for the confederate than girls did, but only in the frustration condition ($p < .05$). After the second phase, no sex differences were found in Ss' ratings.

EXPERIMENT III: **Subjects:** $N = 60$; 8–9 yrs. **Measures:** Same as Experiment I, except that only half of the Ss completed the like-dislike rating scales. **Results:** No sex differences were found in number of times Ss pressed the "slowing" button.

Malouf, R. E., and Dodd, D. H. Role of exposure, imitation, and expansion in the acquisition of an artificial grammatical rule. *Developmental Psychology*, 1972, 7, 195–203.
   Subjects: $N = 84$; 6 yrs. **Measures:** An assessment was made of the effects of various environmental factors (exposure, imitation, and expansion) on Ss' learning of an artificial grammatical rule. **Results:** No sex differences were found in number of errors or number of trials to acquisition.

Manheimer, D. I., and Mellinger, G. D. Personality characteristics of the child accident repeater. *Child Development*, 1967, 38, 491–513.
   Subjects: $N = 8,874$; 4–18 yrs. **Measures:** Each S's history of medically attended injuries was obtained from his medical records. **Results:** Boys' accident rate was higher than that of girls.

Manosevitz, M., Prentice, N. M., and Wilson, F. Individual and family correlates of imaginary companions in preschool children. *Developmental Psychology*, 1973, 8, 72–79.
   Subjects: $N = 222$; 3–5 yrs. **Measures:** Parents completed the Imaginary Companion Questionnaire, designed to provide data about home setting and play activities of Ss. Part II of the questionnaire was answered only by parents whose children had imaginary companions. **Results:** (1) Girls had more imaginary companions than boys did. (2) Boys were more likely to have a male than a female imaginary companion, whereas girls showed only a slight tendency to have same-sex imaginary companions. (3) Parents reported that boys had more fights than girls did.

Markel, N. N., Prebor, L. D., and Brandt, J. F. Biosocial factors in dyadic communication: sex and speaking intensity. *J. Personality & Social Psychology*, 1972, 23, 11–13.
   Subjects: $N = 72$; 18–21 yrs (college). **Measures:** Ss spoke to male and female Es at near and far interpersonal distances. Average speaking intensity was measured. **Results:** (1) Men had a higher speaking intensity than women ($p < .01$). (2) Men Ss had a higher speaking intensity than women Ss when speaking to a woman E. When E was a man, no sex differences were found.

Marks, E. Some situational correlates of recognition-response level. *J. Personality & Social Psychology*, 1967, 6, 102–6.
   Subjects: $N = 722$; 18–21 yrs (college). **Measures:** Ss initially learned the names of 8 line-drawn figures. Ss were then presented with a set of 6 specially constructed test booklets. Pp. 2–5 of each booklet contained drawings that represented parts of 1 of 8 figures learned in the first phase. The drawings ranged from the most incomplete representation of the figures (p. 2) to the complete figures (p. 5). The drawing on p. 2 contained elements common to all 8 figures, the drawing on p. 3 contained elements common to 4 of the figures, and the drawing on p. 4 contained elements common to 2 of the figures. Ss were told to tear off 1 page at a time. When they felt they could identify the figure represented, Ss were instructed to write its name on that page and not tear off any more pages. The response measure was the total number of pages pulled. **Results:** No sex differences.

Marks, E. Personality factors in the performance of a perceptual recognition task under competing incentives. *J. Personality & Social Psychology*, 1968, 8, 69–74.
   Subjects: $N = 760$; 18–21 yrs (college). **Measures:** Ss answered 3 self-report inventories assessing quick and intuitive behavior, lack of forethought, and lack of need for definiteness. Ss also completed 3 self-report scales of concrete thinking, black-white thought processes, and activity level. Scores on the SAT verbal section and the Advanced Vocabulary Test were obtained. **Results:** No sex differences.

Marlatt, G. A. A comparison of vicarious and direct reinforcement control of verbal behavior in an interview setting. *J. Personality & Social Psychology*, 1970, 16, 695–703.
   Subjects: $N = 96$; 18–21 yrs (college). **Measures:** Ss were first exposed to a tape-recorded same-sex model who described personal problems to an interviewer. Ss then discussed their problems in 2 interviews, separated by a 1-week interval. Ss received either positive, negative, or neutral reinforcement from either a male or a female interviewer. The response measures

were number of problems discussed and length of time spent talking. **Results:** (1) No sex differences were found in number of problems discussed. (2) During the first interview, Ss discussed more problems with female interviewers than with male interviewers ($p < .01$). No differences were found during the second interview. (3) Men talked longer than women did in both interviews ($p < .05$). (4) Ss talked more with female interviewers than with male interviewers ($p < .05$ for both interviews).

Marquis, P. C. Experimenter-subject interaction as a function of authoritarianism and response set. *J. Personality & Social Psychology*, 1973, *25*, 289–96.
Subjects: $N = 52$; 18–21 yrs (college). **Measures:** Ss' attitudes on a topic were assessed before and after exposure to a persuasive communication. **Results:** No sex differences were found in attitude change.

Martin, J. C. Competitive and noncompetitive behavior of children in beanbag toss game. Preliminary draft, University of California, 1973.
Subjects: $N = 51$; 7 yrs. **Measures:** Ss could choose to shoot beanbags at any 1 of 4 targets. Targets farther away were higher in value (i.e. worth more marbles) than the targets close by. In the competitive condition, Ss played in same-sex pairs. At the end of the game, the most successful member of each pair was allowed to keep not only the marbles he had won but also his opponent's winnings. In the noncompetitive condition, Ss played alone. **Results:** (1) Girls threw at the closer target more often than boys did. This difference was greatest between Ss who threw after their opponents did in the competitive condition ($p < .05$). (2) No sex differences were found in number of marbles won.

Martin, M. F., Gelfand, D. M., and Hartmann, D. P. Effect of adult and peer observers on boys' and girls' responses to an aggressive model. *Child Development*, 1971, *42*, 1271–75.
Subjects: $N = 100$; 5–7 yrs. **Measures:** Ss observed a male model displaying aggression toward an inflated plastic doll. Ss were observed for 10 minutes of free play in an identical setting with either a male or female, adult or peer observer, or no observer. Imitative and total aggressive behaviors were rated. Afterward, Ss' free-play activities were observed in an identical setting in the presence of either a male or female, adult or peer observer. In a fifth condition, no observer was present. Aggressive responses were recorded. **Results:** Under all conditions, boys displayed more imitative and total aggression than girls ($p < .001$, $p < .001$).

Marvin, R. S. Attachment- and communicative-behavior in two-, three-, and four-year-old children. Unpublished doctoral dissertation, University of Chicago, 1971.
Subjects: $N = 48$; 2–4 yrs and mothers. **Measures:** Ss and their mothers were brought to the testing room. After a 3-minute observation period (Episode 1), Ss were exposed to the following situations: entrance of a stranger (Episode 2); departure of Mo (Episode 3); departure of Str, entrance of Mo (Episode 4); departure of Mo (Episode 5); entrance of Str (Episode 6); departure of Str, entrance of Mo (Episode 7). The presence or absence of the following behaviors was noted: crying, smiling, vocalizing, exploratory locomotion, exploratory manipulation, visual exploration, visual orientation to Mo, visual orientation to Str, and visual orientation to objects in the room other than the toys. In addition, the incidence of each of the following classes of behavior toward Mo was rated on a 7-point scale: proximity- or contact-seeking (e.g. approaching and clambering up, reaching, leaning); contact-maintaining (e.g. clinging, embracing, clutching); proximity-avoiding (e.g. ignoring, looking away, turning away); and searching for Mo following her departure (e.g. following Mo to door, trying to open the door, going to Mo's chair). **Results:** (1) Within each of the 3 age groups, no sex differences were found in smiling, vocalizing, locomotor exploration, searches for Mo following her departure, visual orientation to Mo, visual orientation to Str, or visual orientation to some object in the room other than a toy. (2) Among 2-year-old Ss, boys displayed less manipulatory exploration, less visual exploration (mother-absent episodes only), more crying (beginning with Episode 3), and a greater incidence of contact-maintaining behavior (no difference in average amount), whereas girls exhibited more proximity-avoiding behaviors (significant for Episodes 4 and 7 only). No sex difference was found in the frequency of proximity-seeking behaviors. (3) Among 3-year-old Ss, no sex differences were found. (4) Among 4-year-old Ss, girls displayed less manipulatory exploration, less visual exploration (beginning after Episode 3), more crying (beginning with Episode 4), more proximity-seeking behavior, and a greater average amount of contact-maintaining behavior (no difference in incidence). No sex difference was found in the frequency of proximity-avoiding behavior.

Marwell, G., Schmitt, D. R., and Shotola, R. Cooperation and interpersonal risk. *J. Personality & Social Psychology*, 1971, *18*, 9–32.
EXPERIMENT I: **Subjects:** $N = 64$; 18–21 yrs (college). **Measures:** Ss could choose to perform an individual or a cooperative task. The basic response for either was pulling a plunger. On the individual task, a single pull of the plunger was reinforced. On the cooperative task, Ss could earn money only by coordinating their responses. The mutual choice of cooperation entailed the risk that either S could take some of the other's earnings by pressing a take button. Each press of the take button transferred 1 cent. **Results:** Women pressed the take button more often than men did ($p < .001$). On the last few trials, a similar number of male and female pairs cooperated.
EXPERIMENT II: **Subjects:** $N = 56$; 18–21 yrs (college). **Measures:** Same as Experiment I, except each press of the take button transferred $1.00. No sex differences were found in the number of times Ss pressed the take button or in the number of pairs who reached steady-state cooperation.
EXPERIMENT III: **Subjects:** $N = 22$; 18–21 yrs (college). **Measures:** Same as Experiment II, except ability to take was made available to Ss regardless of task choice. Individual task no longer provided protection. **Results:** (1) Women pressed the take button more often than men did ($p < .001$). (2) No sex differences were found in number of pairs of Ss who eventually established cooperation.
EXPERIMENT IV: **Subjects:** $N = 24$; 18–21 yrs (college). **Measures:** Same as Experiment II, except that Ss were allowed to communicate with each other. **Results:** No sex differences.
EXPERIMENT V: **Subjects:** $N = 20$; 18–21 yrs (college). **Measures:** Same as Experiment II, except that ability to communicate was introduced partway into the experiment. **Results:** No sex differences.

Mascaro, G. F., and Graves, W. Contrast effects of background factors on the similarity-attraction relationship. *J. Personality & Social Psychology*, 1973, *25*, 346–50.
Subjects: $N = 33$; 18–21 yrs (college). **Measures:** After examining an attitude questionnaire completed by a moderately similar stranger, Ss completed the Interpersonal Judgment Scale measure of attraction and a measure of perceived similarity. **Results:** No sex differences.

Massari, D. J., and Mansfield, R. S. Field dependence and outer-directedness in the problem solving of retardates and normal children. *Child Development*, 1973, *44*, 346–50.
Subjects: $N = 104$; 21–25 yrs (high and low MA, field-dependent and -independent retardates). **Measures:** Ss performed a discrimination-learning task with squares that varied in size and color. **Results:** No sex differences were found in the number of trials Ss needed to reach criterion.

Massari, D. J., Hayweiser, L., and Meyer, W. J. Activity level and intellectual functioning in deprived preschool children. *Developmental Psychology*, 1969, *1*, 286–90.
Subjects: $N = 33$; 5 yrs (low SES). **Measures:** Draw-A-Line and Walk-A-Line tests were administered during the first and last weeks of a 6-week preschool program. Ss were instructed to perform both tasks as slowly as possible, and as quickly as possible. In addition, on the Walk-A-Line test, Ss were given a no-instruction condition. **Results:** No sex differences.

Masters, J. C. Effects of social comparison upon subsequent self-reinforcement behavior in children. *J. Personality & Social Psychology*, 1968, *10*, 391–401.
EXPERIMENT I: **Subjects:** $N = 30$; 3–5 yrs. **Measures:** While playing a question game, Ss received either as many tokens as their younger same-sex partners or more or fewer. Ss in 2 control groups played alone. Ss then played a maze game during which they were free to help themselves to rewards (tokens, pennies, and pieces of paper). The response measure was Ss' self-reinforcing behavior during the maze game. **Results:** (1) Sex of Ss had no main effect on number of tokens taken. In control groups, boys took more tokens than girls; in experimental groups (excluding the equal group), girls took more tokens than boys ($p < .05$). (2) Sex of Ss had no main effect on number of pennies taken. Boys took more pennies than girls in the control and equal conditions; girls took more pennies than boys in the low and high experimental conditions ($p < .05$). (3) Sex of Ss had no main effect on number of pieces of paper taken. In the low and high experimental groups, girls took more pieces of paper than boys ($p < .05$); in control groups, boys took more pieces of paper than girls ($p < .05$).
EXPERIMENT II: **Subjects:** $N = 40$; 3–5 yrs. **Measures:** Same as Experiment I, but instead of the maze game, Ss played a second question game without their partners. During this second game each S divided a preset number of tokens between E and himself. In addition,

1 of the 2 control conditions was eliminated. **Results:** Sex of Ss had no effect on the number of tokens Ss took for themselves.

EXPERIMENT III: **Subjects:** $N = 30$; 3–5 yrs. **Measures:** Same as Experiment I, except that Ss played a second question game with their partners, during which the Ss divided a preset number of tokens between themselves and their partners. Both control conditions were eliminated. **Results:** Sex of Ss had no effect on the number of tokens children took for themselves.

Masters, J. C. Social comparison, self-reinforcement, and the value of a reinforcer. *Child Development*, 1969a, *40*, 1027–38.

> **Subjects:** $N = 59$; 4–5 yrs. **Measures:** Ss played a question-and-answer game, either alone or with a younger same-sex partner. In the 3 experimental conditions, Ss received 9 tokens for their performance, while their partners received either 54, 9, or 3. In the 2 control conditions, 54 tokens were placed in a box either for the other children in the nursery school or for no special purpose. As in the experimental conditions, control Ss received 9 tokens, 1 after each question. To assess how valuable the tokens were to each child, Ss played a game called Store. The main response measure was the number of tokens Ss were willing to trade for a shiny new penny. Afterward, Ss played the same question-and-answer game with E. After each question, Ss were given 4 tokens to dispense in any way they wished between themselves and E. The number of tokens Ss kept for themselves was recorded. **Results:** No sex differences.

Masters, J. C. Word association and the functional definition of words. *Developmental Psychology*, 1969b, *1*, 517–19.

> **Subjects:** $N = 72$; 4–9 yrs. **Measures:** Ss were given a word association test and a word definition test. The number of syntagmatic associations and functional definitions Ss produced was recorded. **Results:** No sex differences.

Masters, J. C. Effects of social comparison upon children's self-reinforcement and altruism toward competitors and friends. *Developmental Psychology*, 1971, *5*, 64–72.

> **Subjects:** $N = 120$; 4–5 yrs. **Measures:** In 3 of 5 conditions, Ss played a question-and-answer game with a younger same-sex partner; in the 2 control conditions, Ss played alone. Ss always received 9 tokens for their performance. Their partners in the experimental conditions received either more (54), less (3), or the same number. In the social-comparison control condition, 54 tokens were placed in a box "for all the other children in the nursery school." In the no-comparison control condition, 54 tokens were again dropped in a box, but the box was not designated for any special purpose. Afterward, Ss were provided with the opportunity to give as many of their tokens as they wished to their partner and to a friend, both of whom were absent. In the social-comparison control condition, Ss could donate their tokens "to all the other children in the nursery school." Ss then played the question-and-answer game again, this time with E as their partner. After each question, Ss were given 4 tokens to divide between themselves and E. **Results:** No sex differences were found in the number of tokens Ss gave to their partners or to their friends, or in the number of tokens Ss kept for themselves while playing the question-and-answer game with E.

Masters, J. C. Effects of social comparison upon the imitation of neutral and altruistic behaviors by young children. *Child Development*, 1972a, *43*, 131–42.

> **Subjects:** $N = 80$; 4–5 yrs. **Measures:** Ss played "Paymaster," a question-and-answer game. Each time they answered a question correctly, Ss received 1 token. In 3 of the 5 conditions, Ss played with an adult model (M) who received either more, fewer, or the same number of tokens as Ss. In the 2 remaining conditions, Ss played alone. At the conclusion of the Paymaster game, Ss watched as M played with several toys. Half the children observed a same-sex model and half observed an opposite-sex model. After M departed, Ss played with the toys for 3 minutes. Measures were taken of number of imitative behaviors. **Results:** No sex differences were found. The interaction between sex of S and sex of M did not reach significance.

Masters, J. C. Effects of success, failure, and reward outcome upon contingent and non-contingent self-reinforcement. *Developmental Psychology*, 1972b, *7*, 110–18.

> **Subjects:** $N = 80$; 7–8 yrs. **Measures:** Ss either succeeded or failed (prearranged) on a pursuit rotor task. They received high or low token reward for success. Ss performed either the same or a different task, with as many self-reward tokens available as they "deserved" or as they "wished." **Results:** There were no main sex differences. Boys showed greater self-reinforcement than girls when prior reward had been of low magnitude ($p < .05$).

Masters, J. C. Effects of age and social comparison upon children's noncontingent self-reinforcement and the value of a reinforcer. *Child Development*, 1973, *44*, 111–16.

> **Subjects:** $N = 160$; 4–5 yrs. **Measures:** Same-sex pairs played "Paymaster," a matching task

involving difficult discriminations selected from the Matching Familiar Figures Test; 1 child of pair was the subject, and he received 9 tokens in every condition. Tokens dispensed to partner were either lower than, higher than, or equal to, the number S received. In the control condition, S played by himself and 54 tokens were placed in box for "all the children." Discrepancy in allotment of tokens was either contingent or noncontingent. Ss then completed a maze drawing task for which they reinforced themselves with tokens. Ss were asked to recall distribution of tokens during Paymaster game and were questioned as to how they valued the reinforcer. **Results:** (1) There was no sex effect during social comparison phase. (2) Among younger Ss, girls were more responsive to social comparison manipulation than boys were, as measured by amount of self-reinforcement ($p < .05$). (3) Girls valued tokens less than boys did ($p < .001$).

Masters, J. C., and Christy, M. C. Achievement standards for contingent self-reinforcement: effects of task length and task difficulty. Presented at the meeting of the Society for Research in Child Development, 1973.
    Subjects: $N = 32$; 7 yrs. **Measures:** Ss completed 4 versions (long-easy, long-difficult, short-easy, short-difficult) of a form-discrimination task, a card-sorting task, and an arithmetic task. After completing each task, Ss were allowed to reward themselves with from 0 to 10 tokens. The response measures were the number of tokens taken and the amount of time needed to complete each task. **Results:** (1) No sex differences were found in number of tokens taken. (2) The difference in time taken to complete difficult and easy tasks was greater for boys than for girls ($p < .05$). No main effects were found.

Masters, J. C., and Driscoll, S. A. Children's imitation as a function of the presence or absence of a model and the description of his instrumental behaviors. *Child Development,* 1971, *42,* 161–70.
    EXPERIMENT I: **Subjects:** $N = 48$; 4 yrs. **Measures:** E read Ss a story that described the novel arrangement of 8 toys. In 1 condition, the model in the story (Tarzan) arranged the toys. In a second condition, the model found the toys already arranged. In a third condition, Ss were simply told the model discovered the 8 toys, with no reference to their arrangement. At the end of the story, Tarzan was rewarded by being made "king of the jungle." After listening to the stories, Ss were presented with the same 8 toys and left alone for 3 minutes. The way in which Ss arranged the toys was recorded. **Results:** Boys imitated the novel toy arrangements more than girls did ($p < .05$).
    EXPERIMENT II: **Subjects:** $N = 40$; 4 yrs. **Measures:** Same as Experiment I, except that a fourth condition was added and Tarzan was rewarded with a bag of candy instead of being made king. In the added condition, the novel arrangement of the 8 toys was described, but no mention was made of Tarzan. **Results:** No sex differences.

Masters, J. C., and Mokros, J. R. Effects of incentive magnitude upon discriminative learning and choice preference in young children. *Child Development,* 1973, *44,* 225–31.
    EXPERIMENTS I, II, III, IV: **Subjects:** $N = 234$; 4–5 yrs. **Measures:** Ss performed 2-choice discrimination tasks; high- or low-magnitude incentives were offered in a manner designed to maximize their distracting or satiating effects. **Results:** No sex differences.

Masters, J. C., and Morris, R. J. Effects of contingent and noncontingent reinforcement upon generalized imitation. *Child Development,* 1971, *42,* 385–92.
    Subjects: $N = 56$; 4 yrs. **Measures:** Ss were asked to imitate each of 7 aggressive behaviors performed by a female model. In 1 condition, Ss were rewarded by E after every imitative sequence. In a second condition, no reinforcements were given. In a third condition, a machine dispensed marbles to Ss after every response. In a fourth condition, marbles were given to Ss in a bunch at the beginning of the experiment. Afterward, all Ss were exposed to a male model who exhibited 6 neutral behaviors. The number of imitative behaviors Ss performed following the male model's departure was recorded. **Results:** Boys showed greater imitation of the male model than girls did ($p < .05$).

Masters, J. C., and Peskay, J. Effects of race, socioeconomic status and success or failure upon contingent and noncontingent self-reinforcement in children. *Developmental Psychology,* 1972, 7, 139–45.
    Subjects: $N = 112$; 7–9 yrs (white and black, low and high SES). **Measures:** Ss received success, failure, or neutral feedback about their performance on trials of game. After the game, Ss could self-reward as deserved (contingent condition) or as wanted (noncontingent condition). Number of reward tokens dispensed was determined. **Results:** No sex differences.

Matheny, A. P., Jr. Heredity and environmental components of competency of children's articulation. Paper presented at the Biennial Meeting of the Society for Research in Child Development. Philadelphia, 1973.

Subjects: $N = 22$ opposite-sex twin pairs; 3–8 yrs. Measures: Templin-Darley Screening Test of Articulation. Results: Girls had higher articulation scores than boys ($p < .001$).

Mathews, M. E., and Fozard, J. L. Age differences in judgments of recency for short sequences of pictures. *Developmental Psychology*, 1970, 3, 208–17.

Subjects: $N = 128$; 5, 6, 7, 8, 11, 12 yrs. Measures: Ss were presented with either 7 or 12 pictures, 1 at a time. Afterward, 2 pictures from the set were shown a second time. Ss were asked to judge which of the 2 pictures had been presented to them more recently. Results: No sex differences.

Matlin, M. W. Response competition as a mediating factor in the frequency-affect relationship. *J. Personality & Social Psychology*, 1970, 16, 536–52.

Subjects: $N = 39$; 18–21 yrs (college). Measures: Ss rated their liking for each of 120 words of different frequencies. Results: No sex differences.

Maw, W. H., and Maw, E. W. Differences in preference for investigatory activities by school children who differ in curiosity level. *Psychology in the Schools*, 1965, 2, 263–66.

EXPERIMENTS I, II, III: Subjects: $N = 914$; 10, 11 yrs. Measures: Ss' activity preferences were assessed from their responses to multiple-choice questions. Results: In each of the 3 experiments, boys selected outgoing investigatory activities more often than girls did ($p < .05$, $p < .01$, $p < .0005$).

May, R. R. A method for studying the development of gender identity. *Developmental Psychology*, 1971, 5, 484–87.

Subjects: $N = 75$; 8, 9, 10 yrs. Measures: Ss were asked to write stories about a picture of a male and a female trapeze artist in midair and a picture of a bullfighter alone in the ring. Stories were scored so that more positive scores indicated a more "feminine" pattern (deprivation followed by enhancement) rather than a more "masculine" pattern (enhancement followed by deprivation). Results: Girls' mean score was higher than boys' ($p < .0005$).

Meddock, T. D., Parsons, J. A., and Hill, K. T. Effects of an adult's presence and praise on young children's performance. *J. Experimental Child Psychology*, 1971, 12, 197–211.

Subjects: $N = 64$; 4–5 yrs. Measures: After a baseline minute, Ss performed a nonskill task (marble-dropping) under 4 conditions: supportive or unresponsive E, present or absent E. Performance rate change was assessed. Results: Girls had higher baseline response rates, but there were no sex differences in change scores.

Mehrabian, A. Measures of vocabulary and grammatical skills for children up to age six. *Developmental Psychology*, 1970, 2, 439–46.

Subjects: $N = 127$; 3–5 yrs. Measures: Ss were given a picture vocabulary test, a comprehension of meaningful commands test, a comprehension of meaningless commands test, a sentence-completion test measuring grammatical ability, a test entitled "Judgment of the Grammaticalness of Sentences and Phrases," and a verbal imitation test. Results: No sex differences.

Meichenbaum, D., and Goodman, J. Reflection-impulsivity and verbal control of motor behavior. *Child Development*, 1969, 40, 785–97.

Subjects: $N = 30$; 5–6 yrs. Measures: Ss performed a finger-tapping task and a foot-depression task. Both were designed to assess verbal control of motor behavior. On the first administration of the tapping task, Ss pressed a telegraph key while saying aloud the words "faster" and "slower" for 2 15-second trials each. On the second administration, Ss said the words quietly to themselves. The response measure was the number of taps Ss performed under each of the various conditions. While performing the foot-depression task, Ss were presented with a random sequence of 24 lights (12 blue, 12 yellow). Ss were required to push the toe foot pedal whenever the blue light came on, but not to push it if the yellow light came on. The task was given to Ss twice, first without, then with the instructions to verbalize the meaning of the lights ("push" or "don't push") before responding. The number of accurate responses Ss performed was recorded. Then 2 weeks after the administration of these tasks, Ss were given the Matching Familiar Figures (MFF) test. Results: (1) On the first administration of the foot-depression task, girls incorrectly responded to the appearance of the yellow light by pushing the foot pedal more frequently than boys did. (2) On the MFF, girls had lower response latencies than boys.

There were no sex differences in number of recognition errors. (3) No sex differences were found on any other measure.

Meisels, M., and Guardo, C. J. Development of personal space schemata. *Child Development*, 1969, *40*, 1167–78.

Subjects: $N = 431$; 8–15 yrs. **Measures:** Ss were shown silhouette figures representing same-sex and opposite-sex peers. In the first 2 subsections of the task, the stimulus figure was described as (1) a best friend, (2) an acquaintance, (3) a stranger, (4) someone liked very much, (5) someone disliked very much, (6) someone neither liked nor disliked, (7) someone feared. In the latter 2 subsections, the group stimulus figures were described as (1) friends, (2) strangers, (3) feared peers. For each situation, S was asked to place a silhouette figure representing himself in face-to-face relation to the stimulus figure(s). Interfigure distances were recorded. **Results:** (1) Overall, girls employed greater spatial distances between themselves and "a stranger," "someone neither liked nor disliked," "someone disliked very much," "someone feared," "feared peers," and "strangers," while boys used more distance between themselves and "a friend." (2) For "a friend," "an acquaintance," "a stranger," and "strangers," boys used more space at 8 years and sometimes also at 9 and 10 years, while girls generally used more distance at 11, 12, and 13 years. At 14 and 15 years of age, no sex differences were found. (3) For "someone feared," "feared peers," and "strangers," boys maintained smaller distances from opposite-sex peers than from same-sex peers, while girls maintained the same distances from both sexes.

Mendelsohn, G. A., and Griswold, B. B. Assessed creative potential, vocabulary level, and sex as predictors of the use of incidental cues in verbal problem solving. *J. Personality & Social Psychology*, 1966, *4*, 423–31.

Subjects: $N = 223$; 18–21 yrs (college). **Measures:** Vocabulary test of the Institute of Educational Research Intelligence Scale CAVD, Barron-Welsh Art Scale (BWAS), and Remote Associates Test (RAT). **Results:** Women scored higher than men on the BWAS ($p < .05$). No sex differences were found on the vocabulary test or the RAT.

Mendelsohn, G. A., and Griswold, B. B. Anxiety and repression as predictors of the use of incidental cues in problem solving. *J. Personality & Social Psychology*, 1967, *6*, 353–59.

Subjects: $N = 181$; 18–21 yrs (college). **Measures:** Ss memorized a list of 25 words while another list of 25 words was being played on a tape recorder. Ss then attempted to solve 30 anagrams; 10 of the solution words had appeared on the focal (memory) list, and another 10 words had appeared on the peripheral (interference) list. The response measures were numbers of focal, peripheral, and neutral solutions. Ss also completed the first- and second-factor scales of the MMPI, A and R. **Results:** (1) No sex differences were found in R scores. Women had higher A scores than men ($p < .01$). (2) No sex differences were found in number of focal, peripheral, or neutral solutions.

Messé, L. A., Aronoff, J., and Wilson, J. P. Motivation as a mediator of the mechanisms underlying role assignments in small groups. *J. Personality & Social Psychology*, 1972, *24*, 84–90.

Subjects: $N = 72$; 18–21 yrs (college). **Measures:** Ss responded to a 60-item sentence-completion test (SCT) that assessed the degree to which Ss were concerned with satisfying safety and esteem needs. Only Ss high in one motive and low in the other were selected to participate. Ss were run in 24 3-person groups composed of 2 women and 1 man. All members of a group were homogeneously safety- or esteem-oriented. Ss worked a number of tasks both individually and as a group for 2 hours. Videotapes were made of each group. Ss' behavior was scored as to whether they gave procedural suggestions, suggested solutions, gave opinions, gave orientations, drew attention, or asked opinions. Composite leadership scores were then calculated. **Results:** In two-thirds of the safety-oriented groups, men had higher leadership scores than women ($p < .02$).

Messer, S. B., and Lewis, M. Social class and sex differences in the attachment and play behavior of the year-old infant. *Merrill-Palmer Quarterly*, 1972, *18*, 295–306.

Subjects: $N = 25$; 13 mos (low SES) and mothers. **Measures:** Infants were observed in a playroom containing the following toys: a set of blocks, a pail, a lawnmower, a stuffed dog, a plastic cat, a set of quoits, a wooden mallet, a pegboard, and a wooden pull-toy bug. After receiving a signal from E, mothers removed the infants from their laps and placed them on the floor. For the next 15 minutes, mothers passively watched their infants play. The following infant behaviors were recorded: latency to return to Mo, number of returns to Mo, number of seconds in contact with Mo, number of seconds spent vocalizing to Mo, number of seconds spent looking at Mo, number of looks to Mo, number of activity changes, duration of longest activity, number of squares traversed (the room was marked off into 12 equal squares), number of seconds spent playing with each of the toys, number of seconds spent banging toys, number of seconds spent putting toys into pail, and number of seconds spent playing with nontoys (doorknob, doorstopper, lights, etc.). **Results:** (1) Girls returned to their mothers more quickly and more frequently than boys did ($p < .025$), ($p < .025$). (2) Girls spent more time touching their mothers than boys did ($p < .025$). (3) Girls traversed more squares than boys did ($p < .025$).

Meyer, J. W., and Sobieszek, B. J. The effect of a child's sex on adult interpretations of its behavior. *Developmental Psychology*, 1972, *6*, 42–48.
Subjects: $N = 85$; 18–45 yrs. **Measures:** Each S was shown 2 short videotapes of 2 17-month-old children, with each child sometimes being described as a boy and sometimes as a girl. After viewing each tape, S described the child on a short questionnaire with 24 bipolar items, 17 of which were sex-role-linked. **Results:** (1) Women attributed more qualities to the children than men did ($p < .02$). (2) Men attributed more qualities to the child described as a boy, whereas women attributed more qualities to the child described as a girl ($p < .04$).

Meyer, W. J., and Thompson, G. G. Sex differences in the distribution of teacher approval and disapproval among sixth-grade children. *J. Educational Psychology*, 1956, *47*, 385–97.
Subjects: $N = 78$; 11 yrs. **Measures:** (1) Teacher-pupil interactions were observed for 30 hours in each of 3 classrooms. Each incident in which the teacher expressed either approval or disapproval to a pupil was recorded. (2) Common situations in which pupils receive approval or disapproval from their teacher were described to Ss. For each situation, Ss nominated the 4 pupils in their class whom they viewed as being most likely involved in such an incident. **Results:** (1) Observations: boys received more praise (1 of 3 classrooms) and disapproval (all 3 classrooms) from their teachers than girls did. (2) Peer nominations: both sexes perceived boys as receiving more disapproval from their teachers than girls (2 of 3 classrooms). No differences were found in Ss' perceptions of the frequency of boys' and girls' receiving teacher approval.

Meyers, W. J., and Cantor, G. N. Infants' observing and heart period responses as related to novelty of visual stimuli. *Psychonomic Science*, 1966, *5*, 239–40.
Subjects: $N = 24$; 5 mos. **Measures:** Ss viewed a given stimulus projected on a screen for 4 trials (phase 1). A new stimulus was introduced and the 2 stimuli were each presented 4 times (phase 2). A third stimulus was subsequently added (phase 3) and a fourth (phase 4), each appearing 4 times within a given phase. Cardiovascular responses were recorded for each infant. **Results:** During phases 1 and 2, both sexes exhibited similar heart rate decelerations accompanying stimulus presentation. During the last 2 phases, boys showed increased heart rate decelerations; girls showed decreased heart rate decelerations ($p < .05$).

Meyers, W. J., and Cantor, G. N. Observing and cardiac responses of human infants to visual stimuli. *J. Experimental Child Psychology*, 1967, *5*, 16–25.
Subjects: $N = 44$; 6 mos. **Measures:** Fixation time, heart period change, and latency of heart period change of infants' responses to visual stimuli (ball, clown) were recorded in familiarization and test phases. **Results:** (1) Boys demonstrated longer latencies in the group that viewed the ball; girls demonstrated longer latencies in the group that viewed the clown ($p < .05$). (2) For boys, larger heart period changes occurred in response to the nonfamiliarized stimulus than to the familiarized stimulus; this was not true for girls ($p < .01$).

Mikesell, R. H., Calhoun, L. G., and Lottman, T. J. Instructional set and the Coopersmith Self-Esteem Inventory. *Psychological Reports*, 1970, *26*, 317–18.
Subjects: $N = 21$ boys, 8 girls; 15 yrs. **Measures:** Coopersmith's Self-Esteem Inventory was administered to Ss 3 times. On each administration, Ss received a different instructional set. Ss were requested to either (a) answer honestly, (b) present a favorable impression of themselves, or (c) present an unfavorable impression of themselves. **Results:** No sex differences.

Milburn, T. W., Bell, N., and Koeske, G. F. Effects of censure or praise and evaluative dependence in a free-learning task. *J. Personality & Social Psychology*, 1970, *15*, 43–47.
EXPERIMENT I: **Subjects:** $N = 86$; 18–21 yrs (college). **Measures:** Ss were successively presented with 3 lists of words. Ss were asked to recall as many words as possible from each list. In between lists, Ss received either subtle approval or censure from E. **Results:** Women recalled more words than men did ($p < .01$).
EXPERIMENT II: **Subjects:** $N = 48$; 18–21 yrs (college). **Measures:** Same lists as Experiment

I. Procedures were changed to minimize contact between S and E. **Results:** Women recalled more words than men did ($p < .01$).

Milgram, N. A., and Wolfgang, W. R. Developmental and experimental factors in making wishes. *Child Development*, 1969, *40*, 763–71.
    Subjects: $N = 160$; 6, 9, 12, 15 yrs (white and black, normal and noninstitutionalized retardates). **Measures:** Ss were asked, "If you could make 3 wishes, what 3 wishes would you make?" Wishes were scored on abstract/concrete and adult/child dimensions. **Results:** No sex differences.

Milgram, N. A., Shore, M. F., and Malasky, C. Linguistic and thematic variables in recall of a story by disadvantaged children. *Child Development*, 1971, *42*, 637–40.
    Subjects: $N = 99$; 5–7 yrs (white and black, low and middle SES). **Measures:** An illustrated story was read aloud to Ss. Afterward, they were asked to retell the story in their own words. Ss' stories were scored for (a) total number of words, (b) total number of sentences (each new thought expressed was considered a sentence), (c) total number of relevant sentences (sentences were scored according to whether they were part of the story—mere description of the pictures or elaboration of the material was not credited), and (d) presence of each of 22 themes considered essential to the story. **Results:** No sex differences.

Miller, A. G., and Thomas, R. Cooperation and competition among Blackfoot Indian and urban Canadian children. *Child Development*, 1972, *43*, 1104–10.
    Experiment I: Subjects: $N = 96$; 7–11 yrs. **Measures:** Ss played the Madsen Cooperation Board. Group and individual awards were administered. Cooperative behavior resulted in high rewards for everyone, whereas competitive behavior resulted in low rewards. **Results:** No sex differences.
    Experiment II: Subjects: $N = 96$; 7–11 yrs. **Measures:** Same as Experiment I, except that the inhibition of competitive behavior resulted in individual Ss' being rewarded. **Results:** No sex differences.

Miller, D. J., Cohen, L. B., and Hill, K. T. A methodological investigation of Piaget's theory of object concept development in the sensory-motor period. *J. Experimental Child Psychology*, 1970, *9*, 59–85.
    Subjects: $N = 84$; 6, 8, 10, 12, 14, 16, 18 mos. **Measures:** Ss were given 8 of the 16 tasks of the Uzgiris and Hunt "Visual Pursuit and Permanence of Objects" series. 6- and 8-month-olds were tested on Tasks 1–8; 10- and 12-month-olds on Tasks 4–9; and 11-12, and 14-, 16- and 18-month-olds on Tasks 8–9 and 11–16. For 28 Ss, the procedures used by Uzgiris and Hunt were followed as closely as possible (Replication condition); for the remaining 56 Ss, a considerable number of procedural changes were made (Extension condition). **Results:** Among 14-18-month-olds in the Replication condition, girls exhibited a higher level of performance than boys ($p < .05$). No other sex differences were found.

Miller, L. K. Developmental differences in the field of view during tachistoscopic presentation. *Child Development*, 1971, *42*, 1543–51.
    Experiment I: Subjects: $N = 36$; 7, 11, 20 yrs. **Measures:** Ss were shown a series of displays of letters that were divided by lines to form 4 quadrants. After Ss' fixation time was assessed, they were asked to name the quadrant containing the target letter for each array. **Results:** No sex differences.
    Experiment II: Subjects: $N = 36$; 7, 11, 20 yrs. **Measures:** Same as Experiment I, except that the set of displays eliciting the most marked differences in performance associated with target distance was presented in such conditions as to elicit age differences in overall performance. **Results:** No sex differences.

Miller, P. H. Attention to stimulus dimensions in the conservation of liquid quantity. *Child Development*, 1973, *44*, 129–36.
    Subjects: $N = 100$; 5, 8 yrs (white, middle SES). **Measures:** Ss were given a pretraining session to assess their understanding of "same" and "different" concepts. An attention task followed in which relative saliences of height, width, and quantity of liquids were determined. Ss were then given a liquid conservation task. **Results:** No sex differences.

Miller, R. R. No play: a means of conflict resolution. *J. Personality & Social Psychology*, 1967, *6*, 150–56.
    Subjects: $N = 120$; 18–21 yrs (college). **Measures:** Same-sex pairs of Ss played a modified version of the Prisoner's Dilemma game in which a third choice with an automatic zero-zero payoff (overriding any choice by the other player) was available. **Results:** No sex differences.

Miller, T. W. Communicative dimensions of mother-child interaction as they affect the self-esteem of the child. Paper read at the 79th APA meeting, Washington, D.C., 1971.
Subjects: $N = 203$; 13 yrs and mothers (white and black, urban and suburban). Measures: Ss completed Coopersmith's Self-Esteem Inventory. Mothers answered (1) the Parental Response Inventory, which assessed their reactions to positive and negative children's behaviors, and (2) the Relationship Inventory-B, which assessed their affective and empathic reactions in family interactions. Results: (1) In the inner-city black sample, mothers showed greater empathy, genuineness, and positive regard toward their daughters than toward their sons. (2) Girls showed higher levels of overall self-esteem than boys did ($p < .05$).

Milton, G. A. Sex differences in problem solving as a function of role appropriateness of the problem content. *Psychological Reports*, 1959, 5, 705–8.
Subjects: $N = 48$; 18–21 yrs (college). Measures: Ss were given a set of 20 problems, half with content appropriate to the masculine role and half with content appropriate to the feminine role. Results: Men solved more problems than women did (for "masculine" problems, $p < .001$; for "feminine" problems, $p < .05$). The difference between the men's and women's scores was less when the problems were stated with content appropriate to the feminine role ($p < .05$).

Minard, J. G. Response-bias interpretation of "perceptual defense"; a selective review and evaluation of recent research. *Psychological Review*, 1965, 72, 74–88.
Subjects: $N = 52$; 18–21 yrs (college). Measures: Ss were tachistoscopically presented with slides of emotion-arousing and neutral words. Interspersed among these were smudged blank slides. After each presentation, Ss were asked to name the word that had been on the screen. Results: (1) Neither sex evidenced response bias. (2) Men identified neutral words more accurately than emotional words; for women, the reverse was true ($p < .01$).

Minard, J. G., Bailey, D. E., and Wertheimer, M. Measurement and conditioning of perceptual defense, response bias, and emotionally biased recognition. *J. Personality & Social Psychology*, 1965, 2, 661–68.
Subjects: $N = 52$; 18–21 yrs (college). Measures: Ss identified neutral and emotion-arousing words that were tachistoscopically presented at better-than-chance levels of accurate recognition. Results: Women showed a greater predominance of emotional word responses among accurate stimulus identifications than men did ($p < .05$). No sex differences were found in response bias.

Minor, M. W. Experimenter-expectancy effect as a function of evaluation apprehension. *J. Personality & Social Psychology*, 1970, 15, 326–32.
Subjects: $N = 39$; 18–21 yrs (college). Measures: Ss rated the degree of success or failure experienced by individuals in a series of 10 photographs. Results: Women rated the pictures more negatively than men did ($p < .03$).

Minton, C., Kagan, J., and Levine, J. A. Maternal control and obedience in the two-year-old. *Child Development*, 1971, 42, 1873–94 (and personal communication).
Subjects: $N = 90$; 27 mos (firstborn) and their mothers (low, lower-middle, middle, upper-middle SES). Measures: Each mother-child pair was visited at home on 2 separate occasions. Mothers' reactions to (a) requests and (b) violations of maternal standards were recorded. Results: (1) Boys interacted with their mothers more than girls did. (2) Boys committed more violations of maternal standards than girls did. More of boys' than girls' violations involved the integrity of household goods. In contrast to girls, boys were more often reprimanded for aggressing toward their mothers. Girls, in contrast, were more often reprimanded for failing to perform a task with competence (significant for upper-middle SES sample, personal communication). Girls were more likely than boys to obey their mothers immediately. (3) No sex difference was found in the rate of occurrence of requests. Requests for help were more frequent for girls than for boys ($p < .10$), whereas requests for information and permission were more frequent for boys than for girls ($p < .10$). (4) No differences were found between mothers of boys and girls in the frequency of occurrence of anticipation sequences (mother anticipates the child's violation of 1 of her standards) or commands, or in their display of the following types of responses to violations: simple prohibitions; mildly negative statements; removal of object; explanation; questioning; distraction; physical punishment. In comparison to mothers of girls, mothers of boys were more likely to move their child from the locus of the violation and less likely to use directive prohibitions. (5) Mothers of girls worried more often about personal danger to their child and less often about danger to household goods than mothers of boys.

Miranda, S. B. Visual abilities and pattern preference of premature infants and full-term neonates. *J. Experimental Child Psychology*, 1970, *10*, 189–205.
Subjects: $N = 54$; 3 days (full term), 22 days (premature with gestation age of 8 mos). Measures: Ss were presented with pairs of geometric and facial stimuli. Fixation times were recorded. Results: No sex differences.

Mischel, H. N. Professional sex bias and sex-role stereotypes in the U.S. and Israel. Corrected draft, 1972.
EXPERIMENT I: Subjects: $N = 56$; 17–21 yrs. Measures: Ss were presented with 1 article from the professional literature of each of 4 occupational fields: law, city planning, primary education, and dietetics. Law and city planning were thought to be strongly associated with men, whereas primary education and dietetics were considered primarily feminine fields. Articles were ascribed to either male or female authors. After reading each article, Ss answered a set of 9 evaluative questions. Results: (1) There were no main effects of sex of subject or sex of author. (2) Articles ascribed to male authors in the male fields were rated more favorably than those ascribed to female authors; articles ascribed to female authors in the female fields were rated more favorably than those ascribed to male authors ($p < .01$).
EXPERIMENT II: Subjects: $N = 21$; 18–21 yrs. Measures: Ss were asked to indicate the degree to which each of 10 occupational fields was associated with men or with women. Results: (1) There were no main effects of sex of subject. (2) Law and city planning were perceived as masculine fields, dietetics and primary education as feminine fields ($p < .01$).
EXPERIMENT III: Subjects: $N = 52$; 13–20 yrs (Israel). Measures: Same as Experiment I. Results: No sex differences.
EXPERIMENT IV: Subjects: $N = 74$; 14–17, 25–48 yrs (Israel). Measures: Same as Experiment II. Results: Same as Experiment II ($p < .001$).

Mischel, W., and Grusec, J. Determinant of the rehearsal and transmission of neutral and aversive behaviors. *J. Personality & Social Psychology*, 1966, *3*, 197–205.
Subjects: $N = 56$; 3–5 yrs. Measures: Ss were exposed to an adult female model who displayed aversive and neutral behaviors while playing a game. Afterward, in the model's absence, Ss were given the opportunity to demonstrate the game to a confederate. Measures were taken of Ss' rehearsal of the neutral and aversive behaviors in the model's presence, and of Ss' transmission of these behaviors to the confederate. Results: No sex differences.

Mischel, W., and Grusec, J. Waiting for rewards and punishments: effects of time and probability on choice. *J. Personality & Social Psychology*, 1967, *5*, 24–31.
Subjects: $N = 96$; 9–10 yrs. Measures: Ss chose between smaller immediate and larger delayed rewards and punishments. Results: No sex differences.

Mischel, W., and Liebert, R. M. Effects of discrepancies between observed and imposed reward criteria on their acquisition and transmission. *J. Personality & Social Psychology*, 1966, *3*, 45–53.
Subjects: $N = 54$; 9 yrs. Measures: Ss alternated turns with an adult female model (M) in a bowling game. Ss were guided to adopt a criterion of self-reward that was either consistent or inconsistent with the self-reward criterion modeled by M. Afterward, half the Ss demonstrated the game to a younger child and then performed alone. The remaining half went through the reverse sequence. The response measures were the scores for which Ss rewarded themselves when performing alone and when demonstrating the game. Measures were also taken of the self-reward criteria Ss imposed on the younger children. Results: No sex differences.

Mischel, W., and Liebert, R. M. The role of power in the adoption of self-reward patterns. *Child Development*, 1967, *38*, 673–83.
Subjects: $N = 56$; 7–8 yrs. Measures: Ss played a miniature bowling game for which E controlled the scores. Each S practiced games with the male model, who rewarded himself for high scores and guided S to reward himself. However, the model rewarded himself for some lower scores for which he would not allow S to reward himself. In Phase I, Ss were led to believe that the model would possibly give S a free sample game if S performed well. In Phase II, Ss expected no potential reward. Each S performed the game alone in 2 phases. In the second phase, each S in the experimental group was informed that no sample games were available. The response measure was the occurrence or nonoccurrence of self-reward when S performed alone. Results: No sex differences.

Mischel, W., and Underwood, B. Instrumental ideation in delay of gratification. Unpublished manuscript, Stanford University, 1973.
  Subjects: $N = 80$; 2–5 yrs. Measures: After choosing between 2 rewards, E left Ss alone with instructions that if they waited until he came back, they would be rewarded with their preferred choice. However, they were informed that at any time they could signal him to return and immediately receive the less preferred reward. Results: Girls waited for a longer period of time than boys did ($p < .01$).

Mischel, W., Coates, B., and Raskoff, A. Effect of success and failure on self-gratification. *J. Personality & Social Psychology*, 1968, *10*, 381–90.
  EXPERIMENT I: Subjects: $N = 60$; 7–9 yrs. Measures: After receiving instructions from E to reward themselves for good scores, Ss experienced either repeated success or repeated failure in a miniature bowling game. The response measure was the number of rewards taken. Ss were then given maze designs to solve. While attempting to solve the mazes, Ss were allowed to (noncontingently) help themselves to reward tokens. The response measures were the number of reward tokens taken, number of mazes completed, and amount of time spent working on the mazes. Results: (1) No sex differences were found in the number of rewards or tokens Ss took or in the number of mazes they completed. (2) No main sex differences were found in time spent working on the mazes. Boys who succeeded on the bowling task spent more time on the mazes than boys who failed; for girls, there was no effect ($p < .05$).
  EXPERIMENT II: Subjects: $N = 120$; 8–9 yrs. Measures: Same as Experiment I, except that Ss obtained either success, failure, or neutral (no-score) outcomes on the bowling game. No rewards were made available for good scores. The bowling game and the maze task were presented either sequentially (as in Experiment I) or concurrently. Ss rewarded themselves under conditions of greater privacy and anonymity while working on the maze designs. Results: (1) No sex differences were found in number of maze tokens taken or in number of mazes completed. Girls spent more time in the maze situation (working on mazes, collecting make tokens) than boys did ($p < .05$). (2) In the concurrent treatment group, no sex differences were found in the amount of time that elapsed before Ss first switched tasks, or in the total number of times Ss changed tasks.

Mischel, W., Grusec, J., and Masters, J. C. Effects of expected delay time on the subjective value of rewards and punishments. *J. Personality & Social Psychology*, 1969, *11*, 363–73.
  EXPERIMENT I: Subjects: $N = 36$; 9–10 yrs. Measures: Ss rated the relative value (attractiveness or unpleasantness) of immediate and delayed rewards and punishments. Results: No sex differences.
  EXPERIMENT III: Subjects: $N = 30$; 18–21 yrs (college). Measures: Same as Experiment I. Rewards and punishments were changed to make them appropriate for adults. Results: No sex differences.
  EXPERIMENT IV: Subjects: $N = 51$; 18–21 yrs (college). Measures: Ss indicated their preferences for receiving (a) immediate vs. delayed shocks and (b) shocks requiring less delay vs. shocks requiring more delay. Ss also rated how unpleasant they expected the shocks to feel. Results: No sex differences.

Mischel, W., Mailer, J., and Zeiss, A. Attribution of internal-external control for positive and negative events: developmental and stimulus effects. Unpublished manuscript, 1973.
  EXPERIMENT I: Subjects: $N = 60$; 4–8 yrs. Measures: The Stanford Preschool Internal-External Scale (SPIES) was administered to Ss 3 times. On 1 occasion, Ss answered for themselves. On the other 2 occasions, Ss answered for a liked and disliked peer. The SPIES consists of 14 forced-choice items; 6 describe positive events and 8 describe negative events. For each item, Ss must decide whether to attribute the cause of the event to external or internal forces. Results: No sex differences.
  EXPERIMENT II: Subjects: $N = 40$; 18–21 yrs (college). Measures: Same as Experiment I, except that the Stanford College Internal-External Scale (SCIES) was used instead of the SPIES. The format of the SCIES is identical to that of the SPIES except that the items are worded for adults. Results: When an analysis of variance was performed on the overall data, women were found to attribute more responsibility for negative events to themselves than to others ($p < .05$); for men a nonsignificant trend was observed in the opposite direction.

Mitler, M. M., and Harris, L. Dimension preference and performance on a series of concept identification tasks in kindergarten, first grade and third grade. *J. Experimental Child Psychology*, 1969, *7*, 374–84.
  Subjects: $N = 77$; 5–9 yrs. Measures: Dimension preference (color, form, number) and con-

cept identification were measured by the Wisconsin Card Sorting Test. **Results:** No sex differences.

Mock, R. L., and Tuddenham, R. D. Race and conformity among children. *Developmental Psychology*, 1971, 4, 349–65.
  Subjects: $N = 280$; 9–11 yrs (white, black). **Measures:** Each S made visual-spatial judgments while simultaneously confronted with perceptual stimuli and with supposed information about 4 same-sex peers' judgments on the same stimuli. Information from peers (actually experimenter-controlled) was from 1 to 3 degrees discrepant from normal perception of stimuli. The response measure was the extent to which Ss conformed to the group's judgment. **Results:** Girls were more conforming than boys ($p < .01$).

Modreski, R. A., and Goss, A. E. Young children's initial and changed names for form-color stimuli. *J. Experimental Child Psychology*, 1968, 8, 402–9.
  Subjects: $N = 10$; 3–5 yrs. **Measures:** Ss named stimuli that varied in form and color. **Results:** No sex differences.

Moffatt, G. H. Avoidance conditioning in young children with interruption of a positive stimulus as the aversive event. *J. Experimental Child Psychology*, 1972, 13, 21–28.
  Subjects: $N = 48$; 6 yrs. **Measures:** During a delayed conditioning paradigm, Ss heard recordings of high and low interest value. The interruption of the recordings could be avoided by a hand-pushing response. Half of the Ss could avoid interruption by the pushing response and could escape duration of omission interval by another response. The other half could only avoid interruption but not reinstate the recording. **Results:** (1) There were no sex differences in number of Ss who conditioned or reached extinction. (2) Boys made more avoidance responses than girls did on the first acquisition trial block ($p < .05$).

Monahan, L., Kuhn, D., and Shaver, P. Intrapsychic versus cultural explanations of the "fear of success" motive. *J. Personality & Social Psychology*, 1974, 29, 60–64.
  Subjects: $N = 120$; 10–16 yrs. **Measures:** Ss were asked to make up a story starting with the following sentence: "After first-term finals, Ann (John) finds herself (himself) at the top of her (his) medical school class." Ss' stories were analyzed for positive and negative attitudes expressed toward the actor and toward the achievement. **Results:** There were no sex differences. More Ss responded to the Ann cue than to the John cue with negative attitudes (for boys, $p < .0006$; for girls, $p < .07$).

Monday, L. A., Hout, D. P., and Lutz, S. W. *College Student Profiles: American College Testing Program*. Iowa City: ACT Publications, 1966–67.
  Subjects: $N = 238, 145$; 18 yrs. **Measures:** Ss were given the ACT. The high school grades of most of the sample ($N = 225, 402$) were also obtained. **Results:** (1) On the ACT, women had higher English scores, whereas men had higher Mathematics, Natural Science, and Total Composite scores. No sex differences were found in Social Science scores. (2) Women's high school grades were higher than those of men.

Montanelli, D. S. Multiple cue learning in children. *Developmental Psychology*, 1972, 7, 302–12.
  Subjects: $N = 144$; 8, 10, 12, 14 yrs. **Measures:** Ss were given a multiple-cue learning task. By using the color, form, and border of each of 64 geometric stimuli, Ss were asked to judge how far to move a lever across a slot. Each stimulus was presented twice. **Results:** (1) No main sex differences were found in cue utilization. Boys made greatest use of the most valid cue, whereas girls showed greatest use of the cue of intermediate validity. (2) Boys showed a tendency to use the cues of highest and intermediate validity without regard to their physical characteristics, whereas girls tended to use the form cue in conjunction with the cue of highest validity. (3) No sex differences were found in response latencies.

Montanelli, D. S., and Hill, K. T. Children's achievement expectations and performance as a function of two consecutive reinforcement experiences, sex of subject, and sex of experimenter. *J. Personality & Social Psychology*, 1969, 13, 115–28.
  Subjects: $N = 108$; 10 yrs. **Measures:** During each of 2 sessions, Ss received either praise, criticism, or no reaction from either a male or female E while performing a simple operant task (dropping marbles in holes). Ss' achievement expectancies (AEs) were obtained before and after session 1, and after session 2. Ss' response rates were also recorded. **Results:** (1) Boys had higher initial AEs than girls ($p < .05$). Ss with male Es had higher initial AEs than those with female Es ($p < .05$). (2) No sex differences were found in post-session-1 AEs

or in change from initial AEs to post-session-1 AEs. (3) No sex differences were found in pre-session-2 AEs or in change from post-session-1 AEs to pre-session-2 AEs. Ss with male Es had higher pre-session-2 AEs than Ss with female Es. (4) No sex differences were found in Ss' response rates during the baseline period. Ss with male Es had higher base rates than those with female Es ($p < .01$). (5) No sex differences were found in session 1 or session 2 response rates, holding constant Ss' base rates.

Moore, B. S., Underwood, B., and Rosenhan, D. L. Affect and altruism. *Developmental Psychology*, 1973, *8*, 99–104.

> **Subjects:** $N = 42$; 7–8 yrs. **Measures:** Ss were paid 25 pennies for participation in a "hearing" test. After being told to think of something either happy or sad for 40 seconds, Ss were given a 90-second private opportunity to keep or share their pennies. Control Ss either counted slowly or sat quietly during the affective period. **Results:** There was no main effect for sex in the analysis of mean amounts contributed. Girls' median contributions were higher than those of boys ($p < .05$).

Moore, M. Aggression themes in a binocular rivalry situation. *J. Personality & Social Psychology*, 1966, *3*, 685–88.

> **Subjects:** $N = 180$; 8, 10, 12, 14, 16, 18 yrs. **Measures:** By means of a stereoscope, Ss were simultaneously exposed to paired sets of a violent and a nonviolent picture. The response measure was the number of violent pictures seen. **Results:** Boys perceived more violence than girls ($p < .01$).

Moore, T. Language and intelligence: a longitudinal study of the first eight years. Part 1. Patterns of development in boys and girls. *Human Development*, 1967, *10*, 88–106.

> **Subjects:** $N = 76$; tested at ½, 1½, 3, 5, 8 yrs. **Measures:** (1) Griffiths Scale of Infant Development: GQ, Speech Quotient (tested at 6, 18 mos); (2) Stanford-Binet: IQ, Vocabulary (tested at 3, 5, 8 yrs); (3) while tested on the above measures, Ss were rated for (a) comprehension of language (at 3, 5, 8 yrs), (b) length and complexity of sentences (at 3, 5 yrs), (c) enunciation (at 3, 5 yrs), (d) amount of vocalization (at 6 mos), (e) vocal communicativeness (at 18 mos, 3 yrs). **Results:** Among 18-month-old Ss, girls had higher speech quotients than boys ($p < .01$). No other sex differences were found.

Moran, L. J., and Swartz, J. D. Longitudinal study of cognitive dictionaries from ages nine to seventeen. *Developmental Psychology*, 1970, *3*, 21–28.

> **Subjects:** $N = 280$; 9, 12, 15 yrs. **Measures:** An 80-word free association list was administered to Ss, who were retested with same list after 1- and 2-year intervals. Responses were scored as dimension-referent (contrast as in dark-light, or logical coordinate as in apple-orange), perceptual-referent (sensory predicate as in yellow-banana, or abstract predicate as in eagle-bold), concept-referent (synonym or superordinate), paradigmatic (same part of speech), or syntagmatic (summation of noun-verb, noun-adjective, verb-noun, adjective-noun associates). **Results:** No sex differences.

Morf, M. E., and Howitt, R. Rod-and-Frame Test performance as a function of momentary arousal. *Perceptual & Motor Skills*, 1970, *31*, 703–8.

> **Subjects:** $N = 44$; 18–21 yrs (college). **Measures:** The portable model of the Rod-and-Frame Test was administered to Ss. Palmar sweat fingerprints were obtained from each S during the second block of 8 trials. **Results:** No sex differences.

Morf, M. E., Kavanaugh, R. D., and McConville, M. Intratest and sex differences on a portable Rod-and-Frame Test. *Perceptual & Motor Skills*, 1971, *32*, 727–33.

> **Subjects:** $N = 82$; 18–21 yrs (college). **Measures:** Rod-and-Frame Test (portable model). **Results:** No sex differences were found in the initial block of 8 trials. Men were more field-independent than women on trials 9–16 ($p < .05$).

Morin, R. E., Hoving, K. L., and Konick, D. S. Short-term memory in children: keeping track of variables with few or many states. *J. Experimental Child Psychology*, 1970, *10*, 181–88.

> **Subjects:** $N = 48$; 4 yrs. **Measures:** Ss learned the names of 6 familiar objects in each of 4 categories represented by line drawings. E sequentially presented 1 object from each category, after which he asked Ss about the most recent exposure of a particular category ("which animal did you see?"). Stimuli were presented visually to 1 group and aurally to the other. **Results:** No sex differences were found in number of incorrect responses.

Moss, H. A. Sex, age, and state as determinants of mother-infant interaction. *Merrill-Palmer Quarterly*, 1967, *13*, 19–36.

Subjects: $N = 29$; 3 wks (firstborns) and mothers. 25 Ss were retested at 3 mos. Measures: Home observations were made of infant and maternal behaviors. Results: (1) At both observations (a) boys fussed more than girls; (b) boys were more irritable than girls; (c) girls slept more than boys. (2) At 3 weeks of age (but not at 3 months) (a) boys were passively awake more often than girls; (b) boys were observed in the supine position more frequently than girls. (3) At 3 months of age (but not at 3 weeks), mouthing was more frequent in girls than boys. (4) No differences were found between boys and girls in the following behaviors: crying, drowsiness, vocalizations, smiling, eyes on mother, actively awake. (5) At 3 weeks (but not at 3 months), mothers of boys were higher than mothers of girls on the following behaviors: holds infant distant, attends infant, maternal contact (number of holds and attends), stresses musculature, stimulates/arouses infant. (6) No differences were found between mothers of boys and girls on the following behaviors: holds infant close, total number of holds, feeds infant, stimulates feeding, burps infant, affectionate contact, rocks infant, imitates infant, looks at infant, talks to infant, smiles at infant.

Moss, H. A., and Robson, K. S. Maternal influences in early social visual behavior. *Child Development*, 1968, *39*, 401–8.

Subjects: $N = 54$; tested at 1, 3 mos (firstborns) and mothers (18–34 yrs). Measures: (1) 3 home observations were conducted at the end of the infant's first and third months. The frequency with which mother and child simultaneously looked at one another's faces was recorded. (2) At 3 months of age, each infant was presented with geometric and facial stimuli in a laboratory setting. The response measure was the length of the infant's fixation to each stimulus. Results: (1) No sex differences were found during the 3 home observations. (2) In the visual study at 3 months of age, boys looked at both series of stimuli more than girls did (social stimuli, $p < .01$; geometric stimuli, $p < .001$).

Moss, H. A., and Robson, K. S. The relation between the amount of time infants spend at various states and the development of visual behavior. *Child Development*, 1970, *41*, 509–17.

Subjects: $N = 42$; tested at 1, 3 mos (firstborns) and mothers (18–34 yrs). Measures: At both sessions, Ss were observed in their homes. The frequency of fusses and cries and the amount of time Ss spent in each of 2 states (awake and drowsy) were recorded. Results: At 3 months, boys fussed more than girls. No other sex differences were found.

Moyer, K. E., and von Haller, G. B. Experimental study of children's preferences and use of blocks in play. *J. Genetic Psychology*, 1956, *89*, 3–10.

Subjects: $N = 87$; 3–5 yrs. Measures: Ss were exposed to a set of 300 blocks and were then observed by E. Results: No sex differences were found in the amount of time Ss spent playing with the blocks, in the number of structures they built, or in the number of blocks they used.

Moynahan, E. D. The development of knowledge concerning the effect of categorization upon full recall. *Child Development*, 1973, *44*, 238–46.

Subjects: $N = 144$; 6, 8, 10 yrs. Measures: Ss predicted the relative ease of recalling sets of categorized vs. noncategorized stimuli. Recall was measured. Results: No sex differences.

Moynahan, E. D., and Glick, J. Relation between identity conservation and equivalence conservation within four conceptual domains. *Developmental Psychology*, 1972, *6*, 247–51.

Subjects: $N = 96$; 5–6 yrs. Measures: Ss performed identity and equivalence conservation tasks in 4 domains: length, number, weight, and continuous quantity. Results: Boys' identity, equivalence, and total conservation scores were higher than those of girls ($p < .05$; $p < .01$; $p < .05$).

Mueller, E. The maintenance of verbal exchanges between young children. *Child Development*, 1972, *43*, 930–38.

Subjects: $N = 48$; 3–5 yrs. Measures: After being introduced to each other, pairs of Ss were observed in free play in a room equipped with a variety of toys and games. Each S was paired with a child of the same sex. Response measures were frequency of verbal interaction and number of successful and unsuccessful utterances. An utterance was coded as a success if the listener clearly responded to it. If the utterance failed to elicit any response, it was classified as a failure. Results: Boys talked more than girls ($p < .05$). No other sex differences were found.

Mullener, N., and Laird, J. D. Some developmental changes in the organization of self-evaluations. *Developmental Psychology*, 1971, 5, 233–36.
  Subjects: N = 72; 12, 17, 25–35 yrs. Measures: Ss completed a self-evaluation questionnaire on 40 personal characteristics represented by 5 content areas: achievement traits, intellectual abilities, interpersonal skills, physical skills, and social responsibility. Evaluation scores (sum of ratings for the 8 items in a content area) and variance scores (variance of each S's evaluation scores across content areas) were analyzed. Results: No sex differences.

Mumbauer, C. C., and Gray, S. W. Resistance to temptation in young Negro children. *Child Development*, 1970, 41, 1203–7.
  Subjects: N = 96; 5 yrs (black, father present or father absent). Measures: Ss played a beanbag game with a black male or female E; then they played alone when E was gone. The reward was the prize Ss had chosen. Results: No main sex differences were found.

Mumbauer, C. C., and Miller, J. O. Socioeconomic background and cognitive functioning in preschool children. *Child Development*, 1970, 41, 471–80.
  Subjects: N = 64; 4–5 yrs (low, high SES). Measures: Stanford-Binet IQ test, Paired Associates Learning Task, Kagan's Matching Familiar Figures Test, Motoric Inhibition Test, Children's Embedded Figures Test, and Reactive Object Curiosity Test. Results: No sex differences.

Munroe, R. L., and Munroe, R. H. Effect of environmental experience on spatial ability in an East African society. *J. Social Psychology*, 1971, 83, 15–22.
  Subjects: N = 30; 3–7 yrs. Measures: Observations were made of Ss' distance from home, and the directed or undirected character of their activities. Results: Overall, no sex differences were found in distance from home. During their free time, boys traveled farther away from home than girls ($p < .01$).

Murray, F. B. Acquisition of conservation through social interaction. *Developmental Psychology*, 1972, 6, 1–6.
  Subjects: N = 108; 6 yrs. Measures: Ss took a series of conservation tasks (2-dimensional space, number, substance, continuous quantity, weight, and discontinuous quantity). Ss were tested under 3 conditions: alone, in 3-member group (with the stipulation that all members had to agree on answers), and again alone (with additional stimuli, transformations, and tests for concepts of length and area). Results: No sex differences.

Nachamie, S. Machiavellianism in children: the children's Mach scale and the bluffing game. Unpublished doctoral dissertation, Columbia University, 1969.
  Subjects: N = 72; 11 yrs (Puerto Rican, Chinese, black, white). Measures: Ss completed a modified version of Christie's Likert-type Machiavellianism Scale. 47 Ss with either high or low scores were then paired with a middle Mach child of the same sex. S was given a pair of dice to roll. After each throw, S could either bluff or tell the truth about the outcome. The middle Mach child could then either accept or challenge S's statement. Higher rewards were received for successful bluffs and successful challenges. Results: No sex differences were found in Mach scores or in number of successful bluffs or challenges.

Nakamura, C. Y. Effect of prominence of dissonance associated stimuli during evaluation of the stimuli. *J. Experimental Child Psychology*, 1966, 3, 86–99.
  Subjects: N = 32; 9 yrs. Measures: Criterion measures of dissonance reduction were established on 4 tasks: 1 making a stimulus that was in the rewarded situation most cognitively salient, the other 3 tasks intended to require greater generalization of stimuli in order for dissonance reduction to be manifested in evaluations of the stimuli. Results: There were no main sex differences. Boys took longer to extinguish on task performance following low reward than high reward treatment; for girls the converse was true.

Nakamura, C. Y. Effects of increasing and decreasing reward magnitude and pre-experimental persistence level on focal and incidental responses. *J. Experimental Child Psychology*, 1969, 7, 514–31.
  Subjects: N = 48; 5–6 yrs. Measures: Ss' predisposition to persist were rated by teachers. Persistence on a marble game was measured with increasing, decreasing, and random rewards. Results: (1) Low-persistence boys made more lever strokes (release marbles) than high-persistence boys; the converse was true for girls. (2) Under nonreward conditions, boys took more trials to extinction than girls.

Nakamura, C. Y., and Finck, D. Effect of social or task orientation and evaluative or non-evaluative situations on performance. *Child Development*, 1973, *44*, 83–93.

Subjects: $N = 251$; 9–12 yrs. **Measures:** Ss completed the hypothetical situation questionnaire (HSQ), comprising 18 items describing familiar academic situations. Each item is followed by the question "What would you do if you were the child in that situation?" and 4 response choices. On the basis of their answers, Ss were assigned scores on 3 scales: social orientation, task orientation, and self-assurance. Then 204 of the Ss were given a modified version of Pearson and Maddi's Similes Performance Inventory. Ss' task was to learn the correct endings to 30 easy and 30 difficult simile stems. For each set of stems, the number of trials Ss needed to reach the criterion and the total number of errors they made were recorded. **Results:** No sex differences.

Nakamura, C. Y., and Rogers, M. M. Parents' expectations of autonomous behavior and children's autonomy. *Developmental Psychology*, 1969, *1*, 613–17 (and personal communication).

Subjects: $N = 78$; parents of 39 3-year-olds. **Measures:** The Parent's Expectation Inventory was administered to mothers and fathers. Two 10-item subscales measured parents' expectations of 2 types of autonomous behavior in their child—practical and assertive. **Results:** (1) Fathers of girls had higher expectations of assertive autonomy than fathers of boys did. No difference was found between boys' and girls' mothers. (2) Mothers of boys had higher expectations of practical autonomy than mothers of girls did. No difference was found between boys' and girls' fathers. (3) The overall expectations of mothers of boys were greater than those of fathers of boys. No difference was found between the overall expectations of mothers and fathers of girls.

Nash, S. C. Conceptions and concomitants of sex-role stereotyping. Unpublished doctoral dissertation, Columbia University, 1973.

Subjects: $N = 207$; 11, 14 yrs. **Measures:** E administered the group versions of the Embedded Figures Test (GEFT) and the Differential Aptitudes Test, Space Relations (DAT). Demographic data and standardized arithmetic and reading scores were obtained for all Ss. Sex-role preference and theories of sex differences were assessed from Ss' written reports. Ss were given a Stereotypic Questionnaire (99 bipolar items concerning sex-role characteristics) on which they were asked to describe most men, most women, self, and ideal self. **Results:** (1) Among 11-year-old Ss, there were no sex differences on the DAT or the GEFT. Among 14-year-old Ss, boys scored higher than girls on the DAT ($p < .02$) and the GEFT ($p < .01$). There were no main effects of handedness on either spatial reasoning task. (2) There were no sex differences on the standardized arithmetic and reading tests. (3) In both age groups, girls reported they preferred to be boys (11 years, $p < .01$; 14 years, $p < .05$). More 11- than 14-year-old girls preferred to be boys. (4) Among 11-year-old Ss, girls and boys reported it is better to be a boy ($p < .02$). (5) In both age groups, girls rated more bipolar items stereotypic than boys did (11 years, $p < .05$; 14 years, $p < .05$). (6) Ss who preferred to be boys scored higher on the DAT than Ss who preferred to be girls. There were no sex differences on the DAT among Ss who preferred to be boys.

Natsoulas, T. Locus and orientation of the perceiver (ego) under variable, constant, and no perspective instructions. *J. Personality & Social Psychology*, 1966, *3*, 190–96.

Subjects: $N = 96$; 18–21 yrs (college). **Measures:** (1) While S closed his eyes, a letter of the alphabet (either d, b, p, or q) was traced on the side of his head. S's task was to identify which of the 4 letters had been traced. The response measure was the number of times S assumed an internal perspective. (2) Same as Part I, except that S was asked to assume either an external or an internal perspective. The response measure was the number of correct identifications S made. (3) While S closed his eyes, 45- and 90-degree angles were traced on the side of his head. S's task was to draw the traced figures from either an internal or an external perspective. The response measure was the accuracy of S's drawing. **Results:** No sex differences.

Navrat, M. L. Color tint matching by children. *Perceptual & Motor Skills*, 1965, *21*, 215–22.

Subjects: $N = 160$; 3–10 yrs. **Measures:** 9 different tints of the same color were placed in front of Ss. Ss were then given a tint identical to 1 of the 9. S's task was to match it with its duplicate. **Results:** No sex differences were found in the accuracy of Ss' responses.

Nawas, M. M. Change in efficiency of ego functioning and complexity from adolescence to young adulthood. *Developmental Psychology*, 1971, *4*, 412–15.

Subjects: $N = 125$; 26 yrs (originally tested at 18 yrs). Measures: The Thematic Apperception Test Ego Sufficiency Scale (measuring ability to cope with emotional issues posed by the ambiguous TAT scenes and figures, and mastery of problems Ss get characters involved in) and the Complexity Scale (number of constructs used in Ss stories, i.e. achievement, affiliation, hostility, etc.) were administered to each S. Results: At adolescence, girls' scores for both ego sufficiency and complexity were higher than those of boys. In young adulthood, men's scores exceeded those of women.

Nelsen, E. A., and Rosenbaum, E. Language patterns within the youth subculture: development of slang vocabularies. *Merrill-Palmer Quarterly*, 1972, *18*, 273–85.

Subjects: $N = 1,916$; 12–17 yrs. Measures: Same-sex groups of 4 were asked to list as many slang terms as they could that were associated with each of 9 topic areas. Results: Boys listed more terms than girls for "money" and "autos and motorbikes." Girls listed more terms than boys for "clothes, styles, and appearance," "boys," "a popular person," and "an unpopular person." No sex differences were found for "cigarettes," "alcohol," or "girls."

Nelson, J. D., Gelfand, D. M., and Hartmann, D. P. Children's aggression following competition and exposure to an aggression model. *Child Development*, 1969, *40*, 1085–97.

Subjects: $N = 96$; 5–7 yrs. Measures: Ss observed either an aggressive or a nonaggressive adult model. Subsequent to viewing the model, two-thirds of the Ss either succeeded or failed in competitive games; the remaining Ss engaged in noncompetitive play. All SS were then taken to an experimental room, where they engaged in 10 minutes of free play. The room contained a variety of aggressive and nonaggressive toys, among which were those the aggressive model had used. Displays of imitative and nonimitative aggression were recorded. A total (imitative plus nonimitative) aggression score was then computed. Results: (1) After viewing the nonaggressive model, boys were more aggressive than girls. No sex differences were found following exposure to the aggressive model. (2) No sex differences were found in imitative physical aggression scores. Too few displays of imitative verbal aggression were observed to be analyzed.

Nelson, K. E. Accommodation of visual tracking patterns in human infants to object movement patterns. *J. Experimental Child Psychology*, 1971, *12*, 182–96.

Subjects: $N = 80$; 3–9 mos. Measures: Ss' visual movements were videotaped while they watched a model train travel around a track and in and out of a tunnel. After criterion was reached (4 or 8 visual movements toward end of tunnel after the train entered), a series of reversal trials (direction reversals made in tunnel) and original direction trials were made. Results: No main sex differences.

Nelson, L., and Madsen, M. C. Cooperation and competition in four-year-olds as a function of reward contingency and subculture. *Developmental Psychology*, 1969, *1*, 340–44.

Subjects: $N = 72$; 4 yrs (white and black Head Start programs; white, middle SES nursery school). Measures: Same- and opposite-sex pairs of Ss played Madsen's Cooperation Board under 2 conditions: (1) group-reward, in which it was possible for both subjects to get prizes on every trial, and (2) limited-reward, in which it was possible for only 1 subject to get a prize on a trial. Results: No sex differences.

Nemeth, C. Effects of free versus constrained behavior on attraction between people. *J. Personality & Social Psychology*, 1970, *15*, 302–11.

Subjects: $N = 120$; 15–17 yrs. Measures: After a same-sex confederate either helped or did not help Ss finish a task, Ss completed a questionnaire designed to measure Ss' liking for the confederate and the degree to which Ss felt the confederate liked them. Ss and confederate then participated in a role-playing situation. Ss were asked a standard set of 5 questions by the confederate. The response measure was the amount of time Ss spent talking. Ss then responded to a second questionnaire designed to measure how much they wanted to impress the confederate, and how well they felt they knew him. As Ss were dismissed, Ss were stopped by the confederate and asked to complete a survey. Ss also were asked to take additional surveys for others to complete. The response measures were number of surveys taken (help offered) and number of surveys eventually mailed back (help received). Results: No sex differences.

Newson, J., and Newson, E. *Four years old in an urban community.* Harmondworth, England: Pelican Books, 1968 (and personal communication).
Subjects: $N = 700$; 4 yrs and mothers (England). Measures: Maternal interviews. Results: (1) There were no sex-of-child effects on maternal level of restrictions and demands regarding bedtime, table behavior, neatness, physical mobility. (2) There were no sex-of-child effects on maternal intervention in child's quarrels, or encouragement/permission of aggression toward parents. (3) Mothers were more likely to use physical punishment toward boys than toward girls. Fewer boys than girls were "smacked" less than once a week ($p < .03$). (4) There were no sex differences in bed-wetting. (5) More girls than boys were self-reliant in dressing themselves ($p < .001$).

Nisbett, R. E., and Gordon, A. Self-esteem and susceptibility to social influence. *J. Personality & Social Psychology*, 1967, 5, 268–76.
Subjects: $N = 152$; 18–21 yrs (college). Measures: Ss initially completed 2 self-esteem measures and an intelligence test. At a second session, Ss were informed they had done either extremely well or extremely poorly on the intelligence test. Ss then completed both self-esteem tests for a second time and read various persuasive communications, after which Ss indicated their opinions on the topics dealt with in the communications. Results: No sex differences.

Nisbett, R. E., and Gurwitz, S. B. Weight, sex, and the eating behavior of human newborns. *J. Comparative & Physiological Psychology*, 1970, 73, 245–53.
Subjects: $N = 76$; newborn infants. Measures: Special feedings of the hospital's standard formula and a sweetened version of the formula were given to the infants daily. In a second study, sucking the formula was made difficult by decreasing the diameter of the nipple hole. Results: (1) Girls were more responsive than boys to the difference in taste, i.e. relative to boys, girls consumed more sweetened than unsweetened formula ($p < .02$). (2) Girls consumed less formula when sucking was made difficult; boys showed no change ($p < .025$).

Noble, C. E., and Hays, J. R. Discrimination reaction performance as a function of anxiety and sex parameters. *Perceptual & Motor Skills*, 1966, 23, 1267–78.
Subjects: $N = 200$; 18–21 yrs (college). Measures: Ss' task was to learn to snap the correct toggle switch in response to the lighting of a pair of red and green signal lights. Ss had to choose from among 4 switches. When the correct switch was thrown, a white light turned off. Results: Men had faster reaction times than women ($p < .001$).

Northman, J. E., and Gruen, G. E. Relationship between identity and equivalence conservation. *Developmental Psychology*, 1970, 2, 311 (brief report).
Subjects: $N = 60$; 6–9 yrs. Measures: Ss performed identity and equivalence conservation tasks with liquids. Results: (1) There were no sex differences in identity or equivalence conservation among 6-7-year-old Ss. (2) Among 8-9-year-old Ss, boys made more equivalence and identity conservation responses than girls ($p < .01$).

Novak, D. W., and Lerner, M. J. Rejection as a consequence of perceived similarity. *J. Personality & Social Psychology*, 1968, 9, 147–52.
Subjects: $N = 96$; 18–21 yrs (college). Measures: Ss indicated their willingness to interact with same-sex partners who were presented as either similar or dissimilar to themselves, and as either normal or emotionally disturbed. Ss also rated partners' attractiveness and similarity to themselves. Results: (1) No sex differences were found in willingness to interact with partner. (2) Women rated their partners lower in attractiveness than men did ($p < .01$). (3) Women perceived their partners to be less well adjusted than men did ($p < .05$). (4) No main sex differences were found in perceived similarity. Women perceived partners who had been presented as either similar and/or normal to be more similar to themselves than men did; women perceived partners who had been presented as either dissimilar and/or as emotionally disturbed to be less similar than men did.

Nowicki, S., Jr., and Roundtree, J. Correlates of locus of control in secondary school population. *Developmental Psychology*, 1971, 4, 477–78 (brief report).
Subjects: $N = 87$; 17 yrs. Measures: Ss were asked to list the extracurricular activities they were involved in. Results: Girls were more involved in extracurricular activities than boys ($p < .01$).

Nuessle, W. Reflectivity as an influence on focusing behavior of children. *J. Experimental Child Psychology*, 1972, *14*, 265–76.

   Subjects: $N = 40$; 10 yrs. **Measures:** To study relationship between developmental differences in hypothesis-testing behavior and problem-solving styles, Ss were presented with 16 simultaneous concept identification problems, for which feedback was given on a prearranged random schedule. E recorded stimulus choice (which allowed determination of which problem-solving hypothesis S used) and 2 response-latency measures. **Results:** (1) Girls had a higher probability of repeating a preceding hypothesis after positive feedback than boys ($p < .05$). (2) Girls took a longer time than boys to complete a problem ($p < .05$). Girls' latency between feedback and the next response was longer than that of boys, but girls were not more effective focusers than boys. (3) There were no sex differences in mean proportion of blank-trial sequences with consistent hypotheses used, probability of repeating preceding hypotheses following negative feedback, or efficiency with which Ss used feedback information to solve problems (focusing behavior).

Nunnally, J. C., Duchnowski, A. J., and Knott, P. D. Association of neutral objects with rewards: effects of massed versus distributed practice, delay of testing, age, and sex. *J. Experimental Child Psychology*, 1967, *5*, 152–63.

   Subjects: $N = 144$; 6, 8, 10 yrs. **Measures:** Ss played a conditioning game in which a spin-wheel pointer stopping on 1 nonsense syllable resulted in the winning of 2 pennies, stopping on another syllable meant the loss of 1 penny, and stopping on a third had no consequence. Conditioning effects on the syllables were assessed with 3 response measures: (1) E named each of 3 stick figures "boys" with one of the nonsense syllables, and asked Ss which of the boys would do certain positive, negative, and neutral acts; (2) Ss learned to discriminate among boxes labeled with the different nonsense syllables; and (3) E decided how many times to look at pictures of each of the 3 syllables. Before the experiment, Ss were randomly assigned to 4 levels of practice-massing treatment. **Results:** No sex differences.

Odom, R. D., and Guzman, R. D. Problem solving and the perceptual salience of variability and constancy: a developmental study. *J. Experimental Child Psychology*, 1970, *9*, 156–65.

   Subjects: $N = 144$; 5, 11 yrs. **Measures:** Ss performed concept identification tasks in which both constancy and variability were represented on each trial. For half of the Ss, identification of variability was relevant to solution, whereas for the other half, identification of stimulus constancy was relevant to solution. Number of errors to criterion of 10 successive correct identifications was recorded. **Results:** No sex differences.

Odom, R. D., and Guzman, R. D. The development of hierarchies of dimensional salience. *Developmental Psychology*, 1972, *6*, 271–87.

   Subjects: $N = 408$; 5–19 yrs. **Measures:** Relative dimensional salience was assessed for choice tasks in which all possible 2-dimensional and 3-dimensional combinations of form, color, number, and position were presented. A final task of identity involved the same dimensions, with definite correct and incorrect choices. Choices and response times were recorded. **Results:** (1) On the 2-dimensional task, boys made more position choices than girls ($p < .05$). (2) On the 3-dimensional task, boys had longer response times on form choices than girls ($p < .01$).

Odom, R. D., and Mumbauer, C. C. Dimensional salience and identification of the relevant dimension in problem solving: a developmental study. *Developmental Psychology*, 1971, *4*, 135–40.

   Subjects: $N = 277$; 6–19 yrs. **Measures:** Ss performed a color-form salience task, and were free to choose a comparison stimulus that matched the standard in either form or color. Ss (judged as form-dominant) performed a concept-identification problem with either form or color relevant to the solution. **Results:** No sex differences.

Offenbach, S. I., Baecher, R., and White, M. Stability of first-grade children's dimensional preferences. *Child Development*, 1972, *43*, 689–92.

   Subjects: $N = 42$; 6 yrs. **Measures:** Ss chose which of 2 stimuli was most like a third. Projected images varied in color, shape, and size. There was no reinforcement. Lists were administered 3 times in 6 months as a stability measure. **Results:** No sex differences were found in Ss' dimensional preferences.

Ogletree, E. A cross-cultural examination of the creative thinking ability of public and private school pupils in England, Scotland, and Germany. *J. Social Psychology*, 1971, *83*, 301–2.

Subjects: $N = 1,165$; 8–11 yrs (English, Scottish, German). **Measures:** Ss were given the verbal and figural batteries of the Torrance Tests of Creative Thinking. **Results:** On the verbal battery, girls were superior to boys. On the figural battery, English and German girls were superior to boys; no sex difference was found in the Scottish sample.

Ohnmacht, Fred W., and Robert F. McMorris. Creativity as a function of field independence and dogmatism. *J. Psychology*, 1971, *79*, 165–68.

Subjects: $N = 74$; 18–21 yrs. **Measures:** Remote Associations Test. **Results:** No sex differences.

Okonji, M. O. The differential effects of rural and urban upbringing on the development of cognitive styles. *International J. Psychology*, 1969, *4*, 293–305.

Subjects: $N = 33$; 12 yrs (rural Nigerian). $N = 25$; 21–27 yrs (University of Nigeria, urban upbringing). $N = 65$; adult (rural Nigerian). **Measures:** Rural adolescents were given the Children's Embedded Figures Test (CEFT). Rural adults completed the CEFT and the Rod-and-Frame Test (RFT). Ss in the university sample took the RFT and the Embedded Figures Test (EFT). **Results:** (1) Rural boys were more field-independent on the CEFT than rural girls ($p < .02$). (2) Among university Ss, men were more field-independent than women on the RFT, but not on the EFT. (3) Among rural adults, men were more field-independent than women on the CEFT ($p < .01$), but not on the RFT.

Oltman, P. R. A portable Rod-and-Frame apparatus. *Perceptual & Motor Skills*, 1968, *26*, 503–6.

Subjects: $N = 163$; 18–21 yrs (college). **Measures:** Rod-and-Frame Test (both the portable and the standard model). **Results:** No sex differences.

Omark, D. R., and Edelman, M. Peer group social interactions from an evolutionary perspective. Paper presented at the Society for Research in Child Development Conference, Philadelphia, 1973.

Subjects: $N = 436$; 4–8 yrs. **Measures:** Playground observations were recorded by the "nearest neighbor" method (sex, distance, and nature of interaction with nearest neighbor). The "hierarchy" test was given, in which Ss were asked to rank themselves and classmates on "toughness"). In the Draw A Picture Together test (DAPT), each S in a pair was given a distinctive color crayon, and the pair was asked to make a joint picture. The response measures were integration of theme, integration of color (do both colors appear in the same area?), imitation, dominance of outline, and dominance of territory. **Results:** (1) Boys congregated in larger groups than girls (both maximum and average size of play groups). Girls tended to move in groups of 2 or 3, boys in "swarms." (2) On the DAPT, boys dominated girls with respect to both territory and outline at every grade level except kindergarten (age 5). (3) Among same-sex pairs, little relationship was shown between dominance on the "toughness" hierarchy and dominance in the drawing task. In 2 age groups out of 4 (6 and 8 years old) there was "a slight tendency for the tougher child to dominate" the drawings and to draw the outline of the picture more often.

Omark, D. R., Omark, M., and Edelman, M. Dominance hierarchies in young children. Paper presented at International Congress of Anthropological and Ethnological Sciences, Chicago, 1973.

Subjects: $N = 950$; 4–8 yrs (U.S.), 5–9 yrs (Switzerland), 8–10 yrs (Ethiopia). **Measures:** Playground observations were made of distance from nearest neighbor, sex of nearest neighbor, and nature of interaction between the subject and his neighbor. Ss were asked "who is tougher" concerning their classmates and themselves. Pictures were used to identify classmates for kindergarten Ss; paper-and-pencil form was used for older children. **Results:** (1) In all 3 societies, a child's nearest neighbor was most frequently a same-sex child; this trend appeared earlier among boys than girls. (2) Girls were near the teacher more frequently than boys were. (3) Boys were more frequently engaged in physical interaction with an age-mate than girls were. (4) The frequency of aggressive interaction was greater for boys than for girls in all 3 cultures (i.e. hitting or pushing without smiling). (5) Opposite-sex neighbors were farther apart than same-sex neighbors. Boys maintained a greater distance between self and nearest neighbor than girls did (analyzed for American sample only). (6) Boys covered greater distance per unit time than girls did (analyzed for American sample only). (7) In all 3 cultures, boys were higher than girls in the "toughness" hierarchy. (8) Dominance hierarchy was more fully established (more fully agreed upon) between boy-boy dyads than between cross-sex and girl-girl dyads (analyzed for Swiss and American samples only). (9) Boys more often than girls overrated their own position in the dominance hierarchy (analyzed for Swiss and American samples only).

Oskamp, S., and Kleinke, C. Amount of reward as a variable in the Prisoner's Dilemma game. *J. Personality & Social Psychology*, 1970, *16*, 133–40.

Subjects: $N = 100$; 14–17 yrs. Measures: Ss played the Prisoner's Dilemma game in same-sex pairs; 5 different pay-off matrices were used. Results: (1) Individually, boys were more cooperative than girls ($p < .01$). (2) Girls showed a marked decrease in cooperation between the first and last block of 10 trials; boys' level of cooperation remained constant ($p < .05$).

Osser, H., Wang, M., and Zaid, F. The young child's ability to imitate and comprehend speech: a comparison of two subculture groups. *Child Development*, 1969, *40*, 1063–75.

Subjects: $N = 32$; 4–5 yrs (black, white). Measures: Ss imitated sentences read by E and then chose which of 3 simple drawings was described by each sentence. Figures in the drawings were considered racially neutral. Comprehension and imitation errors were recorded. Results: No sex differences.

Osterhouse, R. A., and Brock, T. C. Distraction increases yielding to propaganda by inhibiting counterarguing. *J. Personality & Social Psychology*, 1970, *15*, 344–58.

Subjects: $N = 160$; 18–21 yrs (college). Measures: After being either distracted or not distracted while listening to a discrepant communication, Ss answered a questionnaire assessing communication acceptance. Ss were then given 3 minutes to express their comments on the issues involved (this was used to obtain an approximate measure of the extent to which Ss had counterargued during communication reception). Results: No sex differences.

Ostfeld, B., and Katz, P. A. The effect of threat severity in children of varying socioeconomic levels. *Developmental Psychology*, 1969, *1*, 205–10.

Subjects: $N = 28$; 4–5 yrs (white nursery school, white and black Head Start Program). Measures: Ss were presented with 5 crayons and 5 toys, and asked to rank-order each group according to preference. Ss were then asked to color pictures of toys with the color of their choice. During a free-play period, Ss were randomly assigned to low- or high-threat conditions (verbally prohibited from playing with their favorite toy). After free play, Ss were again asked to rank toys and crayons, and color pictures of toys. Finally, Ss were asked which toy they would like to buy. Results: No sex differences.

Overton, W. F., and Jordan, R. Stimulus preference and multiplicative classification in children. *Developmental Psychology*, 1971, *5*, 505–10.

Subjects: $N = 120$; 4, 6 yrs. Measures: Ss completed a stimulus-preference test of matching problems, each of which could be paired in 2 ways depending on Ss' preferred dimension (color, form, number, size). A 2×2 matrix test was accompanied by a choice of 4 items, 1 of which completed the matrix correctly. Results: No sex differences.

Palermo, D. S. Racial comparisons and additional normative data on the children's manifest anxiety scale. *Child Development*, 1959, *30*, 53–57.

Subjects: $N = 470$; 9–11 yrs (white, black). Measures: Children's Manifest Anxiety Scale. Results: In both racial groups, girls had higher scores than boys on the Anxiety scale ($p < .01$) and on the Lie scale ($p < .05$).

Palermo, D. S. Characteristics of word association responses obtained from children in grades one through four. *Developmental Psychology*, 1971, *5*, 118–23.

Subjects: $N = 100$; 6–9 yrs. Measures: Ss gave free-association responses to each of 100 words. The words were taken from the Palermo-Jenkins list. Results: Girls gave more popular responses than boys.

Pallak, M. S., Brock, T. C., and Kiesler, C. A. Dissonance arousal and task performance in an incidental verbal learning paradigm. *J. Personality & Social Psychology*, 1967, *7*, 11–20.

Subjects: $N = 39$; 18–21 yrs (college). Measures: Before performing a boring task, Ss were either given or not given the option to leave. The task consisted of copying a list of 10 paired associates 20 times. After completing the task, retention of selected paired associates was measured. Ss also indicated how much choice they felt they had in deciding whether to complete the task or to leave, how interesting and worthwhile the experiment was to them, and how willing they would be to participate in a similar experiment at a later date. **Results:** No sex differences.

Palmer, R. M., and Masling, J. Vocabulary for skin color in Negro and white children. *Developmental Psychology*, 1969, *1*, 396–401.
> **Subjects:** $N = 48$; 8–16 yrs (low SES). **Measures:** A white E asked Ss to describe 16 bubble gum pictures of black and white baseball players. The response measure was number of different color descriptions. After Ss completed this task they were asked to describe 16 blue paint samples in order to determine general verbal fluency for colors. **Results:** No sex differences.

Pancratz, C. N., and Cohen, L. B. Recovery of habituation in infants. *J. Experimental Child Psychology*, 1970, *9*, 208–16.
> **Subjects:** $N = 32$; 15–20 wks. **Measures:** Ss were presented with 10 15-second exposures of 1 of 4 habituation stimuli: a green circle, a blue triangle, a yellow rod, or a red square. Before proceeding to the test phase, half of the Ss were given 20 15-second presentations of a filler stimulus (a black star); for the other Ss, the test phase immediately followed the habituation phase. The test phase consisted of alternate presentations of the familiar stimulus and the novel stimuli (the 3 geometric patterns to which Ss had no previous exposure). **Results:** (1) In the habituation phase, boys showed a response decrement; girls did not ($p < .05$). (2) In the test phase, no main sex differences were found in fixation times to the novel and familiar stimuli.

Paolino, A. F. Sex differences in aggressive content. *J. Projective Techniques & Personality Assessment*, 1964, *28*, 219–26.
> **Subjects:** $N = 84$; 18–21 yrs (college). **Measures:** Ss recorded their dreams as soon as possible after awakening. Later, these reports were analyzed for aggressive content. **Results:** (1) Men involved more of their characters in aggressive actions than women ($p < .01$). (2) Men initiated more aggression in their dreams than women ($p < .01$); no sex differences were found in amount of aggression received. (3) The average intensity of aggression reported by men was higher than the average intensity reported by women ($p < .01$). Men instigated and received more severe aggressive acts than women ($p < .05$, $p < .05$). (4) Men received more aggression from males than women did ($p < .05$); women received more aggression from females than men did ($p < .01$). (5) Men directed more aggression toward male victims than women did ($p < .05$); women directed more aggression toward female victims than men did ($p < .01$). (6) Women received more aggression than men from older people ($p < .01$) and from familiar persons ($p < .01$). Men received more aggression than women from persons whose age was not specified ($p < .01$) and from strangers ($p < .01$).

Papageorgis, D., and McCann, B. M. Effects of characteristic definitions on changes in self perception. *Perceptual & Motor Skills*, 1965, *20*, 717–25.
> **Subjects:** $N = 54$; 18–21 yrs (college). **Measures:** Ss received high hostility scores on a fake group personality test and were then provided with 1 of 3 definitions of hostility (vague, weak, and strong). The vague definition allowed Ss considerable latitude in structuring the meaning of the characteristic on their own; the weak and strong definitions did not. Of these latter 2 definitions, the weak one described hostility in mild, internalized terms, whereas the strong one suggested the definite possibility of overt, disruptive aggressive behavior. Afterward, Ss rated themselves on hostility. **Results:** (1) Men rated themselves more hostile than women did ($p < .01$). (2) Of the male groups, men who received the strong definition rated themselves highest in hostility, whereas men who were provided with the vague definition rated themselves lowest; men who received the weak definition were intermediate. The reverse was true for women ($p < .05$). (3) On a postexperimental questionnaire, men expressed more agreement with their test scores than women did ($p < .01$).

Papousek, H. Experimental studies of appetitional behavior in human newborns and infants. In H. W. Stevenson, E. H. Hess, and H. L. Rheingold, eds., *Early behavior: comparative and developmental approaches.* New York: Wiley, 1967.
> **Subjects:** $N = 130$; birth, 3, 5 mos. **Measures:** Head movements were studied as a conditionable motor complex of infantile appetitional behavior. Conditioning, extinction, discrimination, and reconditioning were studied, using an electric bell and buzzer as the CS and milk as the UCS. Response measures were head-turning and changes in general activity (vocalization, facial response, eye movements, breathing). **Results:** No sex differences.

Parisi, D. Development of syntactic comprehension in preschool children as a function of socioeconomic level. *Developmental Psychology*, 1971, 5, 186–89.
Subjects: $N = 144$; 3–6 yrs. Measures: Ss completed a test of Syntactic Comprehension in which they chose 1 of 4 items for each of 20 syntactic contrasts. Results: No sex differences.

Parke, R. D. Nurturance, nurturance withdrawal, and resistance to deviation. *Child Development*, 1967, 38, 1101–10.
Subjects: $N = 80$; 6, 7 yrs. Measures: In the continuous nurturance condition, E encouraged Ss to draw pictures for 10 minutes. In the nurturance-withdrawal condition, E encouraged Ss to draw pictures for 5 minutes, then ignored Ss for 5 minutes. After the nurturance session, Ss were left alone with 5 attractive but prohibited toys for 15 minutes. E asked Ss to read a book and not touch any toys while E left the room. Results: Boys deviated more often than girls.

Parke, R. D., O'Leary, S. E., and West, S. Mother-father-newborn interaction: effects of maternal medication, labor, and sex of infant. Proceedings of the Eightieth Annual Convention, American Psychological Association, 1972.
Subjects: $N = 19$; tested at birth to 2 days (firstborn) and parents. Measures: Observations were made of parent-infant interactions in mother's hospital room. The following parental behaviors were recorded: looks, smiles, vocalizes, holds, kisses, touches, rocks, imitates infant, explores infant, feeds, hands infant over to other parent. Results: Boy infants were touched by their mothers and fathers more frequently than girl infants.

Parry, M. H. Infants' responses to novelty in familiar and unfamiliar settings. *Child Development*, 1972, 43, 233–37.
Subjects: $N = 48$; 10–12 mos. Measures: Infants were observed in a familiar (home) and a nonfamiliar (laboratory) setting while sitting in their mothers' laps. They were familiarized to 1 strange stimulus (wooden disc) and presented with an incongruous stimulus. Fixation time and manipulation were recorded. Results: No sex differences.

Parsley, K. M., Powell, M., O'Connor, H. A., and Deutsch, M. Are there really sex differences in achievement? *J. Educational Research*, 1963, 57, 210–12.
Subjects: $N = 5,020$; 7–13 yrs. Measures: Ss took the California Reading Achievement Test, the California Arithmetic Test, and the California Test of Mental Maturity; 5 scores were recorded for each S: IQ, Reading Vocabulary, Grade Placement, Reading Comprehension Grade Placement, Arithmetic Reasoning Grade Placement, and Arithmetic Fundamentals Grade Placement. Results: No sex differences.

Parten, M. B. Leadership among preschool children. *J. Abnormal & Social Psychology*, 1933a, 27, 430–40.
Subjects: $N = 34$; 4 yrs (nursery school). Measures: Ss were observed during their free-play hour. Results: No differences were found in the number of boys and girls who directed group activities or who reciprocally directed or shared leadership with another child.

Parten, M. B. Social play among preschool children. *J. Abnormal & Social Psychology*, 1933b, 28, 136–47.
Subjects: $N = 34$; 2–4 yrs (nursery school). Measures: Ss were observed during their free-play hour. Results: (1) Boys preferred boys as playmates, girls preferred girls. (2) Girls played with dolls more than boys did. (3) Excluding doll play, no sex differences were found in number of times Ss "played house." (4) Boys rode on the kiddie car and played with blocks and trains more often than girls did. (5) Girls strung beads, cut paper, painted, and played on the swings more frequently than boys did.

Parton, D. A., and Geshuri, Y. Learning of aggression as a function of presence of a human model, response intensity, and target of the response. *J. Experimental Child Psychology*, 1971, 11, 491–504.
Subjects: $N = 112$; 4–5 yrs. Measures: Half the Ss viewed videotapes of a 6-year-old boy aggressing toward surrogate or nonsurrogate targets. The videotapes shown to the other half of the Ss were the same, except that the model was never visible. Afterward, Ss were asked to perform the behaviors they had observed. For each imitative response, Ss were rewarded with a token. Response measures were frequency and intensity of Ss' imitative responses. After the acquisition test, Ss in the model-present condition were asked to select 1 of 6 amounts of candy to give to the model. Results: (1) Mean frequency of imitative responses was higher for boys than for girls ($p < .05$). No sex differences were reported in the intensity

of Ss' aggressive responses. (2) No sex differences were found in the amount of candy Ss wanted to give to the model.

Pascual-Leone, J., and Smith, J. The encoding and decoding of symbols by children: new experimental paradigm and a neo-Piagetian model. *J. Experimental Child Psychology*, 1969, 8, 328–55.
Subjects: $N = 60$; 5, 7, 9 yrs. Measures: Ss were trained to choose between 2 objects on the basis of a verbal or gestural cue given by E. Ss then reproduced E's role in presenting problems and giving cues. Results: No sex differences.

Patterson, G. R. Parents as dispensers of aversive stimuli. *J. Personality & Social Psychology*, 1965, 2, 844–51.
Subjects: $N = 60$; 7–9 yrs. Measures: Ss dropped marbles into either of 2 holes. Following a baseline period (to identify the more preferred hole), Ss received social disapproval from either their mother or their father contingent upon the occurrence of the more preferred response. The response measure was the increase in frequency of the less preferred response. Results: No sex differences.

Paulson, M. J., Lin, Tien-Teh, and Hanssen, C. Family harmony: an etiological factor in alienation. *Child Development*, 1972, 43, 591–603.
Subjects: $N = 210$; 18–21 yrs (college). Measures: Ss completed a family history data sheet and the Maternal form of the Parental Attitude Research Instrument (Ss were asked to respond as if they were the parent). Results: Among establishment Ss with dominant mothers, men had lower factor scores than women. Women more often than men recalled attitudes of their parents associated with greater degree of maternal warmth and love, environment of intimacy, affectional parental closeness, and lessened parental irritability.

Pawlicki, R. E. The influence of contingent and noncontingent social reinforcement upon children in a simple operant task. *Child Development*, 1972, 43, 1432–38 and personal communication.
Subjects: $N = 170$; 8 yrs. Measures: Ss played a marble-drop game. After base rate was established, Ss heard a noncontingent or contingent, supportive or neutral comment. There was a no-treatment condition. Results: There were no main sex differences. Contingency of comment and supportiveness of comment influenced performance of boys but not of girls.

Pecan, E. V., and Schvaneveldt, R. W. Probability learning as a function of age, sex, and type of constraint. *Developmental Psychology*, 1970, 2, 384–88.
Subjects: $N = 40$; 12–15, 35–45 yrs. Measures: Ss in 1 of 2 conditions guessed which of 2 colors of poker chips would be drawn next for 200 draws. In the noncontingent condition, chips were in 1 container in 80 : 20 ratio. The contingent condition involved a red container with red and blue chips (ratio of 80 : 20). and a blue container with blue and red (ratio of 80 : 20). After starting with a red chip from the red container, subsequent draws were made from the container of the color matching the previously drawn chip. Results: (1) Males reached a higher level of probability learning (predicting the more likely event) than females ($p < .01$). This difference was greatest in later trials ($p < .001$). (2) Females repeated the prediction of an infrequent event (perseverance) as often as they switched to predicting a more frequent event, whereas males were more likely to predict the more frequent event (results held for both conditions). Males tended to repeat the more frequent response (especially when correct) with higher probability than females.

Pedersen, D. M., Shindling, M. M., and Johnson, D. L. Effects of sex of examiner and subject on children's quantitative test performance. *J. Personality & Social Psychology*, 1968, 10, 251–54.
Subjects: $N = 24$; 8 yrs (24 undergraduates served as Es). Measures: The arithmetic subtest of the WISC was administered 3 times by a male proctor and 3 times by a female proctor. Results: (1) No sex differences were found in Ss' scores on the arithmetic subtests. (2) Female Ss tested by female Es did better than male Ss tested by female Es ($p < .05$) and female Ss tested by male Es ($p < .05$). No differences were found between male Ss tested by female Es and male Ss tested by male Es. (3) Owing primarily to the outstanding performance of female Ss when tested by female Es, female Es elicited better performance than male Es ($p < .025$).

Pedersen, F. A., and Bell, R. Q. Sex differences in preschool children without histories of complications of pregnancy and delivery. *Developmental Psychology*, 1970, *3*, 10–15.

Subjects: $N = 55$; 2–3 yrs. **Measures:** Same-sex groups of 5 or 6 were observed in nursery school. (1) During the indoor free-play period, measures were taken of the following behaviors: aggression toward peers, positive social interaction with peers, play with clay and dough, looking and listening, watching peers, manipulation of physical objects. (2) During rest period, Ss were encouraged to lie down on their blankets. Both teachers rested to provide the children with appropriate models. A record was kept of the length of time each child was observed in the following 3 positions: up and about (active nonconformity), sitting down (passive nonconformity), lying down (copies teacher's posture). (3) Rest period was terminated each day by a series of imitation games. The behaviors that Ss imitated were modeled by the teachers. The number of times each child imitated correctly was recorded. (4) Following the imitation games, Ss were tested in the Bell Pull situation. Pairs of Ss were lifted over a gate and sent to pull bells off a nearby rack. The cries of their peers encouraged them to hurry. Occasionally 1 of the 6 bells was attached in such a way that it could not be removed. The persistence (struggling time plus number of tugs) and vigor (strength measured in pounds) exhibited by Ss in attempting to detach the bell were recorded.

In a second experimental situation, desirable toys were surrounded by a fence of light boards and boxes. The rate at which Ss tore down the barrier to get at the toys was recorded. (5) During story and refreshment time, measures were taken of gulping, number of seating changes, amount of solids eaten, and amount of juice consumed. In addition, activity recorders attached to the left foot measured nonfunctional motor responses. (6) During the outdoor free-play period, measures were taken of the following behaviors: smiling, squealing, watching, running, tricycle riding, walking, glider or swing play. Activity recorders attached to the back measured gross motor movements. The amount of time Ss spent in separate activities was also recorded. **Results:** (1) Boys exhibited more walking and more manipulation of physical objects than girls did. Boys were also more aggressive, more active, and more passively nonconforming. (2) Girls exhibited more glider and swing play and more play with clay and dough than boys did. Girls were also more imitative of adult models (copies posture, follows game), ate more solids, and spent more time in single activities before changing.

Pedersen, F. A., and Robson, K. S. Father participation in infancy. *American J. Orthopsychiatry*, 1969, *39*, 466–72.

Subjects: $N = 45$; tested at 8, 9½ mos (firstborn) and their mothers and fathers. **Measures:** The extent and quality of father's involvement with the child was ascertained from interviews with mother. Then 6 measures of paternal behavior were derived: (1) variety and frequency of caretaking activities; (2) investment (emotional involvement with the infant); (3) time spent in play; (4) irritability level (irritability threshold, reactivity to the infant's prolonged fussing or crying); (5) apprehension over infant's well-being; (6) stimulation level of play. When father entered the home after a period of absence, observations were made of the infant's greeting behavior; age of onset and intensity were recorded. **Results:** (1) Fathers were more apprehensive over the well-being of girl infants than boy infants ($p < .01$). No other differences were found between fathers of boys and girls. (2) No sex differences were found in Ss' greeting behavior.

Pederson, D. R. Children's reactions to failure as a function of interresponse interval. *J. Experimental Child Psychology*, 1971, *12*, 51–58.

Subjects: $N = 32$; 7–8 yrs. **Measures:** The time interval between success and failure on a ball-tower task and the signal to pull the lever varied (0.5, 1.0, and 5.0 seconds). Starting and movement speeds were recorded. **Results:** (1) Boys' starting speeds were slower than girls' ($p < .05$). Boys' speeds increased in rough linear fashion as a function of interresponse interval; girls' speeds increased from 0.5 to 1.0 second interresponse, then slightly decreased with the 5.0 second interval ($p < .05$).

Penk, W. Developmental changes in idiodynamic set responses of children's word associations. *Developmental Psychology*, 1971, *5*, 55–63.

Subjects: $N = 100$; 7–11 yrs. **Measures:** Ss were asked to give word associations to 24 words. Ss' responses were classified as either object-referent associates (e.g. scissors-cut; lamp-light), concept-referent associates (e.g. tug-pull; blossom-flower), or dimension-referent associates (e.g. long-short, high-low). Mediational faults (more than 1 response word, no response, delayed response, association identical to stimulus word), reaction times, commonality scores, and Thorndike-Lorge frequency values were also recorded. **Results:** (1) Overall, girls gave more concept-referent and dimension-referent associations than boys. (2) Boys had a higher number of mediational faults than girls. (3) Girls had higher commonality means than boys.

Penney, R. K. Reactive curiosity and manifest anxiety in children. *Child Development*, 1965, *36*, 697–702.
Subjects: $N = 108$; 9–11 yrs. **Measures:** Children's Manifest Anxiety Scale, Peabody Picture Vocabulary Test. **Results:** Girls received higher manifest anxiety scores than boys ($p < .005$). No sex differences on PPVT.

Peskay, J., and Masters, J. C. Effects of socioeconomic status and the value of a reinforcer upon self-reinforcement by children. *Child Development*, 1961, *42*, 2120–23.
Subjects: $N = 80$; 6 yrs (low, high SES). **Measures:** Ss played a maze game in which they could self-dispense rewards of high- and low-incentive value in a noncontingent situation. **Results:** No sex differences.

Peters, L. Verbal mediators and cue discrimination in the transition from nonconservation to conservation of number. *Child Development*, 1970, *41*, 707–21.
Subjects: $N = 131$; 5–6 yrs (low SES). **Measures:** Ss were initially tested on conservation of number, conservation of difference, and conservation of area tasks. Also administered were a language comprehension test designed to evaluate Ss' understanding of several specific aspects of language (e.g. the differences between more and less, same and different, before and after, etc.), and an object sorting task. After receiving training in conservation (control Ss received no training), Ss were retested on the conservation measures. **Results:** No sex differences.

Petersen, A. C. The relationship of androgenicity in males and females to spatial ability and fluent production. Unpublished doctoral dissertation, University of Chicago, 1973.
EXPERIMENT I: Subjects: $N = 75$; 13, 16, 17–18 yrs. **Measures:** 2 cognitive batteries were administered, the Wechsler Bellevue (WB) at ages 13 and 16, and the Primary Mental Abilities (PMA) at ages 17 and 18. The Block Design (WB) and Spatial (PMA) subtests were used as measures of spatial ability; the Digit Symbol (WB) and Word Fluency (PMA) subtests were used as measures of fluency. The physical parameters were: (1) growth during adolescence (age at peak height velocity), (2) measures of androgenicity in body shape (muscle/fat, overall body rating), and (3) ratings of secondary sex characteristics (genital size in males, breast size in females, pubic hair for both sexes). The ratings were assessed from nude photographs of Ss. **Results:** There were no main sex differences. Among 18-year-old, highly androgenized Ss, boys were fluency-dominant and girls were spatially-dominant. Among boys, early maturers tended to be space-dominant at age 18; among girls, the relationship was unclear.

Phares, E. J., Ritchie, D. E., and Davis, W. L. Internal-external control and reaction to threat. *J. Personality & Social Psychology*, 1968, *10*, 402–5.
Subjects: $N = 40$; 18–21 yrs (college). **Measures:** After completing a series of personality tests, Ss received individualized reports containing both positive and negative information about their personalities. Ss checked those interpretations that made them slightly uncomfortable and rated each interpretation on several scales. Ss also rated how committed they were to deal with the problems suggested in the interpretations and how useful they felt the overall experiment was in shedding light on the process of psychotherapy. At the end of the experiment, Ss recalled as many interpretations as they could. **Results:** No sex differences.

Phillips, R. Syntax and vocabulary of mothers' speech to young children: age and sex comparisons. *Child Development*, 1973, *44*, 182–85.
Subjects: $N = 57$; 8, 18, 28 mos and mothers. **Measures:** While mother and child engaged in free play, mother's speech was recorded. E then involved mother in casual conversation for 15 minutes. Mother's speech was scored for syntactic complexity, number of verbs, modifiers per utterance, proportion of function words, proportion of content words, number of verb forms, proportion of Old English verbs, proportion of weak verbs, type-token ratio, and concreteness of nouns. **Results:** No sex differences.

Piliavin, I. M., Rodin, J., and Piliavin, J. A. Good samaritanism. *J. Personality & Social Psychology*, 1969, *13*, 289–99.
Subjects: $N = 4,450$; adults. **Measures:** Either a white or a black male confederate staged a collapse after boarding a New York City subway train. On each trial, an observer noted the race, sex, and location of (a) every rider seated or standing in the immediate area and (b) every person who came to the victim's assistance. **Results:** Men were more likely than women to be the first person to come to the assistance of the victim.

Pilisuk, M., Skolnick, P., and Overstreet, E. Predicting cooperation from the two sexes in a conflict situation. *J. Personality & Social Psychology*, 1968, *10*, 35–43.
Subjects: $N = 176$; 18–21 yrs (college). Measures: Ss played a modified version of the prisoner's Dilemma game in same-sex pairs or against simulated same-sex or opposite-sex others. Results: (1) No sex differences were found in percentage of cooperative responses. (2) Women who played against simulated opposite-sex partners were less cooperative than women who played against simulated same-sex partners ($p < .001$). No such difference was found for men.

Pishkin, V. Concept identification of mnemonic cues as a function of children's sex and age. *J. Educational Psychology*, 1972, *63*, 93–98.
Subjects: $N = 144$; 6–9 yrs. Measures: Ss indicated which category (yes or no) stimuli should be placed in; 3 types of feedback were provided: right cues, wrong cues, or right-wrong cues. The measure of performance was the number of errors committed by each S. Results: (1) Among 8-year-old Ss, girls made fewer errors than boys. (2) 8-year-old girls made fewer errors than 6-year-old girls; 8-year-old boys made more errors than 6-year-old boys ($p < .001$). (3) When provided with either right cues or right-wrong cues, girls made fewer errors than boys; when wrong cues were provided, no sex difference was found ($p < .01$).

Pishkin, V., and Shurley, J. T. Auditory dimensions and irrelevant information in concept identification of males and females. *Perceptual & Motor Skills*, 1965, *20*, 673–83.
Subjects: $N = 120$; 25–50 yrs. Measures: On each trial of a concept-identification task, Ss classified auditory stimuli into 2 categories. The dimension that was relevant was either the tone's duration (1 or 3 seconds), its frequency (1,000 or 3,000 cps), or its laterality (presented to either the right or the left ear). The number of irrelevant dimensions was varied (0, 1, 2, or 3). Results: When laterality was the relevant dimension, men made more errors and required more trials to reach the criterion of 16 correct, consecutive responses than women did. When duration or frequency was the relevant dimension, there were no sex differences in performance.

Pishkin, V., Wolfgang, A., and Rasmussen, E. Age, sex, amount, and type of memory information in concept learning. *J. Experimental Psychology*, 1967, *73*, 121–24.
Subjects: $N = 270$; 10–18 yrs. Measures: Ss were administered a concept-learning task (the Wisconsin Card Sorting Task). On each trial, the results of either the previous 0, 1, or 2 trials were made available for Ss' inspection. Ss in 1 group were informed only when they had made a correct choice, whereas Ss in a second group were informed only when they had made an incorrect choice. Ss in a third group were told on every trial whether they had made the correct or the incorrect decision. Performance measure was number of errors made. Results: (1) Girls made fewer errors than boys when either 0 or 2 previous trials were available to them for inspection ($p < .05$). No sex differences were found in the $N = 1$ condition. (2) When informed of only their incorrect choices, girls made fewer errors than boys ($p < .05$). No sex differences were found in the other 2 conditions.

Platt, J. J., Eisenman, R., and DeGross, E. Birth order and sex differences in future time perspective. *Developmental Psychology*, 1969, *1*, 70.
Subjects: $N = 132$; 18–21 yrs (college). Measures: Ss were given 2 instruments to measure the future time perspective (FTP) dimension of extension (described as the length of the future time span that an individual is able to conceptualize) and 2 to measure the FTP dimension of density (described as a measure of the number of events populating an individual's personal future). Ss also completed the Time Metaphors Test, a measure of directionality. Directionality was defined as a sense of moving forward from the present into the future. Results: (1) No main sex differences were found on the extension instruments. (2) On 1 of the 2 density instruments, women exhibited greater FTP than men. (3) No main sex differences were found in directionality. Later-born women saw the passage of time in a more active way than other Ss, particularly later-born men ($p < .001$).

Podell, J. E. Ontogeny of the locus and orientation of the perceiver. *Child Development*, 1966, *37*, 993–97.
Subjects: $N = 112$; 3, 4, 5, 6, 7, 9, 11 yrs. Measures: Laterally asymmetrical figures were traced on S's forehead and occiput. S was asked to indicate what had been drawn by pointing to 1 of 2 given figures. Results: No sex differences.

Porges, S. W., Arnold, W. R., Forbes, E. J. Heart rate variability: an index of attentional responsivity in human newborns. *Developmental Psychology*, 1973, *8*, 85–92.

Subjects: $N = 24$; 1–3 days. **Measures:** Ss' heart-rate patterns were recorded in response to a moderately intense (75 decibels) auditory stimulus. **Results:** No sex differences.

Porteus, B. D., and Johnson, R. C. Children's responses to two measures of conscience development and their relation to sociometric nomination. *Child Development*, 1965, *36*, 703–11.
> **Subjects:** $N = 235$; 14 yrs. **Measures:** Ss listened to stories in which a male or a female yielded to temptation. Affective or cognitive measures of moral judgment were required. Ss responded to a sociometric test concerning the characters. Responses were scored as mature or immature. **Results:** (1) Girls responded with more guilt (affective measure) to stories of moral deviations than boys ($p < .01$). (2) Girls scored higher than boys on the cognitive measure ($p < .05$).

Portuges, S. M., and Feshbach, N. D. The influence of sex and socioethnic factors upon imitation of teachers by elementary school children. *Child Development*, 1972, *43*, 981–89.
> **Subjects:** $N = 96$; 8–10 yrs (white, black). **Measures:** Ss viewed 2 films of a white teacher giving a lesson on African geography using either positive or negative verbal teaching techniques and incidental gestures. Ss were then asked to teach a similar lesson to boy and girl life-size dolls (ambiguous as to race). Measures were made of Ss' preference for the teachers and of their dependence-independency status (teacher rating). **Results:** Girls imitated the teacher model more than boys did ($p < .01$). No sex differences were found in teacher preference.

Potter, M. C., and Levy, E. Spatial enumeration without counting. *Child Development*, 1968, *39*, 265–72.
> **Subjects:** $N = 58$; 2–4 yrs. **Measures:** Ss were presented with a booklet consisting of 23 pages. On each page were pasted colored stickers of animals, flowers, geometric shapes, etc. Ss were asked to touch each sticker just once and then to turn to the next page. Repeats and omissions were scored as errors. **Results:** No sex differences were found in the average number of errors in the younger group ($N = 29$, median age 41 months). A significant difference was found in the older group ($N = 29$, median age 47 months) in favor of the girls ($p < .02$).

Pratoomraj, S., and Johnson, R. C. Kinds of questions and types of conservation tasks as related to children's conservation responses. *Child Development*, 1966, *37*, 343–53.
> **Subjects:** $N = 128$; 4–7 yrs. **Measures:** Ss were tested on 5 conservation-of-substance problems. **Results:** No sex differences.

Presbie, R. J., and Coiteux, P. F. Learning to be generous or stingy: imitation of sharing behavior as a function of model generosity and vicarious reinforcement. *Child Development*, 1971, *42*, 1033–38.
> **Subjects:** $N = 64$; 6 yrs. **Measures:** Ss observed either a stingy or a generous male model share marbles with a child who was not present (full-faced photographs of either a boy or a girl served to designate the sharee). After the model distributed the last marbles, Ss either did or did not hear E praise the model or the model praise himself. Ss were then given the opportunity to share marbles with the absent child. **Results:** No sex differences were found in the number of marbles given to the sharee.

Prescott, D. Efficacy-related imagery, education, and politics. Unpublished honors thesis, Harvard University, 1971.
> **Subjects:** $N = 70$; 18 yrs (college). **Measures:** Men were asked to write stories, given the following verbal lead: "After first-term finals, John finds himself at the top of his medical school class." For women, "Anne" was substituted for "John." Ss' stories were scored for fear-of-success imagery. **Results:** More women than men wrote stories high in fear-of-success imagery ($p < .001$).

Prescott, G. A. Sex differences in Metropolitan Readiness test results. *J. Educational Research*, 1955, *48*, 605–10.
> **Subjects:** $N = 14,959$; 6 yrs. **Measures:** Metropolitan Readiness test. **Results:** When a subsample of 800 Ss was randomly drawn from the population and matched according to chronological age, girls had higher scores than boys ($p < .05$).

Preston, R. C. Reading achievement of German and American children. *School and Society*, 1962, *90*, 350–54.
> **Subjects:** $N = 2,391$; 9, 11 yrs (Germany, U.S.). **Measures:** 2 reading comprehension tests

were administered, the Frankfurter Test (translated into English for American Ss) and the comprehension subtest of the Gates Reading Survey (translated into German for the German Ss). Reading speed was measured by interrupting the Gates subtest 10 minutes into the test and having Ss mark the paragraph they were then reading. **Results:** (1) Among American Ss, girls were superior to boys on all 3 measures. (2) Among 9-year-old German Ss, girls read faster than boys. No sex differences were found on the comprehension tests. Among 11-year-old German Ss, boys scored higher than girls on all 3 measures. (3) Based on the 3 test scores, a higher proportion of American boys than girls were classified as "retarded" or "severely retarded" in reading ability (9 of 12 comparisons significant at the .05 level). In 10 of 12 comparisons (4 of which were significant at the .05 level), a higher proportion of German girls than boys scored in the "retarded" and "severely retarded" range.

Pruit, D. G. Reward structures and cooperation: the decomposed Prisoner's Dilemma game. *J. Personality & Social Psychology*, 1967, 7, 21–27.
   Subjects: $N = 100$; 18–21 yrs (college). **Measures:** Same-sex pairs of Ss played either the standard Prisoner's Dilemma game (Game 1), 1 of 3 versions (Game 2, 3, or 4) of the decomposed PD game (in a single play of the DPD, each party receives 2 payoffs—one as a result of his own behavior and one as a result of the other's), or an expanded version (Game 5) of the DPD (created by adding intermediate alternatives to Game 4). **Results:** (1) No sex differences were found in Games 1–4. (2) Since Game 5 is a variant of Game 4, the results of these games were compared. In Game 4, men started at a higher level of cooperation than women, whereas in Game 5, women started at a higher level of cooperation than men ($p < .05$). (3) Women in Game 4 and men in Game 5 showed a greater increase in level of cooperation than men in Game 4 and women in Game 5 ($p < .001$).

Pulaski, M. Play as a function of toy structure and fantasy predisposition. *Child Development*, 1970, 41, 531–37.
   Subjects: $N = 64$; 5–7 yrs. **Measures:** Ss were observed during 4 15-minute play sessions. E presented each set of playthings twice. Ss were asked to make up a story or put on a play. Fantasies were scored according to richness, variability, and flexibility. There was a 5-point scale rating behavior correlates. **Results:** (1) Boys scored higher than girls on enjoyment ($p < .05$) and movement ($p < .05$) in toy play sessions. (2) Among low-fantasy Ss, boys showed greater movement in toy play sessions than girls ($p < .05$). (3) Boys played with more movement than girls in all conditions ($p < .05$). (4) More girls than boys played with opposite-sex toys in the highly structured play session ($p < .05$).

Pytkowicz, A. R., Wagner, N. N., and Sarason, I. G. An experimental study of the reduction of hostility through fantasy. *J. Personality & Social Psychology*, 1967, 5, 295–303.
   Subjects: $N = 120$; 18–21 yrs (college). **Measures:** Ss initially rated the frequency with which they experienced each of 120 daydreams. After either being insulted or not being insulted, Ss then completed the Sarason Hostility Scale (a difference score was derived by subtracting scores Ss achieved at the beginning of the quarter from scores Ss achieved following the experimental conditions) and an attitude questionnaire (Ss' responses scored for aggressive content). **Results:** (1) Men expressed more hostility on the attitude questionnaire than women ($p < .01$). Whereas insulted men expressed more hostility than noninsulted men, no similar difference was found among women ($p < .05$). (2) No main sex differences were found in change scores on the Hostility Scale.

Quay, L. C. Language dialect, reinforcement, and the intelligence-test performance of Negro children. *Child Development*, 1971, 42, 5–15.
   Subjects: $N = 100$; 3–5 yrs (black Head Start program). **Measures:** Stanford-Binet Test of Intelligence Form L-M was administered under the following conditions: (a) Standard English, intangible reinforcement (praise); (b) Standard English, tangible reinforcement (candy); (c) Negro dialect, praise; (d) Negro dialect, candy. **Results:** No sex differences.

Quay, L. C. Negro dialect and Binet performance in severely disadvantaged black four-year-olds. *Child Development*, 1972, 43, 245–50.
   Subjects: $N = 50$; 4 yrs (black, low SES). **Measures:** Stanford-Binet Form L-M was administered to 1 group in Standard English and to another group in Negro dialect. **Results:** No sex differences.

Rabbie, J. M., and Howitz, M. Arousal of ingroup-outgroup bias by a chance win or loss. *J. Personality & Social Psychology*, 1969, 13, 269–77.
   Subjects: $N = 112$; 15 yrs (Holland). **Measures:** Groups of 8 same-sex Ss were randomly

Annotated Bibliography

subdivided into 2 groups of 4. As a result of either a toss of a coin, E's decision, or decision of 1 of the group, members of 1 group were rewarded while members of the other group were not. Ss then evaluated own and other groups by rating the personal attributes of both groups' members as well as the attributes of each group as a whole. **Results:** No sex differences.

Rabinowitz, F. M., and DeMyer, S. Stimulus and response alternation in young children. *Developmental Psychology*, 1971, 4, 43–54.
  Subjects: N = 96; 4, 5 yrs. **Measures:** Each S chose between 2 toy cars (black or white, light gray or dark gray) by pressing the window of the car he wanted or pushing the button under it. S was allowed to play with the chosen toy between trials. Choice and response latency were recorded for each trial. **Results:** (1) There were no sex differences in stimulus-alternation (alternation of choices by brightness). (2) There were no main sex differences in response-alternation of position. On trial blocks 1–3, 4-year-old girls repeated responses more than 4-year-old boys did, whereas 5-year-old girls alternated responses more than 5-year-old boys did ($p < .05$).

Radin, N. A comparison of maternal behavior with four-year-old boys and girls in lower-class families. Unpublished manuscript, 1973.
  Subjects: N = 52; 4 yrs (white and black, low SES). **Measures:** (1) Ss took the Peabody Picture Vocabulary Test (PPVT) and the Stanford-Binet Intelligence Scale. While completing the Stanford-Binet, 30 of the Ss were rated on achievement motivation by the psychologists administering the test. (2) Ss were present while interviews were conducted with their mothers. Mothers' behaviors toward their children were recorded and classified as either nurturant or restrictive. (3) Using the Pupil Behavior Inventory, teachers rated Ss on academic motivation. **Results:** (1) No sex differences were found in IQ, PPVT, achievement motivation, or academic motivation scores. (2) Mothers were more restrictive with their sons than with their daughters. No sex differences were found in nurturance or in total number of mother-child interactions.

Raina, M. K. A study of sex differences in creativity in India. *J. Creative Behavior*, 1969, 3, 111–14.
  Subjects: N = 180; 13–15 yrs. **Measures:** Verbal and Figural forms of the Torrance Tests of Creative Thinking. **Results:** (1) Boys were more fluent, elaborated more, and had a higher total verbal score than girls. (2) Boys scored higher than girls on all measures of the Figural form.

Ramirez, M., III, Taylor, C., Jr., and Peterson, B. Mexican-American cultural membership and adjustment to school. *Developmental Psychology*, 1971, 4, 141–48.
  Subjects: N = 600; 12–17 yrs (Mexican-American, Anglo-American). **Measures:** All Ss completed a 62-item scale assessing attitudes toward teachers and education. 120 Ss completed the School Situations Picture Stories test, and a projective test designed to assess needs for power, achievement, affiliation, and rejection. **Results:** Boys scored higher than girls in need for achievement ($p < .01$). Among Anglo-American Ss, boys had higher need for affiliation than girls; Among Mexican-American Ss, the reverse was true, but to a much lesser degree ($p < .01$).

Rapoport, A., and Chammah, A. M. Sex differences in factors contributing to the level of cooperation in the Prisoner's Dilemma game. *J. Personality & Social Psychology*, 1965, 2, 831–38.
  Subjects: N = 420; 18–31 yrs (college). **Measures:** Ss played the Prisoner's Dilemma game in either same-sex or opposite-sex pairs. **Results:** (1) Male pairs were more cooperative than female pairs. No sex differences were found in the frequency of cooperative choices in opposite-sex pairs. (2) No sex differences were found in the percentage of Ss who made the cooperative choice on the first and second trials. More male pairs were exclusively cooperative on the last 25 trials than female pairs. More female pairs were exclusively competitive on the last 25 trials than male pairs.

Ratcliff, R. G., and Tindall, R. C. Interaction of reward, punishment, and sex in a two-choice discrimination task with children. *Developmental Psychology*, 1970, 3, 150 (brief report).
  Subjects: N = 72; 9 yrs. **Measures:** Ss performed a 2-choice discrimination task (60 training and 30 extinction trials) with 1 of 3 reinforcement types: (1) token for each correct response, (2) loud tone for each incorrect response, (3) tone or token for each correct or incorrect response, respectively. The number of correct responses in each block of 5 trials was recorded.

Results: When loud tones were administered for incorrect responses, boys learned faster than girls.

Rau, M., Stover, L., and Guerney, B. G., Jr. Relationship of socioeconomic status, sex, and age to aggression of emotionally disturbed children in mothers' presence. *J. Genetic Psychology*, 1970, *116*, 95–100.
> **Subjects:** $N = 79$; 4–10 yrs (emotionally disturbed) and their mothers. **Measures:** Each mother-child pair was observed during a half-hour play session. Frequency and intensity of aggression with toys and toward mother were recorded. **Results:** Boys were more aggressive than girls ($p < .01$).

Rebelsky, F., and Hanks, C. Fathers' verbal interaction with infants in the first three months of life. *Child Development*, 1971, *42*, 63–68.
> **Subjects:** $N = 10$ (7 boys, 3 girls); 2 wks and fathers. **Measures:** At age 2 weeks, 24-hour tape recordings were made approximately every 2 weeks for a 3-month period by attaching a microphone to the infant. Two coders recorded duration, time of day, and activity occurring each time the father vocalized to his child. **Results:** (1) Fathers spent less time vocalizing to their infants during last half than in first half of study. (2) Fathers of female infants verbalized more than fathers of male infants at both 2 weeks and 4 weeks of age. Fathers of male infants vocalized somewhat more than fathers of female infants at 12 weeks of age (statistics not reported). (3) Fathers of female infants verbalized more during caretaking activities than fathers of male infants did. (4) Number of vocalizations during noncaretaking activities remained the same for fathers of male infants, but decreased somewhat for fathers of female infants.

Reese, A. H., and Palmer, F. H. Factors related to change in mental test performance, *Developmental Psychology Monograph*, 1970, *3*.
> **Subjects:** $N = 622$; tested at 6, 12, 17 yrs. **Measures:** Subsamples of Ss were (longitudinally or cross-sectionally) tested on the Stanford-Binet (S-B) and/or the Wechsler-Bellevue (W-B). **Results:** (1) At ages 6 and 12, no sex differences were found on the S-B. At age 17, boys received higher scores than girls. No sex differences were found in the amount of change in scores between the ages of 6 and 12, or 12 and 17. (2) No sex differences were found in W-B Full Scale or Performance IQs. Boys had higher verbal IQs than girls.

Reese, H. W. Attitudes toward the opposite sex in late childhood. *Merrill-Palmer Quarterly*, 1966, *12*, 157–63.
> EXPERIMENT I: **Subjects:** $N = 318$; 10–13 yrs. **Measures:** Ss were asked to rate their liking for each of their classmates on a 5-point scale. **Results:** Among 10-year-old Ss, girls had more favorable attitudes toward the opposite sex than boys did ($p < .001$). Among 11-, 12-, and 13-year-old Ss, boys had more favorable attitudes toward the opposite sex than girls ($p < .05$).
> EXPERIMENT II: **Subjects:** $N = 255$; 10 yrs (75 Ss from Experiment I). **Measures:** Same as Experiment I. **Results:** Overall, no sex differences were found. In the Experiment I sample (as reported above), girls had more favorable attitudes toward the opposite sex than boys did. In the new sample, boys had more favorable attitudes toward the opposite sex than girls did ($p < .001$).
> EXPERIMENT III: **Subjects:** $N = 102$; 10 yrs. **Measures:** Same as Experiment I. Ss rated their classmates 3 times during the year. **Results:** Overall, no sex differences were found. In September, girls were more favorable toward the opposite sex than boys were; in February and June, the reverse was true ($p < .005$).

Reese, H. W. Imagery in children's paired-associate learning. *J. Experimental Child Psychology*, 1970, *9*, 174–78.
> **Subjects:** $N = 71$; 3–5 yrs. **Measures:** Ss in 4 groups performed a paired-associates task, with groups differing by how responses to the stimulus cards were presented: (1) The object on the response card was verbalized, (2) the stimulus and response card objects were verbalized, (3) Ss saw a picture of the stimulus and response objects interacting, with stimulus and response objects verbalized, and (4) Ss heard a sentence describing the interaction between the stimulus and response items, but only saw the response item (though both were verbalized). The process was repeated 2 weeks later. **Results:** No sex differences.

Reese, H. W. Imagery and multiple-list paired-associate learning in young children. *J. Experimental Child Psychology*, 1972, *13*, 310–23.
> **Subjects:** $N = 48$; 2–6 yrs. **Measures:** Ss learned 4 paired-associate lists in a study-test procedure. Recognition was required on test trials, and reinforcement (flashing red bulbs) was given for correct responses. Retention test with no feedback was given after list learning. **Results:** No sex differences.

Regan, J. W. Guilt, perceived injustice, and altruistic behavior. *J. Personality & Social Psychology*, 1971, *18*, 124–32.
> Subjects: $N = 81$; 18–21 yrs (college). Measures: Ss either were made to feel responsible for ruining an experiment or were only involved as witnesses. No misfortune occurred to Ss in a control group. Half of the Ss were then given an opportunity to reflect on the misfortune and to express their feelings. Afterward, Ss were asked to donate money to a cause only remotely associated with the misfortune. Results: No sex differences were found in Ss' donating behavior.

Reppucci, N. D. Parental education, sex differences, and performance on cognitive tasks among two-year-old children. *Developmental Psychology*, 1971, *4*, 248–53.
> Subjects: $N = 48$; 2 yrs. Measures: E administered an embedded figures task, a 2-choice discrimination-learning task, a vocabulary recognition task, and a vocabulary-naming task. Results: No sex differences.

Rettig, S. Group discussion and predicted ethical risk taking. *J. Personality & Social Psychology*, 1966, *3*, 629–33.
> Subjects: $N = 160$; 18–21 yrs (college). Measures: Ss were presented with a set of descriptions of fictitious situations, each portraying a person (either S himself or a hypothetical other) in a dilemma about whether or not to steal money from a bank. For each situation, Ss predicted whether or not the money would be taken. Half of the Ss made their judgments following group discussion. Results: No sex differences.

Rheingold, H. L., and Eckerman, C. O. The infant's free entry into a new environment. *J. Experimental Child Psychology*, 1969, *8*, 271–83.
> Subjects: $N = 24$; 9–10 mos and mothers (2 experiments). Measures: Ss and their mothers were taken to the smaller of 2 adjacent rooms. Ss were allowed free entry into the larger room, which was marked off into 3-foot squares and contained either 0, 1, or 3 toys. Measures were taken of (1) how quickly Ss entered the larger room, number and duration of entries, number and location of squares entered; (2) onset and duration of contact with mother, manipulation of toys, and manipulation of other objects; (3) number of 10-second periods during which Ss vocalized or fussed. Results: No sex differences.

Rheingold, H. L., and Eckerman, C. O. The infant separates himself from his mother. *Science*, 1970, *168*, 78–83.
> Subjects: $N = 48$; 1, 1½, 2, 2½, 3, 3½, 4, 4½, 5 yrs and mothers. Measures: The distance the child roamed from his mother was observed. Results: No sex differences.

Rheingold, H. L., and Samuels, H. R. Maintaining the positive behavior of infants by increased stimulation. *Developmental Psychology*, 1969, 1,520–27.
> Subjects: $N = 20$; 10 mos and mothers. Measures: Ss were observed in an experimental room for 2 10-minute sessions with their mothers present. During the first observational period, no furniture or toys were present. Measures were taken of the following: latency of fussing, frequency of fussing, frequency of vocalizing, number of lines crossed (the room was marked off with masking tape into squares), latency of touching mother, duration of contact with mother, and duration of object manipulation (drapes, doorstop, Ss' own clothing, etc.). During the second session, 5 toys were made available to half the Ss. For the other 10 children, the room remained unchanged. For each of the measures cited above, Ss' score for the second session was the change in their performance from the first observational period. For experimental Ss, 2 additional measures were recorded: latency and duration of contact with the toys. Results: No sex differences.

Rheingold, H. L., Gewirtz, J. L., and Ross, H. W. Social conditioning of vocalizations in the infant. In S. W. Bijou and D. M. Baer, eds., *Child development: readings in experimental analysis*. New York: Meredith Publishing Co., 1967.
> Subjects: $N = 21$; 3 mos. Measures: Ss were tested on 6 successive days. On days 1, 2, 5, and 6, E leaned over and positioned her head above S's head. S's vocalizations were recorded. On days 3 and 4, procedures were identical except that each vocalization was reinforced by E. E's response consisted of a broad smile, three "tsk" sounds, and a light touch applied to S's abdomen. Results: No sex differences were found in number of vocalizations.

Rhine, R. J., Hill, S. J., and Wandruff, S. E. Evaluative responses of preschool children. *Child Development*, 1967, *38*, 1035–42.
> Subjects: $N = 50$; 2–5 yrs (nursery school). Measures: Ss were shown line drawings of children in activities considered bad, good, or neutral. A female E described the content of each picture as it was shown to Ss. The pictures were then arranged in subsets of 4 containing either

1 good and 3 neutral, 1 bad and 3 neutral, or all neutral pictures. For each of 12 subsets, Ss were asked to point to the picture that showed a good (or bad) activity. The Stanford-Binet picture vocabulary test was also administered to Ss. **Results:** No sex differences.

Ricciuti, H. N. Object grouping and selective ordering behavior in infants 12 to 34 months old. *Merrill-Palmer Quarterly*, 1965, *11*, 129–48.
Subjects: $N = 48$; 1, 1½, 2 yrs. **Measures:** Ss were given 4 different object-grouping tasks, each consisting of 2 kinds of objects. No specific sorting instructions were given; Ss were simply encouraged to play with the objects. The order in which objects were touched or manipulated (selective ordering) and the degree to which similar objects were spatially constituted as groups (object grouping) were recorded. **Results:** No sex differences.

Rickard, H. C., and Joubert, C. E. Subject-model sexual status and observer performance. *Psychonomic Science*, 1968, *10*, 407–8.
Subjects: $N = 40$; 18–21 yrs (college). **Measures:** Ss heard prerecorded tapes of words spoken by either a man or a woman. The first 50 words contained no animal names (the critical response class). Each consecutive 50-word set thereafter contained 9, 21, 33, and 47 animal names, respectively. After every fifth word, the tape recorder was stopped and Ss were asked to say the first word that occurred to them. **Results:** No sex of subject or sex of model differences were found in number of animal names emitted. On the last 10 trials, men who heard the adult female responded with more animal names than men who heard the adult male; for women, the reverse was true ($p < .05$).

Rickard, H. C., Ellis, N. E., Barnhart, S., and Holt, M. Subject-model sexual status and verbal imitative performance in kindergarten children. *Developmental Psychology*, 1970, *3*, 405 (brief report).
Subjects: $N = 40$; 5 yrs. **Measures:** Same as Rickard and Joubert (1968); see preceding item. **Results:** No sex of subject or sex of model differences were found.

Rieber, M. Hypothesis testing in children as a function of age. *Developmental Psychology*, 1969, *1*, 389–95.
Subjects: $N = 120$; 5, 7, 9 yrs. **Measures:** 3-dimensional, 2-choice discrimination problems were individually administered to Ss. The blank trials technique was used to determine the nature of Ss' strategy from a sequence of 5 responses. Ss were randomly assigned to 4 groups that differed in the dimensions and values reinforced. **Results:** No sex differences.

Riegel, K. F., Riegel, R. M., and Levine, R. S. An analysis of associative behavior and creativity. *J. Personality & Social Psychology*, 1966, *4*, 50–56.
Subjects: $N = 48$; 18–21 yrs (college). **Measures:** Ss were administered 13 restricted word-association tasks; the same stimuli (35 nouns) were used for all tasks. For each stimulus, a measure was taken of the number of times Ss gave the same response in 2 different tasks. The degree to which each task overlapped with the remaining 12 was then calculated. **Results:** No sex differences were found in task overlap.

Rigg, M. G. The relative variability in intelligence of boys and girls. *J. Genetic Psychology*, 1940, *56*, 211–14.
Subjects: $N = 10,079$; 8–13 yrs. **Measures:** National Intelligence Test. **Results:** No sex differences were found in variability.

Rileigh, K. K., and Odom, P. B. Perception of rhythm by subjects with normal and deficient hearing. *Developmental Psychology*, 1972, *7*, 54–61.
Subjects: $N = 72$; 10, 15 yrs. **Measures:** Ss saw films of 5- and 10-second black-dot rhythm patterns and reproduced each with a telegraph key; 1 hearing group received white noise through earphones during presentation and reproduction periods. Reproductions were scored for correctness of number of beats reproduced, total duration of patterns, and rhythmic relationships, regardless of errors in total duration. **Results:** (1) There were no sex differences in accuracy of reproducing the number of beats. (2) Boys were more accurate than girls in reproducing the total duration of the sequences. (3) There were no sex differences in accuracy of rhythm reproduction.

Rivenbark, W. H., III. Self-disclosure among adolescents. *Psychological Reports*, 1971, *28*, 35–42.
Subjects: $N = 149$; 9, 11, 13, 15, 17 yrs. **Measures:** A modified version of Jourard and Lasakow's questionnaire was used to measure self-disclosure. For each of the 40 items on the ques-

tionnaire, Ss rated their self-disclosure to each of 4 target persons: mother, father, best male friend, best female friend. **Results:** (1) Girls disclosed more to their best male friends and to their best female friends than boys did. Girls disclosed more to their best female friends than to their best male friends; boys disclosed more to their best male friends than to their best female friends ($p < .001$). (2) Girls disclosed more to their mothers than boys did to their fathers. No sex differences were found in disclosure to the opposite-sex parent.

Roberge, J. J., and Paulus, D. H. Developmental patterns for children's class and conditional reasoning abilities. *Developmental Psychology*, 1971, 4, 191–200.
  Subjects: $N = 263$; 9, 11, 13, 15 yrs. **Measures:** Paulus Conditional Reasoning Test, Paulus-Roberge Class Reasoning Test. **Results:** No sex differences.

Roberts, G. C., and Black, K. N. The effect of naming and object permanence on toy preferences. *Child Development*, 1972, 43, 858–68.
  Subjects: $N = 40$; 1 yr and mothers. **Measures:** In the first session, Ss were presented with 16 toys, 1 at a time, half named and half unnamed. Immediately afterward Ss were given a series of timed preference choices between named and unnamed toy pairs. In the second session, the object permanence and vocal imitation subscales of the Infant Psychological Development Scale were administered. **Results:** There were no main sex differences. Boys showed more differentiation between named and unnamed toys in the visual mode; girls showed more differentiation in the tactile mode. No sex differences were found on the object permanence scale, or on mothers' reports of the children's language development.

Robson, K. S., Pederson, F. A., and Moss, H. A. Developmental observations of dyadic gazing in relation to the fear of strangers and social approach behavior. *Child Development*, 1969, 40, 619–27.
  Subjects: $N = 45$; tested at 8, 9½ mos. **Measures:** Mother-infant pairs were visited in their home by 2 male observers. At the beginning and end of each visit, one observer approached the infant while the mother held him, picked him up, held him for approximately 1 minute, and then returned him to his mother's lap. Ss' responses were rated on a 13-point fear-of-strangers scale. During the unstructured portions of the visit, the amount of approach behavior the infant initiated toward both observers while unrestrained was recorded. Information regarding which month infants first exhibited a clear-cut avoidance response to an unfamiliar adult was obtained during interviews with mothers. **Results:** (1) No sex differences were found in fear-of-stranger ratings. (2) Boys exhibited more approach behavior toward observers than girls did (level of significance not given). (3) Girls displayed fear-of-stranger responses at an earlier age than boys ($p < .01$).

Roll, S. Reversibility training and stimulus desirability as factors in conservation of number. *Child Development*, 1970, 41, 501–7.
  Subjects: $N = 87$; 5–7 yrs (Colombian). **Measures:** Ss performed 6 conservation-of-number tasks. **Results:** No sex differences.

Rollins, H., and Castel, K. Dimensional preference, pretraining, and attention in children's concept identification. *Child Development*, 1973, 44, 363–66.
  Subjects: $N = 72$; 3–5 yrs. **Measures:** Two-thirds of the Ss were pretrained on a matching task—one-third on their preferred dimension and one-third on their nonpreferred dimension. All Ss performed a concept identification task with the preferred or nonpreferred dimension relevant (form, color). **Results:** No sex differences.

Roodin, M. L., and Gruen, G. E. The role of memory in making transitive judgments. *J. Experimental Child Psychology*, 1970, 10, 264–75.
  Subjects: $N = 72$; 5–7 yrs. **Measures:** Ss made transitivity judgments about stick lengths. Half of the Ss used a memory-aid stick for initial comparisons; the other half did not. The performance measure was the number of transitive responses Ss gave. **Results:** No sex differences.

Rosekrans, M. A., and Hartup, W. W. Imitative influences of consistent and inconsistent response consequences to a model on aggressive behavior in children. *J. Personality & Social Psychology*, 1967, 7, 429–34.
  Subjects: $N = 36$; 3–5 yrs. **Measures:** Ss were exposed to an adult female model who was either consistently rewarded, consistently punished, or inconsistently reinforced (by an adult female E) for performing novel aggressive responses with a number of toys. Ss were then allowed to play with the toys in the presence of E. The response measures were the frequency of each of 3 types of aggressive behavior (imitative, partially imitative, and nonimitative) and the elapsed time before the initial occurrence of each. **Results:** No sex differences.

Rosenberg, B. G., and Sutton-Smith, B. A revised conception of masculine-feminine differences in play activities. *J. Genetic Psychology*, 1960, *96*, 165–70.
Subjects: $N = 187$; 9, 10, 11 yrs. Measures: Ss were presented with a list of 181 games and were asked to check only those games they had played. Results: (1) Boys chose the following games more frequently than girls did: bandits, bows and arrows, boxing, building forts, cars, cops and robbers, darts, football, hunting, marbles, making model airplanes, shooting, soldiers, spacemen, snowball throwing, toy trains, using tools, and wrestling. (2) Girls chose the following games more frequently than boys did: blindman's buff, building snowmen, cartwheels, Clue, cooking, crack the whip, dancing, doctors, dolls, dressing up, drop the handkerchief, farmer in the dell, follow the leader, fox and geese, hide the thimble, hopscotch, houses, huckle buckle beanstalk, in and out the window, I've got a secret, jacks, jump rope, leap frog, London bridge, Mother may I, mulberry bush, musical chairs, name that tune, pick up sticks, red rover, ring around the rosy, scrapbook making, see saw, sewing, school, Simon says thumbs up, statues, stoop tag, and store.

Rosenberg, B. G., and Sutton-Smith, B. The relationship of ordinal position and sibling sex status to cognitive abilities. *Psychonomic Science*, 1964, *1*, 81–82.
Subjects: $N = 377$; 19 yrs (college). Measures: American College Entrance Examination. Results: (1) Women had higher language (L) scores than men ($p < .01$). (2) No sex differences were found in quantitative (Q) or total (T) scores. (3) Men had higher Q > L ratios than women ($p < .01$).

Rosenberg, B. G., and Sutton-Smith, B. Sibling association, family size, and cognitive abilities. *J. Genetic Psychology*, 1966, *109*, 271–79.
Subjects: $N = 600$; 18–20 yrs (college). Measures: American College Entrance Examination. Results: (1) Men had higher quantitative (Q) scores than women ($p < .01$). No sex differences were found in language (L) scores. (2) Women had higher total scores than men ($p < .001$). (3) The Q > L ratio was higher for men than for women ($p < .001$).

Rosenberg, B. G., and Sutton-Smith, B. Sibling age spacing effects upon cognition. *Developmental Psychology*, 1969, *1*, 661–68.
Subjects: $N = 1,013$; 19 yrs (college). Measures: American College Entrance Examination. Results: (1) Men had higher quantitative (Q) scores than women ($p < .01$). (2) Women had higher language (L) scores ($p < .01$) and total (T) scores ($p < .01$) than men.

Rosenfeld, H. M. Approval-seeking and approval-inducing functions of verbal and nonverbal responses in the dyad. *J. Personality & Social Psychology*, 1966, *4*, 497–605.
Subjects: $N = 92$; 18–21 yrs (college). Measures: 1 member of each same-sex dyad was secretly instructed to either gain or avoid the approval of his partner. Dyads were then observed in free interaction. Measures were taken of several categories of verbal and nonverbal behavior. Afterward, naïve Ss were asked to rate their partners on a like-dislike scale and to list characteristics of their partners that they liked and disliked. Results: (1) The length of women's speeches was shorter than the length of men's speeches ($p < .05$). (2) The ratio of speech disturbances to total words spoken was higher for men than for women ($p < .05$). (3) Women rated their partners more positively than men did. (4) No sex differences in gestures or number of utterances.

Rosenhan, D., and Messick, S. Affect and expectation. *J. Personality & Social Psychology*, 1966, *3*, 38–44.
Subjects: $N = 116$; 18–21 yrs (college). Measures: For each of 150 trials, Ss guessed which of 2 stimuli (a smiling or an angry face) would next appear. Ss were exposed to 1 of 2 input ratios: 70% smiling faces / 30% angry faces (SA condition) or 70% angry faces / 30% smiling faces (AS condition). Results: No sex differences were found in proportion of responses to the stimulus with the 70% input.

Rosenhan, D., and White, G. M. Observation and rehearsal as determinants of prosocial behavior. *J. Personality & Social Psychology*, 1967, *5*, 424–31.
Subjects: $N = 130$; 9–10 yrs. Measures: Ss observed a male model donate half of his winnings (gift certificates) from a bowling game to charity. Ss then played the bowling game twice, once in the presence of the model and once in his absence. Results: No sex differences.

Rosenhan, D., Frederick, F., and Burrowes, A. Preaching and practicing: effects of channel discrepancy on norm internalization. *Child Development*, 1968, *39*, 291–301.
Subjects: $N = 72$; 8–9 yrs. Measures: Ss played a bowling game with preset scores. A model

explained the game and played the first round of 20 trials with Ss. Ss were randomly assigned to 4 conditions of model behavior: consistent (lenient, strict) and discrepant (child-indulgent, self-indulgent). Extent to which the model verbally instructed and personally exhibited high or low standards of self-reward was varied. Ss played the game alone, and norm violations were scored. **Results:** No sex differences.

Rosenkoetter, L. T. Resistance to temptation: inhibitory and disinhibitory effects of models. *Developmental Psychology*, 1973, 8, 80–84.
  Subjects: $N = 48$; 8–12 yrs. **Measures:** Ss were required to sit where they were unable to see a Woody Woodpecker film after observing either a yielding model (who succumbed to temptation and moved to see the film) or a nonyielding model (who resisted temptation to move). Control Ss observed no models. **Results:** No sex differences.

Rosenkrantz, P. S., and Crockett, W. H. Some factors influencing the assimilation of disparate information in impression formation. *J. Personality & Social Psychology*, 1965, 2, 397–402.
  Subjects: $N = 176$; 18–21 yrs (college). **Measures:** Ss listened as 8 speakers each illustrated 2 traits of a male stimulus person (SP). Of the 8 speakers, 4 described positive traits and 4 described negative traits. Half of the Ss recorded their impressions of the SP after hearing 4 speakers, and again after hearing 8 speakers (using the same measuring instruments on each occasion). The remaining Ss heard all 8 speakers before recording their impressions; 2 measures were derived from Ss' responses to the objective scales: a recency score (number of responses similar in valence to the most recently received set of information) and a change score (number of items on which Ss' final impressions differed from their initial impressions). **Results:** No main sex differences were found.

Rosenthal, T. L., and White, G. M. Initial probability, rehearsal, and constraint in associative class selection. *J. Experimental Child Psychology*, 1972, 13, 261–74.
  EXPERIMENT I: Subjects: $N = 112$; 8 yrs. **Measures:** Ss were presented with 15 stimulus nouns. To the right of each noun were 3 words, 1 of which was a noun, 1 a verb, and 1 a color (e.g. book: page, reads, violet). Ss' task was to pick which of the 3 available responses went best with each stimulus word (baseline phase). Ss then observed an adult model respond to the same stimulus words; afterward, new response sheets were distributed and Ss were asked to imitate the model's choices (imitative phase). Finally, Ss were again asked to express their own preferences to each of the 15 stimulus nouns (preference phase). In each of the last 2 phases, the number of times Ss imitated the model's preferences was recorded. **Results:** No sex differences.
  EXPERIMENT II: Subjects: $N = 96$; 8 yrs. **Measures:** Same as experiment I, except that after observing the model, Ss received instructions urging them neither to imitate the model nor to pick the responses they felt fit the stimulus words best. **Results:** In the baseline phase, girls chose nouns more often than boys. No other sex differences were found.

Rosenthal, T. L., Alford, G. S., and Rasp, L. M. Concept attainment generalization, and retention through observation and verbal coding. *J. Experimental Child Psychology*, 1972, 13, 183–94.
  Subjects: $N = 80$; 7 yrs. **Measures:** After a baseline was established, modeled clustering of stimulus objects was observed. The model displayed either no verbalizations, low-information verbalizations, or high-information verbalizations about her clustering. The response measure was the number of fully correct clusters Ss produced. **Results:** (1) Boys scored more correct clusters than girls ($p < .04$). (2) Boys' performance surpassed girls during imitation ($p < .025$), but not during generalization.

Roskens, R. W., and Dizney, H. F. A study of unethical academic behavior in high school and college. *J. Educational Research*, 1966, 59, 231–34.
  Subjects: $N = 2,871$; 18, 21 yrs (college). **Measures:** Ss completed a questionnaire on academic cheating. **Results:** (1) Among 21-year-old Ss, men reported more cribbing, less plagiarism and ghost-writing; women reported more plagiarism and ghost-writing, less cribbing. (2) Among 18-year-old Ss, more men than women cheated in high school; more women than men expressed concern about cheating.

Ross, B. M. Probability concepts in deaf and hearing children. *Child Development*, 1966, 37, 917–27.
  Subjects: $N = 140$; 7, 9, 11, 13, 15 yrs (normal, deaf). **Measures:** Ss watched as E placed balls of 2 different colors in a box. Ss then shook the box and predicted the color of the ball

they would draw out. Ss continued predicting and drawing out balls until box was empty. Ss were confronted with 3 types of choice situations: (1) "sure thing" choices occurred when balls of only 1 color remained; (2) "uneven odds" choices occurred whenever there were more balls of 1 color than the other; (3) "even odds" choices occurred when both colors were equally represented. **Results:** (1) Among 13-year-old deaf Ss, boys made more correct predictions when confronted with "uneven odds" than girls did ($p < .05$). (2) No sex differences were found for "even odds" or "sure thing" choices.

Ross, B. M., and Youniss, J. Ordering of nonverbal items in children's recognition memory. *J. Experimental Child Psychology*, 1969, 8, 20–32.
  Subjects: $N = 64$; 6, 10 yrs. **Measures:** Ss' task was to recognize 3 picture items (previously pointed out to them) from an array of 9. Either (1) Ss were instructed to point to the items in the original presentation order, or (2) the ordering of responses was not mentioned. There was either a 10-second delay or no delay between presentation and recognition trials. **Results:** No sex differences.

Ross, H. S., Rheingold, H. L., and Eckerman, C. O. Approach and exploration of a novel alternative by 12-month-old infants. *J. Experimental Child Psychology*, 1972, 13, 85–93.
  Subjects: $N = 12$; 11–12 mos and mothers. **Measures:** Two 5-minute trials took place. In Trial 1 Ss were placed with their mothers in the "start" room and allowed to enter 1 test room and play with the toy it contained. In Trial 2 the door to the second test room was opened and Ss were allowed to enter either test room. Test rooms and the toys they contained differed in degree of novelty. Response measures were latency to enter test room, time in test room, latency to contact toy, time contacting toy, toy chosen, and vocalizations. **Results:** There were no main effects of sex of Ss on either trial, and no interaction of sex and novelty.

Ross, S. A. A test of generality of the effects of deviant preschool models. *Developmental Psychology*, 1971, 4, 262–67 (and personal communication).
  Subjects: $N = 48$; 3–5 yrs. **Measures:** Ss were taught how to operate a toy store by a same-age, same-sex model. After the model left, a same-sex peer entered the store and bought 1 toy with play money. Measures were taken of the number of storekeeper behaviors Ss exhibited that were imitative of the mannerisms displayed by the model and of the number of storekeeper behaviors exhibited that were nonimitative. As the customer left the store, the model returned to inform the Ss that they could have 1 toy. Then the model took either 1 or 3 toys for himself and left the room. The number of toys Ss took and any behavioral signs of conflict during toy selection were recorded. **Results:** Boys exhibited more nonimitative storekeeper behaviors (e.g. pointing out the advantage of various toys, asking the customer if the toy was for himself or for a friend, etc.) than girls did ($p < .01$). No sex differences were found in the number of imitative behaviors Ss displayed. (2) Boys were more concerned than girls that the customer select a sex-appropriate toy ($p < .001$). (3) No sex differences were found in the number of behavioral signs of conflict Ss exhibited during toy selection or in the number of Ss who took more than 1 toy.

Rothbart, M. K. Effects of motivation, equity, and compliance on the use of reward and punishment. *J. Personality & Social Psychology*, 1968, 9, 353–62.
  Subjects: $N = 60$; 18–21 yrs (college). **Measures:** Ss were free to administer both promises of monetary reward and threats of monetary punishment as incentives for increasing a confederate's performance. **Results:** No sex differences.

Rothbart, M. K. Birth order and mother-child interaction in an achievement situation. *J. Personality & Social Psychology*, 1971, 17, 113–20.
  Subjects: $N = 56$; 5 yrs and mothers. **Measures:** *Task 1:* While their mothers received instructions, Ss played with a set of toys in an adjacent room. Afterward, mothers asked their children to name all the toys they had seen. *Task 2:* Mothers were given 2 cartoons. They were then asked to explain to their children what was happening in each cartoon. *Task 3:* Ss were shown a picture of 20 zoo animals. After the picture was turned over, mothers asked their children to name as many animals as they could remember. Observers rated the amount of achievement pressure mothers exerted. Before the task was administered, mothers estimated how well their children would perform. *Task 4:* Mothers were given a simple diagram of the workings of a water tap, along with an extremely complicated written description. Mothers were asked to explain to their children how the tap worked. *Task 5:* Mothers supervised their children's performance on a difficult geometric puzzle. Estimates of how quickly the puzzle would be solved were obtained from each mother. Mothers were requested to clean up the room (with the child's help) before E's return. **Results:** (1) No main differences were found between boys'

and girls' performances on Tasks 1, 3, and 5. (2) No main sex differences were found in the extent to which Ss participated in the clean-up of the room. (3) No main sex differences were found in mothers' estimates of their children's performances (Tasks 3 and 5). On the picture task (Task 5), mothers of firstborn girls gave higher estimates than mothers of second-born girls; a weaker trend in the opposite direction was found among mothers of boys ($p < .05$). (4) No sex differences were found in the complexity of mothers' explanations (Tasks 2 and 4). (5) No main sex differences were found in mothers' structuring of Task 3 or 5. Structuring was defined as the amount of information mothers gave to their children concerning what would happen to them in the task and what would be expected of them. Mothers structured Task 5 more for firstborn girls and second-born boys than for their opposite-sex counterparts ($p < .01$). (6) In Tasks 1, 2, and 4, no sex differences were found in the number of questions mothers asked or in the amount of time they spent in conversation or explanation. (7) No main sex differences were found on the 2 maternal measures of pressure for success in Task 3. More pressure for remembering was exerted on firstborn girls and second-born boys than on their opposite-sex counterparts ($p < .01$). (8) In Tasks 2, 3, and 4, no sex differences were found in mothers' use of praise or criticism. (9) In Tasks 1, 2, 3, and 4, no main sex differences were found in the number of times children were told by their mothers that they were correct or incorrect. Firstborn girls and second-born boys were more likely to be told they were incorrect than their opposite-sex counterparts ($p < .05$). (10) Across all tasks, mothers of girls exhibited more anxious intrusiveness than mothers of boys.

Rothenberg, B. B. Conservation of number among four- and five-year-old children: some methodological considerations. *Child Development*, 1969, 40, 383–406.
   Subjects: $N = 210$; 4, 5 yrs (low SES). **Measures:** After a warm-up task, Ss performed a modified conservation of number task. **Results:** No sex differences.

Rothenberg, B. B. Children's social sensitivity and the relationship to interpersonal competence, intrapersonal comfort, and intellectual level. *Developmental Psychology*, 1970, 2, 335–50.
   Subjects: $N = 108$; 8, 10 yrs. **Measures:** After concentrating on 1 of 2 actors in 4 tape-recorded stories depicting 4 common emotions, Ss were asked to describe how an actor felt. Teachers and peers rated Ss on 7 dimensions of interpersonal confidence. Ss completed a self-concept measure, the Peabody Picture Vocabulary Test, Block Designs of the WISC, and a defensiveness measure. **Results:** No sex differences.

Rothenberg, B. B., and Courtney, R. G. Conservation of number in very young children. *Developmental Psychology*, 1969a, 1, 493–502.
   Subjects: $N = 117$; 3 yrs (low, middle SES). **Measures:** On a conservation-of-number task, Ss were tested on the following transformations: collapsing, rotation, expansion, equal addition, and unequal addition. **Results:** No sex differences.

Rothenberg, B. B., and Courtney, R. G. A developmental study of nonconservation choices in young children. *Merrill-Palmer Quarterly*, 1969b, 15, 363–73.
   Subjects: $N = 285$; 2–6 yrs (low, middle SES). **Measures:** On a conservation-of-number task, Ss were tested on the following transformations: equal subtraction, rotation, collapsing, expansion, and addition. **Results:** No sex differences.

Rothenberg, B. B., and Orost, J. H. The training of conservation of number in young children. *Child Development*, 1969, 40, 707–26.
   Subjects: $N = 20$; 5–6 yrs (low, middle SES). **Measures:** Ss were tested on 3 conservation-of-number tasks. Ss received training for 2 sessions, after which they were post-tested. **Results:** No sex differences.

Rotter, J. B., and Mulry, R. C. Internal versus external control of reinforcement and decision time. *J. Personality & Social Psychology*, 1965, 2, 598–604.
   Subjects: $N = 120$; 18–21 yrs (college). **Measures:** Ss performed a difficult matching task in which there were actually no correct matches. Before each trial, Ss rated their probability of success on a 10-point scale. Ss were told they were correct on 75% of the first 8 trials; however, on subsequent trials Ss were consistently told they had made the wrong choice. The response measures were (a) mean decision time, (b) mean expectancy of success for the initial 8 trials, (c) frequency of unusual shifts in expectancies, and (d) number of trials to extinction. Ss were considered extinguished when they stated an expectancy of 0 or 1 on 2 consecutive trials. **Results:** No sex differences.

Routh, D. K., and Tweney, D. Effects of paradigmatic response training on children's word associations. *J. Experimental Child Psychology*, 1972, *14*, 398–407.
Subjects: $N = 60$; 5, 10 yrs. Measures: Ss performed a free-association task before and after receiving training on paradigmatic associates. Results: No sex differences.

Rubenstein, J. Maternal attentiveness and subsequent exploratory behavior in the infant. *Child Development*, 1967, *38*, 1089–1100.
Subjects: $N = 44$; 6 mos and mothers. Measures: Ss were presented with a novel stimulus (Bell Test). The number of seconds Ss spent manipulating (oral and tactile), looking at, and vocalizing to the Bell were recorded. The Bell was then paired with each of 10 novel stimuli (Pairs Test). The number of seconds Ss spent exploring the novel stimuli (looking at, manipulating) minus the number of seconds Ss spent exploring the Bell was recorded. Results: No sex differences.

Rubin, K. H. Relationship between egocentric communication and popularity among peers. *Developmental Psychology*, 1972, *7*, 364 (brief report).
Subjects: $N = 80$; 5, 7, 9, 11 yrs. Measures: (1) Ss were asked to name the 3 children with whom they would most like to spend their free time. (2) Ss were also asked to describe each of 10 nonsense figures in such a way that E (who was visually separated from Ss and had 10 identical figures) could identify which figure was being described. The mean number of distinctive features used by Ss to describe each figure was added to a score based on Ss' response to E's inquiries for further information to yield a score of communicative egocentrism. Results: No sex differences were found in popularity or in egocentrism scores.

Rubin, Z. Measurement of romantic love. *J. Personality & Social Psychology*, 1970, *16*, 265–73.
EXPERIMENT I: Subjects: $N = 158$ couples; 18–21 yrs (college). Measures: Ss completed a love and liking scale first with respect to their dating partner and later with respect to a close, same-sex friend. Results: (1) Women liked their dating partner more than they were liked in turn ($p < .01$). No differences were found between men's and women's love for their dating partners. (2) Women loved their same-sex friends more than men did ($p < .01$). No sex differences were found in Ss' liking for their same-sex friends.
EXPERIMENT II: Subjects: $N = 79$ couples; 18–21 yrs (college). Measures: Ss were paired with either their boyfriends or their girlfriends or with another person's boyfriend or girlfriend. Before the experiment began, Ss' visual behavior was recorded when E was out of the room. Results: Women spent more time looking at the men than men spent looking at the women ($p < .01$).

Ruble, D. N., and Nakamura, C. Y. Task orientation versus social orientation in young children and their attention to relevant social cues. *Child Development*, 1972, *43*, 471–80.
Subjects: $N = 56$; 7–10 yrs. Measures: Ss were given the Gerard rod-and-frame test, 2 object assembly tasks (puzzles) and a concept identification task. Before the object assembly tasks were administered, Ss were assigned to 1 of 2 conditions. In the experimental condition, E assembled and then disassembled puzzle 2, while Ss attempted puzzle 1. Afterward, Ss were given the pieces to puzzle 2 to put together. In the control condition, E simply watched Ss perform. Response measures were number of pieces correctly placed (bonus points were awarded for completing the task quickly) and number of glances away from task. In the concept identification task, Ss had to decide which of 3 squares was correct. The squares varied in color and size. In the first trial block, E repeatedly looked at and leaned very slightly toward the correct choice (always the largest square). In the second trial block, E again directed her attention toward the correct selection, but the largest square was no longer always correct. Rather, the correct answer was randomized over the 3 sizes (small, medium, and large). During the third trial block, no social cue was given. Selection of the small square was always correct. The number of trials Ss needed to reach criterion in each trial block was recorded. Results: No sex differences.

Rule, B. G., and Rehill, D. Distraction and self-esteem effects on attitude change. *J. Personality & Social Psychology*, 1970, *15*, 359–65.
Subjects: $N = 90$; 18–21 yrs (college). Measures: Ss read a communication advocating a position opposite theirs. The response measure was amount of attitude change Ss exhibited on a postexperimental scale. Results: No sex differences.

Ryan, T. J., and Strawbridge, J. E. Effects of observer condition, instructional set, reward schedule, and sex of subject upon performer and observer. *Developmental Psychology*, 1969, *1*, 474–81.

Subjects: $N = 192$; 5–6 yrs. **Measures:** Same-sex pairs of Ss were brought to an experimental room to perform a lever-pulling task; 1 member of each pair was randomly designated as Child A and the other as Child B. Child A Ss were assigned to 1 of 2 main conditions: (a) half were rewarded with a marble after each of 40 lever-pulling responses; the other half were rewarded after every other trial. Child B Ss were also assigned to 1 of 2 conditions. Half performed a lever-pulling response immediately after each of Child A's responses and were rewarded for each response (active observer condition). Ss in the other half (passive observer condition) first observed Child A perform all 40 responses; then, in the presence of Child A, they performed 40 responses, each of which was rewarded. Measures were taken of each child's starting speed and movement speed. **Results:** (1) Starting speeds for Ss designated as Child A: boys with an active observer had higher mean speeds than boys with a passive observer; no effect was found for girls ($p < .05$). (2) Movement speeds of Child A Ss: boys with an active observer had higher mean speeds than girls with an active observer. (3) Starting speeds for Child B Ss: no sex differences. (4) Movement speeds for Child B Ss: in the active observer condition, boys had higher mean speeds than girls; no sex differences were found in the passive observer condition.

Ryan, T. J., and Voorhoeve, A. C. A parametric investigation of reinforcement schedule and sex of S as related to acquisition and extinction of an instrumental response. *J. Experimental Child Psychology*, 1966, *4*, 189–97.

Subjects: $N = 120$; 5 yrs. **Measures:** Ss were divided into 6 groups according to percent of trials reinforced on a lever-pulling task (100%, 70%, 50%, 30%, 0%). Starting and movement time was measured on 40 acquisition trials. After acquisition, groups split into 2 subgroups; one received 30 extinction trials, the other received 30 more acquisition trials. **Results:** No sex differences.

Rychlak, J. F., and Lerner, J. J. An expectancy interpretation of manifest anxiety. *J. Personality & Social Psychology*, 1965, *2*, 667–84.

Subjects: $N = 40$; 18–20 yrs (college). **Measures:** Ss were given 6 performance tests of manual dexterity. Preceding Test 1, Ss stated their expectancy for success. Ss then experienced either success or failure on Tests 1–4. Prior to Test 5, Ss again stated their expectancy for success. Test 5 scores were manipulated so that Ss who previously experienced failure on Tests 1–4 performed well above average on Test 5, whereas Ss who previously experienced success on Tests 1–4 performed well below average on Test 5. Preceding Test 6, Ss stated their expectancy for success for a third time. **Results:** (1) Preceding Test 1, men had a higher expectancy for success than women. (2) No sex differences were found in the change in expectancy for success between Tests 5 and 6.

Saarni, C. I. Piagetian operations and field independence as factors in children's problem-solving performance. *Child Development*, 1973, *44*, 338–45.

Subjects: $N = 64$; 10–15 yrs. **Measures:** Ss performed a Rod-and-Frame Test (RFT) and 2 Piagetian tasks, "specific gravity" and "chemical combination." **Results:** Boys were more field-independent than girls on the RFT. No sex differences were found on the Piagetian tasks.

Sabo, R. A., and Hagen, J. W. Color cues and rehearsal in short-term memory. *Child Development*, 1972, *44*, 77–82.

Subjects: $N = 240$; 8, 10, 12 yrs. **Measures:** Ss were presented with rows of pictures and were asked to remember the location of the picture designated "central." For half of the trials there was a color cue. Rehearsal and nonrehearsal conditions were established. **Results:** No sex differences.

Saltz, E., and Soller, E. The development of natural language concepts. *Child Development*, 1972, *43*, 1191–1202.

Subjects: $N = 72$; 5–6, 8–9, 11–12 yrs. **Measures:** Ss were presented with a concept word (both verbally and in writing) and were asked to match with it as many of 72 picture cards as they thought appropriate. The main categories (concepts) were food, animals, transportation, clothes, toys, and furniture. **Results:** No sex differences.

Saltzstein, H. D., Diamond, R. M., and Belensky, M. Moral judgment level and conformity behavior. *Developmental Psychology*, 1972, *7*, 327–36.

Subjects: $N = 63$; 12 yrs. **Measures:** Following Kohlberg's procedure, individual interviews were conducted to assess each child's moral judgment level. Ss then met in same-sex groups of 6 and participated in a modified Asch-type conformity experiment. Ss' task was to decide which of 3 comparison strips was identical in length to a standard. Afterward, Ss filled out a questionnaire. **Results:** (1) In comparison with boys, girls were overrepresented at Stage 3 and underrepresented at Stages 1–2 and Stages 4–5 ($p < .001$). (2a) On critical trials in the conformity experiment (group choice was incorrect), no sex differences were found in the number of Ss who yielded to the group influence; (2b) on neutral trials (group choice was correct) boys made fewer errors than girls; (2c) on the post experimental questionnaire no differences were found in the number of boys and girls who indicated they thought the experiment was "some kind of trick."

Samorajczyk, J. Children's responsiveness to imagination suggestions during school entry. *Developmental Psychology*, 1969, *1*, 211–15.
  Subjects: $N = 60$; 6 yrs. **Measures:** The Barber Suggestibility Scale (BSS), a scale composed of 8 "make-believe" suggestions, was individually administered to each S. Ss' responses to each of the 8 suggestions (e.g. lowering their arms in response to the suggestion that their arms were feeling heavier, closing their hands in response to the suggestion that their hands were stuck together, etc.) were recorded. Afterward, Ss who exhibited the suggested effect were asked whether they had really felt the effect. **Results:** No sex differences.

Sampson, E. E., and Hancock, F. T. An examination of the relationship between ordinal position, personality and conformity. *J. Personality & Social Psychology*, 1967, 5, 398–407.
  Subjects: $N = 251$; 15–17 yrs. **Measures:** Ss made estimates of (a) the number of circles on a poster held up before them, and (b) the height of a triangle, once before and once after exposure to fictitious group norms. Ss also completed a shortened version of the Mandler-Sarason Test Anxiety Scale, and the need for achievement, need for autonomy, and need for affiliation measures from Edward's Personal Preference Schedule. **Results:** (1) Boys conformed to the group norms more than girls ($p < .05$), an effect almost entirely attributable to the high level of conformity of firstborn sons. (2) No sex differences were found in test anxiety, n achievement, n autonomy, or n affiliation.

Sander, L. Twenty-four-hour distributions of sleeping and waking over the first month of life in different infant caretaking systems. Paper presented at the meeting of the Society for Research in Child Development, Philadelphia, 1973.
  Subjects: $N = 18$; newborns awaiting adoption. **Measures:** Around-the-clock observations were made of 9 infants from days 2 to 25. Data were obtained on the other infants from days 11 to 25. **Results:** Both during the day and night, girls spent more time sleeping than boys did.

Sandidge, S., and Friedland, S. J. Sex role-taking and aggressive behavior in children. Paper presented at the meeting of the Society for Research in Child Development, Philadelphia, 1973.
  Subjects: $N = 40$; 9–10 yrs (low SES). **Measures:** Ss were shown schematic cartoons of a boy or a girl speaking aggressively to another child of the same or opposite sex. Ss were asked to respond as they believed the second child would. Each response was scored either as an antisocial aggressive response or as a neutral-prosocial aggressive response. **Results:** There were no sex of S effects. Ss gave more antisocial aggressive responses when they anwered for girls than when they answered for boys ($p < .01$).

Santrock, J. W. Paternal absence, sex typing, and identification. *Developmental Psychology*, 1970, 2, 264–72.
  Subjects: $N = 60$; 4–6 yrs (black, low SES), father-absent (FA) or father-present (FP), and mothers. **Measures:** Mothers completed a revised Sears, Maccoby, and Levin maternal interview (MI). The children completed a structured doll-play interview (DPI) that assessed dependency (subordinate learning relationship by child doll toward mother and/or father doll, particularly mother), aggression (offensive action by doll same-sex as S), and masculinity-femininity (sex of picture selected during 12 choice sets). **Results:** Boys were more independent (DPI, $p < .05$), more aggressive (DPI, $p < .05$), and more masculine (DPI, $p < .001$; MI, $p < .001$) than girls.

Santrock, J. W. Relation of type and onset of father absence to cognitive development. *Child Development*, 1972, 43, 455–69.
  Subjects: $N = 286$; 12–17 yrs (father-absent). **Measures:** Ss filled out a questionnaire about their fathers. Ss' third- and sixth-grade Otis Quick Scoring IQ and Stanford Achievement Test Scores were obtained from their school's files. **Results:** (1) Boys had lower sixth-grade IQs

than girls did ($p < .05$). (2) Among Ss whose fathers were absent because of divorce, desertion, or separation, boys had lower sixth grade IQs than girls did ($p < .05$). (3) When father absence due to divorce, desertion, or separation occurred in the 12- to 13-year age period, girls had higher sixth-grade IQ scores than boys did ($p < .05$). (4) Among Ss whose fathers were dead, boys scored lower on the sixth-grade achievement test than girls did ($p < .01$). (5) When father absence due to death occurred in the 3- to 5-year age period, girls had higher sixth-grade achievement scores than boys did ($p < .05$).

Sarason, I. G., and Ganzer, V. J. Anxiety, reinforcement, and experimental instructions in a free verbalization setting. *J. Abnormal & Social Psychology*, 1962, 65, 300–307.
  Subjects: $N = 96$; 18–19 yrs (college). **Measures:** Ss were asked to talk about themselves. After a baseline period of 10 minutes, one group of Ss was reinforced for positive self-references (PSRs), while a second group was reinforced for negative self-references (NSRs). A third group of Ss was not reinforced at all. During baseline and conditioning, measures were taken of number of PSRs, NSRs, ambiguous self-references (ASRs), and references to others (ORs). **Results:** The differences between baseline and conditions in percentage of PSRs, NSRs, ASRs, and ORs were similar for men and women. The difference in total number of responses was higher for men than for women ($p < .01$).

Sarason, I. G., and Harmatz, M. G. Test anxiety and experimental conditions. *J. Personality & Social Psychology*, 1965, 1, 499–505.
  Subjects: $N = 144$; 15 yrs. **Measures:** Number of correct responses in 2 serial learning tasks. **Results:** No sex differences.

Sarason, I. G., and Koenig, K. P. Relationships of test anxiety and hostility to description of self and parents. *J. Personality & Social Psychology*, 1965, 2, 617–21.
  Subjects: $N = 48$; 18–21 yrs (college). **Measures:** Ss described themselves in general, themselves in academic situations, their fathers, and their mothers. Ss' descriptions were content-analyzed for positive, negative, and ambiguous evaluations of self and parents. **Results:** (1) Overall, women made more positive references than men did ($p < .05$). (2) No sex differences were found in self-descriptions. (3) For academic self-descriptions, women made more positive references than men did ($p < .05$). (4) Women made more positive references to mothers than men did ($p < .05$). (5) No sex differences were found in descriptions of fathers.

Sarason, I. G., and Minard, J. Test anxiety, experimental instructions and the Wechsler Adult Intelligence Scale. *J. Educational Psychology*, 1962, 53, 299–302.
  Subjects: $N = 96$; 18–21 yrs (college). **Measures:** Ss completed the Vocabulary, Comprehension, Block Design, and Digit Symbol subtests of the WAIS. **Results:** Men scored higher than women on the Block Design subtest ($p < .05$).

Sarason, I. G., and Winkel, G. H. Individual differences among subjects and experimenters and subjects' self-descriptions. *J. Personality & Social Psychology*, 1966, 3, 448–57.
  Subjects: $N = 48$; 18–21 yrs (college). **Measures:** Ss were asked to talk about themselves by either same-sex or opposite-sex peer Es. After Ss presented their self-descriptions, E and S rated each other's behavior. Es' behavior was also rated by observers. **Results:** (1) No sex differences were found in number of positive self-references (PSRs). Male Es elicited more PSRs than female Es did ($p < .05$). (2) Women made more negative self-references (NSRs) than men ($p < .05$). Male Es elicited more NSRs than female Es ($p < .025$). Women made slightly more NSRs than men when E was a female; when E was a male, women made a great many more NSRs than men ($p < .005$). (3) No sex differences were found in number of ambiguous self-references. (4) No sex differences were found in number of positive, ambiguous, or negative references to others or in the number of references to mother, father, or peers. (5) No sex differences were found in the number of statements asking E for further directions. (6) No sex differences were found in number of present-tense, future-tense, or past-tense references. Ss paired with female Es made more past-tense references than Ss paired with male Es ($p < .05$). (7) Men emitted more "ah's" than women ($p < .01$). (8) No sex differences were found in number of incompleted sentences. Women made more incompleted sentences than men when E was a male; men made more incompleted sentences than women when E was a female ($p < .025$). (9) No sex differences were found in number of sentence corrections, serial repetitions of 1 word or more, or stutters. (10) Women laughed more frequently than men ($p < .01$). (11) Women perceived Es to be more pleasant, courteous, encouraging, and interested than men did. Women liked the Es with whom they were paired more than men did ($p < .025$). Ss perceived female Es to be more enthusiastic, more pleasant, more professional, more encouraging, and friendlier than male Es. Men rated male Es as friendlier, more

personal, more relaxed, and more casual than female Es; on these same variables, women rated female Es more favorably than male Es ($p < .05$). (12) Es rated female Ss higher than male Ss on liking of S, S's enthusiasm, S's businesslike air, and body movements. (13) Female Es were rated as looking, smiling and nodding in agreement more frequently than male Es. Female Es were also described as making more hand gestures and placing their hands near their faces more frequently than male Es. Male Es were described as fidgeting and as manipulating objects with their hands more frequently than female Es.

Saravo, A., Bagby, B., and Haskins, K. Transfer effects in children's oddity learning. *Developmental Psychology*, 1970, *2*, 273–82.
    Subjects: $N = 144$; 3–7 yrs. Measures: Ss were given an oddity-learning pretraining problem, 6 oddity-discrimination problems, and either a reversal-oddity or new set oddity transfer test. Results: Girls learned the pretraining task in fewer trials than boys ($p < .025$). No sex differences were found in subsequent phases of the experiment.

Savell, J. M. Generalization of the effects of prior agreement and disagreement. *J. Personality & Social Psychology*, 1970, *15*, 94–100.
    Subjects: $N = 96$; 11–12 yrs. Measures: Ss indicated which of 2 pictures they preferred on each of 20 trials. A female E expressed agreement or disagreement with Ss' choice after each trial. Ss were then presented with an additional set of picture pairs; before calling for Ss' preference, E always announced her own choice first. The performance measure was the number of times Ss conformed to E's choice. Results: No sex differences.

Savitsky, J. C., and Izard, C. E. Developmental changes in the use of emotion cues in a concept formation task. *Developmental Psychology*, 1970, *3*, 350–57.
    Subjects: $N = 50$; 4–8 yrs. Measures: Ss chose the 2 most similar human faces from 96 triads of photographs. Two of each triad contained either common elements of hats or facial expressions of emotion. Results: No main sex differences.

Schaefer, C. E. Imaginary companions and creative adolescents. *Developmental Psychology*, 1969, *1*, 747–49.
    Subjects: $N = 800$; 15–17 yrs. Measures: Ss were asked the following question: "As a child, did you ever have any imaginary companions?" Results: No sex differences.

Schaffer, H. R., and Parry, M. H. Effects of stimulus movement on infants' wariness of unfamiliar objects. *Developmental Psychology*, 1972, *7*, 87 (brief report).
    Subjects: $N = 12$; 1 yr. Measures: Ss were exposed for 4 30-second trials to a 10-centimeter-high metal container with flashing lights and bleeps that were either in an approach movement, in a nonapproach movement (along an arc at a standard distance), or stationary. Latency to make contact was recorded. Results: No sex differences.

Schaie, K. W., and Strother, C. R. Cognitive and personality variables in college graduates of advanced age. In G. A. Talland, ed., *Human aging and behavior*. New York: Academic Press, 1968.
    Subjects: $N = 50$; 70–88 yrs (retired academics and professionals). Measures: Ss completed the Burgess Attitude Scale. Ss also rated how happy their lives had been and how satisfied they were with their accomplishments. Results: (1) No sex differences were found in feelings of happiness as assessed by the Burgess Attitude Scale. (2) No sex differences were found in Ss' self-ratings.

Schell, D. J. Conceptual behavior in young children: learning to shift dimensional attention. *J. Experimental Child Psychology*, 1971, *12*, 72–87.
    Subjects: $N = 72$; 4, 5 yrs. Measures: After an initial session to familiarize them with the task, Ss were trained by E to identify the relevant dimensions in a card-sorting task. During training, the relevant dimension was changed several times. A final testing, during which only 1 dimension was relevant, followed the training session. Measures were taken of the number of trials Ss needed to reach criterion. Results: No sex differences.

Schiff, W., and Dytell, R. S. Tactile identification of letters: a comparison of deaf and hearing children's performances. *J. Experimental Child Psychology*, 1971, *11*, 150–64.
    Subjects: $N = 293$; 7–19 yrs. Measures: Ss were presented with raised capital letters (2 to a page) and were asked to either point out the matching letter from a sheet on which the entire alphabet was printed (hearing and deaf Ss), use the manual alphabet to identify the matching letter (deaf Ss only), or vocally identify the letter (hearing Ss only). Results: No sex differences.

Schneider, F. W. Conforming behavior of black and white children. *J. Personality & Social Psychology*, 1970, *16*, 466–71.

EXPERIMENT I: Subjects: $N = 96$; 12, 13 yrs (white, black). Measures: After receiving erroneous judgments from a unanimous peer majority, Ss judged which of 3 geometric figures was largest in area. The performance measure was the number of times Ss conformed to the majority's choice. Results: No sex differences.

EXPERIMENT II: Subjects: $N = 192$; 12, 13 yrs (white, black). Measures: Ss' attitudes toward the other ethnic group were measured by a modified version of the Miller and Biggs children's social distance scale. Results: No sex differences.

Scholnick, E. K. Inference and preference in children's conceptual performance. *Child Development*, 1970, *41*, 449–60.

Subjects: $N = 108$; 5, 7, 9 yrs. Measures: On each administration of a 2-trial concept-identification task, Ss were presented with a pair of geometric stimuli that varied on 1 of 3 dimensions (color, form, or size). Based on information provided to them by E, Ss had to infer which dimension was relevant and which value was correct. Results: No sex differences were found in number of errors made.

Scholnick, E. K. Use of labels and cues in children's concept identification. *Child Development*, 1971, *42*, 1849–58.

Subjects: $N = 96$; 5, 7 yrs. Measures: Ss were pretested on discriminative and vocabulary skills. They were given sample inference tasks to assure their knowledge of positive and negative instances of relevant cue location; 3 verbalization treatment groups were conducted: stimulus comparison, conjunctive labels, and repetition of locational cues. In the experimental task, Ss were asked to locate a single relevant cue among 4 choices in a 2-stimulus inference task. Results: No sex differences.

Scholnick, E. K., and Osler, S. F. Effect of pretest experience on concept attainment in lower- and middle-class children. *Developmental Psychology*, 1969, *1*, 440–43.

Subjects: $N = 192$; 8 yrs (low, middle SES). Measures: Ss were asked to separate geometric figures into 2 piles. The figures varied on 4 dimensions, only 1 of which was relevant: size (large and small), color (red and blue), form (circle and square), and number (single and double figures). After every correct response, Ss were rewarded with a marble. Measures were taken of the number of trials Ss needed to reach criterion. Results: No sex differences.

Schubert, J., and Cropley, A. J. Verbal regulation of behavior and IQ in Canadian Indian and white children. *Developmental Psychology*, 1972, *7*, 295–301.

Subjects: $N = 211$; 6–15 yrs (central Saskatchewan Indians), 9–14 yrs (white rural and urban Canadians), 11–14 yrs (northern Saskatchewan Indians). Measures: Ss were trained in the use of strategies for solving similarities and Block Design problems from the Wechsler Intelligence Scale for Children and were given a test of verbal regulation of behavior. Results: No sex differences.

Schwartz, D. W., and Karp, S. A. Field dependence in a geriatric population. *Perceptual & Motor Skills*, 1967, *24*, 495–504.

Subjects: $N = 120$; 17, 30–39, 58–82 yrs. Measures: Body Adjustment Test, Rod-and-Frame Test, Embedded Figures Test. Results: Among 17-year-old and 30-39-year-old Ss, men were more field-independent than women on all 3 tests. Among the 58-82-year-old Ss, no sex differences were found.

Schwartz, J. C. Effects of peer familiarity on the behavior of preschoolers in a novel situation. *J. Personality & Social Psychology*, 1972, *24*, 276–84.

Subjects: $N = 57$; 4 yrs. Measures: Ss were placed in a room containing novel and familiar toys, either alone, with a close friend, or with an unfamiliar peer. Ss' free behavior was rated for affect and motility. The amount of time Ss spent near or with each of 4 toys was also recorded. For Ss in the stranger and friend conditions, a record was kept of time spent looking at partner. Results: (1) No sex differences were found for any of the measures. (2) Boys fired the gun mounted on the novel copter toy more often than girls did ($p < .01$).

Schwartz, J. C., and Wynn, R. The effects of mothers' presence and previsits on children's emotional reactions to starting nursery school. *Child Development*, 1971, *42*, 871–81.

Subjects: $N = 108$; 3–5 yrs. Measures: On the first day of school, mothers left their children either immediately or 20 minutes after arriving. Each S's separation reaction was rated on a 6-point scale by a student teacher. During the last 20 minutes of free play, S's locus relative to others ("alone," "with teacher," "with peer") and his activity ("active," "passive," "inter-active") were recorded. Ratings were also made of S's motility and comfort in the classroom. S's emotional reaction to school was assessed on the first day and again 1 week later. **Results:** No sex differences.

Schwartz, S. H., and Clausen, G. T. Responsibility, norms, and helping in an emergency. *J. Personality & Social Psychology*, 1970, *16*, 299–310.
> **Subjects:** $N = 179$; 18–21 yrs (college). **Measures:** Ss were exposed to the tape-recorded sounds of a victim (in an adjoining room) experiencing a seizure. Ss were led to believe that either no other bystanders were present (2-person condition) or that 4 other bystanders were present (6-person condition). Half of the Ss assigned to the 6-person condition were informed that 1 of the other bystanders was medically competent (6-person-competent condition). The response measures were the speed and nature of Ss' response to the victim's cries for help. **Results:** (1) No main sex differences were found in speed of helping. In the 2-person groups, women responded more quickly than men ($p < .05$), whereas in the 6-person-competent condition, men responded more quickly than women ($p < .05$). No sex differences were found in the 6-person condition. (2) No main sex differences were found in the proportion of Ss who did not emerge from their rooms to help the victim. (3) Of these Ss who emerged from their rooms, more women than men said (in a postexperimental interview) that rather than help the victim directly, they intended to report the incident to others, or to simply see what was going on ($p < .05$, 1-tailed). No sex differences were found in the proportion of Ss who said they intended to do nothing. (4) In 6-person-competent groups, men were more likely than women to indicate (on a postexperimental questionnaire) that they had thought action might be made easier because others would join them in helping ($p < .05$). Taking the sample as a whole, women were more likely than men to express uncertainty about what steps to take ($p < .05$), to be more concerned that their actions might be deemed inappropriate ($p < .05$), to think about their lack of capability to help ($p < .01$), and to expect others to join them in helping ($p < .01$).

Seitz, V. R. Multidimensional scaling of dimensional preferences; a methodological study. *Child Development*, 1971, *42*, 1701–20.
> **Subjects:** $N = 144$; 4–6 yrs. **Measures:** Ss chose which of 2 stimuli was more like a third. Stimuli varied in color and form. Forced-choice form, forced-choice color, and nonforced-choice trials were pretested. **Results:** No sex differences.

Seitz, V. R., and Weir, M. W. Strength of dimensional preferences as a predicator of nursery-school children's performance on a concept shift task. *J. Experimental Child Psychology*, 1971, *12*, 370–86.
> **Subjects:** $N = 104$; 4–5 yrs. **Measures:** Ss' dimensional preference strengths for color and shape were scaled by a multidimensional comparison technique. Matched for kind and strength of preference, Ss performed a 2-choice simultaneous discrimination task (1–3 weeks later) with either color or form relevant to the solution. They then performed either intra- or extra-dimensional shift problems. Reinforcement was a marble for "correct" responses and nothing for "incorrect" ones. **Results:** No sex differences.

Self, P. A., Horowitz, F. D., and Paden, L. Y. Olfaction in newborn infants. *Developmental Psychology*, 1972, *7*, 349–63.
> **Subjects:** $N = 32$; 1, 2, 3 days. **Measures:** When respiration was stable and activity minimal, Ss were presented with odors of oil of anise, tincture of asafetida, oil of lavender, and tincture of valerian. Responses were recorded by respirometer and visual observation. **Results:** No consistent sex differences were found in olfactory sensitivity.

Selman, R. L. The relation of role-taking to the development of moral judgment in children. *Child Development*, 1971a, *42*, 79–91.
> **Subjects:** $N = 60$; 8, 9, 10 yrs. **Measures:** Ss completed Kohlberg's Moral Judgment Scale and 2 of Flavell's role-taking tasks. **Results:** No sex differences.

Selman, R. L. Taking another's perspective: role-taking development in early childhood. *Child Development*, 1971b, *42*, 1721–34.
> **Subjects:** $N = 60$; 4, 5, 6 yrs. **Measures:** Ss were given 2 role-taking tasks in which they were asked to predict a peer's responses in a situation in which Ss had more information than the peer. In a second task (designed by DeVries), competitive guessing and hiding behavior changed over time as role-taking ability increased. **Results:** There were no sex differences in verbal role-taking skill.

Semler, I. J., and Eron, L. D. Replication report: relationship of aggression in third grade children to certain pupil characteristics. *Psychology in the Schools*, 1967, *4*, 356–58.

Subjects: $N = 863$; 8 yrs. **Measures:** Each child rated every other child in his classroom on a series of items having to do with specific aggressive behaviors (Peer-Rate Index of Aggression). **Results:** Boys were rated higher in aggression than girls ($p < .001$).

Semler, I. J., Eron, L. D., Meyerson, L. J., and Williams, J. F. Relationship of aggression in third grade children to certain pupil characteristics. *Psychology in the Schools*, 1967, *4*, 85–88.

Subjects: $N = 567$; 8 yrs. **Measures:** Each child rated every other child in his classroom on a series of items having to do with specific aggressive behaviors (Peer-Rate Index of Aggression). **Results:** Boys were rated higher in aggression than girls ($p < .001$).

Serbin, L. A., O'Leary, K. D., Kent, R. N., and Tonick, I. J. A comparison of teacher response to the pre-academic and problem behavior of boys and girls. *Child Development*, 1973, *44*, 796–804.

Subjects: 15 female teachers and their pupils (ages 3–5). Number of children in each class ranged from 12 to 17. **Measures:** Teachers' responses to 2 classes of behavior—disruption (ignoring teacher directions, destruction of materials, and aggression toward others) and dependency (crying, proximity to the teacher, and solicitation of teacher attention—were recorded. Also observed were teachers responses to appropriate participation in ongoing classroom activities. **Results:** (1) Boys emitted more aggressive ($p < .02$) and ignoring ($p < .02$) responses than girls. Girls were observed within arm's reach of their teachers more often than boys ($p < .01$). No sex differences were found in frequency of crying or solicitation of teacher attention. (2) Teacher response to disruptive behaviors: (a) teachers were more likely to respond when boys were aggressive than when girls were ($p < .05$); teachers did not respond at different rates to boys' and girls' ignoring responses; (b) boys received more loud reprimands for disruptive behaviors than girls ($p < .02$); no differences were found between boys and girls in frequency of receipt of soft reprimands (audible only to the child and his neighbors) or other forms of negative attention. (3) Teacher response to dependent behaviors: (a) teachers were more likely to respond to boys when they solicited attention than to girls ($p < .01$); rates of praise, hugging, and brief conversation (nondirectional instruction less than 1 sentence in length) in response to solicitation were not different for boys and girls; 3 classes of teacher response to solicitation—extended conversation, brief direction (telling child to do something), and extended direction (detailed instructions or demonstration intended to teach the child how to do something for himself)—were all given at higher rates to boys than to girls ($p < .05$, $p < .02$, $p < .02$); (b) no difference was found in the rate of teacher attention received by boys and girls for being close; girls received more teacher attention when they were near her than when participating in classroom activities farther away; boys did not ($p < .01$); (c) rate of teacher response to crying could not be analyzed because of the low base rates of this behavior. (4) Teacher response to appropriate participation in ongoing classroom activities: (a) teachers responded at higher rates to boys than to girls ($p < .001$); (b) praise, brief directions, and extended directions were given more often to boys than to girls ($p < .01$, $p < .001$, $p < .01$); (c) boys were hugged more frequently than girls ($p < .02$); (d) teachers engaged in extended conversation more often with boys than with girls ($p < .01$). (5) No sex differences were found in the frequency of the following teacher behaviors: brief conversation, touching, and helping. (6) On a postexperimental questionnaire, teachers reported giving more loud reprimands to boys than to girls. They were not aware of responding differentially to boys and girls, or of giving different amounts of positive or instructional attention to either sex.

Sewell, J. B., III, Bowen, P., and Lieberman, L. R. Projective study of college students' attitudes towards marriage. *Perceptual & Motor Skills*, 1966, *23*, 418.

Subjects: $N = 40$; 18–21 yrs (college). **Measures:** Ss were presented with 24 photographs of young men and women, half of whom were judged to be good-looking, the other half of average attractiveness. Ss were told that 6 of the men and 6 of the women were married. Ss' task was to pick out the married persons. **Results:** Women thought that more of the good-looking males were married than men did.

Seyfried, B. A., and Hendrick, C. When do opposites attract? When they are opposite in sex and sex-role attitudes. *J. Personality & Social Psychology*, 1973, *25*, 15–20.

Subjects: $N = 89$; 18–21 yrs (college). **Measures:** Ss completed the Masculine-Feminine Preferences Test (MFPT), a scale designed to measure sex-role attitudes; 29 Ss who had ambiguous or inverted sex-role preferences on this measure were dropped from the study. Ss then examined two MFPT forms (supposedly completed by strangers) and were asked to evaluate each stranger on several scales; 4 types of stimulus persons were created by E: a masculine male, a masculine female, a feminine male, and a feminine female. **Results:** (1) Men rated strangers with masculine attitudes more similar than strangers with feminine attitudes ($p < .05$). No difference was found in women's ratings. No interaction was found between sex of S and sex of stranger. (2) Men rated masculine males more similar than feminine ($p < .05$). (3) Men's similarity ratings of the masculine female and the feminine female did not differ; nor did women's similarity ratings of the masculine male and the feminine male differ. (4) Men liked the masculine male more than any other stranger (feminine male, $p < .05$; masculine female, $p < .05$; feminine female, N.S.). Men did not differ in their like-dislike ratings of either the feminine female or the masculine female. The feminine male was disliked more than any other stranger. (5) Women liked the masculine male more than any other stranger (masculine female, $p < .05$; feminine male, $p < .05$; feminine female, N.S.). Women did not differ in their like-dislike ratings of the feminine male and the masculine female.

Sgan, M. L. Social reinforcement, socioeconomic status, and susceptibility to experimenter influence. *J. Personality & Social Psychology*, 1967, 5, 202–10.
> **Subjects:** $N = 72$; 6 yrs (low, middle SES). **Measures:** Ss indicated their preference for 1 member of each of 14 pairs of pictures. The response measure was the number of times Ss changed an initial preference to agree with E's stated preference on a subsequent administration of the task. **Results:** (1) No main sex differences were found. (2) Low SES boys changed less often than low SES girls ($p < .05$), middle SES girls ($p < .05$), and middle SES boys ($p < .02$). The latter 2 groups did not differ from each other.

Shantz, C. U. A developmental study of Piaget's theory of logical multiplication. *Merrill-Palmer Quarterly*, 1967a, *13*, 121–37.
> **Subjects:** $N = 72$; 7, 9, 11 yrs. **Measures:** Multiplication of classes was assessed by the revised children's Raven's Progressive Matrices Test. Multiplication of asymmetric logical relations was assessed by a specially constructed multiple-relations test. Multiplication of spatial relations was assessed by a modified version of Piaget's landscape test. **Results:** No sex differences.

Shantz, C. U. Effects of redundant and irrelevant information on children's seriation ability. *J. Experimental Child Psychology*, 1967b, 5, 208–22.
> **Subjects:** $N = 72$; 7, 9, 11 yrs. **Measures:** Ss were presented with a vertical series of 4 geometric figures that systematically varied on at least 2 dimensions (e.g. 1 set of figures decreased in size and increased in color brightness as viewed from top to bottom). Between the third and fourth member of each array was an empty space. Ss' task was to choose from among 12 figures the one that best completed the series. Performance measures were number of correct choices and latency to solution. **Results:** No sex differences.

Shapira, A., and Madsen, M. C. Cooperative and competitive behavior of kibbutz and urban children in Israel. *Child Development*, 1969, 40, 609–17.
> **EXPERIMENT I: Subjects:** $N = 80$; 6–10 yrs (kibbutz, urban). **Measures:** Same-sex groups of 4 were tested on Madsen's Cooperation Board. Prizes were rewarded first on a group and then on an individual basis. In both conditions, cooperation was adaptive. **Results:** No sex differences were found in the group reward condition. In the individual reward condition, no mention was made of a first-order sex difference.
> **EXPERIMENT II: Subjects:** $N = 80$; 6–10 yrs (identical to the sample in Experiment I). **Measures:** Same-sex groups of 4 were tested on Madsen's Cooperation Board. Prizes were rewarded only on an individual basis. The board was altered to make competition adaptive. **Results:** Urban boys were more competitive than urban girls (no significance test was reported). No sex differences were found in the kibbutz sample.

Shapiro, A. H. Verbalization during the preparatory interval of a reaction-time task and development of motor control. *Child Development*, 1973, 44, 137–42.
> **Subjects:** $N = 96$; 5, 8 yrs. **Measures:** Ss in 1 group were initially pretrained with a metronome to either say or whisper the nonsense word "veb"; Ss in a second group were pretrained to either whisper or count aloud the numbers 1 to 10. Control Ss simply listened to the metronome. All Ss participated in a reaction-time task. On each trial, a buzzer was followed 9 seconds later by a chime that served as the "press" signal for Ss. During the 9-second interval between the buzzer and the chime, Ss repeated the cues they had learned during pretraining. Measures were taken of reaction time and number of errors of anticipation (premature key presses during the interval between the buzzer and the chime). Eye movements

and blinks, gross body movement, and EOG (electroculogram) and EMG (electromograph) frequencies were also recorded. **Results:** Whispering either the numbers 1–10 or the nonsense word "veb" up until presentation of the chime hindered girls' performance on the reaction-time task more than it hindered boys'. No other sex differences were reported.

Shapiro, S. S. Aural paired associates learning in grade-school children. *Child Development*, 1966, *37*, 417–24.
> **Subjects:** $N = 80$; 10–11, 13–14 yrs. **Measures:** Ss were tested on a list of 8 aurally presented paired associates. The number of trials Ss needed to reach the criterion of 1 perfect recitation was recorded. **Results:** No main sex differences.

Sharan (Singer), S., and Weller, L. Classification patterns of underprivileged children in Israel. *Child Development*, 1971, *42*, 581–94.
> **Subjects:** $N = 357$; 6 yrs. **Measures:** (1) Ss were presented with 12 familiar objects. E picked up 1 object from the array and put it aside. Ss' task was to select from among the remaining 11 objects those that had some characteristic in common with the 1 chosen by E. This same procedure was followed with each of the 12 objects. After each sort, Ss were asked to explain their selection. (2) Ss were presented with groups of 2 or 3 objects and asked to explain why the objects within each group were alike or went together. Ss' explanations were scored on 2 major dimensions: style of categorization (categorical, inferential, relational-contextual, or descriptive) and grouping ability. (Ss were credited with a grouping response if they mentioned in their explanations all of the objects and at least 1 reason for grouping them together; Ss were charged with a nongrouping response if they failed to mention each of the objects they had grouped together or if they assigned different attributes to 2 or more objects; Ss' responses were classified as nonscorable if no verbal explanation was given or if their reasons were unclear.) (3) Ss were asked to draw a 5½-inch line as slowly as possible. The number of seconds Ss took to draw the line was recorded. **Results:** (1) Boys gave fewer grouping responses and more nonscorable responses than girls ($p < .01$, $p < .01$). (2) Girls employed the descriptive style of categorizing more frequently than boys ($p < .05$). (3) Boys drew the line more quickly than girls ($p < .01$).

Sharma, K. L. Dominance-deference: a cross cultural study. *J. Social Psychology*, 1969, *79*, 265–66.
> **Subjects:** $N = 293$; 18–20 yrs (Asian Indians). **Measures:** A dominance-deference scale, consisting of 10 dominance and 10 deference items, was administered to Ss, who were asked to select the 10 items that best described themselves. Ss' score was the number of dominance items selected. **Results:** No sex differences.

Shaw, J. I., and Skolnick, P. Attribution of responsibility for a happy accident. *J. Personality & Social Psychology*, 1971, *18*, 380–83.
> **Subjects:** $N = 116$; 18–21 yrs (college). **Measures:** After reviewing background data on a fictitious college male, Ss read about an accident (with a pleasant or unpleasant outcome) in which he was involved. A postexperimental questionnaire was administered. **Results:** (1) No sex differences were found in the amount of responsibility Ss attributed to the fictitious male for the accident. (2) Men more than women perceived the fictitious male as trustworthy ($p < .05$), identified with him ($p < .03$), and said they would have been likely to engage in the behavior (mixing chemicals) that led to the accident ($p < .001$).

Shears, L. M., and Behrens, M. G. Age and sex differences in payoff demands during tetrad game negotiations. *Child Development*, 1969, *40*, 559–68.
> **Subjects:** $N = 316$; 8, 9 yrs. **Measures:** Ss were assigned to groups of 4 children of the same age and sex. Each tetrad played 8 rounds of "Sticks and Chips." At the beginning of each round, sticks of different lengths were distributed to the players. The object of the game was for 2 or more players to join together to build the longest stick. Any pair that included the player with the longest stick could win, as could any triple alliance. Members of the winning coalition shared in a prize of 20 chips. The actual division of the chips was determined during the bargaining process. Players suggested possible payoff divisions to other players until a stable winning alliance was formed. **Results:** When holding the longest stick, boys were less accommodative (more exploitative) than girls (8-year-old Ss, $p < .05$; 9-year-old Ss, $p < .01$). No sex differences were found among Ss who held sticks of shorter lengths.

Shechtman, A. Age patterns in children's psychiatric symptoms. *Child Development*, 1970, *41*, 683–93.
> **Subjects:** $N = 546$; 5–8, 9–11, 12–14, 15–17 yrs (outpatients in a mental clinic). **Measures:** Ss' psychiatric records were assessed for 91 deviant behavior traits. **Results:** (1) Among 5-8-

year-old Ss, girls had a higher mean number of deviant behavior traits than boys. (2) Among 9-14-year-old Ss, more boys than girls were classified as externalizers (directing hostility against environment or others) or internalizers (exhibiting conflicts within self).

Shepard, W. O. Word association and definition in middle childhood. *Developmental Psychology*, 1970, *3*, 412 (brief report).
  Subjects: $N = 137$; 9, 11, 13 yrs. Measures: Ss wrote single-word associations to 20 words from the Palermo-Jenkins norms. Ss were also asked to define each word. An association was scored syntagmatic if it was of a different form class or often followed the stimulus word in natural language. A definition was scored simple-functional if Ss gave a way in which the word could be used. Definitions were scored complex-functional if both a synonym and a function were given. Results: (1) Among 9- and 11-year-old Ss, girls gave more syntagmatic responses than boys ($p < .01$). (2) Girls gave more complex definitions than boys ($p < .01$).

Shepard, W. O., and Ascher, L. M. Effects of linguistic rule conformity on free recall in children and adults. *Developmental Psychology*, 1973, *8*, 139 (brief report and personal communication).
  Subjects: $N = 96$; 6, 11, 18–21 yrs (college). Measures: Ss heard meaningful, anomalous (syntax preserved by violation of semantic rules), and unstructured 5-word strings read either normally (conversationally) or with uniform word emphasis. The response measure was the total number of words correctly recalled. Results: Girls recalled more words than boys did.

Sher, M. A., and Lansky, L. M. The It Scale for Children: effects of variations in the sex-specificity of the It figure. *Merrill-Palmer Quarterly*, 1968, *14*, 323–30.
  EXPERIMENT I: Subjects: $N = 32$; 5–6 yrs. Measures: Ss were administered the It Scale for Children (ITSC) with the It figure unconcealed. Results: Boys had higher masculine scores than girls ($p < .05$).
  EXPERIMENT II: Subjects: $N = 24$; 5–6 yrs. Measures: Ss were administered the ITSC with the It figure concealed. Afterward, Ss were asked to attribute a sex first to the concealed It figure and then to the unconcealed It figure. Results: Boys had higher masculine scores than girls ($p < .005$). Boys tended to call the concealed It a boy; girls tended to call the concealed It a girl ($p < .007$, 1-tailed). Of those Ss who made an own-sex attribution to the concealed It figure, more girls than boys changed their attributions upon seeing the It figures ($p < .025$, 1-tailed).
  EXPERIMENT III: Subjects: $N = 21$; 5–6 yrs. Measures: After attributing a sex to the unconcealed It figure, Ss responded to the ITSC for an It of that sex. Results: Girls called It a boy more than boys called It a girl ($p < .025$, 1- tailed). No sex differences were found in Ss' ITSC scores.

Sherif, C. W. Social distance as categorization of intergroup interaction. *J. Personality & Social Psychology*, 1973, *25*, 327–34.
  Subjects: $N = 315$; 18–21 yrs (white and black college). Measures: Ss judged how advisable it would be for a black student to decide to interact with whites in a series of situations, each described briefly. Ss' attitudes were not directly assessed. Rather, Ss classified the descriptions into as many categories as they felt suitable to differentiate among the situations. The response measure was the number of categories used. Upon completing the task, Ss were to label any categories in which they felt "quite uncomfortable" or "definitely uncomfortable," with the option of labeling any other categories if desired. The number of categories not labeled constituted the latitude of noncommitment. Results: (1) Men used fewer categories than women ($p < .01$). The sex difference was greater in the black sample than in the white sample. (2) Women's latitude of noncommitment was greater than men's ($p < .025$).

Shipman, V. C. Disadvantaged children and their first school experiences. Educational Testing Service Head Start Longitudinal Study, 1971.
  Subjects: Total $N = 1,875$; 3–4 yrs (white, black). Only sex differences significant at the $p < .01$ level were reported.
  EXPERIMENT I: Measures: ($N = 1,371$.) Ss were shown a picture of a girl named Jane and a picture of a boy named Johnnie and asked the following questions: (1) If Jane (Johnnie) really wants to be a boy (girl), can she (he) be? (2) If Jane's (Johnnie's) hair were short (long) like a boy's (girl's), then would she (he) be a boy (girl)? (3) If Jane (Johnnie) wore clothes like a boy (girl), then would she (he) be a boy (girl)? (4) If Jane (Johnnie) played with a boy's (girl's) toys, then would she (he) be a boy (girl)? (5) If Jane (Johnnie) had short (long) hair like a boy's (girl's) and wore clothes like a boy's (girl's) and played

with a boy's (girl's) toys, then would she (he) be a boy (girl)? **Results:** (1) Picture of Jane: No sex differences were found in response to question 1. In response to questions 2–5, boys answered in the negative more frequently than girls. (2) Picture of Johnnie: No sex differences were found in Ss' responses.

EXPERIMENT II: **Measures:** ($N = 1,194$.) For 6 trials Ss were shown a slide of 20 chromatic straight lines. On the seventh trial, a picture of chromatic curved lines was presented. The amount of time Ss looked at each picture was recorded after every trial. The response measures were (a) change in fixation time over trials 1–6, and (b) difference in fixation time between trials 6 and 7. Similar procedures were also followed with slides of chromatic and achromatic schematic representations of a family. After the chromatic slide was shown 6 times, the achromatic slide was presented on the seventh trial. **Results:** No sex differences.

EXPERIMENT III: **Measures:** ($N = 1,448$.) ETS Story Sequence Task I: Ss were given sets of drawings depicting animals in a variety of situations. Afterward, stories about the animals were read. Ss' task was to arrange the drawings according to the order in which the animals in the stories encountered situations. **Results:** No sex differences.

EXPERIMENT IV: **Measures:** ($N = 1,371$.) Brown IDS Self-Concept Referents Test: Each S was shown a picture of himself. He was then asked to rate the child in the photograph on 15 bipolar adjectives. **Results:** No sex differences were found in self-concept scores. Girls smiled at the picture of themselves more often than boys did.

EXPERIMENT V: **Measures:** ($N = 1,438$.) Children's Auditory Discrimination Inventory: Ss were presented with 2 pictures and told the name of each. Then E stated the name of only 1 of the pictures. Ss' task was to point to that picture. **Results:** Girls' performance was superior to that of boys.

EXPERIMENT VI: **Measures:** ($N = 1,395$.) Ss were asked to point once, and only once, to each circle in an array. Measures were taken of the number of omissions and repetitions. **Results:** Girls' performance was superior to boys'.

EXPERIMENT VII: **Measures:** ($N = 1,435$.) Educational Testing Service Matched Pictures Language Comprehension Test: Ss were presented with pairs of pictures. Though both pictures in each pair contained identical stimulus elements, they depicted different relationships between the elements. E then told Ss the names of both pictures without indicating which title went with which picture. Ss' task was to match each title with the correct picture. **Results:** No sex differences.

EXPERIMENT VIII: **Measures:** ($N = 1,411$.) Johns Hopkins Perceptual Test: Ss were asked to indicate which of several geometric shapes was identical to a standard. **Results:** No sex differences.

EXPERIMENT IX: **Measures:** ($N = 1,497$.) Hess and Shipman Toy Sorting Task: After being trained by their mothers, Ss were asked to sort a set of toys into groups as their mothers had shown them. Ss then explained why they sorted the toys as they did. **Results:** No sex differences were found in sorting. Girls cooperated with their mothers during training more than boys did.

EXPERIMENT X: **Measures:** ($N = 1,462$.) Same as Experiment IX, but with blocks. **Results:** No sex differences were found in sorting. Girls cooperated with their mothers during training more than boys did.

EXPERIMENT XI: **Measures:** ($N = 1,198$.) Peabody Picture Vocabulary Test, Forms A and B. **Results:** No sex differences.

EXPERIMENT XII: **Measures:** ($N = 1,403$.) Picture Completion subtest of the Wechsler Preschool and Primary Scale of Intelligence: Ss were asked to name or indicate the missing part in each of 23 pictures. **Results:** No sex differences.

EXPERIMENT XIII: **Measures:** ($N = 1,288$.) The Preschool Embedded Figures Test was administered. Measures were taken of the total number of correct items and of the latency of the first response to each item. **Results:** No sex differences.

EXPERIMENT XIV: **Measures:** ($N = 1,474$.) Ss were given the Preschool Inventory, a measure of achievement in areas regarded as necessary for success in school (e.g. listening-comprehension, writing, form copying, arithmetic). **Results:** Girls achieved higher scores than boys.

EXPERIMENT XV: **Measures:** ($N = 1,445$.) Ss were asked to choose between a toy that they could see and a paper bag that contained either 5 toys or none at all. **Results:** Boys chose the uncertain outcome (the paper bag) more frequently than girls.

EXPERIMENT XVI: **Measures:** ($N = 1,274$.) After placing a set of tiles in front of himself, E asked Ss (who previously had been provided with their own set of tiles) to "put out the same number." Measures were taken of the number of tiles Ss put out. E recorded whether Ss arranged their tiles in a pattern identical to the configuration of E's tiles. **Results:** No sex differences.

EXPERIMENT XVII: **Measures:** ($N = 1,470$.) Ss were asked to turn a crank as fast as they could for 15 seconds and to run as quickly as possible across a distance of 12 feet. **Results:** Boys turned the crank faster than girls. No sex differences were found in running speed.

EXPERIMENT XVIII: **Measures:** ($N = 1,091$.) Sigel Object Categorization Test: Ss were presented with 12 familiar objects. On each of 12 trials, E selected 1 of the objects and asked Ss to choose from among the 11 remaining objects those that shared some common property. After each trial, Ss explained why they selected the objects they did. Measures were taken of the adequacy of Ss' explanations and of the latency of their initial responses on each trial. **Results:** No sex differences.

EXPERIMENT XIX: **Measures:** ($N = 1,129$.) Seguin Form Board: Ss were presented with 10 differently shaped blocks and a large board with recesses corresponding to the various shapes, with instructions to place the blocks in their correct spots as quickly as possible. Measures were taken of the number of seconds it took Ss to complete the task and of the number of errors they made. Any attempt Ss made to put a block into the wrong recess on the board was considered an error. **Results:** No sex differences.

EXPERIMENT XX: **Measures:** ($N = 1,460$.) Form Reproduction Test: Ss were asked to make copies of 6 geometric forms. **Results:** Girls made more accurate copies than boys.

EXPERIMENT XXI: **Measures:** ($N = 1,098$.) Massad Mimicry Test, Part 1: Ss heard a tape-recorded model utter nonsense words. Ss were then asked to pronounce each word aloud. **Results:** Girls reproduced words more accurately than boys.

EXPERIMENT XXII: **Measures:** ($N = 1,060$.) Massad Mimicry Test, Part 2: Ss heard a tape-recorded model utter meaningful words. Ss were then asked to pronounce each word aloud. **Results:** No sex differences.

EXPERIMENT XXIII: **Measures:** ($N = 1,399$.) Ss were given the Matching Familiar Figures Test. Response times and error rates were recorded. **Results:** No sex differences.

EXPERIMENT XXIV: **Measures:** ($N = 1,458$.) Ss were asked to choose between a smaller immediate reward and a larger delayed reward. **Results:** No sex differences.

Shomer, R. W. Differences in attitudinal responses under conditions of implicitly manipulated group salience. *J. Personality & Social Psychology*, 1970, *15*, 125–32.
   Subjects: $N = 200$; 18–21 yrs (college). **Measures:** Ss responded anonymously to a questionnaire assessing attitudes toward feminism and child rearing in 1 of 3 group settings: all Ss of the same sex, half of the Ss from each sex, or all Ss of the same sex except one. **Results:** (1) Women were more pro-feminist than men ($p < .001$). No sex differences were found in attitudes toward child rearing. (2) Group composition had no effect on Ss' responses to the child-rearing items. With respect to feminist items, the effect of group composition was significant only for men ($p < .01$). Men who responded in the presence of a lone female member and a male E achieved the highest pro-feminist scores of any group, male or female. All male groups with a male E achieved the highest anti-feminist scores. Remaining male and female groups fell in between these 2 extremes.

Shomer, R. W., Davis, A. H., and Kelley, H. H. Threats and the development of coordination: further studies of the Deutsch and Krauss trucking game. *J. Personality & Social Psychology*, 1966, *4*, 119–26.
   Subjects: $N = 64$; 18–21 yrs (college). **Measures:** Same-sex pairs of Ss played a non-zero sum game formulated in terms of the interaction between 2 trucking firms. The amount of money Ss earned was directly related to the speed with which they achieved a state of cooperation. In order to provide a means for Ss to communicate with one another, half the dyads were provided with 2 buttons, one marked "threat" and the other marked "fine." By pressing the "threat" button, Ss could inform their partners of their intention to deliver a fine. By pressing the "fine" button Ss could impose a fine on their partners. **Results:** (1) Male dyads earned more money than female dyads ($p < .01$). (2) On the postexperimental questionnaire, more male than female dyads perceived and used the threat response as a signal to cooperate ($p < .01$).

Shortell, J. R., and Biller, H. B. Aggression in children as a function of sex of subject and sex of opponent. *Developmental Psychology*, 1970, *3*, 143–44 (brief report).
   Subjects: $N = 48$; 11 yrs. **Measures:** Ss were told they were competing in a reaction time experiment against a boy or a girl (actually E) in another room, and that on each trial the slower person would receive a loud tone. Each S chose the noise level for the "opponent's" tone (in case opponent lost) before each trial. Ss completed a semantic differential-rating scale about the opponents. **Results:** (1) Boys set higher noise level for the opponent to receive than girls did ($p < .05$). (2) Girl opponents had less aggression directed at them

than boy opponents did ($p < .01$). (3) Male opponents were rated as less aggressive ($p < .01$) than female opponents (this effect was due primarily to the low rating boys gave to male opponents). (4) Male opponents were rated as less socially desirable than female opponents ($p < .01$). Boys rated both male and female opponents about equally, whereas girls rated male opponents as less socially desirable than boys did ($p < .01$).

Shrader, W. K., and Leventhal, T. Birth order of children and parental report of problems. *Child Development*, 1968, *39*, 1165–75.
Subjects: $N = 599$; 6–17 yrs. Measures: Parents of Ss filled out a checklist of 237 items and described their child's "problem" area on an open-ended questionnaire (eating, sleep, elimination, speech, psychosomatics, self-destruction, school, sibling relations, self-feeling, fears, depression, passivity control, irresponsibility, motor behavior, psychosis, parent relations, sex, peer relations, and habits). Results: No sex differences.

Shuck, S. Z., Shuck, A., Hallam, E., Mancini, F., and Wells, R. Sex differences in aggressive behavior subsequent to listening to a radio broadcast of violence. *Psychological Reports*, 1971, *28*, 921–26.
Subjects: $N = 40$; 18–21 yrs (college). Measures: Ss were asked to shock a same-sex confederate every time he or she gave the wrong answer in a learning experiment. Results: Men administered higher levels of shock than women ($p < .001$).

Shultz, T. R., Charness, M., and Berman, S. Effects of age, social class, and suggestion to cluster on free recall. *Developmental Psychology*, 1973, *8*, 57–61.
Subjects: $N = 160$; 6, 10 yrs (low, middle SES). Measures: S looked at either 16 or 20 object drawings (younger Ss saw fewer) belonging to 1 of 4 categories (fruit, vehicle, clothing, furniture). Ss were asked for verbal recall after presentation of stimuli, either with specific labels verbalized or with specific labels and conceptual categories verbalized. Results: There were no sex differences in proportion of items recalled or amount of clustering in recall.

Shure, M. B., Spivack, G., and Jaeger, M. Problem-solving thinking and adjustment among disadvantaged preschool children. *Child Development*, 1971, *42*, 1791–1803.
Subjects: $N = 62$; 4 yrs. Measures: Ss were given a preschool interpersonal problem-solving test. Problems involved children of the same sex playing with toys (same toys in all cases except 1: trucks for boys, dolls for girls). Ss heard stories about children of their own sex. Authority problems were presented in the same manner. Ss were given an awareness-of-consequences test and a causality test. Ss were rated by teachers on adjustment. Results: No sex differences.

Sieber, J. E., and Lanzetta, J. T. Some determinants of individual differences in predecision information-processing behavior. *J. Personality & Social Psychology*, 1966, *4*, 561–71.
Subjects: $N = 60$; 18–21 yrs (college). Measures: Ss were exposed to slides designed to present ambiguous information (this was accomplished through the use of unusual and touched-up pictures). Ss' task was to identify the main objects in each slide. Slides were presented tachistoscopically for .01-second durations. Ss were free to observe each slide as frequently as they wished before making a decision. Prior to performing, Ss were trained either to name many possible solutions to given problems or to notice and evaluate relevant information in stimulus pictures. Control Ss received no prior training. The response measures were (a) number of queries (number of times Ss looked at each slide before making a decision), (b) amount of time taken between queries, (c) number of correct decisions, (d) amount of information given with each decision, and (e) amount of uncertainty Ss expressed about the correctness of their identifications. Results: (1) There were no main sex differences. (2) Men who were trained to name many possible solutions to given problems looked at the slides a greater number of times before making a decision than women who received similar training ($p < .05$).

Siebold, J. R. Children's rating responses as related to amount and recency of stimulus familiarization and stimulus complexity. *J. Experimental Child Psychology*, 1972, *14*, 257–64.
Subjects: $N = 72$; 10, 11 yrs. Measures: Ss rated their like or dislike for simple or complex figures from the Welsh Figure Preference Test during familiarization, concurrent testing, and post-testing phases. Results: No sex differences.

Siegel, A. W. Variables affecting incidental learning in children. *Child Development*, 1968, *39*, 957–68.
Subjects: $N = 96$; 8, 14 yrs. Measures: Ss operated a stimulus display and response console

to perform a learning-discrimination series of 3 tasks. Selected-stimuli drawings and incidental drawings were presented on a screen, and Ss had to choose the "correct" picture in order to receive the marble reward. There were 3 conditions in which the stimuli were presented with a varying number of incidental objects. Number of presentations was varied. Errors, incidental learning, and response latencies were measured. **Results:** No sex differences.

Siegel, A. W., and Kresh, E. Children's ability to operate within a matrix: a developmental study. *Developmental Psychology,* 1971, *4,* 232–39.
    Subjects: $N = 80$; 4–8 yrs (black and white). **Measures:** While viewing a covered 3 × 3 matrix and its uncovered attribute cells (defining matrix rows and columns), Ss chose duplicates of the matrix stimuli according to which cell of the matrix E pointed to. In a different order, Ss guessed the shape and color of the objects in each covered matrix cell. Next, with the matrix cells empty and uncovered, and with the attribute cells filled and uncovered, Ss placed matrix stimuli in their correct positions. Finally Ss identified the common attribute defining members of rows or columns. **Results:** No sex differences.

Siegel, A. W., and McBurney, D. H. Estimation of line length and number: a developmental study. *J. Experimental Child Psychology,* 1970, *10,* 170–80.
    Subjects: $N = 96$; 6–13 yrs. **Measures:** Ss were asked to hand-grip a tensiometer apparatus to match line lengths and verbal numbers; i.e. the longer the line or higher the number, the harder the hand grip should be squeezed. **Results:** There were no sex differences in hand grip as a function of line length or number size.

Siegel, A. W., and Stevenson, H. W. Incidental learning: a developmental study. *Child Development,* 1966, *37,* 811–17.
    Subjects: $N = 96$; 7–14 yrs. **Measures:** Ss were given successive-discrimination problems in 3 parts: (1) a 3-choice successive discrimination problem, (2) the presentation of each discriminative stimulus embedded in a stimulus complex with 3 other objects, and (3) a test of incidental learning in which incidental object and discriminative stimuli were presented separately. The response measure was the number of times Ss made response to incidental objects that were correct for stimulus complex in which they were embedded. **Results:** There were no sex differences in incidental learning scores for children.

Siegel, A. W., and Vance, B. J. Visual and haptic dimensional preference: a developmental study. *Developmental Psychology,* 1970, *3,* 264–66.
    Subjects: $N = 64$; 5, 6, 8 yrs. **Measures:** For 8 trials, Ss felt or saw 3 stimuli differing in size, form, and color in the visual condition, and in size, form, and texture in the haptic condition. Ss made judgments on which 2 of 3 stimuli were the same. Dimension preference was assessed. **Results:** (1) In the visual condition, girls had greater form preference than boys ($p < .05$). There were no sex differences in color preference scores or size preference scores. (2) In the haptic condition, there were no significant sex differences in form, texture, or size preference.

Siegel, L. S. The development of the ability to process information. *J. Experimental Child Psychology,* 1968, *6,* 368–83.
    Subjects: $N = 192$; 9, 11 yrs. **Measures:** Ss performed an information-processing task involving digits. **Results:** No sex differences.

Siegel, L. S. The sequence of development of certain number concepts in preschool children. *Developmental Psychology,* 1971, *5,* 357–61.
    Subjects: $N = 77$; 3–5 yrs. **Measures:** Ss were given tests of continuous and discrete magnitude discrimination, equivalence, conservation, ordination, seriation, and addition. **Results:** No sex differences.

Siegel, L. S. Development of the concept of seriation. *Developmental Psychology,* 1972, *6,* 135–37.
    Subjects: $N = 415$; 3–9 yrs. **Measures:** Ss were asked to choose stimuli of varying relative heights (smallest, middle-sized, next to largest, etc.) from 2-, 3-, or 4-choice stimulus arrays to the criterion of 9 out of 10 consecutive correct responses. **Results:** No sex differences.

Siegel, W., and Van Cara, F. The effects of different types of reinforcement on young children's incidental learning. *Child Development,* 1971, *42,* 1596–1601.
    Subjects: $N = 108$; 5, 7, 9 yrs. **Measures:** Ss operated a stimulus-response console involving a 3-part successive discrimination task (original learning, presentation of incidental stimuli,

and a test of recognition and recall of incidental stimuli). There were 3 reinforcement conditions: right-blank, wrong-blank, and right-wrong. **Results:** No sex differences.

Siegelman, M. Evaluation of Bronfenbrenner's questionnaire for children concerning parental behavior. *Child Development,* 1965, *36,* 163–74.
   Subjects: $N = 212$; 9, 10, 11 yrs (low SES). **Measures:** Ss completed Bronfenbrenner's Parent Behavior Questionnaire. **Results:** (1) Boys rated their mothers as using more physical punishment and deprivation of privileges than girls did. No sex differences were found in Ss' ratings of (a) their mothers' use of affective reward, affective punishment, social isolation, expressive rejection, prescription, or principled discipline; (b) their mothers' display of nurturance, instrumental companionship, affiliative companionship, protectiveness, power, or indulgence; (c) the extent of their mothers' achievement demands. (2) Boys rated their fathers as using more physical punishment, deprivation of privileges, expressive rejection, and social isolation than girls did. Girls rated their fathers as using more affective reward than boys did. No sex differences were found in Ss' ratings of (a) their fathers' use of affective punishment, prescription, or principled discipline; (b) their fathers' display of nurturance, instrumental companionship, affiliative companionship, protectiveness, power, or indulgence; (c) the extent of their fathers' achievement demands.

Siegenthaler, B. M., and Barr, C. A. Auditory figure-background perception in normal children. *Child Development,* 1967, *38,* 1163–67.
   Subjects: $N = 100$; 4, 5, 7, 9, 11 yrs. **Measures:** Speech reception threshold (SRT) was measured by the Picture Identification test, a test requiring Ss to point to pictures upon demand. Ss were given the test twice, once in the absence of noise and once in the presence of a tape recording of a jumble of voices (40-db). Shifts in SRT due to the effect of masking noises were recorded. **Results:** Among the 11-year-old Ss, boys showed less of an increase in SRT than girls ($p < .02$).

Signori, E. I., and Rempel, R. Research on the picture titles subtest of the IES Test. *Perceptual & Motor Skills,* 1966, *22,* 161–62.
   Subjects: $N = 182$; 18–21 yrs (college). **Measures:** The Picture Titles Subtest of the IES (Impulse, Ego, Superego). Test consists of 12 pictures depicting I, E, and S activity. Ss' task was to give each picture an appropriate title. Responses based on inconsequential details of the pictures were designated defensive (D). **Results:** There were no sex differences in the number of I, E, and S responses. Boys made more D responses than girls ($p < .02$).

Silverman, I. Role-related behavior of subjects in laboratory studies of attitude change. *J. Personality & Social Psychology,* 1968, *8,* 343–48.
   Subjects: $N = 403$; 18–21 yrs (college). **Measures:** After reading a persuasive message, Ss responded to 4 opinion items. The response measure was the amount Ss were persuaded by the message. **Results:** No sex differences.

Silverman, I., Shulman, A. D., and Wiesenthal, D. L. Effects of deceiving and debriefing psychological subjects on performance in later experiments. *J. Personality & Social Psychology,* 1970, *14,* 203–12.
   Subjects: $N = 98$; 18–21 yrs (college). **Measures:** Ss listened to 4 persuasive communications and then rated their agreement or disagreement with each. Ss also completed the Rotter Incomplete Sentence Blank, Gough and Heilbrun's Adjective Check List, and a measure of responsiveness to implicit demands. **Results:** (1) No sex differences were found in persuasibility, responsiveness to implicit demands, or maladjustment scores on the RISB. (2) No sex differences were found in total number of adjectives checked or in percentage of favorable adjectives checked. Two of the 21 subscales yielded sex differences: men showed less counseling readiness ($p < .01$) and more self-control ($p < .01$) than women.

Silverman, I., Shulman, A. D., and Wiesenthal, D. L. The experimenter as a source of variance in psychological research: modeling and sex effects. *J. Personality & Social Psychology,* 1972, *21,* 219–27.
   Subjects: $N = 224$; 18–21 yrs (college). **Measures:** Male and female Es were filmed while administering a person-perception task to confederates. Ss were then shown these films and asked to rate each E on 22 personality traits. **Results:** (1) Women made more ratings in the vain, competent, and vigorous directions than men ($p < .01$). (2) Female Es were judged as more vigorous, competent, and extraverted, and as less warm than male Es.

Silverman, I. W. Incidence of guilt reactions in children. *J. Personality & Social Psychology*, 1967, 7, 338–40.

Subjects: $N = 199$; 11 yrs. Measures: Ss were given the opportunity to score their own tests. On the basis of their scoring behavior, Ss were classified as either noncheaters (did not falsify any answers), low cheaters (falsified some answers, but not enough to win a prize), or high cheaters (falsified a sufficient number of answers to win a prize). Ss were then invited to volunteer from 1 to 60 minutes of their time for an experiment scheduled at a later date. The response measure was amount of time Ss volunteered. Results: (1) Fewer girls than boys were classified as noncheaters; fewer boys than girls were classified as low cheaters ($p < .01$). No sex difference was found in number of high cheaters. (2) No sex difference was found in the number of minutes volunteered.

Silverman, J., Buchsbaum, M., and Stierlin, H. Sex differences in perceptual differentiation and stimulus intensity control. *J. Personality & Social Psychology*, 1973, 25, 309–18.

Experiment I: Subjects: $N = 30$; 18–22 yrs. Measures: The Rod and Frame Test was administered to Ss. They were then given the EEG averaged evoked response measure of perceptual differentiation. Line segments appearing in 1 of 4 positions of tilt to the right of the vertical (0, 6, 19, and 30 degrees) were presented 512 times. Ss were told to judge whether or not each line was vertical with respect to the walls of the room. They were asked not to make any vocal or motor response. Ss' EEG responses were recorded. Results: (1) Men had lower RFT error scores than women ($p < .02$) No sex differences were found in averaged evoked-response indexes.

Experiment II: Subjects: $N = 31$; 14–17 yrs (patients with behavior disorders), 13–20 yrs (their siblings). Measures: The Rod and Frame Test was administered to Ss. They were then given the EEG averaged evoked response measure of stimulus intensity control. 4 intensities of light flashes were presented to Ss in randomized blocks of 10 of the same intensity for 480 trials. Ss' EEG responses were recorded. The response measure was the rate of increase of averaged evoked-response amplitude in relationship to the intensity of the stimulus. Results: (1) Male siblings had lower RFT error scores than female siblings ($p < .05$). No sex differences were found among patients. (2) Male siblings evidenced lower averaged evoked-response slopes than female siblings ($p < .05$). Male patients evidenced higher averaged evoked-response slopes than female patients ($p < .05$).

Simner, M. L. Newborn's response to the cry of another infant. *Developmental Psychology*, 1971, 5, 136–50 (and personal communication).

Experiment I: Subjects: $N = 94$; 2–3 days. Measures: Ss were exposed to the taped spontaneous cry of a 5-day-old female infant. The duration of Ss' cries was recorded. Results: No sex differences.

Experiment II: Subjects: $N = 25$; 2–3 days (15 Ss from Experiment I). Measures: Same as Experiment I. Results: No sex differences.

Experiment IV: Subjects: $N = 30$; 2–3 days. Measures: At each of 2 testings spaced 24 hours apart, Ss were exposed to the taped spontaneous cry of a 5-day-old female infant. The duration of Ss' cries was recorded. Results: No sex differences were found in cry duration scores. Girls' reactions to the female infant's cries were more stable than boys'.

Experiment IVa: Subjects: $N = 100$; 2–3 days. Measures: Same as Experiment I. Results: No sex differences.

Simon, W. E. Some sociometric evidence for validity of Coopersmith's Self-Esteem Inventory. *Perceptual & Motor Skills*, 1972, 34, 92–94.

Subjects: $N = 129$; 11 yrs. Measures: Coopersmith's Self-Esteem Inventory. Results: No sex differences.

Sistrunk, F. Negro-white comparisons in social conformity. *J. Social Psychology*, 1971, 85, 77–85.

Subjects: $N = 64$; 16–17 yrs (Upward Bound students, black and white). Measures: Ss were presented with a number of statements of fact and asked to indicate their agreement or disagreement with each. Before responding to each item, Ss were informed of the majority judgment of a group of persons who had been questioned previously. The number of times Ss conformed to the inaccurate response of the majority rather than give the correct answer was recorded. Results: Among black Ss, girls conformed more frequently than boys did. Among white Ss, no sex differences were found.

Sistrunk, F., and McDavid, J. W. Sex variable in conforming behavior. *J. Personality & Social Psychology*, 1971, *17*, 200–207.

EXPERIMENT I: Subjects: $N = 80$; 18–21 yrs (college). Measures: On each of 45 statements in a conformity measure constructed to control for the sex relatedness of items, Ss were informed whether the majority of a previous college sample had agreed or disagreed with the statement. The response measure was the number of times Ss conformed to the majority opinion. Results: (1) Overall, there were no sex differences in conformity. (2) By item, there were no sex differences in conformity to masculine items; men conformed to neutral and feminine items more than women.

EXPERIMENT II: Subjects: $N = 90$; 18–21 yrs (college). Measures: Same as Experiment I. Results: (1) Overall, no sex differences were found in conformity. (2) Women conformed to masculine items more than men did. There were no sex differences in conformity to neutral or feminine items.

EXPERIMENT III: Subjects: $N = 40$; 14–17 yrs. Measures: Same as Experiment I. Results: (1) There were no main sex differences. (2) Men conformed to feminine items more than women did; women conformed to masculine items more than men did. There were no sex differences in conformity to neutral items.

EXPERIMENT IV: Subjects: $N = 60$; 18–21 yrs (college). Measures: Same as Experiment I, except that Ss were told the sample on which the normative data were based had been either all male or all female. Results: (1) Neither sex of subject nor sex of influence source was significant as a main effect. (2) Women conformed to masculine items more than men. There were no sex differences in conformity to neutral and feminine items.

Sistrunk, F., Clement, D. E., and Guenther, Z. C. Developmental comparisons of conformity across two cultures. *Child Development*, 1971, *42*, 1175–85.

Subjects: $N = 80$; 9–10, 13–14, 17–18, 20–21 yrs (Brazil, U.S.). Measures: In an Asch-type conformity experiment, Ss judged which of 3 lines was longest. Results: Among Brazilian Ss, girls conformed more at ages 9–10 and 20–21, whereas boys conformed more at ages 13–14 and 17–18 (significance not tested). Among American Ss, no sex differences were found.

Sitkei, E. G., and Meyers, C. E. Comparative structure of intellect in middle- and lower-class four year olds of two ethnic groups. *Developmental Psychology*, 1969, *1*, 592–604.

Subjects: $N = 100$; 3–4 yrs (white and black, low and middle SES). Measures: Ss were given the following tests: (1) Peabody Picture Vocabulary; (2) Action-Agent Convergent (Ss must supply the right word to such sentence stems as "What runs——?"); (3) Comprehension (Ss are tested for their understanding of the WISC comprehension items); (4) Picture Description (Ss are asked to describe pictures); (5) Action-Agent Divergent (Ss must give multiple answers to such questions as "What runs——?"); (6) Orpet Utility (Ss must give multiple uses for objects); (7) Monroe Language Classification (Ss are asked to name as many examples as possible of items belonging in a certain category, e.g. animals); (8) ITPA Vocal Encoding (Ss must provide descriptions); (9) Color-Form Matching, and (10) Figure Matching (both require Ss to quickly but accurately discriminate visually presented material); (11) Pre-Raven Matrices (Ss are asked to select the right fill-in for a missing portion of a visual matrix); (12) Design Discrimination (Ss must select the 1 item in a series that differs from the others); (13) Letter Span, (14) Binet Digits, and (15) ITPA Auditory Vocal Sequencing (Ss are required to memorize sequences of letters or digits); (16) Memory for Sentences (Ss are given the sentences-memory items of the Binet); (17) Paired Pictures, and (18) Picture Memory (after naming objects and pictures, Ss are later asked to recall or identify them); (19) Object Memory, and (20) Visual Sequence Memory (Ss are tested for their memory of objects and nonrepresentational play materials); (21) Cube Test (no explanation given); (22) Picture Description (no explanation given). Results: (1) Among lower SES white Ss, girls were superior to boys on the Pre-Raven Matrices, and boys were superior to girls on the Object Memory Test. (2) Among middle SES white Ss, no sex differences were found. (3) Among lower SES black Ss, girls were superior to boys on the Action-Agent Divergent and the ITPA Vocal Encoding tests, and boys were superior to girls on the Picture Memory test. (4) Among middle SES black Ss, girls were superior to boys on the Action-Agent Divergent, Letter Span, and Memory for Sentences tests.

Skolnick, E. K. Effects of stimulus availability in children's inferences. *Child Development*, 1971, *42*, 183–94.

Subjects: $N = 144$; 5, 7 yrs. Measures: On each trial of a concept identification task, Ss were either sequentially or simultaneously presented with 2 stimuli. Each pair differed in shape (flower or circle) or color (red or green). On the basis of information provided by E, Ss inferred which dimension was relevant and which value was correct. **Results:** No sex differences.

Skolnick, P. Reactions to personal evaluations: a failure to replicate. *J. Personality & Social Psychology*, 1971, *18*, 62–67.

Subjects: $N = 114$; 18–21 yrs (college). **Measures:** Ss were induced to believe they had failed or succeeded on 2 performance tests; a control group was left uncertain as to how they performed. After receiving positive or negative evaluation from a stooge, Ss rated the stooge on a semantic differential scale. Ss then rated themselves on a similar scale and completed a questionnaire designed to measure self-esteem. **Results:** No sex differences.

Slaby, R. G. Verbal regulation of aggression and altruism in children. Paper presented at the First International Conference on the "Determinants and origins of aggressive behavior." Monte Carlo, 1973.

EXPERIMENT I: **Subjects:** $N = 60$; 8–9 yrs. **Measures:** 24 groups of 3 words each were read to Ss. After hearing each group, Ss were asked to select 1 of the 3 words and repeat it out loud. Ss were reinforced for selecting either the aggressive, the neutral, or the helpful word in each triad. Afterward, Ss were tested for aggressive behavior on a punching machine. Ss were told another child was in an adjacent room solving arithmetic problems. Every time the other child made a mistake, Ss were asked to deliver a punch to the other child by pressing a button. The buttons were numbered 1 through 10, with number 1 supposedly delivering a soft punch, number 5 a medium punch, and number 10 a hard punch. The measure of aggressive behavior was the sum of Ss' button-press responses. **Results:** (1) No sex differences were found in Ss' performance on the verbal learning task. (2) Boys had higher aggression scores than girls ($p < .05$).

EXPERIMENT II: **Subjects:** $N = 66$; 8–9 yrs. **Measures:** Same as Experiment I, except that following the verbal training procedure, Ss were tested for altruistic behavior rather than aggressive behavior. As in Experiment I, Ss were told another child was in the next room working on a set of arithmetic problems. Every time the child solved a problem correctly, Ss were asked to reward him with pennies (ranging from 1 to 5). For each trial on which Ss rewarded the child with fewer than 5 pennies, they were allowed to keep the extra money. The response measure was the total number of pennies Ss gave the other child. **Results:** (1) No sex differences were found in Ss' performance on the verbal learning task. (2) No sex differences were found in altruism scores.

Slaby, R. G., and Parke, R. D. Effect of resistance to deviation of observing a model's affective reaction to response consequences. *Developmental Psychology*, 1971, *5*, 40–47.

Subjects: $N = 132$; 5–8 yrs. **Measures:** Each S watched a filmed male peer model play with prohibited toys and display either a positive, negative, or neutral emotional affect upon being socially rewarded or punished. Ss were left alone with identical toys for 15 minutes. **Results:** (1) Among Ss who saw the model rewarded and displaying no affect, boys touched the prohibited toys more often and for longer periods than girls. There were no sex differences on same measures when Ss saw the model rewarded and showing positive affect, or rewarded and showing negative affect. (2) There were no sex differences on number or duration of touches when Ss saw model punished, regardless of model's affect upon being punished. (3) There were no sex differences on latency to first touch of prohibited toys, regardless of consequences to model or model affect.

Slobin, D. I. Antonymic phonetic symbolism in three natural languages. *J. Personality & Social Psychology*, 1968, *10*, 301–5.

Subjects: $N = 46$; 18–21 yrs (college). **Measures:** Ss matched English antonym pairs with antonym pairs from Thai and Kanarese. **Results:** No sex differences.

Slovic, P. Risk-taking in children: age and sex differences. *Child Development*, 1966, *37*, 169–76.

Subjects: $N = 1,047$; 6–16 yrs. **Measures:** Ss at a county fair performed a switch-pulling game as a measure of risk taking. **Results:** (1) Among 11-, 14-, 15-, and 16-year-old Ss, girls stopped more often than boys. (2) Girls won more candy (per person) than boys as a result of their caution.

Smart, M. S., and Smart, R. C. Self-esteem and social-personal orientation of Indian 12- and 18-year-olds. *Psychological Reports*, 1970, *27*, 107–15.

Subjects: $N = 267$; 11–12, 18 yrs. **Measures:** Carlson's measures of self-esteem and social-personal orientation were administered to Ss. **Results:** Among preadolescent Ss, girls had higher self-esteem scores and were more socially oriented than boys. No sex differences were found among 18-year-old Ss.

Smith, C. R., Williams, L., and Willis, R. H. Race, sex and belief as determinants of friendship acceptance. *J. Personality & Social Psychology*, 1967, 5, 127–37.
    EXPERIMENT I: **Subjects:** $N = 119$; 18–21 yrs (college). **Measures:** Ss rated each member of pairs of stimulus persons on friendship potential. Pairs of stimulus persons differed with regard to race, sex, beliefs, or combinations of any 2 of these factors. **Results:** No sex differences.
    EXPERIMENT II: **Subjects:** $N = 167$; 18–21 yrs (black college). **Measures:** Same as Experiment I. **Results:** Relative to race, belief congruence was more important for friendship acceptance among women than among men.

Smith, P. K., and Connolly, K. Patterns of play and social interaction in pre-school children. In N. B. Jones, ed., *Ethological Studies of Child Behavior*, London: Cambridge, 1972, pp. 65–95.
    Subjects: $N = 40$; 2–4 yrs. **Measures:** Observations were made of Ss' indoor and outdoor free-play activities. **Results:** (1) Girls talked to other children more frequently than boys did. (2) Boys made more play noises (e.g. "brr-brr," "bang") than girls did. (3) No sex differences were found in total number of vocalizations. (4) Girls engaged in sucking activities (putting a digit or a toy in contact with 1 or both lips) more often than boys did. (5) Boys engaged in rough-and-tumble play more frequently than girls did. (6) Boys' overall physical activity level was higher than that of girls.

Smith, R. E., Ascough, J. C., Ettinger, R. F., and Nelson, D. A. Humor, anxiety, and task performance. *J. Personality & Social Psychology*, 1971, 19, 243–46.
    Subjects: $N = 215$; 18–21 yrs (college). **Measures:** Ss were given a humorous or nonhumorous form of a course examination under standard classroom conditions. The response measure was Ss' performance on the exam. **Results:** No sex differences.

Smothergill, D. W. Accuracy and variability in the localization of spatial targets at three age levels. *Developmental Psychology*, 1973, 8, 62–66.
    Subjects: $N = 60$; 6–7, 9–10, 18–21 yrs (college). **Measures:** S used his left hand to mark on the underside of a pegboard the position of a target on the top of the pegboard, either while the target was present or 5, 15, or 25 seconds after removal. The target was either S's seen or unseen right index finger or a pencil. **Results:** No sex differences.

Smothergill, D. W., and Dusek, J. B. An attentional analysis of observational learning in preschool children." Unpublished manuscript, Syracuse University, 1973.
    Subjects: $N = 48$; 4 yrs. **Measures:** Models of the same age as Ss and of either the same or opposite sex were presented with 3 pictures of each trial and asked to guess which of the 3 pictures was preferred by E. For half the Ss (correct group), the model was told on 12 of 15 trials that he had guessed correctly and on 3 of 15 trials that he had guessed incorrectly; for the other half of the Ss (incorrect group), the model was told on 12 of 15 trials that he was incorrect and on the remaining trials that he was correct. Afterward, with duplicate pictures in front of them, Ss attempted to recall the models' choices. **Results:** No main sex differences were found. Girls performed better in the correct than in the incorrect condition; no effect was found for boys ($p < .05$).

Snow, C. E., and Rabinovitch, M. S. Conjunctive and disjunctive thinking in children. *J. Experimental Child Psychology*, 1969, 7, 1–9.
    Subjects: $N = 97$; 5–13 yrs. **Measures:** Ss performed conjunctive and disjunctive concept card tasks. Cards were sorted into 2 groups on the basis of some rule, using both positive and negative instances of that rule. **Results:** No sex differences.

Solkoff, N. Race of experimenter as a variable in research with children. *Developmental Psychology*, 1972, 7, 70–75.
    Subjects: $N = 224$; 8–11 yrs. **Measures:** Each S was picked up at home by the same black woman and transported to E's office, where each completed the Sarason Test Anxiety Scale for Children and the Wechsler Intelligence Scale for Children (without maze subtest), administered by either a black or white female E. **Results:** (1) Boys had higher scores on the Picture Completion and Object Assembly performance of WISC than girls. Girls scored higher on Coding performance subtest than boys. (2) No sex differences in test anxiety scores.

Solomon, D., and Ali, F. A. Age trends in the perception of verbal reinforcers. *Developmental Psychology*, 1972, 7, 238–43.

Subjects: $N = 294$; 5, 7, 9, 11, 13, 15, 17, 21–25 yrs (college). Measures: Ss listened to a tape recording of a teacher making evaluative comments to children in her class. The comments were positive, neutral, or negative in content, and were said in a pleased, indifferent, or displeased tone of voice. The tape contained all combinations of content and intonation. After hearing each of the teacher's comments, Ss were asked 3 questions: (1) "What did the teacher mean?" (2) "How does the child feel?" and (3) "Does the teacher like or dislike the child?" Results: (1) In answer to questions 2 and 3, boys displayed more positive perceptions than girls ($p < .01$, $p < .05$). The sex differences were of greatest magnitude among 5-year-old Ss. (2) In answer to questions 1 and 2, girls showed more responsiveness to changes in intonation than boys ($p < .001$, $p < .05$).

Solomon, O., Houlihan, K. A., and Pareluis, R. J. Intellectual achievement responsibility in Negro and white children. *Psychological Reports*, 1969, 24, 479–83.

Subjects: $N = 262$; 9, 11 yrs. Measures: Ss were given the Intellectual Achievement Responsibility Questionnaire, which yielded 2 subscale scores and a total score. The I+ and I— subscales measured Ss' respective tendencies to see themselves as responsible for the positive and negative reinforcement they received in intellectual academic situations. The total I score measured Ss' acceptance of responsibility for the outcomes of their achievement efforts. Results: Among white Ss, girls had higher I+ ($p < .01$) and total I ($p < .01$) scores than boys (high scores in each case represent internal responsibility; low scores represent external responsibility). Among black Ss, no sex differences were found.

Spear, P. S., and Spear, S. A. Social reinforcement, discrimination learning, and retention in children. *Developmental Psychology*, 1972, 7, 220 (extended version of brief report).

Subjects: $N = 192$; 6–7, 10–11 yrs. Measures: Ss performed a series of 2-choice simultaneous discrimination problems with immediate accuracy feedback under 1 of 3 reinforcement conditions: praise, criticism, silence. Retention was tested 8 days later. Results: No sex differences.

Speer, D. C. Marital dysfunctionality and two-person non-zero-sum game behavior. *J. Personality & Social Psychology*, 1972, 21, 18–24.

Subjects: $N = 120$; adult married couples. Measures: Prisoner's Dilemma game. Results: No sex differences.

Speer, D. C., Briggs, P. F., and Gavolas, R. Concurrent schedules of social reinforcement and dependency behavior among four-year-old children. *J. Experimental Child Psychology*, 1969, 8, 356–65.

Subjects: $N = 40$; 4 yrs. Measures: Ss performed a puzzle-completion task. Responses were coded as dependent or competent and were subjected to different schedules of social reinforcement. Results: Girls emitted more dependent responses during extinction than boys did, ($p < .05$). No other sex differences were found.

Spence, J. T. Verbal-discrimination performance as a function of instructions and verbal-reinforcement combination in normal and retarded children. *Child Development*, 1966, 37, 269–81.

Subjects: $N = 192$; 7–9 yrs (normal), 10–19 yrs (retardates). Measures: Ss were given a verbal discrimination task. Ss in the "informed" condition were instructed about the meaning of reinforcers and the meaning of "blank." Ss in the "uninformed" condition received no explanation of reinforcement procedures. Ss were reinforced by "right" after correct choices and nothing after incorrect responses, by "wrong" after incorrect choices and nothing after correct responses, or by "right" or "wrong" after each choice. The task was administered for 16 trials, or until the criterion of 2 successive perfect trials. Results: No sex differences.

Spence, J. T. Do material rewards enhance the performance of lower class children? *Child Development*, 1971, 42, 1461–60.

Subjects: $N = 64$; 5 yrs (black, low SES). Measures: Trained or untrained, Ss performed in a conceptual task and received either symbolic (light flash) or material (M&M) reward. Experiments I and II were identical. Results: No main sex differences.

Spence, J. T. Verbal and nonverbal rewards and punishments in the discrimination learning of children of varying socioeconomic status. *Developmental Psychology*, 1972, 6, 381–84.

Subjects: $N = 200$; 4–5 yrs (low, middle SES). **Measures:** Ss performed a 2-choice discrimination-learning task (choosing pictures) under 1 of 4 conditions: nonverbal reward, nonverbal punishment, verbal reward, and verbal punishment. **Results:** No sex differences.

Spitz, H. H., Goettler, D. R., and Diveley, S. L. A comparison of retardates and normals on the Poggendorff and Oppel-Kundt Illusions. *Developmental Psychology*, 1970, *3*, 48–65.
    Subjects: $N = 112$; 9, 15, 35 yrs. **Measures:** Ss were tested on the Poggendorff and Oppel-Kundt (filled space) illusions. **Results:** No sex differences.

Spitz, H. H., Goettler, D. R., and Webreck, C. A. Effects of two types of redundancy on visual digit span performance of retardates and varying aged normals. *Developmental Psychology*, 1972, *6*, 92–103.
    EXPERIMENT I: **Subjects:** $N = 120$; 9, 13, 20 yrs (normal), 15 yrs (retardates). **Measures:** Ss viewed a digit series under 3 types of redundancy conditions: repetition, couplet, or nonredundancy. Ss were asked for recall. **Results:** No sex differences.
    EXPERIMENT II: **Subjects:** $N = 90$; 8, 17 yrs (normal), 15 yrs (retardates). **Measures:** Same as Experiment I, except that repetition redundancy was emphasized by spatial separation, underlining, and punctuation. **Results:** No sex differences.
    EXPERIMENT III: **Subjects:** $N = 22$; adults. **Measures:** Same as Experiments I and II, except that there was no external organization. **Results:** No sex differences.
    EXPERIMENT IV: **Subjects:** $N = 44$; 14–17 yrs. **Measures:** Half of the Ss received nonredundant digits plus externally organized repetition redundancy. The other half received redundant digits, plus digits containing externally organized couplet redundancy. **Results:** No sex differences.

Stabler, J. R., and Johnson, E. E. Instrumental performance as a function of reinforcement schedule, luck versus skill instructions, and sex of child. *J. Experimental Child Psychology*, 1970, *9*, 330–35.
    Subjects: $N = 64$; 5 yrs. **Measures:** Ss pressed telegraph keys to obtain prizes. They received luck or skill instructions, partial or continuous reinforcement. **Results:** Girls showed more resistance to extinction than boys did.

Stabler, J. R., Johnson, E. E., and Jordan, S. E. The measurement of children's self-concepts as related to racial membership. *Child Development*, 1971, *42*, 2094–97 (brief report).
    Subjects: $N = 60$; 5 yrs (white, black). **Measures:** Ss viewed a black box and a white box and were asked to choose which of the 2 boxes emitted negative or positive self-concept statements. On each trial, the 2 boxes emitted the same statement with equal intensity. **Results:** No sex differences.

Stafford, R. E. Sex differences in spatial visualization as evidence of sex-linked inheritance. *Perceptual & Motor Skills*, 1961, *13*, 428.
    Subjects: $N = 232$; teenagers and their parents. **Measures:** Identical Blocks Test. **Results:** In both age groups, males scored higher than females.

Stanes, D. Analytic responses to conceptual style test as a function of instructions. *Child Development*, 1973, *44*, 389–91.
    Subjects: $N = 60$; 6 yrs. **Measures:** Ss were given the Conceptual Styles Test with varied instructions: choose pictures that "are alike," "go together," or "are alike or go together." **Results:** Boys made more analytic responses than girls.

Stanford Research Institute. Follow-through pupil tests, parent interviews, and teacher questionnaires. Appendix C, 1972.
    Subjects: $N =$ approx. 13,000 (total tested); 5, 7 yrs. **Measures:** Follow-through test batteries were administered to Ss after completion of a Head Start program. Some Ss were tested longitudinally, others were not. **Results:** Girls performed better than boys on the tests of reading knowledge ($N = 13,155$), language ability ($N = 7,101$), and quantitative ability (New York Alpha, $N = 6,607$). Girls also had higher scores on the Wide Range Achievement Test ($N = 7,301$).

Staub, E. A child in distress: the influence of age and number of witnesses on children's attempts to help. *J. Personality & Social Psychology*, 1970, *14*, 130–40.
    Subjects: $N = 232$; 5, 6, 7, 9, 11 yrs. **Measures:** Ss' responses to the tape-recorded sounds of

a child (in an adjoining room) in severe distress were recorded. Ss were either alone or in same-sex pairs. **Results:** No sex differences were found in helping behavior.

Staub, E. A child in distress: the influence of nurturance and modeling on children's attempts to help. *Developmental Psychology*, 1971a, 5, 124–32.
Subjects: $N = 64$; 5 yrs. **Measures:** After interacting with Ss in either a nurturant or non-nurturant manner, E went into an adjoining room either to help a girl who had fallen down (Ss heard tape-recorded sounds of mild distress) or to check on the girl who was in there (no distress cues). After returning to tell Ss what had happened, E left to do some work. Ss' responses to subsequent sounds of severe distress from the adjoining room were recorded. **Results:** No sex differences were found in Ss' helping responses.

Staub, E. Helping a person in distress: the influence of implicit and explicit "rules" of conduct on children and adults. *J. Personality & Social Psychology*, 1971b, 17, 137–44.
Subjects: $N = 40$; 12 yrs. **Measures:** Ss were exposed to tape-recorded sounds of a young girl in distress in an adjoining room. **Results:** No sex differences were found in Ss' responses to the distress cue.

Staub, E. The use of role playing and induction in children's learning of helping and sharing behavior. *Child Development*, 1971c, 42, 805–16.
Subjects: $N = 75$; 5 yrs. **Measures:** Same-sex pairs participated in the first session, opposite-sex pairs in the second. Experimental treatments included role playing (Ss enacted situations in which 1 needed help and 1 provided help), induction (Ss provided verbal solutions to the same situations as in role playing), role playing with induction, and control (Ss acted scenes unrelated to helping). For the specific post-test, Ss heard distress sounds coming from a room in which they knew a child was alone; Ss' behavior following noises was observed for helping responses. Then E played a game with Ss during which E spilled paper clips; Ss' helping behavior was observed with and without E; 1 of the post-tests was delayed 5–7 days. Sharing behavior was assessed by the number of candies Ss were willing to put aside for a poor child. **Results:** In the role-playing group, girls helped the child in distress more than boys, while boys donated more candies than girls ($p < .01$, $p < .01$). There were no other main sex effects.

Staub, E. Effects of persuasion and modeling on delay of gratification. *Developmental Psychology*, 1972, 6, 166–77.
Subjects: $N = 144$; 12 yrs. **Measures:** After a base-rate delay-of-gratification measure was obtained, Ss were exposed to 1 of 4 experimental treatments aimed at changing delay behaviors: persuasion by a "scientist" who had done research on the topic, modeling of delayed choice behaviors by a scientist, a neutral speech by a scientist describing her research (control), or a recommendation that Ss choose larger, more valuable rewards (same basic speech as in control). An immediate post-test was given on behavior and attitude measures. A delayed post-test was given 2 weeks later. **Results:** (1) Overall, girls chose a larger number of delayed objects than boys ($p < .05$). (2) There were no other main sex effects.

Staub, E., and Sherk, L. Need for approval, children's sharing behavior, and reciprocity in sharing. *Child Development*, 1970, 41, 243–53.
Subjects: $N = 90$; 9 yrs. **Measures:** Ss responded to a questionnaire that assessed their need for approval, friendship choices, and candy preferences. Each S listened to a taped story with a same-sex child in the room. S was given a bag of his favorite candy to eat during the story. Sharing behavior was observed. E asked S and the other child to draw a picture about the story, but only gave a crayon to the other child. Again, sharing behavior was observed. **Results:** Boys shared more candy than girls did ($p < .02$). No sex differences in need for approval.

Stayton, D. J., Hogan, R., and Ainsworth, M. D. S. Infant obedience and maternal behavior: the origins of socialization reconsidered. *Child Development*, 1971, 42, 1057–69.
Subjects: $N = 25$; 9–12 mos and mothers. **Measures:** Mother-infant pairs were observed at 3-week intervals in their homes. The degree of harmony in the interaction between mother and child was rated on 3 scales: sensitivity-insensitivity, acceptance-rejection, and cooperation-interference. Mothers were also scored for frequency of verbal commands, frequency of discipline-oriented physical interventions, and extent of floor freedom permitted the child. There were 27 measures of infant behavior recorded: frequency of compliance to maternal commands and frequency of display of self-inhibiting, self-controlling behaviors. Infants were also given the Griffiths Scale of Mental Development. **Results:** No sex differences.

Stayton, S. E. Sensory organization in retardates and normals. *Developmental Psychology,* 1970a, *2*, 66–70.

Subjects: $N = 112$; 16 yrs (normals, retardates). **Measures:** Ss were asked to take marbles, 1 at a time, from a box of 5 white and 5 black marbles and place them in test tubes. The sequence in which Ss transferred the marbles was recorded. The retardates' scores on the Stanford-Binet and the normal Ss' scores on the Science Research Associates Test of Educational Ability were obtained. **Results:** (1) Among normal Ss, boys produced fewer sensory sequences (transferring all 5 marbles of 1 color, then all 5 of the other color) than girls did ($p < .025$). (2) Among retarded Ss, boys produced more sensory sequences ($p < .05$) and fewer alternating sequences ($p < .02$) than girls did. (3) No sex differences were found in normal Ss' ability quotients or in retarded Ss' IQs.

Stayton, S. E. Sensory organization and intelligence: a modification and replication. *Developmental Psychology,* 1970b, *3*, 146.

Subjects: $N = 192$; 17 yrs (retardates). **Measures:** Equal numbers of black and white beads were placed in front of Ss. Ss were told to pick up the beads 1 at a time and make the best bead chain they could. **Results:** No sex differences were found in the frequency of sensory sequences (all beads of 1 color strung first, then all beads of the other color) or of alternating sequences (black-white-black-white, etc.).

Steele, L. P., and Horowitz, A. B. "Looking versus remembering: A comparison of the mediational activity of kindergarten children in three retention tasks." Paper presented at the Society for Research in Child Development Conference, Philadelphia, 1973.

Subjects: $N = 72$; 6 yrs. **Measures:** Ss were told either to look at or to try to remember a series of 12 single-line drawings of common objects. Afterward, retention of the stimuli was tested in 1 of 3 ways. Ss in 1 group were asked to recall the names of as many as possible of the objects. Ss in a second group were asked to choose from among 36 drawings those that they had seen. Ss in a third group listened as E read the names of 36 objects to them. Ss were asked to respond whenever E named an object that had been included in the set of 12 drawings. **Results:** No sex differences.

Stein, A. H. The influence of social reinforcement on the achievement behavior of fourth grade boys and girls. *Child Development,* 1969, *40*, 727–36.

Subjects: $N = 160$; 9 yrs. **Measures:** Ss performed a digit-letter coding task under neutral conditions for 3 minutes, then under 1 of 4 treatment conditions (praise, correct, disapproval, alone) for 7 minutes. In the praise condition, E made general praising statements such as "Good" and "Fine." In the correct condition, E emphasized to Ss the accuracy of their responses (e.g. "You're getting them right"). In the disapproval condition, E made general statements of disapproval (e.g. "You're not doing too well"). In the alone condition, Ss completed the task without E present. Changes in response rates from the neutral to the experimental conditions were recorded. **Results:** (1) Girls had higher response rates in the neutral condition than boys ($p < .01$). (2) No sex differences were found in changes in rates of response. In the disapproval condition, the variance of the girls was larger than that of the boys. (3) Sex of E had no effect on Ss' scores.

Stein, A. H., Pohly, S., Pohly, R., and Mueller, E. The influence of masculine, feminine, and neutral tasks on children's achievement behavior, expectancies of success, and attainment values. *Child Development,* 1971, *42*, 195–207.

Subjects: $N = 96$; 11 yrs. **Measures:** 3 tasks involving digit-letter coding, copying the letters of foreign alphabets, and drawing lines between the double borders of figures were administered to Ss. Each task was presented as masculine, feminine, or neutral. At the beginning of the experiment, Ss stated the score they expected to receive on each task. Ss were then given 10 minutes to complete all 3 tasks. The amount of time Ss spent on each task was recorded. Afterward, Ss were asked (1) how important was it for them to do well on each task (attainment value), (2) which tasks they liked most and least, and (3) which tasks they considered hardest and easiest. **Results:** (1) Boys' expectancy and attainment value scores were highest on masculine tasks and lowest on feminine tasks; girls' expectancy and attainment value scores were lower on masculine tasks than on either feminine or neutral tasks ($p < .01$). (2) Attainment value scores were higher with male Es than with female Es ($p < .05$). Expectancy scores on the feminine task were lower with a female E than with a male E ($p < .05$). (3) Boys spent the greatest amount of time on the masculine task, and the least amount of time on the feminine task ($p < .001$). Girls spent about the same amount of time on all 3 tasks. (4) For boys, the difference between the time spent on masculine and feminine tests was greater with male Es than with female Es. Sex of E did not influence the pattern of time scores for girls. (5) Boys liked the masculine tests most and the feminine tests least ($p < .001$); girls liked the tests equally well. Neither sex group attributed differences in difficulty to the 3 tests.

Stein, H. A., and Smithells, J. Age and sex differences in children's sex-role standards about achievement. *Developmental Psychology*, 1969, *1*, 252–59.

  Subjects: $N = 120$; 7, 11, 17 yrs. Measures: Ss were successively presented with 42 items representing 6 areas of achievement: athletic, spatial and mechanical, arithmetic, reading, artistic, and social skills. 7 items were included for each area: 6 described specific activities, and 1 was a general item intended to portray the area as a whole. Ss judged whether the activity described in each item was more masculine or more feminine. Results: (1) Girls made more feminine choices than boys ($p < .01$). The sex difference was greatest at age 7, intermediate at age 11, and negligible at age 17 ($p < .05$). (2) Among 7-year-old and 11-year-old Ss, boys rated more athletic items as masculine than girls ($p < .01$, $p < .01$). (3) Among 7-year-old Ss, girls rated more reading items as feminine than boys ($p < .01$). (4) No sex differences were found in Ss' rank-orderings.

Stein, K. B., and Lenrow, P. Expressive styles and their measurement. *J. Personality & Social Psychology*, 1970, *16*, 656–64.

  Subjects: $N = 249$; 18–21 yrs (college). Measures: Ss rated their degree of interest in activities that were either motoric, ideational, or sensory-perceptual. Results: Women showed greater interest in sensory-perceptual activities than men ($p < .01$). Men showed a greater interest in motoric activities than women ($p < .01$). No sex differences were found in Ss' preferences for ideational activities.

Stevenson, A. H., and Lynn, D. B. Preference for high variability in young children. *Psychonomic Science*, 1971, *23*, 143–44.

  Subjects: $N = 88$; 3–7 yrs. Measures: Ss' preferences for random shapes of varying number of turns were assessed. Results: Boys had a higher preference for variability than girls ($p < .05$).

Stevenson, H. W., and Odom, R. D. Visual reinforcement with children. *J. Experimental Child Psychology*, 1964, *1*, 248–55.

  Subjects: $N = 192$; 6–7, 10–11 yrs. Measures: Ss performed a simple bar-pressing task. After their base rates were obtained, visual reinforcers were presented for a period of 6 minutes. 3 types of visual reinforcers were used: colored drawings of animals, line drawings of common objects, and hues. A 4-minute extinction phase was introduced immediately after termination of the reinforcement period. Difference scores were computed by subtracting each child's base rate from his response rate during the reinforcement and extinction periods. Results: (1) No sex differences were found in response rates during the baseline period. (2) During the reinforcement period, older boys showed a greater increase in response rate across minutes than older girls did ($p < .001$). (3) During extinction, older boys had higher difference scores than older girls ($p < .025$).

Stevenson, H. W., and Odom, R. D. The relation of anxiety to children's performance on learning and problem-solving tasks. *Child Development*, 1965, *36*, 1003–12.

  Subjects: $N = 318$; 9, 11 yrs. Measures: (1) Test Anxiety Scale for Children (A), (2) Defensiveness Scale for Children (D), (3) Anagrams task, (4) Paired associates learning task. (5) On each trial of a concept identification task, Ss were presented with a pair of geometric shapes that varied in size (large or small) and brightness (black or white). Ss' task was to learn which dimension was relevant, size or brightness, and which value within that dimension was correct. Results: Among 11-year-old Ss, girls had higher A scores and higher D scores than boys ($p < .01$, $p < .01$). Among 9-year-old Ss, girls had higher D scores than boys ($p < .01$). No other sex differences were found.

Stevenson, H. W., Hill, K. T., Hale, G. A., and Moely, B. E. Adult ratings of children's behavior. *Child Development*, 1966, *37*, 929–41.

  Subjects: $N = 862$; 17–23, above 24 (college). Measures: Ss watched a film consisting of 1-minute interviews with each of 20 third-grade children and 20 sixth-grade children. Children were questioned about their activities and interests. Each child was rated by Ss on 7-point bipolar adjective scales. Results: (1) Women rated the children in both grades as being more attractive, definite, friendly, colorful, pleasant, mature, and sociable than men did. (2) On the masculine-feminine scale, women's ratings of boys and girls were more extreme than men's ratings. (3) Girls in both grades were rated as being more feminine, interested, jolly, warm, friendly, pleasant, sensitive and sociable than boys. Among third-grade children, girls were rated as being more calm, mature, colorless, timid, passive, shy, and nonassertive than boys. Among sixth-grade Ss, girls were rated as being more definite, active, agitated, enthusiastic, and bright than boys.

Stevenson, H. W., Hale, G. A., Hill, K. T., and Moely, B. E. Determinants of children's preferences for adults. *Child Development*, 1967, *38*, 1–14.
   Subjects: *N* = 1,930; 5–11 yrs (low, middle SES). Measures: Ss watched films of marble-dropping game in which men and women portraying supportive and neutral roles reinforced the performance of a child playing the game. After viewing each film, Ss were asked to choose which adult they would prefer to play with. 3 types of films were shown: (1) supportive-neutral: Ss chose between same-sex pair of adults on the basis of their role (supportive or neutral) in the film; (2) male-female: Ss chose between a male and a female adult, both of whom were either supportive or neutral; (3) mixed: Ss chose between a male and a female adult, 1 of whom was supportive and the other neutral. Results: For male-female films, all Ss chose the adult of their own sex more frequently than chance (for films in which both adults played a neutral role, $p < .01$; for films in which both adults played a supportive role, no test of significance was reported).

Stevenson, H. W., Hale, G. A., Klein, R. E., and Miller, L. K. Interrelations and correlates in children's learning and problem solving. *Monographs of the Society for Research in Child Development*, 1968a, *33*.
   EXPERIMENT I: Subjects: *N* = 256; 12–14 yrs. Measures: Ss performed the following tasks: anagram, concept of probability regarding faces and pegs, conservation of volume, verbal memory (questions about a story), paired-associates, discrimination learning, and probability-learning and incidental-learning. IQ scores on the Thorndike and Iowa Tests of Basic Skills were obtained. Results: (1) Girls performed better than boys on incidental learning tasks and verbal memory (some IQ groups). (2) Among high-IQ Ss, girls performed better than boys on paired-associates (abstract forms). Boys performed better than girls on concept of probability. (3) Among low-IQ Ss, girls performed better than boys on discrimination-learning, verbal memory, and anagrams.
   EXPERIMENT II: Subjects: *N* = 475; 8–12 yrs. Measures: Similar to Experiment I. Results: Girls did better than boys on incidental learning and anagrams.

Stevenson, H. W., Klein, R. E., Hale, G. A., and Miller, L. K. Solution of anagrams: a developmental study. *Child Development*, 1968b, *39*, 905–12.
   Subjects *N* = 529; 8–14 yrs. Measures: Ss were instructed to make as many English words as possible from a given word ("generation"). Results: At all age levels, girls performed at a higher level than boys.

Stevenson, H. W., Friedricks, A. G., and Simpson, W. E. Learning and problem solving by the mentally retarded under three testing conditions. *Developmental Psychology*, 1970, *3*, 307–12.
   Subjects: *N* = 96; 14 yrs. Measures: Ss performed paired-associates, discrimination-learning, incidental-learning, verbal-memory, and anagram tasks with a male or female E under conditions of group testing, with an individual testing with a neutral E, or with an individual testing with supportive E. Results: (1) During individual testing, girls performed at a higher level than boys in incidental learning ($p < .05$). (2) During group testing, girls performed at a higher level than boys on anagrams ($p < .05$). (3) No sex differences in paired associates or discrimination learning.

Stiller, A., Schwartz, H. A., and Cowen, E. L. The social desirability of trait-descriptive terms among high-school students. *Child Development*, 1965, *36*, 981–1002.
   Subjects: *N* = 465; 14, 17 yrs (low, high SES). Measures: Ss were asked to rate a series of 114 trait-descriptive adjectives along a 7-point scale of social desirability. Results: Girls produced more extreme social desirability ratings and were more variable than boys ($p < .001$, $p < .001$).

Stingle, S. F. Age and sex differences in the cooperative and competitive behavior of children. Unpublished doctoral dissertation, Columbia University, 1973.
   Subjects: *N* = 126; 5, 8, 11 yrs. Measures: Same-sex or opposite-sex pairs of Ss played an unspecified cooperative-competitive task. The task was structured so that cooperative behavior maximized reward achievement. Measures were taken of latency (time per trial), type of goal achieved (individual reward goal, joint reward goal, no goal), and number of rewards. Results:

11-year-old boy pairs were more competitive than all other pairs in terms of latency, but not in terms of rewards achieved.

Stodolsky, S. S. How children find something to do in preschools. Paper submitted for publication, University of Chicago, 1971.

> Experiment I: **Subjects:** $N = 35$; 3–5 yrs (black, low SES; white and black, middle SES). **Measures:** Observations were made of Ss' free-play activities. **Results:** (1) Among low SES black Ss, average length of activity segments was longer for girls than for boys. Girls were observed more often than boys in 1 activity for the entire length of the observation period (15 minutes). Boys changed activities more often than girls. Boys spent less time in activities than girls (an activity was defined as a stream of behavior at least 1 minute in length, with a focus and a beginning, middle, and end). (2) No sex differences were found among middle SES subjects.
>
> Experiment II: **Subjects:** $N = 38$; 4–6 yrs (white and black, middle SES). **Measures:** Same as Experiment I. **Results:** No sex differences.

Stone, L. J., and Hokanson, J. E. Arousal reduction via self-punitive behavior. *J. Personality & Social Psychology,* 1969, *12,* 72–79.

> **Subjects:** $N = 14$; 18–21 yrs (college). **Measures:** Following receipt of a shock, a reward, or neither from a confederate (C), Ss performed 1 of 3 counterresponses: they could deliver a shock or a reward to C or they could shock themselves. During the baseline and extinction phases, C's behavior was random. If Ss pressed the self-shock button following receipt of a shock from C (during the conditioning phase), on the next trial a reward followed from C with a 0.9 probability. Pressing the self-shock button was adaptive in such circumstances, since the self-imposed shock was of a lower magnitude than the shock delivered by C. The response measure was the plethysmographic recovery time on those trials on which Ss received a shock from C. **Results:** No sex differences were found during baseline, conditioning, or extinction. Both sexes showed an increase in the self-shock counterresponse during the conditioning phase.

Stouwie, R. J. Inconsistent verbal instructions and children's resistance to temptation behavior. *Child Development,* 1971, *42,* 1517–31 (and personal communication).

> **Subjects:** $N = 120$; 7, 8 yrs. **Measures:** Ss were placed in a room with 9 toys (previously judged to be of equal attractiveness to boys and girls). Ss were assigned to 1 of 4 conditions. In the first condition both a man and a woman told Ss not to play with the toys. In a second condition the woman told Ss they could play with the toys, and the man prohibited them from doing so. In a third condition the two adults reversed roles. In the fourth condition both adults allowed Ss to play with the toys. Following the adults' departure, Ss were observed for 15 minutes. Measures were taken of latency of S's first deviant response, the number of times he touched the toys, and the amount of time he spent in contact with the toys. **Results:** (1) Boys had shorter latencies than girls. (2) Girls spent less time touching the toys than boys did.

Stouwie, R. J. An experimental study of adult dominance and warmth, conflicting verbal instructions, and children's moral behavior. *Child Development,* 1972, *43,* 959–71 (and personal communication).

> **Subjects:** $N = 112$; 7, 8 yrs. **Measures:** Ss were shown 9 toys previously judged to be equally attractive to boys and girls. Ss were then introduced to an adult male and female, one of whom was dominant, the other warm. After interacting with Ss for 5 minutes, 1 of the adults instructed the Ss not to play with the toys, whereas the other gave Ss permission to do so. Ss were then left alone for 15 minutes. The latency of Ss' first deviant responses, the number of times Ss touched the toys, the total amount of time Ss spent in physical contact with the toys, and the average duration of Ss' deviations were recorded. Weighted scores for each of the last 3 measures were calculated by assigning higher values to toys farthest from Ss. **Results:** (1) No sex differences were found in latency of first deviant response or in number of deviations. (2) Boys had higher weighted duration scores (time spent touching the toys) than girls ($p < .05$). (3) The average duration of boys' deviations was longer than that of girls.

Stouwie, R. J., Hetherington, E. M., and Parke, R. D. Some determinants of children's self-reward criteria. *Developmental Psychology,* 1970, *3,* 313–19.

> **Subjects:** $N = 156$; 8–9 yrs. **Measures:** High and low achievement orientation was determined by the number of seconds Ss used on 5 embedded figures tasks. Ss participated in a bowling game with a male or female adult who set higher standards for Ss' reward than for self-reward. Afterward, Ss played alone. Self-reward standards were assessed. **Results:** (1)

There were no sex differences in achievement orientation. (2) Children who interacted with the female model took fewer rewards than those who interacted with the male model ($p < .05$). (3) There were no sex differences in self-reward standards.

Strain, G. S., Unikel, I. P., and Adams, H. E. Alternation behavior by children from lower socioeconomic status groups. *Developmental Psychology*, 1969, *1*, 131–33.
   Subjects: $N = 48$; 5, 6 yrs (low, middle SES). **Measures:** Ss were successively presented with 5 dishes containing an equal number of 2 different colors of M&M's. Ss were asked to take 1 piece of candy from each dish. Measures were taken of the number of times Ss alternated their choice of colors. **Results:** Among low SES subjects, boys alternated less often than girls ($p < .001$). Among middle SES subjects, no sex differences were found.

Strayer, J., and Ames, E. W. Stimulus orientation and the apparent development lag between perception and performance. *Child Development*, 1972, *43*, 1345–54 (and personal communication).
   Subjects: $N = 40$; 4–5 yrs. **Measures:** All Ss were given a form-board task, a pretraining copying test, programmed discrimination training, and a post-training copying test. Forms to be copied were the same as those presented in the form-board. **Results:** (1) Girls made fewer training errors than boys ($p < .05$), especially on the Rhombus vs. Diamond item ($p < .01$) and on the Left vs. Right Oblique item ($p < .05$). (2) There were no sex differences on form-board errors, latencies, or pretest or post-test copying performance.

Stricker, L. J., Messick, S., and Jackson, D. N. Suspicion of deception: implications for conformity research. *J. Personality & Social Psychology*, 1967, *5*, 379–89.
   Subjects: $N = 190$; 16–17 yrs. **Measures:** After participating in a simulated group version of the Asch situation and responding to questionnaires containing fictitious group norms, Ss completed open-ended questionnaires concerning their perceptions of the purpose and method of each study. Based on their responses, Ss were classified as either suspicious, unsuspicious, or indeterminate. **Results:** Boys were more suspicious than girls about the purpose and method of the simulated group experiment, and about the method of the questionnaire study ($p < .05$). No sex differences were found in Ss' suspicions about the purpose of the questionnaire.

Stricker, L. J., Messick, S., and Jackson, D. N. Conformity, anticonformity, and independence: their dimensionality and generality. *J. Personality & Social Psychology*, 1970, *16*, 494–507.
   Subjects: $N = 190$; 16–18 yrs. **Measures:** Ss both estimated the number of clicks they heard and responded to attitude items in an Asch-type situation. Ss also completed 2 questionnaires (estimating probabilities of events, responding to attitude statements) with the purported average answers for the group provided. Responses from an initial administration of each questionnaire in which Ss answered without knowledge of the ostensible group norms were compared with Ss' responses after exposure to group judgments. Conformity, anticonformity, and independence scores were calculated for each measure. **Results:** No main sex differences were found. Among unsuspicious Ss, girls were less conforming and more independent on the attitude questionnaire, and less anti-conforming on the Asch situations than boys.

Strickland, B. R. Aspiration responses among Negro and white adolescents. *J. Personality & Social Psychology*, 1971, *19*, 315–20.
   Subjects: $N = 120$; 14 yrs (low, middle SES). **Measures:** The Rotter Level of Aspiration Board. **Results:** Among middle SES subjects of both races, boys had higher aspiration levels than girls ($p < .01$). There were no sex differences in frequency of shifts or number of unusual shifts in level of aspiration.

Strickland, B. R. Delay of gratification as a function of race of the experimenter. *J. Personality & Social Psychology*, 1972, *22*, 108–12.
   Subjects: $N = 300$; 11–13 yrs (black, white). **Measures:** For completing a locus-of-control measure, Ss were offered either 1 record as an immediate reward or 3 records if they agreed to wait for E (either a black or white male) to return 3 weeks later. **Results:** No sex differences were found in number of delayed vs. immediate choices.

Stroebe, W., Insko, C. A., Thompson, V. D., and Layton, B. D. Effects of physical attractiveness, attitude similarity, and sex on various aspects of interpersonal attraction. *J. Personality & Social Psychology*, 1971, *18*, 79–91.
   Subjects: $N = 200$; 18–21 yrs (college). **Measures:** Ss' attraction to opposite-sex others of high, medium, or low physical attractiveness, and of similar, moderately similar, or dissimilar

attitudes, was measured in terms of Ss' liking for other, Ss' preference for other as a co-worker, and whether or not Ss would consider other as a dating or a marriage partner. **Results:** (1) There were no main sex effects. (2) On 3 of the 4 variables (working dating, marrying), effects of physical attractiveness were stronger for men than for women. (3) On 2 of the 4 variables (liking, working), women were more influenced by similarity than men were.

Strongman, K. T., and Champness, B. G. Dominance hierarchies and conflict in eye contact. *Acta Psychologica*, 1968, *28*, 376–86.
Subjects: N = 10; 18–21 yrs. **Measures:** Each S was paired with each of the other Ss for a period of 2 minutes. Before meeting their partners, Ss were instructed to use the 2 minutes to "become acquainted." Measures were taken of eye contact, directed gaze, and speech with gaze. **Results:** No sex differences.

Strutl, G. F., Anderson, D. R., and Well, A. D. Developmental trends in the effects of irrelevant information on speeded classification. Paper presented to the Society for Research in Child Development, Philadelphia, 1973.
Subjects: N = 54; 6, 9, 12 yrs. **Measures:** Ss were instructed to sort cards into 2 piles as quickly as possible. In sorting, 1 dimension of the stimuli on the cards was relevant, whereas either 0, 1, or 2 dimensions were irrelevant. Ss were informed which dimension was relevant before beginning. **Results:** Sorting times were lower for girls than for boys, especially at the younger ages.

Stuart, I. R., Breslow, A., Brechner, S., Ilyus, R. B., and Wolpoff, M. The question of constitutional influence on perceptual style. *Perceptual & Motor Skills*, 1965, *20*, 419–20.
Subjects: N = 64; 17–25 yrs. **Measures:** Embedded Figures Test, Short Form. **Results:** No sex differences.

Suchman, R. G. Color-form preference, discriminative accuracy, and learning of deaf and hearing children. *Child Development*, 1966, *37*, 439–51.
Subjects: N = 72; 7–12 yrs. **Measures:** Ss were given 2 tests of color-form preference. Discriminative accuracy was tested within color and form dimensions. Successive discrimination was tested, using form-only problems, color-only problems, and color-form combination problems. **Results:** No sex differences.

Sullivan, E. V., McCullough, G., and Stager, M. A developmental study of the relationship between conceptual, ego, and moral development. *Child Development*, 1970, *41*, 399–411.
Subjects: N = 120; 12, 14, 17 yrs. **Measures:** Hunt and Halverson's Conceptual Level Questionnaire, Kohlberg's Moral Development Test, Loevinger and Wessler's Ego Development Test. **Results:** No sex differences.

Sumners, D. L., and Felker, D. W. Use of the It Scale for Children in assessing sex-role preference in preschool Negro children. *Developmental Psychology*, 1970, *2*, 330–34.
Subjects: N = 30; 5 yrs. **Measures:** The It Scale for Children was administered to Ss twice, once with the It figure as the projective device and once with a picture of a child drawn by Ss as the projective device. **Results:** On both administrations, boys obtained more masculine scores than girls.

Sundberg, N., and Ballinger, T. Nepalese children's cognitive development as revealed by drawings of man, woman, and self. *Child Development*, 1968, *39*, 969–85.
Subjects: N = 807; 6–13 yrs (urban and rural Nepal). **Measures:** Ss were asked to make drawings of man, woman, and self according to directions in the Harris revision of the Goodenough Draw-a-Man Test (translated into Nepali). **Results:** No sex differences.

Suppes, P., and Feldman, S. Young children's comprehension of logical connectives. *J. Experimental Child Psychology*, 1971, *12*, 304–17.
Subjects: N = 64; 4–6 yrs (middle SES, disadvantaged). **Measures:** Ss were given 11 verbal commands to test their comprehension of 3 logical connectives: conjunction, disjunction, and negation. **Results:** No sex differences.

Sutton-Smith, B., and Savasta, M. Sex differences in play and power. Paper presented at the Annual Meeting of the Eastern Psychological Association, Boston, 1972.
Subjects: N = 17; 3–4 yrs. **Measures:** Videotapes were made of Ss' nursery school activities, which either Ss or their peers initiated. **Results:** (1) Boys engaged in more episodes of social

testing and spent more time in such activity than girls did (social testing is an attempt by S to get other players in a game to do what he wanted them to). No sex differences were found in the number of episodes or time spent in exploration, world construction, testing (S asserts something about himself and then does it), contesting (testing against another), imitation (S asserts something about his relationship with another), or sociodrama (imitation involving other children in roles). (2) Behaviors classified as social testing were broken down into those directed at children and at adults. Each of these categories was in turn broken down into 4 subcategories: (a) supplicatory behaviors (S seeks sustenance, aid, etc., from another), (b) inclusive-exclusive behaviors (S attempts to control others by promising inclusion or threatening exclusion), (c) attacks, and (d) dominance behaviors. Within each of these subcategories, Ss' tactics were further classified as to whether a physical, verbal, or strategic modality had been used. By employment of this classification system in a reanalysis of the data, boys were found to attack their peers more; girls were found to exhibit more inclusive-exclusive behaviors. No sex differences were found in supplicatory or dominance behaviors, in the distribution of Ss' tactics across modalities, or in Ss' behavior toward adults.

Sutton-Smith, B., Rosenberg, B. G., and Landy, F. Father-absence effects in families of different sibling compositions. *Child Development*, 1968, *39*, 1213–21.
  Subjects: N = 295, father absent, plus 760, father present; 19 yrs. **Measures:** American College Entrance Examination. **Results:** No sex differences.

Svensson, A. Relative achievement. School performance in relation to intelligence, sex and home environment. Stockholm: Almquist & Wiksell, 1971.
  Experiment I: 1961. **Subjects:** N = 5,828; 13 yrs (Swedish elementary school children). N = 3,077; 13 yrs (Swedish experimental comprehensive school children). **Measures:** Ss completed a verbal and a mathematics achievement test and 2 intelligence tests—Opposites (a test of verbal ability) and Number series (a test of mathematical reasoning ability). **Results:** Boys scored higher than girls on the math achievement test and on Number series, while girls were superior to boys on the verbal achievement test. No sex differences were found on Opposites.
  Experiment II: 1966. **Subjects:** N = 1,550; 13 yrs (Swedish elementary school children). N = 6,144; 13 yrs (Swedish comprehensive school children). **Measures:** Identical to Experiment I. **Results:** (1) Girls' scores were superior to those of the boys on the verbal achievement test. No sex differences were found on Opposites. (2) Among comprehensive school children, boys were superior to girls on the math achievement test and on Number series. No sex differences were found in the elementary school sample.

Swingle, P. G. Exploitative behavior in non-zero-sum games. *J. Personality & Social Psychology*, 1970, *16*, 121–32.
  Subjects: N = 60; 18–21 yrs (college). **Measures:** During the first 100 trials of a non-zero-sum game, Ss were exposed to a 90% cooperative same-sex opponent. During the final 50 trials, the opponent's response matched Ss' previous response 90% of the time. The response measure was the percentage of exploitative responses. **Results:** No sex differences.

Szal, J. A. Sex differences in the cooperative and competitive behaviors of nursery school children. Unpublished master's thesis, Stanford University, 1972.
  Subjects: N = 60; 4–5 yrs. **Measures:** Ss in same-sex or opposite-sex pairs played 2 10-trial sessions of a marble-pull game developed by Madsen. The game is designed in such a way that cooperation is adaptive and competition maladaptive to the goal of acquiring marbles. The number of marbles each pair obtained and the amount of sharing each pair exhibited were recorded. In addition, a running account was kept of Ss' actions and verbalizations. Actions were classified as either cooperative (receptive, permissive, submissive, or general—a category designated for those actions considered adaptive to the goal of obtaining marbles but lacking in the defining affect or history of receptive, permissive, or submissive cooperation), competitive (benign, aggressive, or general), or uncooperative. Verbalizations were similarly judged on the dimensions of cooperativeness, competitiveness, or uncooperativeness; in addition, they were categorized according to their grammatical form (narrative, command, suggestion), and their intended target (undirected, directed to other S, directed to E). **Results:** (1) Pairs of girls were more cooperative than pairs of boys. The measures that yielded differences were number of marbles obtained ($p < .05$), number of marbles shared ($p < .01$), and number of cooperative actions (total, $p < .05$; permissive, $p < .01$). Girl-boy pairs were midway in performance between same-sex pairs. (2) Male pairs were more competitive than female pairs. The measures that yielded differences were number of competitive actions (total, $p < .05$; aggressive, $p < .05$); and number of competitive verbalizations (total, $p < .01$; aggressive, $p < .05$). Opposite-sex pairs were again midway in performance between same-sex pairs.

(3) An examination of the individual performance of Ss in opposite-sex pairs revealed 2 differences: (a) boys exhibited more cooperative actions (total) than girls ($p < .05$), and (b) over sessions, girls increased in competitive verbalizations more than boys ($p < .05$). (4) Boys in opposite-sex pairs shared more marbles than boys in same-sex pairs ($p < .05$). (5) Girls in opposite-sex pairs exhibited more competitive actions (total, $p < .05$; aggressive, $p < .01$) and less cooperative actions (total, $p < .05$) than girls in same-sex pairs.

Taft, R., and Johnston, R. The assimilation of adolescent Polish immigrants and parent-child interaction. *Merrill-Palmer Quarterly*, 1967, *13*, 111–21.
  Subjects: $N = 39$; 15–16 yrs (Australia). Measures: Ss were asked questions about tensions with their parents in 3 areas of assimilation: food, language, and social relations. Results: No sex differences.

Taylor, S. P., and Epstein, S. Aggression as a function of the interaction of the sex of the aggressor and the sex of the victim. *J. Personality*, 1967, *35*, 474–96.
  Subjects: $N = 24$; 18–21 yrs (college). Measures: Aggression was measured by the magnitude of shock the subject set for his opponent to receive in a reaction-time task. Wins and losses on the task and aggressiveness of the opponent were actually programmed by E. Results: (1) There were no sex differences in aggression across conditions. (2) Whereas women were less aggressive in the low provocation condition, they showed a greater increase in aggression with increasing provocation than men did ($p < .001$). (3) All Ss were more aggressive to male than to female opponents ($p < .05$). (4) All Ss demonstrated a greater rise in skin conductance when competing with female rather than male opponents ($p < .05$).

Tedeschi, J. T., Horai, J., Lindskold, S., and Gahagan, J. P. The effects of threat upon prevarication and compliance in social conflict. Proceedings of the 76th Annual Convention of the APA, 1968a, *3*, 399–400.
  Subjects: $N = 96$; 18–21 yrs (college). Measures: Ss played a modified version of the Prisoner's Dilemma game with a simulated partner (E). On selected trials, E threatened Ss with a loss of points unless they made the cooperative response on the next trial. Ss were required to respond with 1 of 3 available messages. Results: (1) Women made the cooperative response more frequently than men ($p < .04$). (2) Women lost less money than men ($p < .04$). (3) After being threatened by E, more men than women made the competitive choice after indicating to E their intention to make the cooperative choice ($p < .003$).

Tedeschi, J., T. Lesnick, S., and Gahagan, J. Feedback and "washout" effects in the Prisoner's Dilemma game. *J. Personality & Social Psychology*, 1968b, *10*, 31–34.
  Subjects: $N = 64$; 18–21 yrs (college). Measures: Ss played 100 trials of the Prisoner's Dilemma game with a simulated other. Results: (1) No sex differences were found in percentage of cooperative responses over 100 trials. (2) On the first 10 trials, women were more cooperative than men ($p < .03$).

Tedeschi, J. T., Hiester, D., and Gahagan, J. P. Matrix values and the behavior of children in the Prisoner's Dilemma game. *Child Development*, 1969a, *40*, 517–27.
  Subjects: $N = 96$; 8, 9 yrs. Measures: Same-sex pairs of Ss played a modified version of the Prisoner's Dilemma game. Results: (1) Girls made more cooperative choices than boys ($p < .01$). Boys made more jointly competitive choices than girls ($p < .01$). No sex differences were found in number of jointly cooperative choices. (2) Girls displayed more trust than boys ($p < .01$). Trust was exhibited when S cooperated on trial ($n + 1$) after both he and his partner made the competitive choice on trial n. (3) Girls were more forgiving than boys ($p < .05$). Forgiveness was exhibited when S cooperated on trial ($n + 1$) after his partner made the competitive choice and he made the cooperative choice on trial n. (4) No sex differences were found in trustworthiness or repentance. Trustworthiness was exhibited when S cooperated on trial ($n + 1$) after both he and his partner made the cooperative choice on trial n. Repentance was exhibited when S cooperated on trial ($n + 1$) after his partner made the cooperative choice and he made the competitive choice on trial n.

Tedeschi, J. T., Lindskold, S., Horai, J., and Gahagan, J. P. Social power and the credibility of promises. *J. Personality & Social Psychology*, 1969b, *13*, 253–61.
  Subjects: $N = 200$; 18–21 yrs (college). Measures: After every tenth trial of the Prisoner's Dilemma game, Ss received a promise of cooperation from a simulated same-sex partner. Ss replied with 1 of 3 available messages. Results: Whereas both sexes were preponderantly truthful, women made the cooperative response more often than men after promising their partners they would ($p < .002$).

Templer, D. I., Ruff, C. F., and Franks, C. M. Death anxiety: age, sex and parental resemblance in diverse populations. *Developmental Psychology*, 1971, 4, 108 (brief report).
    Subjects: *N* = 2,559; 13–21, 17–59, 18–61, 19–85 yrs (students, parents of students, psychiatric patients, low SES hospital aides, high SES apartment dwellers). **Measures:** Ss completed a 15-item true-false Death Anxiety Scale. **Results:** Among apartment house residents, adolescents, and parents of adolescents, women had higher Death Anxiety Scale scores than men. No sex differences were found among hospital aides or psychiatric patients.

Ter Vrugt, D., and Pederson, D. R. The effects of vertical rocking frequencies on the arousal level in two-month-old infants. *Child Development*, 1973, 44, 205–9.
    Subjects: *N* = 64; 1–2 mos. **Measures:** Infants were vertically rocked at 1 of 4 frequencies. Observers rated each S's general level of arousal during the baseline, rocking, and post-rocking phases. **Results:** No sex differences.

Thalhofer, N. N. Responsibility, reparation, and self-protection as reasons for three types of helping. *J. Personality & Social Psychology*, 1971, 19, 144–51.
    Subjects: *N* = 192; 18–21 yrs (college). **Measures:** After reading about a disturbed boy whose teacher had recommended that he be removed to a more punishment-oriented school, Ss were asked to rate the boy on how much he could continue to benefit from his present school experience. Ss had previously been led to believe either that they alone (unique condition) or that others were reading about the boy (nonunique condition). After rating the boy, Ss were informed that a decision had been made to transfer him. Ss were then given the opportunity to (a) offer either time or money to help the boy (labeled help relevant to dependency), and (b) rerate the boy on the same scale used previously in rating (labeled help relevant to harm, measured by computing the difference between the first and second ratings). Ss were free to assume that their second ratings might have some effect on the transfer decision. Ss were asked if they'd be willing to participate in future studies, and to fill out an additional questionnaire (labeled help irrelevant to harm and dependency). **Results:** (1) No main sex effects were found. In the nonunique condition, women offered more help relevant to dependency than men did (*p* < .05). (2) In answer to questions concerning their reactions to the study, women more than men liked the boy they read about, thought that one should help another whom one has harmed, and thought that one should help another who is in need (*p* < .001, *p* < .001, *p* < .001).

Thelen, M. H. Modeling of verbal reactions to failure. *Developmental Psychology*, 1969, 1, 297 (brief report).
    Subjects: *N* = 98; 10–12 yrs (Catholic school). **Measures:** Ss watched an audio-video film in which an adult male model performed a card-sorting task. Experimental Ss observed the model make self-blame or rationalization statements after each failure, which had either positive, negative, or no consequences. The control group observed no model. Ss then performed the same card-sorting task, with E asking for comments after each failure trial. Self-blame or rationalization statements similar to model's were recorded. **Results:** No sex differences.

Thelen, M. H. Long term retention of verbal imitation. *Developmental Psychology*, 1970, 3, 29–31.
    Subjects: *N* = 38; 10–12 yrs. **Measures:** Ss observed a filmed adult male model perform a card-sorting task, failing and making self-blame statements on half of the trials. Ss observed E make either a supportive statement to model (positive consequences of failure) or a critical statement (negative consequences). Ss then performed the identical task. **Results:** There were no sex differences in number of self-blame statements.

Thelen, M. H., Rennie, D. L., Fryrear, J. L., and McGuire, D. Expectancy to perform and vicarious reward: their effects upon imitation. *Child Development*, 1972, 43, 699–703.
    Subjects: *N* = 60; 6, 7, 8 yrs. **Measures:** Ss viewed a film about pushing buttons to light up a clown face. Before the film, Ss were manipulated as to expectancy to perform or not to perform. The model in the film was either rewarded or not rewarded. Ss were asked to recall and imitate the model's behavior. **Results:** No sex differences.

Thoman, E. B., Barnett, C. R., and Leiderman, P. H. Feeding behaviors of newborn infants as a function of parity of the mother. *Child Development*, 1971, 42, 1471–83.
    Subjects: *N* = 271; 12–16 hrs and mothers. **Measures:** Infants of primiparous and multiparous bottle-feeding and breast-feeding mothers were observed during feeding. **Results:** No sex differences were found in (1) time spent in feeding and nonfeeding activities, (2) amount of formula consumed, or (3) number of feeding intervals.

Thoman, E. B., Leiderman, P. H., and Olson, J. P. Neonate-mother interaction during breast feeding. *Developmental Psychology*, 1972, 6, 110–18.
Subjects: $N = 40$; 2 days and mothers. **Measures:** Mothers were observed while breast-feeding their infants. The amount of time mothers devoted to breast-feeding, water feeding, and non-feeding activities was recorded. **Results:** (1) Primiparous mothers spent a greater percentage of the total observation time breast-feeding their sons than their daughters; for multiparous mothers, the reverse was true ($p < .05$). (2) While breast-feeding, primiparous mothers talked to their daughters more than to their sons; multiparous mothers showed no preference ($p < .05$). (3) During nonfeeding activities, no difference was found in the percentage of time mothers talked to their boy and girl infants.

Thomas, L. E. Family correlates of student political activism. *Developmental Psychology*, 1971, 4, 206–14.
Subjects: $N = 60$; 18–21 yrs (college) and parents (liberal, conservative). **Measures:** Parent and child open-ended interviews were coded for family emotional climate (permissiveness, warmth, conflict, family interaction), family political climate (parental dedication to causes, parental political tutoring), student activism, and conventional political activity. **Results:** (1) There were no sex differences in student activism and student political participation within liberal or conservative groups. (2) Among conservative Ss, parents of girls were less permissive than parents of boys ($p < .05$).

Thompson, N. L., and McCandless, B. R. It score variations by instructional style. *Child Development*, 1970, 41, 425–36.
Subjects: $N = 72$; 4–5 yrs (white, black). **Measures:** The It Scale for Children (ITSC) was administered to Ss 3 times. 3 sets of instructions were given: (1) Standard (Ss were asked to answer for the It figure who was visible to them throughout the test); (2) Concealed (Ss were asked to answer for a child named "It"; the It figure was kept concealed in an envelope); (3) "It is you" (the It figure was identified as a child of the same-sex as S). **Results:** On each administration of the ITSC, boys' scores were more masculine than girls'.

Thompson, S. K., and Bentler, P. M. The priority of cues in sex discrimination by children and adults. *Developmental Psychology*, 1971, 5, 181–85 (and personal communication).
Subjects: $N = 240$; 4, 5, 6, over 21 yrs. **Measures:** Ss sorted doll clothes into masculine and feminine types. Ss viewed a nude male or female doll with either long or short hair, and were asked to dress it for party and swimming, identify it as mommy or daddy, and justify their identification. **Results:** (1) There were no sex differences in adults' task performances. (2) Boys had lower scores (dressed dolls more femininely) than girls did ($p < .05$). (3) There were no main sex differences in sex identity classifications. Girls gave more masculine classification to the feminine-bodied short-haired dolls than boys did.

Thompson, S. K., and Bentler, P. M. A developmental study of gender constancy and parent preference. *Archives of Sexual Behavior*, 1973, 65, 211–15.
Subjects: $N = 144$; 4–6 yrs. **Measures:** Ss were asked the following questions: (1) Are you going to be a mommy or a daddy? (2) Could you be a mommy/daddy if you wanted to be? (For this question, Ss were asked if they could be the opposite of their response to the first question.) (3) Do you like your mommy or daddy best? **Results:** (1) All boys were aware that they would become fathers and (with the exception of 1 6-year-old) all girls were aware that they would become mothers. (2) No sex differences were found in the number of Ss who indicated it was possible for them to become an opposite-sex parent. (3) Girls preferred their mothers more than boys did; boys preferred their fathers more than girls did ($p < .01$).

Thomson, G. H. *An analysis of performance test scores of a representative group of Scottish children.* London: University of London Press, 1940.
Subjects: $N = 873$; 9–11 yrs. **Measures:** Manikin Test, Sequin Form Board, Stutsman Picture Test, Red Riding Hood Test, Healy Picture Completion Test II, Knox Cube Imitation Test, Cube Construction Test, Kohs Block Design. **Results:** No sex differences.

Tisher, R. P. A Piagetian questionnaire applied to pupils in a secondary school. *Child Development*, 1971, 42, 1633–36 (and personal communication).
Subjects: $N = 232$; 12–14 yrs. **Measures:** A Piagetian questionnaire and interview tasks concerning invisible magnetism, equilibrium in the balance, and combinations of chemicals were administered to each S. **Results:** No sex differences.

Titkin, S., and Hartup, W. Sociometric status and the reinforcing effectiveness of children's peers. *J. Experimental Child Psychology,* 1965, *2,* 306–15.

Subjects: $N = 84$; 7, 10 yrs. Measures: A nonskill task (marble dropping) was verbally reinforced by a popular, unpopular, or socially isolated peer. The number of marbles Ss dropped was recorded. Difference scores indicated the effects of peer reinforcement on response rate. Results: There were no main sex differences. Among 10-year-old Ss reinforced by unpopular peers, girls showed a substantial increment in marble dropping, whereas boys' rate decreased.

Titley, R. W., and Viney, W. Expression of aggression toward the physically handicapped. *Perceptual & Motor Skills,* 1969, *29,* 51–56.

Subjects: $N = 40$; 17 yrs. Measures: Ss were asked to administer a shock to a same-sex or opposite-sex confederate of an intensity just below what they estimated to be the confederate's pain threshold. The confederate appeared to be either physically disabled or normal. Results: (1) Men delivered a higher intensity of shock than women ($p < .05$). (2) Men delivered more shock to women than to men; the reverse was true for women ($p < .001$). (3) Men delivered more shock to the physically disabled confederate than to the normal confederate; the reverse was true for women ($p < .001$).

Todd, F. J., and Hammond, K. R. Differential feedback in two multiple-cue probability learning tasks. *Behavioral Science,* 1965, *10,* 429–35.

Subjects: $N = 72$; 18–21 yrs (college). Measures: Ss were given a multiple-cue probability learning task. Results: No sex differences.

Todd, J., and Nakamura, C. Y. Interactive effects of informational and affective components of social and nonsocial reinforcers on independent and dependent children. *Child Development,* 1970, *41,* 365–76.

Experiment I: Subjects: $N = 54$; 5–7 yrs. Measures: 3 marble-sorting tasks were administered to Ss. Half the Ss received feedback only when they performed correctly, while the other half were informed only when they performed incorrectly. In 4 of the 6 conditions, Ss heard E say "correct" or "incorrect" in either a positive or negative tone of voice; feedback in the other 2 conditions consisted simply of exposure to light flashes. The response measure was the number of trials Ss needed to reach criterion. Results: No sex differences.

Experiment III: Subjects: $N = 48$; 6–7 yrs. Measures: While cutting out designs, Ss received either positive or negative reinforcement from E. Ss in a third condition were exposed to an E who remained silent until Ss completed the task. All Ss were then administered 3 bead-sorting games. Correct responses were reinforced either by E ("correct" said in a neutral tone of voice) or by a light flash. The number of trials Ss needed to reach criterion was recorded. Results: Boys reached criterion faster than girls did.

Tolor, A., and Orange, S. An attempt to measure psychological distance in advantaged and disadvantaged children. *Child Development,* 1969, *40,* 407–20.

Subjects: $N = 40$; 5–14 yrs. Measures: Using a Psychological Distance Board, Ss had to recreate physical distance between stimulus dyads of simulated persons. Ss also completed the Make-A-Picture-Story test. Results: On 3 out of 12 pairings, girls placed the figures farther apart than boys ($p < .05$).

Torrance, E. P. *Rewarding creative behavior.* Englewood Cliffs, N.J.: Prentice-Hall, 1965.

Experiment I: Subjects: $N = 114$; elementary school teachers. Measures: Teachers were asked to describe incidents in which they believed they had rewarded creative behavior in their classrooms. Results: In 75% of the cases, teachers were able to recall who initiated the rewarded behavior; more boys than girls were mentioned ($p < .01$).

Experiment II: Subjects: $N = 212$; 6–8 yrs. Measures: During the administration of the Product Improvement Task, Ss were rated on the degree to which they manipulated each of the 3 toys: a nurse's kit, a fire truck, and a stuffed toy dog. Results: Among 7- and 8-year-old Ss, boys were more manipulative than girls.

Experiment III: Subjects: $N = 171$; 11 yrs. Measures: Ss completed questionnaires about their reading experiences. Results: (1) No sex differences were found in the number of Ss who liked to read. (2) Boys were less likely than girls to go to the library to check out books. (3) Girls indicated that they read more books per month than boys. (4) Boys reported that they owned more books than girls. (5) Boys were more likely than girls to check on the accuracy of a statement they did not believe. (6) Girls enjoyed giving oral book reports in class more than boys. (7) A greater number of girls than boys reported that they sometimes became so absorbed in what they were reading that they were unable to think of other things they should be doing. (8) Girls indicated they were more likely to become "lost to the world" when beginning a book than boys. (9) Boys expressed a greater preference than girls for books dealing with sports, science, and hobbies, whereas girls expressed a greater preference than boys for fiction, animal stories, fairy tales, classical novels, career stories, drama, poetry, and religion (no tests of significance reported). (10) No sex differences were found in the number of Ss who reported they enjoyed telling others about what they had read or who stated that they sometimes found errors in spelling or grammar while reading.

EXPERIMENT IV: **Subjects:** $N = 75$; 12, 13 yrs (minimum IQ 135). **Measures:** The Ask-and-Guess Test, the Unusual Uses Test, the Product Improvement Test, the Consequences Test, and the figural or nonverbal tests of creative thinking were administered to Ss. Ss also completed make-up arithmetic and social studies problems. **Results:** (1) On the figural tests, boys scored higher than girls on nonverbal fluency ($p < .005$), nonverbal originality ($p < .005$), and nonverbal penetration ($p < .025$). (2) On the Consequences Test, boys scored higher than girls on flexibility ($p < .025$) but not on fluency. (3) Girls performed better than boys on the make-up social studies problems ($p < .005$).

EXPERIMENT V: **Subjects:** $N = 50$; 11 yrs. **Measures:** Parallel Lines Test, Ask-and-Guess Test. **Results:** (1) On the Parallel Lines Test, boys scored higher than girls on originality ($p < .025$), and girls scored higher than boys on elaboration ($p < .01$). No sex differences were found on the fluency or flexibility measures. (2) On the Ask-and-Guess Test, girls scored higher than boys on asking questions ($p < .025$) and on causal hypotheses ($p < .025$). No sex differences were found on consequential hypotheses.

EXPERIMENT VI: **Subjects:** $N = 555$; 6–11 yrs. **Measures:** The Product Improvement Task was administered under competitive and noncompetitive conditions. Ss' responses were scored for fluency, flexibility, and originality. **Results:** (1) Among 8-year-old Ss, boys scored higher in originality (competition condition only) and fluency than girls. (2) Among 9- and 11-year-old Ss, boys had higher originality scores in the competitive condition than girls. (3) Among 10-year-old Ss, girls had higher fluency and flexibility scores than boys.

EXPERIMENT VII: **Subjects:** $N = 320$; 6–11 yrs. **Measures:** The Pictures Construction Task and the Incomplete Figures Task were administered to Ss. During practice sessions preceding each test, half the Ss received positive, constructive evaluation from E. The other half of the Ss received encouragement from E but no evaluation. **Results:** (1) Picture Construction Test: (a) Among 6-year-old Ss, girls had higher originality scores than boys; (b) among 8-year-old Ss, girls had higher elaboration scores than boys; boys had higher originality scores than girls (unevaluated condition only); (c) among 9-year-old Ss, girls had higher elaboration scores than boys (evaluated condition only); (d) among 10-year-old Ss, girls had higher elaboration scores than boys in the unevaluated condition, whereas the reverse was true in the evaluated condition; (e) among 11-year-old Ss, girls had higher elaboration scores than boys (evaluated condition only). (2) Incomplete Figures Test: (a) among 8-year-old Ss, girls had higher originality scores than boys; boys had higher closure scores than girls (unevaluated condition only); (b) among 10-year-old Ss, girls had higher elaboration scores than boys (unevaluated condition only); (c) among 11-year-old Ss, girls had higher elaboration scores and higher closure scores (evaluated condition only) than boys.

Torrance, E. P., and Aliotti, N. C. Sex differences in levels of performance and test-retest reliability on the Torrance Tests of Creative Thinking Ability. *J. Creative Behavior*, 1969, 3, 52–57.

Subjects: $N = 118$; 10 yrs. **Measures:** Ss, responses to Forms A and B of the figural and verbal batteries of the Torrance Tests of Creative Thinking Ability were scored for fluency, flexibility, originality, and elaboration. **Results:** (1) On the figural tests, boys were superior to girls in flexibility (Form A, $p < .05$; Form B, NS) and originality ($p < .01$, $p < .05$). Girls scored higher than boys on elaboration ($p < .001$, $p < .001$). No sex differences were found in fluency. (2) On the verbal tests, girls were superior to boys in fluency ($p < .01$, $p < .002$), flexibility ($p < .01$, $p < .002$), and originality ($p < .01$, $p < .002$).

Touhey, J. C. Comparison of two dimensions of attitude similarity on heterosexual attraction. *J. Personality & Social Psychology*, 1972, 23, 8–10.

Subjects: $N = 250$; 18–21 yrs (college). **Measures:** Men and women in a computer-dating study were matched on the basis of maximal or minimal similarity in either religious or sexual attitudes. Ss' impressions of their dates were assessed on a modified version of Byrne's Interpersonal Judgment Scale. **Results:** (1) Women were more attracted to their dates than men were ($p < .05$). (2) Women were more attracted to men with religiously similar attitudes; men were more attracted to women with sexually similar attitudes ($p < .05$).

Tuddenham, R. D. A study of reputation: children's evaluations of their peers. In G. G. Thompson, F. J. DiVesta, and J. Horrocks, eds., *Social development and personality.* Somerset, N.J.: Wiley, 1971.
> **Subjects:** $N = 1,439$; 6, 8, 10 yrs. **Measures:** Ss were asked questions about their classmates (in answering each item, Ss were free to name themselves). **Results:** (1) Among 6-year-old Ss, girls were judged to be more popular, and less quarrelsome than boys. (2) Among 8-year-old Ss, girls were judged to be more popular, more quiet, less quarrelsome, and less bossy than boys. Girls were also rated more favorably than boys on the "doesn't get mad—gets mad easily" dimension. (3) Among 10-year-old Ss, girls were judged to be more quiet and tidy than boys; boys were judged to take more chances, to be bigger show-offs, and to be better at games than girls. (4) Girls voted for others more often than boys did. Boys mentioned themselves more frequently than girls did. Girls judged others of the same sex more favorably than boys did. Boys gave more favorable self-evaluations than girls did. No tests of significance were reported.

Tulving, E., and Pearlstone, Z. Availability versus accessibility of information in memory for words. *J. Verbal Learning & Verbal Behavior,* 1966, 5, 381–91 (and personal communication).
> **Subjects:** $N = 929$; 15–17 yrs. **Measures:** Ss learned lists of words in specific conceptual categories. Immediate recall and cued-recall category name tests followed. **Results:** Girls showed greater recall than boys.

Turiel, E. A comparative analysis of moral knowledge and moral judgment in males and females. To appear in L. Kohlberg and E. Turiel, eds., *Recent research in moral judgment.* New York: Holt, Rinehart & Winston, 1973.
> **Subjects:** $N = 210$; 11, 14, 17 yrs. **Measures:** Ss were individually given a moral judgment interview consisting of 5 stories. In 1 form of the interview the stories involved male protagonists, while in the second form the stories involved female protagonists. Each S was assigned a moral maturity score based on Kohlberg's Scale. A few days later, Ss were given a moral knowledge test composed of 30 statements, each describing a transgression committed by either a boy (for male Ss) or a girl (for female Ss). Ss rated the degree of wrongness of each transgression. **Results:** (1) At ages 11 and 14, girls had higher moral maturity scores than boys; at age 17, boys had higher scores than girls ($p < .05$). (2) No sex differences were found in the moral knowledge test.

Turkewitz, G., Moreau, T., Birch, H. G., and Crystal, D. Relationship between prior head position and lateral difference in responsiveness to somesthetic stimulation in the human neonate. *J. Experimental Child Psychology,* 1967, 5, 548–61.
> **Subjects:** $N = 51$; 1–3 days. **Measures:** With infants lying on their backs, their heads held in midline position with no lateralized pressure detectable on E's fingers, the touch of a camel's hair brush was applied for 1-second trials to the area around the mouth. Mock presentation consisted of moving brush toward mouth but not making contact. On all trials, direction of first head movement after removal of brush was recorded. **Results:** No sex differences.

Turnure, C. Response to voice of mother and stranger by babies in the first year. *Developmental Psychology,* 1971, 4, 182–90.
> **Subjects:** $N = 33$; 3, 6, 9 mos. **Measures:** Ss heard tape recordings (normal, slightly distorted, and grossly distorted) of their mothers' voices. Half of the Ss then heard an additional sequence of auditory stimuli consisting of (a) the voice of an unfamiliar person and (b) more presentations of their mothers' voices (normal and distorted). Movies taken of Ss were scored for limb movement. **Results:** First phase of the experiment in which all Ss participated: (1) at 3 months, girls showed more limb movements to the slight distortion and to the gross distortion of their mothers' voices than boys did ($p < .05$); (2) at 9 months, girls showed more limb movement to their mothers' normal voices than boys did ($p < .05$); (3) no sex differences were found when mean limb movement during the 15 seconds immediately preceding each stimulus presentation was subtracted from mean limb movement during the stimulus period. No sex differences were found in the second phase of the experiment ($N = 15$).

Turnure, J. E. Children's reactions to distractors in a learning situation. *Developmental Psychology,* 1970, 2, 115–22.
> **Subjects:** $N = 90$; 5–7 yrs. **Measures:** Ss performed oddity discrimination problems with either visual distraction, auditory distraction, or no distraction. Correct responses and glances away from the task were recorded. **Results:** No sex differences.

Turnure, J. E. 'Control of orienting behavior in children under five years of age. *Developmental Psychology*, 1971, *4*, 16–24.
Subjects: $N = 40$; 3, 4 yrs. Measures: Ss performed 2-choice discrimination tasks under conditions of distraction and no distraction. E recorded Ss' glances away from the task. Results: There were no main sex differences. Girls made greater gains in correct responses over trials than boys ($p < .05$).

Tyron, A. F. Thumbsucking and manifest anxiety: a note. *Child Development*, 1968, *39*, 1159–61.
Subjects: $N = 104$; 7–14 yrs (current thumbsuckers and non-thumbsuckers). Measures: Children's Manifest Anxiety Scale. Results: No sex differences.

Unikel, I. P., Strain, G. W., and Adams, H. E. Learning of lower socioeconomic status children as a function of social and tangible reward. *Developmental Psychology*, 1969, *1*, 553–55.
Subjects: $N = 144$; 5–6 yrs (Head Start program). Measures: Ss played a simple discrimination-learning game under 1 of 3 conditions: tangible reward (candy), social reward, and no reward (control). Results: (1) There was no main effect for sex of S. (2) Ss performed better with a female rather than with a male E ($p < .05$).

Unruh, S. G., Gross, M. E., and Zigler, E. Birth order, number of siblings, and social reinforcer effectiveness in children. *Child Development*, 1971, *42*, 1153–63.
Subjects: $N = 144$; 6, 7, 8 yrs. Measures: Ss played a marble game designed to be tedious, so that social reinforcement would become the main determinant of how long Ss played. E either did or did not support Ss' performance. Results: No sex differences.

Vassiliou, V., Georgas, J. G., and Vassiliou, G. Variations in manifest anxiety due to sex, age, and education. *J. Personality & Social Psychology*, 1967, *6*, 194–97.
Subjects: $N = 400$; adults (Greek). Measures: Taylor Manifest Anxiety Scale. Results: Women had higher anxiety scores than men ($p < .01$).

Vaughan, G. M., and White, K. D. Conformity and authoritarianism reexamined. *J. Personality & Social Psychology*, 1966, *3*, 363–66.
Subjects: $N = 312$; 18–21 yrs (college). Measures: Berkowitz and Wolkon's forced-choice version of the authoritarian F scale. Results: No sex differences.

Vaught, G. M. The relationship of role identification and ego strength to sex differences in the Rod-and-Frame Test. *J. Personality*, 1965, *33*, 271–83.
Subjects: $N = 180$; 18–21 yrs (college). Measures: Rod-and-Frame Test. Results: Men were more field-independent than women ($p < .01$).

Vernon, D. T., Foley, J. M., and Schulman, J. L. Effect of mother-child separation and birth order on young children's responses to two potentially stressful experiences. *J. Personality & Social Psychology*, 1967, *5*, 162–74.
Experiment I: Subjects: $N = 32$; 2–5 yrs. Measures: Ss were brought to a hospital for surgery and put through standard admission procedures, with their mother either present or absent. Both before and after admission procedures, Ss were placed in a free-play activity situation. Ss were rated for quality of play, aggression, and mood. Results: No sex differences.
Experiment II: Subjects: $N = 32$; 2–5 yrs. Measures: Prior to anesthesia induction, Ss were placed in a free-play activity situation, with their mothers present. Estimates were made of Ss' mood both during the free-play period and during anesthesia induction. After Ss were released from the hospital, their mothers completed a post-hospital behavior questionnaire. Mothers' descriptions of their child's behavior were scored for (a) general anxiety and regression, (b) separation anxiety, (c) sleep anxiety, (d) eating disturbance, (e) aggression toward authority, and (f) apathy withdrawal. Results: No sex differences.

Very, P. S. Differential factor structures in mathematical abilities. *Genetic Psychology Monographs*, 1967, *75*, 169–207.
Subjects: $N = 355$; 18–21 yrs (college). Measures: A battery of mathematical, verbal, and spatial tests. Results: (1) Women scored higher than men on Logical Reasoning, Number Comparisons, Visual Motor Velocity, Moore-Castore Vocabulary. Moore-Castore Paragraph Reading, and English Placement Vocabulary. (2) Men scored higher than women on Division, Arithmetic Reasoning, Mathematical Aptitude, General Reasoning, Spatial Relations, Cards, Cubes, Spatial Orientation, Judgment, Moore-Castore Arithmetic, and Moore-Castore Algebra.

(3) There were no sex differences in Addition, Subtraction, Arithmetic Computation, Number Arrangement, Ship Destination, Practical Estimation, Math Puzzles, Nonsense Syllogisms, Deductive Reasoning, Letter Concepts, Inductive Reasoning, Picture Concepts, and Letter Reasoning.

Voissem, N. H., and Sistrunk, K. F. Communication schedule and cooperative game behavior. *J. Personality & Social Psychology*, 1971, *19*, 160–67.
Subjects: $N = 96$; 18–21 yrs (college). **Measures:** Same-sex pairs of Ss played the Prisoner's Dilemma game, with or without opportunities for communication. **Results:** No sex differences were found in percentage of cooperative responses.

Vondracek, S. I., and Vondracek, F. W. The manipulation and measurement of self-disclosure in pre-adolescents. *Merrill-Palmer Quarterly*, 1971, *17*, 51–58.
Subjects: $N = 80$; 11 yrs. **Measures:** Ss were asked to disclose things about themselves that ordinarily they would reveal only to a few special people. Ss' statements were scored for degree of intimacy. **Results:** No sex differences.

Wagman, M. Sex differences in types of daydreams. *J. Personality & Social Psychology*, 1967, *7*, 329–32.
Subjects: $N = 206$; 18–21 yrs (college). **Measures:** Ss reported the frequency of their daydreams in 24 content categories. **Results:** Men reported a higher frequency of aggressive, sexual, hostile, and heroic or self-aggrandizing daydreams than women. Women reported a higher frequency of passive, affiliative, narcissistic, oral, physical attractiveness, practical, and planning daydreams than men.

Walberg, H. J. Physics, femininity, and creativity. *Developmental Psychology*, 1969, *1*, 47–54.
Random subsamples of 2,074 students taking a new high school physics course were tested.
EXPERIMENT I: **Subjects:** $N = 1,050$; 16–17 yrs. **Measures:** (1) The Science Process Inventory and the Test on Understanding Science, (2) the Physics Achievement Test, (3) the Pupil Activity Inventory. **Results:** (1) Girls scored higher than boys on the Science Process Inventory and on the Test on Understanding Science. Boys scored higher than girls on the Physics Achievement Test. (2) On the Pupil Activity Inventory, girls indicated greater participation in nature study and applications of science. Boys indicated greater participation in cosmological activities and tinkering activities.
EXPERIMENT II: **Subjects:** $N = 450$; 16–17 yrs. **Measures:** (1) Henmon-Nelson Intelligence Test, Form B, 12 grade level, (2) The Study of Values: Theoretical, Economic, Aesthetic, Social, Political, and Religious, (3) Personality measures of dogmatism, authoritarianism, rigidity, need for achievement, need for order, need for affiliation, and need for change. **Results:** (1) Girls scored higher than boys on the IQ test. (2) Girls scored higher than boys on the Social, Aesthetic, and Religious scales; boys scored higher than girls on the Economic, Political, and Theoretical scales. (3) Girls scored higher than boys on the need for affiliation and need for change measures; boys scored higher than girls on the dogmatism measure.
EXPERIMENT III: **Subjects:** $N = 850$; 16–17 yrs. **Measures:** Using semantic differential scales, Ss rated each of 4 physical science concepts: (1) universe, (2) physics, (3) laboratory experiments, and (4) myself as a physics student. **Results:** (1) Girls rated universe as more friendly and beautiful than boys did. (2) Girls rated physics as less safe than boys did. (3) Boys rated laboratory experiments as less important and more simple than girls did. (4) As physics students, girls saw themselves as less facile and as "more apt to be starting" than boys did.
EXPERIMENT IV: **Subjects:** $N = 455$; 16–17 yrs. **Measures:** Ss indicated their agreement or disagreement with items describing characteristics of the socio-emotional climate of learning in the school classroom. **Results:** (1) Girls rated their classes more satisfying, egalitarian, and diverse in their goals than boys did. Girls also perceived more intimacy among the class members than boys did. (2) Boys felt more friction among class members, perceived greater social differences among their fellow students, felt more constrained about what could be said in class, and saw a greater degree of group subservience than girls did.

Waldrop, M. Longitudinal and cross-sectional analyses of seven-and-a-half-year-old peer behavior. Unpublished manuscript, National Institute of Mental Health, 1972.
Subjects: $N = 62$; 7½ yrs. **Measures:** Mothers were asked to keep a diary of their children's activities for a period of 1 week. To supplement these written reports, mothers were individually interviewed at the end of the week. Objective counts were made of hours with peers, hours with 1 peer, and hours with more than 1 peer. The age and sex of each child's play-

mates were also recorded. **Results:** When with peers, highly social boys had extensive peer relations (i.e. they usually played with groups of boys), whereas highly social girls had intensive peer relations (i.e. they usually played with 1 other girl).

Walker, R. N. Some temperament traits in children as viewed by their peers, their teachers, and themselves. *Monographs of the Society for Research in Child Development*, 1967, *32*.
    Subjects: *N* = 450; 8–11 yrs. **Measures:** (1) 406 children rated themselves on 96 self-descriptive statements, 16 for each of 6 traits: energetic, surgent, social, stable, fearful, and aggressive. (2) All 450 children were rated by their teachers on each of the 6 traits. **Results:** Teachers viewed boys and boys viewed themselves as more aggressive and energetic and as less stable and fearful than girls.

Wallach, M. A., and Mabli, J. Information versus conformity in the effects of group discussion on risk taking. *J. Personality & Social Psychology*, 1970, *14*, 149–56.
    Subjects: *N* = 108; 18–21 yrs (college). **Measures:** Based on Ss' responses to Wallach and Kagan's choice-dilemmas battery, 36 3-person groups were formed, composed of either a risky majority and a conservative minority or vice versa. Groups were homogeneous with respect to sex. Effects of group discussion on risk taking were assessed by measuring shifts from initial decisions (on the choice-dilemmas instrument) to group consensus decisions, and from initial decisions to postconsensus person decisions. **Results:** No sex differences.

Wallach, M. A., and Martin, M. L. Effects of social class on children's motoric expression. *Developmental Psychology*, 1970, *3*, 106–13.
    Subjects: *N* = 283; 6, 7, 9, 11 yrs (low, middle SES). **Measures:** Ss were asked to draw designs on a piece of paper. The amount of area that their drawings covered was used as an index of motoric construction-expansiveness. **Results:** Among middle SES 9-year-old Ss, girls were more expansive than boys. No other sex differences were found.

Walls, R. T., and Cox, J. Disadvantaged and nondisadvantaged children's expectancy in skill and chance outcomes. *Developmental Psychology*, 1971, *4*, 299.
    Subjects: *N* = 80; 8–9 yrs. **Measures:** Ss placed as many pegs into a board as possible under 1 of 4 treatments, which varied as to Ss' perceptions about and actual existence of amount of chance and skill. Ss then completed the Internal-External Locus of Control Scale for Children and answered questions concerning occupational aspiration. **Results:** (1) There were no sex differences in pegboard task performance. (2) More disadvantaged than nondisadvantaged girls had a general external expectancy on Internal-External Locus of Control measure; the opposite was true for boys. (3) Among disadvantaged Ss, boys displayed a more internal locus, whereas girls displayed a more external locus. (4) Girls expected to hold more prestigious jobs but earn less money than boys.

Walls, R. T., and DiVesta, F. J. Cognitive factors in the conditioning of children's preferences. *Developmental Psychology*, 1970, *2*, 318–24.
    Subjects: *N* = 108; 6 yrs. **Measures:** Ss matched descriptive adjectives with Greek letter stimuli (as a measure of stimulus preference) before and after conditioning sessions involving 1 or 2 marble reinforcement procedures: reinforced stimuli remaining the same or differing over sessions. **Results:** There were no sex differences in preferences for stimuli on final rating day.

Walster, E. Assignment of responsibility for an accident. *J. Personality & Social Psychology*, 1966, *3*, 73–79.
    Subjects: *N* = 88; 18–21 yrs (college). **Measures:** Ss rated the degree to which a young man was responsible for an accident. Real and possible consequences of the accident varied. **Results:** (1) There were no main sex differences. (2) Men judged the young man to be more responsible when he seriously injured another person than when he might have done so; women judged the young man to be equally responsible in both conditions ($p < .05$). (3) Women judged the young man to be more responsible ($p < .001$) when he might have seriously injured another person than when he might have demolished his own car. Men did not assign more responsibility to the young man as the possible consequences of the accident increased.

Wapner, S. Age changes in perception of verticality and of the longitudinal body axis under body tilt. *J. Experimental Child Psychology*, 1968, *6*, 543–55.
    Subjects: *N* = 192; 7–16 yrs. **Measures:** Positions of apparent vertical location of the longitudinal axis of the body and their relation were assessed under erect and 30-degree left and right body tilt. **Results:** (1) The effect of starting position was greater for girls than for boys (apparent vertical). (2) Girls showed a greater shift of apparent body axis than boys. (3) The effect of starting position was greater for girls than for boys (apparent body axis).

Ward, W. C. Creativity in young children. *Child Development*, 1968a, *39*, 736–54.

Subjects: $N = 87$; 4–6 yrs. Measures: 3 measures of creativity were administered to Ss: the Uses test, the Patterns test, and the Instances test. Ss' responses were scored for fluency and originality. Results: No sex differences.

Ward, W. C. Reflection-impulsivity in kindergarten children. *Child Development*, 1968b, *39*, 867–74.

Subjects: $N = 87$; 5 yrs. Measures: (1) Ss were given Forms A and B of the Peabody Picture Vocabulary Test. The items of the PPVT were arranged in order of increasing difficulty, and the test was administered until Ss missed 6 of any 8 consecutive items. The mean response latency of Ss' last 6 errors was used as a measure of reflectiveness. (2) Ss were shown cards with a vertical line drawn down the center of each. On both halves of each card was an array of dots. Ss' task was to decide which half had more dots. The number of errors Ss made and the latencies of their responses to the most difficult items were recorded. (3) Ss were presented with 6 figures and were asked to indicate which of the 6 was identical to a standard. The number of incorrect matches that each S made was recorded. (4) Ss were given 2 tests based on Kagan's Matching Familiar Figures procedure. Response latency and number of errors were recorded. Results: Girls made fewer errors on the dot tests than boys did ($p < .01$). No other sex differences were found.

Ward, W. C. Creativity and environmental cues in nursery school children. *Developmental Psychology*, 1969, *1*, 543–47.

Subjects: $N = 55$; 4 yrs (nursery school). Measures: In a barren experimental room, Ss were individually given the Uses test (name all the uses for a newspaper, knife, cup, and coat hanger) and the Patterns test (interpret 8 simple abstract patterns). 2½ months later, Ss were given the Instances test (name instances of round things, soft things, and red things) under 1 of 2 conditions: in a barren experimental room or in a cue-rich environment containing 38 objects chosen to be relevant to the test. The response measures were fluency (total number of ideas given) and uniqueness (number of ideas given only by 1 child in the sample). Results: No sex differences.

Ward, W. C., and Legant, P. Naming and memory in nursery school children in the absence of rehearsal. *Developmental Psychology*, 1971, *5*, 174–75 (note and extended report).

EXPERIMENT II: Subjects: $N = 20$; 3–4 yrs. Measures: On each of 10 trials, Ss were shown 2 pictures. Ss either verbally named them or remained silent. After a 20-second delay with no opportunity for covert rehearsal, Ss were instructed to choose those 2 pictures from an array of 9. Results: No sex differences.

EXPERIMENT III: Subjects: $N = 29$; 4 yrs. Measures: Same as Experiment II, except that picture stimuli were alternated with color stimuli. Results: No sex differences.

Ward, W. D. Variance of sex-role preference among boys and girls. *Psychological Reports*, 1968, *23*, 467–70.

Subjects: $N = 48$; 4–7 yrs. Measures: Ss were presented with pictures of 15 pairs of toys, 1 masculine and 1 feminine, and were asked to indicate which toy in each pair they would like to play with. The sex-role preference measure was the number of times Ss chose own-sex toy. Results: (1) Girls showed greater group variance than boys ($p < .01$). (2) Boys preferred boys' toys more than girls preferred girls' toys ($p < .01$).

Ward, W. D. Process of sex-role development. *Developmental Psychology*, 1969a, *1*, 1963–68.

Subjects: $N = 32$; 5–8 yrs. Measures: (1) Sex-role preference was assessed by having Ss choose pictures of masculine and feminine toys on the Toy Preference Test (TPT). (2) A Pointer Game (PG) was devised to determine the extent to which boys and girls would imitate or adopt the responses of either a man or a woman. (3) Identification was measured by S's perceived similarity to parent on the Polar Adjectives Test (PAT). Results: (1) On the TPT, boys and girls preferred their own-sex toys (the main effect was accounted for by the older Ss). (2) On the PG, boys imitated the man and girls imitated the woman. (3) Among younger Ss, there was no perceived similarity with either parent on the PAT; among older Ss, both sexes saw themselves as similar to their mother.

Ward, W. D. The withholding and the withdrawing of rewards as related to level of aspiration. *Child Development*, 1969b, *40*, 491–97.

Subjects: $N = 36$; 5, 6, 7 yrs. Measures: Ss tossed a ball on the floor, and tried to make it land on certain lines. The withholding group started the game without tokens, and received tokens as rewards. The withdrawing group started with 50 tokens, which were taken away whenever S "failed." Level of aspiration was assessed. **Results:** No sex differences.

Ward, W. D., and Furchak, A. F. Resistance to temptation among boys and girls. *Psychological Reports*, 1968, *23*, 511–14.

Subjects: $N = 24$; 5, 7 yrs. **Measures:** E encouraged Ss to play with a collection of uninteresting, broken-down toys, and told them not to play with a group of attractive toys. Afterward, E left Ss alone in the playroom. The length of time Ss refrained from touching the attractive toys was recorded. **Results:** Girls showed greater resistance to temptation than boys ($p < .02$).

Ware, C. K. Cooperation and competition in children: a developmental study of behavior in Prisoner's Dilemma and maximizing differences games. Yale University, 1969.

Subjects: $N = 216$; 6, 9, 12 yrs. **Measures:** Same-sex and opposite-sex pairs of Ss played 1 of 2 games; each was in the form of the Prisoner's Dilemma. **Results:** (1) Girl-girl pairs made more cooperative responses than either boy-boy or girl-boy pairs. (2) No sex differences were found in initial readiness to cooperate. (3) Girls in girl-girl pairs were more likely to cooperate after making a competitive response than Ss in girl-boy or boy-boy pairs. No differences were found among girl-girl, girl-boy, or boy-boy pairs in tendency to cooperate after making a cooperative response.

Warren, V. L., and Cairns, R. B. Social reinforcement satiation: an outcome of frequency of ambiguity? *J. Experimental Child Psychology*, 1972, *13*, 249–60.

Subjects: $N = 100$; 7 yrs. **Measures:** On each trial in a discrimination-learning task, Ss were free to press either of 2 buttons. Every time Ss pressed the "correct" button, E responded with verbal approval (e.g. "right"). The number of times Ss selected the "correct" button was recorded. **Results:** No sex differences.

Wasik, H., and Wasik, J. L. Performance of culturally deprived children on the concept assessment kit—conservation. *Child Development*, 1971, *42*, 1586–90.

Subjects: $N = 117$; 6–9 yrs (white and black, low SES). **Measures:** The Concept Assessment Kit—Conservation was administered to Ss. 8 areas of conservation were measured: 2-dimensional space, number, substance, continuous quantity, weight, discontinuous quantity, area, and length. **Results:** No sex differences were found.

Wasserman, S. A. Values of Mexican-American, Negro, and Anglo blue-collar and white-collar children. *Child Development*, 1971, *42*, 1624–28.

Subjects: $N = 180$; 4 yrs (middle class, working class). **Measures:** Ss were questioned about pictures depicting value conflict situations. The questions pertained to what the persons in the pictures should do. Measures were obtained of Ss' preferences for 4 humanitarian values (helpfulness, cooperation, concern for others, and sharing) and 4 success values (competition, status, expertise-seeking, and task completion). **Results:** No main sex differences were found. Middle SES boys scored higher on humanitarian values (total score) than girls did ($p < .05$).

Watson, J. S. Perception of object orientation in infants. *Merrill-Palmer Quarterly*, 1966, *12*, 73–94.

EXPERIMENT II: **Subjects:** $N = 48$; 7–8, 13–14, 19–20, 25–26 wks and mothers. **Measures:** After being placed in a supine position, S was exposed to 3 orientations each of his mother's (M's) face, of E's face, and of a multicolored cloth mask worn by E. The 3 orientations were a normal (0°) view (E's or M's eyes directly above S's eyes, E's or M's chin directly above S's chin), a sideways (90°) view, and an upside-down (180°) view (E's or M's forehead directly above S's chin, E's or M's chin directly above S's forehead). The response measure was the average time spent smiling to the 0° orientation minus the average time spent smiling to the 90° and 180° orientations. **Results:** No sex differences.

EXPERIMENT III: **Subjects:** Same as Experiment II. **Measures:** Ss were simultaneously presented with 2 orientations (0° and 180°) of a schematic face. The response measure was the time spent fixating on the 0° orientation minus the time spent fixating on the 180° orientation. **Results:** No sex differences.

Watson, J. S. Operant conditioning of visual fixation in infants under visual and auditory reinforcement. *Developmental Psychology* 1969, *1*, 408–16.

EXPERIMENT I: **Subjects:** $N = 32$; 14 wks. **Measures:** Visual fixation on 2 blank targets was differentially reinforced with contingent visual (face) and auditory (soft tones) stimuli. The frequency of fixation on the 2 target positions was recorded by an observer blind to the specific target on which fixation was being reinforced and to the modality and duration of the reinforcement. **Results:** There were no main sex differences in baseline fixation rates or learning scores. Learning was better under visual than auditory reinforcement for boys; the opposite was true for girls.

EXPERIMENT II: **Subjects:** $N = 24$; 10 wks. **Measures:** S was given a 10-minute conditioning session that was divided into several periods involving 3 different types of reinforcement: auditory alone, visual alone, and a simultaneous presentation of both visual and auditory. The response measures were the same as for Experiment I. **Results:** No main sex differences. The relation between sex and effective modality of reinforcement found in Experiment I was not replicated.

Weber, D. S. A time perception task. *Perceptual & Motor Skills*, 1965, *21*, 863–66.
Subjects: $N = 72$; 16–25 yrs (college). **Measures:** Ss were asked to identify from among 9 flashing lights the 1 light containing interflash intervals of a fixed duration. **Results:** Men made more correct identifications than women ($p < .05$).

Weener, P. Language structure and the free recall of verbal messages by children. *Developmental Psychology*, 1971, *5*, 237–43.
EXPERIMENT I: **Subjects:** $N = 90$; 5–8 yrs. **Measures:** Ss heard tapes of word strings with 2 levels of syntax and associativity: with syntax/with associativity (e.g. "swift deer jump high fences"), with syntax/without associativity (e.g. "last foxes sail silver gardens"), without syntax/with associativity (associativity sentences word orders reversed), without associativity/without syntax (word order of without-associativity sentences reversed). Ss were asked to recall words without regard to order. **Results:** No sex differences.
EXPERIMENT II: **Subjects:** $N = 69$; 5–8 yrs (same as Experiment I, 4 months later). **Measures:** Additional stimulus items were constructed by adding intonation to all word strings from Experiment I that had syntax. Ss were only tested on these items; scores were compared to without-intonation scores. **Results:** No sex differences.

Wei, J. D., Lavatelli, C. B., and Jones, R. S. Piaget's concept of classification: a comparative study of socially disadvantaged and middle-class young children. *Child Development*, 1971, *42*, 919–27.
Subjects: $N = 80$; 5, 7 yrs. **Measures:** Ss performed 4 Piagetian classification tasks (changing criteria, classification, class inclusion, and matrices). **Results:** No sex differences.

Weinberg, S., and Rabinowitz, J. A sex difference in the Wechsler IQ vocabulary scores as a predictor of strategy in a probability-learning task performed by adolescents. *Developmental Psychology*, 1970, *3*, 218–24.
Subjects: $N = 48$; 12–19 yrs. **Measures:** Ss predicted which of 2 stimuli would be presented in each trial of a series. Unknown to Ss, stimuli had an 8 : 2 ratio. Prediction strategies were analyzed through choices and questioning. Before predictions, Ss completed the Block Design and Vocabulary subtests of the Wechsler Intelligence Scale for Children. **Results:** (1) More boys than girls used a maximizing strategy (predicted the more frequently appearing stimulus); more girls than boys used matching strategy (attempted to match the sequence exactly). (2) There were no sex differences on Block Design and Vocabulary scores.

Weiner, B. Achievement motivation and task recall in competitive situations. *J. Personality & Social Psychology*, 1966, *3*, 693–96.
Subjects: $N = 70$; 18–21 yrs (college). **Measures:** Ss attempted to complete more puzzle tasks than their same-sex or opposite-sex opponents. Recall of incompleted and completed tasks was assessed later. Ss also completed the Achievement Risk-Preference Scale (ARPS). **Results:** (1) There were no main sex differences. (2) Men recalled relatively more incompleted than completed tasks when competing against a woman than when competing against a man ($p < .01$). No similar difference was found for women. (3) Men who obtained high scores on the ARPS recalled relatively more incompleted than completed tasks than men who obtained low scores on the ARPS ($p < .01$). No similar difference was found for women.

Weinheimer, S. Egocentrism and social influence in children. *Child Development*, 1972, *43*, 567–68.
Subjects: $N = 160$; 5–8 yrs. **Measures:** Ss were presented with 9 stimuli. After each was shown, they reported what they had seen to E. E then informed Ss of the responses previously reported by a group of alters (3 male or female adults or peers) who had been seated at the opposite end of the table. The stimuli that were described were placed in the middle of the table so that Ss saw them from a different perspective than that of the alters. Afterward, Ss judged the correctness of their own and alters' responses. Ss' judgments were classified into 3 categories:

reconciling, conforming, and independent. **Results:** (1) Girls conformed more than boys (p < .01). Girls conformed more in the presence of male adult alters than boys did in the presence of female adult alters (p < .001). (2) Boys were more independent than girls (p < .01). (3) No sex differences were found in number of reconciling responses.

Weinraub, M., and Lewis, M. Infant attachment and play behavior: sex of child and sex of parent differences. *Educational Testing Service Research Bulletin*, Princeton, N.J., 1973.
> **Subjects:** $N = 18$; 2 yrs. **Measures:** Ss were tested in a free-play situation twice, once in the presence of their mothers and once in the presence of their fathers. Parents were instructed to respond to their children, but not to initiate any interaction. The number of seconds Ss spent in sustained toy play and the number of seconds Ss engaged in each of 4 attachment behaviors (touching the parent, proximity to the parent, looking at the parent, and vocalizing to the parent) were recorded. **Results:** (1) No sex-of-child or sex-of-parent differences were found in amount of time spent in sustained play. Girls showed more sustained play in the presence of their mothers than in the presence of their fathers; no such difference was found for boys (p < .01). Girls played more than boys in the presence of their mothers (p < .01); no sex differences were found in the presence of fathers. (2) No sex differences were found in attachment behaviors.

Weisbroth, S. P. Moral judgment, sex, and parental identification in adults. *Developmental Psychology*, 1970, 2, 396–402.
> **Subjects:** $N = 78$; 21–39 yrs (college graduates). **Measures:** Ss completed Kohlberg's moral judgment test. **Results:** No sex differences.

Weiss, R. F., Lombardo, J. P., Warren, D. R., and Kelley, K. A. Reinforcing effects of speaking in reply. *J. Personality & Social Psychology*, 1971, 20, 186–99.
> **Subjects:** $N = 418$; 18–21 yrs (college). **Measures:** After listening to a tape of another person's viewpoint on a topic, Ss were told to press a switch if they wanted to reply to the other person. During the acquisition phase, Ss were allowed to speak either on every trial on which they pressed the switch or on only 50% of the trials. During the extinction phase, no opportunity was given to reply to the other person. The response measure was the elapsed time between the presentation of the signal "Press switch if you wish to comment" and Ss' response. **Results:** No sex differences.

Weizmann, F., Cohen, L. B., and Pratt, R. J. Novelty, familiarity, and the development of infant attention. *Developmental Psychology*, 1971, 4, 149–54.
> **Subjects:** $N = 32$; tested at 6, 8 wks. **Measures:** Beginning at age 4 weeks, each S was placed in a bassinet and exposed to a stabile 30 minutes a day for a period of a month. At 6 weeks and again at 8 weeks of age, half the Ss were observed for 2 1-minute periods in each of 4 conditions (double observation group); the other half of the Ss were observed only at 8 weeks of age (single observation group). The 4 conditions were (1) familiar bassinet–familiar stabile; (2) familiar bassinet–novel stabile; (3) novel bassinet–familiar stabile; (4) novel bassinet–novel stabile. Fixation times to the stabiles were recorded. **Results:** (1) In the double observation group, boys had longer fixation times than girls; in the single observation group, no sex differences were found. (2) In the familiar bassinet, boys fixated on the novel stabile longer than girls.

Weller, G. M., and Bell, R. Q. Basal skin conductance and neonatal state. *Child Development*, 1965, 36, 647–57.
> **Subjects:** $N = 40$; 2–4 days. **Measures:** Basal skin conductance, level of arousal, respiration rate, and regularity of respiration (standard deviation of respiration rate data) were recorded between feeding periods. **Results:** Girls had higher skin conductance than boys. No other sex differences were found.

Weller, L., and Sharan (Singer), S. Articulation of the body concept among first-grade Israeli children. *Child Development*, 1971, 42, 1553–59.
> **Subjects:** $N = 362$; 6 yrs. **Measures:** Ss were asked to draw a human figure. Drawings were scored for degree of articulation of the body concept. **Results:** (1) Among lower SES Ss whose parents were born in Yemen, and among middle SES Ss whose parents were born in Poland, girls showed greater body articulation than boys. (2) No sex differences were found among lower SES Ss whose parents were born in Poland or Iran, or among lower or middle SES Ss whose parents were born in Iraq.

Wenar, C. Executive competence and spontaneous social behavior in one-year-olds. *Child Development*, 1972, 43, 256–60.

Subjects: N = 26; 12–15 mos and mothers. **Measures:** Child's executive competence activity was scored for duration, intensity, and level, as well as for kind and intensity of affect. Spontaneous social response was scored for kind, duration, and intensity. Overall executive competence was scored for persistence. **Results:** No sex differences.

Werden, D., and Ross, L. E. A comparison of the trace and delay classical conditioning performance of normal children. *J. Experimental Child Psychology*, 1972, 14, 126–32.

Subjects: N = 48; 4–6 yrs. **Measures:** Ss were conditioned to pure tones under trace-and-delay conditions for 250 single-cue eyelid-conditioning trials. **Results:** Boys conditioned better than girls (p < .05).

Werner, E. E., Honzik, M. P., and Smith, R. S. Prediction of intelligence and achievement at ten years from pediatric and psychological examinations. *Child Development*, 1968, 39, 1063–75.

Subjects: N = 639; tested at 20 mos, 10 yrs. **Measures:** A Perinatal Stress Score, a psychological appraisal, the Cattell Infant Intelligence Scale, and the Doll's Vineland Social Maturity Scale were given at 20 months. The Science Research Associates Primary Mental Abilities Test (PMA), the Wechsler Intelligence Scale (for Ss who scored below mean on the PMA), and a teacher's summary of school achievement were given at age 10. An SES rating was obtained for each family. **Results:** (1) Both pediatricians and psychologists rated a larger proportion of boys than girls "low normal" or "retarded." (2) Among average and below-average SES Ss, girls obtained higher scores than boys on the Cattell Scale. (3) Among below-average SES Ss, girls obtained higher scores than boys on the PMA.

Wheeler, R. J., and Dusek, J. B. The effects of attentional and cognitive factors on children's incidental learning. *Child Development*, 1973, 44, 253–58.

Subjects: N = 144; 5, 8, 10 yrs. **Measures:** Incidental and central learning were tested. Ss viewed paired drawings of animals and household objects, either spatially separated or contiguous, under labeling or nonlabeling conditions. **Results:** Overall, girls had greater recall on central learning than boys. There were no sex differences on incidental learning.

White, G. M. Immediate and deferred effects of model observation and guided and unguided rehearsal on donating and stealing. *J. Personality & Social Psychology*, 1972, 21, 139–48.

Subjects: N = 210; 9–10 yrs. **Measures:** Following exposure to an altruistic model, Ss either did or did not rehearse charitable behavior (placing gift certificates in a charity box) in the model's presence. Immediately afterward, half of the Ss were given the opportunity to donate certificates in the absence of the model (Session I), and then again 2 days later (Session II). The remainings Ss only performed during Session II. The response measure was the number of certificates donated. **Results:** (1) No sex difference was found when the Session I performance of Ss playing immediately was compared with the Session II performance of Ss playing later. (2) When the Session II performances of both groups were examined, girls were found to donate more than boys. (3) When the Session I and Session II performances of Ss playing immediately were compared, girls were found to be more stable givers than boys (p < .002). (4) No sex differences were found in the donating behavior of control Ss.

White, K. M. Conceptual style and conceptual ability in kindergarten through the eighth grade. *Child Development*, 1971, 42, 1652–56.

Subjects: N = 150; 5–6, 7, 9, 11, 13 yrs. **Measures:** Ss were presented with 48 drawings of humans, animals, and objects. Ss were asked to make 10 different groups, placing together those drawings with some characteristic in common. Ss were free to place a drawing in more than 1 group. Ss' groupings were classified as either inferential, descriptive, or relational. **Results:** No sex differences.

White, W. F., Anderson, H. E., Jr., and Cryder, H. The emerging self-concept in relation to select variables of secondary school students. *J. Social Psychology*, 1967, 72, 81–88.

Subjects: N = 225; 13–17 yrs. **Measures:** Ss were administered the McKinney Sentence Completion Blank (a self-concept inventory). Ss' responses were classified by 3 judges into the following categories: (a) Sense of Bodily Self, (b) Sense of Continuing Self-Identity, (c) Sense of Self-Esteem, Pride, (d) Sense of Self-Extension, (e) Sense of Self-Image, (f) Sense of Self as a Rational Coper, and (g) Sense of Self as a Propriate Striver. **Results:** Girls made more responses that fell into categories (b), (d), and (g) than boys. Boys made more responses that fell into category (e) than girls.

Whiteman, M. Children's conceptions of psychological causality. *Child Development*, 1967, *38*, 143–55.
Subjects: $N = 42$; 5–6, 8–9 yrs (black, Puerto Rican). **Measures:** 7 stories were read to Ss. In each, a young girl exhibited 1 of 7 mechanisms of adjustment: displacement, wishful dreaming, projection, repression, regression, rationalization, or denial. After each story, Ss were asked to explain why the young girl acted as she did. Ss were rated on how well they explained the girl's behavior. **Results:** No sex differences.

Whiting, B., and Pope, C. A cross-cultural analysis of sex differences in the behavior of children aged three to eleven. *J. Social Psychology*, 1974, in press. (Further analysis of the data originally appearing in B. B. Whiting, ed., *Six cultures: studies of child rearing*. New York and London: John Wiley & Sons, 1963.)
EXPERIMENT I: Subjects: $N = 134$; 3–11 yrs (Nyansongo, Kenya; Taira, Okinawa; Khalapur, India; Toronj, Philippines; Juxtlahuaca, Mexico; Orchard Town, U.S.A.). **Measures:** Over a period of 2 years (1954–56) each child was observed in natural settings an average of 17 different times. **Results:** Though the data were analyzed separately for each culture, only the overall results of the combined sample are reported here. (1) Among younger (3-6-year-old) Ss, girls sought help more frequently than boys. No sex difference was found among older Ss. (2) Among 7-11-year-old Ss, boys sought attention more frequently than girls. No sex difference was found among younger Ss. (3) Among younger Ss, girls were observed to seek or offer physical contact more often than boys. No sex difference was found among older Ss. (4) No sex differences were found in sociability. (5) No sex differences were found in the frequency with which Ss withdrew from aggressive instigations. Among older Ss, boys more often than girls reacted with counteraggression after being attacked by peers; among younger Ss, no sex differences were found. (6) No overall sex differences were found in compliance to prosocial and egotistically dominant instigations. Among older Ss, girls were more compliant than boys to their mothers' commands and suggestions. (7) No sex differences were found in the proportion of acts that were self-instigated. (8) Among older Ss, girls offered help and support to others more frequently than boys. No sex differences were found among younger Ss. (9) Among 3-6-year-old Ss, girls offered responsible suggestions more frequently than boys. No sex difference was found among older Ss. (10) Among younger Ss, boys were more dominant than girls. No sex difference was found among older Ss. (11) Boys engaged in more rough-and-tumble play than girls. (12) Boys were more verbally aggressive than girls. (13) Assaulting with the intent to injure was not observed frequently enough to make any definitive statement. (14) Among older Ss, girls took care of children under 18 months of age more frequently than boys. (15) Girls interacted with adult women more frequently than boys. Boys interacted with peers more frequently than girls.
EXPERIMENT II: Subjects: $N = 57$; 3–10 yrs (Ngecha, Kenya). **Measures:** Observations were made of Ss for periods of 30 minutes over the course of 2 years. **Results:** (1) Among 3-6-year-olds, boys were more sociable than girls. (2) No sex differences were found in the frequency with which Ss offered help and support to others or in the frequency with which they sought attention from others. (3) There were no sex differences in the number of times Ss engaged in rough-and-tumble play.

Wicker, A. W., and Bushweiler, G. Perceived fairness and pleasantness of social exchange situations: two factorial studies of inequity. *J. Personality & Social Psychology*, 1970, *15*, 63–75.
Subjects: $N = 142$; 18–21 yrs (college). **Measures:** Ss responded to 18 hypothetical situations derived from all possible combinations of the following statements: (a) I (like, dislike) my co-worker, (b) I believe myself to be (more, equally, less) valuable to my employer than my co-worker, (c) I make (more, the same, less) money per hour (than) my co-worker. Ss were asked to rate the pleasantness and fairness of each situation. **Results:** No main sex differences.

Wilcox, B. M., and Clayton, F. L. Infant visual fixation on motion pictures of the human face. *J. Experimental Child Psychology*, 1968, *6*, 22–32.
Subjects: $N = 6$ boys, 4 girls; 5 mos. **Measures:** Ss' fixation times to silent motion pictures of a woman's face were recorded. Each S had 60-second exposures to smiling, frowning, and neutral, moving and nonmoving faces. **Results:** No sex differences.

Willerman, L., Broman, S. H., and Fiedler, M. Infant development, preschool IQ, and social class. *Child Development*, 1970, *41*, 69–77.
   Subjects: $N = 3,037$; tested at 8 mos, 4 yrs. **Measures:** Ss were given the Collaborative Research Form of the Bayley Scales of Mental and Motor Development at age 9 months and Form L-M of the Stanford-Binet IQ test at 4 years. **Results:** (1) Girls scored higher than boys on the Motor Scale ($p < .01$). No sex differences were found on the Mental Scale. (2) Girls scored higher than boys on the Stanford-Binet ($p < .001$).

Williams, J. E. Connotations of racial concepts and color names. *J. Personality & Social Psychology*, 1966, *3*, 531–40.
   Subjects: $N = 520$; 18–21 yrs (white and black college). **Measures:** Ss rated race-related color-person concepts (brown, yellow, red, white, black person) and ethnic-national concepts (Asiatic Indian, Oriental, American Indian, Caucasian, and Negro) on 12 scales, 6 of which reflected an evaluation factor, 3 a potency factor, and 3 an activity factor. **Results:** No sex differences.

Williams, J. F., Meyerson, L. J., Eron, L. D., and Semler, I. J. Peer-rated aggression and aggressive responses elicited in an experimental situation. *Child Development*, 1967, *38*, 181–90.
   Subjects: $N = 120$; 8 yrs. **Measures:** Ss whose scores on the Peer-Rate Index of Aggression were either 1 standard deviation above or below their class mean were assigned to same-sex triads. Each triad was asked to turn off a set of lights by pressing buttons situated directly below the lights. Each triad was led to believe it was competing against other teams for a prize and that the team reaching criterion first (i.e. performing the task correctly 3 times in a row) would win. On each of the first 15 trials, each S was informed that both his partners had performed incorrectly. He was then given the opportunity to let his partners know by pressing 1 of 10 buttons, each of which produced a noxious sound in their earphones. Buttons to the right produced louder sounds than buttons to the left. Measures were taken of latency, duration, intensity, and frequency of Ss' responses. **Results:** Among high-aggression Ss, boys delivered more intense sounds than girls did. A similar difference was found between low-aggression boys and girls. No sex differences were found in latency, frequency, or duration.

Williams, R. L., and Byars, H. Negro self-esteem in a transitional society. *Personnel & Guidance Journal*, 1968, *47*, 120–25.
   Subjects: $N = 310$; 14–17 yrs (black, white). **Measures:** Tennessee Self-Concept Scale. **Results:** Among black Ss, boys had lower scores on the Self-Criticism Scale than girls, implying that they were more defensive than girls about their reported self-esteem.

Williams, T. M., and Fleming, J. W. Methodological study of the relationship between associative fluency and intelligence. *Developmental Psychology*, 1969, *1*, 155–62.
   Subjects: $N = 36$; 3–4 yrs. **Measures:** The Peabody Picture Vocabulary test and a verbal and a visual associative task were administered to Ss under both an evaluative and a play atmosphere. On the verbal associative task, Ss were asked to name uses for a common object and to give examples of objects that have some particular characteristic. On the visual associative task, Ss were shown 7 simple, black line drawings. For each item, Ss were asked to name all the things they thought it could be. A total score (number of responses given) and a fluency score (total score minus number of responses that were incomprehensible, obscure, or repetitious) were obtained for each associative-task item. **Results:** No sex differences.

Willis, F. N. Initial speaking distance as a function of the speaker's relationship. *Psychonomic Science*, 1966, *5*, 221–22.
   Subjects: $N = 755$; adults. **Measures:** Distances between individuals who were classified as either strangers, acquaintances, friends, or close friends were recorded at the moment conversation began. **Results:** (1) Women were approached more closely than men ($p < .01$). (2) Compared to men, women stood closer to good friends, but farther away from friends ($p < .01$).

Willis, R. H., and Willis, Y. A. Role playing versus deception: an experimental comparison. *J. Personality & Social Psychology*, 1970, *16*, 472–77.
   Subjects: $N = 96$; 18–21 yrs (college). **Measures:** Ss in same-sex pairs ranked 10 stimulus photographs according to aesthetic value. Ss were then informed of the scores earned by their own and partner's rankings, and received a copy of partner's ranking. Ss' subsequent reranking

of the stimuli was compared with partner's initial ranking to yield a net conformity score. **Results:** No sex differences.

Willoughby, R. H. Field-dependence and locus of control. *Perceptual & Motor Skills,* 1967, *24,* 671–72.
Subjects: $N = 76$; 18–21 yrs (college). **Measures:** Hidden Figures Test. **Results:** No sex differences.

Wilson, P. R., and Russell, P. N. Modification of psychophysical judgments as a method of reducing dissonance. *J. Personality & Social Psychology,* 1966, *3,* 710–12.
Subjects: $N = 60$; 18–21 yrs (college). **Measures:** After being blindfolded, Ss lifted a heavy and a light weight the same vertical distance (Ss were unaware of this fact). Afterward, Ss were asked to estimate how high they had lifted each weight. Response measure was the difference between Ss' estimates. **Results:** No sex differences.

Wilson, R. S., and Harpring, E. B. Mental and motor development in infant twins. *Development Psychology,* 1972, *7,* 277–87.
Subjects: $N = 261$ pairs of twins; tested at 3, 6, 9, 12, 18, 24 mos. **Measures:** Bayley Scales of Infant Development. **Results:** At 9 months, girls scored higher than boys on the motor scale ($p < .05$). At 18 months, girls scored higher than boys on the mental scale ($p < .05$).

Wilson, R. S., Brown, A. M., and Matheny, A. P. Emergence and persistence of behavioral differences in twins. *Child Development,* 1971, *42,* 1381–98.
Subjects: $N = 232$ pairs of same-sex twins; 3–72 mos and mothers. **Measures:** Interviews were conducted with mothers on a regular basis. For each of 17 behavioral variables, mothers were asked whether both twins displayed the behavior to an equal degree (concordance), or whether 1 twin exhibited the behavior to a greater degree than the other (discordance). **Results:** A higher proportion of female twins than male twins were reported concordant in quality of vocalization at 24, 36, and 72 months of age.

Wilson, W., and Insko, C. Recency effects in face-to-face interaction. *J. Personality & Social Psychology,* 1968, *9,* 21–23.
Subjects: $N = 158$; 18–21 yrs (college). **Measures:** After playing a modified version of the Prisoner's Dilemma game with a confederate of the same sex, Ss rated the confederate on the following traits: generosity, cooperativeness, fairness, willingness to accommodate, willingness to compromise, greed, kindness, and meanness. The response measure was the sum of the ratings on these traits. **Results:** No sex differences.

Winitz, H. Language skills of male and female kindergarten children. *J. Speech & Hearing Research,* 1959, *2,* 377–86.
Subjects: $N = 150$; 5 yrs. **Measures:** The Wechsler Intelligence Scale for Children, Ammons Full-Range Vocabulary Test, and the Templin Screening Test of Articulation were administered. Verbal responses elicited from Ss after the presentation of the Children's Apperception Test Cards were scored for length of responses, number of words in the 5 longest responses, number of 1-word responses, standard deviation, number of different words, and structural complexity. 4 measures of word fluency were also obtained: Ss were asked to name as many children's names, as many adults' names, as many names of things, and as many words that rhymed with certain sounds as they could think of. **Results:** (1) Girls had higher WISC Performance Scale IQs than boys ($p < .02$). No sex differences were found in WISC Full Scale IQ or WISC Verbal Scale IQ. (2) No sex differences were found in vocabulary and articulation tests. (3) For the verbal response measures, the 5 longest responses ($p < .01$) and the standard deviation ($p < .05$) were both higher for girls than for boys. (4) Girls named more children's names than boys did ($p < .01$). No sex differences were found on the other 3 word fluency measures.

Winkel, G. H., and Sarason, G. Subject, experimenter, and situational variables in research on anxiety. *J. Abnormal & Social Psychology,* 1964, *68,* 601–8.
Subjects: $N = 144$; 18–21 yrs (college). **Measures:** Ss who were either high or low in test anxiety were presented with 12 nonsense words for 15 trials in a word-anticipation task. After completing the task, Ss were informed by E that they had performed either extremely well or extremely poorly. Ss were then given a second list of 12 nonsense words for 15 trials. The 24 male Es who administered the tasks were either high or low in anxiety (as assessed by the Test Anxiety Scale). **Results:** (1) Women made more correct anticipations than men (List 1, $p < .05$; List 2, $p < .01$). (2) Women performed better under low-anxiety Es than under high-anxiety Es, whereas the reverse was true for men (List 1, $p < .01$; List 2, $p < .05$).

Wispé, L. G., and Freshley, H. B. Race, sex, and sympathetic helping behavior. *J. Personality & Social Psychology*, 1971, *17*, 59–65.
> EXPERIMENT I: **Subjects:** $N = 176$; adults (white, black). **Measures:** S's responses to a black or white female accomplice who dropped a bag of groceries in front of S as S left a supermarket were classified as either helping or nonhelping. **Results:** More black men helped the female accomplice than black women did ($p < .02$). No sex difference was found in the white sample.
> EXPERIMENT II: **Subjects:** $N = 48$; adults (observed Ss in Experiment I refuse to help female accomplice). **Measures:** Helping behavior of observers. **Results:** More men helped the female accomplice than women did ($p < .05$).

Witkin, H. A., Goodenough, D. R., and Karp, S. A. Stability of cognitive style from childhood to young adulthood. *J. Personality & Social Psychology*, 1967, *7*, 291–300.
> **Subjects:** $N = 515$; 8, 10–13, 15, 17, 18–21 yrs (cross-sectional study). $N = 47$; tested at 8, 13 yrs. $N = 51$, tested at 10, 14, 17 yrs. **Measures:** Series 3 of the Rod-and-Frame Test was administered to all Ss. Ss in the cross-sectional study were also given the Embedded Figures Test (EFT) and the Body Adjustment Test (BAT) of the Tilting-Room-Tilting-Chair Test. **Results:** (1) In the cross-sectional study, boys were more field-independent on the RFT and EFT than girls. No sex differences were found on the BAT. (2) In the 5-year longitudinal study, boys were more field-independent than girls at both ages. In the 7-year longitudinal study, no sex differences were found.

Witkin, H. A., Birnbaum, J., Lomonaco, S., Lehr, S., and Herman, J. L. Cognitive patterning in congenitally totally blind children. *Child Development*, 1968, *39*, 768–86.
> **Subjects:** $N = 53$; 12–19 yrs (blind, sighted). **Measures:** Ss completed a tactile embedded figures test, an auditory embedded figures test, 2 analytic-ability problem-solving tasks (the tactile block design task and the tactile matchsticks task), a clay-modeling body-concept test, and the verbal section of the Wechsler intelligence scales. **Results:** Girls performed better than boys on the tactile matchsticks task. No sex differences were found on the other tests.

Wittig, M. A., and Weir, M. W. The role of reinforcement procedure in children's probability learning as a function of age and number of response alternatives. *J. Experimental Child Psychology*, 1971, *12*, 228–39.
> **Subjects:** $N = 80$; 4–5 yrs. **Measures:** Ss performed either a 2- or a 4-choice probability-learning task under either contingent or noncontingent reinforcement procedures. On each trial, Ss were told to guess which of 2 (or 4) buttons would light up by pressing that button. The buttons were arranged in a horizontal row. **Results:** (1) No sex differences were found in the number of times Ss chose the higher probability alternative. (2) On the 2-choice task, there were no sex differences in the frequency with which Ss exhibited either of the following simple response patterns: left button–right button–left button or right button–left button–right button. (3) On the 4-choice task, boys in the contingent reinforcement condition emitted more left-to-right or right-to-left sequences of responses than did their female counterparts ($p < .01$). No sex differences were found in the noncontingent reinforcement condition.

Wohlford, P. Extension of personal time, affective states, and expectation of personal death. *J. Personality & Social Psychology*, 1966, *3*, 559–66.
> **Subjects:** $N = 147$; 18–21 yrs (college). **Measures:** Before providing descriptions of a future event (either a pleasant or unpleasant experience or their death), Ss completed a personal association test. For each association, Ss were requested to give temporal referents. Dates were converted to scale scores to yield measures of extension (the length of the time span encompassed by Ss' cognition), protension (Ss' extension of personal time into the future), and retrotension (Ss' extension of personal time into the past). **Results:** Women had higher retrotension scores than men ($p < .01$). No sex differences were found in protension and extension scores.

Wohlford, P., Santrock, J. W., Berger, S. E., and Liberman, D. Older brothers' influence on sex-typed, aggressive, and dependent behavior in father-absent children. *Developmental Psychology*, 1971, *4*, 124–34.
> **Subjects:** $N = 66$; 4–6 yrs (black, low SES, father-absent). **Measures:** Ss responded to forced-choice picture pairs of male- or female-typed activities, people or scenes, doll-play situations that elicited aggressive responses, and doll-play situations that were scored for dependency. Mothers were interviewed on Ss' masculinity-femininity, aggression, and dependency. **Results:** (1) Boys' sex-typed behavior was more masculine than girls' on the forced-choice masculinity-

femininity measures ($p < .001$). (2) There were no sex differences in maternal report of masculinity-femininity. (3) Boys displayed more intense aggression (i.e. hitting as opposed to threatening to hit) in the doll-play interview than girls ($p < .03$). Boys were also higher on frequency of doll-play interview aggression ($p = .02$), but no sex difference was found on the mother-interview report of aggression. (4) There were no sex differences in dependency on either doll-play or maternal interview measures.

Wohlwill, J. F. Texture of the stimulus field and age as variables in the perception of relative distance in photographic slides. *J. Experimental Child Psychology*, 1965, 2, 163–77.
Subjects: $N = 96$; 6, 9, 13, 16 yrs. Measures: Photographic slides of stimulus fields were taken at an angle to convey the impression of depth. The fields varied in texture density and in the regularity of patterning of their texture elements. Each field featured a toy cow in the foreground and a toy horse in the background; a toy fence was placed at varying distances in between. Ss' task was to judge which of the two stimuli, the cow or the horse, was closer to the fence. Results: No sex differences.

Wolf, T. M. Effects of live modeled sex-inappropriate play behavior in a naturalistic setting. *Developmental Psychology*, 1973, 9, 120–23.
Subjects: $N = 60$; 7–11 yrs. Measures: Ss viewed a male or female peer model play with a toy judged to be sex-inappropriate for the child observer (for boys, a toy oven; for girls, a truck). Following exposure to the model, Ss were observed in free play for 5 minutes. Latency to touch the inappropriate toy and total time spent playing with it were recorded. Ss were then asked whether they liked or disliked the model. Results: (1) No main sex differences were found on either the latency or duration measure. Boys played with the oven longer following exposure to a boy than to a girl model. Girls played with the truck more quickly following exposure to a girl than to a boy model. (2) Boys and girls did not differ in their liking of the models. Boys liked same-sex models more than opposite-sex models; no difference was found for girls.

Wolf, T. M. Response consequences to televised modeled sex-inappropriate play behavior. Submitted for publication, *Developmental Psychology*, 1974.
Subjects: $N = 140$; 5–9 yrs. Measures: Each S viewed a videotape of a boy or girl model playing with a toy judged to be sex-inappropriate for S (a doll for boys, a fire engine for girls). Models were either praised, criticized, or not reinforced while playing with the toy. After completion of the filmed sequence, Ss were observed in free play for 5 minutes. Latency to touch the sex-inappropriate toy and total time spent playing with it were recorded. Ss were then asked to exhibit as many of the unusual responses performed by the model as possible. During both the free play and recall phase, measures were taken of the number of different unusual responses displayed by each child. Liking for the model was also assessed. Results: (1) Girls touched the inappropriate toy longer and more readily than boys did. Both sexes played with the toy longer after being exposed to a same-sex model than after viewing an opposite-sex model. (2) During the recall task, boys displayed more unusual responses than girls. No sex differences were found during the free play phase. (3) Girls liked the model more than boys did. The same-sex model was liked more by girls than the opposite-sex model; no difference was found for boys.

Wolfensberger, W. P., Miller, M. B., Foshee, J. G., and Cromwell, R. L. Rorschach correlates of activity level in high school children. *J. Consulting Psychology*, 1962, 26, 269–72.
Subjects: $N = 100$; 13–17 yrs. Measures: While Ss listened to music, their activity level was measured with a ballistograph. Results: 44 Ss who had either the highest or the lowest activity levels were selected to participate in a second study. Of these 44 Ss, more boys than girls were hyperkinetic ($p < .01$).

Wolff, P. The role of stimulus-correlated activity in children's recognition of nonsense forms. *J. Experimental Child Psychology*, 1972, 14, 427–41.
EXPERIMENT I: Subjects: $N = 67$; 4–7 yrs. Measures: Ss performed a task involving a visual recognition of nonsense forms with voluntary haptic activity. Results: No sex differences.
EXPERIMENT II: Subjects: $N = 30$; 4–5 yrs. Measures: Same as Experiment I, except that Ss were trained in haptic activity. Results: No sex differences.

Wolff, P., and Wolff, E. A. Correlational analysis of motor and verbal activity in young children. *Child Development*, 1972, 43, 1407–11.
Subjects: $N = 55$; 4–5 yrs. Measures: Teachers rated their pupils on gross motor activity, fine motor activity, manual dexterity, verbal output, and verbal skill. Results: No sex differences.

Wolman, R. N., Lewis, C., and King, M. The development of the language of emotions: conditions of emotional arousal. *Child Development*, 1971, *42*, 1288–93.
Subjects: $N = 256$; grade school. Measures: Ss were interviewed about their feelings and emotions: hunger, thirst, sadness, sleepiness, happiness, anger, fear, and nervousness. If Ss indicated they had experienced an emotion, they were asked, "When do you get it?" Ss' responses were classified as either internal (e.g. "I get hungry when my stomach feels empty") or external (e.g. "I get hungry when it is time for lunch"). Results: Among older Ss (age range not given), boys reported that the conditions eliciting their emotions occurred more frequently within themselves and less frequently outside themselves than girls did (level of significance not reported).

Woodruff, D. S., and Burren, J. E. Age changes and cohort differences in personality. *Developmental Psychology*, 1972, *6*, 252–59 (and personal communication).
Subjects: $N = 77$; 16, 18–21 yrs (college). $N = 85$; 43–46 yrs (previously tested at 18–21 yrs). Measures: The California Test of Personality was administered to Ss; 43-46-year-old Ss were tested twice: (1) In the self-condition, Ss described themselves. (2) In the retrospective condition, Ss answered the test as they thought they had responded in 1944. Results: (1) No main sex differences were found among 16- or 18-21-year-old Ss. (2) No main sex differences were found in the 1944 scores of the 43-46-year-old sample, nor were there any sex differences in their 1969 scores in either the self or retrospective condition.

Woods, M. G. The unsupervised child of the working mother. *Developmental Psychology*, 1972, *6*, 14–25.
Subjects: $N = 108$; 10 yrs (black). Measures: Ss indicated whether or not they were supervised by adults during the critical periods of the school day (breakfast, lunch hour, and after school until dinner). Results: More girls than boys reported a lack of supervision ($p < .02$).

Worchel, S., and Brehm, J. W. Effect of threat to attitudinal freedom as a function of agreement with the communicator. *J. Personality & Social Psychology*, 1970, *14*, 18–22.
Subjects: $N = 73$; 18–21 yrs (college). Measures: S filled out attitude questionnaires before and after reading a persuasive speech. Speeches were either for or against S's position, and were designed to either threaten or not threaten S's freedom to decide for himself. The response variable was the amount of change in attitude either toward or away from S's advocated position. Results: No sex differences.

Wright, D. Social reinforcement and maze learning in children. *Child Development*, 1968, *39*, 177–83.
Subjects: $N = 80$; 10, 11 yrs. Measures: Ss attempted to solve a maze task twice. Social reinforcement was given in 3 conditions: positive, negative, and mixed. The control group received no reinforcement. The measure of learning was the number of trials to criterion. Results: Boys were better at learning the maze task than girls ($p < .05$). This effect appears due to the presence of girls in the control group; girls in the experimental groups tended to do slightly better than boys.

Wyer, R. S., Jr. Self-acceptance, discrepancy between parents' perceptions of their children, and goal-seeking effectiveness. *J. Personality & Social Psychology*, 1965, *2*, 311–16.
Subjects: $N = 889$; 18 yrs and parents. Measures: Ss rated (their acceptance of) themselves on each of 24 adjectives. Using the same set of adjectives, parents recorded their feelings about their children. Results: (1) No sex differences were found in self-acceptance. (2) Mothers' acceptance ratings of their daughters were higher than their ratings of their sons. No sex differences were found in fathers' acceptance ratings.

Wyer, R. S., Jr. Effects of incentive to perform well, group attraction, and group acceptance on conformity in a judgmental task. *J. Personality & Social Psychology*, 1966, *4*, 21–26.
Subjects: $N = 80$; 14–17 yrs. Measures: Ss estimated the number of dots presented on slides. Judgments were made both before and after exposure to fictitious group norms. The response measure was the degree of conformity. Results: No sex differences.

Wyer, R. S., Jr. Behavioral correlates of academic achievement: conformity under achievement- and affiliation-incentive conditions. *J. Personality & Social Psychology*, 1967, *6*, 255–63.
EXPERIMENT I: Subjects: $N = 2,000$; 18 yrs (college). Measures: Ss' scores on the Ameri-

can College Testing Service Entrance Examination (ACTS) and their first-term freshman grade-point averages (GPA) were obtained. **Results:** No sex differences.

EXPERIMENT II: **Subjects:** $N = 128$; 18 yrs (same as Experiment I). **Measures:** Ss selected from the larger sample were either high-high, high-low, low-high, or low-low in performance (GPA) and aptitude (ACTS). Before and after exposure to fictitious group norms, Ss (in groups of 7–10) estimated the number of dots on each of 10 slides. Ss were tested under 2 conditions: achievement-incentive (Ss were told that their performance would reflect their achievement potential) and affiliative-incentive (group attractiveness was made salient while the importance of the task was deemphasized). The response measure was the degree to which Ss conformed to the fictitious group norms. **Results:** (1) There were no main sex differences. (2) Conformity scores for men were higher in the affiliative-incentive condition than in the achievement-incentive condition; conformity scores for women showed the reverse trend ($p < .05$).

Wyer, R. S., Jr. Effects of task reinforcement, social reinforcement, and task difficulty on perseverance in achievement-related activity. *J. Personality & Social Psychology*, 1968, 8, 269–76.

Subjects: $N = 70$; 3–6 yrs. **Measures:** Ss were asked to perform an objectively easy or difficult task. The response measure was Ss' perseverance on the task. Ss were then shown a series of 5 games, 1 of which was described as easy for other children to perform and the other as difficult. Ss' relative preferences for the easy and difficult games were recorded. **Results:** No sex differences.

Wylie, R. C., and Hutchins, E. B. Schoolwork ability estimates and aspirations as a function of socioeconomic level, race, and sex. *Psychological Reports*, 1967, Monographic Supplement 3-V21.

Subjects: $N = 3,422$; 12–17 yrs. **Measures:** 11 groups of senior high school students (ranging in size from 39 to 448) and 6 groups of junior high school students (ranging in size from 34 to 149) were asked (1) whether they thought they were in the top or bottom half of their homerooms in ability to do schoolwork; (2) whether they felt they had the ability to do college work; (3) whether they were interested in going to college; (4) whether they were planning to go to college; (5) whether their parents had encouraged them to attend college; (6) whether their same-sex close friends would admire them for trying to do well in their schoolwork; and (7) if they thought their grade averages for the year were in the top half of their homerooms. Ss were also questioned about their grade aspirations and career plans. **Results:** Following each result below are 2 numbers. The first gives the fraction of subgroups that exhibited the stated sex difference. The second gives the number of subgroups in which this difference was significant. (1) More boys than girls placed themselves in the top half of their homerooms in ability: junior high school (JHS), 6/6, 0; senior high school (SHS), no trend emerged. (2) More boys than girls felt they had the ability to do college work: JHS, 6/6, 0; SHS, no trend emerged. (3) More boys than girls wanted to go to college: JHS, 6/6, 1; SHS, 7/8, 3. (4) More boys than girls planned to go to college: SHS, 3/3, 3. (5) More boys than girls reported that their parents had encouraged them to attend college: JHS, 5/5, 1; SHS, 11/11, 6. (6) More girls than boys indicated that their friends would admire them if they tried to do their best in their schoolwork: JHS, 5/6, 1; SHS, 3/3, 3. (7) More girls than boys judged that their grade average for the year was in the top half of their homerooms: JHS, no trend emerged; SHS, 6/6, 3. (8) More girls than boys had high career aspirations: JHS, 5/6, 1. More boys than girls had high career aspirations: SHS, 7/11, 4. (9) More girls than boys aspired to high grades: JHS, no trend emerged; SHS, 6/6, 3.

Yamamoto, K. Development of ability to ask questions under specific testing conditions. *J. Genetic Psychology*, 1962, 101, 83–90.

Subjects: $N = 780$; 6–17 yrs. **Measures:** Ask and Guess Test. **Results:** (1) Among 9-year-old Ss, girls asked twice as many "Be?" questions as boys ($p < .01$). (2) Among 10-year-old Ss, girls asked 3 times as many "Where?" questions as boys. Boys asked twice as many "Be?" questions as girls ($p < .01$). (3) Among 12-year-old Ss, boys asked 3 times as many "What?" questions as girls ($p < .01$).

Yando, R. M., and Kagan, J. The effect of teacher tempo on the child. *Child Development*, 1968, 39, 27–34.

Subjects: $N = 160$; 6 yrs. **Measures:** The Matching Familiar Figures Test was administered to Ss twice—once in the fall and once in the spring. **Results:** At the initial testing, no sex differences were found in response time. At the spring testing, boys and girls exhibited similar changes in scores.

Yando, R. M., and Zigler, E. Outerdirectedness in the problem-solving of institutionalized and noninstitutionalized normal and retarded children. *Developmental Psychology*, 1971, 4, 277–88.

Subjects: $N = 192$; 5–6, 9–10 yrs. **Measures:** Ss performed a 3-choice discrimination-learning task and an imitation task. On each trial of the discrimination task, Ss received a marble after choosing the largest of 3 squares. On each trial of the imitation task, Ss either watched E make a design, viewed a slide of a design projected onto a screen, or did both. Ss were then given the opportunity to make any design they wanted to. **Results:** (1) No main sex differences were found in the number of errors on the discrimination-learning task. (2) Both sexes exhibited a similar degree of imitation of the model's and of the projector's designs.

Yando, R. M., Zigler, E., and Gates, M. The influence of Negro and white teachers rated as effective or noneffective on the performance of Negro and white lower-class children. *Developmental Psychology*, 1971, 5, 290–99.

Subjects: $N = 144$; 8 yrs. **Measures:** (1) Ss were given 3 tasks assessing social approach and avoidance tendencies; 2 of these required Ss to place free forms on a large felt panel. After each trial, the distance of Ss' placement from E's end of the panel was recorded. The third task offered Ss the choice of looking through 1 of 4 Viewmasters that varied in distance from E. A record was kept of Ss' choice of Viewmasters. Ss also completed the Peabody Picture Vocabulary Test and a curiosity measure. All 5 tests were administered by black or white female teachers who were judged by a school psychologist to be either highly effective or noneffective. Both classroom teachers and teacher Es rated each child on (a) his classroom achievement (or in the case of the teacher E, his "probable" achievement), (b) the amount of fear he displayed in his interaction with adults, and (c) the frequency with which he displayed positive and negative attention-seeking behaviors. **Results:** (1) No main sex differences were found on the social approach and avoidance tasks. On trial 1 of 1 of the 2 placing tasks, girls placed the felt forms closer to white Es than boys did. (2) Among Ss in the white sample, boys obtained higher scores on the PPVT than girls did. No sex difference was found in the black sample. (3) Among Ss in the black sample, boys showed less curiosity than girls. No difference was found between white boys and girls. (4) Teacher Es rated girls as more fearful than boys. No other sex differences were found in their ratings. (5) Among white Ss, boys were rated by their classroom teachers as displaying more positive and negative attention-seeking behavior than girls; among black Ss, no sex differences were found. No differences were found between teachers' fearfulness or achievement ratings of black or white boys and girls.

Yang, R. K., and Douthitt, T. C. Newborn responses to threshold tactile stimulation. *Child Development*, 1974, in press.

Subjects: $N = 43$; 2 days. **Measures:** Air puffs of increasing intensities were presented to Ss' abdomens until a motor response occurred. Changes in heart rate were recorded. **Results:** No sex differences.

Yarrow, L. J., Rubenstein, J. L., and Pedersen, F. A. Dimensions of early stimulation: differential effects on infant development. Paper presented at the meeting of the Society for Research in Child Development, 1971 (and personal communication).

Subjects: $N = 41$; tested at 5, 6 mos (black) and their primary caretakers. **Measures:** At 5 months of age, 2 home observations were made of infants and their primary caretakers. Infants were scored for frequency of positive vocalization, frequency of fussing and crying, and amount of time spent in focused exploration of their environment. Caretakers were scored for proximity to infant, level and variety of social stimulation, contingency of response to the infant's positive vocalizations, and contingency of response to the infant's distress calls. Measures were also taken of the variety, complexity, and responsiveness of the objects available to the infant. During the fifth month, a research form of the Bayley Tests of Infant Development was also administered. The Bayley yields a Mental Developmental Index, a Psychomotor Index, and 8 more differentiated clusters: Social Responsiveness, Language Development, Fine Motor, Gross Motor, Goal Orientation, Reaching and Grasping, Secondary Circular Reaction, and Object Permanence. A ninth cluster, Problem Solving, was developed from 4 supplementary items administered after the Bayley. At 6 months of age, Ss were given a structured situational test designed to assess exploratory behavior and preference for novel stimuli. Ss were first presented with a novel toy (a bell) for 10 minutes. Durations of manipulating, looking, and vocalizing to the bell were recorded. Then a series of 10 new toys were presented 1 at a time. Each was paired with the bell. Two measures were taken: (1) time spent looking at the novel toy minus time spent looking at the bell, and (2) time spent manipulating the novel toy minus time spent manipulating the bell. **Results:** (1) Boys received higher levels and a greater variety of social stimulation than girls did ($p < .05$, $p < .01$). Boys' gross motor responses were encouraged more than girls' ($p < .05$). (2) Boys scored higher than girls on Goal Orientation and Object Permanence ($p < .05$). (3) Girls looked at the bell more than boys did ($p < .05$).

Yarrow, M. R., and Scott, P. M. Imitation of nurturant and non-nurturant models. *J. Personality & Social Psychology*, 1972, 23, 259–70.
Subjects: $N = 118$; 3–5 yrs. Measures: Ss participated in small mixed-sex play groups under the supervision of either a nurturant or nonnurturant female caretaker, who performed a variety of neutral, nurturant, and nonnurturant behaviors. Imitative displays of the models' behavior were recorded. **Results:** No sex differences.

Yarrow, M. R., Waxler, C. Z., and Scott, P. M. Child effects on adult behavior. *Developmental Psychology*, 1971, 5, 300–311.
Subjects: $N = 118$; 3–5 yrs. Measures: Child-woman and child-peer interactions were observed in a nursery school setting for 4 30-minute play sessions. Ss were in play groups of 6–8 members with either a high- or low-nurturant adult caretaker. **Results:** There were no sex differences in frequency of bids for adult attention.

Yee, A. H., and Runkel, P. J. Simplicial structures of middle-class and lower-class pupils' attitudes toward teachers. *Developmental Psychology*, 1969, 1, 646–52.
Subjects: $N = 209$; 9–12 yrs (low, middle SES). All classes had male teachers. Measures: The About My Teacher Inventory was administered to Ss to assess their attitudes toward their teachers on 5 dimensions: affective (e.g. Is your teacher fun to be with?), cognitive (e.g. Does your teacher explain your lesson clearly?), disciplinary (e.g. Does your teacher succeed in keeping the pupils under control?), innovative (e.g. Does your class go on field trips that help you understand what you are studying?), and motivational (e.g. Does your teacher make you feel like learning a lot on your own?). **Results:** No sex differences.

Yelen, D. R. Identification: the acquisition of evaluative connotations. *J. Personality & Social Psychology*, 1969, 12, 328–32.
Subjects: $N = 96$; 18–21 yrs (college). Measures: 1 member (model) of each same-sex pair of Ss was conditioned to associate either positive or negative connotations with nonsense syllables. Afterward, the model (M) and his partner (P) rated the nonsense syllables on semantic scales. M responded first by saying 1 of the scale numbers aloud. P then indicated his choice. Each time that P imitated M's rating, he was reinforced by E. Imitation was defined as a rating on the same side of the scale as the M's rating. Before and after the imitation trials, P was presented with the nonsense syllables followed by pairs of bipolar evaluative words. For each item, P indicated which of the 2 words had a meaning most similar to that of the nonsense syllable. **Results:** (1) No sex differences were found on the pre-imitation test. (2) No sex differences were found in models' ratings. (3) Women imitated model's ratings more than men did ($p < .05$). (4) On the post-imitation test, women acquired more reinforced evaluative connotations than men did ($p < .05$).

Youniss, J., and Murray, J. P. Transitive inference with nontransitive solutions controlled. *Developmental Psychology*, 1970, 2, 169–75.
Subjects: $N = 64$; 5, 8 yrs. Measures: Ss performed 20 transitivity judgments of stick lengths in 3 paradigms. **Results:** No sex differences.

Youssef, Z. I. The role of race, sex, hostility, and verbal stimulus in inflicting punishment. *Psychonomic Science*, 1968, 12, 285–86.
Subjects: $N = 120$; 18–21 yrs (college). Measures: Ss administered shocks to either a black or white, male or female confederate. Ss also completed a scale composed of items from Cook and Medley's Hostility Scale and Siegel's Manifest Hostility Scale. **Results:** (1) Men inflicted more intense shocks than women ($p < .05$). (2) Male confederates received higher levels of shock than female confederates ($p < .05$). (3) Men scored higher than women on the hostility scale ($p < .01$).

Zander, A., and van Egmond, E. Relationship of intelligence and social power to the interpersonal behavior of children. *J. Educational Psychology*, 1958, 49, 257–68.
Subjects: $N = 418$; 7, 10 yrs. Measures: Ss were randomly assigned to 4-person groups. Every group worked on 4 tasks, each of which required a group decision as a first step toward completion of the task. The number of times Ss exhibited the following behaviors was recorded: (a) attempts to influence others; (b) successful influence attempts; (c) un-

successful influence attempts; (d) demanding influence attempts; (e) suggestions; (f) evaluation of another child's behavior (positive or negative); (g) aggressive acts; and (h) affect-laden acts (friendly and unfriendly). **Results:** (1) Boys engaged in the following behaviors more often than girls: attempt to influence others, successful influence attempts, unsuccessful influence attempts, demanding influence attempts, and aggressive acts. (2) No other sex differences were found.

Zander, A., Fuller, R., and Armstrong, W. Attributed pride or shame in group and self. *J. Personality & Social Psychology*, 1972, *23*, 346–52.
> **Subjects:** $N = 88$; 18–21 yrs (college). **Measures:** S rated the amount of pride or shame he would have in his group or himself, after his group had earned each of 5 gradated scores on an unspecified task. **Results:** (1) Men had higher pride-in-self ratings than women ($p < .02$). (2) No sex differences were found in pride-in-group ratings.

Zelazo, P. R. Smiling to social stimuli: eliciting and conditioning effects. *Developmental Psychology*, 1971, *4*, 32–42.
> **EXPERIMENT I: Subjects:** $N = 20$; 3 mos. **Measures:** After base-rate smiling to unresponsive E was recorded, E responded contingently to S's smiles by smiling back and talking while touching S's abdomen. Number of contingently stimulated smiles (when E was not interacting with S), elicited smiles (during interaction time), and total smiling were recorded. **Results:** No sex differences.
> **EXPERIMENT II: Subjects:** $N = 30$; 3 mos. **Measures:** After base-rate smiling data were recorded, E administered social stimulation under contingent (same as Experiment I), non-contingent (social stimulation administered at random without regard to occurrence of infant smiling), or unresponsive control conditions. All smiling during 3-second periods was recorded as 1 smile. **Results:** No sex differences.

Zern, D. The "mental step" hypothesis in solving verbal problems: effects of variations in question-phrasing on a grade school population. *Developmental Psychology*, 1971, *4*, 103–4 (brief report).
> **Subjects:** $N = 69$; 7, 9–12 yrs. **Measures:** Ss answered 72 questions, each of which was similar in form to the following: "The answer was 27. Is it or is it not true that the answer was not an even number?" Measures were taken of the number of errors that Ss made and the latencies of their responses. **Results:** No sex differences.

Zern, D., and Taylor, A. L. Rhythmic behavior in the hierarchy of responses of preschool children. *Merrill-Palmer Quarterly*, 1973, *19*, 137–45.
> **Subjects:** $N = 41$; 2–4 yrs (nursery school). **Measures:** Classroom observers noted S's rhythmicities, i.e. rhythmical repetitive body movements, exclusive of goal-directed behavior. **Results:** No sex differences were found in frequency of oral or non-oral rhythmicities.

Zigler, E. Motivational aspects of change in culturally deprived nursery school children. *Child Development*, 1968, *39*, 1–14.
> **Subjects:** $N = 52$; 3–4 yrs (white, black). **Measures:** Stanford-Binet IQ Test. **Results:** No sex differences.

Zigler, E., and Balla, D. Developmental course of responsiveness to social reinforcement in normal children and institutionalized retarded children. *Developmental Psychology*, 1972, *6*, 66–73.
> **Subjects:** $N = 50$; mental ages 8, 11 yrs. **Measures:** Ss performed a monotonous task (Marble-in-the-Hole Game), receiving predetermined verbal and nonverbal reinforcement. The Zigler Social Deprivation Scale was used to assess preinstitutional social histories of retarded Ss; 4 measures of maintenance of contact with family and friends were collected. Length of institutionalization, percentage of life institutionalized, and age at time of institutionalization were obtained. **Results:** No sex differences (data of youngest mental-age group were not analyzed).

Zigler, E., and Yando, R. Outer directedness and imitative behavior of institutionalized and noninstitutionalized younger and older children. *Child Development*, 1972, *43*, 413–25.
> **Subjects:** $N = 192$; 7, 11 yrs. **Measures:** Before each trial in a marble-sorting task, Ss observed either a female E or a marble dispenser drop a marble into 1 of 4 quadrants of a wooden bowl. Measures were taken of the number of times Ss displayed imitative behavior (i.e. chose a marble of the same color and dropped it into the same quadrant as did E or the machine). **Results:** No sex differences.

Zigler, E., Levine, J., and Gould, L. Cognitive challenge as a factor in children's humor appreciation. *J. Personality & Social Psychology*, 1967, *6*, 332–36.
  Subjects: *N* = 60; 8, 10, and 12 yrs. **Measures:** After exposure to cartoons varying in level of difficulty, Ss rated the cartoons for humor. A measure of comprehension was obtained by asking Ss what they found particularly funny about each cartoon. Spontaneous mirth responses were recorded. **Results:** No sex differences.

Zigler, E., Abelson, W. D., and Seitz, V. Motivational factors in the performance of economically disadvantaged children on the Peabody Picture Vocabulary List. *Child Development*, 1973, *44*, 294–303.
  EXPERIMENT I: **Subjects:** *N* = 82; 4–5 yrs. **Measures:** Peabody Picture Vocabulary Test (Form B). **Results:** No sex differences.
  EXPERIMENT II: **Subjects:** *N* = 96; 3–5 yrs. **Measures:** Same as Experiment I, with new E. Whether E played with S before testing varied. **Results:** No sex differences.

Zillmann, D., and Cantor, J. R. Directionality of transitory dominance as a communication variable affecting humor appreciation. *J. Personality & Social Psychology*, 1972, *24*, 191–98.
  Subjects: *N* = 40; 18–21 yrs (college). **Measures:** Ss were presented with cartoons and jokes involving expressions of interpersonal hostility and aggressiveness. Ss rated each communication for its humorous content and novelty. **Results:** No sex differences.

Zimmerman, B. J. Effects of modeling and reinforcement on the acquisition and generalization of question-asking behavior. *Child Development*, 1972, *43*, 892–907.
  Subjects: *N* = 36; 7 yrs (Mexican-American). **Measures:** In the first phase of the study, Ss were asked to pose questions to their teachers about pictures shown to them. During the second phase, two-thirds of the Ss were praised for asking questions; the remaining 12 Ss received no reinforcement. Of the 24 Ss who received praise, 12 were additionally exposed to a model who exhibited question-asking behavior. During Phases 3 and 4, procedures identical to Phases 1 and 2 were followed. **Results:** There were no main sex differences. During Phase 4, boys asked more questions than girls; no sex differences were found during the other 3 phases ($p < .05$).

Zimmerman, B. J., and Bell, J. A. Observer verbalization and abstraction in vicarious rule learning, generalization, and retention. *Developmental Psychology*, 1972, *7*, 227–31.
  Subjects: *N* = 84; 9–12 yrs. **Measures:** Ss in 3 conditions (verbal description, passive observation, irrelevant verbalization) observed a model's task performance exemplifying either an associative or a conceptual rule. Ss then performed the task. **Results:** No sex differences.

Ziv, A. Sex differences in performance as a function of praise and blame. *J. Genetic Psychology*, 1972, *120*, 111–19.
  Subjects: *N* = 240; 13 yrs. **Measures:** The Raven Matrix was administered to all Ss at the beginning and at the end of a 4-hour testing session. Ss received either positive, negative, or neutral reinforcement from either a male or female E prior to the second administration of the matrix. **Results:** (1) There were no main sex differences. (2) Boys' scores increased when E was a male; girls' scores increased when E was a female ($p < .05$).

Zurich, M., and Ledwith, B. E. Self-concepts of visually handicapped and sighted children. *Perceptual & Motor Skills*, 1965, *21*, 771–74.
  Subjects: *N* = 58; 8–9 yrs (visually handicapped, sighted). **Measures:** Lipsitt's self-concept scale. **Results:** (1) Among visually handicapped Ss, girls rated themselves higher than boys did on the adjectives friendly, happy, likable, trusted, cooperative, and cheerful. Boys rated themselves higher than girls did on the adjective polite. (2) Among sighted Ss, girls rated themselves higher than boys did on the adjectives good, courteous, obedient, and clean. Boys rated themselves higher than girls did on the adjectives happy, kind, honest, likable, trusted, and proud.

Zussman, J. U. Sex differences in parental discipline techniques. Manuscript in preparation, Stanford University, 1973.
  Subjects: *N* = 44; 10 yrs and mothers. **Measures:** Ss were questioned about their parents' disciplinary techniques. Interviews were also conducted with mothers. **Results:** (1) Parents practiced love withdrawal (e.g. isolation, acting hurt or upset) more frequently with boys than with girls (mothers' reports, $p < .05$; Ss' reports, $p < .01$). (2) Parents used teaching techniques (e.g. reasoning, discussion, role-taking) more often with girls than with boys

(mothers' reports, $p < .05$; Ss' reports, NS). (3) No sex differences were found in parental use of power-assertive techniques (e.g. spanking, withdrawal of privileges).

Zussman, J. U., and Reimer, D. G. An exploration of two processes of empathy. Unpublished manuscript, Stanford University, 1973.
  Subjects: $N = 64$; 9, 10 yrs. **Measures:** After watching 2 puppet monologues, Ss were asked to recall as much of each monologue as they could. **Results:** No sex differences.

Zytkoskee, A., Strickland, B. R., and Watson, J. Delay of gratification and internal versus external control among adolescents of low socioeconomic status. *Developmental Psychology*, 1971, *4*, 93–98.
  Subjects: $N = 132$; 14–17 yrs (white, black). **Measures:** Ss completed the Bialer Locus of Control Scale and a delay-of-reward measure. **Results:** No sex differences.
  No sex differences.